SPECIAL EDITION
USING

Microsoft®

Office Word
2007

Faithe Wempen

Nicholas Chase

Kathy Jacobs

Karen McCall

Joyce J. Nielsen

Patrick Schmid

®

800 East 96th Street

Indianapolis, Indiana 46240 USA

SPECIAL EDITION USING MICROSOFT® OFFICE WORD 2007

International Standard Book Number: 0-7897-3608-X

Printed in the United States of America

First Printing: December 2006

10   09   08   07   06   4   3   2   1

Trademarks

All terms mentioned in this book that are known to be trademarks or service marks have been appropriately capitalized. Que Publishing cannot attest to the accuracy of this information. Use of a term in this book should not be regarded as affecting the validity of any trademark or service mark.

Microsoft and Windows are registered trademarks of Microsoft Corporation.

Bulk Sales

Que Publishing offers excellent discounts on this book when ordered in quantity for bulk purchases or special sales. For more information, please contact

> **U.S. Corporate and Government Sales**
> **1-800-382-3419**
>
> **corpsales@pearsontechgroup.com**

For sales outside of the U.S., please contact

> **International Sales**
> **international@pearsoned.com**

  This Book Is Safari Enabled

The Safari® Enabled icon on the cover of your favorite technology book means the book is available through Safari Bookshelf. When you buy this book, you get free access to the online edition for 45 days.

Safari Bookshelf is an electronic reference library that lets you easily search thousands of technical books, find code samples, download chapters, and access technical information whenever and wherever you need it.

To gain 45-day Safari Enabled access to this book:

- Go to http://www.quepublishing.com/safarienabled
- Complete the brief registration form
- Enter the coupon code D1QF-P7NQ-EWM2-Q2P5-81CI

If you have difficulty registering on Safari Bookshelf or accessing the online edition, please e-mail customer-service@safaribooksonline.com.

Library of Congress Cataloging-in-Publication Data

Wempen, Faithe.
  Special edition using Microsoft Office Word 2007 / Faithe Wempen.
    p. cm.
  Includes index.
  ISBN 0-7897-3608-X
  1. Microsoft Word. 2. Word processing. I. Title. II. Title: Using Microsoft Office Word 2007.
  Z52.5.M52W465 2007
  005.52—dc22

                                    2006038295

Associate Publisher
Greg Wiegand

Acquisitions Editors
Michelle Newcomb
Stephanie McComb

Development Editor
Todd Brakke

Managing Editor
Gina Kanouse

Project Editor
Lori Lyons

Copy Editor
Bart Reed

Indexer
Erika Millen

Proofreader
Water Crest Publishing

Technical Editors
Joyce J. Nielsen
Vince Averello
Bill Coan
Mark Hall

Publishing Coordinator
Cindy Teeters

Book Designer
Anne Jones

Composition
Gloria Schurick

CONTENTS AT A GLANCE

CONTENTS

VII Customizing and Extending Word

ABOUT THE AUTHOR

Faithe Wempen, M.A., is a Microsoft Office Master Instructor and an adjunct instructor of Computer Information Technology at Indiana University/Purdue University at Indianapolis, specializing in Microsoft Office and PC hardware. She is the author of more than 90 books on PC hardware and software, and teaches online courses in Office applications for corporate clients including Hewlett-Packard, Gateway, and Sony. She also owns and operates Sycamore Knoll Bed and Breakfast (www.sycamoreknoll.com).

ABOUT THE CONTRIBUTING AUTHORS

Nicholas Chase has been involved in Web site development for companies such as Lucent Technologies, Sun Microsystems, Oracle, and the Tampa Bay Buccaneers. Nick has been a high-school physics teacher, a low-level radioactive waste facility manager, an online science fiction magazine editor, a multimedia engineer, an Oracle instructor, and the Chief Technology Officer of an interactive communications company. He is the author of several books, including *XML Primer Plus* (Sams), and is currently a partner in the Backstop Media technical content production firm (http://www.backstopmedia.com).

Kathy Jacobs, Microsoft MVP in PowerPoint and OneNote, has been using Office since its earliest days. She started out using Word for newsletters, letters, books, and other documents in the late 1980s. She added PowerPoint and Excel to her areas of expertise in the early 1990s. She has been an active beta tester for Office since the 2002 release, and has been working with Office 2007 for many months. Kathy specializes in helping people from all backgrounds and all walks of life learn to use Office to make their lives easier. As a PowerPoint and OneNote consultant, trainer, and writer, she has written on Office topics for her own site (www.OnPPT.com), Office On-Line, LockerGnome, IndeZine, and the PowerPoint FAQ. She presents regularly on a variety of subjects at the Phoenix PC User Group, where she is currently vice president. She has been actively involved in PPT Live (the PowerPoint conference for users) since its inception. She has written a PowerPoint book, *Kathy Jacobs on PowerPoint*, and co-written a OneNote book, *Unleash the Power of OneNote*. She is the creator of Keystone learning's OneNote 2003 training DVD. Right now, she specializes in helping people solve their Office emergencies through her service, Call Kathy Solutions.

Karen McCall is a respected author and speaker with extensive expertise in software accessibility and usability. She trains software and web design professionals around the world on techniques to improve the digital experience for people with disabilities. Her current book, *Logical Document Structure Handbook: Word 2003*, is the first in a series focusing on designing and generating accessible and usable word processed documents. She currently lives in Canada, sharing adventures with Barnaby Edmund and Olivia Zane.

Joyce J. Nielsen is the author or coauthor of more than 35 computer books and has edited several hundred more. She has worked in the publishing industry for 17 years as an author, development editor, technical editor, and project manager. Joyce also worked as a research analyst for a shopping mall developer, where she developed and documented computer applications used nationwide. She graduated with a B.S. degree in Quantitative Business Analysis from Indiana University and now resides in Arizona.

Patrick Schmid has been a OneNote MVP since 2006 and can be found constantly in many Microsoft Office community newsgroups. During the Office 2007 beta, he became an expert in RibbonX. His website and blog at http://pschmid.net are a premier resource for customizing the Office 2007 Ribbon. Patrick is currently a Ph.D. Candidate in Computer Science at Lehigh University in Bethlehem, Pennsylvania.

DEDICATION

To Margaret, for the usual reasons.

—Faithe

To Bruce, who reads every word three times over and who made sure there was a server for me to learn on. You make me great!

—Kathy

ACKNOWLEDGMENTS

A big thanks to the great team at Que for another job well done, including Michelle Newcomb, Stephanie McComb, Todd Brakke, Lori Lyons, Bart Reed, Erika Millen, Sarah Kearns, and Gloria Schurick. Thanks also to my contributors:

Kathy Jacobs, who wrote about online collaboration in Chapter 29

Nicholas Chase, who shared his expertise of XML in Chapter 32

Patrick Schmid, who added his knowledge of RibbonX to the book in Chapter 35

Karen McCall, who provided the accessibility expertise in Appendix C

Joyce Neilsen, who checked the entire book for technical accuracy and was a great help during our last-minute scramble to make sure the book was up-to-date

WE WANT TO HEAR FROM YOU!

As the reader of this book, *you* are our most important critic and commentator. We value your opinion and want to know what we're doing right, what we could do better, what areas you'd like to see us publish in, and any other words of wisdom you're willing to pass our way.

As an associate publisher for Que Publishing, I welcome your comments. You can email or write me directly to let me know what you did or didn't like about this book—as well as what we can do to make our books better.

Please note that I cannot help you with technical problems related to the topic of this book. We do have a User Services group, however, where I will forward specific technical questions related to the book.

When you write, please be sure to include this book's title and author as well as your name, email address, and phone number. I will carefully review your comments and share them with the author and editors who worked on the book.

Email: feedback@quepublishing.com

Mail: Greg Wiegand
       Associate Publisher
       Que Publishing
       800 East 96th Street
       Indianapolis, IN 46240 USA

READER SERVICES

Visit our website and register this book at www.quepublishing.com/register for convenient access to any updates, downloads, or errata that might be available for this book.

INTRODUCTION

Welcome to *Special Edition Using Microsoft Office Word 2007*! This book is designed to be your one-stop reference for Microsoft Word 2007, from the basics of Ribbon usage to the intricacies of forms, fields, and customization tools. Whether you're just getting started, are upgrading, or are already a Word whiz, this book can help you move up to the next level in expertise.

HOW THIS BOOK IS ORGANIZED

Special Edition Using Microsoft Office Word 2007 is organized into these parts.

PART I: WORKING WITH TEXT DOCUMENTS

This part starts by touring the new Word 2007 interface and explaining the new features such as the Ribbon, tabs, and galleries. You'll learn how to create and save documents, type and edit text, check your spelling and grammar, and print and fax documents. These basic skills will pave the way to more extensive editing later in the book.

PART II: FORMATTING A DOCUMENT

In this part, you'll learn how to format documents on several levels: character, paragraph, and document-wide. You'll learn how to automate formatting with styles and themes, how to set up sections that enable different margin, column, and header/footer information in different parts of a document, and how to use and create project templates that streamline the process of formatting documents that you frequently re-create. You'll also learn how to create some nonstandard documents, such as banners, envelopes, and greeting cards.

PART III: TABLES AND GRAPHICS

This part explains how to create and format data in tabular format, and how to insert and format a variety of special-purpose graphical elements including clip art, drawings, charts, SmartArt, and mathematical equations. Most of these graphic types have formatting controls in common, so after you've learned how to format one type of object, the other types become much easier.

PART IV: COLLECTING AND MANAGING DATA

In this part, you'll learn how to use Word to collect data, and to use data to automate tasks. You'll learn how to mail-merge labels, letters, envelopes, and catalogs, and how to use fields and data entry forms to display and collect information.

PART V: LONG DOCUMENTS

This part covers the many tools Word provides for managing lengthy manuscripts such as research papers and books. You'll learn how to outline and summarize documents, how to create master documents that combine several files into a single unit, and how to generate tables of contents and other listings. This part also includes information about the new citation management features in Word 2007, and explains how to create effective indexes.

PART VI: COLLABORATION AND ONLINE SHARING

In this part, you'll learn about the tools that Word 2007 provides for sharing your work with others, both while it is in the development stages and when it is finalized. You'll find out how to collaborate on documents with a team, how to protect and secure your files, and how to use Office Live and SharePoint Team Services. This part also covers blogging and emailing via Word, and generating web and XML content.

PART VII: CUSTOMIZING AND EXTENDING WORD

This part explains how you can make Word easier to use by adding features such as macros and add-ins, and by customizing the Word interface. You'll even learn about the XML-based RibbonX utility for customizing the Ribbon.

PART VIII: APPENDIXES

The appendices for this book provide an assortment of reference guides, including help for recovering and repairing problems, converting from other word processing systems, creating documents that are accessible to people with disabilities, and setting up and modifying Word. You'll also find a command reference here that maps the commands from Word 2003 to Word 2007.

CONVENTIONS USED IN THIS BOOK

Here's a quick look at a few structural features designed to help you get the most out of this book. To begin with, you'll find the following features:

TIP

> Tips are designed to point out especially quick ways to get the job done, good ideas, or techniques you might not discover on your own.

NOTE

> Notes offer even more insight into features or issues that may be of special interest, without distracting you from the meat-and-potatoes answers you're looking for.

CAUTION

> Cautions, as you'd expect, warn you away from potential pitfalls and problems, and point out fixes for common issues.

Often, when a subject is covered in greater detail, you'll find a marker like this, which points you to the location where the topic can be found:

→ For more information about Word's automated spelling and grammar checker, **see** "Performing an Interactive Spelling and Grammar Check," **p. 98**.

Each chapter concludes with a Troubleshooting section that addresses several of the most common issues people have with Word 2007's features. In these Troubleshooting sections, you'll learn how to work around program limitations, interpret error messages, and more.

Que's *Special Edition* conventions are designed to be completely predictable. It's easy to understand what you're reading and what you're supposed to do.

For example, whenever you should press multiple keys together, in this book they are written separated by a plus sign, like this: Ctrl+B. That means hold down the Ctrl key, press the B key, and then release both keys.

Terms introduced and defined for the first time are formatted in *italic*.

Text that you are supposed to type in is formatted in bold type, as in the following example:

Run Setup using a command such as **setup.exe /q1 /b1**.

That's all you need to know to get the most out of this book. Now fire up your copy of Word 2007 and let's have a go at it.

WORKING WITH TEXT DOCUMENTS

CHAPTER 1

INTRODUCING WORD 2007

In this chapter

IT'S A WHOLE NEW WORD

Word 2007 is an amazing, powerful program that can meet all your word processing needs, from 1000+ page dissertations to family newsletters. But at first glance, it might seem a bit intimidating.

If you're an upgrader from an earlier version of Word, there's a lot to like in this new version—but also a lot to get used to. Word 2007 is not like any other word processing program you've probably seen before, and it represents a huge departure from earlier versions in its user interface (UI). There's definitely a learning curve in getting up to speed with it. But once you've mastered Word 2007, the new features and interface will outshine earlier versions in both power and usability.

Those who are new to word processing with Word 2007 will catch on quickly. Microsoft has spent hundreds of hours doing usability testing of the new interface to ensure that it is intuitive and easy for beginners to master.

In this chapter, I'll explain some of what makes Word 2007 so special—and so different from any other word processing system. You'll learn about the new user interface, and you'll find out how to change the view and access the Help system—essential survival skills for the rest of the book.

TIP

> Word 2007 is part of the Microsoft Office 2007 suite, and most of the applications in the suite use the same basic type of user interface. Therefore, if you spend the time to learn the new Word 2007 interface, you're 80% of the way to learning other applications, such as Excel 2007 and PowerPoint 2007.

TABS AND THE RIBBON

The first thing you might notice when you fire up Word 2007 is the lack of menus. There do appear to be some menu names across the top, but when you click one, no menu appears. The toolbar just changes.

Those words that seem to be menu names are actually tab names, and what you're accustomed to calling a toolbar is now called the *ribbon*. Clicking a tab brings a different page of the ribbon to the forefront. Each one of these pages is called a *tab*. Figure 1.1 shows the Home tab. Notice that the commands on the tab are divided into named *groups*. The Home tab has groups for Clipboard, Font, Paragraph, Styles, and Editing, for example.

A small toolbar floats above the tab names. This is the Quick Access toolbar. This is the only customizable portion of the user interface (unless you want to get into XML modifications, described in Chapter 35); you can add buttons to the Quick Access toolbar for any activities you frequently perform. For example, if you frequently do a spell-check, you could add the button for spell checking there. The commands and buttons that appear on the ribbon depend on which tab you have selected, but the Quick Access toolbar always appears the same, no matter what tab you're using.

Figure 1.1
The ribbon and the Quick Access toolbar appear at the top of the Word window.

The Home tab is displayed
Quick Access toolbar
Tab names
Ribbon

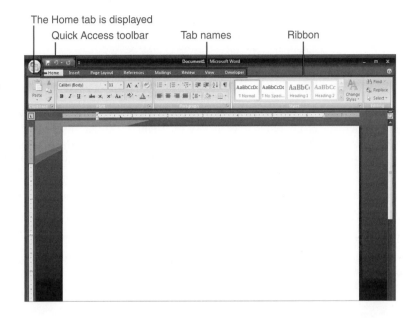

TIP

To add any command or button from any tab to the Quick Access toolbar, right-click the button or command and choose Add to Quick Access Toolbar from its shortcut menu. To remove a button from the Quick Access toolbar, right-click it on the Quick Access toolbar and choose Remove from Quick Access Toolbar.

Some tabs are always available, such as Home and View. Others come and go depending on what you're doing. Those are *contextual tabs*. For example, when you're working with a table, two additional tabs appear, Design and Layout, under a Table Tools heading (see Figure 1.2). When you move the insertion point out of the table, those tabs go away.

Table Tools tab group
Design and Layout tabs

Figure 1.2
Contextual tabs appear only when an object is selected that requires them.

The contents of the tabs change somewhat depending on the size of the Word window. All the controls are always available, but not always in the same format.

For example, when the Word window is fairly wide (say, around 1100 or more pixels), each of the items in the Page Background group on the Page Layout tab appears as a large button, as shown on the left side of Figure 1.3. When the window decreases a bit (say, to around 1024 pixels), each of those buttons becomes a smaller, horizontal one, as shown on the right side of Figure 1.3.

Figure 1.3
Certain groups on certain tabs change their look as the window changes width.

Not only do the sizes and shapes of buttons change based on the window width, but some groups actually change their content. All the items are still available, but instead of them being separate buttons, they become a single button with a menu. For example, on the Review tab, the Proofing group could be quite expanded (see Figure 1.4, left), moderately compressed but still with separate buttons for everything (see Figure 1.4, center), or completely compressed with just a Proofing button that opens a menu (see Figure 1.4, right).

Figure 1.4
Some groups collapse completely, except for a single button when the window is very narrow.

NOTE

It's important to know about this collapsing of groups because if you are running Word in a window size other than what was used to create the graphics in this book (1024×768), sometimes your tabs will not look exactly like the ones shown in the book, and occasionally a step-by-step procedure might be slightly different. For example, you might have an extra step where you have to click a collapsed group's button to access a button, or you might *not* have to click a collapsed group's button when the book shows that you do. It's not a big deal, but be aware.

THE OFFICE MENU

There is one real menu in Word 2007: the *Office menu*.

To access the Office menu, click the round graphic in the top-left corner of the Word window. On the Office menu are various commands for starting, opening, closing, saving, and printing files. Some of the commands on the Office menu have right-pointing arrows next to them. Pointing to such commands opens a submenu to the right, from which you can choose additional commands (see Figure 1.5).

There are two slightly different types of these commands with arrows next to them. Notice that when you point to Save As or Print, a divider appears between the main portion of the button and the arrow, as in Figure 1.5. This indicates that the main button (in this case, Print) is clickable on its own. You can simply choose Office, Print instead of choosing a command from the submenu. Other commands, such as Prepare, Send, and Publish, have arrows but do not have that divider bar. These commands are not selectable on their own; you must choose from the submenu for them.

Click here to open the Office menu

Figure 1.5
The Office menu contains commands for working with document files.

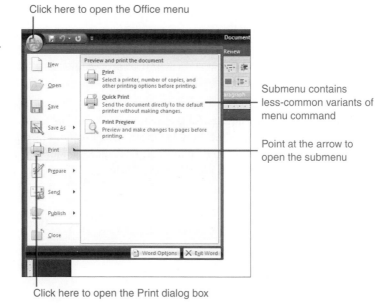

Submenu contains less-common variants of menu command

Point at the arrow to open the submenu

Click here to open the Print dialog box

When none of the submenus is displayed, the right side of the Office menu displays a list of recently used files. This is equivalent to the recently used file list that used to appear at the bottom of the File menu in earlier Word versions. Each filename has a pushpin icon next to it (see Figure 1.6). You can click that icon to "pin" the filename to the list so that it never scrolls off, even if other files were more recently opened. Click the pushpin again to unpin the file.

Figure 1.6
The right side of the Office menu displays the recently used files when it is not displaying a submenu.

Click a pushpin to pin the file to the list

Pinned file (shaded pushpin)

THE MINI TOOLBAR

One of the annoyances in earlier versions of Word was that the Formatting toolbar was so far away from the text being edited that you had to move your mouse a great distance each time you wanted to format some text. Word 2007 improves upon this situation by providing a pop-up Mini Toolbar when working with text.

To display the Mini Toolbar, select some text and then hover the mouse over the selection. The Mini Toolbar appears as a semitransparent "ghost" above and to the right of the selected text. If you then move the mouse pointer over the ghosted image, the Mini Toolbar appears full-strength, as in Figure 1.7. This floating toolbar enables you to apply some of the most common formatting changes to text, including selecting a font, size, and color and applying highlighting. (Those text-formatting commands can also be applied from the Home tab on the ribbon.)

Figure 1.7
The Mini Toolbar provides quick access to common formatting tools.

TIP

Another way to display the mini-toolbar is to right-click the selected text. A shortcut menu appears, but so does the mini-toolbar, above the shortcut menu.

→ To learn about the specific buttons and lists on the mini-toolbar, **see** Chapter 6, "Applying Character Formatting," **p. 155**.

GALLERIES AND DIALOG BOXES

Some of the buttons on the ribbon open dialog boxes, the same type of dialog boxes that you are probably familiar with from other Windows-based programs and from earlier versions of Office. For example, the Find button on the Home tab opens the Find and Replace dialog box, largely unchanged from Word 2003. Ditto with familiar features such as Spelling & Grammar, which are now located on the Review tab.

In other cases, part of the functionality that used to be accessed from a dialog box is now available from a button's drop-down list. For example, on the Page Layout tab, the Orientation button opens a menu containing Portrait and Landscape, as shown in Figure 1.8. Having common options available directly from a tab, rather than having to open a dialog box to access them, is one of the major usability improvements in Word 2007.

Some buttons' menus contain *galleries*, which are collections of presets you can apply. In some cases, you can also save custom settings to create your own presets that appear on these menus. For example, on the Insert tab, the Header button opens a Header Gallery from which you can select a preformatted document header. You can remove or edit one of these presets by right-clicking it and selecting from its shortcut menu, as shown in Figure 1.9.

Figure 1.8
Many buttons, such as this one, open drop-down lists containing the most common settings.

Notice also the command at the bottom of that menu—you can add the selected text in the document to the gallery as a new header preset, which will then appear on this menu.

Figure 1.9
Some buttons open galleries of presets.

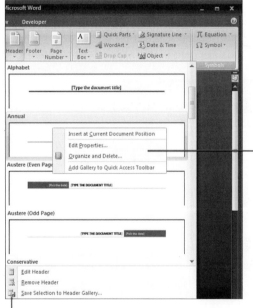

Right-click a gallery entry for its menu

Add selected text from the document to the gallery

Some galleries—or at least the first line of them—appear directly on a tab. If you want to select one of the items that appears in that first row, you simply click it from the tab. For example, in Figure 1.10, you can apply one of the four style examples from the Styles group on the Home tab by clicking it. To see the rest of the gallery, you can either click the single down-pointing arrow to scroll down to the next row of the gallery, or open the full gallery by clicking the More button (the down arrow with the line over it).

Click here for the next row of gallery entries

Figure 1.10
Some galleries appear
directly on a tab.

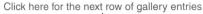
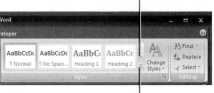

Click the More button to open
the full gallery as a list

Sometimes even with all the gallery entries, however, the presets aren't enough and you need the full dialog box. Most of the dialog boxes from Word 2003 are still available in Word 2007, and can easily be accessed from the ribbon.

Some buttons that have drop-down lists have a command at the bottom for opening the associated dialog box. For example, in Figure 1.11, notice that the Columns button not only contains some presets, but also a More Columns command. Clicking More Columns opens the Columns dialog box, from which you can choose less-common column settings, such as unequal widths.

Figure 1.11
Select the "More"
command from a but-
ton's list to open its
dialog box.

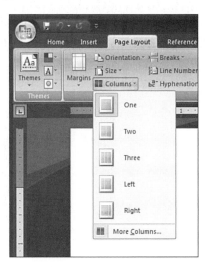

In addition, some of the groups have dialog boxes associated with them. Look in the bottom-right corner of a group for a dialog box launcher icon. If a group has one of these, you can click the icon to open a dialog box from which you can control settings applicable to that group. For example, in Figure 1.12, notice that most of the groups on the Home tab have these. Each one opens a different dialog box.

Figure 1.12
Some groups have
dialog boxes associ-
ated with them.

Dialog box launcher icons

> Despite the name, not all of the dialog box launcher icons open actual dialog boxes. For example, the one in the Clipboard group in Figure 1.12 opens the Clipboard task pane, and the one in the Styles group opens the Styles task pane.

SHAPE STYLES

Just as text styles can be applied to text paragraphs to ensure consistency, now in Word 2007 *shape styles* can be applied to graphic objects. Word provides a variety of interesting styles that include gradients, tints, borders, and shadows. These effects can be applied to virtually any graphic object created within Word, including AutoShapes, SmartArt diagrams, charts, and WordArt. This is yet another way in which Word's 2007 interface saves you time—you no longer have to set up shape formatting such as gradients, borders, and colors manually for each object.

Shape styles are available from the Format tab, which is present only when a graphic object is selected. As with other galleries, you can select one of the styles displayed in the first row, as in Figure 1.13, or you can click the More arrow to open the full gallery.

Click a shape style

Figure 1.13
Apply shape styles to graphic objects such as AutoShapes.

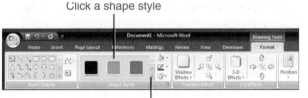

Click here for the entire gallery

NOTE

> As you work with the various galleries, such as the shape styles just described, *Live Preview* is in effect. When you hover the mouse pointer over a gallery object, in most cases the selected text or object is previewed using its formatting. So, for example, if you're looking for a shape style, you can run your mouse pointer over the available styles and see how each one will look before you commit to one.

→ To learn more about formatting graphic objects, **see** "Formatting Drawn Objects," **p. 427**.

FORMATTING THEMES

Themes are like styles, except they apply to the entire document as a whole, not just one particular type of text or object. For each text or graphic object, you can manually format it, or you can leave its formatting set to automatic. When an object's formatting is automatic, it derives its formatting from whatever the theme specifies. You can then change the entire document's appearance at once by applying a different theme.

Themes contain three formatting aspects: theme colors, theme fonts, and theme effects.

Theme colors are a set of color placeholders. As you are assigning colors to text and objects in your document, you have a choice of assigning a fixed color or a placeholder color. If you assign a placeholder color, then when the color theme changes, that object's color changes too. Figure 1.14 shows a typical color picker in Word 2007. The top row of colors are the colors in the current theme; the tints and shades beneath each color are those same colors with light/dark modifiers applied. Beneath the theme colors are standard colors; these do not change when you change the color theme.

Figure 1.14
When selecting a color, you can apply theme colors or fixed colors.

To switch to a different color theme, select one from the Theme Colors list, found in the Themes group on the Page Layout tab.

Theme fonts are a pair of fonts applied to text depending on the paragraph style. The *Heading font* applies to all text to which a heading style is applied; the *Body font* applies to all text to which a body style is applied. Theme fonts are used only if the text does not have some other font applied to it. If you have selected some text and manually chosen a font for it, for example, the theme fonts will not apply. Similarly, if you have created a style and defined a certain font for it, and that style is applied to a paragraph, that paragraph will not use the theme fonts.

So when will theme fonts be applied, then? Theme fonts are applied whenever the text has the font set to either Heading or Body rather than a specific font. By default in the Normal template, the Normal style's font is Body, and the styles for the built-in headings are set to Heading. Perhaps you've noticed that in brand-new documents, the font listed in the Font group on the Home tab is Calibri (Body). That means that the Body placeholder is in effect, and that Calibri happens to be the font specified by the font theme currently in use. To change to a different font theme, choose one from the Theme Fonts list, in the Themes group on the Page Layout tab.

The third and final type of theme is *theme effects*. This type of theme applies to graphic objects such as SmartArt and charts, and applies different textures and shapes to the objects that comprise a chart or diagram. For example, some theme effects apply rounded corners to the bars on a bar chart, or make them look like shiny plastic.

You can apply themes for effects, fonts, and colors separately using their individual buttons on the Page Layout tab (in the Themes group), or you can use the Themes button's gallery to select an overall theme to the document that is a combination of all three (see Figure 1.15).

Themes
Color themes
Font themes
Effect themes

Figure 1.15
Apply themes from
the Page Layout tab.

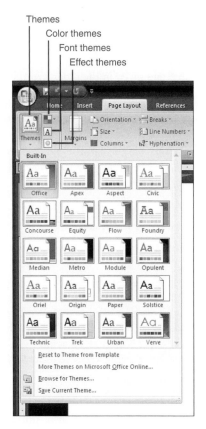

→ To learn more about themes, **see** "Working with Themes," **p. 256**.

NEW FILE FORMATS

From Word 97 through Word 2003, there was a common file format (doc). This made it very easy to exchange documents between versions, but it also held back the innovators at Microsoft who wanted to put new features into Word that the old file format would not support.

In Word 2007, there's a whole new file format, with a new extension: docx. This file format is quite a departure from earlier ones in many ways, but perhaps the biggest difference is that it's based on eXtensible Markup Language (XML). You'll learn more about this in the section "Selecting an Appropriate File Format" of Chapter 2, "Creating and Saving Documents." Basically, though, it means two things: smaller file size and files that are less prone to unrecoverable corruption. So this move to XML is a good thing.

Word 2007 also has full support for the earlier file format, though, and you can even set the 97-2003 format to be the default one if you frequently need to share documents with others who have not yet upgraded to Word 2007 (or downloaded an Office 2007 Compatibility update to make docx files readable in older versions of Word). If you use the older file format, though, you miss out on many of the coolest new features in Word. Which brings me to the next point….

SUPPORT FOR LEGACY FEATURES

Word 2007 implements familiar features in some very different ways. All the graphics in items such as charts and SmartArt, for example, are based upon a brand-new graphics engine called Escher 2.0. Those graphics can't be created and saved in the older Word 97-2003 file format.

To get around this problem, Word 2007 offers fairly good support for the earlier versions of most of the graphics-manipulation tools from Word 2003. For example, charts in Word 2003 were created by a program called Microsoft Graph. If you create a chart in Word 2007 while working in a file that's in Word 97-2003 file format, the old Microsoft Graph tools appear within the Word 2007 user interface. The same goes for other parts of the program, such as the equation editor and diagrams.

In a few parts of this book, I'll cover both the new Word 2007 and the legacy methods of doing things, but mostly I'll assume you're going full-speed ahead with the Word 2007 file format and its benefits.

NOTE

> If at any point in this book you run into a situation where the tools you see onscreen are radically different from what's shown, check to make sure you are not working in Compatibility Mode, which is the mode for Word 97-2003 documents. If you see Compatibility Mode in the title bar of the Word window, choose Office, Convert to convert the document to Word 2007 format.

BUILDING BLOCKS

Users of Word 2003 and earlier versions are perhaps familiar with AutoText, a feature that stored stock text phrases and even entire paragraphs for easy insertion into multiple documents. AutoText was very popular with law offices, for example, because certain boilerplate clauses could be inserted into contracts with no retyping.

The Building Blocks feature in Word 2007 is like AutoText on steroids (only legal). You can use it to save text blocks, but that's just the beginning. You can also save entire pages, including multiple graphic objects, and you can create your own galleries of headers, footers, watermarks, cover pages, and more. To access building blocks, click the Quick Parts button on the Insert tab and then choose Building Blocks Organizer.

→ For more information on Building Blocks, **see** "Working with Building Blocks," **p. 90**.

CITATION TOOLS

Any student who has ever had to write a research paper and use correct MLA or APA citation format will really appreciate this next feature. Word 2007 contains a brand-new Manage Sources feature that keeps track of each of the sources you refer to in your research paper, and then generates a properly formatted bibliography automatically. No more looking up obscure citation formatting in dusty reference books! The feature supports all the most popular citation formats (plus some you've probably never heard of!), including APA, MLA, Chicago Manual of Style, GOST, and Turabian.

→ To learn about the Manage Sources feature, **see** "Understanding Sources and Citations," **p. 720**.

CUSTOMIZATION

If you like to customize Word, there's some good news and some bad news in Word 2007.

First some good news: Certain aspects of Word are highly customizable. For example, you can fine-tune the status bar at the bottom of the Word window to display any of a wide variety of statistics about the document and its status. Just right-click the status bar and toggle items on/off from the menu that appears. Many other aspects of the program can be customized by choosing Office, Word Options.

Then there's some bad news: The ribbon portion of the user interface (that is, the buttons that appear on the tabs, and the tabs themselves) is much less customizable in Word 2007 than in earlier versions. Word no longer provides a convenient, easy-to-use way of creating and customizing toolbars and menus. You can add and remove buttons from the Quick Access toolbar, but that's about the extent of it.

Then some semi-good news: Microsoft offers a method of customizing the ribbon called RibbonX. It's an XML-based utility that enables you to create custom groups on ribbons and even entire custom ribbons.

More bad news: RibbonX is very difficult to use unless you have XML programming experience, and incorporating your customized tabs into the Word ribbon is awkward to set up.

And now the best news of all: As an owner of this book, you have a couple of great resources at your disposal:

- Chapter 35, "Using RibbonX," provides a guide to using RibbonX and doesn't assume any prior experience with XML. Armed with this chapter, you should be able to do your own ribbon customization, although it might take some time and effort.
- Patrick Schmid, who wrote the "Using RibbonX" chapter, is also a talented programmer, and has written a handy utility for automating the ribbon-customization process. You'll find a free copy of it on this book's CD. So while you might enjoy reading Chapter 35 and learning something about how ribbons work behind the scenes, you might prefer to use Patrick's automated tool.

WORKING WITH VIEWS

Setting an optimal view for your needs can make a tremendous difference in Word's usability. Not only can you choose among various document views (such as Draft, Print Layout, and so on), but you can zoom in and out within those views. You can also display or hide onscreen elements such as rulers and gridlines, and display multiple document windows simultaneously. The following sections explain these viewing options.

SWITCHING DOCUMENT VIEWS

Word 2007 offers five views:

- **Print Layout view**—Shows most document features as they will print, including headers, footers, graphics, and columns. You see the entire page, all the way to the edges of the paper, so you can gauge the margins visually.

CAUTION

Print Layout is not always completely accurate in showing how the document will print. For a fully accurate picture, use Print Preview (Office, Print, Print Preview).

- **Full Screen Reading view**—Shows the document in two book-style columns, with large font, and with the ribbon and other screen elements hidden. You can use the right- and left-arrow keys to move between pages. There is also a variety of special reading tools available here, as explained in the section "Working in Full Screen Reading View" of Chapter 27, "Working with Comments and Revision Tracking."
- **Web Layout view**—Shows the document as it will appear in a web browser. This view is suitable for creating web pages and email messages.
- **Outline view**—Shows the document as collapsible levels of headings, so you can see the document's structure at a glance. To learn more about the tools available in this view, see the "Outline Basics" section of Chapter 22, "Outlining and Summarizing Documents."
- **Draft view**—Shows just the main text of the document; you don't see graphics, headers, footers, or multiple columns. Also, page breaks and section breaks are represented by horizontal lines rather than actual breaks. This view uses less memory than others to draw the display, and can make a performance difference on a very slow PC.

NOTE

If you try to create graphics or work with other document elements that aren't supported in Draft view, Word automatically switches to Print Layout view.

The quickest way to switch views is to click one of the view buttons in the bottom-right corner of the Word window (see Figure 1.16).

Print Layout
Web Layout
Draft

Figure 1.16
Switch views from the status bar.

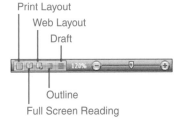

Outline
Full Screen Reading

You can also switch views from the View tab; each view has its own button in the Document Views group (see Figure 1.17). (This View tab figures heavily into the view customizations described in the following sections as well.)

Figure 1.17
The View tab provides a variety of viewing options, including Document Views.

SHOWING OR HIDING ONSCREEN ELEMENTS

The Show/Hide group of the View tab has several check boxes that turn special elements on/off:

- **Ruler**—In Print Layout, Web Layout, and Draft views, this option displays a horizontal ruler across the top of the document, with markers for margins, indents, and tab stops. If you're in Print Layout view, you also get a vertical ruler along the left side of the document.

- **Gridlines**—A nonprinting grid of squares that fills the area within the margins. It can be useful to help align graphic objects more precisely.

- **Message Bar**—When a document information bar is available for the document, such as when you're working with Information Rights Management, that bar can be toggled on or off here.

- **Document Map**—An outline of the document headings that appears in a separate pane to the left of the main document. It can provide you with a way of seeing the outline and the full document simultaneously, and you can click a heading in the document map to jump to that portion of the document.

- **Thumbnails**—A set of small pictures (thumbnails) of each page of the document, in a separate pane to the left of the main document. You can scroll through the thumbnails and click the page to which you want to jump. This is useful if the pages have content that, visually, is easily recognizable.

→ To learn more about the document map or thumbnails, **see** "Locating Specific Content," **p. 79**.

CHANGING THE ZOOM

The zoom is the size of the document within the document window. It is an onscreen setting only; it has no effect on the printed version. A higher zoom percentage (such as 400%) makes everything very large, and you can't see very much at once. A lower zoom percentage (such as 50%) makes everything small so you can see entire pages at once (but you'll probably find them harder to read).

The easiest way to adjust the zoom is to drag the Zoom slider on the status bar, or to click the minus or plus button at either end of the Zoom slider (see Figure 1.18).

Decrease zoom   Increase zoom

Figure 1.18
Change the zoom by
dragging the Zoom
slider or incrementing
its setting by clicking a
button at one end or
the other.

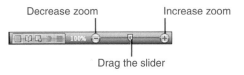

Drag the slider

You can also adjust the zoom from the View tab, shown in Figure 1.17. The One Page, Two Pages, and Page Width buttons do just what their names imply: They adjust the zoom level for optimal viewing depending on the size of your Word window. For example, if your Word window is maximized on a 1024×768 resolution display, a One Page zoom would be 55%. On a higher-resolution display, a One Page zoom would be a higher percentage than that.

The Zoom button on the View tab opens a Zoom dialog box, in which you can enter an exact zoom percentage (see Figure 1.19).

Figure 1.19
Use the Zoom dialog
box to set an exact
zoom amount.

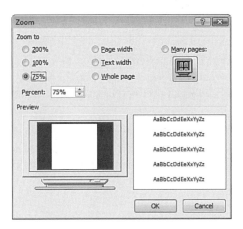

DISPLAYING MULTIPLE DOCUMENTS AND WINDOWS

Word allows multiple documents to be open at once, each in its own window. By default, only one window appears at once, but you can arrange the windows so that several are visible at once, as you would arrange any other windows. Each document has its own ribbon and other controls in its window.

NOTE

In earlier versions of Word, it was possible to have multiple documents open in subwindows within a single copy of the Word window. This is not possible in Word 2007. Each document has its own full set of Word controls.

To switch between open Word documents, select the desired document from the Windows task bar, or click the Switch Windows button on the View tab in Word and choose from the list of open documents (see Figure 1.20). (This is the same list that was on the Window menu in earlier Word versions.)

Figure 1.20
The Switch Windows button lists all the open documents so you can switch between them.

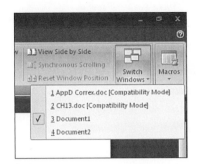

In addition to manually arranging document windows onscreen, you can use some arrangement shortcuts that are built into Word (on the View tab):

- **New Window**—Opens a second window containing a copy of the active document. The copies are joined, so changes made in one copy are automatically reflected in the other copy. You can use the second copy to scroll to a different spot in the document, so you can view multiple locations simultaneously.

- **Split**—Creates a split line within the active document, and provides separate scroll bars on each side of the split. That way, you can scroll to two different parts of the documents at once without opening a whole separate Word window.

- **Arrange All**—Arranges all open Word document windows so that each one takes up an equal amount of space onscreen.

- **View Side by Side**—Arranges the active document and one other document of your choice, side by side. If there are only two documents open, it uses those two; if there are more than that, a dialog box appears asking what you want the second document to be.

- **Synchronous Scrolling**—When View Side by Side is active, this option locks the scrolling of the two documents so that scrolling in one also scrolls in the other an equal amount (if possible).

- **Reset Window Position**—When View Side by Side is active, this option resets the arrangement of the two windows to the original size and shape—with each window side by side, taking up half the available space each.

USING THE HELP SYSTEM

Over the years and versions, Microsoft has tried many different ways of helping users access the onscreen documentation, trying to figure out what works best. Each version of Word has had a radically redesigned Help system, and Word 2007 is no exception.

The entryway to the Help system in Word 2007 is the Help icon, the small blue circle with a question mark in the upper-right corner of the Word window. Either click it or press F1 to open the Word Help window.

Help is context-sensitive, so depending on what you were doing when you asked for help, a different listing might appear. If you were not doing anything that triggers a certain section of help, a general Browse Word 2007 Help window appears, as in Figure 1.21. From here you can click any topic to see subtopics, and eventually you'll arrive at specific instructions for doing something.

Figure 1.21
Browse help topics from the main Word Help window.

TIP

> If the Help window takes a long time to display its content, try switching it offline. To do so, click Connected to Office Online in the status bar to open a menu. On the menu, click Show Content Only from This Computer. Only the basic Word help information will be available, but it'll be available more quickly.

The following buttons are available in the Word Help window:

Use the Back arrow button to move back to the previous Help screen.

After using Back, use the Forward arrow button to move forward again.

Click Stop to stop a page from loading (for example, if it is loading from the Web and is taking too long).

Click Refresh to refresh the display of the page (for example, if it is located online and did not load properly the first time).

To return to the general index of topics, click the Home button.

Click the Print button to print the displayed topic.

Click the Change Font Size button to open a list of font sizes, and select the one that works best for your vision.

Click Show Table of Contents to open a Table of Contents pane at the left, from which you can browse the same topics as on the main page shown in Figure 1.21 without leaving the current page you're looking at.

Click the Keep On Top button to toggle the Word Help window between always being on top and being an ordinary stackable window.

Another way to get help is to search for topics or keywords of interest. To do this, type a word in the Search box at the top of the Word Help window and then press Enter or click Search. For example, Figure 1.22 shows the list of topics when searching for "numbering."

Figure 1.22
Search the help system for the topic you need help with.

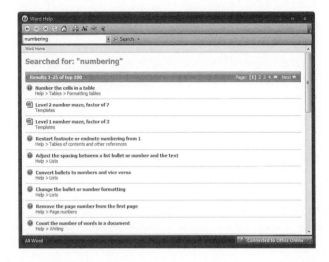

Within a help article, blue or brown words are hyperlinks. Point at one and it becomes underlined. Click it to go to a different topic. The color of the hyperlink depends on whether or not it has been visited (that is, previously clicked on).

TROUBLESHOOTING

HELP SEARCHES ARE SLOW OR PROVIDE TOO MANY RESULTS

Sometimes Word can be *too* helpful when it comes to finding help information. Every time you search for even the simplest thing, it does a full-scale search, including web resources.

If you just want the basic steps for performing tasks, restrict the help search to only Word Help. To do so, in the Word Help window, click the down arrow to the right of the Search button, and on the menu that appears, choose Word Help (see Figure 1.23).

Figure 1.23
Confine the scope of help searches to make them faster and more targeted.

I CAN'T FIND CERTAIN COMMANDS FROM WORD 2003

You're not alone. Lots of features have shifted in Word 2007. Fortunately, though, there are many resources for finding the lost features. Start with Appendix D, "Command Reference: Word 2003 to Word 2007." If you don't find your answer there, consult the Help system:

1. Click the Help button.

2. In the Search box, type **Word 2003** and press Enter.

3. In the search results, click Reference: Locations of Word 2003 Commands in Word 2007.

Microsoft has also made an interactive utility available for finding features. Press F1 for the Help system, and then click **What's New**. Click **Reference: Location of Word 2003 Commands in Word 2007**. Scroll down to the bottom of the page and click **Interactive: Word 2003 to Word 2007 Command Reference Guide**.

CHAPTER 2

CREATING AND SAVING DOCUMENTS

In this chapter

STARTING A NEW DOCUMENT

When Word starts, it displays a single blank document, ready for editing. This blank document is set up with generic settings that are appropriate for a variety of uses; it has single-spaced, 11-point text and standard margins of 1" on all sides. You can use this document or you can create another one.

 If the default new documents do not have those settings, see "New Documents Are Using Word 2003 Settings" in the Troubleshooting section at the end of this chapter.

CREATING A BLANK DOCUMENT

To create a new, blank document with the same settings as the one that appears automatically when Word starts, press Ctrl+N or do the following:

1. Choose Office, New.

 To access the Office menu, click the circular graphic in the top-left corner of the Word window.

2. In the New Document dialog box (see Figure 2.1), click Blank Document and then click Create.

Figure 2.1
The New Document dialog box contains a Blank Document icon for creating a new blank document.

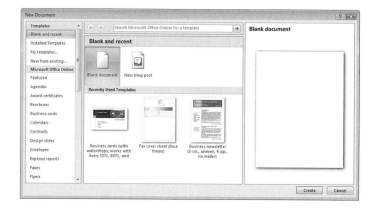

TIP

To add a shortcut for the New Document dialog box to the Quick Access toolbar, open the Office menu, right-click New, and click Add to Quick Access Toolbar.

Blank documents are based on the Normal.dotm template. Notice the *m* at the end of the template name; this stands for "macro-enabled." In Word 2007, there are three types of Word templates: Word 97-2003 templates for backward compatibility (.dot extension), regular Word templates (.dotx extension), and macro-enabled templates (.dotm extension). You will learn more about these in Chapter 10, "Using and Creating Project Templates."

NOTE

Normal.dotm is a hidden file. Depending on your Windows version, it is stored either in Users*username*\Application Data\Microsoft\Templates (Windows Vista) or in Documents and Settings*username*\Application Data\Microsoft\Templates (Windows XP), where *username* is the currently logged in Windows user. A separate copy is maintained for each local user of the PC (based on Windows login).

→ To learn more about template types, **see** "About Templates," **p. 298**.

Adding a Toolbar Button for a New Blank Document

In earlier versions of Word, there was a New Document button on the toolbar that created a new blank document based on Normal.dot, without going through a dialog box. Word 2007 does not have that button by default, although its shortcut key combination remains usable (Ctrl+N). Here's how to add it to the Quick Access toolbar:

1. Choose Office, Word Options.
2. Click Customize.
3. In the Choose Commands From list, choose All Commands.
4. Click New Blank Document on the list of commands.
5. Click Add to add it to the Quick Access toolbar.
6. Click OK.

→ To learn more about customizing the Quick Access toolbar, **see** "Customizing the Quick Access Toolbar," **p. 936**.

CREATING A DOCUMENT BASED ON A TEMPLATE

In addition to the basic blank document template, Word also offers dozens of specialized templates for items such as resumes, newsletters, and business cards. Most of the templates have sample text and graphics in them, as well as styles and other formatting set up to facilitate the chosen document type. For example, the Screenplay template has styles called Dialogue, Character, Action, and so on.

→ For more information about styles, **see** "Understanding Styles," **p. 228**.

Word 2007 installs a few simple templates on your hard disk for items such as letters and reports, and it makes many other templates available via Office Online. Here are the steps to access these templates:

1. Choose Office, New. The New Document dialog box opens.
2. To access the locally stored templates, click Installed Templates.

   To access the Office Online templates, click one of the categories listed under Microsoft Office Online (see Figure 2.2).
3. Click the desired template. (For some Office Online template categories, you might need to click through one or more layers of subcategories to get to the templates.)

4. Click Create or Download to start the document.

   The command differs depending on the template's location; a local template shows Create, whereas a template from Office Online shows Download.

Figure 2.2
Create a document based on a Word template by selecting from the Office Online categories.

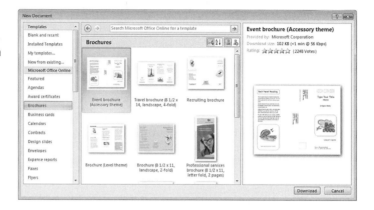

TIP

> One of the installed templates, Office Word 2003 Look, creates documents with the same settings as the default blank document from Word 2003. It's essentially the same as the Normal.dot file from earlier Word versions.

The installed templates include not only templates, but also *wizards*. A wizard is a dialog box interface that walks you through the process of creating a complex document. You just fill in the blanks presented to you. You can distinguish them from regular templates by the word *Wizard* in the name, such as Newsletter Wizard.

Templates you create yourself are stored in the default template folder, which is Users*username*\Application Data\Microsoft\Templates if you are running Windows Vista, or Documents and Settings*username*\Application Data\Microsoft\Templates if you are running Windows XP.

To access these local templates, follow these steps:

1. Choose Office, New. The New Document dialog box opens.
2. Click My Templates. The New dialog box opens (see Figure 2.3). Icons appear for the templates stored in the default template folder.
3. Click a template and then click OK to create a new document based on it.

→ To create your own templates, **see** "Creating Your Own Templates," **p. 310**.

Figure 2.3
Use templates you've created yourself by selecting My Templates.

CAUTION

The templates stored in the default template storage location are specific to the user logged into Windows. If some other user logs into the same PC, that user will not have access to these templates. To make a template available to all users on the local PC, place it in the workgroup template folder.

→ To set up a workgroup template folder, **see** "Accessing Workgroup Templates," **p. 304**.

SAVING A DOCUMENT

"Save early, save often," as the saying goes, to avoid losing any work due to unexpected power outages or program crashes. Word 2007 offers many saving options, including saves in different formats and to different locations.

The basic save is the same as in any other program. Use any of these methods:

- Click the Save button on the Quick Access toolbar.
- Press Ctrl+S.
- Choose Office, Save.
- Exit Word (Office, Exit Word) without saving the document and then click Yes when asked if you want to save your changes.

For an unsaved document, the Save As dialog box opens, and you specify the file's name, location, and type. For a previously saved document, the changes are automatically saved (no dialog box opens).

If you simply open the Office menu and click Save As, the Save As dialog box reopens as it did initially. However, if you pause on the arrow to the right of the Save As command, a submenu appears from which you can choose to save in Word 97-2003 format (see Figure 2.4).

Figure 2.4
The Save As command opens a fly-out menu with shortcuts to common "Save As" activities.

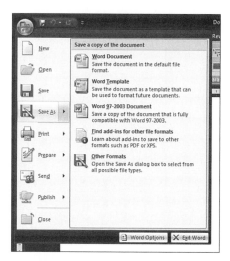

The Save As dialog box is different depending on whether you are running Word under Windows XP or Windows Vista, especially when it comes to navigating between locations. The following sections explain the procedures for each version separately.

NOTE

The navigation techniques explained in the following sections also apply to the Open dialog box, as well as to almost all other dialog boxes in which you select files within Word 2007.

CHANGING THE FILE SAVE LOCATION (WINDOWS VISTA)

With Vista, the Save As dialog box has a navigation bar across the top with *breadcrumbs* on it that point to the path of the location shown. You can click the arrow to the right of one of those folder names to open a menu of other locations you can jump to at that level, as shown in Figure 2.5. To see a top-level list of locations (such as Computer, Network, etc.), click the arrow to the right of the leftmost item. (In Figure 2.5, the leftmost item is a folder icon.)

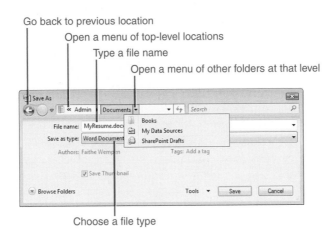

Go back to previous location

Open a menu of top-level locations

Type a file name

Open a menu of other folders at that level

Figure 2.5
The Save As dialog
box under Windows
Vista has a new way
of changing locations.

Choose a file type

> **TIP**
>
> The Save As dialog box is resizable (larger only, not smaller); just drag its bottom-right corner.

Select the desired save location, enter a name for the file, select a file type, and then click Save. After a document has been saved, you can resave it with different settings using the Office, Save As command.

> **NOTE**
>
> Save Thumbnails saves a preview of the first page of the document so that the preview will appear rather than a generic icon when browsing for files to open in the Open dialog box.

Notice in Figure 2.5 that there is no pane displayed for browsing folders by default. That's because you don't necessarily need to see a list of existing files in order to save a new one.

If you prefer to see a list of existing files in the chosen location, or if you want to work with some file management tools within the dialog box, click the Browse Folders button to display extra controls. With Browse Folders open, as in Figure 2.6, several additional areas become available:

- A Favorite Links pane, from which you can select among common locations like Computer or Desktop.
- A file list displaying the contents of the currently selected location.
- A toolbar containing an Organize menu, a Views menu, and a New Folder button.

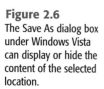

Manage files from the Organize menu
Use Views to change the file listing
Click to create a new folder

Figure 2.6
The Save As dialog box under Windows Vista can display or hide the content of the selected location.

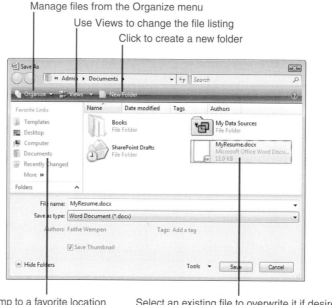

Jump to a favorite location   Select an existing file to overwrite it if desired

---

Managing Files in the Save As Dialog Box

While you're in the Save As dialog box (or the Open dialog box, for that matter), you can do some simple file management tasks. Most of these work in both the Windows Vista and Windows XP versions of the dialog boxes.

The Organize menu (in Windows Vista only) contains commands for many common file operations; click the Organize button shown in Figure 2.6 to access it.

You can also use shortcut keys or right-click operations to work with files. To copy a file or folder, select it and press Ctrl+C (or right-click it and choose Copy), then move to the desired location and press Ctrl+V (or right-click an empty area and choose Paste).

To move a file or folder, select it and press Ctrl+X (or right-click it and choose Cut), move to the desired location, and press Ctrl+V (or right-click an empty area and choose Paste).

To delete a file or folder, select it and press Delete (or right-click it and choose Delete).

CHANGING THE FILE SAVE LOCATION (WINDOWS XP)

Under Windows XP, Word 2007's Save As dialog box is very much the same as it was in earlier Word versions. To display a different location in the Save As dialog box, open the Save In drop-down list and select the desired location. If it doesn't appear on the list, select the drive and then drill down until you get to the desired folder within it (see Figure 2.7).

Figure 2.7
Under Windows XP, the Save As dialog box works as it did in Word 2003.

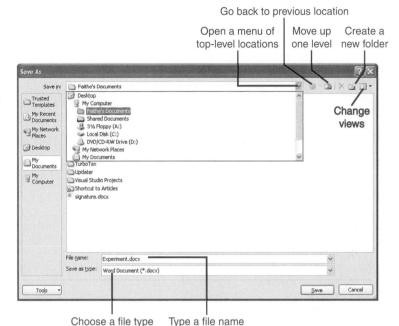

Go back to previous location

Open a menu of top-level locations

Move up one level

Create a new folder

Change views

Choose a file type   Type a file name

SAVING TO REMOTE LOCATIONS

The preceding sections covered saving to your local hard disk or other local drives, but what about when you need to save to drives on other systems, such as network drives, Web servers, or FTP locations? The following sections address some of these special situations.

SAVING TO A NETWORK LOCATION

A *network location* is one that's accessible from your personal or business LAN, without connecting to the Internet. Under either Windows Vista or Windows XP, there are two ways to select a network location. You can either choose a network favorite shortcut that has already been set up on the system, or you can browse the entire network for valid locations to which to save.

For Windows Vista:

- To choose an existing network shortcut, click Browse Folders to display the Favorite Links list, select Network Shortcuts from that list, and then select the desired shortcut's icon.
- To browse the entire network, click the arrow to the left of the leftmost (topmost) level in the path and choose Network from the menu that appears (see Figure 2.8). Then browse the entire network via the icons that appear for available network resources.

Click here to open the top-level menu
Choose Network

Figure 2.8
Select Network to browse all network resources.

For Windows XP, start out by clicking My Network Places on the Favorites bar, or selecting My Network Places from the Save In list. After that:

■ To choose an existing network shortcut (called a Network Favorite under XP), double-click any of the shortcuts that appear on the My Network Places list.

■ To browse the entire network, double-click the Entire Network icon and then navigate to the desired network location.

Some networks have mapped drives, so certain network locations appear as drive letters on the local PC. Treat these like any other drive.

SAVING TO A WEB LOCATION

To save to a web location, type the URL in the File name text box and press Enter. A prompt will appear for your username and password. Enter them, and the folders on that web server will appear like local folders on your hard disk. Check with the hosting company to make sure you know the correct folder in which to save.

SAVING TO AN FTP SITE

FTP stands for *File Transfer Protocol*, an older way of transferring files on the Internet. Word 2007 can save directly to an FTP server using Windows' built-in FTP protocols.

In Windows Vista, follow these steps to save to an FTP location:

1. Choose Office, Save As.

2. In the File name box, type the complete path to which you want to save. For example, if the server is ftp.wempen.com and the file name to use is myfile.docx, the path would be ftp://ftp.wempen.com/myfile.docx.

3. Click Save. The FTP Log On dialog box opens.

4. Click the User button, and enter your user name and password for the FTP server.

5. Click OK.

In Windows XP, the FTP capabilities are actually a bit more robust than in Windows Vista, in that you can save FTP locations as favorites. Follow these steps:

1. Click Office, Save As.

2. Open the Save In drop-down list.

3. If the FTP site you want already appears on the list, select it and skip to step 7. Otherwise, choose Add/Modify FTP Locations.

4. In the Add/Modify FTP Locations dialog box, fill in the information needed for the connection:

   ■ **Name of FTP site**—Include the full FTP address here, such as ftp.que.com.

   ■ **Log on as**—Click User and then type the username.

   ■ **Password**—Enter the password given to you for logging into this server.

5. Click Add to add this FTP site to the list of sites.

6. Click OK.

7. On the FTP server, navigate to the folder where you want to save and then continue saving normally.

CHANGING THE LOCATIONS IN THE FAVORITE LINKS LIST OR FAVORITES BAR

Depending on the Windows version you have, there is either a Favorite Links List or a Favorites bar available for providing quick access to the most common locations.

CHANGING THE FAVORITE LINKS LIST (WINDOWS VISTA)

If you have Windows Vista, a Favorite Links List appears in the Save As and Open dialog boxes, as well as most other related dialog boxes that browse for files to open. This list provides shortcuts for the locations to which you most frequently save. You can add a folder to it by dragging any folder from the folder list into the Favorite Links List pane, or remove a folder from it by right-clicking its shortcut and choosing Remove Link.

CHANGING THE FAVORITES BAR (WINDOWS XP)

If you have Windows XP, a Favorites bar appears to the left of the file listing in the Save As and Open dialog boxes. It contains shortcuts to commonly selected locations.

The Windows XP Favorites bar starts out with six shortcuts: Trusted Templates, My Recent Documents, My Network Places, Desktop, My Documents, and My Computer. You can add your own favorite locations to this list. Here's how:

1. Display the location for which you want to create an icon.

2. Right-click the Favorites bar and choose Add *location*, where *location* is the folder name.

To remove a shortcut from the Favorites bar, right-click it and choose Remove. To rename an item, right-click it and choose Rename. Then type the new name. Both of those activities work only with items you have added to the bar yourself, not with the default items there.

To rearrange the order of the items in the Favorites bar, right-click an item and choose Move Up or Move Down. Any of the items can be rearranged, even the default ones.

> **TIP**
>
> You can fit more items on the Favorites bar at once if you display them as small icons, but they look more like they did in earlier versions of Word if you display them as large icons. To switch the icon size, right-click the Favorites bar and choose Large Icons or Small Icons.

SELECTING AN APPROPRIATE FILE FORMAT

Word 2007's file format, like those in other Office 2007 applications, is based on eXtensible Markup Language (XML). XML is a type of markup language in which plain text is used to express both the literal text of the document and the coding that specifies what to do with that text. It is a close cousin to Hypertext Markup Language (HTML), the markup language used on the web. (In fact, the latest version of HTML, called XHTML, is actually created with XML.)

There are many good reasons for Word 2007's adoption of a new file format based on XML:

- The files are smaller than in previous version formats.
- When a file is corrupted, it is easier to extract the data from it because the content can be separated from the formatting.
- Using XML makes it possible for third-party developers to build application solutions that can work with Office data.
- Files can include many types of objects, such as graphics and charts, and still be fully XML-compatible. In Office 2003, an XML format was available but it didn't fully support all the graphic object types that the applications could create or import.

When I first encountered the new Word 2007 format, known as WordML, I tried to open the file in a text editor. After all, I thought, regular XML files open in a text editor, and these are XML, so why shouldn't it work?

Well, it didn't work, and here's why. WordML files are not plain XML files. They are actually compressed archives (ZIP files, to be exact) that contain multiple XML files. You can open one using a plain text editor, but first you have to extract the files from it.

If you want to give it a try, follow these steps:

1. Create a new Word 2007 document. Type a few lines of text in it, and then save it and exit Word.

2. In Windows, browse to the folder where you saved the file. Select the file, copy it (Ctrl+C), and paste the copy (Ctrl+V).

3. Make sure the display of file extensions is enabled. See "I Can't See the File Extensions" in the Troubleshooting section at the end of this chapter for instructions on turning them on.

4. Right-click the copy of the file and choose Rename. Rename the file to test.zip. A warning appears; click Yes. Now the file has a different icon.

5. Double-click the file to open it in a Windows Explorer window. There'll be a [Content_Types].xml file, plus three folders: _rels, docProps, and word.

6. Double-click the Word folder, and then double-click document.xml. The document opens in Internet Explorer showing the XML markup. Scroll down through the file and locate the text you typed in the document. Figure 2.9 shows an example.

7. Close Internet Explorer and delete the copy you created.

Figure 2.9
The XML source code behind the document text for a Word 2007 document.

Besides being an interesting exercise that helps you understand the new format, the preceding steps can also be used to help you recover text from a corrupted file. You can always open a Word 2007 document this way and manually copy-and-paste text out of it.

→ To learn other ways of recovering the content of corrupted files, **see** Appendix A, "Recovering Files and Repairing Word," **p. 975**.

NOTE

Microsoft is doing something revolutionary with file extensions in Office 2007: They're breaking out of the three-character extension limit. The original limit was imposed by MS-DOS's 8-3 naming convention; files were limited to eight characters for the name and three characters for the extension. To maintain backward compatibility with MS-DOS systems, files had to adhere to that limitation. Backward compatibility with such systems is still possible by using one of the older formats, but the new formats will work only under operating systems that support long filenames. (Both Windows 9x forward and the Mac OS do.)

For many previous versions, Word used the same file format for its documents, which made it easy to transfer files between PCs of different versions. That format is called Word 97-2003, a nod to the fact that the format didn't change over all those versions: Word 97, Word 2000, Word XP, and Word 2003.

However, Word 2007's new XML-based file format changes all this. The new format is not backward-compatible with earlier Word versions—or for that matter, with any other word processing application. (Microsoft does offer a compatibility pack for free download that can enable earlier Word versions to open Word 2007 files, but you can't assume that everyone—or even most people—will have it.) Therefore, it's important to choose an appropriate file format for a document based on the needs of others who might be working with it.

Table 2.1 lists a summary of the file format options that Word 2007 provides.

TABLE 2.1 SAVE FILE FORMATS IN WORD 2007

Format	Extension	Notes
Word Document	.docx	The default format for Word 2007, supporting all the latest features of the program.
Word Macro-Enabled Document	.docm	A Word document that supports macro usage; the new .docx format does not, for security reasons.
Word 97-2003 Document	.doc	A backward-compatible document format, for exchanging documents with earlier versions of Word.
Word Template	.dotx	The new Word 2007 format for full-featured document templates.
Word Macro-Enabled Template	.dotm	The same as .dotx, but macros can be stored in it. As with the regular Word files, the standard template does not store macros for security reasons.
Word 97-2003 Template	.dot	A backward-compatible template format, useful when creating templates that will be used across multiple Word versions.
Single-File Web Page	.mhtml, .mht	A web page in which all the graphics and other helper files are embedded. Useful for creating HTML-based email.
Web Page	.html, .htm	A web page that retains all the coding it needs for full use in Word plus all the coding it needs for full use on the Web; graphics and other helper files are placed in a support folder.

Format	Extension	Notes
Web Page, Filtered	.html, .htm	A web page that contains only standards-compliant HTML code, and no Word coding. Graphics and other helper files are placed in a support folder.
Rich Text Format	.rtf	A widely accepted generic word processing format, supported by almost any word processing program (including WordPerfect). Retains basic features such as tables and text formatting.
Plain Text	.txt	As the name implies, this format saves the text only, with no formatting at all.
Word XML Document	.xml	A document in eXtensible Markup Language, easily integrated with XML projects.
Word 2003 XML Document	.xml	A document in the Word 2003 version of XML.
Works 6.0 - 9.0	.wps	Another really old document format, this one for swapping data with early versions of the Microsoft Works word processor.

NOTE

If you upgraded to Word 2007 from an earlier version, you might have other file formats available besides the ones shown in the preceding table.

If backward compatibility is not an issue, use the default Word document format. The files will open only in Word 2007, but you'll have access to all of Word 2007's features.

Saving in Web Format

Word 2007 is not a full-featured web development tool, but it does save in three different web-based formats:

- **Web Page**—The default web format is a *round-tripping* format. In other words, it not only contains all the codes needed to display as HTML in a browser, but it also contains all the codes needed to retain its status as a full-fledged Word document. You can save it as a web page, and then open it in Word again and save it as a document file, without losing any Word functionality at all. As you might expect, such a file is much larger than either a pure Word version or a pure HTML version.

- **Web Page, Filtered**—For files that will be exported to HTML and not reimported into Word, Word provides a pure-HTML save format. This format consists only of standards-compliant HTML coding, and the file size is dramatically smaller. Such a file is also much easier for someone accustomed to working with HTML code to understand and modify in a text editor.

- **Single-File Web Page**—Web pages are text-only files that do not contain any graphics. Instead they have hyperlinks to the graphic files, which are pulled in by the Web browser when the page is displayed. Therefore, when you save in either of the aforementioned web formats, Word pulls out any graphics as separate files and stores them in a support folder. That's fine if the page will be published on a web server, but it's a problem for pages that will be distributed via email. To solve this problem, Word offers the Single-File Web Page format, a.k.a. MIME-encoded HTML (MHTML). This file type embeds the graphics into the web page for easy transport. The drawback with using MHTML is that very old browsers (pre-Internet Explorer 4.0) cannot view the files. As time goes by, however, it becomes less and less likely that anyone viewing a page will have a browser that old.

The only difference between saving in regular Word format and saving in one of these web-based formats is the addition of the Page Title option in the Save As dialog box. The *page title* is the text that appear in the title bar.

By default, Word chooses a page title based on the first line of text in the document. Click the Change Title button in the Save As dialog box to change it to something else, as shown in Figure 2.10.

Figure 2.10
Set a page title when saving a document in a web format.

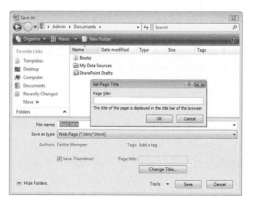

NOTE

Word 2003 had a separate Save as Web Page command on the Office menu, but this has been removed in Word 2007. It was redundant anyway because selecting a web format from the regular Save As dialog box has the same effect as that command.

→ To learn how to customize how Word saves web pages to support a specific web browser, **see** "Options for Web Page Saving," **p. 863**.

SAVING A DOCUMENT AS AN IMAGE

Word documents can also be saved as image files, in either TIFF or MDI format.

 If Microsoft Office Document Image Writer does not appear as a printer, see "Image Writer is Not Available" in the Troubleshooting section at the end of this chapter.

TIFF stands for Tagged Image File Format; it is an old, well-supported format commonly used in faxing software and for digital photography. Saving a document in TIFF format enables you to import the document as an attachment in almost any faxing application. TIFF files in general can be either color or monochrome, but the ones created via Word are always monochrome.

MDI is the proprietary Microsoft Document Image Writer format, used in Microsoft applications. Its advantage over TIFF is that it enables any images in the document to be compressed, making the file size smaller. (TIFF files can be extremely large.) It can also save in color. Its disadvantage is that not all graphics programs can open MDI files, whereas TIFF is an extremely common format.

To save in either of these two formats, you don't actually use the Save command in Word; instead you print to the Microsoft Office Document Image Writer virtual printer. This printer driver is installed in Windows automatically when you install Office 2007.

Follow these steps to save the document as an image:

1. Choose Office, Print. The Print dialog box opens.
2. On the Name list, select Microsoft Office Document Image Writer.
3. Click the Properties button to open the Properties dialog box for the printer driver.
4. On the Advanced tab, select an output format: MDI or TIFF (see Figure 2.11).

Figure 2.11
Choose which format to use for the image output.

5. If you're saving in TIFF format, select a resolution: Standard, Fine, or Super-Fine. Higher resolutions result in less grainy images, but larger file sizes.
6. Click OK to return to the Print dialog box.
7. Click OK to send the document to the driver. The Save As dialog box opens.

8. Enter a name in the File Name box. Change the location if needed.

   The default location is My Documents in Windows XP or Documents in Windows Vista.

9. Click Save. The file is created, and it opens for your inspection in your default graphics program associated with that file format.

> **NOTE**
>
> Word 2007 can save in PDF and XPS formats, but you must download the add-ins for them To do so, open a Web browser and go to http://r.office.microsoft.com/r/ rlidMSAddinPDFXPS. Follow the prompts on the page that appears to acquire the add-ins. (You might need to allow the browser to install the Microsoft Genuine Advantage ActiveX component to validate your copy of the software in order to perform the download. If a Security Warning box appears for that, click **Install**.) Then on the Web page, click **Download**, and in the next security box that appears, click **Run**. This installs the add-ins.
>
> After the add-ins have been installed, the Save As submenu changes to show a PDF or XPS option. Click it and then use the Publish as PDF or XPS dialog box that appears to create one of those files. (Change the Save as Type setting to switch between PDF and XPS.) Click the **Options** button in the dialog box to fine-tune the settings, such as saving with different variants of PDF for example; then click **Publish** to create the file.

CONVERTING A DOCUMENT TO WORD 2007 FORMAT

When a Word document created in an earlier version is open in Word 2007, a Convert command appears on the Office menu. Use this command to update the file to Word 2007 format. The downside, of course, is that the file won't be usable in any earlier Word version, or in any other non–Office 2007 application.

> **TIP**
>
> Although you can't by default open Word 2007 files in earlier Word versions, there's a workaround. Microsoft has a free compatibility pack available at http://office.microsoft. com that will install Office 2007 filters in earlier versions to enable them to open Office 2007 files.

When you issue the Convert command, a confirmation box appears explaining that upgrading will enable you to use new Word 2007 features and will decrease the size of the document file. Click OK to perform the upgrade. If you don't want to see the confirmation box in the future, mark the check box labeled Do Not Ask Me Again About Converting Documents. To find out more about the conversion process, click the Tell Me More button.

OPENING A DOCUMENT

The purpose of saving a file, of course, is to open it at some point in the future. This section discusses ways of opening files, looks at the types of files you can open, and more.

OPENING A RECENTLY USED DOCUMENT

If you have recently saved a new document or opened an existing one in Word, it appears on the Office menu's list of recent documents. "Recently" here is a relative term; the list shows the nine files you most recently worked on, regardless of how long ago that was. To open a recently used file, select it from the Office menu's list, as shown in Figure 2.12.

Figure 2.12
Recently used files appear on the Office menu.

> **TIP**
>
> The number of files that appear on the Office menu's list can be customized; the default is nine. To change this setting, choose Office, Word Options, click Advanced, scroll down to the Display section, and set a Show This Number of Recent Documents value.

New in Word 2007 is the ability to "pin" a recently used file to the listing so that it never disappears from the list even if other files were more recently used. Notice the little pushpin icon next to each filename in Figure 2.12? Click a pushpin to lock the corresponding file onto the list.

Another way to access recently used documents is by selecting Office, Open and then clicking the My Recent Documents shortcut in the Favorites bar (Window XP), or the Recently Changed shortcut in the Favorite Links list (Windows Vista). This listing shows all files that Word can open (including HTML files, document templates, and so on) according to their Last Modified dates, whereas the Office menu's list shows only the files you have actually opened and edited with Word.

Opening a Document with the Open Dialog Box

If the file you want doesn't appear on one of the recently used lists, use the Open dialog box to locate and select it. Choose Office, Open and then navigate to the folder containing the file. The navigational controls are the same for the Open dialog box as for the Save As dialog box, covered earlier in this chapter. There are major differences in the dialog box depending on whether Word 2007 is running under Windows Vista or Windows XP.

← To review file navigation techniques for the Open and Save As dialog boxes, **see** "Changing the File Save Location (Windows Vista)", **p. 32** or "Changing the File Save Location (Windows XP)", **p. 34**, depending on your Windows version.

Figure 2.13 shows the Open dialog box under Windows Vista. It's a bit less cramped than the Save As dialog box, and the extra space is allocated to the file listing. Whereas in the Save As dialog box under Vista, it was not that important to see a list of existing files, in the Open dialog box, that's the whole reason you're there. Navigate to the desired location, and then click the desired file and click Open, or just double-click the file you want.

Figure 2.13
The Open dialog box shares many features with the Save As dialog box.

To open more than one file at once, select multiple files in the Open dialog box. To select a contiguous group, click the first one and hold down Shift as you click the last one.

To select a noncontiguous group, hold down Ctrl as you click each one you want. This works only if all the files are stored in the same folder.

You can also open files from a network or web location, the same as with saving files to those locations. Refer to "Saving to a Network Location" or "Saving to a Web Location" earlier in this chapter; the same information applies to opening as to saving.

→ To save or open a file on an OfficeLive document workspace, **see** "Using OfficeLive Document Workspaces," **p. 824**.

→ To save or open a file on a SharePoint team site, **see** "Working with SharePoint Team Services," **p. 833**.

CHANGING THE FILE LIST VIEW IN THE OPEN DIALOG BOX

Sometimes changing the View setting in the Open dialog box can help you locate the file you need.

Under Windows Vista, a Views button appears near the top of the Open dialog box. Click the Views button and then select a view from the list by dragging the slider, as in Figure 2.14.

- **Icons** (various sizes)—Displays file icons at the specified size. Available sizes are Extra Large Icons, Large Icons, Medium Icons, or Small Icons. The name appears below the icon for all except Small Icons; for Small Icons the name appears to the right.

- **Details**—Shows the file listing in a single column along with information about each file (type, author, and so on).

- **Tiles**—Shows the icon for each file medium-sized with its name to its right.

Figure 2.14
Drag the slider to change the view of the file listing.

The icon that appears for each file is either a generic Word icon or a preview of the document, depending on whether or not you saved a thumbnail with the document when you saved the document itself. In the Save As dialog box, when the Browse Folders area is expanded, a Save Thumbnails check box appears. If you mark this check box, then the file's preview is created during the save operation. Files that were saved this way show their preview as the icon in the Open dialog box; files that were not saved this way show a generic Word icon.

Under Windows XP, there is also a Views button, but its menu contains different options. The various icon sizes are split out separately and given different names, and there is a separate view for seeing previews of the documents that is not dependent on whether a preview has been saved with the document or not.

OPENING OTHER FILE TYPES

The file type in the Open dialog box is set by default to show all supported file types (All Word Documents) for maximum flexibility. The file type appears to the right of the File Name box under Windows Vista, or on a separate Files of Type line beneath the file name under Windows XP.

Word 2007 can open several more file types than it can save in; for example, it can open files from many different WordPerfect versions. This enables users to convert from other word processors to Word. (But conveniently for Microsoft's sales of Word, not back again!)

The Files of Type selection merely serves as a filter based on file extension; it does not prevent you from opening any files. If you are working with a folder containing hundreds of files and you want to quickly find just the ones with the .wps extension (Microsoft Works word processor files), you could set the Files of Type selection to Works 6.0 - 9.0 and all the other files would be hidden on the listing. Similarly, the default setting of All Word Documents filters out files with extensions that Word doesn't recognize.

TIP

> By default, Word converts from other file types silently, without asking for confirmation. If you would rather know when a conversion is occurring, choose Office, Word Options. Click Advanced, and in the General section, mark the Confirm File Format Conversion on Open check box.

 If you can't open a file because Word doesn't support its format, see "I Need to Open a Non-supported File Type" in the Troubleshooting section at the end of this chapter.

OPENING A FILE IN READ-ONLY OR COPY MODE

You can choose to open a file in Read-Only mode, which restricts you from overwriting the original file with your changes. You are still free to use Save As to save it with a different name, type, and/or location. Read-Only mode is useful if it's important that the original file be retained in its current state and you don't trust yourself to get trigger-happy with the Save button.

A related mode is Open as Copy. It also preserves the original, but Open as Copy actually creates a copy of the original file in the same location as the original and then opens the copy for editing. The file is not read-only.

To use either of these opening modes, click the down arrow to the right of the Open button in the Open dialog box and select the desired mode from the drop-down list (see Figure 2.15).

These special modes are useful only if the person opening the files knows to utilize them, of course. If you are concerned about people making changes to a file and you don't trust them to remember to use Open Read-Only or Open as Copy, consider making the document itself read-only. You can do this from outside of Word, or from the file listing in the Save As or Open dialog box:

1. Right-click the filename and choose Properties.
2. In the Properties dialog box, mark the Read-Only check box (see Figure 2.16).
3. Click OK.

Figure 2.15
You can open a file as read-only or as a copy if you are concerned about preserving the document's original state.

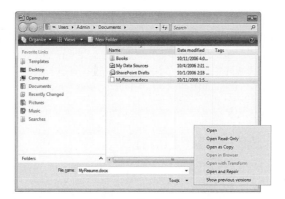

Figure 2.16
To set a file to be read-only, modify its properties.

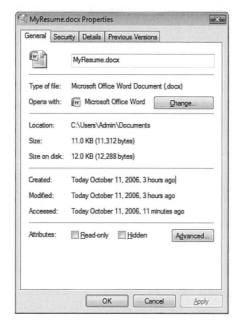

→ To learn more about protecting a file from changes, **see** "Protecting a Document," **p. 806**.

OPENING EARLIER VERSIONS OF A FILE

Word 2003 had a Versions feature built into it that enabled you to save and reopen earlier versions of a document, for archival purposes and to protect yourself against making bad changes. Word 2007 does not have a Versions feature, but there are a couple of alternatives available.

If your operating system is Windows Vista, a Previous Versions button is available in Windows Explorer if the file is stored on a drive that uses the NTFS 5 file system (the default file system for Windows Vista). You can select a file and then click Previous Versions to access *shadow copies* of earlier versions of it.

Regardless of your operating system, you can also set up Word to create automatic backup copies of files. Every time you save a file, the previous version is saved into a backup file, a Word file with the same name as the original but with "Backup of" at the beginning of the name.

→ For information about turning on the automatic backup feature, **see** "Creating Automatic Backup Copies," **p. 979**.

WORKING WITH FILE PROPERTIES

All files have properties, such as their size, their type, their extension, the date they were last modified, and whether or not they are read-only. You can see a file's properties in Windows by right-clicking the file and choosing Properties, as you did in the preceding section.

But in Word, the term *properties* has a separate meaning. A document's Properties settings in Word store information users can enter and edit, such as subject, category, and keywords. This information can then be used to organize and find files on a document management server, or even on your own hard disk.

There are two levels of properties in Word: Standard and Advanced. The Standard properties consist of some text boxes into which you can enter information that will be helpful for filing purposes, such as author, title, category, and so on. To access the Standard properties, choose Office, Prepare, Properties. A Document Properties bar appears across the top of the document, as shown in Figure 2.17.

Figure 2.17
The standard properties for a document.

A few notes about some of the Standard properties:

- The Author field is filled in automatically for you if you specified a username when you set up Word. If you did not, you can do so at any time. Choose Office, Word Options, click Popular, and enter your name and initials in the text boxes provided for them. The Author name will then be pre-entered for all new documents you create.

- The Title property is not the same as the filename. The document title is used when creating a web page; it's the text that appears in the title bar of the web browser when the page is displayed. If you have ever saved this document as a web page, the Title field will be filled in with the title you used then; otherwise, the text of the first line of the document appears.

■ The Subject, Keywords, Category, and Status fields are all free-form fields; you can put whatever you want in them. However, if you are participating in a corporate document server, or if you share files with others on your network, you might want to find out if there are any established conventions for using these fields in your company.

TIP

> If you use the AutoSummarize feature (covered in Chapter 22, "Outlining and Summarizing Documents"), the keywords it generates are automatically placed in the Keywords property field; otherwise, that field is blank by default.

To see the Advanced properties, click the down arrow next to Document Properties, and click Advanced Properties. A Properties dialog box appears for the document. It is similar to the Properties dialog box accessible from Windows, but it has more tabs and more detail:

■ **General**—Contains the same basic information as in the Windows version of the Properties dialog box (refer to Figure 2.16). The file attributes (read-only, hidden, and so on) are not editable from within Word.

MS-DOS Names

One interesting and unique piece of information on the General tab is the MS-DOS name. Earlier in the chapter, I mentioned that MS-DOS limited filenames to eight characters for the name and three for the extension. If a file that does not meet that specification is placed on an MS-DOS system, it won't be accessible. To get around this problem, Windows stores an MS-DOS name for each file along with its long name that strips out any spaces and trims the name to eight and three (8-3) characters. If the long name is already 8-3 or less, the MS-DOS name is the same as the long name. Otherwise, the MS-DOS name consists of the first six letters of the filename (or as many letters as it has, if less than six) followed by a tilde symbol (~) and a number starting with 1 for the first file with this name, then 2, and so on. The number helps account for the fact that several files might begin with the same six letters in their names. If you plan on using the file on an MS-DOS system, it might be useful to know what its name will be when it gets there, for easier retrieval.

■ **Summary**—Contains the same text boxes as the Standard view of the properties, plus a few additional text boxes such as Manager and Company. It also tells what document template is assigned to the document. The Save Thumbnails for All Word Documents check box generates a thumbnail of the first page of the document and shows it as the file's icon in the Open dialog box (under Windows Vista) or places it in the Preview pane of the Open dialog box (under Windows XP).

■ **Statistics**—Lists the dates and times of the file's creation, modification, and last access and printing. It also tells who last saved the file, how many revisions there have been, and how much time has been spent editing it. Finally, document statistics appear here, such as the number of pages, paragraphs, lines, words, and characters (see Figure 2.18).

Figure 2.18
The Statistics tab summarizes the document's editing history and size.

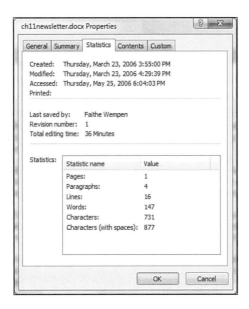

- **Contents**—If you marked the Save Thumbnails for All Word Documents check box on the Summary tab, the Contents tab shows a snapshot of the document headings here. Otherwise, it shows only the document title.

- **Custom**—On this tab, you can define values for less commonly stored facts about the document, again useful for doing searches on document servers and in large collections of documents.

DEFINING CUSTOM PROPERTIES

Custom properties are special-purpose fields that you can choose to use in managing your documents on an as-needed basis. You can enter and edit them on the Custom tab of the Properties dialog box.

Here are the steps to follow to define a custom property:

1. Click the Custom tab in the Properties dialog box.

2. On the Name list, click the property you want to use.

3. Select the type of data to be stored in that field from the Type drop-down list. The most generic type is Text; it will accept everything. You might use a more specific type, such as Date, to prevent invalid entries.

4. In the Value field, enter the value for that property for the current document.

5. Click the Add button. The property, type, and value appear in the Properties list, as shown in Figure 2.19.

Figure 2.19
Add a custom property to the document.

To edit a custom property, select it from the Properties list at the bottom of the dialog box and then change the value in the Value box.

Automatically Updating Custom Properties

Custom properties are usually static; their values remain set at whatever you specify for them. To create a custom property that automatically updates based on some text in the document, define that text as a bookmark, as you'll learn in Chapter 19, "Copying, Linking, and Embedding Data," and then mark the Link to Content check box on the Custom tab. (That check box isn't available unless the document has at least one bookmark in it.)

The Value field changes to the Source field, which is a drop-down list of all the bookmarks in the document.

Finding a Document to Open

Word 2003 had a File Search feature (on the File menu) that helped users search for files based on their names, contents, or properties. This feature has been removed in Word 2007, but if you are running Word 2007 on Windows Vista, you can access the Windows Vista search engine from within the Open dialog box.

To search for a file containing a certain word or phrase, follow these steps:

1. Choose Office, Open. The Open dialog box appears.
2. Navigate to the location at which you want to begin searching. Word will search that location and everything subordinate to it. To search all drives on the whole system, choose Computer as the starting location.

3. In the Search box, type the word or phrase.

4. Click the Search button or press Enter. A list of files containing that word or phrase appear.

5. Select the file you want, and open it as you would any other file.

TIP

> If you have Windows XP, you can still search for files, but you must do it from outside of Word 2007. From the Start menu, choose Search, and use the Windows XP Search feature to look for the file you want.

SETTING FILE-HANDLING PREFERENCES

One of Word 2007's strengths is its customization capability. If you don't like how something works, you can change it. Here are some tips for configuring Word to better reflect the way you want to save and open files.

SETTING THE DEFAULT SAVE LOCATION AND FILE TYPE

Word's default save location is Documents on a Windows Vista system or My Documents on Windows XP. That folder appears by default in the Save As and Open dialog boxes. Beginners should leave this at the default so that they never have to remember where they stored a file—it's always in that location. More advanced users may want to save files in other locations, though, and might even want one of those other locations to be the default.

NOTE

> The default save location in Office 2007 is the Documents or My Documents folder for the currently logged-in user. That folder's path is Users*username*\Documents (in Windows Vista) or Documents and Settings*username*\My Documents (in Windows XP), where *username* is the user. Therefore, when a different person logs into the computer, a different location will be accessed in Office 2007 applications.

You can also change the default file format in which files are saved. If you are using only Word 2007, leave the default file format set to Word Document, but if you frequently need to exchange files with people using earlier versions, set the default format to one that's compatible with those other users' PCs.

Both of these defaults are set in the same location.

To set up file location preferences, follow these steps:

1. Choose Office, Word Options.

2. Click Save.

3. Open the Save Files in This Format drop-down list and choose the desired file format (see Figure 2.20).

Figure 2.20
Set the default file location and type here.

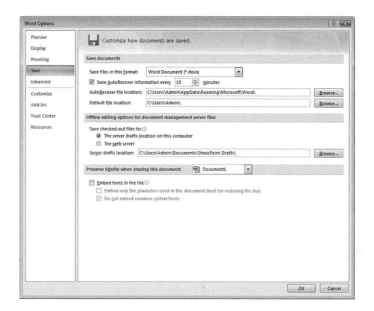

4. In the Default File Location box, enter the path to the desired location, or use the Browse button to locate it.

5. (Optional) To set the file locations for other types of files, such as templates, do the following:

   a. Click Advanced, and scroll all the way to the bottom.

   b. Click File Locations. The File Locations dialog box opens.

   c. Click a file type, and click Modify. The Modify Location dialog box opens.

   d. Navigate to the desired location, and then click OK. The location changes in the Location column for that file type.

   e. Repeat steps c-d for other file types, or click OK to return to Word Options.

6. Click OK to close the Word Options dialog box.

SETTING AN AUTORECOVER INTERVAL

Word automatically saves a temporary copy of each document every 10 minutes (that's the default interval). This way, if Word crashes or your computer shuts down unexpectedly, you won't have lost more than 10 minutes' worth of work. When you restart Word after such a crash, the saved backup file(s) open automatically.

To change the interval at which Word saves backups, or to turn off the feature entirely, do the following:

1. Choose Office, Word Options.

2. Click Save, mark or clear the Save AutoRecover Information Every ___ Minutes check box to turn the feature on or off. To change the save interval, type a different number in the text box (refer to Figure 2.20).

3. To change the location where Word stores these temporary backup files, click the Browse button and browse to a different location, or type a new path directly into the AutoRecover File Location text box.

4. Click OK to close the Word Options dialog box.

TROUBLESHOOTING

I NEED TO OPEN A NON-SUPPORTED FILE TYPE

If Word doesn't appear to support the file type you want to open, you have several options. One is just to try opening it anyway by changing the Files of Type setting to All Files. Another is to go back to the original application and resave it in a format that Word can recognize. Rich Text Format (RTF) is supported in almost all word processing programs, for example. If all else fails, save it as a plain text file, or open the original program alongside Word 2007 and then copy and paste the text from one application to another.

If the file's extension does not represent the file type accurately, rename that file in Windows before attempting to open it in Word. Word's converter works much better when it knows what type of document it should expect. If you don't want to take the time to do that, though, you can set the Files of Type setting to All Files so that all file types are displayed in the dialog box, and then either rename that file on the fly (right-click it and choose Rename) or just try to open it as is.

If none of that does the trick, consider a third-party file conversion application such as Dataviz Conversions Plus.

→ For more information about opening different file types, see "Converting from Other Word Processing Systems," **p. 985**.

I CAN'T SEE THE FILE EXTENSIONS

By default, Windows does not display the file extensions for file types that it recognizes. This is ostensibly to shield the beginning user from the scary-looking extensions, but it's a hindrance to advanced users who want to see what they're doing. Here's how to turn on the display of all file extensions:

Windows Vista: Open Computer (or any file management window) and choose Organize, Folder and Search Options. On the View tab, clear the Hide Extensions for Known File Types check box and click OK.

Windows XP: Open My Computer (or any file management window) and choose Tools, Folder Options. On the View tab, clear the Hide Extensions for Known File Types check box and click OK.

NEW DOCUMENTS ARE USING WORD 2003 SETTINGS

On a brand-new install of Word or Office 2007, the default font is set for +Body (Calibri), 11 point, and the margins are set for 1" on all sides. If you have upgraded from Word 2003 or earlier, however, or if you chose to leave Word 2003 installed on your PC alongside Word 2007, the default settings for Word 2003 might remain in effect.

This happens because Word 2007 does not delete any old version of the default template from earlier versions (Normal.dot), and furthermore, if such a template exists, Normal.dotm copies its settings.

If you want to continue using the default settings from Word 2003, just let it be. If you don't, however, here's how to fix it:

1. Close all versions of Word.
2. Navigate to the folder containing user templates:

   C:\Users*username*\Application Settings\Microsoft\Templates (Windows Vista) or C:\Documents and Settings*username*\Application Settings\Microsoft\Templates (Window XP) where *username* is the logged-in Windows user.
3. Delete Normal.dot and Normal.dotm.
4. Restart Word. The settings will now be the defaults described at the beginning of this chapter.

IMAGE WRITER IS NOT AVAILABLE

By default, the Microsoft Document Image Writer driver is not installed, although it might already be present if you upgraded to Office 2007 from an earlier version. To install it, see "Modifying or Repairing Your Office Installation" in Appendix E, and set Office Tools, Microsoft Document Imaging, Microsoft Office Document Image Writer to Run from My Computer.

CHAPTER **3**

TYPING AND EDITING TEXT

In this chapter

3

TEXT ENTRY AND EDITING BASICS

A blank document starts out with a flashing insertion point, which looks like a small vertical bar. In addition, if you're working in Draft or Outline view, a horizontal bar (not flashing) appears as an end-of-file marker (see Figure 3.1). Initially the two markers are together because there's nothing in the file, but the end-of-file marker moves further down on the page as you add more text to your document.

Figure 3.1
The insertion point is a flashing vertical line; the end-of-file marker (appearing only in Draft or Outline view) is a horizontal, non-flashing line.

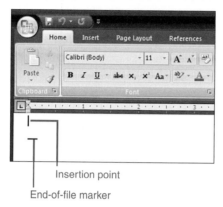

Insertion point
End-of-file marker

→ To switch between views, such as Draft and Print Layout, **see** "Switching Document Views," **p. 20**.

Text you type always appears at the insertion point. (You can move it around, as you will learn later in the chapter.) To enter text, just type as you would in any program. The following keys have specific functions:

- **Enter**—Press this key to start a new paragraph.
- **Shift+Enter**—Press this key combination to start a new line within the same paragraph.
- **Ctrl+Enter**—Press this key combination to start a new page.
- **Tab**—Press this key to move to the next tab stop (by default every 0.5").
- **Backspace**—Press this key to delete a single character to the left of the insertion point.
- **Delete**—Press this key to delete a single character to the right of the insertion point.

You can also delete a text selection of any size, including text and/or other objects, by pressing the Delete or Backspace key.

Line Breaks Versus Paragraph Breaks

A surprising number of people have trouble understanding the difference between a new paragraph and a new line. Yes, starting a new paragraph does also start a new line, so on the surface they seem to be doing the same thing. But if you turn on the Show/Hide ¶ feature (on the Home tab), you'll see that two completely different symbols are inserted.

A paragraph break (¶ symbol) creates a whole new paragraph, which can have its own indentation, bullets and numbering, line spacing, and other paragraph-level settings.

A line break (↵ symbol) is like any other character of text within the paragraph, except instead of printing a letter on the screen, it moves the insertion point to the next line. The text after the line break has the exact same paragraph-level formatting as the text before the break, because it's all one paragraph.

Line breaks come in handy whenever you don't want the stylistic attributes of multiple paragraphs. For example, suppose you want to create a bulleted list of mailing addresses, with each complete address as a separate bullet point. If you press Enter between the lines of each address, each line will have its own bullet character, like this:

- John Smith
- 240 W. Main Street
- Macon, IL 62544

By using line breaks instead, you can create a single bulleted item with multiple lines, like this:

- John Smith
  240 W. Main Street
  Macon, IL 62544

SWITCHING BETWEEN INSERT AND OVERTYPE MODES

When editing text, Insert mode is on by default, meaning that any text you type to the left of existing text will cause the existing text to scoot over to the right to make room for it. The alternative, Overtype mode, types over any existing text to the right of the insertion point.

To toggle between Insert and Overtype mode, follow these steps:

1. Choose Office, Word Options.
2. Click Advanced.
3. Under Editing Options, mark or clear the Use Overtype Mode check box.
4. Click OK.

CAUTION

> You cannot change the status of the Use Overtype Mode check box when Track Changes is enabled on the Review tab. Furthermore, even if the active document does not have Track Changes enabled, you still cannot access that check box if *any* open document is tracking changes. You can, however, change the overtype status in one of the non-tracked open documents using one of the methods described next.

If you find yourself frequently switching between Insert and Overtype, you might want to set up an easier method for performing the switch. There are two such methods available: remapping the Insert key, and adding an Insert/Overtype indicator to the status bar.

By default, the Insert key works as a shortcut for the Paste command on the Home tab. If you prefer, you can change its mapping so that it instead switches between Insert and Overtype modes.

→ To learn about using the Insert key as a pasting shortcut, **see** "Using Paste Options," **p. 76**.

To make the Insert key toggle between Insert and Overtype views, follow these steps:

1. Choose Office, Word Options.
2. Click Advanced.

3. Under Editing Options, mark the Use the Insert Key to Control Overtype Mode check box.

4. Click OK.

Now the Insert key functions as a toggle between Insert and Overtype modes. To make it more obvious which mode you are in, you might want to turn on the Insert/Overtype mode indicator on the status bar.

To add the indicator to the status bar:

1. Right-click the status bar.

2. Click to place a check mark next to Overtype.

Insert (or *Overtype*) appears in the status bar. You can then click that word to toggle between them.

UNDOING, REDOING, AND REPEATING

Whenever you make a mistake, such as accidentally deleting or overwriting something, you can easily reverse it with Word's Undo feature. To undo, press Ctrl+Z, or click the Undo button on the Quick Access toolbar.

The Undo feature retains a list of actions you've recently taken, and you can undo any number of them. The effect is cumulative. In other words, you can undo, for example, the last five actions you took, but you can't pick-and-choose among those five; you must undo the intervening four in order to undo the fifth one. To undo multiple levels, repeat Ctrl+Z or repeatedly click the Undo button on the Quick Access toolbar, or click the down arrow to the right of the Undo button to open a menu and then select the actions to undo from that list.

After you have undone one or more actions, the Redo button becomes available on the Quick Access toolbar. It reverses undo operations, and comes in handy when you accidentally undo too much. Ctrl+Y is its keyboard shortcut. Figure 3.2 shows the Undo and Redo buttons.

Undo⌐ ⌐Redo

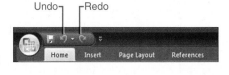

Figure 3.2
The Undo button undoes the last action when clicked; it also has a drop-down list from which you can choose to undo multiple actions at once.

The Repeat feature enables you to repeat an operation such as typing, formatting, inserting, and so on. The Repeat button looks like a U-turn arrow, and appears in place of the Redo button on the Quick Access toolbar, when available. Its shortcut is also Ctrl+Y; this works because Repeat and Redo are not available at the same time (see Figure 3.3).

Repeat

Figure 3.3
The Repeat button
makes it easy to
repeat the last action
you took.

INSERTING SYMBOLS AND SPECIAL CHARACTERS

The computer keyboard is very limited in the characters it can produce, and people often need other characters to produce typeset-quality documents. For example, the copyright (©) and trademark (™) symbols are frequently used in business documents, and an attractively typeset page uses em dashes (—) rather than two hyphens together (--) to represent dashes in sentences.

INSERTING SYMBOLS WITH KEYBOARD SHORTCUTS OR AUTOCORRECT

Some of the most popular symbols have keyboard shortcuts and/or AutoCorrect shortcuts. AutoCorrect is a feature used most often for correcting common spelling errors, but it is also useful for generating certain common symbols on the fly. To use an AutoCorrect shortcut, type the text shown and press the spacebar once, and Word converts the shortcut text to the specified symbol. Table 3.1 summarizes both the keyboard shortcuts and the AutoCorrect entries for some common symbols.

TABLE 3.1   KEYBOARD AND AUTOCORRECT SHORTCUTS FOR SYMBOLS

Symbol	Keyboard Shortcut	AutoCorrect Shortcut
— (em dash)	Ctrl+Alt+Num – (minus sign on the numeric keypad)	
– (en dash)	Ctrl+Num – (minus sign on the numeric keypad)	
© (copyright)	Ctrl+Alt+C	(c)
® (registered trademark)	Ctrl+Alt+R	(r)
™ (trademark)	Ctrl+Alt+T	(tm)
… (ellipsis)	Ctrl+Alt+. (period)	...
' (single opening quote)	Ctrl+`,` Hold down Ctrl and press the grave accent key (`) twice. It is above the Tab key.	
' (single closing quote)	Ctrl+',' Hold down Ctrl and press the apostrophe key twice. It is to the left of the Enter key.	
" (double opening quote)	Ctrl+`," Hold down Ctrl and press the grave accent key (`) once, and then type a quotation mark.	

continues

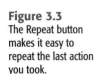

3

Symbol	Keyboard Shortcut	AutoCorrect Shortcut
" (double closing quote)	Ctrl+'," Hold down Ctrl and press the apostrophe key once, and then type a quotation mark.	
← (typographical left arrow)	None	<—
→ (typographical right arrow	None	—>
← (thick typographical left arrow)	None	<==
→ (thick typographical right arrow)	None	==>
↔ (double-headed arrow)	None	<=>

TABLE 3.1   CONTINUED

NOTE

The single and double quotation marks in Table 3.1 are typographical—that is, they differ depending on whether they are at the beginning or end of the quoted phrase. This is different from the straight quotation marks and apostrophes that you can directly type from the keyboard.

Notice that in Table 3.1, there are no AutoCorrect entries for the dashes and the quotation marks. That's because they're not needed. Word automatically converts straight quotes to typographical ones (Word calls these "smart quotes") and two hyphens in a row to a dash. If you don't want that change to occur, using Undo (Ctrl+Z) immediately after Word makes the change to reverse it. Undo also reverses any of the AutoCorrect conversions as well if you catch them immediately after they occur.

→ To disable an AutoCorrect entry, **see** "Automating Corrections with AutoCorrect," **p. 111**.

→ To learn how to disable the automatic conversion of straight quotes to smart quotes, or two hyphens to a dash, **see** "Setting AutoFormat As You Type Options," **p. 183**.

INSERTING SYMBOLS WITH THE SYMBOL DIALOG BOX

Another way to insert a symbol is with the Symbol button on the Insert tab. Click Symbol to open a drop-down list of some common symbols (see Figure 3.4). (This list has some overlap with the ones in Table 3.1, but is not the same list. There are more math symbols here, for example.)

Figure 3.4
Symbols can be inserted from the Symbol drop-down list on the Insert tab.

If the symbol you want doesn't appear, click More Symbols to open the Symbol dialog box, shown in Figure 3.5. From here you can select any character from any installed font, including some of the alternative characters that don't correspond to a keyboard key, such as letters with accent symbols over them.

Figure 3.5
The Symbol dialog box can be used to insert any character from any font.

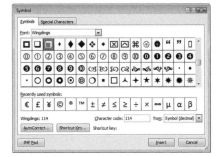

> **TIP**
>
> For a wide choice of interesting and unique symbols, check out the Wingdings fonts, which you can select from the Font drop-down menu.

You can also find a symbol by its character code, which is a numeric identifier of a particular symbol in a particular coding system. The two main coding systems are ASCII and Unicode. ASCII is the older system, and characters can be identified using either decimal or hexadecimal numbering in it. Unicode is the Windows standard for character identification, and it uses only hex numbering. Select the desired coding system from the From drop-down list and then type the character code in the Character Code box.

On the Special Characters tab of the dialog box are some of the most common typographical characters, along with reminders of their keyboard shortcuts. If you need to insert one of these common characters, finding it on the Special Characters tab can be easier than trying to wade through all the characters in a font for it.

TIP

> If you want a special character such as an accented letter or copyright symbol to blend in smoothly with the rest of the paragraph, make sure (normal text) is selected from the Font drop-down list in the Symbol dialog box. You won't always be able to do this, though, because not all symbols are available in all fonts. When you select symbols from the Special Characters tab, they are automatically in the (normal text) font.

AUTOMATING SYMBOL ENTRY

To make it easier to insert the same symbol again later, you might want to set up an AutoCorrect entry or a shortcut key combination for it.

To create an AutoCorrect entry, follow these steps:

1. From the Symbol dialog box, click the symbol for which you want to create the entry.
2. Click AutoCorrect. The AutoCorrect dialog box opens with a new entry already started.
3. Type the text that should represent the symbol. It is customary to enclose one or two characters in parentheses for AutoCorrect symbol insertion, but this is not required. For example, to create an entry for the ± sign, you might choose (+) as the text to enter (see Figure 3.6).
4. Press Enter. The new entry appears on the list.
5. Click OK to return to the Symbol dialog box.

Figure 3.6
Add an AutoCorrect entry for a symbol.

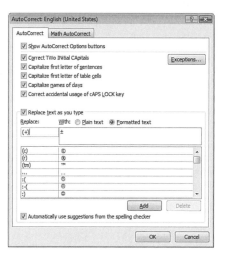

To assign a shortcut key combination to a symbol, follow these steps:

1. From the Symbol dialog box, click the symbol for which you want to create the shortcut.
2. Click Shortcut Key. The Customize Keyboard dialog box appears.

3. Click in the Press New Shortcut Key text box and then type the key combination you want to use. If that key combination is currently assigned to something else, a Currently Assigned To line will appear, as in Figure 3.7. (You can overwrite a default shortcut key assignment if desired.)

4. By default, the change will be saved to the Normal.dotm template; if you want it saved only to the open document, open the Save Changes In list and choose the document.

5. Click the Assign button.

6. Click Close to return to the Symbol dialog box.

Figure 3.7
Map a keyboard shortcut to a symbol.

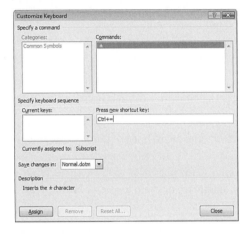

→ To learn more about creating AutoCorrect entries, **see** "Automating Corrections with AutoCorrect," **p. 111**.

MOVING AROUND IN A DOCUMENT

In a short document, moving around is easy. You can use the keyboard's arrow keys to move the insertion point, or click the mouse to place the insertion point where you want it.

But when a document grows to several pages or more, those basic methods can be insufficient. In the following sections, you'll learn some shortcuts and alternative methods for moving around in a document.

SCROLLING

Vertical and horizontal scroll bars are available at the right and bottom of the Word window, respectively, whenever there is more content than will fit in the window. You're probably already familiar with these from other applications, but here's a quick review:

- **Arrows**—Click an arrow to scroll a small amount in that direction, or click and hold on an arrow to scroll quickly.

- **Scroll box**—This is the light part of the bar; drag it to scroll quickly without moving through each page on the way there. The scroll box is context-sensitive; the more undisplayed content, the smaller the bar will be. For example, if 50% of the document appears onscreen and the other 50% is not shown, the scroll box will take up approximately 50% of the scroll bar.
- **Scroll bar**—This is the dark part, behind the scroll box. Click above the scroll box to move up one screenful, or click below the scroll box to move down one screenful.

Many mice and trackballs have a wheel between the left and right buttons. Roll this toward you or away from you to scroll vertically in the document. Some of these wheels can also be pushed to the left or right to scroll horizontally.

MOVING THE INSERTION POINT WITH CLICK AND TYPE

The Click and Type feature enables you to place text anywhere on the page. If the location you choose is outside the current document, extra tab stops and/or empty paragraphs are added to allow the insertion point to reach that spot.

So what does "outside the current document" mean? Recall from the beginning of this chapter that each document has an end-of-file marker, a small horizontal line that marks where the last line of the document ends. This marker is visible only in Draft and Outline view, but it's always there, enforcing the boundary of the document. As you type lines of text, this marker moves further down the page.

Before the days of Click and Type, you could not move the insertion point past this end-of-file marker via normal methods (such as by pressing the arrow keys or by clicking). That meant if you wanted to place text further down on the page than the end-of-file marker, you had to press Enter, adding blank paragraphs, until the document had sufficiently expanded so that the desired area was part of the document.

Click and Type provides an alternate method for placing text outside the document's current borders—and for starting text at horizontal locations other than the left margin. With Click and Type, you simply double-click to place the insertion point, rather than the usual single-clicking.

If the location you chose is outside the end-of-file marker, Word automatically inserts the needed blank paragraphs so that the area is within the document.

If the location you chose is not at the left margin, Word inserts a tab stop at the chosen spot and tabs over to it for you. If the text you type is longer than will fit on one line, Word wraps the next line to the left margin. To make all the text line up under the first line you typed, select the paragraph and press Ctrl+Shift+T to create a hanging indent.

NOTE

If you find yourself accidentally enabling Click and Type when you don't want it, turn the feature off. To do so, choose Office, Word Options, click Advanced, and in the Editing Options section, clear the Enable Click and Type check box.

You can even get different text alignments on those tab stops that Word creates with Click and Type. Notice the mouse pointer changes as you move over different areas of the page. When you are in an area where Click and Type can be used, the mouse pointer has a text alignment symbol on it. Over the left side of the page, it's a left-align symbol, as in Figure 3.8. In the center it's a center-align symbol, and as you approach the right margin, it's a right-align symbol. Whatever symbol is shown when you double-click determines whether it will be a left-aligned or right-aligned tab stop that's created.

Figure 3.8
The tab stop's alignment depends on the area of the page in which you are using Click and Type.

→ To change the tab stop's alignment, **see** "Working with Tab Stops," **p. 201**.

NAVIGATING WITH KEYBOARD SHORTCUTS

Table 3.2 lists some keyboard shortcuts for moving the insertion point in Word 2007.

TABLE 3.2	KEYBOARD SHORTCUTS FOR NAVIGATION
Keyboard Shortcut	**Moves to:**
Alt+down arrow	Next object
Alt+End	End of the row
Alt+F1 (or F11)	Next field
Alt+F6	Next window
Alt+F7	Next misspelled word
Alt+Home	Start of the row
Alt+Page Down	Bottom of the current column
Alt+Page Up	Top of the current column
Alt+Shift+F1 (or Shift+F11)	Previous field
Alt+Shift+F6	Previous window
Alt+up arrow	Previous object
Ctrl+Alt+Page Down	Bottom of the window
Ctrl+Alt+Page Up	Top of the window
Ctrl+Alt+Z (or Shift+F5)	Previous location of the insertion point
Ctrl+down arrow	Next paragraph or next table cell
Ctrl+End	End of the document

continues

TABLE 3.2 CONTINUED	
Keyboard Shortcut	**Moves to:**
Ctrl+F6 (or Alt+F6)	Next window
Ctrl+Home	Beginning of the document
Ctrl+left arrow	One word to the left
Ctrl+Page Down	Next item (based on the Browse Object setting)
Ctrl+Page Up	Previous item (based on the Browse Object setting)
Ctrl+right arrow	One word to the right
Ctrl+Shift+F6	Previous window
Ctrl+up arrow	Previous paragraph
End	End of the current line
F6	Next pane or frame
Home	Beginning of the current line
Page Down	Next screen
Page Up	Previous screen
Shift+F6	Previous pane or frame
Shift+Tab	Previous cell in a table
Tab	Next cell in a table, or starts a new table row if already in the last cell

SELECTING TEXT AND OTHER OBJECTS

Like most applications, Word works using the selection/action system. First you select some text or other data, and then you act upon that selection by issuing a command. For example, first you select text to be copied, and then you issue the command to copy it.

There are many ways of selecting text and other objects in a Word document, and you can use any combination of methods. However, some methods are much more convenient and well-suited for certain situations.

The most basic way to select text with the mouse is to drag across the text (with the left mouse button down). The selected text becomes highlighted.

By default, Word extends your selection to the nearest entire word, and includes the paragraph marker at the end of a selected paragraph. If you do not want this, see "I Don't Want Word to Extend Selections" in the Troubleshooting section at the end of this chapter.

There are also shortcuts for selecting certain objects or amounts of text with the mouse and keyboard, as described in Tables 3.3 and 3.4, respectively. To use keyboard shortcuts, first position the insertion point at the starting point for the selection and then use the keys indicated to extend the selection.

TABLE 3.3   MOUSE SHORTCUTS FOR SELECTING

To select...	Do This:
From the insertion point to any other point	Position the insertion point, then hold down Shift and click the end point for the selection.
The entire document	Triple-click in the left margin.
A word	Double-click the word.
A sentence	Ctrl+click the sentence.
A paragraph	Triple-click the paragraph or double-click in the left margin next to it.
A line	Click in the left margin next to it.
A table	Click in the table and then click the Table Selection box (looks like a four-headed arrow) in the top-left corner of the table grid.
A table cell	Click the left edge of the cell.
A table row	Point the mouse pointer to the left of the row, so the pointer turns into a white arrow, and then click.
A table column	Point the mouse pointer at the top gridline of the column, so the pointer turns into a black arrow, and then click.
A graphic	Click the graphic.
A text box	Click any outer edge of the text box.
A rectangular block (unrelated to paragraph or column divisions)	Hold down Alt and drag across the area to select.
Multiple noncontiguous selections	Make the first selection and then hold down Ctrl as you drag across additional selections.
Multiple graphics or non-text objects	Click the first object, and then hold down Ctrl as you click additional objects.

TABLE 3.4   KEYBOARD SHORTCUTS FOR SELECTING

To select...	Press This:
The entire document	Ctrl+A
The bottom of the window	Ctrl+Alt+Shift+Page Down

continues

TABLE 3.4 CONTINUED

To select...	Press This:
The top of the window	Ctrl+Alt+Shift+Page Up
The end of the paragraph	Ctrl+Shift+down arrow
The beginning of the paragraph	Ctrl+Shift+up arrow
The end of the document	Ctrl+Shift+End
The beginning of the document	Ctrl+Shift+Home
A rectangular block (unrelated to paragraph or column divisions)	Ctrl+Shift+F8+arrow keys
The beginning of the word	Ctrl+Shift+left arrow. Press the left arrow key again, still holding Ctrl+Shift, to extend to subsequent words.
The end of the word	Ctrl+Shift+right arrow. Press the right arrow key again, still holding Ctrl+Shift, to extend to subsequent words.
The entire line above	Shift+up arrow
The entire line below	Shift+down arrow
The end of the line	Shift+End
The beginning of the line	Shift+Home
One character, line, or table cell in any direction	Shift+arrow keys

TIP

Here's a trick you can do with the F8 key for selecting: Press F8 to turn Extend mode on, and then press it again to select the current Word. Pressing it a third time selects the current sentence, and pressing it a fourth time selects the entire document. You can also use F8 with the arrow keys to extend the selection one character or line at a time in the arrow's direction. Use Shift+F8 to reduce the size of the selection.

MOVING AND COPYING TEXT AND OBJECTS

Perhaps the most important benefit of word processing over typewriter use is the ability to move and copy objects and blocks of text. There are many ways of accomplishing move and copy operations in Word, so you can select whatever method is most comfortable for you or makes the most sense in a particular situation. The following sections explain the various move and copy operations and the differences between them.

Moving or Copying Text with Drag-and-Drop

Drag-and-drop operations are popular because they most closely resemble the way you do things outside the computer. (Yes, there really is a life outside the computer!) When you want to move something in your living room, you pick it up and reposition it. Or if it's heavy, like a piece of furniture, you drag it and drop it. You can do the same thing with objects and with blocks of selected text in Word.

For a standard drag-and-drop operation, follow these steps:

1. Select the text or object(s) you want to move or copy.
2. (Optional) To copy, hold down the Ctrl key. You don't have to hold anything down if you want to move.
3. Position the mouse over the selection, and then click and hold down the left mouse button on it.
4. Still holding down the left mouse button, drag the selection to a new location. Then release the mouse button.

There are additional drag-and-drop options; to see them, use the right mouse button rather than the left one in the preceding steps. (Don't hold down the Ctrl key if you are using the right mouse button.) When you release the mouse button in step 4, a shortcut menu appears with these choices on it:

- **Move Here**—The default operation; the same as regular dragging with the left mouse button.
- **Copy Here**—The same as holding down the Ctrl key with the left-mouse-button drag.
- **Link Here**—Creates a copy that retains a link to the original location, such that if the original changes, this copy changes too.
- **Cancel**—Cancels the current drag-and-drop operation.

Using Cut, Copy, and Paste

One of the complaints that many people have with drag-and-drop is that they are simply not coordinated enough to manage positioning the mouse pointer in exactly the right spot while holding down keys and mouse buttons. People who have this problem may prefer to use the Cut, Copy, and Paste commands instead.

Cut and Copy are very similar operations. Cut removes the selection from the document and places it on the Clipboard, which is a hidden holding area; Copy leaves the selection as is and places a copy of it on the Clipboard. After a Cut or Copy operation, you can then use Paste to place the Clipboard's content at the insertion point location.

NOTE

There are actually two Clipboards—the Windows Clipboard and the Office Clipboard. The Windows Clipboard holds only one item at a time; when you place a second item on that Clipboard, the first item is erased from it. The Office Clipboard has multiple slots for holding content. It uses the Windows Clipboard for one slot, but it can also hold 23 other items at the same time. I explain more about the Office Clipboard later in the chapter.

Word offers ribbon, keyboard, and right-click methods for issuing the Cut, Copy, and Paste commands. Table 3.5 summarizes them.

TABLE 3.5   CUT, COPY, AND PASTE METHODS

	Cut	Copy	Paste
Click these buttons on the Home tab:	✄	🗐	📋
Press these shortcut keys:	Ctrl+X	Ctrl+C	Ctrl+V
Right-click your selection and then choose one of these commands:	Cut	Copy	Paste

TIP

Experienced users generally end up using the keyboard shortcut methods most frequently because they are the fastest.

 If you would like to save something from the Clipboard so that it can be used later, but you don't want to save it in Word, see "I'd Like to Save Clipboard Content for Later Use" in the Troubleshooting section at the end of this chapter.

PASTING WITH PASTE SPECIAL

The Paste Special command enables you to define the format of the pasted copy, and in some circumstances also create a dynamic link to the original.

To use Paste Special instead of Paste, open the drop-down menu below the Paste button and select Paste Special from that menu, as in Figure 3.9.

Doing so opens the Paste Special dialog box, shown in Figure 3.10.

Figure 3.9
Select Paste Special from the Paste button's options.

Figure 3.10
Use the Paste Special dialog box to paste in a different way than the default.

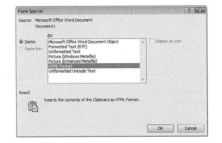

3

For a normal (nonlinked) paste, select a paste format from the As list. The choices on the list depend on the type of content you cut or copied. For example, if you copied some text from another document that had some unusual formatting, you could choose to keep that formatting by selecting Formatted Text (RTF), or you could choose to discard that formatting by selecting Unformatted Text.

CAUTION

If you paste text in one of the Picture formats, it is no longer editable as text; you can edit it only with a picture-editing program.

Pasting in a format whose name ends with "Object" creates an embedded copy that retains its link to the original program. This is not especially relevant for copying text within and between Word documents because the original program is Word itself, but it makes a difference when copying multimedia content, such as graphics from a graphics program, into Word, for example. When you choose an "Object" format, the selection is placed in its own separate frame from the rest of the document, and you can edit that object in its native program later by double-clicking it.

Under some circumstances, a Paste Link option is also available. For Paste Link to be available, the selection must have been copied from some other document or file than the one in which it is being pasted, and the document/file from which it came must have been saved at least once (so it has a filename, not just the generic "Document1" name a file gets before it is saved). Paste Link creates a dynamic link between the original and the copy so that when the original changes, the copy also changes.

CAUTION

> Don't use Paste Link unless you can actually benefit from it, because it makes the file size larger, and if the original file ever is deleted or moved, an error message will appear in the file containing the copy.

→ To learn more about linking and embedding, **see** "Embedding Data," **p. 615** and "Linking to Data in Other Files," **p. 620**.

USING PASTE OPTIONS

After you have pasted something in Word, a Paste Options button appears next to it. You can click this button to open a menu of choices governing the paste operation, as shown in Figure 3.11. Here are the choices:

- **Keep Source Formatting**—The object retains its look from its original location.
- **Match Destination Formatting**—The object is stripped of any previous formatting and the formatting of the new location is applied.
- **Keep Text Only**—The object is stripped of any previous formatting and remains stripped in the new location.

Figure 3.11
Choose options for the paste operation just performed.

The Set Default Paste command opens the Word Options dialog box (same as Office, Word Options) and displays the Advanced options. From here you can set a variety of paste options in the Cut, Copy, and Paste section, as shown in Figure 3.12:

Figure 3.12
Paste options are controlled in the Word Options dialog box.

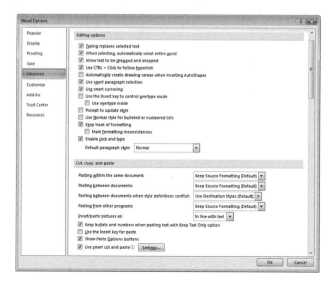

- **Pasting Within the Same Document**—Choose how formatting is applied to the copy when copying within a document. You can choose Keep Source Formatting, Match Destination Formatting, or Keep Text Only.

- **Pasting Between Documents**—Choose how formatting is applied to the copy when styles are not an issue (for example, when both the source and destination use the same style defined the same way).

- **Pasting Between Documents When Style Definitions Conflict**—Choose how formatting is applied to the copy when you are copying between documents and the style applied in the source document differs from that applied at the insertion point location in the destination document.

- **Pasting From Other Programs**—Choose how formatting is applied to the copy when the text is coming from some other application than Word.

- **Insert/Paste Pictures As**—Choose how non-text objects are placed in the document. In Line with Text means the object is treated as a text character at the insertion point, and will move with the surrounding text. The other options are all various wrapping settings for floating objects.

→ For more on picture/text wrap settings, **see** "Setting Text Wrap Properties," **p. 402**.

- **Keep Bullets and Numbers When Pasting Text with Keep Text Only Option**— Just like the name says. If you have set one of the previous settings to Keep Text Only, but you are copying a bulleted or numbered list, this setting determines whether the bullet or number is preserved.

- **Use the Insert key for Paste**—Mark this if you want the Insert (Ins) key on the keyboard to be remapped to be a shortcut for the Paste command. This check box is paired with the Use the INS Key to Control Overtype Mode check box (on the same tab); only one or the other can be chosen at once.

- **Show Paste Options Buttons**—Clear this check box if you don't want that Paste Options button to appear next to pasted selections. (Sometimes it can get in the way.)

- **Use Smart Cut and Paste**—Enables Word to apply a rather complex set of rules to determine how selections should be pasted. To fine-tune these rules, click the Settings button to display the Settings dialog box (see Figure 3.13). Note that you can choose default options for Word 2002-2007 or for Word 97-2000, or go your own way with custom settings.

Figure 3.13
Fine-tune the paste options here.

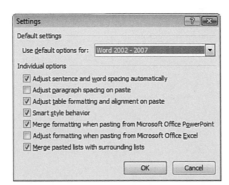

USING THE OFFICE CLIPBOARD

The Office Clipboard is an expanded version of the Windows Clipboard. It can hold up to 24 selections, and you can choose which item to paste with each operation.

NOTE

> If you are copying or cutting between an Office application and a non-Office application, the two Clipboards talk to each other, but only via the first position on the Office Clipboard. The other 23 possible positions on the Office Clipboard are simply ignored.

To access any clips other than the last one stored, you must display the Office Clipboard task pane. To view the Office Clipboard task pane, click the dialog box launcher for the Clipboard group on the Home tab.

The Office Clipboard appears to the left of the main document window, as shown in Figure 3.14.

Figure 3.14
Use the Clipboard task pane to access the Office Clipboard's 24 separate areas for storing clips.

NOTE

> By default, the Clipboard pane is fixed in location and size, but you can click the down arrow in its top-right corner for a menu from which you can move and resize it.

Each time you copy something to the Clipboard, it is added to the Clipboard task pane's list, with the most recently added items at the top. To paste an item from it, position the insertion point and then click that item in the Clipboard task pane. To paste all the items at once, click Paste All.

To remove a single item from the Clipboard task pane, right-click the item and click Delete (see Figure 3.15). (Alternatively, you can point at the item until a down arrow appears to its right. Click that down arrow to open the same menu as with right-clicking; then click Delete.)

Figure 3.15
Delete an item from the Clipboard.

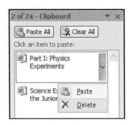

To clear the entire Clipboard at once, click the Clear All button at the top. Clearing the Office Clipboard also clears the Windows Clipboard.

To fine-tune how the Office Clipboard works, click the Options button. A menu appears with these options on it:

- **Show Office Clipboard Automatically**—Displays the Office Clipboard automatically when copying items.

- **Show Office Clipboard when Ctrl+C Pressed Twice**—Displays the Office Clipboard when Ctrl+C is pressed twice.

- **Collect Without Showing Office Clipboard**—Copies items to the Office Clipboard but does not show the task pane unless you specifically call for it (by pressing Ctrl+C twice, for example).

- **Show Office Clipboard Icon on Taskbar**—Displays an Office Clipboard icon in the notification area of the taskbar (near the clock) whenever the Office Clipboard is active. You can double-click that icon to display the Office Clipboard in the active application. (Remember, all Office apps share the Office Clipboard.)

- **Show Status Near Taskbar When Copying**—Pops up a message near the Office Clipboard icon when something has just been copied to the Clipboard.

LOCATING SPECIFIC CONTENT

Word offers many ways of jumping quickly to certain content in a document. This content can be actual data that you've typed, or can be an object such as an image, a caption, a bookmark, or even a certain type of formatting. In the following sections, you'll learn about several ways to browse or search a document to find specific items.

FINDING AND REPLACING

The Find feature in Word helps locate instances of a specified text string. That text string can be anything you care to look for—a product name, a person, a string of numbers, or whatever. You can even use it to find specific formatting or a nonprinting symbol or code, such as a tab or a paragraph break. For example, suppose you are looking for a phone number in a document. You don't remember what page it's on, but you know it starts with a (317) area code. You could search for (317) to locate it.

The Replace feature works hand-in-hand with Find; it performs the Find operation but then replaces the found item with a different text string you specify. As with Find, you can also use Replace with formatting and with nonprinting symbols and codes. For example, suppose you are drawing up a contract for a Ms. Smith, when you find out that she has recently become Mrs. Brown. You can perform a Replace operation to change all instances of Smith to Brown, and all instances of Ms. to Mrs. (Be careful with that one, though, because there might be more than one person in the document who uses Ms. as a prefix.)

FINDING A TEXT STRING

Here's how to do a basic Find in which you examine each instance of the text, one instance at a time:

1. Press Ctrl+F, or click Find on the Home tab.

   TIP

   > If you use Find frequently, consider adding a button for it to the Quick Access toolbar. To do this, right-click the Find button on the Home tab and choose Add to Quick Access Toolbar. That way you can access it no matter which tab is currently displayed.

2. Type the text string into the Find What box. (To find other things besides text strings, such as special characters or formatting, see the next several sections.)
3. Click Find Next. The display jumps to the first instance of that text (see Figure 3.16).
4. Keep clicking Find Next until you find the instance you are interested in, or until a message appears that Word has finished searching the document.

Figure 3.16
Find a text string in a document.

SELECTING ALL INSTANCES OF FOUND TEXT

If you prefer, you can have Word select all instances at once, and then you can page through the document to examine them. This method actually selects the text strings, as if you had held down Ctrl and dragged across them to select them yourself with the mouse. Clicking anywhere in the document will deselect them, so you can't do any editing of individual instances here without disturbing the selection. However, what you *can* do is perform some global formatting command upon them all, such as making them all bold or a different font or color.

To select all instances of the found text, follow these steps:

1. Press Ctrl+F, or click Find on the Home tab.
2. Type the text string into the Find What box.
3. Click Find In. On the menu that opens, click Main Document. Word selects each instance of the text string.
4. Without closing the Find and Replace dialog box, scroll through the document to examine all the instances. If desired, apply a formatting command to them as a group.

→   To learn more about text formatting, **see** "Applying Character Formatting," **p. 155**.

5. When you are finished, click Close to close the Find and Replace dialog box.

HIGHLIGHTING ALL INSTANCES OF FOUND TEXT

The preceding procedure selects the instances only for as long as the Find and Replace dialog box is open and you have not clicked to select anything else. Their selection is pretty tenuous, in other words. If you want more durable marking of each found instance, try this instead:

1. Press Ctrl+F, or click Find on the Home tab.
2. Type the text string into the Find What box.
3. Click Reading Highlight. On the menu that opens, click Highlight All.
4. Close the Find and Replace dialog box and examine all the found instances at your leisure.
5. When you are finished examining all the found instances, reopen the Find and Replace dialog box (Ctrl+F).
6. Click Reading Highlight. On the menu that opens, click Clear Highlighting. This clears the highlighting applied from the Find and Replace dialog box, but does not clear highlighting applied with the Highlight feature on the Home tab.
7. Close the Find and Replace dialog box.

CUSTOMIZING A FIND OPERATION

The Find operation has many options available for customizing the search. To access them, click the More >> button in the Find and Replace dialog box. The dialog box that appears is shown in Figure 3.17.

Figure 3.17
Customize the Find command using these search options.

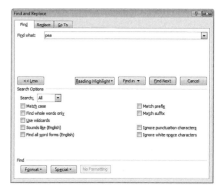

You can set any of these options as needed:

- **Search**—Choose Down, Up, or All to determine in what direction from the insertion point the Find operation will proceed.

- **Match Case**—The search is limited to the letter case you used for typing the Find What entry. For example, if you are searching for *butter*, it will not find *Butter*.

- **Find Whole Words Only**—The search is limited to whole words that match the search string. For example, if you are searching for *butter*, it would not find *butterfly*.

- **Use Wildcards**—You can use wildcard designators in your searches to find any character (^?), any digit (^#), or any letter (^$). If you forget these codes, you can select them from the Special menu.

- **Sounds Like (English)**—The search will include words that are pronounced similarly to the word you are searching for. This is good to have if you aren't sure how to spell a word but you know how it sounds.

- **Find All Word Forms (English)**—The search will contain forms of a word even if they are not spelled the same. For example, a search for *is* would find words such as *am, is, are, was, were,* and *be.*

- **Match Prefix**—Finds the string only if it appears at the beginning of a word.

- **Match Suffix**—Finds the string only if it appears at the end of a word.

- **Ignore Punctuation Characters**—Omits punctuation from the search. For example, a search for *three and* would find *three, and* (note the comma) if this option is turned on.

- **Ignore White-Space Characters**—Omits white space from the search. For example, a search for *living room* would find *livingroom.*

With all these options showing, the Find and Replace dialog box becomes rather large and cumbersome. You can shrink it again by clicking the <<Less button.

REPLACING A TEXT STRING

Click the Replace tab in the Find and Replace dialog box for access to the Replace tools. If the dialog box is not already open, you can open it and display that tab on top by pressing Ctrl+H or selecting Replace on the Home tab.

After entering text in the Find What and Replace With boxes, click Find Next to find the first instance of the string, and then click Replace to replace that instance, or click Find Next again to skip that instance (see Figure 3.18).

Figure 3.18
Replace one text string with another on the Replace tab.

If you're really brave, click Replace All to do all instances at once. Be aware, though, that this can have unintended consequences if there are instances you didn't anticipate. For example, suppose you are replacing all instances of *White* with *Brown*. But somewhere in your document you talk about the whitening power of a laundry product. The word *whitening* would become *brownning*, which is clearly not what you want.

FINDING AND REPLACING FORMATTING

In addition to finding text strings, Find and Replace can also find formatting. You can use this to find certain strings that are formatted in a certain way, or you can simply find the formatting itself and not include any text in the search.

To find (and optionally replace) certain formatting, follow these steps:

1. Make sure the additional controls are displayed in the Find and Replace dialog box. Click the More >> button to display them if they are not.

2. Click in the Find What box to place the insertion point in it. (Optional) If you want to limit the search to certain text, type that text.

3. Click the Format button. A menu opens.

4. Click the type of formatting you want to specify. For example, to specify character formatting such as a font, click Font.

5. In the dialog box that appears, specify the formatting you want to find and then click OK. The dialog box will be different depending on the type of formatting you chose in step 4. For example, in Figure 3.19, the Find Font dialog box is shown.

   Notice that the Effects check boxes have a solid fill in them, meaning that their setting will not be an issue in the search. If you click one of them, it becomes selected with a check mark, meaning the search will find text only with that attribute on. Click it again and it becomes cleared, meaning the search will find text only with that attribute off. Click it a third time to cycle back to the solid fill again.

Figure 3.19
Find Font is just one example of the dialog boxes for specifying formatting to find.

Back in the Find and Replace dialog box, a line now appears beneath the Find What text box stating the formatting that has been chosen.

6. (Optional) Repeat steps 3–5 to specify more formatting criteria for the text to be found.

7. (Optional) If you want to specify formatting for the replacement, click in the Replace With box and then repeat steps 3–5.

> **NOTE**
> If you make a mistake in specifying formatting, click in either the Find What or the Replace With text box and click No Formatting to clear it.

8. Continue the find operation normally. You can use the Find Next button for an interactive find, or use Replace, Replace All, Find In, or Reading Highlight. (The latter two are available only on the Find tab.)

FINDING AND REPLACING SPECIAL CHARACTERS

Sometimes the text you need to find is not really text at all, but a layout character such as a paragraph break, page break, or tab. It's actually a fairly common need. For example, suppose you download some unformatted text from the Internet in a plain-text file that uses two paragraph breaks per paragraph—one to end a paragraph and one to create an extra line break between paragraphs. You want to get rid of the extra paragraph breaks, but it's a 100-page document. No problem. For the Find What field, enter two paragraph breaks by selecting Paragraph Mark from the Special menu twice in a row. In the Replace With box, enter a single paragraph mark. In other words, you're replacing every instance of two paragraph marks with one paragraph mark.

As you select a symbol from the Special menu, a caret code is entered into the Find What or Replace With box. It's called a caret code because each of these codes begins with a caret (^) symbol. If you happen to remember the code for what you want, feel free to type it in manually. Table 3.6 lists the codes for all the available special characters. Some of these are available only to find, not to replace, so they will not be available on the list when the insertion point is in the Replace With box.

TABLE 3.6   CARET CODES FOR SPECIAL CHARACTERS IN FIND AND REPLACE OPERATIONS

Symbol	Code	Where Available
Paragraph break	^p	Find What/Replace With
Tab character	^t	Find What/Replace With
Any character	^?	Find What
Any digit	^#	Find What
Any letter	^$	Find What
Caret character	^^	Find What/Replace With
Section character (§) (not an actual section break)	^%	Find What/Replace With
Paragraph character (¶, not an actual paragraph break)	^v	Find What/Replace With
Clipboard contents	^c	Replace With
Column break	^n	Find What/Replace With
Em dash (—)	^+	Find What/Replace With
En dash (–)	^=	Find What/Replace With
Endnote mark	^e	Find What
Field	^d	Find What
Find What text	^&	Replace With
Footnote mark	^f	Find What
Graphic	^g	Find What
Manual (hard) line break	^l	Find What/Replace With
Manual (hard) page break	^m	Find What/Replace With
Nonbreaking hyphen	^~	Find What/Replace With
Nonbreaking space	^s	Find What/Replace With
Optional hyphen	^-	Find What/Replace With
Section break	^b	Find What
White space	^w	Find What

3

In addition to the "caret codes" that refer to individual symbols, there are a variety of special codes that can refer to multiple characters. Table 3.7 lists the available codes and their usage.

TABLE 3.7   TEXT STRING CODES FOR FIND AND REPLACE OPERATIONS

To find...	Use This:	Example
Text at the beginning of a word	<	<(new) finds newton but not renew; same as match Prefix.
Text at the end of a word	>	>(new) finds renew but not newton; same as Match Suffix.
Any single character of a list of characters	[ ]	f[ai]n finds fan and fin but not fun
Any single character in a range	[-]	s[a-o]ng finds sang, sing, and song, but not sung.
Any single character except the specified character range	[!]	s[!a-o]ng finds sung but not sang, sing, or song
An exact number of occurrences of the preceding character or expression	{n}	we{2}d finds weed but not wed
At least a number of occurrences of the preceding character or expression	{n,}	we{1,}d finds both weed and wed
Any single character	{n,m}	5{1,4} finds 50, 500, 5000, and 50000
One or more occurrences of the preceding character or expression	@	50@ finds 50, 500, 5000, and higher numbers of zeros

USING SELECT BROWSE OBJECT

The Select Browse Object feature provides an efficient way to scroll through a document when you are looking for a specific type of content. For example, suppose you want to scroll through a large document so you can check the captions on the graphics. You could use Select Browse Object to scroll to the graphics, skipping over any screens that don't contain graphics.

Start by clicking the Select Browse Object button, which is the round icon below the lower arrow on the vertical scroll bar. (Alternatively, press Ctrl+Alt+Home.) A fly-out palette of choices appears. You can point to each choice to see a description. (Table 3.8 also describes each one.) Click one of the choices to specify what to browse for (see Figure 3.20).

Figure 3.20
Choose what Word should browse for.

After selecting the browse type, use the blue double arrows above and below the Select Browse Object button (or press Ctrl+Page Down or Ctrl+Page Up) to move to the next or previous instance of the chosen item.

TABLE 3.8   SELECT BROWSE OBJECT TYPES

Button	Object Type
→	Opens the Go To tab in the Find and Replace dialog box
🔍	Opens the Find tab in the Find and Replace dialog box
✎	Browse by edits (if tracking changes)
☰	Browse by heading
🖼	Browse by graphic
▦	Browse by table
{a}	Browse by field
📑	Browse by endnote
📑	Browse by footnote
💬	Browse by comment
🗔	Browse by section
🗋	Browse by page

USING GO TO

Go To is useful when you want to go to a particular instance of a content type, not just browse all instances. For example, perhaps you don't want to go through the document page by page, but instead want to jump immediately to page 100. Go To lets you enter the desired page number and go to it. It does this not just with pages, but with many other types of items as well, such as comments, bookmarks, graphics, and so on.

As you saw in Table 3.8, you can access the Go To tab of the Find and Replace dialog box via the Select Browse Object feature. You can also access it by clicking Find and selecting Go To on the Home tab (see Figure 3.21).

Figure 3.21
Select Go To on the
Home tab.

On the Go To tab, select the item type and then enter the information about it. Depending on the type of item, either a text box or a drop-down list appears. Figure 3.22 shows an example of browsing for a particular section, for example.

Figure 3.22
Go to a specified instance of a particular type of item with the Go To tab.

→ To learn about the other tabs of the Find and Replace dialog box, **see** "Finding and Replacing," **p. 79**.

DISPLAYING A DOCUMENT MAP

In a document that uses heading styles, you can display a document map that lists the headings, like a mini-outline view. You can click a heading in the document map to jump quickly to that heading within the document itself.

To display the document map, select the Document Map check box on the View tab. Then click an item on the map to jump to it in the document.

You can customize the document map to show only certain heading levels if you wish. To do so, right-click an empty area of the document map and click the desired outline level, as shown in Figure 3.23. Alternatively, you can click a particular heading that has subheadings beneath it and then right-click and choose Expand or Collapse to show more or fewer levels in only a section of the outline.

Figure 3.23
Display a document map that shows all the headings and bookmarks.

To turn off the document map, click the Close (X) button in the top-right corner, or clear the Document Map check box on the View tab again to toggle the feature off.

→ To learn about heading styles, **see** "Understanding Styles," **p. 228**.

→ To change the outline level at which a style appears in the document map, **see** "Setting a Style's Outline Level," **p. 688**.

DISPLAYING PAGE THUMBNAILS

Thumbnails are small images of each page. They are useful in situations where you want to move to a certain page based on what it looks like. (Maybe it has a distinctive graphic on it, for example.)

To display or hide page thumbnails, mark or clear the Thumbnails check box on the View tab. Or, if the document map is already open, use the drop-down list at the top of the document map to switch to Thumbnails view.

INSERTING DUMMY TEXT

Dummy text is generic text that is inserted so you can see the document's formatting. This is especially useful when creating multicolumn frame-based layouts such as in a brochure or newsletter.

Different applications use different words for dummy text; some programs repeat the same sentence over and over, use nonsense words, or use Greek phrases. (The latter is an inside joke born of the fact that in typesetting, when lines are placed where text will eventually go, it's called *greeking*, as in "It's all Greek to me.")

Word 2007, however, has real English language paragraphs that it uses, and they even make sense! Word use three paragraphs with text that discusses the galleries feature. If you insert more than three paragraphs, they start repeating.

To insert dummy text, you use a random function such as the following, where p represents the desired number of paragraphs:

=rand(p)

You just type this directly into the document, and when you press Enter, Word replaces what you typed with the paragraphs.

By default, each paragraph has three sentences in it. If you want more or fewer sentences per paragraph, add another argument to the function, like this:

=rand(p,s)

Here, s is the desired number of sentences. For example, to get eight paragraphs with four sentences each, use =rand(8,4).

3

CAUTION

> This function works only when it is typed as a paragraph all to itself. It doesn't work when typed as part of an existing paragraph, or at any position other than the beginning of a paragraph.

WORKING WITH BUILDING BLOCKS

Earlier versions of Word had a feature called AutoText that stored and retrieved snippets of text. Word 2007 has greatly expanded this capability into a new feature called *building blocks*. Building blocks are stored snippets that can contain formatted text, graphics, and other objects. They can be inserted into any document at any time.

NOTE

> Word 2007 still nominally supports something called AutoText, in that one of the building block galleries is named AutoText and you can place items into it. However, AutoText is now part of the building block functionality.

Building blocks are categorized by their function and are organized in *galleries*. The gallery in which a building block is stored is a matter of preference, but different galleries do show up in different places in the program. For example, if you place a building block in the Quick Parts category, it will appear on the Quick Parts drop-down list on the Insert tab.

Building blocks are stored in templates. To make a block accessible to all new documents based on Normal.dotm, you can store it in that template. Alternatively, you can store a building block in a template called Building Blocks.dotx, designed specifically for holding them. The Building Blocks.dotx template is always available, no matter what template is applied to the body of the document.

NOTE

> The difference in file extensions between the two templates is part of Word 2007's new system of file naming. A .dotm template supports macros; a .dotx template does not.

CREATING A BUILDING BLOCK

A building block can contain text (formatted or unformatted), graphics, objects such as text frames, diagrams, or WordArt, and more. Anything you create in Word can be saved in a building block.

To create a building block, first create the content and then do the following:

1. Select all the content that should be included in the document part.
2. On the Insert tab, choose Quick Parts, Save Selection to Quick Part Gallery. The Create New Building Block dialog box opens (see Figure 3.24).

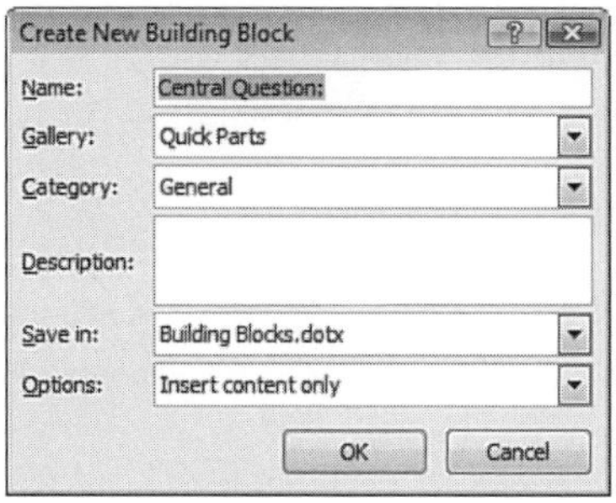

Figure 3.24
Create a new building block and specify which gallery it belongs to.

3. In the Name box, change the default name if desired. This name will appear on lists of building blocks. By default, the name is the first few words of the text.

4. Change the Gallery setting if desired.

   By default, the Gallery is set to Quick Parts. Items placed in this gallery will be accessible via the Quick Parts menu, so they'll be very convenient. However, if you add too many items to the Quick Parts gallery, it might become unwieldy to work with the list. Various galleries are used for features you will learn about in other chapters throughout the books, including headers and footers, page numbers, and cover pages.

5. (Optional) Assign a category to the item. You can stick with the default General category or choose Create New Category to build your own system of categories.

6. Type a description of the building block in the Description box if desired.

7. Change the Save In setting if desired. The default is Building Blocks.dotx.

> **TIP**
>
> The items in Building Blocks.dotx are available via the Building Blocks Organizer regardless of what template is in use.

8. Select the desired insertion method from the Options list:
   - **Insert content only**—Places the item at the insertion point.
   - **Insert content in its own paragraph**—Places the item in a separate paragraph.
   - **Insert content in its own page**—Places the item on a new page.

9. Click OK to create the new building block entry.

The new building block will now be available for insertion, as explained in the next section.

INSERTING A BUILDING BLOCK

A building block's insertion method depends on the gallery in which you placed it when you created it. If you chose to place it in the Quick Parts gallery, it appears on the Quick Parts list (see Figure 3.25).

Figure 3.25
Building blocks appear on different menus depending on the gallery in which they were placed.

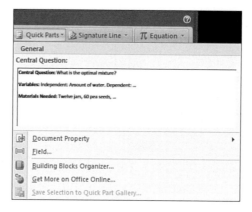

If the desired building block does not appear in either location, you can select it from the Building Blocks Organizer, as follows:

1. From the Insert tab, click Quick Parts and then click Building Blocks Organizer. The Building Blocks Organizer dialog box appears.

2. Click an item to preview it (see Figure 3.26).

3. When you find the item you want to insert, click Insert.

Figure 3.26
Insert an item from the Building Blocks Organizer.

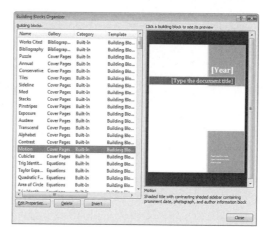

NOTE

You might have some different building blocks than shown in Figure 3.26. If you upgraded from an earlier version of Word, for example, you will have some of the AutoText entries from the previous version available.

DELETING BUILDING BLOCKS

You can delete any building blocks, both those that you have created yourself and those stored in the Building Blocks.dotx template that comes with Word. To delete a building block, follow these steps:

1. From the Insert tab, choose Quick Parts, Building Blocks Organizer. The Building Blocks Organizer dialog box appears.
2. Click the item to delete.
3. Click the Delete button.
4. When you are finished deleting blocks, click Close.

CHANGING A BUILDING BLOCK'S PROPERTIES

All of a building block's properties are editable, including its gallery, its template location, and so on. Follow these steps to edit building block properties:

1. From the Insert tab, choose Quick Parts, Building Blocks Organizer. The Building Blocks Organizer dialog box appears.
2. Click the item and then click Edit Properties. The Modify Building Block dialog box opens. It is much the same as the dialog box you used to create the building block initially (refer to Figure 3.24).
3. Make any changes as needed, and then click OK.
4. A confirmation box appears; click Yes.

TROUBLESHOOTING

I DON'T WANT WORD TO EXTEND SELECTIONS

By default, Word uses smart paragraph selection. In other words, if you drag across a paragraph to select it, Word will automatically include the hidden end-of-paragraph marker in the selection area. This is for your own good, because it prevents you from leaving behind the paragraphs' marker inadvertently. Word also automatically selects an entire word when you drag across selections, so your selection doesn't stop in the middle of a word.

If you dislike either of these features, you can turn them off. Choose Office, Word Options, click Advanced, and in the Editing Options section, clear the Use Smart Paragraph Selection check box and/or the When Selecting, Automatically Select Entire Word check box.

I'D LIKE TO SAVE CLIPBOARD CONTENT FOR LATER USE

By far the easiest way to save something from the Clipboard is to paste it into Word (or some other application) and then save it in that application's native file format. But you can also save, organize, and recall items from the Windows Clipboard.

With a default installation of Office, a utility is installed called Microsoft Clip Organizer. It is primarily for managing clip art, but you can also use it to save items to and from the Clipboard.

You'll find it on the Start, All Programs, Microsoft Office, Microsoft Office Tools menu. Start it up, and then choose Edit, Paste to copy the current contents of the Windows Clipboard into the organizer. The pasted item appears as a thumbnail image there. You can drag it into any of the various collections on the Collection List, assign keywords to it, place it back on the Clipboard (with Edit, Copy), and more.

One thing you *can't* do with the Microsoft Clip Organizer, however, is to save the clip as a separate file. To do this, you need a different utility—the ClipBook Viewer. This is a Windows XP utility, not Office. (It is not available in Windows Vista.) In Windows XP, you can find it at this path: Windows\System32\clipbrd.exe. (Use the Run command to run it.)

The ClipBook Viewer starts out with a single, minimized window called Clipboard that contains the current contents of the Windows Clipboard. Restore this window and then choose Office, Save As to save that clip as an NT Clipboard File (with a .clp extension). To recall a saved Clipboard item, use Office, Open. This places the content of the file onto the Windows Clipboard, displacing what was there before.

The Building Blocks.dotx File is Corrupted

If you see a warning about the Building Blocks.dotx file being missing or corrupted, click OK. If asked whether you want to recover the data from the file, choose No. Then close Word, and use Windows to do a search for the file Building Blocks.dotx. Delete all instances of that file and reopen Word. Word will re-generate a fresh copy of the file. You will lose any building blocks you have created, however.

CHAPTER **4**

USING SPELLING, GRAMMAR, AND RESEARCH TOOLS

In this chapter

CORRECTING SPELLING AND GRAMMATICAL ERRORS

Word has a built-in, automatic spelling and grammar checker that compares every word and sentence to a built-in dictionary and grammar guide and then lets you know which words, phrases, and sentences are questionable—not necessarily wrong, but worthy of a second look.

There are two ways of checking spelling and grammar in a document. You can check individual words and phrases on a case-by-case basis, or you can run a complete spelling and grammar check of the entire document. Each technique is explained separately in the following sections.

CHECKING THE SPELLING OF AN INDIVIDUAL WORD

In an open text document, a wavy red or blue underline (nonprinting) indicates a word that Word can't identify. It might be misspelled, or it simply might not be in Word's dictionaries for some reason.

The difference between the red and the blue underlines is context. A red underlined word is not in the dictionary at all. For example, in the following sentence, *luse* would be red-underlined:

> You've got nothing to luse.

A blue underline represents a word that is in the dictionary but might be used improperly in its current context. For example, in the following sentence, *loose* would be blue-underlined:

> You've got nothing to loose.

Right-click a red-underlined or blue-underlined word to see a menu, as shown in Figure 4.1, that contains these options:

- **Spelling corrections**—These are suggestions for the spelling correction. Click a suggestion to apply it. If the correct spelling for the word does not appear on the list, you can manually edit the word, as you would any other text in the document.

- **Ignore**—Ignores only this instance in the current document. The word is still flagged elsewhere in the document.

- **Ignore All**—Ignores this and all other instances of the word within the current document only. The word is still flagged in other documents.

- **Add to Dictionary**—Adds the word to the custom dictionary so that it is not flagged in future documents (or in any instances in the current document). This one is not available for blue-underlined words.

- **AutoCorrect**—Opens a submenu containing all the words that were suggested at the top of the menu so that you can quickly set up an AutoCorrect entry that always changes your misspelling to that word. This option does not appear if there are no spelling suggestions on the list, or if the word is blue-underlined.

→ To learn more about AutoCorrect settings, **see** "Automating Corrections with AutoCorrect," **p. 111**.

→ If Word isn't checking spelling correctly because it thinks a passage of text is written in some other language, **see** "Word Marks Passages of Text as the Wrong Language" in the Troubleshooting section at the end of this chapter.

- **Language**—Enables you to set a different language for the word so that it will be evaluated using a different dictionary (if you have multiple language dictionaries installed).

- **Spelling**—Opens the Spelling dialog box, discussed fully in the next section.

Figure 4.1
Right-click a red-underlined word to get spelling assistance for it.

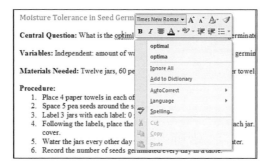

It's important to note that a red-underlined word is not always wrong. It's just not in any of the dictionaries that Word consulted. It could be a proper name, such as the name of a person or product, or it could be a model number, serial number, or some other type of code.

FIXING INDIVIDUAL GRAMMATICAL ERRORS

A possible error in grammar or punctuation appears with a green wavy underline. Word finds many types of grammatical errors, ranging from double punctuation (such as two commas in a row) to a lack of subject/verb agreement.

Right-clicking a green-underlined phrase produces a shortcut menu with one or more grammar suggestions or options. The exact content of the menu depends on the type of error, but as shown in Figure 4.2, here are some of the options you might see:

- **Grammar corrections**—These are suggestions for the grammar correction. Click a suggestion to apply it.

- **Ignore Once**—Ignores this grammar rule in this instance but continues to check for this grammar rule elsewhere in the document.

- **Grammar**—Opens the Grammar dialog box, described in the next section.

- **About This Sentence**—Opens a Help window explaining the grammar rule that is (perhaps) being violated.

- **Look Up**—Opens the Research pane, which provides information from various reference sources such as dictionaries.

4

Figure 4.2
Right-click a green-underlined phrase to get grammar help.

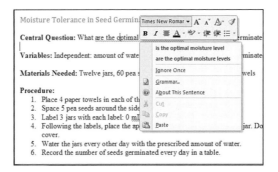

CAUTION

Word is good at finding possible errors and suggesting corrections, but it can't substitute for a human proofreader. Grammar is a lot more subjective than spelling, and Word makes more mistakes with grammar. In some cases, it even suggests changes that will make the grammar out-and-out wrong. If you don't know whether something is grammatically correct, don't take Word's word for it; look it up or ask a friend.

PERFORMING AN INTERACTIVE SPELLING AND GRAMMAR CHECK

An interactive spelling and grammar check can save some time when you have a large document to check. It uses a dialog box interface to jump to each possible spelling and grammatical error, one by one, so you don't have to scroll through the document looking for the red and green underlines.

To perform an interactive check, follow these steps:

1. Display the Review tab and click Spelling & Grammar to open the Spelling and Grammar dialog box. (F7 is a shortcut.)

2. (Optional) To perform only a spell check (not grammar too), clear the Check Grammar check box.

3. If a spelling error is found, examine the word that appears in red in the Not in Dictionary box (see Figure 4.3). Then do one of the following to respond to it:

Figure 4.3
Check spelling via the Spelling and Grammar dialog box.

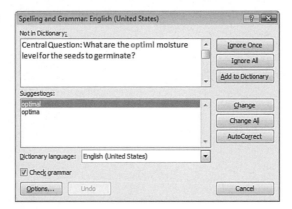

- Click Ignore Once to skip this instance but continue to flag other instances in the current document.

- Click Ignore All to ignore this and all instances of the word in the current document.

- Click Add to Dictionary to add the word to the custom dictionary.

- Click a word on the Suggestions list and then click Change to change this one instance only to the chosen word, or click Change All to change all instances.

- Click in the Not in Dictionary box to move the insertion point into it, type a correction there manually, and then click the Change button.

- Click a word on the Suggestions list and then click AutoCorrect to create an AutoCorrect entry for it.

4. If a grammatical error is found, examine the phrase that appears in green in the Grammatical Error box (see Figure 4.4) and then do one of the following to respond to it:

Figure 4.4
Check grammar via the Spelling and Grammar dialog box.

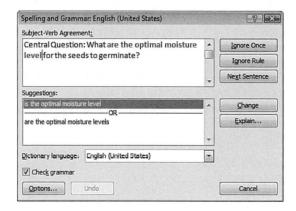

- Click Ignore Once to skip this instance but continue to flag other instances in the current document.

- Click Ignore Rule to ignore this and all instances of the grammar rule in the current document.

- Click Next Sentence to skip this sentence, not making any changes.

- Click a suggestion in the Suggestions list and then click Change to change this instance as recommended. If no automatically applicable suggestion is available (for example, if the suggestion is to revise the sentence so that it is no longer a fragment), the Change button will be unavailable.

- Click Explain to see a Help window with a description of the error found.

5. Continue the spelling and grammar check until the entire document has been checked, or click Cancel or Close to end the check early.

FINDING PROOFING ERRORS

When a document contains one or more spelling errors, the Proofing Errors icon appears in the status bar, as shown in Figure 4.5. Click that icon to jump to the first error (starting at the current insertion point position) and display a shortcut menu with suggestions of how to deal with it. It's like doing a Search for red and green wavy underlines.

Figure 4.5
Click the Proofing Errors icon on the status bar to jump to an error and see suggestions for correcting it.

Proofing Errors icon

When no more proofing errors exist in the document, the button changes to a No Proofing Errors one (a blue check mark).

CUSTOMIZING SPELLING AND GRAMMAR OPTIONS

The spelling and grammar checker is very customizable. For example, you can choose not to check certain types of words (such as words in all uppercase or those that contain numbers), you can turn the wavy red and green underlines on and off, and much more. You can even specify a level of "strictness" for the grammar checker to enforce.

To access the spelling and grammar options, choose Office, Word Options and then click Proofing (see Figure 4.6).

Figure 4.6
Control spelling and grammar settings in the Word Options dialog box.

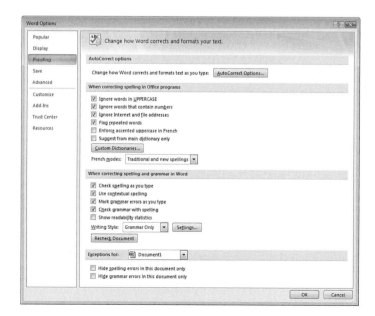

TIP

You can also access the spelling and grammar options from the Spelling and Grammar dialog box (or the individual Spelling or Grammar boxes) by clicking the Options button.

→ To learn more about AutoCorrect settings, **see** "Automating Corrections with AutoCorrect," **p. 111**.

Basic spelling options are found in the When Correcting Spelling in Office Programs section. These are applied globally in all Office applications (Word, Excel, PowerPoint, and so on):

- **Ignore Words in UPPERCASE**—This refers to words that are all-uppercase, not just words that begin with a capital letter.

- **Ignore Words That Contain Numbers**—This refers to words that contain digits, such as *BR549*, not words that spell out numbers, such as *sixteen*.

- **Ignore Internet and File Addresses**—This excludes URLs, email addresses, and file paths (such as C:\Windows) from being checked.

- **Flag Repeated Words**—This marks a possible misspelling when the same word appears twice in a row.

- **Enforce Accented Uppercase in French**—This marks a possible misspelling in text marked as French when uppercase letters that normally require accents do not have them.

- **Suggest from Main Dictionary Only**—This confines the Suggestions list to the words found in Word's main built-in dictionary. Any words you have added to the custom dictionary will not be suggested.

- **Custom Dictionaries**—This opens the Custom Dictionaries dialog box.

→ To learn how to mark a passage of text as French, or any other language, **see** "Checking Spelling and Grammar in Multiple Languages," **p. 108**.

→ To work with custom dictionaries, **see** "Managing the Spelling Dictionaries," **p. 103**.

The When Correcting Spelling and Grammer in Word section's options are specific to Word only:

- **Check Spelling As You Type**—Turn this off to stop Word from checking spelling (and red-underlining words) on the fly. To check spelling when this is turned off, you must use the interactive spelling and grammar check (F7).

- **Use Contextual Spelling**—Turn this off to stop Word from blue-underlining words that might be used improperly in the current context.

- **Mark Grammar Errors As You Type**—Turn this off to stop Word from checking grammar (and green-underlining words and phrases) on the fly. To check grammar when this is turned off, you must use the interactive spelling and grammar check (F7).

- **Check Grammar With Spelling**— Turn this off to stop Word from checking grammar when using the Spelling and Grammar dialog box.

- **Recheck Document**—Click this button to run the spelling and grammar check again after changing the grammar settings to see if any additional errors or concerns are flagged.

- **Show Readability Statistics**—Turn this on to display a box with readability information at the end of a spelling and grammar check with the Spelling and Grammar dialog box. Readability statistics are covered later in this chapter, in the section "Evaluating Readability."

- **Writing Style**—Set the level of grammar check you want here; you can have it check for grammar only, or also check stylistic conventions. Examples of style issues include contractions, clichés, commonly misspelled words, and unclear phrasing. (To fine-tune these settings, see the next section.)

The Exceptions For section enables you to select any open document from the drop-down list and then set these options:

- **Hide Spelling Errors in This Document Only**—This does not turn off the spell checking as you type, but it does prevent the wavy red underlines from appearing onscreen.

- **Hide Grammar Errors in This Document Only**—Same thing. It does not turn off the grammar checking as you type, but it suppresses the green underlines.

CUSTOMIZING GRAMMAR AND STYLE RULES

It can be really annoying when Word insists on marking a certain grammatical or stylistic convention as "wrong" when you know it's right. To avoid situations like that, you can adjust the grammar and style rule application settings to match the way you want to write.

The grammar settings are controlled from the Proofing tab of the Word Options dialog box, which you saw in Figure 4.6. Choose Office, Word Options, click Proofing, and then scroll down to the When Correcting Spelling and Grammar in Word section, and click the Settings button. The Grammar Settings dialog box appears, as in Figure 4.7.

Figure 4.7
Fine-tune the grammar and style settings to your specifications here.

In the Grammar Settings dialog box, open the Writing Style list and select the writing style to customize—either Grammar Only or Grammar & Style.

Then in the Require section, turn on any of the checks you want to use:

- **Comma Required Before Last List Item**—This is called the "serial comma" in the professional editing world. When you have three or more items in a list, some writing styles (such as in academic writing) prescribe a comma between the last two, like this: *bread, butter, and milk*. In other writing styles (such as journalism), the comma is omitted, like this: *bread, butter and milk*. Because style conventions vary, Word's default is not to check this. Your other choices are Always and Never.

- **Punctuation Required with Quotes**—Some writing styles prescribe that punctuation should fall within the quotation mark when both occur at the end of a sentence, like this: Tom is "angry at his father." In other writing styles, the punctuation falls outside the quotes. Your choices here are Don't Check, Inside, and Outside. (Inside is the more common convention.)

- **Spaces Required Between Sentences**—Some writing styles prescribe one blank space between sentences; others prescribe two. (Generally speaking, in monospace fonts such as Courier, two spaces is used, whereas with proportionally spaced fonts, one space is used.) You can choose 1 or 2 here to make Word enforce one convention or the other.

In the Grammar section, clear the check boxes for any of the options you don't want. They are all marked by default.

In the Style section, mark or clear check boxes as desired. They are almost all marked if you chose Grammar & Style as the writing style setting; they are all cleared if you chose Grammar Only.

After making the changes to the settings, click OK to close the Grammar Settings dialog box. Then, back in the Word Options dialog box, click the Proofing tab and click Recheck Document to check it using the new settings you just specified.

MANAGING THE SPELLING DICTIONARIES

The main dictionary in Word is not editable, so when you add words to the dictionary, those words have to be stored somewhere else. That's where custom dictionaries come into the picture.

The default custom dictionary is a plain-text file called custom.dic, stored in the \Users*username*\AppData\Roaming\Microsoft\UProof folder (Windows Vista) or the \Documents and Settings*username*\Application Data\Microsoft\UProof folder (Windows XP). Because it is stored in the folder set for the individual user logged into the PC, it will be available only to that one user; each user has his or her own custom.dic file.

NOTE

If you happen to have a custom.dic file in the \Users*username*\AppData\Roaming\Microsoft\Proof folder (Windows Vista) or the \Documents and Settings*username*\Application Data\Microsoft\Proof folder in Windows XP (that's Proof, not UProof), it's a leftover file from an earlier version of Word. The custom.dic file for Word 2007 was created based on that older file when you upgraded, but any changes you've made to the custom dictionary in Word 2007 since then will be reflected only in the copy in the UProof folder.

ADDING FLAGGED WORDS TO THE CUSTOM DICTIONARY

To add a word that has been identified as a possible error to Custom.dic, right-click the red-underlined word and choose Add to Dictionary, or in the Spelling and Grammar dialog box, click Add to Dictionary.

EDITING A CUSTOM DICTIONARY'S WORD LIST

You can also add words to a custom dictionary (such as Custom.dic) without having them appear in the document. Here's how to do this:

1. Choose Office, Word Options.
2. Click Proofing.
3. Click Custom Dictionaries.
4. Select the desired custom dictionary from the list. As shown in Figure 4.8, only one dictionary appears (custom.dic).

Figure 4.8
Edit custom dictionaries from the Custom Dictionaries dialog box.

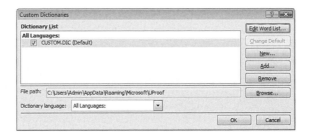

5. Click Edit Word List. A dialog box appears listing all the words currently in that dictionary.
6. To add a new word, type it in the Word(s) box and click Add. Words can be no longer than 64 characters.

CAUTION

> Type only one word per entry; multiword entries are accepted, but are entered that way in the list, and spellings consisting of only part of the entry are not recognized. For example, you could enter Roberto Sanchez, but the spell-checker would not recognize Roberto or Sanchez by itself. On the other hand, if you enter them as separate words, they are accepted either separately or together.

7. To delete a word, select it and click Delete. To clear the entire dictionary, click Delete All.
8. Click OK three times to close all open dialog boxes when you are finished editing the custom dictionary.

CHANGING THE ASSOCIATED LANGUAGE FOR A CUSTOM DICTIONARY

By default, a custom dictionary's language is set to All Languages, meaning that Word uses it no matter what language is specified for the text. You can limit a dictionary's use to a certain language by changing its Dictionary Language setting in the Custom Dictionaries dialog box (refer to Figure 4.8).

→ To specify the language to be used when checking a block of text, **see** "Checking Spelling and Grammar in Multiple Languages," **p. 108**.

ADDING MANY WORDS AT ONCE TO A CUSTOM DICTIONARY

The procedure in the preceding section adds only one word at a time. If you have a lot of words to add, the process can be really tedious. You might instead prefer to manually edit the custom dictionary file from outside of Word. Dictionary files are plain-text files with one word per line, so they are easy to edit in the Windows Notepad. You can even combine two or more dictionary files into a single file by copying-and-pasting lists of words between them.

To manually edit a dictionary file, follow these steps:

1. Exit Word and use the Windows File Explorer (click Start, Computer) to browse to the folder containing the dictionary files:

   In Windows XP: \Documents and Settings*username*\Application Data\Microsoft\UProof.

   In Windows Vista: \Users*username*\AppData\Roaming\Microsoft\UProof.

2. Right-click the dictionary file to edit (such as CUSTOM.DIC) and choose Open. (If needed, select Notepad as the program with which to open it.) The file opens in Notepad (see Figure 4.9). The word list will be different from what's shown in Figure 4.9 depending on what words you have added.

3. Edit the list, deleting and adding words as desired. Copy words from other files if needed.

4. Choose File, Exit. When prompted to save your changes, click Yes (or Save).

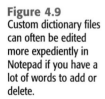

Figure 4.9
Custom dictionary files can often be edited more expediently in Notepad if you have a lot of words to add or delete.

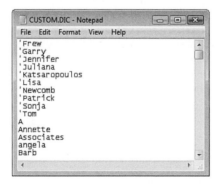

CREATING A NEW CUSTOM DICTIONARY

A custom dictionary can contain a maximum of 5,000 words and can be no larger than 64KB in file size. If you need a larger custom dictionary, create another dictionary.

TIP

> You might also want to create additional custom dictionaries to keep sets of words separate for different projects. For example, suppose you are doing work for a client that uses an alternative spelling for certain words. You don't want those words marked in documents for that client, but you do want them marked in documents for all other clients. You can create a custom dictionary just for that client, and then enable/disable that dictionary as appropriate for the current document. You might even write a macro that enables and disables that custom dictionary, and you can assign a shortcut key combination to it.

→ To enable or disable a dictionary, **see** "Enabling and Disabling Custom Dictionaries," **p. 107**. To record a macro, **see** "Recording a Macro," **p. 908**.

Follow these steps to create a custom dictionary:

1. Choose Office, Word Options.
2. Click Proofing and then click Custom Dictionaries.
3. Click New.
4. When the Create Custom Dictionary dialog box appears, navigate to the location in which you want to store the dictionary. Here are some recommendations:
   - To make the dictionary accessible to all users of the PC, store it in C:\Program Files\Microsoft Office\Office12\Dictionaries. If the folder does not already exist, create it.
   - To make the dictionary accessible to only the current Windows user, store it here:
     In Windows XP: \Documents and Settings*username*\Application Data\Microsoft\UProof.
     In Windows Vista: \Users*username*\AppData\Roaming\Microsoft\UProof.

NOTE

> As long as Word knows where you have stored the dictionary, you can put it anywhere you like; the above locations are just suggestions.

5. Type a name for the dictionary in the File name box.
6. Click Save.

The new dictionary now appears on the Dictionary List in the Custom Dictionaries dialog box.

→ To add someone else's dictionary file to your copy of Word, **see** "Adding an Existing Custom Dictionary to Word," **p. 108**.

Enabling and Disabling Custom Dictionaries

All spell checks use the main dictionary plus all the dictionaries that are selected on the Dictionary List. To disable a certain dictionary from being used, clear its check box in the Custom Dictionaries dialog box (refer to Figure 4.8).

Setting the Default Custom Dictionary

All enabled custom dictionaries are checked automatically during the spell-checking process, but newly added words are placed only in the default custom dictionary. To set the default dictionary, select a custom dictionary in the Custom Dictionaries dialog box and then click the Change Default button.

Using an Exclusion Dictionary

With an exclusion dictionary, you can specify words that appear in the main dictionary that you nevertheless want to be flagged as possible misspellings. An exclusion dictionary is the opposite of a custom dictionary, in that it forces normally correct words to be considered incorrect.

For example, perhaps your company has a product that has an unusual spelling that's similar to a common word in the dictionary, like Tek. Since your employees commonly forget about the unusual spelling and write "Tech" instead, you might add "Tech" to the exclusion dictionary so it will be flagged as a potential misspelling. That way the writer can take a second look at each instance to ensure that it is correct.

The default exclusion dictionary is named ExcludeDictionaryEN0409.lex (for U.S. English versions). If you delete this file, Word re-creates it the next time you start the program. By default the file is empty, but you can add words to it as follows:

1. From Windows, navigate to this folder:

   In Windows XP: \Documents and Settings*username*\Application Data\Microsoft\UProof.

   In Windows Vista: \Users*username*\AppData\Roaming\Microsoft\UProof.

2. Open ExcludeDictionaryEN0409.lex in Notepad. (See the following sidebar for help with that if needed.) If you haven't already modified this file, it is empty.

3. Type the words you want to exclude, one per line.

4. Save and close the file.

Opening a .lex File in Notepad

If you have previously opened .lex files in Notepad on this computer, you can simply right-click the ExcludeDictionaryEN0409.lex file and choose Edit.

If the Edit command does not appear on the right-click menu, you need to set up Notepad as the default application for editing .lex files. To do this:

   a. On the right-click menu, choose Open With.

   b. Click Select a Program from a List of Installed Programs and click OK.

   c. Click Notepad and click OK.

4

ADDING AN EXISTING CUSTOM DICTIONARY TO WORD

You can download new dictionaries from the Microsoft Office website and also buy them from third-party sources. For example, you can purchase dictionaries for medical, pharmaceutical, legal, and academic writing, sparing you the trouble of adding the many words unique to that profession individually to custom dictionaries.

When you get a new dictionary, you must then integrate it into Word. You must also do this for each Word user if you want to share a dictionary among multiple users. For example, log in as one local Windows user, make the change in Word, log out, log in as someone else and repeat, and so on.

To add an existing dictionary to Word, follow these steps:

1. Outside of Word, copy the custom dictionary file where you want it. If it should be accessible by only one user, copy it here:

    In Windows XP: \Documents and Settings*username*\Application Data\Microsoft\UProof.

    In Windows Vista: \Users*username*\AppData\Roaming\Microsoft\UProof.

    If it should be accessible to multiple users, copy it to C:\Program Files\Microsoft Office\Office12\Dictionaries. (If the folder is not already there, add it.)

2. In Word, choose Office, Word Options.

3. Click Proofing and then click Custom Dictionaries.

4. Click Add. The Add Custom Dictionary dialog box opens.

5. Navigate to the folder containing the dictionary to be added and select it.

6. Click Open. The dictionary appears on the Dictionary List in the Custom Dictionaries dialog box.

To remove a custom dictionary from the list, select it and click Remove. This does not delete the dictionary file; it only removes it from the listing in Word.

CHECKING SPELLING AND GRAMMAR IN MULTIPLE LANGUAGES

By default, the spelling and grammar check is performed in the native language for your copy of Word. For example, if you bought your copy of Word in the United States, then English (U.S.) is the default language.

The country designation is significant because many languages have slightly different spelling and grammar rules in different countries. For example, in the United Kingdom (U.K.), words such as *realize* and *customize* are spelled with an *s* instead of *z* (*realise* and *customise*). Word 2007 has default AutoCorrect entries that change those words (and others) to the U.S. spellings, so if you specifically need the U.K. spellings, you need to mark the text as being in a different national language.

When you right-click a spelling error, one of the choices on the menu is Language. It opens a submenu from which you can select the desired language module with which to check the word. At first there is only one language module on the list, but you can easily add others.

To add a language, follow these steps:

1. Select the text that should be checked in a different language.

2. On the Review tab, click the Set Language button. (Or, if you are setting a single word to a different language, and that word currently has a wavy red underline, right-click it and choose Language, Set Language.)

3. In the Language dialog box, select the desired language. Languages for which support is installed on your PC are indicated by a check mark icon, as shown in Figure 4.10. (The English-language versions of Word include support for all variants of English, Spanish, and French; you can buy additional language packs separately.)

Figure 4.10
Choose a language to be made available for spell checking.

4. (Optional) If you want Word to simply ignore the selected text, mark the Do Not Check Spelling or Grammar check box. Otherwise, Word will attempt to check the text using the rules defined for the chosen language.

5. (Optional) If you want Word to try to detect languages and mark text passages with the correct language automatically, leave the Detect Language Automatically check box marked.

TIP

Detect Language Automatically sounds like a good idea, but Word makes mistakes in identification. If you find that passages in U.S. English are not getting properly checked because Word is misidentifying them as some other variant of English, for example, you might want to turn that option off.

6. (Optional) To make a different language the default for future spell checks (including those in all new documents based on the Normal.dotm template), select it and click the Default button.

7. Click OK.

The text is now marked as being in the chosen language.

EVALUATING READABILITY

Readability refers to the ease with which people can read what you have written. It's determined using some basic statistics about the document, such as counts (word, character, paragraph, sentence) and averages (sentences per paragraph, words per sentence, characters per word). Those counts and averages are then fed into formulas that provide numeric evaluations of your writing.

Word supports two types of readability evaluation:

- **Flesch Reading Ease**—A number between 0 and 100. The higher the number, the easier it is to comprehend.

- **Flesch-Kincaid Grade Level**—An estimate of the approximate grade level of education someone would need to be able to understand your writing with ease. For example, a score of 9 means someone who can read at a ninth-grade education level or higher should be able to read it.

How Is Readability Calculated?

Word does the calculation for you, so you don't have to worry about calculating readability yourself. Just in case you are interested, though, here's how it's done. For each of the following formulas, ASW refers to average syllables per word and ASL refers to average sentence length (in words).

For the Flesch-Kincaid Grade Level:

$(0.39 \times ASL) + (11.8 \times ASW) - 15.59$

For the Flesch Reading Ease scale:

$206.835 - (1.015 \times ASL) \times (8.46 \times ASW)$

To get readability statistics for a document, turn on the feature as follows:

1. Choose Office, Word Options.
2. Click Proofing.
3. Scroll down to the When Correcting Spelling and Grammar in Word section and mark the Show Readability Statistics check box.
4. Click OK.

From that point on, every interactive spelling and grammar check will end with a Readability Statistics dialog box being displayed, as shown in Figure 4.11.

Figure 4.11
Display readability statistics about a document at the end of the spelling and grammar check.

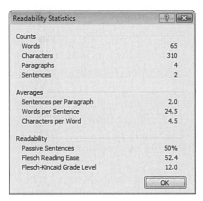

VIEWING WORD COUNT

Many a student struggling to come up with a 1,000-word essay has appreciated Word's ability to do a quick word count!

Word count statistics are similar to readability statistics, in that they have some measurements in common. However, whereas readability statistics are evaluative, word count statistics are simply numeric counts of various items (pages, words, characters excluding spaces, characters including spaces, paragraphs, and lines).

 To display the document's statistics, display the Review tab and click the Word Count button (see Figure 4.12).

Figure 4.12
Word count statistics.

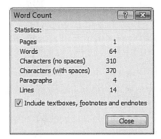

AUTOMATING CORRECTIONS WITH AUTOCORRECT

AutoCorrect is a service that automatically replaces all instances of a certain text string with another. There are many uses for AutoCorrect, several of which you've seen in previous chapters. For example, you can quickly insert symbols with AutoCorrect, such as by typing (r) for the ® symbol. AutoCorrect also works with the spelling checker to automatically fix common misspellings, as you saw earlier in the chapter.

AutoCorrect isn't a command that needs to be explicitly issued; it just happens automatically. You can set its options or turn it off, though, and you can manage the list of AutoCorrect entries.

REJECTING AN AUTOMATIC CORRECTION

When an automatic correction occurs, a small blue box appears when you rest your mouse pointer near the text. Point to the blue box, and an AutoCorrect Options button appears. Click that button, and a menu opens, as shown in Figure 4.13. From here you can do the following:

- Change back to the original usage for this instance only.
- Stop correcting this particular word or phrase. Choosing this adds the word or phrase to the Exceptions list, covered in the next section.
- Open the AutoCorrect Options dialog box, also covered in the next section.

Figure 4.13
The AutoCorrect Options button appears next to an automatic correction in the document.

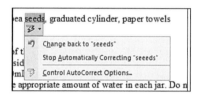

There are also shortcut keys you can use for rejecting an automatic correction. They all appear to do the same thing, but there is a difference:

- Ctrl+Z (Undo) undoes the correction, but Word does not remember that preference.
- Backspace or the left-arrow key undoes the correction and adds it to the Exceptions list.

> **NOTE**
>
> For Backspace or the left-arrow key to add items to the Exceptions list, the Automatically Add Words to List check box must be marked in the AutoCorrect Exceptions dialog box on the tab for the applicable error type. You'll learn about this in the next section.

SETTING AUTOCORRECT OPTIONS

To access the AutoCorrect options (see Figure 4.14), choose Office, Word Options. Click Proofing and then click the AutoCorrect Options button.

Figure 4.14
The AutoCorrect Options button appears next to an automatic correction in the document.

The top portion of the AutoCorrect tab contains check boxes for enabling/disabling certain features:

- **Show AutoCorrect Options Buttons**—Clear this to prevent the AutoCorrect Options button from appearing after an AutoCorrect action (as in Figure 4.13).

- **Correct TWo INitial CApitals**—In a word that starts out with two capital letters and then switches to lowercase, AutoCorrect will lowercase the second letter.

- **Capitalize First Letter of Sentences**—AutoCorrect will capitalize the first letter of the first word that comes at the beginning of a paragraph or after a sentence-ending punctuation mark.

- **Capitalize First Letter of Table Cells**—AutoCorrect will capitalize the first letter of the first word in each table cell.

- **Capitalize Names of Days**—AutoCorrect will capitalize days of the week, such as Monday, Tuesday, and so on.

- **Correct Accidental Usage of cAPS LOCK Key**—When this feature is enabled, AutoCorrect notices when you have left the Caps Lock on and will turn it off and correct the text that was erroneously capitalized.

To set up exceptions to some of the features, click the Exceptions button. The AutoCorrect Exceptions dialog box opens (see Figure 4.15).

Figure 4.15
Manage the exceptions list for automatic corrections.

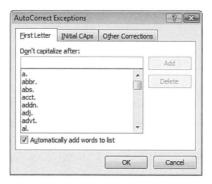

For each tab, use Add and Delete to manage the list of exceptions. You can type new words or phrases and click Add, or select existing items on the lists and click Delete.

- **First Letter tab**—These are situations where the first letter after a sentence-ending punctuation mark (such as a period) should not be capitalized. For example, you would not always want a capitalized first letter after an abbreviation such as "etc."

- **INitial CAps tab**—These are situations where two initial caps in a row should be left alone. For example, when talking about student "IDs," it is perfectly proper that the first two letters be capitalized.

- **Other Corrections tab**—These are words that should not be automatically corrected, even though they appear on the Replace Text as You Type list. For example, perhaps you want to accept U.K. spellings of certain words as well as U.S. spellings.

For each tab, mark or clear the Automatically Add Words to List check box. When this is marked, words are added to the appropriate list whenever you press Backspace or the left-arrow key to undo an AutoCorrect operation immediately after it occurs.

The bottom part of the AutoCorrect tab contains a list of AutoCorrect entries. Word comes with a large list of common spelling corrections and symbol insertions, and you can add or remove entries from it on your own as well, as the following sections explain.

CHANGING OR REMOVING AN AUTOCORRECT ENTRY

Most of the time, the AutoCorrect entries that come with Word are useful, but occasionally you might find one that interferes with your writing. For example, by default (c) is the AutoCorrect entry for the copyright symbol, but Que Corporation, the publisher of this book, happens to use (c) to indicate a heading in a manuscript. Someone working for that employer would want to remove or change the copyright symbol's AutoCorrect entry.

To edit an entry, open the AutoCorrect dialog box, as you learned in the preceding section, and then scroll through the Replace Text as You Type list to locate the desired entry. (You can type the first few letters of the entry in the Replace box to jump to that portion of the list quickly.) When the entry appears in the Replace and With boxes, you can edit the text in either box to change the entry. To remove an entry entirely, select it and click the Delete button.

ADDING A PLAIN TEXT AUTOCORRECT ENTRY

You saw earlier in the chapter how to add an AutoCorrect entry via the Spelling and Grammar checker. When correcting the spelling on a word, the AutoCorrect entry appears, offering to make that correction an automatic one.

An alternative is to manually type a new text entry in the AutoCorrect dialog box. Type the text into the Replace box, deleting whatever is already there, and type the desired replacement into the With box (also deleting what is already there). Then click Add to add it to the list. This type of entry is a Plain Text one, and is limited to 255 characters.

AutoCorrect can be used not only for simple spelling corrections, but also for inserting blocks of text that you type frequently. For example, you could set up an AutoCorrect entry that replaces your initials in parentheses with your full name. You don't have to use the parentheses, but they help prevent regular typing from unintentionally triggering the automatic correction.

ADDING A FORMATTED OR GRAPHICAL AUTOCORRECT ENTRY

When typing text into the With box for an AutoCorrect entry, there's no way to include formatting, graphics, or line/paragraph breaks. However, using an alternative method, you can create formatted entries that include all these things, plus special characters and symbols that you cannot directly type into the With box.

Follow these steps to create a formatted entry:

1. In a document, type the full text that you want to paste into the With box in an AutoCorrect entry.
2. Select the text (and graphics if desired). No need to copy it to the Clipboard.
3. Open the AutoCorrect dialog box (Office, Word Options, Proofing, AutoCorrect Options). The text you selected appears in the With box, as formatted text. (If the Formatted Text option button is not already selected, select it.)
4. In the Replace box, enter the code that should represent the selection. (Avoid using anything that you might type for other reasons.)
5. Click Add.

CONFIGURING MATH AUTOCORRECT

Word 2007 has a whole separate AutoCorrect database for mathematical entries. These entries serve as shortcuts for creating various math-related symbols. For example, instead of hunting around in the Symbol dialog box for the not-equal-to symbol ($\neq$), you could simply type **\neq** and Word would automatically AutoCorrect it into that symbol.

To work with math AutoCorrect options, click the Math AutoCorrect tab in the AutoCorrect dialog box (see Figure 4.16).

4

Figure 4.16
Math AutoCorrect is a separate set of AutoCorrect entries that create math symbols.

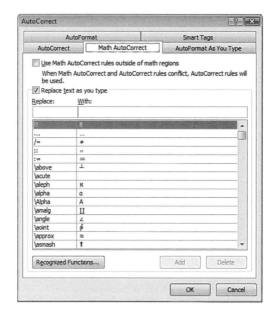

By default, Math AutoCorrect is in effect only within what Word calls "math regions," which are areas created with the Equation Editor. You can change this behavior so that Math AutoCorrect entries are universally applied by marking the Use Math AutoCorrect Rules Outside of Math Regions check box. This would be useful, for example, if you were writing a document on the subject of mathematics and needed to discuss certain principles in sentence form.

You can add and remove entries from the Math AutoCorrect tab in the same way as on the regular AutoCorrect tab.

→ For more information about the Equation Editor, **see** "Creating Math Formulas with the Equation Editor," **p. 552**.

Within the Equation Editor, any text you type is assumed to be a variable and is therefore italicized. When you are referencing a function, however, you won't want that automatic italicizing to occur. Word maintains a list of recognized functions that are not italicized when they appear as text in an equation. To edit that list, click the Recognized Functions button on the Math AutoCorrect tab. Then in the Recognized Math Functions dialog box (see Figure 4.17), add or remove functions from the list. To add a function, type it and click Add. To remove a function, select it and click Delete.

Figure 4.17
Add or remove function names from the list. Items on this list will not be italicized when used in the Equation Editor.

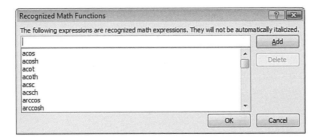

CONTROLLING HYPHENATION

When a long word does not quite fit at the right edge of a paragraph, it wraps to the next line, and you end up with a short line of text. In a paragraph where some lines are dramatically shorter than others, the right margin can look distractingly ragged.

Employing hyphenation can help. When the word is allowed to break at a hyphenation point, the paragraph's right edge looks more uniform and you can fit more text on the page. Figure 4.18 shows the difference.

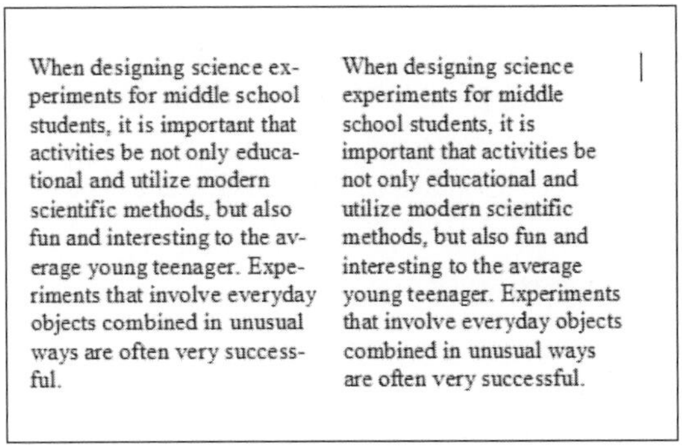

Figure 4.18
A paragraph with and without hyphenation.

> When designing science experiments for middle school students, it is important that activities be not only educational and utilize modern scientific methods, but also fun and interesting to the average young teenager. Experiments that involve everyday objects combined in unusual ways are often very successful.
>
> When designing science experiments for middle school students, it is important that activities be not only educational and utilize modern scientific methods, but also fun and interesting to the average young teenager. Experiments that involve everyday objects combined in unusual ways are often very successful.

Word has two types of hyphenation: automatic and manual. Automatic hyphenation applies a uniform set of hyphenation rules, whereas manual hyphenation provides more control on a case-by-case basis.

ENABLING OR DISABLING AUTOMATIC HYPHENATION

To turn on automatic hyphenation for a document, display the Page Layout tab and then choose Hyphenation, Automatic. To turn hyphenation off, choose Hyphenation, None.

If there is a specific part of the document that you *don't* want to hyphenate, do the following to exclude a paragraph (or more) from the hyphenation settings:

1. Select the paragraph(s) to affect.
2. On the Home tab, click the dialog box launcher in the bottom-right corner of the Paragraph group, opening the Paragraph dialog box.

3. On the Line and Page Breaks tab, mark the Don't Hyphenate check box (see Figure 4.19).

4. Click OK.

Figure 4.19
You can exclude certain paragraphs from hyphenation via the Paragraph dialog box.

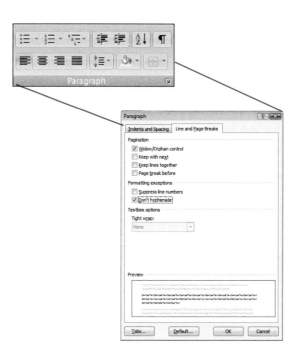

HYPHENATING A DOCUMENT MANUALLY

Manual hyphenation works by inserting discretionary hyphens in certain words. A discretionary hyphen is one that *can* appear if the word happens to fall near the end of a line and needs to be hyphenated, but otherwise does not appear. Discretionary hyphens are better than hyphens you would type with the minus key because if you happen to add or remove text that makes the paragraph line breaks shift, you aren't stuck with extraneous hyphens to try to track down and delete.

To manually hyphenate a document, follow these steps:

1. On the Page Layout tab, choose Hyphenation, Manual. The Manual Hyphenation dialog box appears, showing the first word that is a candidate for hyphenation.

   In the Hyphenate At box (shown in Figure 4.20), all the available hyphen points for the word are shown with hyphens in them; the suggested hyphenation point is highlighted.

Figure 4.20
Evaluate the hyphen-
ation suggestion for
the word.

2. Do one of the following:

   ■ Click Yes to accept the default hyphenation point for that word.

   ■ Click one of the other hyphens in the word to select it as the hyphenation point, and then click Yes.

   ■ Click No to decline to hyphenate that word.

3. Continue evaluating words until the Hyphenation is Complete message appears; then click OK.

CAUTION

> Words that have been manually hyphenated might be flagged as possible spelling errors (wavy red underline). They are not really errors, of course, and "correcting" them removes the discretionary hyphens.

You can also insert discretionary hyphens into words as symbols, unrelated to the hyphen-ation feature. To do so, click where you want to place a discretionary hyphen in a word and then press Ctrl+- (that is, hold down Ctrl and type a minus sign). Alternatively, on the Insert tab, choose Symbol, More Symbols. On the Special Characters tab, click Optional Hyphen and then click Insert.

WORKING WITH SMART TAGS

A *Smart Tag* is a pop-up that appears when you hover the mouse over certain text. Depending on the text, a Smart Tag might offer to perform any of a variety of services on that text, such as looking up an address, scheduling a meeting, or getting a stock quote. Smart Tags are "smart" in that Word is able to determine the type of content by its format and offer appropriate choices. For example, Word is able to distinguish dates and telephone numbers from ordinary numbers based on their patterns. (They also make you "smart" in that you have more information at your fingertips!)

Here are the types of data that can have Smart Tags assigned and the choices you have on each type's menu:

■ **Addresses**—You can add a contact to Outlook, or display a map or driving directions.

■ **Dates and times**—You can schedule a meeting in Outlook and/or display the Outlook calendar.

■ **Financial symbols**—You can retrieve stock quotes from MSN MoneyCentral, get com-pany reports, and read news about the company.

- **People**—You can send email or instant messages, schedule meetings, open contact information in Outlook (or create new contact information), and insert addresses.
- **Places**—You can display a map or driving directions.
- **Telephone numbers**—You can add a phone number to an Outlook Contact list entry.

Other Smart Tags are available—some for free and some for an additional charge. To see what's available, click the More Smart Tags button on the Smart Tags tab of the AutoCorrect dialog box (see Figure 4.22, later in this chapter). Then follow the hyperlinks to the various services to learn about their benefits and costs.

CAUTION

After you install more Smart Tags, the new tags might not be available until you exit and restart Word.

FOLLOWING A SMART TAG

A Smart Tag appears in a document as a dotted purple underline. Point to it, and a Smart Tag Actions button appears. Click that icon for a menu of activities you can perform (see Figure 4.21).

Figure 4.21
Follow a Smart Tag by clicking its Smart Tag Actions button and selecting from the menu.

CONFIGURING SMART TAG SETTINGS

The specific Smart Tag labels are controlled via the AutoCorrect dialog box. Here you can choose what type(s) of recognizers to use. A *recognizer* is a type of data, such as Date, Financial Symbol, Place, and so on. Follow these steps to configure Smart Tag settings:

1. Choose Office, Word Options.
2. On the Proofing tab, click AutoCorrect Options.
3. In the AutoCorrect dialog box, click the Smart Tags tab.
4. To turn the Smart Tag labels on or off as a whole, mark or clear the Label Text with Smart Tags check box. (It is on by default.)

5. Place a check mark next to each recognizer type you want to use (see Figure 4.22).

6. Click OK.

Figure 4.22
Choose which recognizers you want to use as Smart Tags in your documents.

REMOVING SMART TAGS

To remove a specific Smart Tag instance in the document, open the menu for a Smart Tag and click Remove this Smart Tag (refer to Figure 4.21).

That takes care of that instance, but Word will continue to recognize that same text again in future documents as a Smart Tag–eligible item. To exclude the text from being marked again, choose Stop Recognizing *text* (where *text* represents the text that has been tagged).

You can also remove all the Smart Tags from the current document as well as prevent the currently tagged text from being tagged in future checks. To do this, follow these steps:

1. Open the menu for any Smart Tag, as in Figure 4.21, and choose Smart Tag Options. A custom version of the AutoCorrect dialog box appears showing Smart Tag options (see Figure 4.23).

2. To remove all Smart Tags, click Remove Smart Tags.

3. A warning message appears; click Yes.

4. Click OK.

Figure 4.23
Remove all Smart Tags from the document.

After Smart Tags have been removed, they will not reappear for that text, but they will reappear for other similar text. For example, if you remove all the Smart Tags from a list of phone numbers, retyping any of those phone numbers later will not result in a Smart Tag being placed, but typing a different phone number that was not on the earlier list *will* result in a Smart Tag.

Using Research Tools

In addition to the spelling- and grammar-checking features, Word has a variety of research and translation features that can help you improve your document. These tools are significant because they represent a shift from mechanics to meaning. Not only is Word helping you with the mechanics of your document (such as spelling and punctuation), but it is actually helping you write stronger and more accurate content by helping you choose the right words and present accurate facts and figures.

All the research tools use the same Research pane, and you can switch between them freely within that pane.

TIP

> You can also use the Research pane in Internet Explorer. From IE, choose View, Explorer Bar, Research.

Checking a Word's Definition with a Dictionary

Word's Research tools include the Encarta Dictionary, which you can use to look up quick definitions of words. (Encarta, as you may know, is Microsoft's encyclopedia tool, and it's covered in more detail in the next section.)

CAUTION

> Most of Word 2007's research tools, including the dictionaries and encyclopedias, rely on the Internet for their data; these tools do not work very well (or at all in some cases) unless you are online.

To look up a word in the dictionary, follow these steps:

1. Select the word in the document. If you select more than one word, the dictionary looks up only the first one.

2. On the Review tab, click Research. The Research pane opens.

3. Open the drop-down list under the Search For box and choose Encarta Dictionary: English (North America). Or, if you are in some other part of the world, choose whatever is applicable to your location and language.

   Information about the word appears, including its definition, its pronunciation, and its hyphenation, as shown in Figure 4.24.

Figure 4.24
Look up a word's definition in the dictionary.

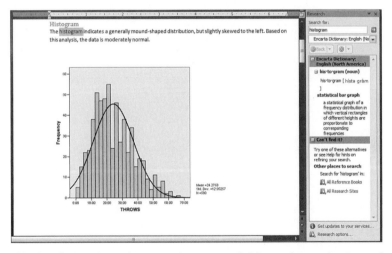

→ To learn how to add other dictionaries to the Research pane, **see** "Adding and Removing Research Providers," **p. 129**.

NOTE

> The default dictionary depends on the language and country set as your default. To use a different dictionary, click Research Options at the bottom of the Research pane and select a different dictionary from the Reference Books list.

FINDING WORDS WITH A THESAURUS

A *thesaurus* is a book (or service) that lists the synonyms and antonyms of common words, to help you improve and diversify your word choices. A *synonym* is a word that means roughly the same thing as another word (such as *happy* and *glad*); an *antonym* is a word that means the opposite of another word (such as *happy* and *sad*).

One way to look up a synonym is to right-click it and use the shortcut menu. To look up a word from your document in the thesaurus, follow these steps:

1. Select the word.

2. Right-click the word and point to Synonyms. A quick list of synonyms for the word appears (see Figure 4.25).

3. To substitute any of the found words for the selected word, click the desired word.

Figure 4.25
Get quick synonyms.

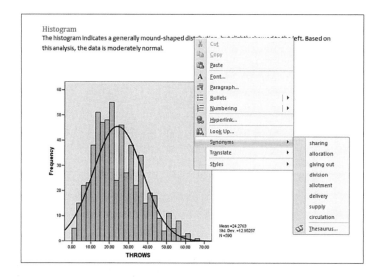

Another way to look up a synonym is with the Research pane:

1. Select the word.

2. On the Review tab, click Thesaurus.

   The Research pane appears to the right of the document, with synonyms and antonyms for the word. (Antonyms are clearly marked as such, as in Figure 4.26.)

3. (Optional) To replace the instance in the document with one of the found words, right-click the found word and click Insert.

4. (Optional) To copy the word to the Clipboard, right-click the found word and click Copy.

5. (Optional) To look up synonyms and antonyms for one of the found words, double-click it. (Use the Back button on the Research pane to return to the results for the previous word.)

Figure 4.26
Look up synonyms and antonyms in the thesaurus.

TIP

> By default, the thesauruses are enabled for each of the languages you have enabled in the Set Language tool. You can enable/disable the various thesauruses, such as for different languages and different nationalities within a language, by clicking Research Options at the bottom of the Research pane and marking/clearing check boxes in the Reference Books list.

LOOKING UP INFORMATION AT A RESEARCH SITE

Word 2007 offers several very good research sites at no additional charge to users:

- **Encarta Encyclopedia**—An all-purpose encyclopedia, suitable for academic, family, and business use.

- **Factiva iWorks**—A Dow Jones/Reuters service with business news and information collected from more than 9,000 authoritative sources. This is a good source of accurate, up-to-date information.

- **HighBeam Research**—A research library of more than 3000 library publications, including 35 million magazines, journals, and other resources one might find at an academic library.

- **MSN Search**—This is the web search engine associated with the very popular MSN portal. (Note that data from MSN search is not authoritative or even necessarily correct; it just finds what's out there on the Web.)

All of these require Internet connectivity for use.

To look up a word or phrase at one of these sites, start the process the same as with the dictionary lookup, but specify one of the research sites instead of the dictionary as the site:

1. Select the word or phrase in the document.

2. On the Review tab, click Research. The Research pane opens, with results from all reference books.

3. Open the drop-down list under the Search For box and choose any site within the All Research Sites portion of the list (see Figure 4.27).

Figure 4.27
Look up a word or phrase in an encyclopedia or other research archive.

TRANSLATING TEXT INTO OTHER LANGUAGES

Word 2007 can translate from almost any language to almost any other language, a real boon for those who need to communicate internationally. Of course, the translation won't be as good as if it were done by a real person, and it might even be unintentionally hilarious to the recipient of it! But in most cases, you can at least make yourself understood.

Word has two different means of translation available, depending on the languages you are translating to/from. For these languages, the U.S. English version of Word has built-in bilingual dictionaries, and translates word-for-word between English and the following languages:

French	Korean
German	Chinese (PRC)
Italian	Chinese (Taiwan)
Japanese	Spanish

For all other language pairs, Word uses online machine translation by a website called WorldLingo. Using this service, it can translate between any two of the following languages:

Chinese	Italian
Dutch	Japanese
English	Korean
French	Portuguese
German	Russian
Greek	Spanish

TRANSLATING WITH THE RESEARCH PANE

The Research pane provides full-service access to the translation services in Word. From there, you can choose different languages, set translation options, and more.

There are two ways of opening the Research pane and displaying the Translation services:

- Alt+click any word in the document to open up that word in the Research pane; then select Translation from the drop-down list at the top of the pane. (By default, it is set to the most recently used reference tool.)

- Select the word or phrase to translate and then on the Review tab, click Translate.

Once the translation services are displayed, you can select the desired From and To languages, and the translation appears in the Research pane (see Figure 4.28). Depending on the languages you chose, the translation appears from the bilingual dictionaries in Word or from the WorldLingo service.

Figure 4.28
Translate text into any of several language choices.

You can also translate an entire document:

1. With the Research pane open and the translation services displayed, click the right-arrow button next to Translate the Whole Document.

2. In the Translate Whole Document dialog box, click Yes to use the WorldLingo service to translate the document. A web page opens, showing the translated text.

3. (Optional) Select the translated text, copy it (Ctrl+C), and paste it into Word (Ctrl+V).

TRANSLATING WITH SCREENTIPS

Here's another way to use translation services. As you are typing text, right-click any word and choose Translate, and then choose the desired language. This enables ScreenTips (pop-up messages) with translation information from the bilingual dictionary. Then point to any word, and a ScreenTip pops up with the word's dictionary definition and translation in the language you chose (see Figure 4.29).

English word

Figure 4.29
Translation ScreenTips help you look up words quickly in a bilingual dictionary.

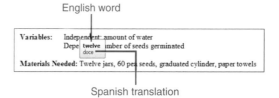

Spanish translation

To turn off the translation ScreenTips, right-click any word and choose Translate, Turn Off Translation ScreenTip.

SETTING TRANSLATION OPTIONS

Click Translation Options in the Research pane to see a list of dictionaries and services available, as shown in Figure 4.30.

In the Bilingual Dictionary section, these options are available:

- **Use Online Dictionary**—Enables Word to access the Web for dictionary lookups.

- **Use Only When the Installed Dictionary Is Unavailable**—Uses local dictionaries whenever possible, relying on the web version only when the local dictionary is not available.

- **Available Language Pairs**—Each bilingual dictionary installed in Word is listed here. Clear a check box to disable a dictionary. Doing so will force Word to use machine translation (such as WorldLingo) for that language pair.

Figure 4.30
Select dictionaries and translation services for each language pair.

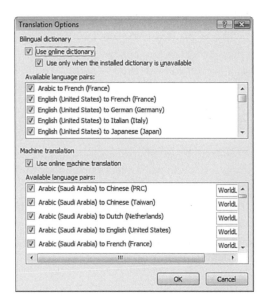

In the Machine Translation section, you can choose whether or not to use online machine translation when bilingual dictionaries are not available (or when you are translating more than a few words at a time). Mark or clear the check box for each language pair as desired.

By default, Word is set up to access only one translation service: WorldLingo. If you install other translation services through third-party vendors, you can choose which service should be employed for each language pair by changing its drop-down list setting to the desired service.

CUSTOMIZING AND EXTENDING THE RESEARCH TOOLS

The Research tools in Word are fully customizable. You can choose exactly which services you want to use, and you can even add new services and implement parental control limits.

ADDING AND REMOVING RESEARCH PROVIDERS

One thing that really separates Microsoft Word from the competition is the full array of tools included with it. At no extra charge, you get access to valuable research and reference services such as Encarta, HighBeam Research, Factiva iWorks, encyclopedias, dictionaries, translation services, and more. No other word processor offers anywhere near that much.

Even with all these tools, however, there's still more to wish for. For example, legal offices might want to add FindLaw, an online version of the West Legal Directory, and LexisNexis's lexisONE research service, covering state and federal case law and other legal news. Many third-party research tools are available for academic, business, and professional use.

Typically these for-pay providers have their own setup utility that copies the needed files to your hard disk and sets up the link to the Research pane in Office. After running the setup utility for a tool, restart Word, and the new tool appears on the list of services in the Research pane. In some cases, however, you will need to point Word to the new service. To do so, follow these steps:

1. From the Research pane, click Research Options.

2. In the Research Options dialog box, click Add Services.

3. Type the URL of the provider in the Add Services dialog box. (The service provider should have given you this information when you signed up for the service.)

4. Click Add.

5. Follow the prompts that appear for the selected service.

You can also remove a provider from the list. Removing a provider removes all the research services from that provider; you can't pick and choose. (However, you can enable or disable individual services, as you'll learn in the next section.)

Here's how to remove a provider:

1. From the Research pane, click Research Options.

2. In the Research Options dialog box, click Update/Remove.

3. Select a provider. All the services for that provider will automatically be selected.

4. Click Remove and then follow the prompts for removal.

Enabling or Disabling Research Services

Some research services are not enabled by default because they are for some other language or nationality. For example, you might have access to the North American version of Encarta by default, but not the U.K. and Canada versions. You can enable any of these additional services by following these steps:

1. From the Research pane, click Research Options.

2. In the Research Options dialog box, mark the check boxes for any additional services you want to use.

3. Clear the check boxes for any services you don't want.

4. Click OK.

Updating Installed Services

Sometimes a service provider adds or changes its service offerings. To get the latest information, and set up any additional services that might be available, do the following:

1. From the Research pane, click Research Options.

2. In the Research Options dialog box, click Update/Remove.

3. Select a provider. Word automatically selects all the services for that provider.

4. Click Update. Word checks for updates via the Web, downloads them, and offers to install any updates or additions it finds.

5. Follow the prompts to update the service. When the update is complete, click OK at the confirmation message.

USING PARENTAL CONTROLS TO LIMIT A RESEARCH SERVICE

Parental controls can be configured to prevent the research services from delivering any search results that might be offensive. This can be useful for parents with children who use the Research pane, and also for people who just want to make sure they don't accidentally encounter anything that offends them.

> **NOTE**
>
> The tools used in the Research pane are already pretty well scrubbed, generally speaking. Most are business and research oriented, so there won't be much sex or violence in the results. The only exception might be the general MSN search tool, which searches the entire Web, not just research sites.

To set up parental controls for research, follow these steps:

1. From the Research pane, click Research Options.

2. In the Research Options dialog box, click Parental Control. The Parental Control dialog box appears.

3. Mark the Turn on Content Filtering... check box (see Figure 4.31).

Figure 4.31
Enable content filtering here.

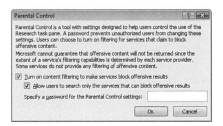

4. (Optional) Type a password for parental control setting changes. (If you don't do this, anyone can turn off the parental controls.)

5. Click OK. A Confirm Password dialog box appears.

6. Retype the password and click OK. A notice now appears in the Research Options dialog box stating that parental controls are active and that some of the services on the list are now unavailable. (The unavailable services are those that do not use content filtering.)

7. Click OK to close the Research Options dialog box.

CAUTION

Most of the research sites will be unavailable if you turn on parental controls, including the Encarta Encyclopedia. Even though these research services contain little or no material that anyone might object to, the filtering programs block the sites because their content constantly changes and cannot be guaranteed to be completely sanitized at all times. This can be a hindrance to children trying to do research reports for school because the encyclopedia contains such good information on the topics that students are frequently assigned to cover.

TROUBLESHOOTING

ADDED RESEARCH SERVICE DOES NOT APPEAR IN THE RESEARCH PANE

Exit and restart Word. Any changes you make to the research services will not show up until you do so.

WORD MARKS PASSAGES OF TEXT AS THE WRONG LANGUAGE

This is actually fairly common: Word decides for some reason that a passage of text in U.S. English is actually in U.K. English, and marks it as such. It's not a huge problem, but it does prevent the spelling checker from identifying words that use British spellings rather than American.

One way around this problem is to mark the entire document as U.S. English and then prevent Word from identifying the language of future passages. Here's how:

1. Select the entire document.
2. On the Review tab, click the Set Language button.
3. In the Language dialog box, choose the desired language—in this case, English (U.S.).
4. Click the Default button. A confirmation box appears.
5. Click Yes to confirm that you want the chosen language to be the default.
6. Clear the Detect Language Automatically check box.
7. Click OK.

CHAPTER 5

PRINTING AND FAXING DOCUMENTS

In this chapter

PRINTING A DOCUMENT

Even in this age of electronic communication, the best way to distribute a document is still often the hard-copy printout. Most legal contracts are valid only when printed and signed, for example, and printouts help you reach audiences that don't have computer access.

Printing a document can be as simple or as complex as you make it. You can do a quick print job with default settings with just a single mouse click, or you can delve deep into the print setup options to get special effects, custom ranges, and more.

USING QUICK PRINT

For a quick printout consisting of a single copy of the entire active document on the default printer, choose Office, Print, Quick Print.

You can also do a Quick Print from *outside* of Word. In Windows, browse to the folder containing the document to print and then right-click the document and choose Print. The document opens in Word, prints, and then closes again, all in the blink of an eye.

PRINTING THE CURRENT DOCUMENT

To specify basic properties of the print job, such as number of copies, page range, printer to use, and so on, choose Office, Print or press Ctrl+P to display the Print dialog box (see Figure 5.1).

Figure 5.1
Use the Print dialog box to specify how you want the document to be printed.

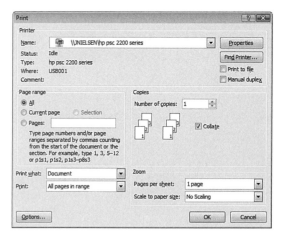

SELECTING THE PRINTER

The default printer appears in the Name box. To choose a different printer, open the drop-down list and pick one. For example, you might have a color printer that has a rather expensive per-page cost of ink, so for drafts you might want to print instead to a monochrome laser printer.

Information about the selected printer appears below the Name list in the Print dialog box. For example, you can see the printer's status and type, and how it is connected to the computer (either directly, or remotely via a local area network).

The default printer gets its designation from Windows, not from Word. To change the default printer:

- In Windows Vista: Choose Start, Control Panel. Choose Printer (under Hardware and Sound). Right-click a printer and choose Set as Default Printer.
- In Windows XP: Choose Start, Printers and Faxes. Right-click a printer and choose Set as Default Printer.

SPECIFYING A PAGE RANGE

In the Page Range section of the Print dialog box, you can choose among these ranges:

- **All**—All pages of the current document (the default).
- **Current page**—The page in which the insertion point lies.
- **Selection**—The content that was selected when you opened the Print dialog box. If no content was selected beforehand, this option is unavailable.
- **Pages**—A page range that you specify:

  For a contiguous page range, use a hyphen between the first and last number, as in 1-4.

  For noncontiguous pages or ranges, separate them by commas, as in 2, 5, 7-10.

  For sections, precede the number by an s to indicate you are talking about sections, not pages, as in s2-s4.

  For pages within sections, use p for page and s for section, as in p1s2.

→ To learn about sections, **see** "Working with Sections," **p. 264**.

5

CHOOSING COPIES AND COLLATION

The number of copies defaults to 1; you can type a value here or increment the current value up or down with the arrow buttons.

If you set the number of copies to greater than 1, collation becomes an issue. When collation is off, all the copies of page 1 print, followed by all the copies of page 2, and so on. When collation is on, full sets print, ready to be stapled.

PRINTING SPECIAL ELEMENTS

The Print What drop-down list (see Figure 5.2) enables you to print things other than the document itself. It offers the following choices:

- **Document**—The document itself (the default).
- **Document properties**—Information about the document, as defined in its Properties box. See "Working with File Properties," p. 50.
- **Document showing markup**—The document along with any changes that have been made to it with revision marks. See "Using Revision Tracking," p. 790.

- **List of markup**—A list of the changes made to the document via revision tracking, but *not* the document itself.
- **Styles**—A list of the styles used in the document and their definitions. See "Understanding Styles," p. 228.
- **Building Blocks entries**—The building block entries that are available in the current document. See "Working with Building Blocks," p. 90.

CAUTION

Printing building block entries prints not only your own entries you've created, but also all the entries provided in Building Blocks.dotx too, so it will take many pages to print them all.

- **Key assignments**—A list of any shortcut key assignments you've set up for the current document. See "Defining Shortcut Keys," p. 937.

Figure 5.2
Print other elements in the document by selecting them from the Print What list.

PRINTING ON BOTH SIDES OF THE PAPER

Most printers can print on only one side of the paper, so if you need two-sided printouts, you must reinsert the printed pages for printing on the second side. This is known as *manual duplexing*.

To do manual duplexing in Word, mark the Manual Duplex check box in the Print dialog box and then print normally. Only the odd-numbered pages will print, and a message will appear onscreen telling you to reinsert the pages and click OK. Do so, and Word prints the reverse sides of the pages.

The trick to this procedure is making sure you understand how paper feeds into your printer. One good way to determine this is to draw an up-pointing arrow on a blank page with a marker or pencil, and then insert it into the paper tray face-up, with the arrow facing into the printer. Then print the first page of your document on it. This will show you the relationship between how the paper goes in and how the printout is made. You can then adjust the paper orientation accordingly to make sure you are printing the second side of your duplex job on the correct side, and that it's not upside-down on the second side.

An alternative to the Manual Duplex option is the Print drop-down list (see Figure 5.3). Its choices are All Pages in Range (the default), Odd Pages, and Even Pages. Printing only the odd or even pages might be helpful if you eventually do want to do a duplex print but you want to wait until later to print the second half of the job.

Figure 5.3
Manual duplex prints all pages—first the odd, then the even. You can also choose to print only the odd or even pages from the Print list.

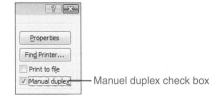 —— Manuel duplex check box

PRINTING MULTIPLE PAGES PER SHEET

The Zoom section of the Print dialog box enables you to shrink pages so that more than one page fits on a single sheet of paper. This can be useful for creating thumbnail summaries of a long report (perhaps for speaking notes), or for creating a booklet.

To get multiple pages per sheet, simply set the number of Pages Per Sheet to the desired value in the Print dialog box. The pages will be shrunk to fit automatically; you do not have to specify a shrinkage amount.

SCALING TO A DIFFERENT PAPER SIZE

The Scale to Paper Size setting is useful in situations where you need the print job to fit on a smaller size area than the paper you are actually using. For example, perhaps all you have is legal-sized paper at the moment, but you want to print a document that will be eventually copied onto letter-sized paper with a copier. Set the Scale to Paper Size drop-down box to the paper size target, and Word will confine the printout to that area, even if you are printing on a larger piece of paper.

SETTING PRINT OPTIONS FOR WORD DOCUMENTS

The settings in the Print dialog box apply only to the current document. To set options that affect all documents printed in Word, click the Options button in the Print dialog box. This opens the Display settings in the Word Options dialog box (see Figure 5.4). At the bottom are printing options.

In the Printing Options section, mark or clear any of these check boxes to control what happens when the Print command is executed:

- **Print drawings created in Word**—This option includes drawings created using Word's drawing tools, including AutoShapes, in the printout. They are printed by default. The option to exclude them is available because sometimes people use those drawing tools to create annotations (circles, arrows, and so on) that they don't want to print.

- **Print background colors and images**—A dark page background that looks great on screen can look terrible on a printout, especially a black-and-white one. Background colors and images are not printed by default for this reason.

- **Print document properties**—When this is marked, the document properties will print in addition to the document itself. (This is in contrast to the Print What setting in the Print dialog box, through which you can choose to print the document properties *or* the document itself.)

5

- **Print hidden text**—One of Word's text-formatting options is the Hidden attribute. You can set hidden text to be displayed or hidden onscreen, independent of its print setting. Here, you can choose whether or not to print hidden text as well.

- **Update fields before printing**—This is applicable only if the document contains fields (which are covered in Chapter 20, "Working with Fields"). It ensures that the fields contain the most recent values available.

- **Update linked data before printing**—This is applicable only if the document contains links (covered in Chapter 19, "Copying, Linking, and Embedding Data"). It retrieves a fresh copy of the linked data before printing.

Figure 5.4
Set print options that apply to all Word documents here.

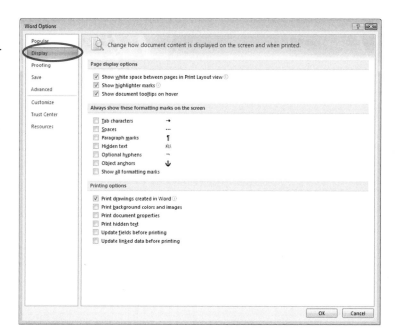

CAUTION

In some cases, you might not want links and fields updated. For example, if you are reprinting an archival copy of a memo that used a date field code, you would not want the date updated to today when printing the document; you would want the field value to stay at its original value.

Additional printing options are found on the Advanced tab of the Word Options dialog box, shown in Figure 5.5.

Figure 5.5
More printing options are available on the Advanced tab.

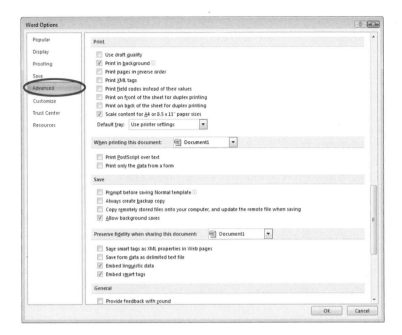

Click Advanced, scroll down to the Print section, and configure these controls:

- **Use draft quality**—Prints the document at a lower resolution, resulting in a smaller, faster print job.

- **Print in background**—Returns control to Word after a print job has been started, so you can continue working while you are waiting for it to finish. If you disable this option, Word will be locked up until the print job has finished spooling.

- **Print pages in reverse order**—This is useful for printers that spit out the pages face-up rather than face-down; it ensures that the printout pages will be in the same order as in the document.

CAUTION

Don't reverse the page order both in Word and in the printer's driver properties, or the two settings will cancel each other out. (The reverse of the reverse is the same as the original.)

- **Print XML tags**—When you're working with an XML document (see Chapter 32, "Preparing XML Content"), this option includes the tags in the printout. They are hidden by default.

- **Print Field codes instead of their values**—When you're working with a document containing fields (Chapter 20, "Working with Fields"), by default the values in those fields print. Marking this option makes the field codes print instead of the values.

- **Print on front of the sheet for duplex printing**—Enables printing on the front of a sheet on a printer that supports duplex.

- **Print on back of the sheet for duplex printing**—Enables printing on the back of the sheet on a printer that supports duplex printing.

- **Scale content for A4 or 8.5"×11" paper size**—Scales the document content to the appropriate size if the printer paper doesn't match the paper size specified in Word.

- **Default tray**—This setting specifies which paper tray to use for the document, if more than one is available. For example, for a letter, you might want the tray that contains your letterhead stationery.

These last two options are applicable only for individual documents. Select the document from the When Printing This Document list and then mark or clear these check boxes:

- **Print PostScript over text**—This option enables watermarks or other PostScript-specific content to be printed. When this option is not selected, PostScript overlays will be printed beneath the text rather than on top of it. It's applicable only when printing on a PostScript-compatible printer.

- **Print only the data from a form**—This setting is applicable only if the document contains form controls (covered in Chapter 21, "Creating Forms"). When this option is marked, only the data from the filled-in fields appears on the printout. When cleared, both the text labels and the data print.

SETTING OPTIONS FOR A CERTAIN PRINTER

Each printer has its own set of properties in Windows. These properties affect all print jobs from all applications, not just Word. You can access these properties from within Word, but it's important to remember that these are not Word settings.

To access a printer's properties, first select the printer from the Name list in the Print dialog box and then click the Properties button. A dialog box for that printer appears.

Figure 5.6 shows one example, but there is little standardization in these dialog boxes because their options are provided by the printer's manufacturer (or whoever wrote the printer driver). Color printers have different options from black-and-white; inkjet printers have different options from lasers; PostScript printers have different options from non-PostScript.

Here are a few settings that almost all printers have, though:

- **Copies**—Like the setting in the Print dialog box, this controls the number of copies of the print job. Be aware, however, that this is a separate setting, and it functions as a multiplier with the Copies value in the Print dialog box. If you set them both to 2, for example, you'll end up with four copies.

- **Orientation**—This switches between portrait and landscape modes. The orientation set in Word overrides the orientation set here. This setting is applicable mainly in programs that don't enable you to set the orientation.

Figure 5.6
Each printer has its own set of properties you can adjust.

- **Paper size**—Choose the paper size that's in the printer's input tray. For printers that have multiple trays, you can choose which tray to pull paper from, or leave it set to Automatically Select. (In Figure 5.6, there's a Paper tab for this and the next option.)

- **Paper type**—Most printers have a paper type setting, but it's an important issue mostly on inkjet printers, which print at different resolutions depending on the paper type. On such printers, setting a paper type also sets the print quality.

- **Print quality**—If the printer has a separate setting for this from the paper type, specify a value in dots per inch (dpi). The lower the dpi (down to about 300 dpi), the faster the printing; the higher the dpi, the better the quality. (In Figure 5.6, there's a Print Quality tab for this option.)

- **Color adjustment**—Most color printers have color adjustments you can make, such as color correction, balance, and/or matching.

- **Utilities (or Tools)**—Inkjet printers typically have utilities built into their printer drivers, for cleaning and aligning the print heads. Unless you are experiencing color problems, such as stripes or missing colors, you can ignore these.

> **TIP**
>
> Do your own quality comparison. Print a page containing both text and graphics at various dpi settings that your printer supports. (You won't notice much difference on the text; the graphics are usually the deciding factor.) If you can't tell any difference between them, go with the lower setting and get faster printing.

STORING DIFFERENT PROPERTIES FOR A SINGLE PRINTER

What Windows calls a "printer" is actually a printer driver. You can have multiple drivers installed that refer to the same printer, making it possible to quickly switch among printer settings. For example, if you have a color laser printer, you could have two copies of its driver—one that prints in black-and-white only and one that prints in color. Then depending on the demands of the print job at hand, you could choose one or the other.

To set up additional drivers for a printer that is already installed, use the Add New Printer Wizard in Windows (from the Printers and Faxes window), but do not automatically detect the printer; instead select it from the list provided or insert the driver disk that came with the printer. After setting up a duplicate copy of the same printer, change the properties for one of the copies.

USING PRINT PREVIEW

Print Preview helps you save paper—and wear and tear on your printer—by showing you onscreen exactly how the printout will appear on paper. It's great for catching unattractive page breaks, awkward placement of headings and artwork, inconsistent indentation, unbalanced columns, and more.

To access the Print Preview tab, choose Office, Print, Print Preview. The shortcut key for Print Preview is Ctrl+F2 or Ctrl+Alt+I. Figure 5.7 shows Print Preview view.

Figure 5.7
Use Print Preview to check out your print job before sending it to the printer.

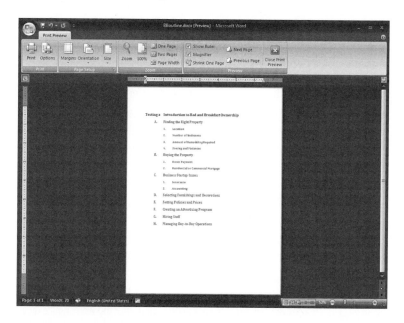

> **TIP**
>
> Previous versions of Word had a Print Preview button on the Standard toolbar. Although that button is gone in Word 2007, you can add it to the Quick Access toolbar; right-click the Print Preview command and choose Add to Quick Access Toolbar.

On the Print Preview tab, you'll find the following controls:

- **Print**—Opens the Print dialog box.
- **Options**—Opens the Display page of the Word Options dialog box, where many printer settings are located (as you learned earlier in this chapter).
- **Margins**—Opens a Margins list, from which you can change the document's margins. See "Changing Page Margins" in Chapter 9.
- **Orientation**—Opens an Orientation list, from which you can choose Portrait or Landscape. See "Setting Page Orientation" in Chapter 9.
- **Size**—Opens a Size list, from which you can change the paper size. See "Setting Paper Size" in Chapter 9.
- **Zoom**—Opens a Zoom dialog box, from which you can choose a zoom level at which to display the page. See "Switching Views" in Chapter 1. You can also adjust the zoom by dragging the Zoom slider in the bottom-right corner of the Word window.
- **One Page, Two Pages, and Page Width**—Use these buttons to zoom the corresponding amounts.
- **Show Ruler**—Displays or hides the ruler. You can use the ruler to adjust margins and indents, as covered in Chapter 7, "Formatting Paragraphs and Lists."
- **Magnifier**—When this control is selected, the mouse pointer is a magnifier that zooms in and out on the document with a click. When it's not selected, the mouse pointer is a normal arrow and insertion point with which you can edit the document.
- **Shrink One Page**—Each time you click this button, the font size used in the document shrinks in order to make the document fit on one fewer page. This change affects the document permanently, even after you have left Print Preview.

NOTE

Use Undo (Ctrl+Z) to reverse a Shrink One Page operation if you don't want the change to be permanent.

- **Next Page and Previous Page**—Click these buttons to scroll between pages in Print Preview. You can also page through the document with the scroll bar or the Page Up/Page Down keys on the keyboard.

- **Close Print Preview**—Returns you to regular viewing.

You can edit the document in Print Preview, including not only changing the text, but also changing the page setup, page background, and paragraph settings. Just make sure the Magnifier option is turned off to enable editing.

→ To learn about the options available on the Page Layout tab, **see** "Formatting Paragraphs and Lists," **p. 191** and "Formatting Documents and Sections," **p. 263**.

PRINTING TO A PRINTER (.PRN) FILE

When you print a document, the application sends the document to a printer driver, which in turn translates it into codes that the printer understands. Then it sends those codes to the printer. Those codes can be intercepted and instead placed in a file that can then be submitted to the printer later. This is called *printing to a file*. It's the same thing as printing to a printer except instead of the codes going to the printer, they go to a file. This is useful when the desired printer is not available for some reason.

There are a few gotchas with printing to a file:

- To print a file for a certain printer, that printer's driver must be installed in Windows. If it's not, you must add it using the Add Printer Wizard in Windows before printing to the file.

- When it's time to actually send the job to the printer, the printer must be connected to the PC via a local legacy parallel (LPT) interface. USB printers will not work, which is unfortunate because most home printers these days are USB-only and most offices print to a network printer.

- The name of the print job file should conform to DOS naming limitations (no more than eight characters, no spaces) if you are going to copy it to a printer port via a command-line interface.

To print to a file, follow these steps:

1. Choose Office, Print. The Print dialog box opens.
2. Set up the print job as you normally would, choosing the printer, the page range, the number of copies, and so on.
3. Mark the Print to File check box.
4. Click OK. The Print to File dialog box opens. It's like a Save As dialog box, but you're creating a printer file (.prn extension) instead of a document.
5. Type a name for the print job in the File name box. Limit the name to eight characters (no spaces).
6. (Optional) Change the save location if desired.
7. Click OK.

Of course, printing to the file is only half the equation. When the printer becomes available, you must copy the print job to it. Follow these steps to do this via a command-line interface:

1. Identify the complete path to the print job file. For example, if you stored a print job called draft.prn in a folder called Books on your C: drive, the complete path would be C:\Books\draft.prn.
2. Open a command prompt:

   In Windows Vista: Open the Start menu, type CMD in the Search box, and press Enter.

   In Windows XP: Open the Start menu, click Run, type CMD, and press Enter.

3. At the command prompt, type the following command, as shown in Figure 5.8:

```
COPY C:\folder\filename.prn LPT1: /B
```

where *C:\folder\filename.prn* is the complete path you identified in step 1.

4. Press Enter.

Figure 5.8
Copy the print job file to the printer using the COPY command.

> **NOTE**
>
> A USB printer will not work because you must specify an LPT port for the destination. (Most systems have only one LPT port, which is LPT1.) The /B switch stands for "binary" and indicates that the file being sent is a binary file (not plain text only).

So if it's so much hassle to print to a file and then copy it to a port, and if it only works with LPT ports, why is this feature even there? In a word, *PostScript*. Some professional printing companies like for you to submit your work to them in a .prn file that references a PostScript printer. Then they copy the file directly to their high-powered PostScript printer, either via the COPY method I just showed you or using a printer utility program.

→ To learn how to convert a .prn file for a PostScript printer to a PDF file, **see** "What Does This .PRN File Contain?" **p. 150**.

PRINTING TO A PDF DOCUMENT

Adobe Acrobat has for years been the leading program in creating PDF files. It's a third-party program that you purchase separately from Windows, and it consists of an Adobe Acrobat editing program and an Adobe Acrobat printer driver (which can be used from any program that prints, not just Acrobat). To create a PDF file from any application, you simply "print" to that printer.

Making the PDF conversion a printing function causes it to be immediately available to all applications. If it were handled as a Save operation, Adobe would have needed to provide utilities for every Windows-based application that someone might conceivably want to create a PDF from—an administrative nightmare. It's easy to see why Adobe implemented PDF creation via the print subsystem.

Creating PDF files from Word documents is a very welcome new feature in Word 2007, but this creation takes place as a Save operation, not as a Print operation. Microsoft has no interest in providing PDF support to every application, only its own Office 2007 applications. Therefore, in Office programs such as Word, PDF creation is built into the Save function.

5

If you already have Adobe Acrobat installed, you can continue to use its printer driver to create PDF files via "printing," or you can use the save method described in Chapter 2, "Creating and Saving Documents." You get the same result either way (except for some very minor differences in settings).

→ To save a Word document in PDF format, **see** "Saving to PDF or XPS Format," **p. 44**.

PRINTING IRON-ON TRANSFERS

Iron-on transfer paper is available at any office supply or computer store, and enables you to create your own transfers for T-shirts, hats, tote bags, and anything else made of cloth. There's just one gotcha, though—everything on a transfer is backward, a mirror image of the final design.

What you need, then, is a way to create a mirror image of your design in Word. If your printer supports mirroring (flipping), that's the easy way to go. Open the properties for the printer and look for a Mirror Image (or similar) check box. Figure 5.9 shows one example.

Figure 5.9
Some printers have a Mirror Image option you can set in the printer's properties.

Mirror image check box

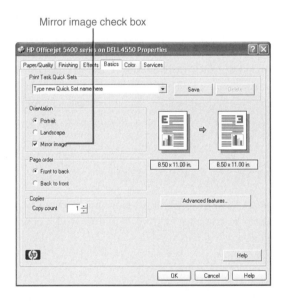

If your printer does not have a Mirror feature, but your design is graphics-only (no text), you can flip it by selecting all the objects and then using the Flip Horizontal command in Word. This doesn't work with text, though, because Word does not mirror text. (It does work with WordArt.)

→ To learn how to flip objects, **see** "Rotating and Flipping Objects," **p. 464**.

If having text on your transfer is important, consider using some other application to create the transfer, such as Photoshop or Paint Shop Pro. These programs let you create text as a graphic and then it can be rotated or flipped as freely as any other graphic would.

MANAGING A PRINT QUEUE

Each printer installed in Windows has its own print queue, where documents wait their turn to be printed (from all applications, not just Word). Although this is not part of Word per se, it does affect your work in Word. A print spooler service in Windows manages this queue.

The print spooler accepts the print job from Word and holds it in the queue until the job can be sent to the printer. The spooler communicates with the printer and sends the job as quickly as the printer can accept it. If the printer reports a problem, it tells the print spooler, which in turn displays a message to you in Windows. The print spooler relieves the applications of the responsibility of ensuring that the print job has completed, so the application can be freed up to continue working. If the print spooler did not exist or were turned off, Word would lock up until the document had finished printing.

Most of the time, the print spooler does its job in the background, and users don't even notice it's there. You might notice a printer icon flash briefly in the notification area in Windows, as the job enters and exits the queue. It's only when a problem occurs that the print queue gets attention.

When there is a problem with a print job, an icon appears in the notification area (by the clock) indicating that the printer is waiting for help. Usually it is a printer icon with a question mark on it. A pop-up balloon is usually also present, reporting an error condition.

To open a print queue, double-click its icon in the notification area. Or, if the icon does not appear there, open Printers (Windows Vista) or Printers and Faxes (Windows XP) from the Control Panel and double-click the printer in question.

The print queue window lists the jobs that are waiting to be printed. Normally jobs come and go very quickly here—almost instantaneously—so most of the time when you open the print queue window, it will be completely empty.

If you want to get a good look at a print job, pause the print queue and then submit a print job. To pause the queue, choose Printer, Pause Printing. Figure 5.10 shows a print queue that has been paused. To resume the queue, choose Printer, Pause Printing again.

Figure 5.10
A paused print queue, with one job waiting to be printed.

When an error occurs, the job's status will show Error. Usually you cannot recover from such an error; you'll need to delete the print job. To do so, select the print job and press the Delete key, or choose Document, Cancel.

However, sometimes deleting a print job can leave extraneous codes in the printer that also doom all the print jobs coming after it to pages of gibberish. Therefore, when other jobs are waiting to be printed behind the one with the error, it's best to pause those other jobs until the problem can be cleared. To pause a print job, select the job and choose Document, Pause. To resume it, repeat this selection.

To delete all the print jobs in the queue, choose Printer, Cancel All Documents. This is a quick way to delete all jobs at once instead of canceling each one individually.

TIP

> Have you ever accidentally printed a huge document? Rather than eating up all that paper unnecessarily, cancel the print job. To do so, first take the printer offline. (Press its Online button, or pull out the paper tray to interrupt it.) Then cancel the print job from the print queue. Finally, on the printer itself, use its LED panel (if it has one) to issue the command to cancel the current print job, or just unplug it, wait a few seconds, and plug it back in.

FAXING DOCUMENTS

For quick document delivery, faxing is an attractive alternative to mailing a hard copy. (So is email, discussed in Chapter 30, "Using Word as an Email Editor.")

Faxing is an old technology, but it's still very viable. The standard fax method is to use a fax modem on both ends of the conversation, connected via a dial-up telephone connection. The sending and receiving fax machines send codes that negotiate a mutually acceptable speed and protocol, and then the pages are transferred. With standard faxing, the pages are black-and-white only (no grayscale, no color), and herein lies the primary drawback of faxing. Because all colors and gray tones are reduced to either black or white (whichever they are nearest to), most artwork ends up as shapeless blobs. Color and grayscale-compatible fax machines and services are available, but the machines at both ends need to have that capability.

There are also Internet-based faxing services that can deliver black-and-white or color faxes to any fax machine (or any other Internet faxing service) without you having to actually own a fax modem of any type.

FAXING A DOCUMENT WITH A FAX MODEM

A fax modem is the same thing as a regular dial-up modem that you might use for a dial-up Internet connection. Faxing services have been included with dial-up modems for over a decade now, so if you have a dial-up modem, you have a fax modem. However, if you have a cable or DSL modem, you do *not* have faxing capabilities built into it. These are not really modems, but rather terminal adapters that connect you to Internet services.

Most fax modems come with basic faxing software that you can install in Windows, and Windows also has a faxing client you can use.

FAXING WITH WINDOWS VISTA

A Windows Fax and Scan utility is built into Windows Vista; you do not have to do anything special to set it up. A Fax driver is automatically installed as a printer; just print to it to start faxing.

The first time you print to the Fax driver, a Fax Setup dialog box opens; work through the prompts provided to set up your fax account.

After setting up the fax account, a New Fax window opens with the current document shown as an attachment. Create your cover sheet in the New Fax window by filling in the fields provided, and then click Send to send the fax (see Figure 5.11).

Figure 5.11
Use the New Fax window to prepare and send a fax in Windows Vista.

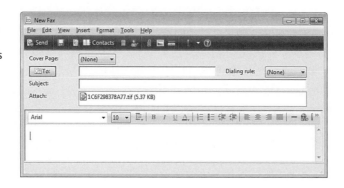

FAXING WITH WINDOWS XP

Windows XP has a fax client called Microsoft Fax. It is not installed by default, but you can easily add it.

To add Microsoft Fax to your system in Windows XP, follow these steps:

1. Open the Control Panel and open Add or Remove Programs.
2. Click Add/Remove Windows Components.
3. If Fax Services does not have a check mark next to it already, mark it, and then click Next.
4. Follow the prompts to install the faxing service. You will probably be prompted to insert your Windows CD.
5. After installing Fax Services, choose Start, All Programs, Accessories, Communications, Fax Console. The Fax Configuration Wizard runs.
6. Work through the wizard to configure the fax settings on your PC, including entering your contact information and selecting the modem to use.

After fax services have been configured in Windows XP, you can send a fax from Word by printing to the Fax printer driver that was set up when you installed Fax Services. Follow these steps:

1. Choose Office, Print.
2. Open the Name list and choose Fax as the printer name.

5

3. Click OK. The Send Fax Wizard runs.

4. Work through the wizard, entering the recipients and other information required to send the document as a fax.

TIP

> If you have a third-party faxing program you would rather use to send the fax, save the Word document as a TIFF file, as you learned in the section "Saving a Document as an Image" in Chapter 2, and then attach the TIFF file to the fax job in your faxing program.

DISTRIBUTING DOCUMENTS VIA INTERNET FAX

If you don't own a fax machine or fax modem, and don't want to buy one, you might want to consider an Internet faxing service. These services send your faxes over the Internet, for delivery to regular fax machines or to other Internet fax service accounts. (Such services are not free; they typically charge monthly or per-fax fees.)

To get started, choose Office, Send, Internet Fax. If you have not yet signed up with a fax provider, a message to that effect appears; click OK. You will then be redirected via a web browser interface to a page at Microsoft.com that describes the available fax providers and offers links through which you can sign up for them.

TROUBLESHOOTING

WHAT DOES THIS .PRN FILE CONTAIN?

Suppose someone gives you a .prn file on a disk, but they don't tell you what printer it's for. Without that information, you have no idea what printer to send it to. So what do you do then?

Well, if the .prn file happens to refer to a PostScript-type printer, and you have Adobe Acrobat (the full version, not just the reader), you have a utility called Acrobat Distiller that can convert .prn files to PDF files. Open up Acrobat Distiller and follow these steps:

1. Choose File, Open. The Open PostScript File dialog box appears.

2. Open the Files of Type drop-down list and choose All Files.

3. Navigate to the folder containing the .prn file and select it.

4. Click Open. The file is translated to PDF format.

5. Double-click the PDF file for the printer file you converted to open it in Adobe Acrobat. From there you can print it directly to a printer.

If that doesn't work, or if you don't have Acrobat Distiller, try opening up the .prn file in a text editor such as Notepad. The codes near the top of the file indicate what printer the file is designed to be printed on. Look for a text string that follows a "ModelName" marker.

AN EXTRA BLANK PAGE PRINTS AT THE END

It's possible that you simply have an extra page in your document composed of nothing but empty paragraph breaks. Switch to Draft view and then position the insertion point immediately after the final text in your document and press the Delete key until you see the end-of-file marker (horizontal line).

¶ You can also turn on the display of paragraph markers (on the Home tab) and look for extraneous paragraph marks to delete.

While you're in Draft view, look also for any extra hard page breaks you might have inserted at the end of the document. These appear as horizontal lines running across the whole width of the page in Draft view. (In Print Layout view, you see the actual pages rather than break markers.)

FONTS ARE NOT DISPLAYED CORRECTLY IN A DOCUMENT CREATED ON ANOTHER PC

Each PC has its own installed fonts, and if a document uses a font that the PC doesn't have, the PC tries to substitute a similar font for it. Sometimes it gets pretty close—other times not.

Here are some ways of dealing with this problem:

- Apply a different font to the affected text. This is the easiest way, but it doesn't preserve the original font designation, so in the future if you open the document on a PC that actually does have the original font, the text won't show in it.
- Set up font substitution. To do this, choose Office, Word Options, and click Advanced. In the Show Document Content section, click the Font Substitution button and specify a different font for the missing one. This substitution will take place only on this PC, and the document opened on a PC that does have the original font will appear as it did originally.

PART

II

FORMATTING A DOCUMENT

CHAPTER 6

APPLYING CHARACTER FORMATTING

CHANGING TEXT FONT, SIZE, AND COLOR

Character formatting is formatting that can be applied to individual characters of text. There are other types of formatting too, which I address in other chapters. *Paragraph formatting* is formatting that applies to entire paragraphs (for example, line spacing), and *page formatting* is formatting that applies to entire pages (for example, page margins and paper size).

Each character has a certain font (typeface) and size applied to it that govern how the letter appears. You can change the font and/or the size for a single character or any size block of text, often dramatically changing the look of the document.

NOTE

In Microsoft Office and Windows, the term *font* is synonymous with *typeface*; it refers to a style of lettering, such as Arial or Times New Roman. (Windows itself also uses this definition; if you add or remove fonts, you are actually adding/removing typefaces.) This usage is not universal, however. Some programs refer to a typeface as a *font family*, and a typeface at a certain size with certain attributes (such as bold) as a *font*. Modifiers such as bold and italic are called *font styles*.

UNDERSTANDING HOW FONTS ARE APPLIED

When you type some text in Word, how does Word know what font to use for it? And how can you change that font choice? The answers to those questions are surprisingly complex.

There are three ways that you can assign a font to text:

- The font can be applied manually to the text. You select the text and then choose a font from the Home tab or the Font dialog box. Manual font choices override styles and themes.

- Each paragraph has a paragraph style assigned to it; the default paragraph style is called Normal. The style's definition can include a font, such that any paragraphs with that style applied will appear in the specified font unless manual formatting has been applied to override it.

- In Word 2007 documents (not backward-compatible ones), instead of assigning a specific font to a style, you can assign a Body or Heading placeholder. Then you can specify a theme on the Page Layout tab that changes what font those placeholders will represent, or choose a Quick Style Set from the Home tab.

→ To learn how to change the font assigned to a style, **see** "Modifying a Style Definition," **p. 249**.

→ To change to a different set of fonts by changing the document's theme, **see** "Working with Themes," **p. 256**.

→ To change to a different set of fonts by applying a Quick Style Set, **see** "Changing the Quick Style Set," **p. 231**.

In the default Normal.dotm template, the default paragraph font is defined using the Body placeholder. The default theme applied is called Office, and it defines the Body placeholder as Calibri 11-point text. As a result, Calibri 11-point is the default font and size in new documents. You can change this by switching to a different theme, by redefining the Normal style to use a specific font, or by selecting the desired text and manually applying a font.

In most cases, it is best to change the font at the style or theme level and let the change trickle down to the individual instances. This helps ensure consistency throughout a document. However, sometimes you just want one certain block of text to change, independently of the rest of the document. For that type of formatting, you must select the text and make the change manually.

If you select a block of text and then change the font, Word places invisible beginning and ending codes around that block of text.

For example, suppose you type **ACME Industries** and then select it and apply Arial font. Codes are inserted at the beginning and end of the selection to indicate what font to use, like this:

> **[begin font Arial]**ACME Industries**[end font Arial]**

That's just a conceptual example; the actual codes are hidden deep within the file's coding and not available to end-users except by manually deconstructing the XML coding.

How WordML Applies Font Formatting

If you would like to see the actual codes that WordML (Word XML) uses to apply manual formatting, make a copy of your document file and rename the copy with a .ZIP extension. Then double-click it to open it as a folder. Locate the word\document.xml file and open it in Internet Explorer to view its contents.

In WordML, there are two parts to the process of applying a font manually. First a code sets up Arial to use:

```
<w:rFonts w:ascii="Arial" w:hAnsi="Arial" w:cs="Arial" />
```

Then the text to be formatted is surrounded by a pair of codes that call the font specified:

```
<w:t>ACME Industries</w:t>
```

If you change the font without first selecting any text, Word puts beginning and ending font codes around the insertion point, so that whatever you type next will appear in that font (as long as you don't move the insertion point outside of the codes):

> **[begin font Arial]***(insertion point)***[end font Arial]**

It's important to understand the placement of those codes because if you move the insertion point outside of the coded area (by clicking or by using the arrow keys, for example), the font choice is no longer in effect.

CAUTION

> WordPerfect users may be accustomed to that program's Reveal Codes feature, which shows you the actual codes that mark the beginning and ending of the formatting. Word does not have such a feature, but it does have a Reveal Formatting task pane that displays information about selected text. To display it, press Shift+F1.

→ To learn more about the Reveal Formatting feature, **see** "Revealing and Comparing Formatting," **p. 181**.

6

CHANGING THE FONT AND SIZE

As I mentioned earlier, the default font assigned to the Normal style in the Normal.dotm template is Calibri. It is a clean, easy-to-read font, suitable for a wide variety of document types, but you are free to change any or all text to another font at any point in the document-creation process.

To manually change the font, position the insertion point or select the block of text to affect, and then choose from the Font drop-down list on the Home tab (see Figure 6.1). You can also right-click or point to the selection to display the mini-toolbar and then select a font from there instead.

NOTE

The mini toolbar is available only in Word 2007 documents; it does not work in a Word 97-2003 document, or while working in Compatibility Mode. It can be displayed in two ways. You can right-click the selection, which displays both the mini-toolbar and a shortcut menu, or you can point at the selection. When you point at it, a faint version of the mini-toolbar appears; move your mouse onto it to make it bright (and available).

Figure 6.1
Select a font from the Font drop-down list on the Home tab.

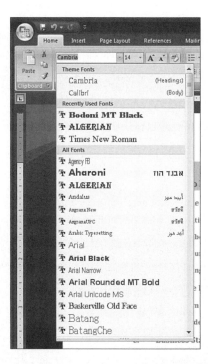

Notice that each font appears in its actual lettering style (where possible), making it easy to browse the available choices. For some fonts, it is not possible to view the names in the actual fonts because the fonts contain no letters; Wingdings is a symbols-only font, for example.

The Font drop-down list displays fonts in three areas:

- **Theme Fonts**—When you choose Body or Heading as the font choice rather than selecting a specific font, you allow the chosen theme (selected from the Page Layout tab) to control the font choices. Selecting one of the fonts in this section of the list sets the text to draw its font choice from those placeholders, so that changing the theme (on the Page Layout tab) will change the font.

→ To apply and modify themes, **see** "Working with Themes," **p. 256**.

- **Recently Used Fonts**—Fonts that you have recently applied appear here, for easy reselection.

- **All Fonts**—A complete list of the available fonts appears in this area.

The fonts appear in alphabetical order in the All Fonts part of the list. To quickly jump to a certain area of the list, start typing the first few letters of the font's name.

Font sizes are measured in points. A *point* is 1/72 of an inch on the printed page. (Because zoom settings and monitor sizes vary, the font size has no fixed relationship to the size of the text onscreen.)

To change the font size, select from the Font Size drop-down list. You are not limited to the sizes that appear on this list, though; you can type any size (including decimal numbers, such as 10.5) into the text box at the top of the list area (see Figure 6.2). You can enter a font size of up to 1638 points here. In addition, the Home tab has Grow Font and Shrink Font buttons that increase and decrease, respectively, to the next larger or smaller size on the Font Size list. (Depending on the font and the current size, this could be 1 point or it could be more. Notice, for example, that there are big jumps between the larger sizes, such as 48 and 72.)

Grow Font

Type a specific size / Shrink Font

Figure 6.2
Choose a font size from the list, or type a custom font size.

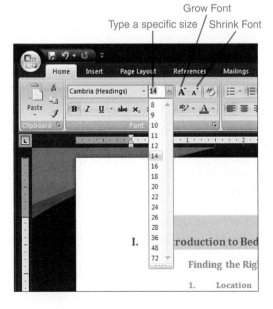

6

There are also shortcut keys for changing the font size (see Table 6.1).

TABLE 6.1   SHORTCUT KEYS FOR ADJUSTING FONT SIZE

Shortcut	Effect
Ctrl+]	Increases the font size by 1 point.
Ctrl+[	Decreases the font size by 1 point.
Ctrl+Shift+>	Increases the font size to the next larger size in the Font Size list. Sometimes this is 1 point; sometimes it's more.
Ctrl+Shift+<	Decreases the font size to the next smaller size in the Font Size list.
Ctrl+Shift+P	Opens the Font dialog box with the Size list selected; you can then use the up and down arrow keys to select a font size and press Enter to close the dialog box.

New in Word 2007, you can also access font and size controls by right-clicking or pointing at a text selection. When you do so, the mini-toolbar appears, containing a Font drop-down list and the Grow Font and Shrink Font buttons (see Figure 6.3).

Figure 6.3
Use the mini-toolbar for quick access to the Font list and to the buttons for increasing and decreasing font size.

One more method: You can use the Font dialog box to change both the font and the size. To display the Font dialog box shown in Figure 6.4, do any of the following:

- Press Ctrl+D.
- Click the dialog box launcher ▣ in the bottom-right corner of the Font group on the Home tab.
- Right-click the selected text and choose Font from the shortcut menu that appears.

Figure 6.4
The Font dialog box offers a wide variety of character-formatting options, including font and size choices.

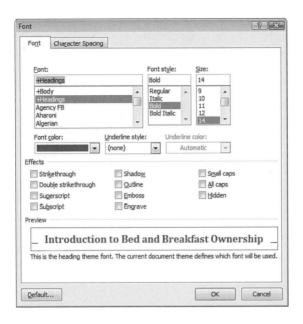

The Font dialog box is useful as a one-stop shop for all types of character formatting—not only fonts and sizes, but also attributes such as bold, italic, underline, strikethrough, and so on, as well as character spacing. You'll learn about all these things as this chapter progresses. For font and size selection, however, the Font dialog box offers little benefit over the tab method, and in fact has several drawbacks. Fonts appear on the dialog box's list in plain text, rather than as the actual fonts, so you must look to the Preview area to see a sample of the font you have chosen. The Font list in the dialog box also does not pull out theme fonts or recently used fonts separately, making them more difficult to find. Finally, the Font list here does not show icons indicating the font types.

SETTING THE DEFAULT FONT

If you don't like the default font of Calibri—for whatever reason—you can easily change it. This change is made to the Normal.dotm template, so that all new documents are affected.

There are two ways to set a default font. If you always want a certain font, you can set the default definition of the Normal style to a fixed choice. If you prefer to maintain the flexibility of working with the Body and Heading placeholders, so you can use themes to format the fonts later if desired, you can define a set of theme fonts and then set them as the default.

SPECIFYING A FIXED DEFAULT FONT

Notice in the Font dialog box (refer to Figure 6.4), a Default button appears in the bottom-left corner. Select the desired default font and size, and then click the Default button. A confirmation box appears; click Yes, and your choice of font and size becomes the default.

Here's another way of doing the same thing: Apply the desired font to some text, and select that text, and then on the Home tab, click Change Styles and click Set as Default.

6

TIP

> If you change the default font and then regret it, you can easily change it again. If you've forgotten what the original settings were, see "I Accidentally Modified Normal.dotm and Now All New Documents Are Messed Up" in the Troubleshooting section at the end of this chapter.

Setting Different Default Theme Fonts

You'll learn about themes in Chapter 8, but here's a quick walkthrough of how to change the default definition for Body and Heading by creating a new theme font set and then setting it to be the default:

1. On the Home tab, click Change Styles, point to Fonts, and click Create New Theme Fonts.

2. In the Create New Theme Fonts dialog box, specify a font for Body and for Heading.

3. Type a name for the new font theme in the Name box.

4. Click Save.

5. Click Change Styles again, and click Set as Default.

→ For more information about theme font sets, **see** "Working with Themes," **p. 256**.

More About Font Types

The vast majority of the fonts used in Windows are scalable OpenType or TrueType fonts. These are *outline fonts*, which means they consist of unfilled mathematically created outlines of each character. When you assign a size, you are sizing the outline; then the outline is filled in with black (or whatever color you choose) to form each character. Such fonts look good at any size.

TrueType fonts, which Microsoft and Apple jointly developed, have been around since the late 1980s; they're good basic scalable fonts that you can use on any printer. OpenType was created as a joint venture between Microsoft and Adobe (the makers of PostScript), so OpenType fonts have many of the characteristics and benefits of both TrueType fonts and Adobe Type 1 fonts, including the capability of storing more than 65,000 characters in a single font file. For example, OpenType fonts typically store ligatures, alternative characters, typeset-style ordinals, and built fraction sets, as well as characters for many different written languages.

Not all fonts are created equal, however. The simple fact of a font being OpenType does not necessarily make it better than a TrueType font, because both amateurs and experts create both types. In the end, the quality and versatility of a font depends in large part upon who created it. The best commercial OpenType fonts, such as those that Adobe has produced, have several alternative character sets in them, plus alternative characters for superscript and subscript numbers, fractions, ligatures, and so on. And although Word cannot access this feature, most commercial OpenType fonts have several weights of lettering, such as light, normal, semi-bold, bold, and extra bold. A free, amateur-created font might have only the basic keyboard letters, numbers, and symbols.

6

Word's Font list does not differentiate between TrueType and OpenType fonts; both appear with TT icons to their left. To find out which fonts are which, open the Fonts folder (from the Control Panel in Windows; use the Classic View) and check the icon for the font in question. An OpenType font has an O icon; a TrueType font has a TT icon (see Figure 6.5).

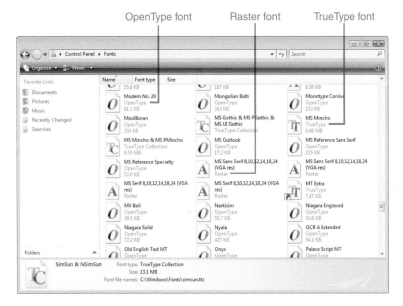

Figure 6.5
TrueType, OpenType, and Raster icons in the Fonts list in Windows.

You might also have a handful of nonscalable fonts available on your system. These fonts are *raster* or *bitmap fonts*; each letter at each size consists of a tiny graphic. Such fonts are available at only a few sizes (such as 8, 10, 12, 14, 18, and 24 point, for example). Examples of these include MS Sans Serif and MS Serif. These fonts do not appear on the list of font choices in Word, but they do appear in the Fonts folder in Windows (with A icons).

> **NOTE**
>
> Serifs are the little tails on the letters. Fonts that use them are called serif fonts, like this. Fonts that don't are called sans serif, like this.

Finally, depending on the default printer, you might have some printer-resident fonts available. These fonts do not appear in the Fonts folder in Windows. The printer driver tells Windows (and Word) about their existence, and the fonts become available on Word's list. For example, most PostScript-compatible printers have 35 or more printer-resident fonts. In Word, printer-resident fonts appear with a printer icon to their left. The available printer-resident fonts on the Fonts list change when you set a different printer to be the default in Windows.

CAUTION

> Try not to use printer-resident fonts when creating documents that you intend to save in PDF format. There are reports of PDF documents not being searchable when created using printer fonts. It probably has something to do with the way the PDF file format embeds the font information; PDF files know how to handle TrueType, OpenType, and Adobe Type 1 fonts, but not printer-resident fonts.

Printer-resident fonts do not usually have Windows equivalents, so the version you see onscreen may not exactly match the version you see printed. With a TrueType or OpenType font, on the other hand, what you see onscreen is what you get on the printout.

ADDING MORE FONTS TO YOUR SYSTEM

Fonts, like printers, are installed Windows-wide. Different word processing and desktop publishing applications come with different fonts, so your font choices depend on what other programs you have installed besides Word.

Office 2007 comes with a large selection of fonts, but you can also buy more (or acquire them for free online in many cases). After acquiring one or more new fonts, install them in Windows to gain access to them in all applications (including Word).

Here are the steps to take in Windows XP:

1. Open the Control Panel. If not already in Classic view, click Switch to Classic View.
2. Double-click Fonts. The Fonts folder opens.
3. Choose File, Install New Font. The Add Fonts dialog box opens.
4. If needed, open the Drives list and change to the drive containing the fonts.
5. In the Folders list, navigate to the folder containing the fonts. The available fonts appear under List of Fonts (see Figure 6.6).

Figure 6.6
Add new fonts to your system in Windows XP.

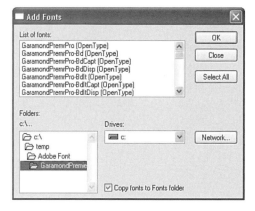

6. In the list of fonts, click the font(s) to install. To select more than one, hold down the Ctrl key as you click each one, or hold down Shift as you click the first and then the last one in a contiguous group. To select all the fonts in that location, click Select All (or press Ctrl+A).

7. Click OK. Windows XP installs the fonts.

In Windows Vista, here are the steps to follow:

1. Open the Start menu and click Control Panel.

2. Click Appearance and Personalization.

3. Click Fonts.

> **TIP**
>
> If you are using the Classic view of the Control Panel, you can skip step 2, and double-click instead of single-click Fonts.

4. Press the Alt key to display a menu bar.

5. On the menu bar, choose File, Install New Font.

6. If needed, open the Drives list and change to the drive containing the fonts.

7. In the Folders list, navigate to the folder containing the fonts. The available fonts appear under List of Fonts (see Figure 6.6).

8. In the list of fonts, click the font(s) to install. To select more than one, hold down the Ctrl key as you click each one, or hold down Shift as you click the first and then the last one in a contiguous group. To select all the fonts in that location, click Select All (or press Ctrl+A).

9. Click Install. Windows Vista installs the fonts.

EMBEDDING AND SUBSTITUTING FONTS

One potential problem when sharing documents with other people is that not everyone has the same fonts installed on their PCs. When a document is opened on a PC that does not have the correct font, the name of the font appears in the Font box on the Home tab, but the actual font does not appear; instead the text appears in whatever Word considers to be a close match for the font. (Often it is not a close match at all, but a generic-looking font such as Courier.) The text remains marked as using the missing font, so if the document is later opened on a different PC with the correct font installed, it will appear as originally intended.

To get around this problem, in some cases you can embed the font in the document so that the font travels with it. This works only if there is no prohibition against embedding built into that font. (Some font designers disallow embedding to keep the font from being distributed without their permission.)

6

To embed fonts in a document, follow these steps:

1. Choose Office, Save As. The Save As dialog box opens.
2. Click Tools and choose Save Options. The Word Options dialog box opens.
3. Mark the Embed Fonts in the File check box.
4. Select either or both of the options provided:
   - **Embed only the characters used in the document**—This embeds only the letters in use; do not do this if there will be any editing of the document later.
   - **Do not embed common system fonts**—This prevents fonts from being embedded that come with Windows, such as Times New Roman and Arial.
5. Click OK.
6. Continue saving normally.

If the person who created the document did not have the foresight to embed the needed fonts, you aren't completely stuck; you can change the font substitution table so that the missing fonts are at least displayed in a font of your choice. To modify the font substitution table for the document, follow these steps:

1. Choose Office, Word Options. The Word Options dialog box opens.
2. Click Advanced.
3. Scroll down to the Show Document Content section and click Font Substitution.

   If no fonts needs to be substituted, a message appears to that effect and you're done. Otherwise, the Font Substitution dialog box opens, listing the missing and substituted fonts (see Figure 6.7).

Figure 6.7
View and change font substitutions.

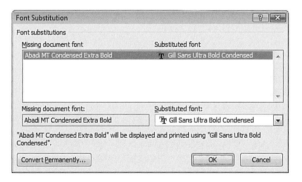

4. Click a font on the list, and then select a different font from the Substituted Font drop-down list. Repeat for each font.
5. (Optional) To permanently convert all instances of the missing font to the chosen substitution, click Convert Permanently and then click OK to confirm.
6. Click OK to close the Font Substitution dialog box, and then OK to close the Word Options dialog box.

If you are sharing the document with others, be wary of converting fonts permanently. You might be the only one who is missing the chosen font, and the original font choice might be important to maintain (for example, to match the company's official document-formatting standards).

CHANGING FONT COLOR

The default setting for font color in Word is Automatic (not black, as many people assume). Automatic makes the text appear either black or white, depending on which would most sharply contrast with the background on which it is placed. By default, the background is white, so text appears black. However, if you change the background to a dark color (or to black), the text changes to white. You can change the font color to any color you like—including fixed black or fixed white.

To understand the font color choices in Word 2007, you must know something about themes. A *theme* is like a style that applies to the entire document. Themes include colors, fonts, and object effects (for formatting drawn lines and shapes). There are 12 color place-holders in a theme. By changing the theme, you can change what colors are populated into those placeholders.

→ To change themes, **see** "Applying a Theme," **p. 256**.
→ To learn more about object effects, **see** "Changing the Theme Effects for the Entire Document," **p. 546**.

When specifying the color for text (or for an object), you can either choose a fixed color or a theme color. A fixed color does not change, regardless of the theme applied. A theme color does not actually apply a color to the selection, but rather a link to one of the theme's color placeholders. Then whatever color happens to be assigned to that placeholder trickles down to the selection. That way, you can have elements in your document that change color automatically when you switch themes.

You do not necessarily have to apply a theme color at full strength; you can instead apply a *tint* or *shade* of it. A tint is a scaled-back version of a color, derived by blending the color with white. Tints are described in percentages, such as a 25% tint, a 50% tint, and so on. Shades are darkened versions, derived by blending the color with black. Shades are also described in percentages, such as a 50% shade.

Color formatting works like font formatting, in that if you select the text first, it applies only to the selected block. If you do not select anything, the formatting applies to the insertion point's current position.

To change the font color, do the following:

1. If desired, select text to affect. Otherwise, the change will apply to new text typed at the insertion point's current location.
2. On the Home tab, open the Font Color button's drop-down list (see Figure 6.8).

6

Figure 6.8
Select a font color—
either a fixed color or
one from the current
theme.

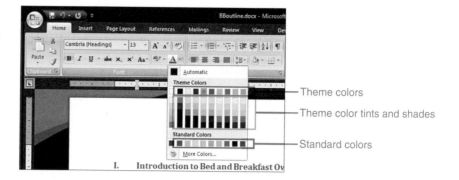

Theme colors

Theme color tints and shades

Standard colors

TIP

This same Font Color list is also available in the Font dialog box. You can also point to or right-click the selected text and use the Font Color button on the mini toolbar.

3. Do one of the following:

- Click Automatic.
- Click a theme color (top row).
- Click a tint or shade of a theme color.
- Click a standard (fixed) color (bottom row).

If none of the color choices please you, choose More Colors from the Color drop-down list and select a color from the Colors dialog box. This dialog box has two tabs: Standard and Custom.

On the Standard tab, you can click any of the colored hexagons, as shown in Figure 6.9.

Figure 6.9
Select one of the stan-
dard colors from the
Standard tab.

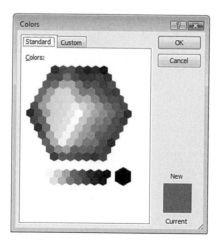

On the Custom tab, you can define a color precisely using its numeric value from either the RGB or the HSL color model. These numeric color models can be useful when you are trying to match a color exactly; for example, many corporations have official colors to be used in all company correspondence and publications.

RGB stands for Red/Green/Blue; colors are defined with values ranging from 0 to 255 for each of those three colors. Equal amounts of each color results in varying shades of black-gray-white.

HSL stands for Hue/Saturation/Luminosity. These are also 0-to-255 values, but H is for all hues (0 and 255 are both red; the numbers in between are the other colors of the rainbow), S is for saturation (the intensity of the color, as opposed to neutral gray), and L is for the lightness/darkness (white to black). As you can see in Figure 6.10, you can click any spot on the color grid to select that color, or you can drag the vertical slider up or down.

Figure 6.10
Define a color numerically on the Custom tab.

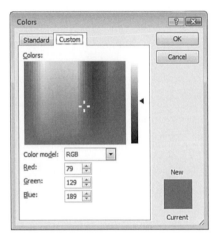

BOLD AND ITALIC: APPLYING FONT STYLES

Font styles are modifiers that affect the shape and/or thickness of the characters. In Word, a font's style can be set to Regular, Italic, Bold, or Bold Italic. The way font styles are applied depends on the particular font. Some fonts that appear as single entries in Word's Font list are actually four separate font files behind the scenes—one for each style. This is the ideal, because the shapes of the letters can be subtly different for each style. Other fonts have only one font definition, and Word must simulate "bold" by fattening up the characters or "italic" by skewing them to the right slightly. In some programs, this skewing is called *false italics.*

6

CAUTION

Do not confuse font styles with character styles. A *character style* is a Word-defined style that applies to individual characters, covered in Chapter 8, "Creating and Applying Styles and Themes."

Word makes no distinction between true italics and false ones, or between true bold and simulated bold, but you can see the difference for yourself by experimenting with the various fonts on your system. For example, in Figure 6.11, the Broadway and Times New Roman fonts are shown in both regular and italic. Notice that the Broadway font's letters are simply tilted to the right, but the Times New Roman letters are actually different in shape and thickness.

Figure 6.11
Some fonts are merely tilted for italics; others have completely different character shapes.

You can also tell which fonts have separate files for the various styles by opening the Fonts folder from the Control Panel. In the Fonts folder, open the View menu and make sure that Hide Variations is not marked. Then browse the font icons that appear, looking for fonts that have separate icons for regular, bold, italic, and bold italic. Some professional-quality fonts might even have more icons than that—they might have separate sets for light, normal, demi-bold, bold, and so on. Word recognizes and uses only one level of bold, however.

As with other formatting, you can select the text first and then apply bold and/or italic, or you can apply the font style to the insertion point position.

To quickly apply bold or italic to text, use one of these methods:

- Click the Bold or Italic button on the Home tab, as shown in Figure 6.12.
- Right-click the selected text and use the Bold or Italic button on the mini toolbar (if not in Compatibility Mode).
- Use shortcut keys: Ctrl+B for bold or Ctrl+I for italic.

All these methods are on/off toggles. To remove bold or italic, click the button again or use the shortcut key again. (You can also strip off all formatting from text, including bold and italic, by selecting it and pressing Ctrl+spacebar.)

Figure 6.12
Apply bold or italic from the Home tab.

Bold   Italic

→ To learn about clearing text formatting, **see** "Clearing Formatting," **p. 180**.

You can also apply bold or italic from the Font dialog box:

1. On the Home tab, click the dialog box launcher 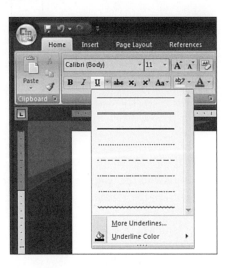 in the lower-right corner of the Font group, or press Ctrl+D. The Font dialog box opens.

2. On the Font Style list, click your preference: Regular, Italic, Bold, or Bold Italic.

3. Click OK.

UNDERLINING TEXT

Word enables you to apply a variety of underline styles and colors to text. Unlike bold and italics, underlining does not modify the basic shape or weight of the text itself; it's an additive element.

To apply the default underline style (a plain, solid single line, Automatic color), click the Underline button on the Home tab. The Underline button on the Home tab also has a drop-down menu associated with it for choosing alternate underline styles, as shown in Figure 6.13. To pick an underline color from the menu, point to Underline Color for a flyout menu of color choices.

Figure 6.13
Apply underlining from the Home tab.

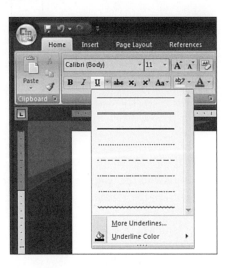

6

For even more underline options, choose More Underlines from the menu to display the Font dialog box (see Figure 6.14). From here, open the Underline Style drop-down list and select a style. A variety of line styles are available, including solid, dotted, dashed, single, double, and wavy. While you're here, open the Underline Color list and select a color. (The choices for colors are the same as for font colors.)

NOTE

There are shortcut keys for some of the most popular underline styles:

- **Single plain underline**–Ctrl+U
- **Words Only underline**–Ctrl+Shift+W
- **Double underline**–Ctrl+Shift+D

Figure 6.14
Apply underlining from the Font dialog box.

APPLYING FONT EFFECTS

Font effects are additives or modifiers applied to the text, such as strikethrough, shadow, or superscript. Some of these are available from the Home tab; others must be applied via the Font dialog box (refer to Figure 6.14). Table 6.2 summarizes the effects and shows the Home tab buttons and/or the shortcut keys where applicable.

TABLE 6.2	FONT EFFECTS		
Effect	**Home Tab Button**	**Shortcut Key**	**Usage Example(s)**
~~Strikethrough~~	abc	——	Text to be marked for deletion.
~~Double strikethrough~~	——	——	Text to be marked for deletion.
Sub$_{script}$	x₂	Ctrl+= (equal sign)	Chemical formulas.
Super^{script}	x²	Ctrl+Shift++ (plus sign)	Exponents, footnotes.
Shadow	——	——	Decorative effect.

Effect	Home Tab Button	Shortcut Key	Usage Example(s)
Outline	—-	—-	Decorative effect.
Emboss	—-	—	Page watermark, decorative effect.
Engrave	—-	—-	Page watermark, decorative effect.
SMALL CAPS	—-	Ctrl+Shift+K	Headings, emphasis. Letters already capitalized appear full size; letters not already capitalized appear capitalized in shape but about 20% smaller than normal capitals.
ALL CAPS	—-	Ctrl+Shift+A	Headings, emphasis. All letters appear as full-size caps regardless of their previous state. This does not actually change the letters; if you remove the All Caps effect, the letters go back to their previous capitalization.
Hidden (makes text nonprinting)	—	Ctrl+Shift+H	Text that should not appear in printed copies.

As the name implies, the Hidden effect hides the text. Marking text as hidden is useful when you don't want it in the current draft but you might eventually want it again. For example, in a boilerplate contract, you could hide text that doesn't apply to a certain client. Hidden text will not print under any circumstances, but you can choose whether or not it should appear onscreen. The easiest way to do this is to click the Show/Hide ¶ button on the Home tab; this turns on the display of all hidden text and characters. If you don't want all the other hidden characters, but just hidden text, customize the viewing options as follows: Choose Office, Word Options, and on the Display tab, mark the Hidden Text check box if you want hidden text to show onscreen.

Font effects can be combined, but there are a few exceptions. The following are mutually exclusive:

- Strikethrough and double strikethrough
- Superscript and subscript
- Shadow, outline, emboss, and engrave
- Small caps and all caps

CHANGING TEXT CASE

In the ASCII character set, which is the basic set of characters used in English-language writing (as well as many other languages), upper- and lowercase versions of the same letter

6

are considered two completely separate characters. For example, a capital *A* has no inherent relationship to a lowercase *a*. Therefore, generally speaking, if you accidentally type *A* instead of *a*, you must retype it.

There are cases where you don't have to retype text to change its case, however. As you learned in Chapter 4, "Using Spelling, Grammar, and Research Tools," Word's AutoCorrect feature turns off the Caps Lock feature and corrects any text that you have accidentally typed with it on. AutoCorrect also fixes instances of two capital letters at the beginning of an otherwise-lowercased word.

You can also use Word's Change Case feature to change the case of some text. Here are the choices:

- **Sentence case**—Text is capitalized as in an English-language sentence (first letter of the first word only).
- **Uppercase**—All letters of all words are capitalized.
- **Lowercase**—All letters of all words are lowercased.
- **Capitalize Each Word**—The first letter of each word is capitalized.
- **Toggle case**—The current case of each letter is reversed.

CAUTION

The Capitalize Each Word option is not "smart" or contextual. It simply capitalizes the first letter in every word. Modern English usage dictates that certain words such as *of* and *in* should not be capitalized in titles, so you will need to edit what Word has done to conform to that standard usage. However, the grammar checker will fix such problems, so running a grammar check immediately after changing text to Title Case should do the trick.

To change the text case of some text, select the text and then click the Change Case button on the Home tab. Select the desired case from the menu, as shown in Figure 6.15. Alternatively, you can toggle through uppercase, lowercase, and sentence case by pressing Shift+F3.

Figure 6.15
Change case from the Home tab.

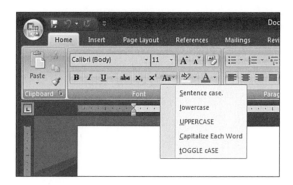

The All Caps font effect covered in the preceding section does make the text *appear* to be in all caps, but this is just an illusion. The letters have not changed; they have just had a mask placed over them that makes them appear as their uppercase cousins. That's not the same thing as actually changing the text's case. It's useful, for example, if you want to make a heading all-caps for a certain appearance effect, but you want to retain the flexibility of going back to the original capitalization later without retyping.

Highlighting Text

Students have long known that a highlighter marker can be of great help in marking important passages of a textbook. Word's highlighting feature lets you do the same thing to Word documents. You can use highlighting to call attention to text, or to color-code various passages (for example, to mark text that's the responsibility of a certain writer or reviewer).

There are two ways to highlight text:

- Select the text first, and then select a highlight color from the Text Highlight Color button's drop-down list on the Home tab (see Figure 6.16).

- Select a highlight color first, and then drag across text to be highlighted with that color. Press Esc to turn off the highlight when finished.

Figure 6.16
Select a highlight color.

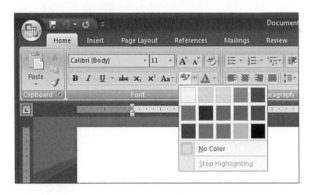

To remove a highlight, select the text and then open the Text Highlight Color button's list and choose No Color.

Highlighting is the one type of character formatting that is *not* removed by the Clear Formatting command (Ctrl+spacebar or the Clear Formatting button on the Home tab). Highlighting can be removed only with the Text Highlight Color button.

6

ADJUSTING CHARACTER SPACING

Have you ever wondered why ordinary word processing documents don't look as polished and professional as book or magazine pages? It's the spacing. A professional designer knows how to subtly manipulate spacing to create more readable and attractive pages.

Word enables you to adjust text spacing to achieve the same professional-looking effects that professionals enjoy who use very expensive page layout programs. Although Word's controls are perhaps not as exhaustive in function, they are adequate for most projects.

To change character spacing, use the Font dialog box. Follow these steps:

1. Select the text to affect, or position the insertion point where you will type new text that will have this formatting.

2. On the Home tab, click the dialog box launcher ▣ in the bottom-right corner of the Font group to open the Font dialog box.

3. Click the Character Spacing tab.

4. Adjust any of the character spacing settings, as described following these steps, and as shown in Figure 6.17.

5. Click OK.

Figure 6.17
Set spacing options on the Character Spacing tab of the Font dialog box.

TIP

To redefine the defaults in Normal.dotm, click the Default button in the Font dialog box.

Here are some details about the options on the Character Spacing tab:

- **Scale**—This is the size of the text in relation to its baseline size (as specified via the Font Size setting). Scale can be used to subtly adjust the size of certain characters—for example, to make an @ sign or punctuation mark slightly larger or smaller than the surrounding text. A drop-down list of common percentages is provided, but you can manually enter any value from 1% to 600%.

> Setting scaling for a character is preferable to setting its font size because its size shifts proportionally if you later change the font size definition for the style on which it is based. For example, suppose the Body style is defined as 12 point, and you choose to make a particular character 120% of that size. That character ends up 14.4 point in size. If you redefine the Body style to be 10 point, the character changes to 12 point (120% of 10 point).

- **Spacing**—This is an increase or decrease of the space between letters compared to a baseline size of Normal. This setting does not change the letters themselves, but only the space between the letters. In some programs, this is called *tracking*. You choose either Expanded or Condensed and then specify a number of points. (One point is 1/72 of an inch.) The increment arrows move the value up one point at a time, but you can manually type values in as fine a detail as 1/20th of a point (for example, 1.05 points).

- **Position**—This is a raising or lowering of the characters compared to the baseline of Normal. This setting is called *baseline shift* in some desktop publishing programs. You choose either Raised or Lowered and then specify a number of points. As with spacing, you can use the increment arrows to go up or down one point at a time or manually enter values in as fine a detail as 1/20th of a point. This can be used to make a manual adjustment to the height of a superscript or subscript character, for example.

- **Kerning**—This is a spacing adjustment between certain pairs of letters based on their shapes. For example, when the letters *A* and *V* appear adjacent to one another, they can afford to be closer together because their shapes fit into one another: AV. You can turn kerning on or off, and you can specify a minimum font size at which kerning should occur.

  Kerning is more useful at larger sizes; with very small text, however, kerning can actually backfire and make letters look like they are *too* close together. Kerning also slows down the computer's performance somewhat, especially noticeable on a PC that is slow to begin with. If you notice a difference in performance with kerning turned on for body text sizes (say, 10 point and up), but you want to kern text that size, consider doing all the editing on the document with kerning turned off and then turning it back on right before you print.

> Kerning may cause spacing to shift, and in some cases might cause text to float from one page to another.

6

Many OpenType and TrueType fonts have kerning tables built into them that determine how much space should be left between letters when kerning is turned on for maximum readability and attractiveness. This table can contain as many as 500 *kerning pairs* (pairs of letters with rules established for kerning them when they appear together). If the font has such a table, Word uses it; otherwise, Word tries to kern based on the letter shapes.

TIP

High-end desktop publishing programs enable you to manually adjust the kerning values between specific letter pairs. Word does not offer this feature, but you can simulate such an adjustment by changing the spacing between two letters with the Spacing setting. For example, if you think a particular *A* and *V* are too close to each other, select the *V* and change its spacing to Expanded by a certain value (perhaps 0.5 point to start with) and then adjust up or down as needed.

Creating Your Own Built Fractions

A *built fraction* is one that looks typeset, like this:

½

as opposed to a regular typed fraction like this:

[1/2]

Most fonts have built fractions for 1/2 and 1/4; you can access them via the Symbol command (on the Insert tab). However, when you have some odd fraction such as 23/54, the font can't realistically be expected to have a built-in symbol for it.

To create a built fraction manually in Word, use a combination of font size, superscript, and position:

1. Type the fraction normally. You might want to zoom in on it to see it more clearly.

2. Select the numerator and make it superscript (from the Home tab).

3. Select the divider line (/) and the denominator and change their font size to two-thirds of the original size. For example, if the original size was 12, set the size to 8.

4. Select the divider line and change its Position to Raised by 1 point.

The end result won't fool a professional typesetter, but it'll be good enough that casual readers won't be able to tell the difference, especially at body text size.

6

CREATING A DROP CAP

A *drop cap* is an enlarged capital letter at the beginning of a paragraph, "dropped" down into the paragraph. Drop caps are used to call attention to the beginning of a chapter, section, or article; they say to the reader "begin here."

There are two basic styles of drop cap: Dropped and In-Margin. The Dropped style places the letter in the paragraph itself, so that the lines move over to accommodate its presence. An In-Margin drop cap places the letter to the left of the paragraph, and does not interfere with any line positions (see Figure 6.18).

Figure 6.18
Dropped-style drop
cap versus in-margin
style.

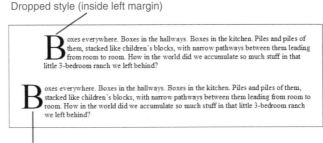

Dropped style (inside left margin)

In-margin style (outside left margin)

To create a drop cap for a paragraph, click in the paragraph. Then on the Insert tab, click the Drop Cap button and choose the type of drop cap you want: Dropped or In-Margin (see Figure 6.19). To remove a drop cap from a paragraph, choose None.

Figure 6.19
Apply a simple drop
cap from the Drop
Cap button's menu.

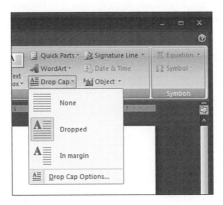

For a drop cap with custom settings, choose Advanced. The Drop Cap dialog box opens (see Figure 6.20). From here, you can select the following options:

- **Font**—By default, whatever font was previously applied to that letter is used. Sometimes a different font can make for a more interesting drop cap, though; for example, an Old English or handwriting style font can be attractive.

- **Lines to Drop**—The default is three lines. The larger the value here, the larger the drop cap will be and the further down into the paragraph it will drop.

- **Distance from Text**—The default is 0". Increase this value to increase the spacing around the drop cap.

6

Figure 6.20
Create custom drop caps with the Drop Cap dialog box.

TIP

If you increase the Distance from Text setting, the drop cap will appear somewhat indented compared to the rest of the paragraph. To counteract this, adjust the first-line indent for the paragraph. A quick way to do this is to drag the first-line indent marker to the left on the horizontal ruler.

→ To learn about adjusting paragraph indentation, **see** "Indenting Paragraphs," **p. 197**.

CLEARING FORMATTING

Sometimes it's easier to format text by starting from scratch rather than wondering what formatting has been applied to it. To quickly strip off all the character formatting from some text (except for highlighting), select the text and press Ctrl+spacebar, or click the Clear Formatting button on the Home tab.

NOTE

Ctrl+spacebar is an old trick that Word has offered for many versions now, but few people knew about it because there was no menu command for it. The Clear Formatting button is new in Word 2007, and it serves to make the feature more obvious.

COPYING FORMATTING WITH FORMAT PAINTER

Formatting can be copied from one block of text to another, which can save a tremendous amount of time in situations where text has multiple formatting actions applied to it. For example, instead of individually making multiple blocks of text 16 point *and* bold *and* italic *and* red, you can format one block of text that way and use Format Painter to copy all that formatting to other blocks.

To copy the formatting from one block of text to another, follow these steps:

1. Select the text that is already formatted correctly. You can select as little as a single character. If you do not select any text, Format Painter will copy the text settings that are in effect at the insertion point's current location.

2. Click the Format Painter button on the Home tab, or click the Format Painter button on the mini toolbar. The mouse pointer changes to show a paintbrush.

3. Drag across the text to receive the formatting.

Format Painter turns itself off automatically when you release the mouse button. If you would like Format Painter to stay on, so you can copy the same formatting to additional selections, double-click instead of clicking the button in step 2.

REVEALING AND COMPARING FORMATTING

The Reveal Formatting task pane is Word's partial response to requests from WordPerfect users who missed that program's Reveal Codes feature after moving to Word. To display the Reveal Formatting pane, press Shift+F1. The pane describes the formatting applied to the currently selected text, or to the insertion point's current location (see Figure 6.21).

Figure 6.21
The Reveal Formatting task pane describes the formatting of the selected text.

Notice the underlined headings in the Reveal Formatting task pane, in sections such as Font, Language, Alignment, and Indentation. Each of those headings is a hyperlink to the dialog box in which that setting can be changed.

The Reveal Formatting task pane also has two check box options:

■ **Distinguish Style Source**—When this is marked, information appears about where the formatting comes from. For example, if the font choice comes from the paragraph style applied to it, that source is noted. It's good to know that a particular formatting attribute is part of the style (or not) so you know whether to change the style's definition or apply manual formatting over it.

- **Show All Formatting Marks**—When this is marked, nonprinting characters such as end-of-paragraph markers appear. This can be helpful in sorting out where one paragraph ends and the other begins, and where manual line breaks (Shift+Enter) have been inserted.

The Reveal Formatting pane can also be used to compare the formatting between two blocks of text. Here's how to do this:

1. With the Reveal Formatting task pane open, select the first text to compare.
2. Mark the Compare to Another Selection check box.
3. Select the second text to compare. The differences appear on the Formatting Differences list in the task pane, as shown in Figure 6.22.

The differences are indicated with -> arrows. For example, under Font, it indicates that the first text uses 14 pt, whereas the second text uses 13 pt.

Figure 6.22
The Reveal Formatting task pane can also be used to compare formatting.

If you want to select different text for the initial selection, clear the Compare to Another Selection check box and then start the steps over again.

USING AUTOFORMAT

There are actually two different features called AutoFormat in Word:

- **AutoFormat As You Type**—Automatically makes formatting changes for you, such as changing two minus signs in a row to a dash and converting straight quotes to curly ones. These options work behind the scenes in every document. You can turn individual options on or off.

- **AutoFormat**—Sets up headings and lists and applies some styles automatically. AutoFormat can be done all at once (in a single pass) or interactively (where you confirm or decline each change).

The latter AutoFormat has been deemphasized in Word 2007, to the point where there is not even a button for it on any of the tabs. You have to know the shortcut key combo for it (Ctrl+Alt+K) or add a button for it to the Quick Access toolbar. It's still around, however, and still useful.

SETTING AUTOFORMAT AS YOU TYPE OPTIONS

Most AutoFormat As You Type options are enabled by default in Word, so setting options consists mostly of turning off the ones you don't want. To access these options and make your selections, follow these steps:

1. Choose Office, Word Options. The Word Options dialog box opens.
2. Click Proofing, and then click AutoCorrect Options.
3. Click the AutoFormat As You Type tab (see Figure 6.23).
4. Mark or clear check boxes to make your selections.
5. Click OK to close the AutoCorrect dialog box, and then click OK to close the Word Options dialog box.

Figure 6.23
Set AutoFormat As You Type options.

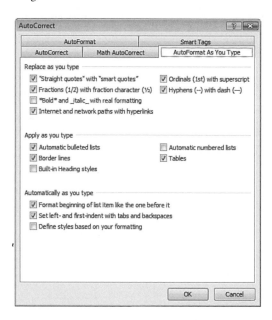

As shown in Figure 6.23, the options are broken down into three major categories:

- **Replace As You Type**—A set of options for inserting typographical symbols to substitute for plain typing. These provide shortcuts for items such as ordinals, fractions, quotation marks, and dashes.

- **Apply As You Type**—A set of options for applying automatic formatting at the paragraph level, including bulleted and numbered lists, borders, headings, and tables.
- **Automatically As You Type**—A set of options for tidying up text as you type, including, formatting list items in a parallel fashion and defining styles based on formatting.

As in many other dialog boxes in Word, you can click the ? button in the top-right corner to get detailed information about its options, so I won't belabor each of the options here. However, I do want to point out a couple of things that are especially useful.

With the Tables option under Apply As You Type, you can create a table by typing plus and minus signs. Type a row that begins with a plus sign, and use minus signs for spaces and plus signs where column breaks should occur. When you press Enter at the end of the line, Word creates a table with the columns in the spots you indicated.

Another item of interest is Format Beginning of List Item Like the One Before It. When this option is on, Word pays attention to special formatting you apply at the beginning of a list item, such as a bold word or phrase preceding the rest of the text in a bullet point. When you press Enter to start a new bulleted paragraph, Word will automatically format the first words of the paragraph to match whatever formatting you applied in the previous item.

> **TIP**
>
> You might also want to experiment with Define Styles Based On Your Formatting. (This is one of the few settings that's off by default.) It generates new styles based on the manual formatting you apply as you work. Some people find that it results in too many unwanted styles being created, but try it for yourself and see what you think.

FORMATTING A DOCUMENT WITH AUTOFORMAT

All those AutoFormat As You Type options apply only to new text that you type. If you import existing text, such as from a plain-text version of a document, AutoFormat As You Type won't help you. Instead, you must rely on the regular AutoFormat command.

There are two types of AutoFormat you can run—an automated type (by pressing Ctrl+Alt+K) and an interactive type. We'll look at each of these in more detail shortly, but first you need to know how to access them.

MAKING AUTOFORMAT AVAILABLE ON THE QUICK ACCESS TOOLBAR

As mentioned earlier, Word 2007 still includes AutoFormat, but it has been deemphasized. There's no way to launch either the automated or interactive AutoFormat command from any of the tabs.

The automated AutoFormat still retains its shortcut key combo, Ctrl+Alt+K. However, there is no keyboard shortcut for the interactive AutoFormat. Fortunately, you can customize the Quick Access toolbar to add buttons for either or both.

To add the button(s) to the Quick Access toolbar, follow these steps:

1. Choose Office, Word Options. The Word Options dialog box opens.
2. Click Customize.
3. Open the Choose Commands From list and choose All Commands.
4. Scroll through the list and locate AutoFormat. There are four AutoFormat entries on the list:

   AutoFormat...—The interactive (dialog box-based) AutoFormat.

   AutoFormat As You Type—The AutoFormat As You Type options from the AutoCorrect dialog box.

   AutoFormat Now—The Ctrl+Alt+K automatic version of AutoFormat.

   AutoFormat Options—The AutoFormat options from the AutoCorrect dialog box.

   Click the one you want (probably AutoFormat...) and then click Add >> to add it to the Quick Access toolbar (see Figure 6.24).
5. Repeat step 4 for another button if desired.
6. Click OK.

Figure 6.24
Add the AutoFormat command(s) to the Quick Access toolbar.

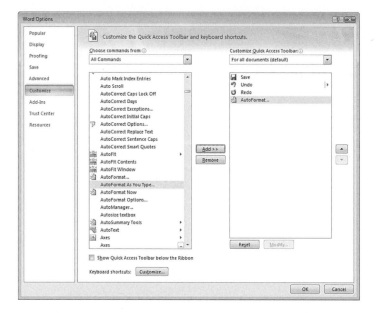

NOTE

If you add both AutoFormat... and AutoFormat Now to the Quick Access toolbar, they arrive there with identical icons. However, you can hover the mouse over them to see ScreenTips that differentiate between them.

6

SETTING AUTOFORMAT OPTIONS

The AutoFormat options are similar to the AutoFormat As You Type ones (refer to Figure 6.23). They are all turned on by default, so setting options consists mainly of disabling any you don't want.

To access the AutoFormat options, follow these steps:

1. Choose Office, Word Options. The Word Options dialog box opens.
2. On the Proofing tab, click AutoCorrect Options.
3. Click the AutoFormat tab.

> **TIP**
>
> If you placed the AutoFormat... button on the Quick Access toolbar in the preceding section, then as an alternative to steps 1–3 here, you can open the AutoFormat dialog box (from the button) and click Options.

4. Mark or clear check boxes to make your selections. As shown in Figure 6.25, the options are broken down into four categories:

Figure 6.25
AutoFormat options govern what happens when you issue the AutoFormat command.

- **Apply**—Various types of styles that can be automatically applied, such as headings, lists, and bullets.
- **Replace**—Typographical symbols, formatting, and hyperlinks that can replace plain text.
- **Preserve**—Only one option here, Styles. Leave this marked to leave any styles that are already applied to the text.

- **Always AutoFormat**—Only one option here, Plain Text WordMail Documents. Leave this marked to let AutoFormatting occur when using Word as an email editor.

→ To use Word as an email editor, **see** "Sending Email from Word," **p. 855**.

5. Click OK twice to close open dialog boxes.

APPLYING AUTOFORMAT (AUTOMATED MODE)

In automated mode, AutoFormat applies all the selected options (from the preceding section) to the entire document as best it can. There is no prompt. To AutoFormat a document, press Ctrl+Alt+K, or if you placed a button on the Quick Access toolbar for the command, click that button.

If there's anything it does that you don't like, undo the operation (press Ctrl+Z or click the Undo button on the Quick Access toolbar). Then open up the AutoFormat options again, deselect any options you want to omit, and then try the AutoFormat again.

APPLYING AUTOFORMAT (INTERACTIVE MODE)

In interactive mode, you can review each AutoFormat change. As mentioned earlier, you must add the AutoFormat Dialog command to the Quick Access toolbar to get access to this feature in Word 2007.

Follow these steps to AutoFormat interactively:

1. Click the AutoFormat Dialog button on the Quick Access toolbar (assuming you placed it there in the earlier section). The AutoFormat dialog box appears (see Figure 6.26).

Figure 6.26
Perform an interactive AutoFormat.

2. Click AutoFormat and Review Each Change.

3. The default document type is General Document. If you are composing a letter or email, open the drop-down list and select one of those types instead.

4. Click OK. A message appears that the formatting is completed.

5. Click Review Changes. A markup of the document appears. Additions appear red and underlined; deletions appear red and strikethrough.

6. Click one of the Find buttons. A change appears. The change is described in the Review AutoFormat Changes dialog box (see Figure 6.27).

Figure 6.27
Review each change.

7. To accept the change, click a Find button to move past it. To reject the change, click the Reject button. Continue through the document until you have reviewed all changes.

8. Click Cancel to close all open dialog boxes as needed.

USING THE STYLE GALLERY TO REFORMAT TEXT

A Style Gallery button appears in the AutoFormat dialog box. You can click this button to automatically format the document based on other templates than the default (Normal.dotm).

When you click Style Gallery, a Style Gallery dialog box appears, with all the available templates listed at the left. Click one of those templates to see how the document will look when AutoFormatted with that template's styles (see Figure 6.28).

Figure 6.28
Use the Style Gallery to format a document based on some other template.

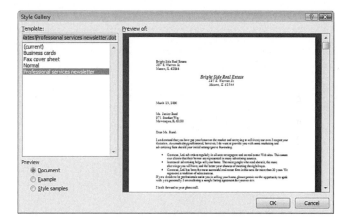

The Style Gallery does not actually change the template applied to the document; it only simulates the look of the template by updating the style definitions to match those of the chosen template. Note that this only works with the built-in style names in Word, such as Body Text, Heading 1, Heading 2, and so on; if the document is formatted with custom style names, those paragraphs will not be affected by Style Gallery AutoFormat changes.

→ To learn about built-in and custom styles in Word, **see** "Understanding Styles," **p. 228**.

TROUBLESHOOTING

ONLY ONE OR TWO FONTS APPEAR IN THE FONT LIST

This problem is usually caused by not having a default printer selected in Windows, or by a corrupt driver for the default printer. Make sure you have set a default printer. If you have two or more printers, try a different printer as the default. If that helps, remove and reinstall the driver for the printer that was formerly the default.

THE FONT ONSCREEN IS NOT THE FONT THAT PRINTS

Some printers that have many built-in fonts (such as PostScript printers) have font-substitution tables built into their drivers. Such tables enable the printer to use one of its built-in fonts rather than a soft font (that is, one that the PC sends to the printer as needed) whenever there is a close match between one of the Windows fonts and one of the printer's own fonts. It is advantageous to use a printer-resident font rather than a soft font because it makes the job print faster. However, if the substituted font is not exactly the font you want, it can cause a problem.

Open the Printers folder (or Printers and Faxes in Windows XP) and then right-click the printer icon and choose Properties. Then locate the font substitution information for your printer and modify it. Font substitution data is stored in different locations depending on the printer model. There might be a Fonts tab on which it is displayed, for example, or there might be a Device Settings tab on which there is a Font Substitution Table entry. Some printers do not have a font substitution option at all. (It is more common on lasers than on inkjets because lasers have more fonts built in.)

THE FONT NAME APPEARS AS BODY (CALIBRI)

In Word 2007, some styles do not specify a font; instead they use either Body or Heading. This allows the style to pick up whatever font is assigned by the theme (Page Layout tab). The "Calibri" part of the designation exists because Calibri is the +Body font assignment in the default theme. It's a big change from earlier versions of Word.

This will make more sense when you get to Chapter 8, "Creating and Applying Styles and Themes," and start working with styles. For now, just accept it as "situation normal."

I ACCIDENTALLY MODIFIED NORMAL.DOTM AND NOW ALL NEW DOCUMENTS ARE MESSED UP

If you just want to change the default font, open the Font dialog box, choose the font settings you want, and click the Default button. That should overwrite the settings in Normal.dotm.

If you've really messed things up badly and just want to go back to the way Normal.dotm was originally, delete it. Normal.dotm is custom-created for each user, and if Word doesn't find a copy when it starts up, it creates a new copy with the default settings.

Close Word and then navigate to C:\Documents and Settings*username*\Application Data\Microsoft\Templates (Windows XP) or C:\Users*username*\AppData\Roaming\ Microsoft\Templates (Windows Vista), where *username* is the name under which you are logged into Windows. Select Normal.dotm and press the Delete key on the keyboard—or, if you're feeling a little timid about the process, rename the file to something like Normal.old. The next time you start Word, Normal.dotm will be re-created anew.

By the way, don't be shocked if you browse for the newly created Normal.dotm and can't find it. Unless you make a change to Normal.dotm, it doesn't actually exist as a separate file from Word; Word simply uses its internal version of this file. Make a change to the default settings, however, and a file named Normal.dotm will appear.

If you've deleted Normal.dotm and things still haven't gone back to normal, go back in and look for a Normal.dot, a leftover template from a previous version of Word. Delete it, too, to prevent its settings from carrying over.

In this chapter

HOW WORD HANDLES PARAGRAPHS

A *paragraph* is a block of text that ends with a paragraph marker (¶), which you create by pressing the Enter key on the keyboard. The marker symbol does not print, and it does not show up onscreen unless you have configured Word to display nonprinting characters.

> **TIP**
>
> To toggle between displaying nonprinting characters, such as the paragraph marker, click the Show/Hide ¶ button on the Home tab or press Ctrl+*.

Pressing Enter starts a new paragraph (and ends the previous one), but not all line breaks are paragraph breaks. You can create a line break that does *not* start a new paragraph by pressing Shift+Enter. A line break is represented by the nonprinting symbol ↵. (Again, the symbol doesn't appear onscreen unless Word is displaying nonprinting characters.) Figure 7.1 shows examples of paragraph breaks and line breaks.

Click here to toggle the display of nonprinting characters.

Figure 7.1
Paragraph and line breaks are nonprinting characters; they can be displayed or hidden onscreen.

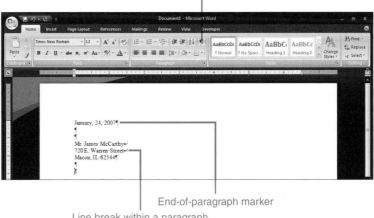

End-of-paragraph marker

Line break within a paragraph

Starting a new paragraph by pressing Enter carries over the same paragraph settings as were in the preceding paragraph. So, for example, if the preceding paragraph has a 1-inch left indent, the new paragraph will too.

Paragraph formatting is stored as part of the end-of-paragraph marker, so deleting the paragraph marker between two paragraphs combines them into a single paragraph that has the paragraph formatting settings of the second of the two paragraphs. (Any settings that were stored in the first paragraph's marker are deleted along with the marker itself.)

It's important to remember that paragraph formatting is stored in the marker because when you are copying or moving text, you might or might not also want to copy or move the paragraph formatting along with it. To preserve the paragraph formatting, make sure the end-of-paragraph marker is included in your selection. To make the pasted text conform to the paragraph settings in its new destination, do *not* include the paragraph marker in the selection.

Customizing Which Nonprinting Characters Appear

When you click the Show/Hide ¶ button on the Home tab, it toggles *all* the nonprinting characters on and off, including the little dots representing each space. If you want to see only certain nonprinting characters, use this method instead:

1. Toggle *off* all the nonprinting characters with the Show/Hide ¶ button.
2. Choose Office, Word Options and click Display.
3. Mark the check boxes for the nonprinting characters you want to see: tab characters, spaces, paragraph marks, hidden text, optional hyphens, and object anchors. (Notice that you cannot separately control line breaks created with Shift+Enter. They are lumped in the paragraph breaks for this setting.)
4. Click OK. Now only the marks you've selected appear, and they appear regardless of the Show/Hide ¶ toggle setting.

Each paragraph has a paragraph style applied to it from which it inherits its basic properties. These basic properties include not only paragraph characteristics such as line spacing and indentation, but also character-formatting defaults such as font, size, and color.

To change a paragraph's appearance, you can apply a different paragraph style to it, change the definition of the paragraph style that's applied, or apply manual paragraph formatting that overrides the style's formatting.

In this chapter, you'll learn how to apply manual paragraph formatting that overrides the paragraph's style. Learning these techniques enables you to format paragraphs without worrying about style definitions. These techniques also familiarize you with the basic paragraph controls you can use to make changes to the paragraph styles in Chapter 8, "Creating and Applying Styles and Themes."

SETTING LINE SPACING

Line spacing is the vertical spacing of the paragraph's lines. It can be expressed as a fixed amount in points, or as a percentage of the line height. You can set line spacing to any amount you like, as described in the following sections. You can also set different line spacing for different paragraph styles. (Paragraph styles are discussed in Chapter 8.

CHOOSING A LINE SPACING MULTIPLIER

 You can quickly switch a paragraph among a few common line-spacing settings with the Line Spacing button on the Home tab. The choices are measured in multiples of the text height: 1.0, 1.15, 1.5, 2.0, 2.5, or 3.0. The default setting for body text is 1.15.

Since line spacing depends on the font size; it changes as the font size does. For example, if the text in the paragraph is 12 points in size, a setting of 1.5 would add 6 points of extra space between lines (see Figure 7.2). (The "1" is the line itself, and the ".5" is the extra space.)

7

Figure 7.2
Make quick line spacing selections from the Home tab.

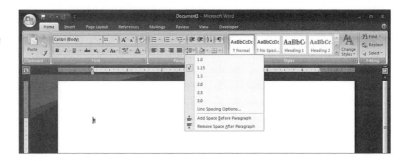

NOTE

When a paragraph has multiple font sizes, each line of the paragraph controls its own height independently based on the size needed for the largest font used on that line.

Resetting the Default Line Spacing to Single

Some users of earlier Word versions are distressed that single spacing is no longer the default. The 1.15 line spacing works great for some things, like large body paragraphs, but for short lines it can spread out the text too much.

You can easily reset this default to single spacing by following these steps:

1. Type a few words in a new paragraph.
2. Set the line spacing multiplier to 1.0, as explained in the following section.
3. On the Home tab, click the dialog box launcher button in the bottom-right corner of the Styles group. The Styles pane opens.
4. Right-click Normal and choose Update Normal to Match Selection.
5. Right-click Normal and choose Modify.
6. Click New Documents Based on This Template.
7. Click OK.

Normal is now redefined in the Normal.dotm template to use single line spacing, in this and future documents based on that template.

SETTING A PRECISE LINE-SPACING VALUE

The Line Spacing Options command on the line spacing button's menu opens the Paragraph dialog box (see Figure 7.3).

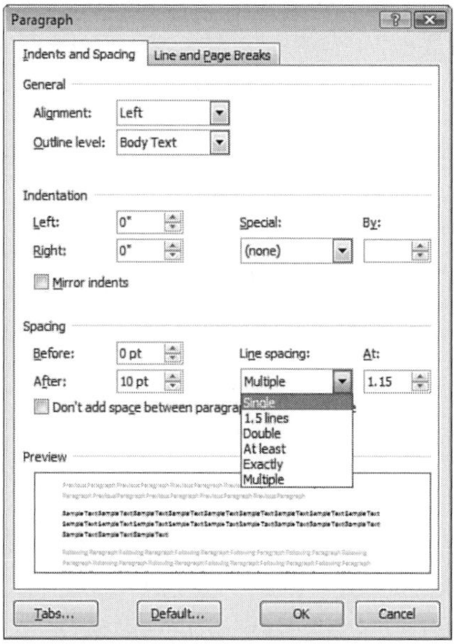

Figure 7.3
More spacing options are available in the Paragraph dialog box.

The Line Spacing drop-down list in the Paragraph dialog box offers these choices:

- **Single**—Single spacing. No extra space between lines. Same as "1.0" on the button's menu.

- **1.5 Lines**—One-and-a-half spacing, an extra half-height blank line between each printed line of the paragraph. Same as "1.5" on the button's menu.

- **Double**—Double-spacing, an extra blank line between each printed line of the paragraph. Same as "2.0" on the button's menu.

- **At Least**—A minimum line height to be used. (You specify the amount.) If the single-space line height is greater than the amount specified, single spacing will be used for that line. Otherwise, the At Least value will be used.

- **Exactly**—A precise line height to be used. (You specify the amount.) Be careful with this setting; if you specify a size that's smaller than the largest font size used in the paragraph, the large letters will be truncated on top.

- **Multiple**—A multiple of single spacing. (For example, enter 3 for triple spacing.) You can enter any value from 0 to 132, in decimal increments of 0.01. This is how the default setting of 1.15 is created.

Desktop publishing programs typically call line spacing by another name: leading (rhymes with "bedding"). The term *leading* technically refers to the amount of blank space between the lines, not to the total line height. For example, in a desktop publishing program, a leading value of 4 points would add 4 points of vertical space between each line of the paragraph, regardless of the total line heights.

7

In Word, you cannot directly set leading. The At Least and Exactly settings are the closest things to it, but they're calculated differently. The At Least and Exactly values are expressed in total line height, not blank space height. For example, an Exactly setting of 16 pt, when used on a paragraph that has 12-point text in it, would result in a 4-point vertical space between lines. However, that same setting, when used with 10-point text, would have a 6-point vertical space between lines. And when used with 20-point text, there would be no vertical space between lines and the tops of the larger letters would be cut off.

When the line spacing setting specifies more height than is needed for a line of text (given its largest font size), the extra spacing appears *below* the text. This is useful to keep in mind because it affects the amount of space that follows the paragraph. If you have two consecutive double-spaced paragraphs, there will also be double spacing between them because the extra space for the last line of the first paragraph will appear at its bottom. However, if a double-spaced paragraph follows a single-spaced one, there will only be single spacing between them because the single-spaced paragraph specified no extra space below each line.

SETTING SPACING BEFORE OR AFTER A PARAGRAPH

The quickest way to add spacing before or after a paragraph is to choose Add Space Before Paragraph or Remove Space After Paragraph from the Line Spacing button's menu on the Home tab (refer to Figure 7.2). This adds the same amount of space, either before or after the paragraph, as the paragraph's font size. For example, if the font size is 12, choosing Add Space Before Paragraph adds 12 points of space before it.

If you need different spacing than that, use the Paragraph dialog box (refer to Figure 7.3). It has Before and After settings that add space before and after the paragraph, respectively. Enter the number of points of extra space you want.

The After setting is cumulative with the line-spacing setting. For example, if you have a paragraph with 12-point text and its line spacing is set to Double, and then you add an After value of 5 pt, there will be 17 points of space between that paragraph and the next one.

Before and After values are also cumulative with one another. If two consecutive paragraphs have Before values of 10 and After values of 10, they will have 20 points of space between them (not counting any extra space coming from the Line Spacing setting).

TIP

> Because all these cumulative effects can be potentially confusing, I recommend using only After spacing (not Before spacing) when creating space between paragraphs. That's a somewhat arbitrary decision; you could just as easily stick with the Before setting and never use the After setting. However, because line spacing applies itself below each line of a paragraph (including the last line), it makes marginally more sense to go with After.

The Page Layout tab also has Before and After boxes that work the same as their counterparts in the Paragraph dialog box. Use the increment arrows or type values directly into the text boxes there (see Figure 7.4).

Spacing before paragraph

Figure 7.4
Set Before or After spacing from the Page Layout tab.

Spacing after paragraph

If you're in a hurry, it can be tempting to simply create extra space between paragraphs by pressing Enter a few extra times. That technique backfires in longer documents, however, because it results in spacing that is inflexible and difficult to modify. Each time you press Enter, you get exactly one line of space—what if you want more or less than that? And each of the spaces between the paragraphs is actually its own individual blank paragraph, so you can't change the spacing by applying paragraph styles to the text.

On the other hand, by applying spacing to a paragraph with the After setting (or Before, whichever you like), you make the spacing an integral part of the paragraph itself. That way, you can easily define that paragraph's settings as a new style, and apply that style to other paragraphs to achieve a consistent look. You can also modify the style at any time to change the amount of spacing between paragraphs to tighten up or spread out a page as needed.

→ To change the line spacing for a paragraph style, **see** "Modifying a Style Definition," **p. 249**.

INDENTING PARAGRAPHS

Indentation is the amount of horizontal space between the margin and the paragraph. Indentation is used for a variety of stylistic purposes. For example, left and right indents often set off long quotations, and first-line indents are commonly used in newspapers and magazines to help readers' eyes track the beginnings of paragraphs.

Paragraph indentation can be set with keyboard shortcuts, with buttons on the Home tab, with the Paragraph dialog box, or with the ruler. Although they all achieve the same basic results, they create them somewhat differently.

SETTING PRECISE INDENT VALUES

For maximum control and precise numeric entry, use the Paragraph dialog box method. Select the paragraph(s) and then open the Paragraph dialog box by clicking the dialog box launcher icon 🔲 in the bottom-right corner of the Paragraph group on either the Home tab or the Page Layout tab.

As you can see in Figure 7.5, the Paragraph dialog box offers three types of indents:

- **Left**—The indentation between the left margin and the left side of the paragraph.
- **Right**—The indentation between the right margin and the right side of the paragraph.

7

- **Special**—A list from which you can select one of two types:
  - **First Line**—The indentation of only the first line of the paragraph, in relation to the general left indent. For example, if the paragraph has a 1" left indent and a 0.5" first-line indent, the first line starts at 1.5" and all other lines start at 1".
  - **Hanging**—The indentation of all the lines of the paragraph except the first one. Like First Line, this setting is cumulative with the Left indent setting.

Figure 7.5
Set indents in the Paragraph dialog box.

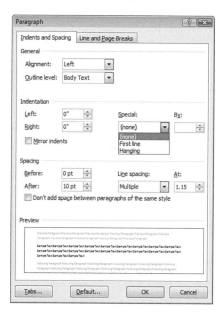

The Page Layout tab also has Left and Right indent controls that correspond with the Left and Right settings in the Paragraph dialog box. Enter amounts or use the increment arrow buttons (see Figure 7.6).

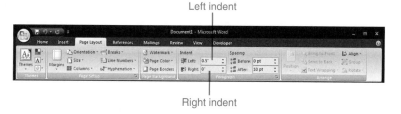

Left indent

Right indent

Figure 7.6
Left and right indents can be set from the Page Layout tab.

Indents can be either positive or negative numbers. A negative indent forces the paragraph outside of the document margins. For example, in a document with a 1" left margin, a setting of –0.25" would place the paragraph 0.75" from the edge of the paper.

Each indent type can be specified in increments as small as 0.01 inches. Note that indents are measured in inches, not points, as with vertical spacing. There is no fixed limit for the maximum amount of indentation you can specify, but if the indents are so large that they squeeze the text out entirely, an error message appears telling you that you have chosen indents that are too large.

QUICK INDENTING WITH BUTTONS AND SHORTCUTS

To quickly increase or decrease the left indent of a paragraph by 0.5", select the paragraph(s) to affect and then click the Increase Indent or Decrease Indent button on the Home tab (see Figure 7.7).

Decrease Indent   Increase Indent

Figure 7.7
Use the indent buttons on the Home tab to quickly increase or decrease a paragraph's left indent.

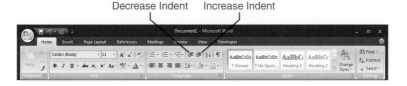

There are corresponding shortcut keys for these buttons: Ctrl+M for Increase Indent and Ctrl+Shift+M for Decrease Indent.

There are also shortcut keys for increasing or decreasing hanging indents, although there are no corresponding buttons on the tab: Ctrl+T is used to increase the hanging indent 0.5", and Ctrl+Shift+T is used to decrease it.

NOTE

> An indent can be decreased only to zero with the Home tab buttons or the shortcut keys; the paragraph cannot be forced outside of the document margins. If you need to do that, for example, to create a one-time hanging indent, use the Paragraph dialog box method described in the preceding section or the ruler method described next.

VISUALLY INDENTING WITH THE RULER

Sometimes it is easier to set an indent by "eyeballing it" with drag-and-drop. By dragging the indent markers on the ruler, you can do just that.

TIP

> If the ruler does not appear across the top of the document, turn it on by marking the Ruler check box on the View tab.

The ruler has four indent markers on it (see Figure 7.8). At the left end are these three:

- **Left indent**—Controls the left indent for all lines of the paragraph.
- **Hanging indent**—Controls all lines except the first line. On the ruler, it is inseparable from the left indent marker.
- **First-line indent**—Controls the first line of the paragraph.

7

At the right end is a single marker:

Right indent—Controls the right indent for all lines of the paragraph.

Figure 7.8
Indent markers on the ruler.

Hanging   Left   First line   Right

Indent changes apply only to the selected paragraph(s), so make your selection before working with the indent markers.

The first-line indent marker can be dragged separately from the others to create a different first line from the rest, just like when you enter a hanging indent value in the Paragraph dialog box. The zero mark on the ruler represents the document's left margin; you can drag the first-line marker to the left of zero to create a negative indent that forces the paragraph past the margin.

The hanging indent works differently on the ruler than it does in the Paragraph dialog box. With the ruler method, dragging the hanging indent marker also moves the left indent marker, so the hanging indent is not cumulative with the left indent. A paragraph's left indent is always the same as its hanging indent; the first-line indent can either match up with them or can be offset to the left or the right.

When you drag the left indent marker (the rectangle), the first-line and hanging markers move along with it, without losing their relationship to each other. So, for example, if the hanging and left indent markers are at 1" and the first-line indent marker is at 0", moving the left indent marker to 2" moves the first-line indent marker to 1".

There is also an alternative method of setting the first-line indent and left indent on the ruler: Use the tab stop controls. (You'll see these in detail in the next section.) Here's how that works:

1. Select the paragraph(s) to affect.
2. At the far-left end of the ruler is the Tab Stop Type button. Click it until the first-line indent marker appears on the button's face, as shown in Figure 7.9.
3. Click on the ruler where you want to move the first-line indent marker.
4. Click the Tab Stop Type button again. Now the left indent marker appears on its face.

NOTE

> The ScreenTip calls the marker in step 4 the hanging indent marker, but that's not wrong; it's just that the left indent marker and the hanging indent marker function as a single entity when setting them this way.

5. Click on the ruler where you want to move the left indent marker (and the hanging indent marker; remember they move together).

Figure 7.9
You can set the first-line and left indents using a tab stop method.

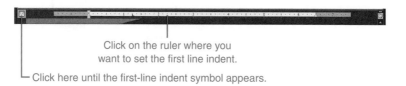

Click on the ruler where you want to set the first line indent.

└─ Click here until the first-line indent symbol appears.

WORKING WITH TAB STOPS

Tab stops are nonprinting markers that tell the insertion point where to stop when you press the Tab key. By default, a paragraph has tab stops every 0.5" in Word, but you can create your own custom tab stops to replace or supplement these.

Back in the days of the typewriter, the best (and only) way to create a multicolumn layout was to use tab stops. In Word 2007, there are many alternatives to that, such as creating newspaper-style columns with the Columns feature and creating a multicolumn tabular layout with the Tables feature. Nevertheless, tab stops remain a viable option for simple multicolumn lists, and they even have some advantages that those other options can't match.

→ To create a document with newspaper-style columns, **see** "Working with Multiple Columns," **p. 290**.

→ To create a document with tabular columns, **see** "Creating a Table," **p. 354**.

> **TIP**
>
> Each paragraph maintains its own tab stop settings, just like it does with line spacing and indentation. If you want the entire document to have the same tab stops, select the entire document (Ctrl+A) before setting the tab stops, or better yet, include tab stops in the definitions of the styles you apply to the paragraphs.

→ To modify a style's tab stop settings, **see** "Modifying Styles," **p. 248**.

When setting up a tabbed list, many beginners end up pressing Tab multiple times, moving through the default tab stops until they reach the desired position. With nonprinting characters displayed, that might look something like Figure 7.10.

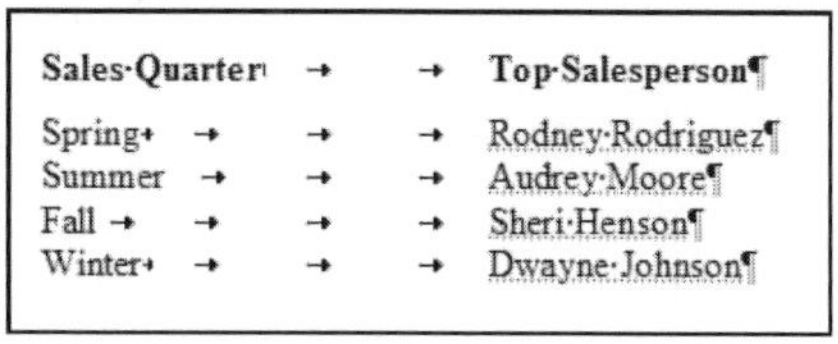

Figure 7.10
Some people press Tab multiple times to move through the default tab stops.

Sales·Quarter	→	→	Top·Salesperson¶
Spring◆	→	→	Rodney·Rodriguez¶
Summer	→	→	Audrey·Moore¶
Fall →	→	→	Sheri·Henson¶
Winter◆	→	→	Dwayne·Johnson¶

A better way, though, is to simply set a custom tab stop where you want the insertion point to stop and then press Tab only once to get to it. (When you set a custom tab stop, all the default tab stops to its left disappear.) With a single tab stop creating the full amount of space, as in Figure 7.11, it's easy to modify the list later by adjusting that one tab stop's position.

7

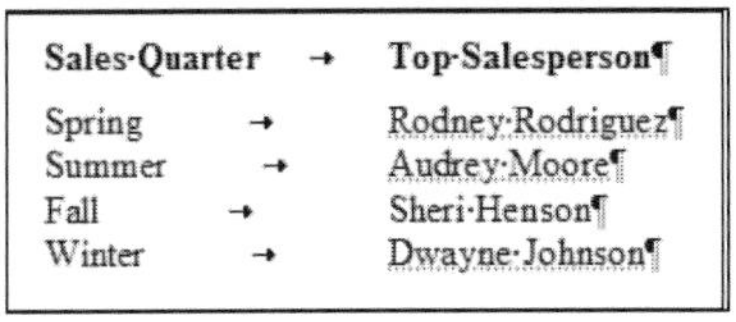

Figure 7.11
A better use of tab stops is to create a single stop exactly where you want it.

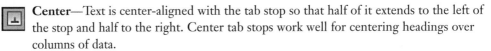

TYPES OF TAB STOPS

The default tab stop type is Left, the traditional "typewriter-style" stop. That's not the only type of stop available, though; here is a full list of the tab stop types. Figure 7.12 shows examples of several types.

Left—Text is left-aligned and extends to the right of the stop. This general-purpose tab stop is the staple of most lists.

Center—Text is center-aligned with the tab stop so that half of it extends to the left of the stop and half to the right. Center tab stops work well for centering headings over columns of data.

Right—Text is right-aligned and extends to the left of the tab stop. This type is good for aligning text at the right margin, for example.

Decimal—The first decimal (period) in the text is aligned at the tab stop position; anything that comes before it is right-aligned, and anything that comes after it is left-aligned. This one is great for lining up columns of numbers that have differing numbers of digits before and after the decimal point.

Bar—This one is not really a tab stop in the same sense as the others. When a bar stop is set at a particular position, pressing Tab to move to that spot places a vertical line there, the height of that line of text. When several of these appear in consecutive lines, they form a solid vertical divider line, making the tabbed list resemble a table.

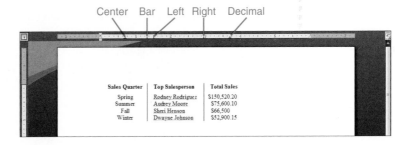

Figure 7.12
Tab stop examples.

PLACING AND REMOVING TAB STOPS ON THE RULER

Each time you click the Tab Stop Type button (to the far left of the ruler), the button cycles through the tab stop types listed in the preceding section. (There are actually two other items within the cycle—First Line Indent and Left Indent—but they are for setting indents, not tabs.)

→ To learn about setting the first-line and left indents using the Tab Stop Type button, **see** "Visually Indenting with the Ruler," **p. 199**.

→ If you're having trouble placing a tab stop at the same spot as an indent marker on the ruler, **see** "I Can't Place a Tab Stop Over an Indent Marker" in the Troubleshooting section at the end of this chapter.

When the Tab Stop Type button face shows the type of stop you want, click on the ruler to place it at the desired location. To remove a tab stop from the ruler, drag the stop off the ruler (up or down) and drop it.

To reposition a tab stop on the ruler, drag the stop to the left or right. As you drag, a dotted vertical line appears to help you line up the stop appropriately with the content in your document.

TIP

As you are dragging a stop to reposition it, hold down the Alt key to see measurements of the current tabbed column widths. This is useful if you need to create tabbed columns with exact width measurements. That's different from the exact positions on the ruler you get when creating tab stops with the Tabs dialog box (covered next), because this feature tells you the width of each column individually, whereas the Tabs dialog box tells you the ruler position of each stop. (Sure, you could calculate the width of a column from the ruler positions, but why bother when Word does it for you?)

DEFINING TAB STOPS WITH THE TABS DIALOG BOX

The Tabs dialog box is useful for setting tab stops when you need precise positions or when you need a leader character. A *leader* is a repeated character that extends from typed text to the next tab stop. Leaders are commonly used in tables of contents, for example, as shown in Figure 7.13.

Figure 7.13
A tab leader example.

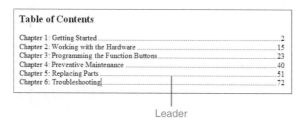

→ To generate tables of contents in Word, **see** "Creating a Table of Contents," **p. 748**.

There are two ways to open the Tabs dialog box:

- Double-click any custom tab stop on the ruler.
- Open the Paragraph dialog box and click the Tabs button.

The Tab Stop Position list shows all the custom tab stops that are set for the selected paragraph(s). Tab stops are identified by their position on the ruler, in inches. The ruler begins with 0" as the left margin.

To remove a single tab stop from the list, click it and click Clear. To remove them all, click Clear All.

To create a new tab stop, enter a new value in the Tab Stop Position box, select an Alignment for it, and optionally select a leader for it (see Figure 7.14). Then click the Set button to create the tab stop.

Figure 7.14
Control custom tab stops in the Tabs dialog box.

Every aspect of a tab stop can be changed. Select the stop from the Tab Stop Position list and then change its numeric value (position), its alignment, and/or its leader setting.

CHANGING THE DEFAULT TAB STOP INTERVAL

Word provides soft tab stops every 0.5" in a paragraph. By "soft" I mean they exist only when necessary—that is, when you press the Tab key. Otherwise, you would never know they're there.

You can change this interval for the entire document by doing the following:

1. Display the Tabs dialog box (refer to Figure 7.14).
2. In the Default Tab Stops box, increase or decrease the value.
3. Click OK to close the Tabs dialog box.

> **TIP**
>
> A change to the default tab stop interval affects all paragraphs in the current document. To make the change to all new documents, open the Normal.dotm template and make the change there.

CONVERTING A TABBED LIST TO A TABLE

Tabbed lists work great when they contain small amounts of text, but what if some text in one of the columns needs to wrap to an additional line or two? In cases like that, you're faced with the thorny task of manually splitting up lines of text and trying to figure out how much text will fit between the tab stops.

When items of text must wrap to multiple lines in the list, go for a table instead. Fortunately you don't have to start from scratch when you make the discovery that you should have used a table; you can convert a tabbed list to a table very easily:

1. Select the entire tabbed list.

2. On the Insert tab, click the Table button. A menu appears.

3. On the menu, click Convert Text to Table. The Convert Text to Table dialog box opens (see Figure 7.15).

4. Confirm the number of columns. If the number is not what you expected, click Cancel, check that you have an equal number of tab stops in each line, and then try again.

5. Click OK. The tabbed list is now a table, and the Table Tools tab appears.

Figure 7.15
Converting a tabbed list to a table.

→ To control the table's size, or adjust row heights or column widths, **see** "Sizing a Table," **p. 367**.

→ To format the table, **see** "Formatting a Table," **p. 370**.

COPYING TAB STOP SETTINGS BETWEEN PARAGRAPHS

Because tab stops are somewhat time-consuming to set up, you will probably want to reuse the settings wherever possible rather than reset the stops for each paragraph. One way to facilitate this is to select multiple paragraphs before you set the tab stops in the first place. But let's suppose for the moment that you forgot to do that.

When you start a new paragraph by pressing Enter at the end of a paragraph, the tab stops carry over automatically.

To manually copy the tab stop settings (and other paragraph formatting too) from one paragraph to another, use the Format Painter tool you learned about in Chapter 6, "Applying Character Formatting," but instead of selecting specific text, follow these steps:

1. Click anywhere within the paragraph that contains the tab stops to be copied.

2. On the Home tab, click the Format Painter button.

3. Click anywhere within the paragraph to receive the tab stops.

7

If you need to copy the stops to more than one paragraph, double-click the button in step 2 rather than single-clicking, and then you can click multiple paragraphs, one by one, in step 3. Alternatively, you can drag over a group of paragraphs in step 3 instead of clicking within one.

SETTING PARAGRAPH ALIGNMENT

Alignment, also called *justification*, is the way that text aligns horizontally within its assigned area. In a regular paragraph, that area is the space between the right and left margins (or between the right and left indent markers, if set). In a table or text box, that area is the cell or the box.

The choices for paragraph alignment are as follows:

- Left
- Centered
- Right
- Justified

All are self-explanatory except perhaps that last one. *Justified*, also called *Full* in some programs, aligns the text at both the right and left margins. To accomplish this, Word inserts small amounts of space between words and characters so that shorter lines come out the same length as longer ones.

Left alignment is usually the best choice for business letters, reports, booklets, and other print publications. Left alignment results in the easiest-to-read text.

CAUTION

> Some people use Justified alignment for all their documents, thinking it makes the documents look more polished. Well, it does make for a pretty page, which is nice in a brochure or glossy handout, but it often impedes readability. For text-heavy documents such as letters, business reports, and research papers, stick with Left alignment.

To set a paragraph's alignment, select the paragraph(s) to affect and then click one of the alignment buttons on the Home tab.

You can also select paragraph alignment from the Paragraph dialog box, although there is no advantage to doing so unless you already happen to have that dialog box open. Use the Alignment drop-down list on the Indents and Spacing tab.

CREATING NUMBERED AND BULLETED LISTS

Bulleted and numbered lists help break up text into more manageable chunks, and make it easier to read and skim. Just take a look at the text in this book! Regular paragraphs and headings are interspersed liberally with lists to better help you understand the material being presented.

TIP

> Some people use bulleted and numbered lists interchangeably, but that's not always appropriate. When the order of the items is significant, such as in step-by-step driving directions, use numbering. When the order is not significant, such as in a grocery list, use bullets.

Bulleted and numbered lists almost always use hanging indents, so that the bullet or number character "hangs" to the left of the rest of the paragraph. Back in the days of the typewriter, such formatting was done rather awkwardly with tab stops, but Word's Bullets and Numbering feature makes list making as simple as clicking a button.

→ To number an outline, **see** "Numbering Outline Items," **p. 690**.

TYPING A QUICK NUMBERED OR BULLETED LIST

For a quick and simple bulleted or numbered list, use the Bullets or Numbering button on the Home tab, as shown in Figure 7.16.

Bullets   Numbering

Figure 7.16
The Bullets and Numbering buttons on the Home tab turn on/off list formatting quickly.

There are two ways to use these buttons:

- Type the entire list, select all the text, and then click the Bullets button or the Numbering button.
- Click one of the buttons first and then start typing the list. Each time you press Enter, a new bulleted or numbered paragraph is created. Press Enter twice in a row to turn off the list formatting and return to normal text.

The bullet character or numbering style applied with these buttons is whatever you most recently used. The default is a plain round black bullet or Arabic numerals (1, 2, 3) in the same font and size as the paragraph text. Later in this chapter, you will learn how to change the bullet character or number style, and after you make such a change, Word will remember your setting and will use that new setting for all future lists.

CREATING LISTS WITH AUTOFORMAT AS YOU TYPE

Recall from Chapter 6 that AutoFormat As You Type allows Word to apply certain types of formatting for you, on the fly, as you work. The feature includes help for creating bulleted and numbered lists, too.

First, make sure the options are enabled for numbered and bulleted lists by doing the following:

7

1. Choose Office, Word Options. The Word Options dialog box opens.

2. Click Proofing, and then click AutoCorrect Options. The AutoCorrect dialog box opens.

3. Click the AutoFormat As You Type tab.

4. In the Apply As You Type section, make sure Automatic Bulleted Lists and Automatic Numbered Lists are marked.

5. Click OK to close the AutoCorrect dialog box, and then click OK to close the Word Options dialog box.

Then just start typing a list in Word. For a bulleted list, type an asterisk followed by a tab, and then the text for the paragraph. Or for a numbered list, type a number followed by a tab or period. Word automatically converts the list to use its own Bullets and Numbering feature.

To the left of the new number or bullet, an AutoCorrect Options icon appears. Open its menu and choose Undo Automatic Numbering or Undo Automatic Bullets if you did not intend for AutoFormat As You Type to kick in for that instance (see Figure 7.17). You can also press Ctrl+Z or click Undo to undo the autoformatting immediately after it occurs.

Figure 7.17
The AutoCorrect Options icon's menu lets you reverse an AutoFormatting action.

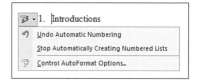

If you decide you do not like the automatic bullets and numbering, you can turn off either or both. Use the preceding steps to go back to the AutoCorrect Options dialog box and clear one or both check boxes, or on the AutoCorrect Options icon's menu shown in Figure 7.17, choose Stop Automatically Creating Numbered Lists (or Bulleted Lists, as the case may be).

→ To learn more about AutoFormat As You Type, **see** "Setting AutoFormat As You Type Options," **p. 183**.

RESTARTING OR CONTINUING LIST NUMBERING

When one paragraph of a numbered list immediately follows another, Word continues the list without incident. But when there is intervening text, Word can sometimes get confused.

Fortunately, Word *knows* it can get confused, so it asks for your help in the form of an AutoCorrect Options icon. In Figure 7.18, Word has guessed that the third numbered item is actually a brand-new list, and it has restarted the numbering at 1. But whatever Word guesses, it gives you the option of sending it the other way. Click the AutoCorrect Options icon, and on its menu, click Continue Numbering.

7

Figure 7.18
Word gives you the option of continuing the preceding numbered list.

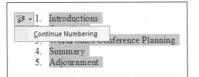

The AutoCorrect Options icon remains next to the paragraph after you switch to Continue Numbering, but its menu choice changes to Restart Numbering so you can go back if needed.

If you don't see an AutoCorrect Options icon, there's an alternate way. Follow these steps:

1. Do one of the following to open the Set Numbering Value dialog box (see Figure 7.19):

   - Click in the paragraph to affect. Then on the Home tab, click the down arrow to the right of the Numbering button, opening a menu, and then click Set Numbering Value.

   - Right-click the paragraph to affect, and on the menu that appears, point to Numbering and then click Set Numbering Value.

Figure 7.19
Control numbering by starting a new list, continuing a list, or setting a specific value.

2. Click Start New List or click Continue from Previous List.

3. Click OK.

STARTING A LIST AT A CERTAIN NUMBER

Besides starting or continuing a list, you can also assign a specific number to a numbered list item. A list need not start with 1; it can start with any number you want, including 0. That can be useful when you are enumerating items that have unusual numbering (for example, the interrupts on a PC are numbered 0 through 23), or when you're continuing a list from another document.

To set a specific number, display the Set Numbering Value dialog box (refer to Figure 7.19), as in the preceding section, and then enter a specific number in the Set Value To box.

CAUTION

If you are using some other style of numbering, such as letters or roman numerals, don't enter that style in the Set Value To box; enter simple Arabic numbers there (1, 2, 3, and so on).

7

CHANGING THE NUMBER FORMAT

A *number format* is the specification that defines how the numbering for the numbered list will appear. A number format consists of the following aspects:

- **Number style**—What type of number characters will be used? Choices include Arabic (1, 2, 3), uppercase or lowercase roman (I, II, III or i, ii, iii), and uppercase or lowercase letters (A, B, C or a, b, c).

- **Font**—In what font, size, and color will the numbers appear? By default they appear in whatever way is defined by the paragraph's style, but you can modify that.

- **Extra text or symbols**—What text or symbols will precede or follow the number character? Common symbols to follow a number include a period or a closing parenthesis. Some numbered lists also have text preceding the number, as in Chapter 1, Chapter 2, Chapter 3.

- **Alignment**—What type of tab stop will be used to separate the numbers from the paragraph? The choices are left, right, and centered. The choice determines how the numbers align.

Alignment is not much of an issue when all the numbers are the same length (such as an Arabic list of fewer than 10 items), but it's a big issue in longer lists or lists that use roman numerals. Figure 7.20 illustrates the difference between Left and Right number alignment.

Figure 7.20
Alignment governs the tab stop type at which the numbers align.

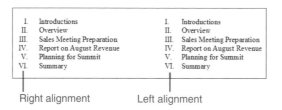

SELECTING FROM THE NUMBERING LIBRARY

The quickest way to change number formats is with the Numbering Library, available from the Numbering button's drop-down list on the Home tab (see Figure 7.21). You can also access the Numbering Library by right-clicking the selected list and pointing to the Numbering command. Just click the number format you want.

Your number format choice remains in effect (within the current document only) until you select a different number format. Subsequent numbered lists within the document use your chosen format automatically when you create them by clicking the Numbering button on the Home tab.

When you move to a different document (or start a new one), the default numbering reverts to regular Arabic style, but your previous choice remains easily accessible from the Recently Used Number Formats area of the Numbering button's drop-down list.

Figure 7.21
Select one of the built-in number formats from the Numbering Library list.

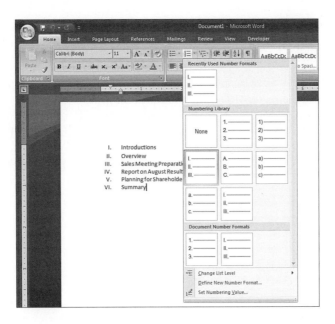

DEFINING A CUSTOM NUMBER FORMAT

If none of the choices in the Numbering Library is right, you can define a custom number format instead. Follow these steps:

1. Select the numbered list to affect.

2. Open the drop-down menu for the Numbering button on the Home tab and click Define New Number Format. (Alternatively, right-click the numbered list and choose Numbering, Define New Number Format.) The Define New Number Format dialog box opens (see Figure 7.22).

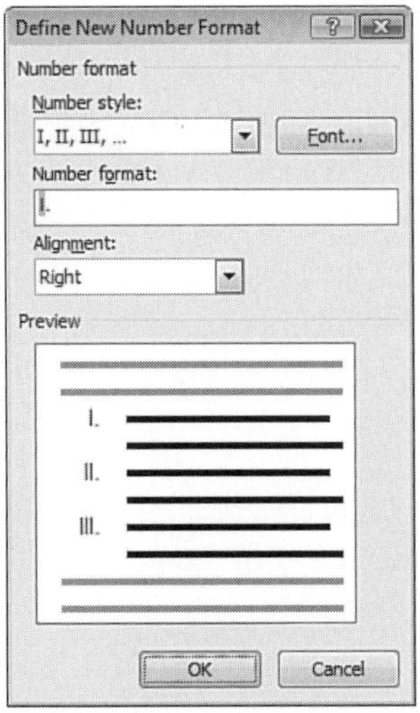

Figure 7.22
Define your own number format here.

3. Open the Number Style list and select the desired style. Notice that this list contains some additional options that were not in the Numbering Library, such as ordinals (1st, 2nd, 3rd) and text numbering (One, Two, Three).

4. Click the Font button. The Font dialog box appears.

It is just like the regular Font dialog box, except some of the Effects check boxes are filled with solid squares. These squares indicate "no selection" for those effects. In other words, for those effects, the numbers will inherit the settings from the style. Leave these alone unless you need one of the effects to always be on or off for the numbers; if so, then click the check box to cycle through its settings (see Figure 7.23).

Figure 7.23
Specify different font formatting for the numbers if desired.

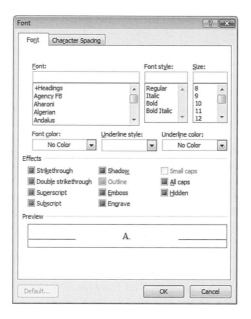

5. Select a different font, font style, size, color, and so on for the numbers if desired; then click OK to return to the Define New Number Format dialog box.

6. In the Number Format box, a code for the number appears shaded in gray. You can't change that. Click in the Number Format box, though, and place any extra text on either side of that code, such as a period or parenthesis after it or some text such as "Chapter" or "Section" before it.

7. Open the Alignment list and select an alignment for the numbering.

8. Click OK. The new numbering format is applied to the numbered list in your document.

After you've defined a new number format, it appears in the Numbering Library. It continues to appear there even if you start a new document, or close and reopen Word. To remove it from the gallery, right-click it and choose Remove.

7

CHANGING THE BULLET CHARACTER

With numbering formats, there's a limit to the creativity because numbers have to be…well, *numbers.* And there are only so many ways of expressing them. However, with bullet characters, the sky's the limit. Virtually *anything,* text or graphic, can be used as a bullet character.

The Bullets button on the Home tab has a drop-down list containing a small library of bullet characters. To apply one of these bullets to your list, select the list and then open the button's drop-down list and click a bullet (see Figure 7.24).

Figure 7.24
Select a bullet from the Bullet Library.

If you don't like any of the bullets in the Bullet Library, choose Define New Bullet from the menu. This opens the Define New Bullet dialog box, shown in Figure 7.25. From here you can choose one of two types: Symbol or Picture.

Figure 7.25
Create a new bullet.

CREATING A SYMBOL (TEXT) BULLET

Symbols are text characters. You can select any character from any font installed on your PC—even one of the characters that doesn't correspond to any of the keyboard keys. To select a symbol bullet, click the Symbol button and then select from the Symbol dialog box (see Figure 7.26). First choose the desired font from the Font list, and then click the desired character within that font.

7

NOTE

If you happen to know the numeric code for a particular symbol, you can enter it in the Character Code box to locate and select it quickly.

Figure 7.26
Select a symbol to use as a bullet.

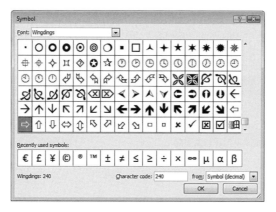

Any font is a potential source of symbols, but some are much better suited than others. You wouldn't typically want to use a regular letter or number as a bullet, for example, and most fonts are mostly letters and numbers. Look instead at the specialty fonts such as Symbol, Wingdings, Webdings, Marlett, and so on. Not sure which fonts contain potential bullet characters? Open the Font drop-down list on the Home tab and scroll through, looking for fonts where sample characters appear to the right of the name. Such fonts are good candidates.

After selecting a symbol as your bullet, click the Font button to change the font formatting for it. You can make all the same changes as for numbers, as you saw back in Figure 7.23. One of the most common changes is to increase or decrease the font size for the bullet, for example.

CREATING A PICTURE BULLET

To use a picture bullet, click the Picture button in the Define New Bullet dialog box. The Picture Bullet dialog box opens (see Figure 7.27). This dialog box is actually a filtered version of the Clip Organizer, set up to show only clip art images that are suitable for use as bullet characters. Click one of the bullet pictures to select it, and then click OK.

A few notes on the picture bullet selection process:

■ Some bullets have a little yellow star icon in the bottom-right corner. These are animated bullets; when they appear on a web page, they will have some type of animation associated with them.

■ By default, the Picture Bullet dialog box does not access Office Online (a source of additional bullets) because on PCs with slow Internet connections, it makes the list slow to scroll. If you have a fast connection and want additional bullet choices, mark the Include Content from Office Online check box.

■ The Search Text box at the top of the Picture Bullet dialog box lets you search for a bullet picture by keyword. However, in practice, most of the bullets have the same keywords, so this feature is of limited usefulness.

■ To use a graphic of your own design for a bullet, click the Import button in the Picture Bullet dialog box, and then select the graphic file and click Add. You can add any graphic this way, of any size. Valid graphic formats for bullets are .gif, .bmp, and .jpg (or .jpeg). Simple graphics work best because of the small size.

■ Unlike with a symbol bullet, you cannot directly modify the size of a picture bullet. The picture bullet's size is determined by the paragraph's font size.

Figure 7.27
Select a picture bullet.

TIP

Here's a workaround for picture bullet size. Global settings for a paragraph are stored in its end-of-paragraph marker, so by changing the formatting on that marker, you can affect the bullet character size. Make sure end-of-paragraph markers are displayed onscreen, so you can see what you're doing, and then select the marker only. (Position the insertion point to the left of the marker, hold down Shift, and press the right arrow key once.) Then change the font size from the Font Size list on the Home tab. The picture bullet's size will change.

CHANGING THE LIST LEVEL

Word supports up to nine levels of list nesting—that is, placing a subordinate list within a list. You can combine bulleted lists and numbered lists within the same nested structure, too. For example, in Figure 7.28, a numbered procedure has a bulleted list nested under one of the steps, and one of those bullet points has its own nested numbered list.

7

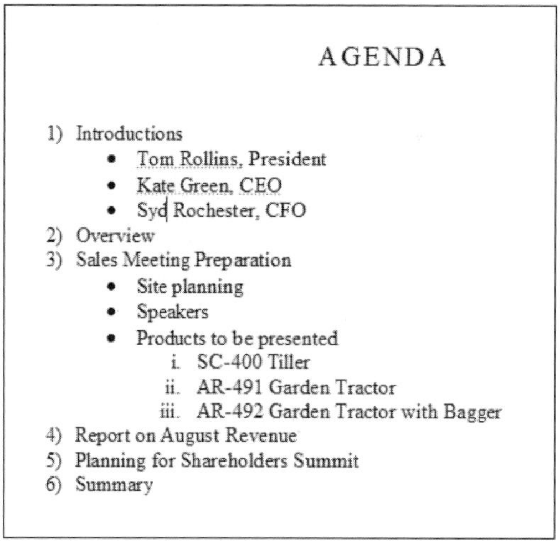

Figure 7.28
Word supports up to nine levels of list nesting.

```
                           AGENDA

   1)  Introductions
              •  Tom Rollins, President
              •  Kate Green, CEO
              •  Syd Rochester, CFO
   2)  Overview
   3)  Sales Meeting Preparation
              •  Site planning
              •  Speakers
              •  Products to be presented
                     i.  SC-400 Tiller
                    ii.  AR-491 Garden Tractor
                   iii.  AR-492 Garden Tractor with Bagger
   4)  Report on August Revenue
   5)  Planning for Shareholders Summit
   6)  Summary
```

Here's the easiest way of creating a nested list: Start typing the main list normally, and press Enter for a new paragraph, and then press the Tab key. An indented, subordinate list item is created, ready for the text to be typed.

When the subordinate list is complete and you want to go back to the main list level, press Enter again to start a new paragraph, and then either press Enter again or press Shift+Tab. Both do the same thing: They promote that paragraph to next-higher level.

NOTE

> Tab and Shift+Tab control list levels only if you press them when the insertion point is at the beginning of the paragraph, and only when bullets or numbering is turned on. Otherwise, pressing Tab simply tabs over to the next tab stop.

Another way to switch among list levels is with the Change List Level submenu, found on the drop-down list for both the Bullets and the Numbering buttons on the Home tab. Open the submenu and click the desired level for the selected paragraph(s), as shown in Figure 7.29.

Figure 7.29
Switch among list levels via the Change List Level submenu.

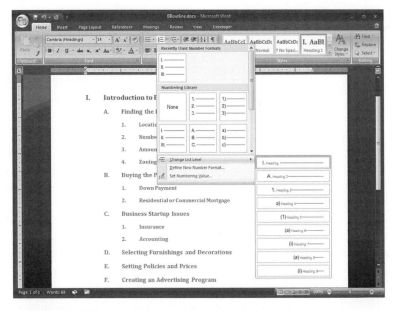

→ For more information about multi-level numbered lists, especially when used in outlines, **see** "Numbering Outline Items," **p. 690**.

ADJUSTING BULLET OR NUMBER SPACING AND INDENTS

In earlier versions of Word, you could customize bullet and number formats by specifying a bullet position and text position. These positions defined the left indents and tab stop positions for the first line and subsequent lines.

You can still define bullet and text indents in Word 2007, but not as part of the bullet or number format. Instead, you make those changes as you would with any other paragraph, through the Paragraph dialog box or with the ruler.

→ To review the procedures for controlling indents, **see** "Indenting Paragraphs," **p. 197**.

APPLYING PARAGRAPH BORDERS

A *border* is a visible line around one or more sides of a paragraph (or around a group of paragraphs). Borders help create separations in the text to make it easier to read and skim. You can see borders at work in this book, for example, in the tips, notes, and cautions.

A border can be placed on any or all sides of a paragraph. The most common usage is to place the border around all sides, creating a box, but interesting effects can also be achieved applying the sides more selectively. For example, in Figure 7.30, a bottom-only border is used under each heading, and notes are marked with top and bottom borders.

7

Figure 7.30
Examples of borders applied to only certain sides of paragraphs.

TIP

Although it is possible to manually apply borders to individual paragraphs, as you will learn in this section, it is often more efficient to create a paragraph style that includes the desired border and apply that paragraph style to the desired text.

→ To create a paragraph style, **see** "Creating a New Style by Example," **p. 241**.

→ If the border continues past the paragraph that you want it to surround, **see** "I Wanted a Border on a Single Paragraph Only, But the Border Keeps Expanding as I Type" in the Troubleshooting section at the end of this chapter.

APPLYING AND REMOVING BORDERS

For a basic border (solid, black, thin), select the paragraph(s) and then use the Borders drop-down menu on the Home tab. It contains options for borders on various sides of the selection (see Figure 7.31).

Figure 7.31
Apply a basic border to one or more sides of the selected paragraph(s).

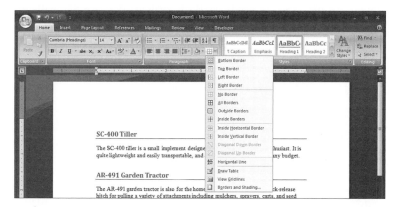

Table 7.1 provides a summary of the border choices, along with some notes on their usage.

Table 7.1	Border Types
Menu Selection	**Notes**
No Border	Removes all borders from all sides of the selected paragraph(s).
All Borders	Turns on all borders on all available sides of the selected paragraph(s). This includes the borders between each pair of paragraphs in a multiparagraph selection.
Outside Borders	Turns on all borders on all outer sides of the selection. If the selection is a single paragraph, the effect is the same as with All Borders. If the selection is multiple paragraphs, no lines will appear between the paragraphs.
Inside Borders	In a single-paragraph selection, this does nothing. In a multiparagraph selection, it places borders between the paragraphs but not around the outsides.
Top, Bottom, Left, and Right Border	These settings individually turn on each side. Settings can be combined; select Top and then reopen the menu and select Bottom, for example.
Inside Horizontal	In regular paragraphs, this is the same as Inside Borders. In a table, this adds the inside borders between rows only, not between columns.
Inside Vertical	In regular paragraphs, this does nothing. In a table, this adds the inside borders between columns only, not between rows.
Diagonal Down and Diagonal Up Border	In regular paragraphs, these settings do nothing. In a table, they draw diagonal lines through the selected cell(s).

Formatting Borders

The Borders button enables you to turn borders on and off, but it doesn't help you format them. So, if you want a border that's a different thickness, color, or line style (such as dotted or dashed), you must use the Borders and Shading dialog box.

To format a border, follow these steps:

1. Select the paragraphs(s) to affect. They can already have a border applied to them or not—it doesn't matter.
2. Open the Borders button's drop-down list and click Borders and Shading. The Borders and Shading dialog box opens with the Borders tab displayed (see Figure 7.32).
3. Select a border type from the Setting icons along the left side of the dialog box:
   - **None**—Turns off all borders.
   - **Box**—Places an outside border in which all sides are the same thickness.
   - **Shadow**—Places an outside border, and also places a shadow effect along the bottom and right sides.

7

Figure 7.32
Format paragraph borders from the Borders tab of the Borders and Shading dialog box.

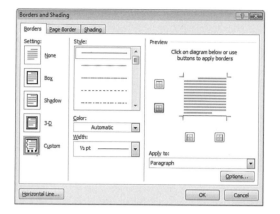

TIP

The Shadow effect that the Borders and Shading dialog box applies is quite limited. You can't change its size or color, and you can't shift it to other sides of the paragraph. If you need a more complex shadow, consider placing the text in a text box and then applying a shadow to the text box. That way you get a full range of shadow-formatting tools.

- **3-D**—Places an outside border with a 3D effect—in theory, anyway. In most cases there is no difference in the end result between Box and 3D.
- **Custom**—Enables you to select and format each side individually. (You can start with any of the other settings, and when you start to change individual sizes, the setting changes to Custom automatically.)

4. On the Style list, select a line style.

5. On the Color list, select a line color. (Color selection works the same here as with any other colored object.)

→ For an explanation of Word's color choices, **see** "Changing Font Color," **p. 167**.

6. On the Width list, select a line thickness.

7. (Optional) If you want to remove the border on certain sides, click the corresponding button in the Preview area. (There is a button for each of the four sides.)

NOTE

If you remove the border on one or more sides and a Shadow effect was chosen in step 3, the Shadow effect is removed and the Setting type changes to Custom.

8. (Optional) To control how far the border appears from the text on each side, click the Options button and then enter values (in points) in the Border and Shading Options dialog box (see Figure 7.33). Then click OK to return to the Borders tab.

Figure 7.33
Adjust spacing between the text and the border if desired.

9. Click OK to accept the new border.

After having applied border formatting as in these steps, the next border(s) you apply with the Border button's drop-down list are formatted in the same way. For example, if you chose a light-green double border in the preceding steps, all new borders you apply will also be light green and double until you change to something else (within the current document only).

Applying Different Formatting on Each Side

You can create some interesting effects by varying the borders on certain sides. To do this, first turn off the sides in the Preview area of the Borders and Shading dialog box by clicking them. Next, change the formatting selected in the Style, Color, and/or Width lists, and then click those sides again in the Preview area to reenable them with the new formatting.

For example, for a (somewhat) 3D effect, apply a thick solid border to the bottom and right sides, and then apply the same style and thickness to the top and left sides but in a lighter color (perhaps a tint of the same theme color you used on the bottom and right).

APPLYING PARAGRAPH SHADING

Paragraph shading places a colored background behind the entire paragraph. Shading—like borders—helps make the text stand out from the crowd. You might make the shading on an important warning bright orange, for example, to point out its urgency.

NOTE

Don't confuse paragraph shading with highlighting (from Chapter 6, "Applying Character Formatting"). Highlighting is applied to individual characters within a paragraph; highlighting cannot exist in areas where there is no text (for example, at the ragged right margin of a paragraph). Paragraph shading, on the other hand, extends all the way to the edges of the paragraph on all sides in a neat rectangular form.

7

To apply a simple solid-fill shading, follow these steps:

1. Select the paragraph(s) to affect.

2. On the Home tab, open the Shading button's drop-down list and click the desired color (see Figure 7.34). To try out different colors before committing, point to a color to see a preview of it.

Figure 7.34
Select a solid shading color.

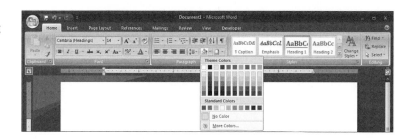

→ For an explanation of Word's color choices, **see** "Changing Font Color," **p. 167**.

Patterned shading is another option. A *pattern* is a two-tone background that consists of one basic color (the Fill color) overlaid with a pattern of the second color. That pattern can be very subtle, such as a spray of fine dots, or very dramatic, such as strong stripes. The two colors can sharply contrast for a strong effect or can be very nearly the same for a subtle one.

To create a pattern fill, follow these steps:

1. Select the paragraph(s) to affect.

2. On the Home tab, open the Borders button's drop-down list and click Borders and Shading. The Borders and Shading dialog box opens.

3. Click the Shading tab.

4. Open the Fill drop-down list and choose the desired color.

5. Open the Style drop-down list and select the pattern style desired (see Figure 7.35).

6. Open the Color drop-down list and choose the color for the pattern.

7. Click OK to apply the pattern.

Figure 7.35
Select a pattern for the shading if desired.

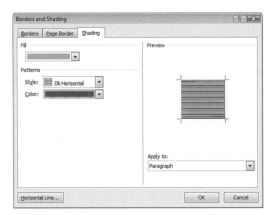

CAUTION

Patterns make the text more difficult to read, especially the very bold ones with strongly contrasting colors. Use patterned shading sparingly and strategically.

PREVENTING PARAGRAPHS FROM BREAKING

In multipage documents, paragraphs don't always break gracefully. Sometimes a single line of a paragraph appears either at the bottom or the top of a page. These stray lines are called *widows* and *orphans*, and you can easily prevent them from occurring.

NOTE

There is debate over which situation constitutes a "widow" and which an "orphan." If a single line is left behind at the bottom of a page, is it orphaned, or is it widowed? The point is mostly moot because Word uses a single setting for avoiding single lines at both the top and the bottom of a page. However, Word Help defines an orphan as a single line at the bottom of a page, and a widow as a single line at the top.

Word has several settings for controlling how (or if) paragraphs are allowed to break between pages. All are found in the Paragraph dialog box, on the Line and Page Breaks tab.

Follow these steps to examine and change the break settings for a paragraph:

1. Select the paragraph(s) to affect. To affect the entire document, press Ctrl+A.
2. Open the Paragraph dialog box and click the Line and Page Breaks tab (see Figure 7.36).

7

Figure 7.36
Specify options for keeping lines together.

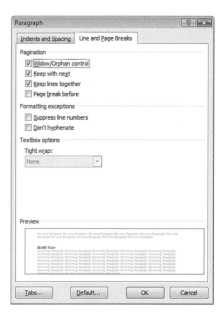

3. Mark or clear any of these check boxes as desired:

- **Widow/Orphan Control**—Ensures that if a paragraph breaks across pages, at least two lines of the paragraph will appear on each page. If this is not possible, the paragraph floats completely to the next page.

- **Keep with Next**—Ensures that the paragraph will not be on a different page from the paragraph that follows it. This is useful for keeping a heading together with the body paragraph that follows it.

- **Keep Lines Together**—Prevents a paragraph from breaking at all. If it will not fit at the bottom of a page, the whole paragraph moves to the next page. This is especially useful in tables, where a page break that interrupts the text in a table cell can create confusion.

- **Page Break Before**—Starts the paragraph on a new page. This is useful for chapter and section titles, for example.

4. Click OK.

TIP

Why use Page Break Before when you could just insert a hard page break before the paragraph? Well, if it's a one-time instance, that would be fine, but if you are setting up a paragraph style to be reused for multiple headings, all of which should start on a new page, you can save some time by adding the formatting to the style.

7

NOTE

If you want to change the widow/orphan setting for all text, including any new text you type later, modify the paragraph style, as you'll learn to do in Chapter 8. Line and page breaks can be specified in style definitions just like any other paragraph formatting.

→ To create styles, **see** "Creating a New Style by Example," **p. 241**.

TROUBLESHOOTING

TAB STOPS DON'T WORK IN A TABLE

You can have tab stops in table cells, but how do you move the insertion point to them? Pressing the Tab key within a table cell moves the insertion point to the next cell, not to the tab stop. Try using Ctrl+Tab instead.

I CAN'T PLACE A TAB STOP OVER AN INDENT MARKER

When you click on the ruler to place a tab stop, it doesn't work if there is already an indent marker at that spot. To get around this, temporarily drag the indent marker to another location, place the tab stop, and then drag the indent marker on top of the tab stop. Alternatively, place the tab stop in a different location and then drag it on top of the indent marker.

I WANTED A BORDER ON A SINGLE PARAGRAPH ONLY, BUT THE BORDER KEEPS EXPANDING AS I TYPE

Remember, by default when you press Enter to start a new paragraph, Word continues the same settings into the new paragraph. Therefore, if the original paragraph had a border, the new ones will too. This is by design.

To stop this, select the paragraph containing the unwanted border and then, on the Home tab, open the Borders button's drop-down list and click No Border.

I DON'T SEE SOME OF MY CUSTOM TAB STOPS ON THE RULER

When multiple paragraphs are selected and they don't all have the same tab stops, tab stops will not appear on the ruler. You can set new tab stops that will then apply to all selected paragraphs, but any tab stops that are specific to only certain paragraphs within the selection are inaccessible.

THE DEFAULT BULLET CHARACTER APPEARS AS A CLOCK FACE

The default bullet character comes from the Symbol font (symbole.fon). If that font is damaged or has been removed from the system, Word falls back on the Wingdings font.

Each character within a font has a certain numeric value; when you change to a different font, the numeric value stays the same but the character changes. (That's why, for example, you get a different-looking capital *F* when you change to a different font, but it doesn't change to a capital *Z*.) Between fonts that contain letters and numbers, there is little difference between the characters represented by the same number, but within fonts designed primarily for use as symbols and bullet characters, there is a great difference.

As you might surmise by all that, the clock symbol in the Wingdings font happens to correspond to the plain bullet symbol in the Symbol font. So if Symbol isn't available, all your bullets look like clocks.

To fix the problem, look in the Fonts folder for the Symbol font (symbole.fon). To access the Fonts folder, go through the Control Panel or browse to C:\Windows\Fonts. If the Symbol font is there, delete it. If it's not there, someone has already deleted it. Replace it by copying the font file from the Windows CD, or from another PC that has Windows installed, into the Fonts folder.

→ To install a font, **see** "Adding More Fonts to Your System," **p. 164**.

7

CHAPTER 8

CREATING AND APPLYING STYLES AND THEMES

In this chapter

UNDERSTANDING STYLES

Styles are named formatting definitions that you can apply to text to ensure consistency within a document. For example, you could apply the Heading 1 style to all headings in the document, and all the headings would be formatted in exactly the same way.

Styles also make it easier to make global changes to the formatting in a document; you make a change to the style, and all text based on that style is automatically changed. Suppose you decide you want all the headings to be underlined—just turn on underlining for the Heading 1 style and you're done.

Word uses styles not only to standardize document formatting, but also to control the organization in outlines, tables of contents, and master documents. Investing time in learning about styles will pay off many times over as you explore Word's advanced features later in the book.

TYPES OF STYLES

Word supports several types of styles, each suitable for a specific formatting task.

The most common style type is *paragraph style*, which can apply both paragraph and character formatting to entire paragraphs. All paragraphs have a paragraph style; the default one is called Normal, and it carries the default settings for body paragraphs in the document. There are also built-in paragraph styles for headings, such as Heading 1, Heading 2, and Heading 3, each presenting a different heading level.

A *character style* is a style that contains only character-level formatting and that applies to individual characters. The default character style is Default Paragraph Font, which is derived from the character formatting defaults from the Normal paragraph style.

Two popular built-in character styles are Strong and Emphasis. By default, Strong makes text bold, and Emphasis makes text italic. At first it might seem strange that there are character styles that basically do the same thing as Bold and Italic manual formatting. The benefit in using them is not in the initial application, but in the possibility they create for easy change later. For example, suppose you know that you want to set off certain new vocabulary words in a document in some way, but you haven't decided on the exact formatting yet. If you've made them all bold with the Bold button, and then later decide to use italics instead, you would have to manually change each instance. (Using the Find and Replace feature could help somewhat.) On the other hand, suppose you format all the vocabulary words as Strong using the character style. Then if you decide to make the words italic, you simply modify the definition of Strong so that it is italic rather than bold.

In addition to character and paragraph styles, there are also *linked styles*. Linked styles are nearly identical to paragraph styles, except for their behavior when applied to a selection of text (rather than to an entire paragraph).

Suppose you select one sentence within a paragraph, and then apply a paragraph style. The entire paragraph receives that style's character and paragraph formatting equally. If you apply a linked style, however, then the character aspects of the style apply only to the selected text. (The paragraph aspects of the style apply to the entire paragraph as usual.) Throughout this chapter, everything you learn about paragraph styles also applies to linked styles, unless otherwise noted.

Paragraph styles can be applied to text within table cells, but not to the cells themselves. To format table cells, use a *table style*. Table styles store table cell formatting such as background color, vertical and horizontal alignment, and cell border.

→ To format tables, **see** "Formatting a Table," **p. 370**.

A *list style* applies settings specific to bulleted and numbered lists. List formatting, such as bullet and numbering styles, can also be stored in paragraph styles, but the List type has the advantage of storing up to nine levels of numbering or bullet formatting in a single named style. That way, if a list item changes in level, it need not have a different style applied to it.

Order of Style Application

When multiple types of styles are applied to the same text and one layer contradicts another, the formatting is determined by the last-applied style. Styles are applied in this order: table, list, paragraph, character. Therefore, any conflict between a paragraph style and a character style will always result in the character style winning. However, attributes that the later-applied style does not specify are inherited from the earlier-applied style.

For example, suppose the Heading 1 style (a paragraph style) is set for Arial font, italic, 14-point, and red. Further, suppose the Emphasis style (a character style) is set for bold and green. If you apply the Emphasis style to a word within a Heading 1 paragraph, that word will appear in Arial, bold, italic, 14-point, and green. Notice that because the Emphasis style doesn't specify the font type, italicization, or the size of the lettering, the word instead inherits those attributes from the Heading 1 style.

METHODS OF APPLYING STYLES

There are many ways of applying styles in a document, and much of the first half of this chapter is devoted to explaining those methods. Here's a quick summary:

- **Select a Quick Style from the Home tab**—A fast and easy way to use styles, but not all the available styles are represented. See "Working with Quick Styles," p. 230. To change which styles appear on the Quick Style Gallery, see "Removing or Adding a Style in the Quick Style Gallery," p. 232.

- **Choose a style from the Apply Styles pane**—Use a handy floating pane to access a drop-down list of styles. See "Using the Apply Styles Pane," p. 234.

- **Choose a style from the Styles pane**—Use the full-size Styles pane, as in earlier versions of Word, for full access to all styles. See "Using the Styles Pane," p. 233.

- **Press a shortcut key combination assigned to a style**—You can assign keyboard shortcuts to any style for quick application; see "Applying a Keyboard Shortcut to a Style," p. 246.

METHODS OF CREATING AND MODIFYING STYLES

The built-in styles are useful, but most people find that they need more or different styles for their projects. You can create new styles and/or modify the definitions of existing ones. Here's a quick reference to those skills I cover in this chapter:

- **Change the Quick Style set**—You can quickly change the look of the paragraphs that have the built-in Quick Styles applied by changing the Quick Style set. These sets alter the definitions of the built-in styles automatically for you. See "Changing the Quick Style Set," p. 231.

- **Create a new style based on existing formatting**—You can quickly define a new style that mimics some manual formatting that's already applied in the document; see "Creating a New Style by Example," p. 241.

- **Define a new style**—You can precisely define every aspect of a new style, everything from the font choice to the spacing and indentation. It takes longer, but you have more control. See "Creating a New Style by Definition," p. 243.

- **Make a style change automatically**—If you like, you can set up styles such that when you apply any manual formatting to text that has that style applied, the style changes its definition to match, so there is no manual formatting in your document. See "Updating a Style Automatically," p. 248.

- **Change a style to match a selection**—You can apply manual formatting to some text and then update the text's style to match it. See "Updating a Style to Match a Selection," p. 248.

- **Modify a style definition**—You can precisely define the changes you want to make to the style. See "Modifying a Style Definition," p. 249.

WORKING WITH QUICK STYLES

Quick Styles, a new feature in Word 2007, enables you to apply certain styles from a sample-based menu system called the Quick Style Gallery on the Home tab.

The first row of styles appears on the tab without opening the menu. Click a style there to apply it (see Figure 8.1).

If the style you want doesn't appear, click the down arrow to open the full menu (see Figure 8.2).

Quick Styles Gallery

Figure 8.1
The Quick Style Gallery is located on the Home tab.

Click here to open menu

Figure 8.2
Select a style from the Quick Style Gallery.

8

In Print Layout or Web Layout view, as you roll the mouse over the various styles, the text in the document changes to show a preview of that style, so you can experiment with the various styles before you commit to one.

TIP

> To quickly apply one of the built-in heading styles (Heading 1 through Heading 3), press Ctrl+Alt plus the number corresponding to the heading level. For example, for Heading 1, press Ctrl+Alt+1. To quickly apply the Normal style, press Ctrl+Shift+N.

→ To create your own styles for use on the Quick Formatting list, **see** "Creating a New Style by Example," **p. 241**.

→ To designate whether or not a style appears on the Quick Styles list, **see** "Removing or Adding a Style in the Quick Style Gallery," **p. 232**.

CHANGING THE QUICK STYLE SET

In earlier versions of Word, each style had only one definition per template. If you wanted to change the definition of the Normal style, for example, you had to either change the style manually or apply a different template to the document.

In Word 2007, however, you can apply Quick Style sets that redefine the built-in styles in various ways, all within the current template. You can quickly switch among the various Quick Style sets to create very different looks without having to modify any styles or change any templates.

Here's how to select a different Quick Style set:

1. From the Home tab, click the Change Styles button.

2. Point to Style Set and then point to one of the style sets. The document is previewed in that style set (see Figure 8.3).

Figure 8.3
Browse the Quick
Style sets.

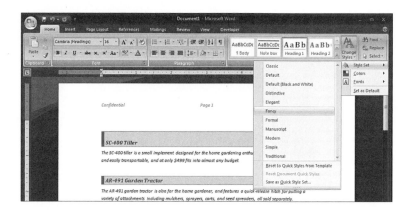

3. When you find a style set that you like, click it to apply it. The built-in styles change to reflect the new choice.

NOTE

> You can create your own quick style sets by setting up the formatting the way you want it and then choosing Change Styles, Style Set, Save as Quick Style Set.

If you have any styles you've created yourself, they will not be updated by changing to a different Quick Style set unless they are based on one of the built-in styles. For example, if you have a Big Normal style that is based on the Normal style but is 14 point, and the Quick Style set redefines the font and size of Normal, the font change will cascade down to Big Normal but the size change will not because Big Normal has its own size definition.

→ To learn more about basing one style on another, **see** "Working with Cascading Styles," **p. 250**.

TIP

> You can prevent users from switching Quick Style sets in a document by doing the following: Click the Styles dialog box launcher in the bottom-right corner of the Styles group (on the Home tab) to display the Styles pane. Click the Manage Styles button at the bottom. In the Manage Styles dialog box, click the Restrict tab and then mark the Block Quick Style Set Switching check box.

REMOVING OR ADDING A STYLE IN THE QUICK STYLE GALLERY

Ideally the Quick Style Gallery should show only the styles you use most often. Keeping the list streamlined makes it easier to apply your favorite styles without wading through a large assortment. For example, if you never use heading levels deeper than Heading 1, you could remove the other heading levels.

To remove a style from the Quick Styles list, open the list and right-click a style; then choose Remove from Quick Style Gallery.

If you change your mind and want to re-add the style to the list later, display the Styles pane (as you'll learn in the next section) and then right-click the style and choose Add to Quick Style Gallery.

USING THE STYLES PANE

The Styles pane is equivalent to the Styles and Formatting task pane in earlier Word versions. It shows a list of styles (optionally with a preview), and you can click a style to apply it to the selected text.

To display the Styles pane, click the dialog box launcher in the bottom-right corner of the Styles group on the Home tab. It can be docked, as shown in Figure 8.4, or dragged into the center to turn it into a floating window.

Click here to open
the Styles pane

Figure 8.4
The Styles pane.

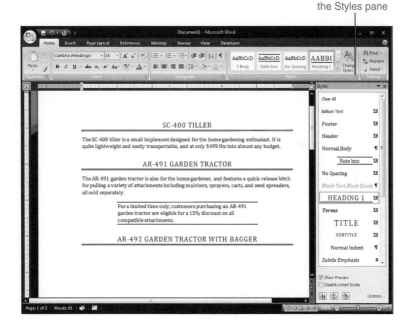

NOTE

Why use the Styles pane, when the Quick Style Gallery is so much more convenient? The Quick Style Gallery is somewhat limited in the styles it shows, for one thing. Not all styles are Quick Styles—nor should they be. Quick Style designation is reserved for the few most frequently used styles that you need to keep closest at hand. Heavy-duty style work is best done in the Styles pane.

To see a complete description of a style's definition, point at the style with the mouse (see Figure 8.5).

8

Figure 8.5
View a description of
the style's formatting.

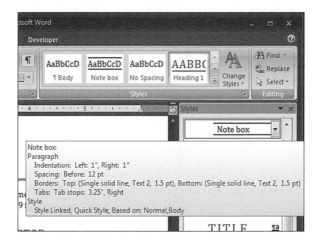

Each style has its own drop-down list in the Styles pane, which you can access either by right-clicking the style name or by pointing at it and then clicking the down arrow that appears to its right. On this menu are these options:

- **Select All x Instances**—Enables you to quickly select all instances of the style in the entire document. This makes it easy to apply manual formatting to all instances at once (although that's not really a good idea; it would be better to update the style definition to make such a global change). If the style is not currently in use, this option will be unavailable and will read Select All: Not Currently Used.

- **Modify**—Opens the Modify Style dialog box in which you can edit the style's definition. (More on this later in the chapter.)

- **Delete** *stylename*—Deletes the style. Works only on user-created styles; you cannot delete built-in styles.

- **Remove from Quick Style Gallery**—Keeps the style on the Styles pane's list, but removes it from the list on the Home tab.

- **Update** *stylename* **to Match Selection**—Changes the style's definition to match the formatting of the currently selected text.

USING THE APPLY STYLES PANE

An abbreviated version of the Styles pane is also available: the Apply Styles pane. To display it, open the Quick Style Gallery menu and click Apply Styles, or press Ctrl+Shift+S.

The Apply Styles pane is a small floating pane from which you can choose styles from a drop-down list (see Figure 8.6). Its buttons are described in the following list:

- **Reapply**—After selecting a style from the list, click this button to apply it to text. It's equivalent to clicking a style on the Styles pane.

- **Modify**—Click this button to modify the style's definition (which you'll learn to do later in this chapter). It's equivalent to right-clicking a style and choosing Modify on the Styles pane.

Figure 8.6
The Apply Styles pane.

→ Another way to avoid moving the mouse to apply styles is to use shortcut key assignments for common styles. **See** "Applying a Keyboard Shortcut to a Style," **p. 246**.

CUSTOMIZING THE STYLES PANE

The controls at the bottom of the Styles pane offer several ways of customizing its appearance and functionality.

When Show Preview is enabled, the style names appear in the actual styles they represent, as nearly as possible. This makes it easier to remember what a style represents, but it makes the list somewhat less compact and can slow down performance somewhat on a slow PC.

When Disable Linked Styles is enabled, linked styles behave like paragraph styles. For example, when you select some characters of text and then apply a linked style, only those characters receive the character-level formatting from the style. If you disable linked styles, however, that character-level formatting would apply to the entire paragraph regardless of the selection. Click the Options hyperlink to display the Style Pane Options dialog box (see Figure 8.7).

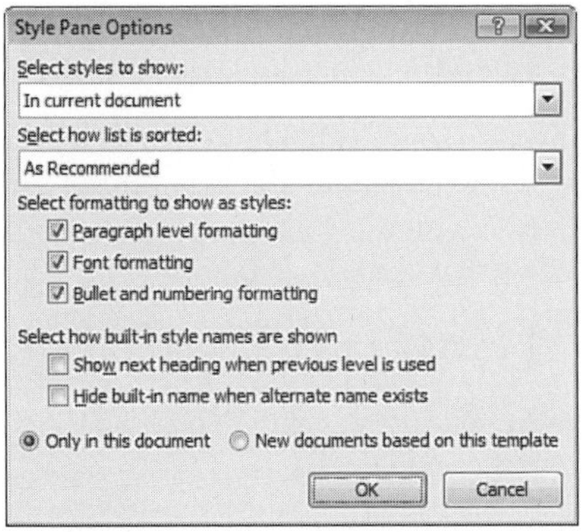

Figure 8.7
Set Styles pane options.

The Select Styles to Show setting controls which styles will appear on the Styles pane, and also in the Apply Styles pane. Here are the choices:

- **Recommended**—Only styles marked as Recommended appear.

→ To choose which styles are marked as Recommended, **see** "Sorting the Styles List," **p. 252**.

- **In Use**—Only styles that are currently in use appear.
- **In Current Document**—Only styles that have been applied in this document appear. (Heading 1 through Heading 3 and Normal always appear even if they are not in use.)
- **All Styles**—All available styles appear.

The Select How List Is Sorted setting controls how styles will be arranged on the list. You can choose from the following options:

- **Alphabetical**—From A to Z by name.
- **As Recommended**—Styles marked as Recommended appear first, followed by the others, alphabetically within each section of the list.
- **Font**—Arranged according to the font choice, alphabetically by font.
- **Based On**—Arranged according to the style on which each is based, and alphabetically within that list.
- **By Type**—Arranged according to paragraph style versus character style, and alphabetically within those categories.

In the Select Formatting to Show as Styles section, specify how you want entries to appear in the Styles pane for manual formatting that has occurred but has not yet been officially designated as a style. This can be handy because it can help you create styles more quickly out of existing formatting.

In the Select How Built-in Style Names Are Shown section, specify whether you want built-in names to appear only if the previous level is used (for example, show Heading 5 only if Heading 4 is in use), and whether to hide built-in names when an alternate name exists.

Finally, you can choose to have these options apply Only In This Document or in New Documents Based on This Template. If you choose the latter, these settings are saved with the template; otherwise, they are saved with the document.

CLEARING STYLES AND FORMATTING

There are several ways of clearing formatting, depending on how extreme you want the removal to be:

- To clear all manual formatting and remove all styles, reverting the text to Normal style, choose Clear All from the Styles pane's list.
- To remove the manual formatting from text, leaving only the style's formatting, in the Apply Styles pane select the style name and click Reapply, or open the Quick Style Gallery menu and click Clear Formatting.

- To remove all the manual formatting and also all the character styles, leaving only the paragraph formatting, select the text and press Ctrl+Spacebar.
- To strip off any manually applied paragraph formatting, leaving only the paragraph formatting specified by the paragraph style, select the text and press Ctrl+Q.

New in Word 2007, you can also use a feature called the *Style Inspector*, a floating pane that can help you examine the formatting for text and strip off anything you don't want.

 To activate the Style Inspector, click the Style Inspector button in the Styles pane.

The Style Inspector consists of two sections: Paragraph Formatting and Text Level Formatting. Each section has two eraser buttons. The upper button in each section removes the style (paragraph style and character style, respectively), and the lower button in each section strips off any manual formatting but leaves the style intact (see Figure 8.8).

Figure 8.8
Use the Style Inspector to examine and remove formatting.

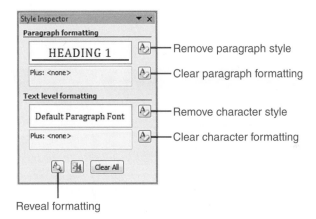

Each of the areas in the Style Inspector also has a menu, similar to the menus available by right-clicking the style names in the Styles pane or the Quick Style Gallery (see Figure 8.9). What's different here is that you can access the paragraph style and the character style separately for the same text; this is very useful in situations where manual formatting has been overlaid over character styles that have in turn been overlaid on paragraph styles.

TIP

> You can drag the Style Inspector window to the far left or right edge of the Word window to dock it there as a full-size pane.

Figure 8.9
All the usual menu commands for the styles appear here.

The Reveal Formatting button, pointed out in Figure 8.8, opens the Reveal Formatting pane that you learned about in Chapter 6, "Applying Character Formatting." It shows the exact formatting applied to the selected text (see Figure 8.10).

Figure 8.10
Use the Reveal Formatting pane to further examine the text formatting.

The Reveal Formatting pane

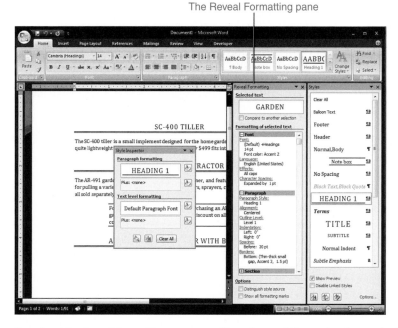

→ For more information about the Reveal Formatting pane, **see** "Revealing and Comparing Formatting," **p. 181**.

VIEWING THE STYLE AREA

In Draft view (accessible from the View tab), you can optionally display a Style area to the left of the document. Next to each paragraph, the assigned paragraph style name appears, so you can easily locate any paragraphs that do not have the desired styles applied (see Figure 8.11).

Figure 8.11
The Style area.

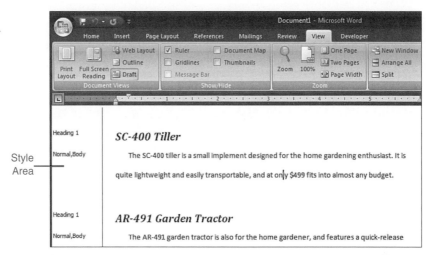

To turn on the Style area, do the following:

1. Choose Office, Word Options.

2. Click Advanced.

3. Scroll down to the Display section, and in the Style Area Pane Width in Draft and Outline Views box, enter a value greater than 0, in inches. The larger the number, the wider the Style area will be (see Figure 8.12). (Figure 8.11 shows a width of 1", which is typical.)

4. Click OK.

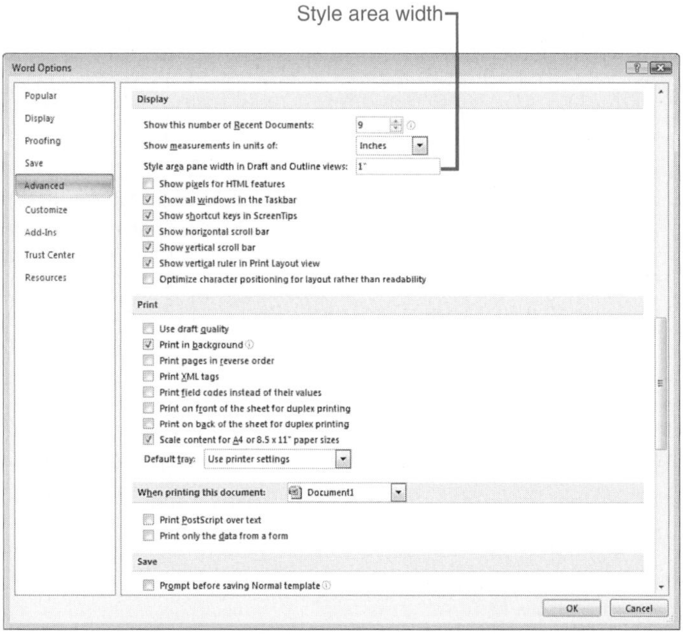

Figure 8.12
Display the Style area in Draft view by specifying a width for it.

8

CREATING AND DELETING STYLES

There are several ways to create styles, ranging from simple example-based techniques to powerful and specific definitions. The following sections look at the ins and outs of style creation, naming, and deletion.

STYLE NAMING AND ALTERNATE NAMES

Before you start creating styles, spend some time thinking about the rules you will use for deciding on the names. Many a beginner has started out with a naming scheme that proved unwieldy, only to have to rename dozens of styles later to fix the problem.

Create style names based on the intended usage for the style, not based on the formatting. For example, Article Title is a much better name than Arial 16-point because you might decide later that the title should be a different font or size.

To create clusters of styles, name them with the same first few characters so that they appear together in alphabetically sorted listings. For example, to keep several bulleted and numbered list styles together alphabetically, you might name them List Bullet A, List Bullet B, List Number A, and List Number B.

Strategic naming is an issue only for the new styles you create yourself, because Word does not allow you to rename a built-in style. You can, however, create *alternate names* (aliases) for them.

To create an alternate name, follow these steps:

1. From the Styles pane or the Quick Styles list, right-click a style and choose Modify.
2. In the Name box, click to place the insertion point at the end of the current name. Then type a comma and then the alternate name. For example, to alias Heading 1 as H1, type the following:

   Heading 1,H1
3. Click OK. The style name now appears in all listings with both names.

> **NOTE**
>
> With built-in styles, you can actually just delete the name that appears in the Name box and replace it entirely with the alternate name. When you click OK, Word will reinsert the original name before the name you typed, with a comma separator.

Creating the alternate name is in itself not that useful because lists continue to be sorted by the real names. However, you can then set up the Styles list to show the alternate names of styles *instead of* the real names. Follow these steps:

1. In the Styles pane, click Options. The Style Pane Options dialog box opens.
2. Mark the Hide Built-In Name When Alternate Name Exists check box (see Figure 8.13).
3. Click OK. Now, if a style has an alternate name, that name appears instead of the real name in the Styles list.

Figure 8.13
Set the Styles list to show only alternate names when they exist.

CREATING A NEW STYLE BY EXAMPLE

Creating a style by example is useful if you already have some text that's formatted in the correct way and you want to apply that same formatting consistently throughout the document.

Here's how to create a new style and place it on the Quick Style Gallery list:

1. Format text the way you want the style to be, and select that text. If creating a paragraph style, select the entire paragraph.

2. On the Home tab, open the Quick Style Gallery and choose Styles, Save Selection As a New Quick Style. Alternatively, right-click the selected text and choose Save Selection As a New Quick Style. The Create New Style from Formatting dialog box opens.

> **NOTE**
>
> The Modify button in Figure 8.14's Create New Style from Formatting dialog box opens a larger version of the same dialog box. This larger version opens by default when you create the new style from the Styles pane, as in the next set of steps. In it, you can make changes to the style definition. You'll learn about these changes later in the chapter.

3. In the Name box, type a name for the style (see Figure 8.14).

4. Click OK. The new style appears on the Quick Styles list.

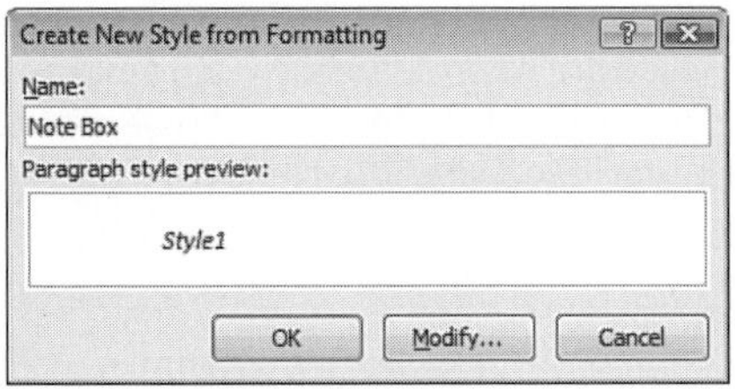

Figure 8.14
Create a new style by example.

8

You can also create a new style by example with the Styles pane:

1. If the Styles pane is not already open, display it (by clicking the dialog box launcher in the bottom-right corner of the Styles group in the Home tab).

2. Format text the way you want the style to be, and select that text. If creating a paragraph style, select the entire paragraph.

3. In the Styles pane, click the New Style button. The Create New Style from Formatting dialog box opens (see Figure 8.15).

Figure 8.15
This dialog box is a more complex version than the one for Quick Styles (refer to Figure 8.14).

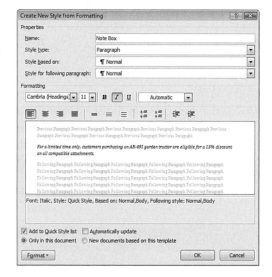

4. In the Name box, type a name for the style.

5. (Optional) Make any changes desired to the style definition. (You'll learn about such changes in the next section.)

6. (Optional) If you want this to be a Quick Style, mark the Add to Quick Style List check box.

7. (Optional) If you want the style to automatically update, mark the Automatically Update check box.

CAUTION

You probably don't want to use Automatically Update because it can get you into unintended messes. This feature updates the style's definition whenever you make manual formatting changes to text that has that style applied. For example, if you have a heading level that is bold but not italic, and you apply italics to one instance, the style itself changes so that it includes italics and all instances change.

8. (Optional) If you want the new style to be saved in the template, click New Documents Based on This Template.

9. Click OK. The new style appears in the Styles pane.

CREATING A NEW STYLE BY DEFINITION

Creating a style by definition means constructing the style's specifications based on dialog box settings rather than based on an example. That's somewhat misleading as a definition, though, because technically *every* new style definition starts out as a "by example." When you open the dialog box for constructing a new style, the default settings within it come from whatever style was in effect at the insertion point position when you opened the dialog box. The main point of differentiation, then, is whether you make modifications to the settings or just accept what the example provided.

To define a style, you use many of the skills you acquired in Chapter 6, "Applying Character Formatting," and Chapter 7, "Formatting Paragraphs and Lists," for applying character and paragraph formatting to individual blocks of text. The same controls—or at least similar ones—are used for the style definition in many cases.

To create a new style by definition, it is preferable to start out with as much of a "blank slate" as possible example-wise, so click in an area of the document that has the Normal style applied, or apply that style to an area. (Ctrl+Shift+N is a shortcut for applying the Normal style.) Then do the following:

1. If the Styles pane is open, click the New Style button. If not, on the Home tab open the Quick Styles list and click Save Selection As a New Quick Style. Then click the Modify button. Either way, the larger version of the Create New Style from Formatting dialog box appears.

2. Type a name for the new style in the Name box.

3. Select a style type from the Style Type list. The dialog box controls change to show formatting appropriate for the type chosen:

   - **Paragraph**—Contains paragraph-level formatting, and can optionally also contain character-level formatting that applies to the entire paragraph.

   - **Character**—Contains character-level formatting only.

   - **Linked**—Contains both paragraph-level and character-level and can be applied as either a Paragraph or Character style.

   - **Table**—Contains formatting specific to tables, and can include elements of paragraph and character formatting as well, as it applies to table cells.

   - **List**—Contains formatting specific to bulleted or numbered lists, somewhat like an outline numbered list.

NOTE

A list style contains paragraph formatting for up to nine levels of bulleted or numbered list elements in a single style. This is useful because you can use the same style for an entire multilevel list, and items can be promoted and demoted without having their styles changed.

4. Select a parent style from the Style Based On list. Anything that is not specifically defined for the new style will be copied from this style. The most common style to base other styles on is Normal. This option is not available for List styles.

5. (Paragraph and Linked types only) Make a selection in the Style for Following Paragraph list. This determines the style of the next paragraph that appears when you press Enter at the end of a paragraph. For a heading style, it would be appropriate for the next paragraph to be a body style such as Normal; for a body style, it would be appropriate to have another paragraph of the same style.

6. In the Formatting section, use the controls to define formatting for the style.

The controls are different for each style type. Figure 8.16 shows them for a Paragraph style, for example.

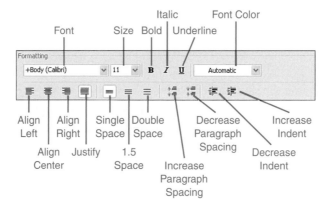

Figure 8.16
Creating a new Paragraph type of style.

If you want to be able to change the text appearance by applying formatting themes, don't specify a certain font or color for a style. Instead, set the font to +Body for a body style or +Heading for a heading style, and set the color to Automatic.

The Linked style type's controls are the same as in Figure 8.16, and the Character type's controls are a subset of those. (The Character type includes only the controls that apply to individual characters, such as font, size, and color.)

The Table style type's controls are shown in Figure 8.17, and the List style type's in Figure 8.18.

7. For the List type only, open the Apply Formatting To list and choose a list level (1st through 9th). Then specify the formatting for that level, and go on to the next level until you have set up all levels (refer to Figure 8.18).

8. If any formatting is needed that isn't available in the Formatting section, click the Format button to open a menu of formatting categories and then click the appropriate category.

8

Figure 8.17
Creating a new Table type of style.

Border Width   Border Color   Scope of formatting

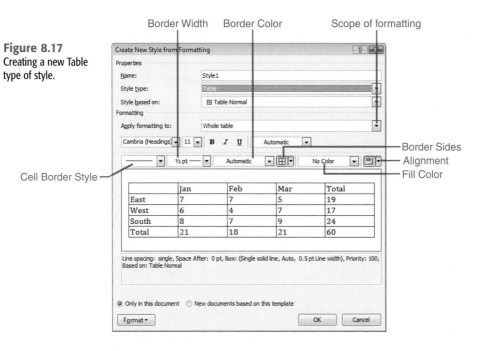

Cell Border Style

Border Sides
Alignment
Fill Color

Figure 8.18
Creating a new List type of style.

Starting number

Bullet/Numbering Style

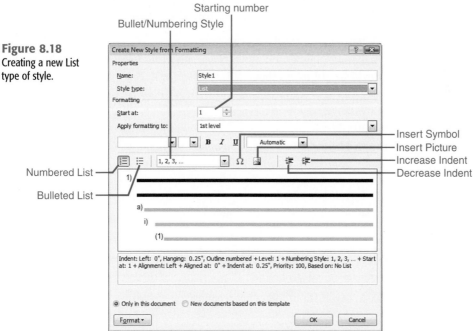

Numbered List
Bulleted List

Insert Symbol
Insert Picture
Increase Indent
Decrease Indent

Then set up the formatting in the dialog box that appears and click OK to return to the Create New Style from Formatting dialog box. The dialog boxes are the same as the ones you learned about in Chapters 6 and 7 for the individual formatting categories (Font, Paragraph, Tabs, and so on).

8

For example, to create a hanging indent for the style, you would need to select Paragraph and then set the Special indent on the Indents and Spacing tab.

→ Each of the choices on the Format button's menu corresponds to a dialog box covered elsewhere in the book:

For Font, **see** "Changing the Font and Size," **p. 158**.

For Paragraph, **see** "Setting Line Spacing," **p. 193**.

For Tabs, **see** "Working with Tab Stops," **p. 201**.

For Border, **see** "Applying Paragraph Borders," **p. 217**.

For Language, **see** "Checking Spelling and Grammar in Multiple Languages," **p. 108**.

For Frame, **see** "Setting Text Wrap," **p. 402**.

For Numbering, **see** "Creating Numbered and Bulleted Lists," **p. 206**.

9. If you want this style to appear on the Quick Styles list, mark the Add to Quick Style List check box. (This is not available for Table or List styles.)

10. If you want the style to automatically update its definition when you reformat text in the document that has that style applied, mark the Automatically Update check box. (This option is for Paragraph and Linked styles only.)

11. Select how the new style will be available: either Only in This Document or New Documents Based on This Template.

12. Click OK to create the new style.

APPLYING A KEYBOARD SHORTCUT TO A STYLE

Keyboard shortcuts make style application much faster and easier because you don't have to take your hands off the keyboard to use them.

Certain built-in styles already have keyboard shortcuts assigned to them:

- **Normal**—Ctrl+Shift+N.

- **Heading 1 through Heading 3**—Ctrl+Alt+*number* (for example, Ctrl+Alt+1 for Heading 1).

You can also assign keyboard shortcuts to other styles as desired. Keyboard shortcuts can be assigned as you are creating the styles or can be added later.

NOTE

Shortcut keys cannot be assigned to Table styles.

To assign a shortcut key combination, follow these steps:

1. Do one of the following:

   - To assign while creating a new style, start the new style as you learned in the preceding section, so that the large version of the Create New Style from Formatting dialog box is open.

   - To modify an existing style, right-click the style on the Quick Styles list or in the Styles pane and choose Modify.

8

NOTE

Different dialog boxes open when you're creating a new style versus modifying an existing one, but they are virtually identical except for their names.

2. Click the Format button and then choose Shortcut Key. The Customize Keyboard dialog box opens.

3. Click in the Press New Shortcut Key box and then press the key combination to assign (see Figure 8.19).

Key combinations usually involve some combination of the Ctrl or Alt key plus one or more numbers and/or letters, or a function key (F1 through F12). Many key combinations are already assigned; if you pick one that is taken, the Currently Assigned To indicator shows its existing assignment. You can assign an already-assigned combination, but the new assignment overrides the old one.

Figure 8.19
Assign a keyboard shortcut to a style.

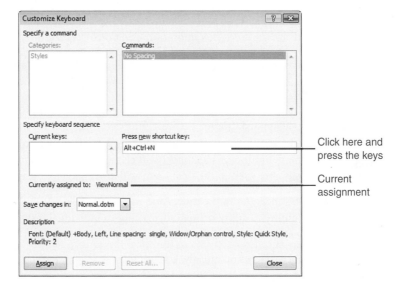

Click here and press the keys

Current assignment

4. Open the Save Changes In list and choose where to store the keyboard shortcut—either in the current template or the current document.

5. Click Assign to assign the keyboard shortcut.

6. Click Close.

NOTE

To remove a keyboard shortcut from a style, repeat steps 1–2, select the shortcut in the Current Keys list, and then click Remove.

DELETING A STYLE

Built-in styles such as Normal and Heading 1 through Heading 9 cannot be deleted. (They can be redefined, though, as you'll learn in the next section.)

To delete a user-created style, right-click it (either from the Quick Styles list or the Styles pane) and choose Delete *name*, where *name* is the style name.

If the style is based on some other style than Normal, rather than a Delete command, you'll instead see a Revert To command. This command not only deletes the style but converts the formatting on any text to which it is assigned to the parent style. For example, if you have a style called Modified Heading 1 that is based on the Heading 1 style, selecting Revert to Heading 1 will delete Modified Heading 1, and all text that was formatted with it becomes formatted with Heading 1 instead.

MODIFYING STYLES

Styles can be modified in several ways. You can set styles to update automatically, update a style by example, or revisit the style's definition using dialog box interfaces.

UPDATING A STYLE AUTOMATICALLY

As you saw when creating styles earlier in the chapter, an Automatically Update option is available. This option changes the style's definition whenever you apply manual formatting to text with that style applied. So, for example, suppose you select a Heading 1–styled paragraph and change the font for it. If the Automatically Update check box is marked for the Heading 1 style, the definition of Heading 1 will change to reflect the new font choice, and all instances of Heading 1 used in the document will also change.

It sounds like a good idea, but in practice, Automatically Update can cause problems because it takes away your ability to apply manual formatting to individual instances within a document. Therefore, be cautious with this option.

Here's how to turn on/off Automatically Update for a style:

1. Right-click the style on the Quick Style Gallery or in the Styles pane and choose Modify.
2. Mark or clear the Automatically Update check box.
3. Click OK.

UPDATING A STYLE TO MATCH A SELECTION

As long as Automatically Update is not enabled (see the preceding section), you retain the ability to manually format some text in a manner that's different from its style's definition. If you then choose to incorporate that new formatting into the style's definition, you can use Update to Match Selection to do so.

To update a style to match the formatting of selected text, right-click the style on the Quick Styles list or in the Styles pane and choose Update *name* to Match Selection, where *name* is the style name.

MODIFYING A STYLE DEFINITION

The same process you learned earlier in "Creating a New Style by Definition" can also be used to modify the style later. This method uses a set of dialog boxes for defining the formatting.

To access the Modify Style dialog box, right-click the style and choose Modify. The Modify Style dialog box is identical to the Create New Style from Formatting dialog box, except for the name. Then use the same controls as when creating a style. The basic formatting can be set in the Formatting section; for more options, click the Format button to open a menu of categories.

REDEFINING THE NORMAL (DEFAULT) STYLE

The Normal style is the basis for most other styles in the document, so modifying it will trickle down changes throughout many styles.

The Normal style can be modified the same as any other style, but there is also a special location in which you can set a definition of Normal, either for the document or for the template. This is a rather basic definition, but it includes the essentials: font, size, color, paragraph position and indentation, and paragraph spacing (before, after, and between lines).

To modify the default settings for the Normal style, follow these steps:

1. Display the Styles pane and then click the Manage Styles button. The Manage Styles dialog box appears.
2. Click the Set Defaults tab.
3. Change any settings as desired (see Figure 8.20).

> **TIP**
>
> If you want to retain the ability to have a theme change the body text's font, make sure you set the Font to +Body rather than a specific font. The same goes for color: If you want themes to be able to specify body color, set the Font Color to Automatic.

4. (Optional) If you want the changes to apply to the template, click New Documents Based on This Template.
5. Click OK.

8

Figure 8.20
Redefine the default
Normal style settings
for the document or
template.

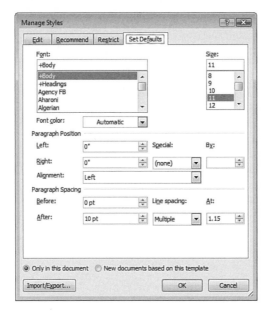

RENAMING STYLES

To rename a style, open the Modify Style dialog box (right-click the style and choose Modify) and type a different name in the Name box. You cannot rename the built-in styles, only the user-created ones. (However, see the section "Style Naming and Alternate Names" earlier in the chapter to learn how to assign an alternate name to a built-in style.)

Style name changes are automatically populated throughout the document. Any text that is formatted with the renamed style remains so, but the style name associated with it changes to match the new name.

WORKING WITH CASCADING STYLES

Documents look best when all the styles are coordinated to give a unified impression. (That's the basic idea behind the Themes feature, covered later in this chapter.) When you make a change to one style in your document, you might end up needing to make the same change to all the styles to keep the document's look consistent, and this can be time-consuming.

To avoid having to make changes to multiple styles, consider setting up all the styles in the document as cascading versions of one central style, such as Normal. Then if you want to change a certain aspect of the formatting, you make the change to Normal, and the change trickles down to all styles based on it. This is known as *cascading* style definitions. You could even have multiple levels of cascading. Style C could be based on Style B, and Style B based on Style A, and Style A based on Normal.

Or, at the other end of the spectrum, perhaps you don't want every style to update based on your changes to Normal. Perhaps there's a certain style that should never change at all. You can set up such a style to be based on No Style, locking it into its own definition.

To set the style's basis, follow these steps:

1. Right-click the style and choose Modify.

2. Open the Style Based On list and select a style, or choose (No Style) from the top of the list.

3. Click OK.

Changing the basis does not change the style's definition, but it changes whether and how it *will* (or *will not)* change later. For example, if a style is no longer based on Normal, then changes to Normal will not affect it in the future.

MODIFYING THE STYLES IN THE CURRENT TEMPLATE

Word 2007 makes it very easy to modify the styles in the template. You do not even have to open the template for editing in order to do so—just work from within any document based on that template.

To modify the style definitions in the current template, start modifying a style and make sure you select the New Documents Based on This Template option in the Modify Style dialog box. This saves the style change to the template itself, not just to the current document.

You can also open the template file itself (Office, Open and then select All Word Templates as the file type to open), but there's not much advantage in that in Word 2007 because you can so easily save styles to the current template from within any document.

MODIFYING STYLES IN THE MANAGE STYLES DIALOG BOX

If you need to modify a lot of styles, you might find the Manage Styles dialog box to be a more efficient interface for doing so than the Quick Style Gallery or the Styles pane.

 To access the Manage Styles dialog box, display the Styles pane and click the Manage Styles button at the bottom.

The Manage Styles dialog box has four tabs. We're most interested in the Edit tab at the moment, shown in Figure 8.21. It lists all available styles in the document.

From the Edit tab, you can do the following:

- **Specify that changes be saved in the template**—Click New Documents Based on This Template before making changes.

- **View style definitions**—Click a style and examine the Preview area's sample and definition.

- **Modify a style's definition or name**—Click the style and click Modify, and use the Modify Style dialog box.

- **Delete a style (except built-in styles)**—Click the style and click Delete.

■ **Create a new style**—Click the New Style button and use the Create New Style from Formatting dialog box.

Figure 8.21
Manage the entire Styles list from one interface in the Manage Styles dialog box.

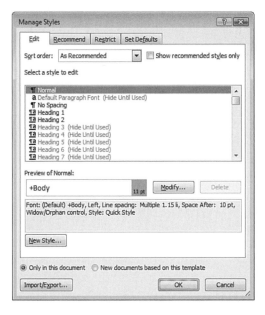

One handy feature of the Manage Styles dialog box is that it identifies styles that are set for Automatically Update with an (AutoUpdate) indicator following their names. This is a good way to see at a glance which styles are being automatically updated, and to remove that designation if needed.

→ To import or export styles, **see** "Copying Styles Between Documents," **p. 255**.

→ To learn about the Recommend tab in the Manage Styles dialog box, **see** "Sorting the Styles List," **p. 252**.

SORTING THE STYLES LIST

An alphabetical list of styles, such as the one that appears in the Styles pane, is perhaps not the most efficient list. If a frequently used style happens to begin with a Z, for example, and the Styles list is long, you end up needing to scroll through the Styles pane's list every time you want to apply that style. It would be much nicer to be able to prioritize the list so that your favorite styles appear near the top of the list, for easy selection.

The Recommend feature enables you to do just that. You can set up a Recommend level for a style between 1 and 99, and then set the list's sort order to As Recommended. Within a certain level, entries are sorted alphabetically.

NOTE

If you set the Recommend level to greater than 99, the style is set for Last, which means it will appear at the bottom of the list.

To view the current Recommend level assignments, follow these steps:

1. From the Styles pane, click the Manage Styles button. The Manage Styles dialog box opens.

2. Click the Recommend tab. All the styles available in the current document appear. (This includes both styles inherited from the template and styles you might have created uniquely in this document.)

3. Scroll through the list. The number that appears to the far left is the Recommend level (see Figure 8.22).

Figure 8.22
Set a Recommend level for each style.

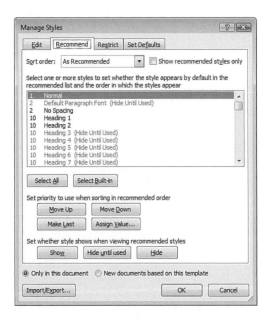

4. To change a level, select the style and then click one of the following buttons:

   - **Move Up**—Promotes it one level (if not already 1).
   - **Move Down**—Demotes it one level (if not already Last).
   - **Make Last**—Sets it to Last.
   - **Assign Value**—Opens a dialog box in which you can type the number desired.

   TIP

   > You can set the level for more than one style at once. Select multiple styles by holding down Ctrl as you click each one, or use the Select All or Select Built-In button. Be aware, however, that if either All or Built-In includes one or more unchangeable styles, you won't be able to change the value for that group.

5. Click OK.

8

Now make sure the Styles list is set to be sorted by the Recommend level. Here's how to do this:

1. On the Styles pane, click Options. The Style Pane Options dialog box opens (see Figure 8.23).

2. On the Select How List Is Sorted list, make sure As Recommended is selected.

3. Click OK.

Figure 8.23
Set viewing options for the Styles list.

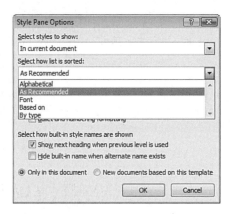

FILTERING THE STYLES LIST

Besides the style sort order, the Recommend list also controls which styles will appear on a list that is filtered to show only recommended styles. The term "Recommended" in this context does not have anything to do with the Recommend level number you assigned in the preceding section. Instead, it has to do with which of three statuses are configured for the style on the Recommend tab of the Manage Styles dialog box (refer to Figure 8.22):

- **Show**—The style appears on the list whether the list is filtered or not.
- **Hide Until Used**—The style appears on the list whether the list is filtered or not, but only if the style is in use in the document.
- **Hide**—The style does not appear on a filtered list.

To set a style's status, follow these steps:

1. From the Styles pane, click the Manage Styles button. The Manage Styles dialog box opens.

2. Click the Recommend tab. All the styles available in the current document appear.

3. Select a style, and then click the Show, Hide Until Used, or Hide button.

4. Repeat for each style to control whether it will appear on a filtered list.

5. Click OK.

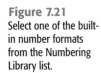

Choose a sort order

Figure 10.4
Templates from Office
Online can be sorted
within a category.

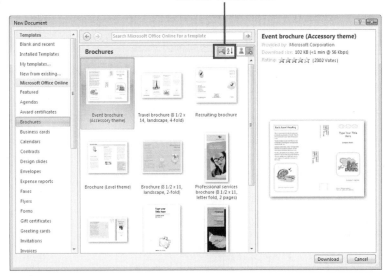

10

USING A USER TEMPLATE

A *user template* is one that you or another user have created. Templates you create are stored in the default template folder:

In Windows Vista: Users*username*\\AppData\\Roaming\\Microsoft\\Templates

In Windows XP: Documents and Settings*username*\\Application Data\\Microsoft\\Templates

where *username* is the name with which you have logged into Windows. To make a template available that you have received from someone else, place it in that folder.

CAUTION

If you log into Windows as a different user, you will not have access to your user templates. See "Accessing Workgroup Templates" later in this chapter to learn how to share templates with all the local users of the PC and how to change the default storage location for both workgroup and user templates.

Here's how to access these local templates:

1. Choose Office, New. The New Document dialog box opens.
2. Click My Templates. The New dialog box opens (see Figure 10.5). Icons appear for the templates stored in the default template folder. The templates that appear on the list will be different depending on what templates you have already created, if any.

3. Click a template and then click OK to create a new document based on it.

→ To create your own templates, **see** "Creating Your Own Templates," **p. 310**.

Figure 10.5
Use templates you've created yourself by selecting My Templates.

USING AN EXISTING DOCUMENT

You do not have to convert a document to a template in order to create other documents based on it. Any document can function as a makeshift template. When you start a new document based on a template, Word makes a copy of the document and opens that copy in an unsaved document window.

To base a new document on an existing one, follow these steps:

1. Choose Office, New. The New Document dialog box opens.

2. Click New from Existing. The New from Existing Document dialog box opens. It's just like the Open dialog box except for the name.

3. Select the document on which to base the new one.

4. Click Create New. The new document is created, with all the same settings and text as the document you chose.

ACCESSING WORKGROUP TEMPLATES

As mentioned earlier in the chapter, user templates are stored on a per-user basis. Each Windows user has his or her own template storage location.

If you need to make user-created templates publicly available, store them in the workgroup templates folder. When you start a document from My Templates (in the New Document dialog box), all the templates from both your personal template folder and the workgroup templates folder appear integrated on the same list. Any user of these templates cannot tell that they are coming from two different places.

First, find out if you have a workgroup templates folder set up. If you don't, define one.

Follow these steps:

1. Choose Office, Word Options. The Word Options dialog box opens.

2. Click Advanced.

3. Scroll down to the General section and click the File Locations button. The File Locations dialog box opens.

4. Look at the Workgroup Templates line to see what folder has been defined for workgroup templates. In Figure 10.6, for example, C:\Templates has been defined.

Figure 10.6
Note the location defined for workgroup templates, and change it if desired.

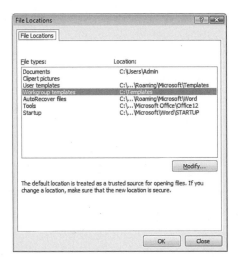

5. (Optional) Change the assigned folder by doing the following:

   a. Double-click Workgroup Templates, or click Workgroup Templates and then click Modify.

   b. Navigate to the folder you want to use. (It can be either a local or network location.)

   c. Click OK.

6. Click OK to accept the new location.

7. Click OK to close the Word Options dialog box.

> **TIP**
>
> You can use that same procedure to change the default location for user templates if you like; choose User Templates in step 5 instead of Workgroup Templates.

Next, move all the templates you want to share into that folder. You can do so from a Windows file management interface such as Windows Explorer. For example, to move templates from your personal template storage to the workgroup storage, follow these steps:

1. In Windows, open Computer (Windows Vista) or My Computer (Windows XP).

2. Navigate to the location where your user templates are stored:

   In Windows Vista: Users*username*\\AppData\\Roaming\\Microsoft\\Templates.

   In Windows XP: Documents and Settings*username*\\Application Data\\Microsoft\\Templates, where *username* is the name with which you have logged into Windows.

3. Select the desired template files. Hold down Ctrl as you click each one to select multiple files.

4. Cut the files to the Clipboard by pressing Ctrl+X (or use any other method you prefer).

5. Navigate to the folder you specified for workgroup templates.

6. Paste the files from the Clipboard by pressing Ctrl+V (or use any other method you prefer).

As you create new templates, as described later in this chapter, save them in either the personal or the workgroup location, depending on whether or not you want to share them.

DOWNLOADING TEMPLATES FROM OFFICE ONLINE

As you learned earlier in the chapter, you can access a large library of templates from Microsoft via the New Document dialog box. Those online templates are readily available whenever you are connected to the Internet, but not everyone is always connected. If you want to make sure that a certain template is always available, even offline, you might prefer to download it to your hard disk.

To make a template available offline, you must access the template library via a Web interface. Visit the Templates home page on Office Online by selecting the Feature category in the Microsoft Office Online section, and then clicking the Templates hyperlink at the bottom of the New Document dialog box (see Figure 10.7).

Figure 10.7
Click the Templates hyperlink to go to the Templates section of Office Online.

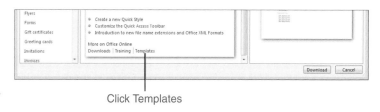

Click Templates

On the Templates home page, browse for a template that interests you and click the link for one. Figure 10.8 shows the web page for a calendar template.

Figure 10.8
Locate a template that you want to download.

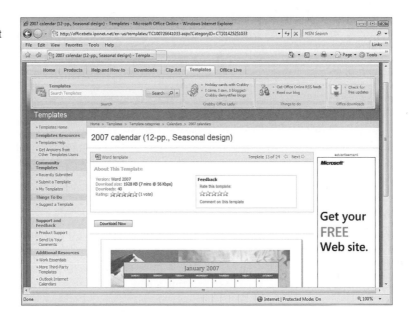

Here's what you can do, as shown in Figure 10.8:

- **Version**—Check what versions of Word the template will work with.
- **Download size**—See how long the template will take to download and how much disk space it will consume.
- **Feedback**—Click the stars to rate the template (ostensibly after you have used and evaluated it).
- **Download Now**—Click this button to begin the download.

If you get a message that the template could not be downloaded automatically, directions will appear on the error message page that explain how you can manually download it. This involves downloading a compressed file (.cab) and then extracting the template file from it.

If the template does download successfully, a new document opens based on it in Word. From here, save the file as a template to an appropriate folder. Here are the folders to use:

- **Personal user template**—If using Windows Vista, save to Users*username* \\AppData\\Roaming\\Microsoft\\Templates.

  If using Windows XP, save to \\Documents and Settings*username*\\Application Data\\Microsoft\\Templates, where *username* is the name with which you have logged into Windows.

- **Workgroup user template**—Save to the folder you have designated as the workgroup template folder.

- **Microsoft-installed template**—Save to \\Program Files\\Microsoft Office\\Templates\\1033.

NOTE

> 1033 is the country code for the United States. If you have a version for some other country, the country code will be different. You will find only one folder with a four-digit number as the name, however, so that'll be the one.

In the Save As dialog box, make sure you set the Save as Type setting to Word Template (*.dotx) or Word Macro-Enabled Template (*.dotm); otherwise, it'll be saved as a regular document. You don't need to use the macro-enabled type unless you plan to store any macros in it (and most people don't).

MODIFYING TEMPLATES

The easiest way to get comfortable with creating templates is to modify an existing template. For example, suppose Word provides a calendar template that you really like, but you wish the colors were different. You can make the color changes and then save your work, either overwriting the previous version or creating a new file.

CAUTION

> When you edit an existing template, you're making a permanent change to it, so do this with caution. Even if you open the template with intentions of saving it under another name, it's easy to forget and click the Save button and accidentally overwrite the original version. For this reason, the safest route is to create a backup folder into which you can put copies of the original template files that you can restore later, if needed.

TEMPLATE STORAGE LOCATIONS

To open a template, you must know where it's stored. As you learned earlier, a template can potentially be stored in several locations, depending on the type of template it is:

- **Personal user templates**—For Windows Vista, Users*username*\\AppData\\Roaming\\Microsoft\\Templates.

  For Windows XP, Documents and Settings*username*\\Application Data\\Microsoft\\Templates, where *username* is the name with which you have logged into Windows.

- **Workgroup user templates**—The folder you specified in Word Options, if any.

- **Microsoft-installed templates**—\\Program Files\\Microsoft Office\\Templates\\1033.

If you can't find the Application Data folder in the path, see "Can't Find the Application Data or AppData Folder" in the "Troubleshooting" section at the end of this chapter.

If Normal.dotm does not appear in the personal user templates folder, see "Normal.dotm Is Missing" in the "Troubleshooting" section at the end of this chapter.

If you want to get back the original version of Normal.dotm after editing it, see "I Want the Original Version of Normal.dotm" in the "Troubleshooting" section at the end of this chapter.

Opening a template is like opening any other Word file. By default, the Open dialog box displays all files that Word can open, including templates, but you might find it easier to filter the files to show only a certain type of template. To do that, change the Files of Type setting in the Open dialog box, as shown in Figure 10.9.

Figure 10.9
Filter the Open dialog box's file listing to show only templates.

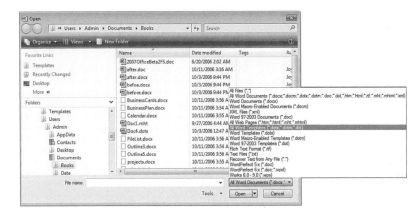

MODIFYING A TEMPLATE BY MODIFYING THE CURRENT DOCUMENT

You can also modify a template by editing a document based on it. When you add a style or macro to a document, for example, you're prompted for a storage location. You can choose to store it either in the current document or in the current template. If you choose to store it in the template, the template is modified when you save your work.

A message might appear asking whether you want to save your changes to the document template, or the changes might be saved behind the scenes. You can specify whether you want changes to Normal.dotm to be made "silently" or not by doing the following:

1. Choose Office, Word Options. The Word Options dialog box opens.

2. Click Advanced.

3. Scroll down to the Save section and mark or clear the Prompt Before Saving Normal Template check box (see Figure 10.10).

4. Click OK.

Figure 10.10
Choose whether or not to be prompted when changes are made to Normal.dotm.

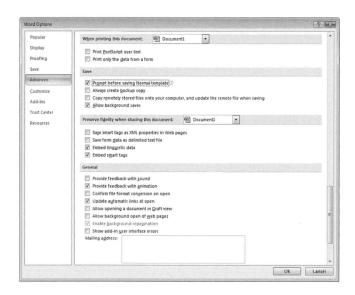

CAUTION

It is convenient to have changes silently saved to Normal.dotm, but some macro viruses infect Normal.dotm by making changes to it that you might not be aware of. Forcing Word to prompt you before making changes to that file is an extra layer of security.

PROTECTING TEMPLATES

Templates can be protected from changes, just like regular documents. See "Protecting a Document," in Chapter 28, "Protecting and Securing Documents," for information about password-protecting and encrypting templates, making them read-only, and preventing them from being copied or emailed using Information Rights Management (IRM).

CREATING YOUR OWN TEMPLATES

One way to create a template is to save a modified template or document under a different name. That way, you can base the new template on an existing one and save yourself some time.

To create a template, you must first decide on the type to use. Review the template types explained in "About Templates" at the beginning of this chapter. Word 97-2003 templates are best when compatibility is an issue with earlier Word versions. Use the Word Template type for a template that will not need to include any macros; use the Word Macro-Enabled Template type for one that will.

Follow these steps to create a template:

1. Open the template or document on which you want to base the new template and then make any changes to it.

2. Choose Office, Save As. The Save As dialog box opens.

3. Open the Save as Type list and choose the desired template type (see Figure 10.11).

Figure 10.11
Set the Save as Type setting to reflect the desired template type.

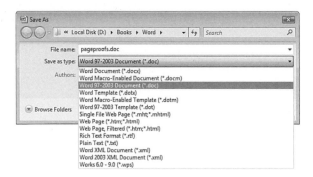

4. Navigate to the location in which you want to save the template. Refer to the locations listed in the preceding section, "Modifying Templates."

5. Click Save. The template is created.

When you choose to create a new document based on My Templates, the New dialog box appears. As you saw in Figure 10.5, by default this dialog box consists of a single tab: My Templates.

If you have a lot of templates to manage, consider creating additional tabs in this dialog box and grouping the templates into categories. To do this, create subfolders within the Templates folder, each with the name you want to assign to a tab, and then place the templates in the subfolders.

Follow these steps to create an additional tab and move some templates onto it:

1. Using the Windows Explorer, navigate to the folder where user templates are stored:

   For Windows Vista: Users*username*\\AppData\\Roaming\\Microsoft\\Templates.

   For Windows XP, Documents and Settings*username*\\Application Data\\Microsoft\\Templates, where *username* is the name with which you have logged into Windows.

2. Right-click an empty area of the window and choose New, Folder. A new folder appears.

3. Type a name for the new folder and press Enter.

4. Drag and drop one or more of the templates onto the icon for the new folder to move them into that folder.

Now return to Word 2007 and start creating a new document based on a user template. The New dialog box will now have an additional tab for the subfolder you created, and the template(s) you placed in that subfolder will appear on that tab.

CHANGING A DOCUMENT'S TEMPLATE

Most of the time, you'll start a document based on the template you want it to use. If you change your mind later, though, you can switch templates without having to re-create the document. You can also make additional templates available, so you can use any macros or building blocks from them, without changing the primary template assigned to the document.

Follow these steps to apply a different template to the document:

1. If the Developer tab does not appear, do the following to display it:

   a. Choose Office, Word Options.

   b. Click Popular.

   c. Click Show Developer Tab in the Ribbon.

   d. Click OK.

2. On the Developer tab, click the Document Template button. The Templates and Add-Ins dialog box opens, shown in Figure 10.12.

Figure 10.12
Use the Templates tab to change the template assigned to the document.

3. On the Templates tab, click Attach. The Attach Template dialog box appears.

4. Select the desired template from the Attach Template dialog box. (Navigate to the location containing the template.)

5. Click Open to return to the Templates tab.

6. (Optional) If you want the style definitions to update automatically to match the new template's definitions, mark the Automatically Update Document Styles check box.

7. Click OK.

If you use the Templates and Add-Ins dialog box frequently, consider adding a shortcut to it to the Quick Access toolbar. To do so, display the Developer ribbon, right-click the Document Template button, and choose Add to Quick Access Toolbar.

CAUTION

> Automatically updating document styles works only if the styles in the new template have the same names as the styles already applied to the text. If the new template uses different names for styles, you'll need to do a Find-and-Replace operation to replace all instances of the old style name with the new style name. See "Finding and Replacing" in Chapter 3, "Typing and Editing Text," for more information on Find-and-Replace operations.

APPLYING GLOBAL TEMPLATES

A *global template* is a template that makes its features available to all documents, not just when it is specifically applied. Some examples of global templates include Normal.dotm and Building Blocks.dotx; their content is available no matter what template is assigned to the current document.

→ For more information about building blocks, **see** "Working with Building Blocks," **p. 90**.

You can also make other templates available globally. For example, if you have a template that has some handy macros stored in it, you can designate that template to be global and have access to those macros in all documents.

To make a template global, follow these steps:

1. On the Quick Access toolbar, click the Templates and Add-Ins button. The Templates and Add-Ins dialog box opens, as shown in Figure 10.12.

   If the Templates and Add-Ins button does not appear on the Quick Access toolbar, add it, as you learned earlier in this section.

2. In the Global Templates and Add-Ins section of the Templates tab, click Add. The Add Template dialog box appears.

3. Select the template to add globally and click OK. It appears on the list (see Figure 10.13).

Figure 10.13
Add global templates to include their functionality in all documents.

4. (Optional) To enable or disable global templates, mark or clear their check boxes on the list. Or to remove a template from the list completely, select it and click Remove.

> **TIP**
>
> It is usually better to disable a global template than to remove it because it can be more easily reenabled later.

5. Click OK.

 If a template loads automatically at startup, you can't remove it from the list in the Templates and Add-Ins dialog box using the Remove button. See "I Can't Remove a Global Template from the List" in the "Troubleshooting" section at the end of this chapter.

Global templates remain enabled for as long as Word is running. If you close Word and reopen it again, the global template(s) you specified will still be on the list on the Templates tab (see Figure 10.13). However, their check boxes will not be marked. You must reopen the Templates and Add-Ins dialog box and re-mark their check boxes in each Word session.

ENABLING GLOBAL TEMPLATES AT STARTUP

If you find yourself reenabling the same global template(s) every time you start up Word, here's a shortcut. Copy the template into the Startup folder for Word: Users*username*\AppData\Roaming\Microsoft\Word\Startup (Windows Vista) or \Documents and Settings*username*\Application Data\Microsoft\Word\Startup (Windows XP). Doing so forces the template to load globally at startup. You can disable it if needed from the Templates and Add-Ins dialog box on a case-by-case basis.

 If unwanted global templates are loading at startup, see "Templates Are Loading at Startup That I Don't Want" in the "Troubleshooting" section at the end of this chapter.

AUTOMATICALLY CHANGING THE TEMPLATE OF ALL DOCUMENTS OPENED

Suppose your organization has been using a certain template for all documents, but now you've been given a new template and a directive to switch over all your documents to this new template.

One way to do that is to open each document and then manually switch the template assigned to the document and save/close it. An easier way, however, is to create a special macro called AutoOpen. Whatever commands you place in AutoOpen run automatically whenever you open a document. Save the AutoOpen macro in Normal.dotm.

Macro recording is covered in Chapter 33, "Add-Ins and Macros," but here's a quick overview:

1. Make sure you have already created a button for the Templates and Add-Ins dialog box on the Quick Access toolbar.

2. Click the Macro Recording button on the status bar (the document with the red circle). If you do not see this button on the status bar, right-click the status bar and click Macro Recording.

3. In the Record Macro dialog box, type **AutoOpen** as the macro name.

4. In the Store Macro In list, make sure All Documents (Normal.dotm) is selected.

5. Click OK to begin the recording.

6. Click the Templates and Add-Ins button on the Quick Access toolbar.

7. Click the Attach button, select the template to attach, and click Open.

8. Mark the Automatically Update Document Styles check box.

9. Click OK.

10. Click the Stop Macro button (the blue square that replaced the document with the red dot in the bottom-left corner of the Word window).

The macro is now created. To try it out, open a document that uses some other template, and then note whether the document's template changes.

To see what template a document is using, choose Office, Prepare, Properties, and then open the Document Properties menu and choose Advanced Properties. On the Summary tab of the dialog box that appears, you can find the template's name near the bottom of the dialog box.

To stop the macro from running automatically at startup, delete or rename the AutoOpen macro. For information about deleting and renaming macros, see "Renaming and Deleting Macros" in Chapter 33.

TROUBLESHOOTING

NORMAL.DOTM IS MISSING

If you have not made any changes to the default settings in Word, such as changing the default font, Normal.dotm will not appear in a file listing. In its default state, it is built into Word. It appears as a separate file only if you have changed it in some way.

To force it to appear, make some sort of change to the default settings. For example, on the Home tab, open the Font dialog box, change the font, and click the Default button. When prompted to change the default font, click Yes.

Normal.dotm will then appear in the default location for user templates. To browse to its folder, you might need to turn on the display of hidden files. See the next section for details.

CAN'T FIND THE APPLICATION DATA OR APPDATA FOLDER

The path for personal templates stored on your hard disk is:

Windows Vista: Users*username*\\AppData\\Roaming\\Microsoft\\Templates.

Windows XP: Documents and Settings*username*\\Application Data\\Microsoft\\Templates.

However, if you try to navigate to this folder in Windows, you might not be able to find it. That's because the Application Data or AppData folder is hidden by default.

To display hidden folders, follow these steps:

1. From any file management window:

   In Windows Vista: Choose Organize, Folder and Search Options.

   In Windows XP: Choose Tools, Folder Options.

   The Folder Options dialog box opens.

2. Click the View tab.

3. Click Show Hidden Files and Folders.

4. Click OK.

STYLES DO NOT UPDATE WHEN CHANGING THE TEMPLATE

Simply changing the template does not automatically change the formatting. For example, suppose the Heading 1 style is defined as 18-point Arial in the current document, and you apply a template that defines Heading 1 as 20-point Times New Roman. The existing Heading 1 text will not change automatically, but if you reapply Heading 1 to the text, it will change at that point. In addition, any new headings you create with the Heading 1 style will have the new definition.

To force the existing Heading 1 text to change, mark the Automatically Update Document Styles check box in the Templates and Add-Ins dialog box as you are applying the new template.

If that doesn't help, you can force all the styles in the document to update themselves in each instance by selecting the entire document (Ctrl+A) and then pressing Ctrl+Q.

NOT ALL STYLES FROM THE NEW TEMPLATE APPEAR ON THE STYLES LIST

Unless you mark the Automatically Update Document Styles check box in the Templates and Add-Ins dialog box, only the styles that are currently in use will appear on the Styles list for the new template. Go back and reapply the template, and this time mark the check box.

I WANT THE ORIGINAL VERSION OF NORMAL.DOTM

If you make changes to Normal.dotm that you later decide were ill-advised, or if Normal.dotm gets corrupted, you might want to go back to the original Normal.dotm that came with Word.

To revert to the original Normal.dotm, simply delete your customized copy of it. The next time you restart Word, it creates a fresh copy of Normal.dotm.

I CAN'T REMOVE A GLOBAL TEMPLATE FROM THE LIST

Global templates that are set to load at startup reside in:

In Windows Vista: Users*username*\\AppData\\Roaming\\Microsoft\\Word\\Startup

In Windows XP: Documents and Settings*username*\\Application Data\\Microsoft\\Word\\Startup

where *username* is the name with which you have logged into Windows.

These startup templates cannot be removed from the list in the Templates and Add-Ins dialog box (although they can be disabled from there). To remove one of these, you must delete it from the Startup folder outside of Word.

TEMPLATES ARE LOADING AT STARTUP THAT I DON'T WANT

Some third-party applications such as Adobe Acrobat set up Word templates to load at startup to provide tighter integration with other programs. In the case of Adobe Acrobat, the automatically loaded template provides a macro for creating a new PDF document using Acrobat.

If you see items in the Templates and Add-Ins dialog box that you don't recognize and don't want, and they appear to be marked by default at startup, here's how to get rid of them:

1. Exit from Word.
2. In Windows, navigate to the folder containing the startup templates:

   In Windows Vista: Users*username*\\AppData\\Roaming\\Microsoft\\Word\\Startup

   In Windows XP: Documents and Settings*username*\\Application Data\\Microsoft\\Word\\Startup

   where *username* is the name with which you have logged into Windows.
3. Delete the unwanted templates, or copy them elsewhere, or rename them so that they do not have a template file extension anymore (and therefore Word won't recognize them as templates).
4. Restart Word and then confirm that the templates no longer automatically load.

CHAPTER 11

WORKING WITH NONSTANDARD DOCUMENT LAYOUTS

In this chapter

CREATING TEXT BOX LAYOUTS

Word is obviously well-suited to writing ordinary documents such as reports, letters, and memos, but it also has some other uses that most people never get a chance to explore. In this chapter, you'll learn about some of the interesting things Word can do with nonstandard layouts.

Text box layouts are layouts in which text is not typed directly onto the page, but instead placed in floating text boxes. This type of page layout has many advantages, and in fact that's the standard operating mode for most professional-quality desktop publishing programs, including Adobe InDesign and QuarkXpress, as well as consumer-level publishing programs such as Microsoft Publisher and presentation programs such as PowerPoint. Each text box can be moved around on the page freely, so the text need not follow a strict top-to-bottom flow. Figure 11.1 shows an example of a page layout constructed with text boxes.

Figure 11.1
Text boxes make it possible to place text precisely where you want it on the page.

T I P

Text boxes are single-column by nature. Need a multicolumn text box? Use a table instead. **See** Chapter 12, "Creating and Formatting Tables."

INSERTING A TEXT BOX

Word 2007 includes a variety of text box building blocks for quickly inserting preformatted boxes with sample text. (Yes, it's the same building blocks feature as is used with AutoText, headers and footers, and page numbering.)

To insert a preset text box, display the Insert tab, click Text Box, and then click one of the presets on the menu (see Figure 11.2). Then click inside the text box and edit the sample text as desired.

Figure 11.2
Select a text box preset.

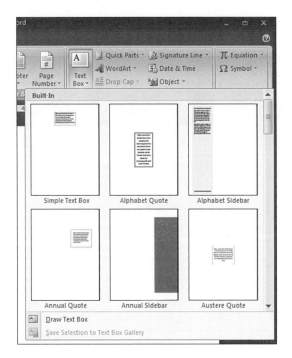

If none of the presets are to your liking, you can draw your own text box anywhere on the page, and then format it and place text in it later. To draw a text box, follow these steps:

1. From the Insert tab, click Text Box and then click Draw Text Box. The mouse pointer changes to a crosshair.

2. Drag to draw a text box on the page. When you release the mouse button, the text box appears and the Format tab appears.

   The default text box style is a thin solid black border and a white fill.

3. Click inside the text box and type text into it.

CAUTION

Text boxes can hold almost anything that the document itself can hold—text, graphics, tables, fields, and so on. There are a few exceptions, however. Text boxes cannot contain multiple columns or column breaks, page breaks, drop caps, comments, footnotes, endnotes, or markings for indexes and tables of contents.

If you need to use comments, footnotes, endnotes, or index/TOC markings in a text box, convert it to a frame, as described later in the chapter. (Unfortunately, frames do not accept multiple columns, page breaks, and drop caps, so using one will not help you with those items.)

To select a text box, click it. When a text box is selected, it has its own indent markers on the ruler; set those as you would in any document (see Figure 11.3).

Indent markers for text box

Figure 11.3
A text box has its own ruler settings.

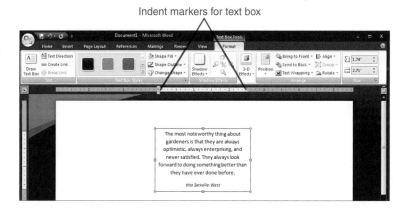

When a text box is selected, a Format tab appears containing options for formatting the text box. The following sections explore those options.

MOVING AND RESIZING A TEXT BOX

To move a text box, select it by clicking it so that a border with selection handles appears around it (see Figure 11.4). Then to move the text box, drag it by its border (but not by a selection handle), or to resize it, drag any selection handle. If you need the text box to be a precise size, enter values in the Height and Width boxes on the Format tab.

Set an exact width

Set an exact height

Figure 11.4
Move or resize a text
box by dragging.

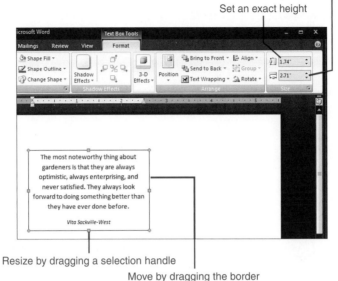

Resize by dragging a selection handle

Move by dragging the border

Another way to enter height and width values is via the text box's Properties box:

1. Right-click the border of the text box and choose Format Text Box. The Format Text Box dialog box appears.

2. Click the Size tab.

3. Enter values in the Height and Width sections. If the Absolute option button is not already selected in each section, select it, so absolute measurements are entered (see Figure 11.5).

4. Click OK.

NOTE

Absolute is the default for both height and width for drawn text boxes, but for some of the preset ones, the width value is set to Relative and set at a percentage of the page width. (A relative width enables the same building blocks to be used on different paper sizes and take up the same proportional amount of space.)

11

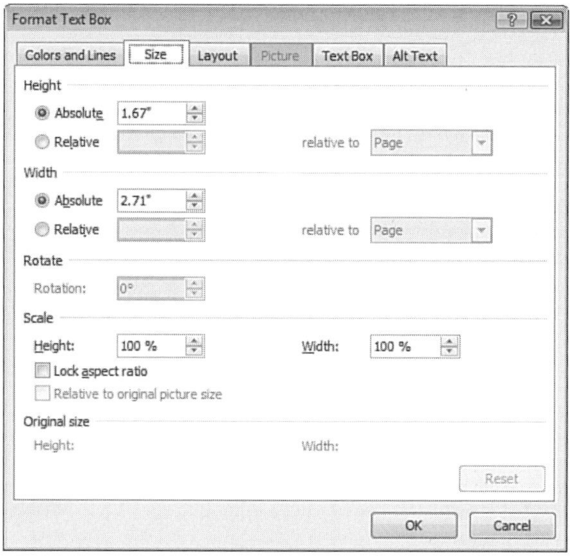

Figure 11.5
Specify a height and width in the properties for the text box.

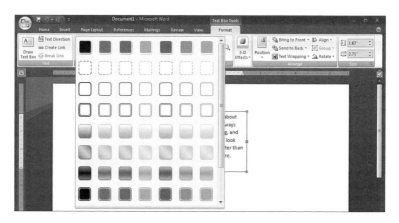

APPLYING AND REMOVING TEXT BOX BORDERS AND FILLS

Word 2007 provides a wide variety of style presets that can be applied to text boxes. There are 10 different styles, and each is available in seven different colors. Select the text box and then open the Text Box Styles list from the Format tab and make your selection, as shown in Figure 11.6.

Figure 11.6
Select a formatting style for the text box.

> **TIP**
>
> To copy formatting from one text box to another, use the Format Painter button on the Home tab.

→ To learn about Format Painter, **see** "Copying Formatting with Format Painter," **p. 180**.

If you're using text boxes for document layout, rather than as decorative aids, you probably don't want to do much with their formatting, and in fact you probably want most text boxes to be invisible (no border, no fill).

By default, drawn text boxes have visible borders; here's how to turn off the border on a text box:

1. Select the text box.
2. Display the Format tab.
3. Open the Shape Outline button's list and choose No Outline.

And here's how to remove the fill, if one is applied:

1. Select the text box.
2. Display the Format tab.
3. Open the Shape Fill button's list and choose No Fill.

Need more control? There's a whole lot you can do to fine-tune the text box's line and fill. Display the Format tab, and use the Shape Fill, Shape Outline, 3-D Effects, and Shadow Effects controls. These controls work the same for text boxes as they do for AutoShapes, so I won't cover them here; instead, flip over to Chapter 15, "Working with Drawings and WordArt," for the details.

→ To learn about line, fill, shadow, and 3D options, **see** "Creating and Modifying a WordArt Object," **p. 484**.

CHANGING THE TEXT BOX SHAPE

Text boxes are rectangular by default, but can be converted to any of a variety of shapes— rounded rectangles, circles, ovals, parallelograms, diamonds, and more.

Technically, when you change the shape of a text box, it ceases to be a text box, and becomes instead an AutoShape.

NOTE

After you've changed the shape, right-clicking the border no longer offers a Format Text Box command; instead, the command is Format AutoShape. It doesn't radically change any properties of the text box.

Here's how to change the shape of a text box:

1. Select the text box.
2. On the Format tab, click Change Shape and then click the desired shape (see Figure 11.7).

Figure 11.7
Select a shape for the text box.

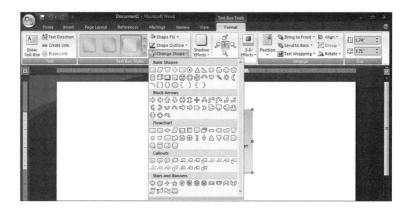

Even though the text box may have an asymmetric shape, the text within it still conforms to a rectangular area. For example, in a parallelogram in Figure 11.8, the lines do not begin at different positions to hug the borders of the shape; instead, the text is confined to a small area in the center that does not overlap any borders.

Figure 11.8
A text box with a parallelogram shape.

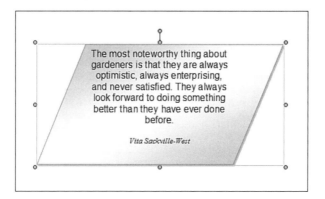

The most noteworthy thing about gardeners is that they are always optimistic, always enterprising, and never satisfied. They always look forward to doing something better than they have ever done before.

Vita Sackville-West

SETTING TEXT BOX MARGINS AND VERTICAL ALIGNMENT

By default, a text box has 0.1" left and right internal margins and 0.05" top and bottom internal margins. These margins allow the text to fill the text box completely but not quite touch the border lines.

Vertical alignment is the placement of the text within the text box vertically. If there is not enough text to fill the entire text box vertically, where will the blank space occur? Text boxes have a default vertical alignment of Top, so any blank space appears at the bottom.

To change either of these settings, use the Format Text Box dialog box (or Format AutoShape, if you have changed the text box's shape). Follow these steps:

1. Right-click the border of the text box and choose Format Text Box (or Format AutoShape).

2. Click the Text Box tab.

3. Change the Left, Right, Top, and/or Bottom internal margin settings (see Figure 11.9).

4. Change the vertical alignment setting if desired. The choices are Top, Center, and Bottom.

5. Click OK.

Figure 11.9
Set internal margins and vertical alignment for the text box.

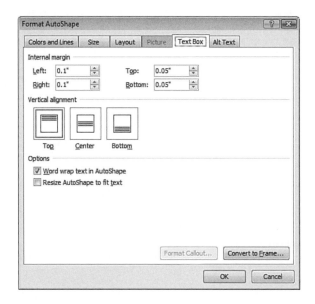

WRAPPING TEXT AROUND A TEXT BOX

When a text box overlaps with regular document text, it interacts with it according to the Text Wrapping setting you specify. These are the same text-wrapping settings as for AutoShapes, photos, clip art, and all other types of content. These wrap settings are covered in detail in "Setting Text Wrap" in Chapter 13, "Working with Photos," but here's a quick summary of the process:

1. Select the text box, and display the Format tab for it.

2. Click the Text Wrapping button, opening a menu of wrap choices.

3. Click the desired wrapping style:

   - **Square**—Wraps text around both sides of the text box in a rectangular shape.

   - **Tight**—For a rectangular text box, this is the same as Square. For a text box with some other shape (as covered in the preceding section), it wraps the text around the shape.

   - **Behind Text**—The text box is placed behind the text, so the text runs over the top of it. This one is not recommended for text boxes.

   - **In Front of Text**—The text box is placed on top of the text, so the text runs behind it. Usually not a great choice because the text is obscured.

- **Top and Bottom**—The text wraps around the text box above and below it, but the space to the left and right of the text box remains empty.

- **Through**—Same as Tight except somewhat tighter if it's an irregular-shaped object like a piece of clip art

You can also choose Advanced Layout for a dialog box with a few other choices, or choose Edit Wrap Points to manually edit the points around which the text wraps.

→ To edit wrap points or use advanced wrapping options, **see** "Setting Text Wrap," **p. 402**.

LINKING TEXT BOXES

In magazine and newspaper publishing lingo, all the text for a particular article is called a *story*. When a story fills up one text box and continues to another, the two text boxes are said to be *linked*.

A story-based layout with text boxes in Word is accomplished by creating multiple text boxes and linking them together with the Link Text Box command, as follows:

1. Create all the text boxes needed for the story.

   NOTE

   If the text for the story is already typed, it should all appear in the *first* text box. All other text boxes must be empty or it won't work. Many people find it easier to create the story in a separate document and then cut and paste it into the set of linked text boxes after the links have been configured.

2. Right-click the border of the first text box and choose Create Text Box Link. The mouse pointer turns into an upright pitcher.

   TIP

   As an alternate method for step 2, you can click the Create Text Box Link button on the Text Box Tools tab.

3. Position the mouse pointer over the center of the text box that will be linked next in the chain. The mouse pointer turns into a tilted pitcher (see Figure 11.10).

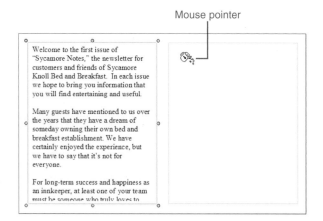

Figure 11.10
The tilted pitcher mouse pointer indicates the link is ready to be "poured" into the text box.

4. Click to create the link.

5. If there are more text boxes to link, right-click the second text box and then link it to the third, then the third to the fourth, and so on until all text boxes are linked.

6. Type the story, starting in the first text box.

   Alternatively, paste the story into the first text box, and it will flow into the others automatically.

Unlike in some other desktop publishing programs, Word does not have an indicator to show overflow text, so if there is nowhere for excess text to go (for example, no subsequent linked text boxes), it is simply truncated. The text still exists, though, and if you enlarge the text box or link another box to it, the truncated text will reappear.

MOVING BETWEEN LINKED BOXES

As you are typing and editing text in a linked set of text boxes, you can right-click a text box's border and choose Next Text Box or Previous Text Box to quickly jump from box to box. This is especially handy if the boxes are not on the same page. (Often in a magazine or newsletter, a story is continued many pages away from the first page, for example.)

BREAKING THE LINK

If a story does not run as long as you expected, you might want to delete the unneeded boxes, or break the link to the unused boxes so they can be used for some other story.

To break a link, do the following:

1. Display the text box that should be the last box in the chain. (All boxes after this one will be unlinked.)

2. Right-click the text box border and choose Break Forward Link.

CHANGING THE TEXT DIRECTION

One advantage of a text box is that you can set the text to run vertically in it. This enables you to create interesting special effects, such as a newsletter title that runs vertically along the left side of the page, as in Figure 11.11.

Text Direction button

Figure 11.11
Vertical text in a text box.

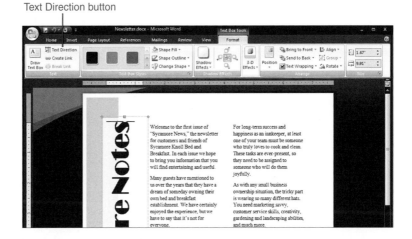

Word supports three text directions: Horizontal, Vertical (Top to Bottom), and Vertical (Bottom to Top). To toggle between these, click the Text Direction button on the Format tab.

TIPS FOR CREATING TEXT BOX LAYOUTS

In desktop publishing programs such as Publisher, Adobe InDesign, and QuarkXpress, it is easy to place the text boxes in the same spots on every page because you can place nonprinting guide lines on each page. Word does not have guide lines per se, but it does have a non-printing grid you can toggle on and off.

To toggle the grid, on the View tab mark or clear the Gridlines check box. Gridlines appear in Print Layout view only.

In addition, here are some other ways to ensure consistent placement of objects between pages:

■ Use the Height and Width controls on the Format tab to make sure that each text box is the same size, and then use the Align and Distribute controls (also on the Format tab) to place them evenly on the page.

→ To learn about Align and Distribute, **see** "Aligning and Distributing Objects," **p. 471**.

■ Create one text box the way you want it and then copy it to create the others, ensuring consistent size and shape. To copy a text box, hold down Ctrl as you drag its border (not a selection handle).

■ Create one page the way you want it, with all the text boxes in place, and save that page as a building block. On the Insert tab, click Quick Parts and then choose Save Selection to Quick Part Gallery. Make sure to change the Options setting to Insert Content in Its Own Page. You can then insert that page as many times as needed to duplicate the page layout.

→ To create your own sample pages with building blocks, **see** "Saving Content as a New Cover Page," **p. 275**.

- Create temporary content to serve as guides. For example, if you want guides for creating three equal-sized columns, set Columns to 3 (Page Layout tab), set the paragraph background shading to a color, and then press Enter enough times to fill an entire page. The result is three empty-but-shaded columns. Then drag your text boxes on top of those, and remove the shading when finished.

WORKING WITH FRAMES

A text box is technically a graphic object, not part of the main document. That's fine in most cases, and in fact it provides some formatting benefits. For example, as you saw earlier, you have access to all the same line and fill formatting options as with AutoShapes, including 3D and shadow effects.

However, there are certain special-purpose cases in which the fact that text box text resides in the graphics layer can be problematic. One is that you can't use any automatically numbered reference elements in a text box, such as footnotes, comments, and captions. You also can't use certain fields that automatically number things based on their position in the document, such as AUTONUM and AUTONUMLGL. That makes sense if you think about it—if each text box is a separate graphical unit, it has no relationship to the document's main body.

NOTE

Here's a complete list of the fields that work only in frames, not in text boxes: AUTONUM, AUTONUMLGL, AUTONUMOUT, TC, TOC, RD, XE, TA, and TOA.

The solution in these cases is to convert the text boxes into frames. Frames are part of the text layer, so they can use all the aforementioned reference elements, but the frames are sectioned off from the main text (which can wrap around them).

CAUTION

With a frame, you give up some of the formatting functionality of a text box, and you lose the ability to link. A linked text box cannot be converted to a frame. You must remove the link first.

To convert a text box to a frame, follow these steps:

1. Right-click the text box's border and choose Format Text Box.
2. Click the Text Box tab and then click the Convert to Frame button.
3. A warning appears; click OK. The text box becomes a frame.

You cannot convert from a frame to a text box; you must create a new text box and then cut and paste the text from the frame into it.

The most immediately apparent difference between a frame and a text box is that on a frame, the selection handles are black squares, whereas on a text box, they are greenish-blue circles. The black squares indicate that the frame is an inline object in the document, part of the text.

To format a frame, right-click its border and choose Format Frame. The Frame dialog box opens, as shown in Figure 11.12. From here you can do the following:

- Set the text wrapping around the frame. However, it is limited to None (same as Top and Bottom for a text box) or Around (same as Square for a text box).

- Set the size of the frame, either to exact measurements or to Auto (to change the frame size based on the contents).

- Set the horizontal and vertical positions of the frame, in relation to the margin, column, or page.

- Specify whether or not the frame should move with the text. For example, if you add more text above the frame, should the frame shift down, or should it stay static?

- Specify whether to lock the frame's anchor. The anchor marks the position on the page.

Figure 11.12
Set frame properties in the Frame dialog box.

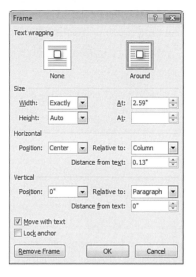

The Frame dialog box also contains a Remove Frame button. Use this to place the frame's text into the main document as regular text and delete the frame. The text from the frame is placed at the location of the frame's anchor point.

CREATING BANNERS

Word is perhaps not the best program for creating large-format items such as posters and banners because it doesn't have any special features in that regard. Microsoft Publisher, if available, is a more satisfactory solution. However, Word will serve in a pinch, and this section explains how to make that happen.

The challenge when working with large-format items is that most people don't have a large-format printer, so they end up printing pieces of the document on separate sheets and then knitting them together with tape or staples. Most printers have a "dead" area of about 1/4" around all sides of a printed page, so when creating pages designed to be pasted together, you'll need to figure in at least 1/2" of overlap area between them (1/4" on each page where two pages come together). In practice, however, it is better to leave even more space than that for overlap to simplify the connections.

Each panel of a multisheet banner is a separate page in Word. The pages can be Landscape in orientation for a banner that is 8.5" high or Portrait for a banner that is 11" high.

→ To switch between portrait and landscape page orientation, **see** "Setting Page Orientation," **p. 269**.

The best way to create a banner in Word is to start with a Microsoft-provided template, and then modify it as dictated by the needs of your project. The Microsoft templates have divider lines that show where the copies will join, taking the guesswork out of the overlap. Once you've used the template a few times and have an idea of how things work, you can create your own from-scratch versions. Search the Office Online templates for the word *banner* to locate appropriate templates to use.

→ To review how to create a document by using a template, **see** "Starting a New Document Based on a Template," **p. 300**.

Figure 11.13 shows a birthday banner in Print Preview, created from a template. Notice that each panel is a separate page, and that each page has dotted vertical lines on it showing where the pages should be overlapped. You can either fold the pages or cut along the dotted lines to prepare them.

Figure 11.13
A multisheet banner created in Word.

When it comes time to create your own banner designs, here are some tips:

■ For graphic elements that repeat on each page, such as the colored bar below the letters in Figure 11.13, place them in the page header and footer rather than copying them onto every sheet individually.

■ Use the drawing tools in Word to draw the vertical dotted lines that will guide your cutting or folding. To make it less obvious if you don't cut the lines quite right, use a very light color for the lines, such as pale gray.

■ Use text boxes to place the text on the banner rather than placing the text directly onto the page. To make sure the text boxes are the same size and position on every page, use the Clipboard to copy a text box from one page and paste it on another page.

■ Try to make page breaks wherever there are natural breaks in the text, such as between letters or words.

■ Do not attempt a patterned background; it's too hard to get the pieces lined up. In fact, it's best to just stick with a plain background. Use colored paper if you want.

ADDRESSING ENVELOPES

There are two ways to print envelopes in Word: You can print a single envelope at a time (or multiple copies, but all addressed to the same person), or you can do a mail merge and print lots of envelopes at once, all addressed to different people. The latter is a huge topic all its own, and it's covered separately in Chapter 18, "Performing Mail and Data Merges." In this chapter, you'll learn about creating single envelopes, storing addresses for them, and placing them in letter documents.

ADDING AN ENVELOPE TO A LETTER

Ready to generate an envelope for the letter you've just typed? Word can do it automatically. It even pulls out the delivery address from the letter and places it on the envelope.

Follow these steps to create an envelope layout:

1. In the letter you've composed, select the complete delivery address.
2. On the Mailings tab, click Envelopes. The Envelopes and Labels dialog box appears, with the recipient's address in the Delivery Address box (see Figure 11.14).
3. If your return address does not already appear in the Return Address box, type it there. (Word remembers it after you enter it initially.)

   Or, if you are going to print on an envelope with a preprinted return address, mark the Omit check box.

Figure 11.14
Word identifies the recipient address and places it in the Delivery Address box.

4. Change the envelope size if needed. (This is covered in the next section.)

5. Click Add to Document. Word creates a new section above the main letter, with an appropriate page size for the envelope size you chose and with the delivery and return addresses filled in (see Figure 11.15).

Figure 11.15
An envelope is its own section in the document, with its own page size.

11

NOTE

> If you don't need the envelope to be stored with the document, click Print to send the envelope directly to the printer instead of adding it to the document.

SETTING THE ENVELOPE SIZE

The default envelope size is Size 10, which is a regular business envelope in the United States (4 1/8"×9 1/2"). To change to a different size, click the Options button in the Envelopes and Labels dialog box. Then in the Envelope Options dialog box, select a different Envelope Size setting from the list provided (see Figure 11.16).

Figure 11.16
Choose an envelope size.

If none of the sizes matches your envelope, choose Custom Size. The Envelope Size dialog box opens, in which you can enter the exact dimensions of the envelope you have.

CHANGING THE ADDRESS POSITION

Usually the default address positions work well; Word places the return address in the upper-left corner of the envelope, about 1/2" from the top and left edges, and places the delivery address in the center horizontally and slightly lower than center vertically.

To change the position of either of these addresses, click the Options button in the Envelopes and Labels dialog box and then change the From Left and From Top values as needed.

CHANGING THE ENVELOPE FONT

If you add the envelope to the document, you can then select the addresses and change their font formatting afterward.

However, if you choose not to add the envelope to the document—that is, if you send it directly to the printer with the Print button—then there is no opportunity to change the font after the fact, so you must set the desired font within the Envelope Options dialog box.

From the Envelopes and Labels dialog box, click Options, displaying the Envelope Options dialog box (refer to Figure 11.16). Then in the Delivery Address area, click Font. The Envelope Address dialog box opens, which looks very much like the Font dialog box you worked with in Chapter 6, "Applying Character Formatting." Change the font, style, size, color, and so on, and then click OK to accept the changes (see Figure 11.17). Then do the same thing for the return address.

Figure 11.17
Choose font formatting for the delivery address.

PRINTING AN ENVELOPE

To quickly print the envelope, click the Print button in the Envelopes and Labels dialog box. (You can reopen the dialog box by clicking the Envelopes button again on the Mailings tab if needed.) One copy of the envelope (only) prints on the default printer. It happens immediately; the Print dialog box does not appear.

Do you need more control than that? Perhaps you need multiple copies of the envelope, or a different printer than the default? For this, you must have added the envelope to the document. Just click the envelope (moving the insertion point onto its page), and choose Office, Print. In the Print dialog box, set the Page Range to Current Page, choose the desired printer and number of copies, and click OK to print.

CONTROLLING HOW ENVELOPES FEED INTO YOUR PRINTER

Word recommends an envelope feed orientation based on the default printer's driver information. That recommendation appears in the Feed area of the Envelopes and Labels dialog box.

Sometimes, however, the default envelope feed orientation won't work for some reason. For example, perhaps it is based on having an envelope tray that feeds the envelopes in centered, but you don't have such a tray so you're feeding the envelopes in at the left edge of the paper guide. Or perhaps the default orientation is to feed the envelope in head-first, but the printer's paper carriage width isn't wide enough for a large envelope.

To change the envelope printing orientation, follow these steps:

1. In the Envelopes and Labels dialog box, click the picture in the Feed area. The Envelope Options dialog box opens with the Printing Options tab displayed.

2. Click a picture that best represents the feed orientation needed (see Figure 11.18).

Figure 11.18
Choose an envelope feed orientation.

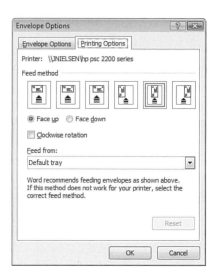

3. Click the Face Up or Face Down button, as appropriate. (This setting doesn't change which side of the page Word prints on, except if you have a duplex-capable printer, but it does change the graphic shown to help you remember how to place the envelopes in the paper tray.)

4. If you're feeding the envelope in sideways, if the return address prints to the right, click Clockwise Rotation.

5. (Optional) Select a different paper tray in the Feed From list if needed.

6. Click OK.

STORING AND RETRIEVING ADDRESSES

After you've entered a return address, Word offers to save it as the default return address. If you click Yes, it fills in that same return address automatically for all future envelopes.

You can also select an address from the Address Book that is used in Windows Mail and Microsoft Outlook 2007. To do so, follow these steps:

1. Click the Insert Address icon above either the Delivery Address or Return Address box in the Envelopes and Labels dialog box.
2. If prompted to select a mail profile, choose the desired profile and click OK.
3. In the Select Name dialog box, addresses appear from your Outlook contact list or from the mail system associated with the profile you chose in step 2.

   Depending on the mail programs installed, you might have more than one address book available. Select from the Address Book drop-down list at the top-right corner of the dialog box.
4. Click OK. The address is filled into the Delivery Address or Return Address box.

ADDING GRAPHICS TO AN ENVELOPE

There's no special feature for adding envelope graphics, but all the regular graphics tools can be used to place a graphic on an envelope that has been added to the document. You can use clip art, logo graphics, WordArt, and so on. Here's a quick list of cross-references for learning about various graphic types:

- **Graphics from files**—**See** "Inserting Pictures from Files," **p. 401**.
- **Clip art**—**See** "Finding and Inserting Clip Art," **p. 428**.
- **WordArt**—**See** "Creating and Modifying a WordArt Object," **p. 484**.
- **AutoShapes**—**See** "Drawing an AutoShape," **p. 456**.

After inserting a graphic on the envelope and positioning it appropriately, you might find it useful to save the graphic (and optionally the return address with it) as a building block. You can then insert that building block into future envelope layouts, saving yourself the trouble of reimporting the graphic each time. See "Creating a Building Block" in Chapter 3, "Typing and Editing Text," for more information.

USING E-POSTAGE WITH WORD

If you use a third-party postage service such as Stamps.com, it can be accessed via Word's Envelope feature. Such systems save you trips to the post office by enabling you to print government-approved postage directly onto your envelopes. You then pay your monthly postage bill by credit card through the service.

First, of course, you must sign up for a service. When you mark the Add Electronic Postage check box (or try to) in the Envelopes and Labels dialog box, and you haven't yet installed any postage software on your PC, a message appears offering to open the Microsoft Office website so you can find out more about e-postage. Click Yes to visit that page and find a link for signing up.

Once you've signed up and the postage software is installed, the Envelopes and Labels dialog box will allow you to mark the Add Electronic Postage check box, and the E-Postage Properties option will become available. (Click E-Postage Properties to set up options such as certified or registered mail or insurance.)

11

The exact steps for adding e-postage depend on the service you are using. For example, Stamps.com's service checks the delivery address you entered to make sure it is valid, makes corrections if needed, and prompts you for the weight and mailing date. Just follow the self-explanatory prompts to complete the postage purchase.

CREATING LABELS

As with envelopes, there are two ways of printing labels in Word. You can print individual labels (or a sheet containing multiple copies of the same label), or you can do a mail merge that creates one label apiece for a whole list of addressees. The latter is covered in Chapter 18, "Performing Mail and Data Merges." In this chapter, you'll learn how to create and print individual labels only.

To print labels, you will need special label paper. There are many brands and sizes of labels; most come in full 8.5"×11" sheets, with perforated peel-off labels. Word recognizes the model numbers for many popular brands and sizes, and you can also set up custom labels in situations where none of Word's presets are appropriate.

CAUTION

> Make sure you buy the type of label sheets designed for your printer type. Labels designed for inkjet printers cannot withstand the heat generated by the laser printing process, and might become curled or wrinkled—or worse yet, peel off or melt inside the printer—if used with a laser printer. Laser labels will work okay in inkjet printers, but the ink might not stick to them quite as well because laser label paper tends to be less porous.

PRINTING A FULL PAGE OF THE SAME LABEL

One common use of the Labels feature is to create return address labels for packages and other mailings. You can get really creative with these and include graphics, photos, colors, fancy fonts, and so on, or you can go strictly utilitarian.

NOTE

> It doesn't matter whether you start from an existing document or a new one when creating labels because Word automatically creates a new document to hold the labels.

To print a basic label, follow these steps:

1. On the Mailings tab, click Labels. The Envelopes and Labels dialog box opens with the Labels tab displayed (see Figure 11.19).

Figure 11.19
Set up a label for printing.

2. In the Address box, type the address to appear on the label. (It doesn't really have to be an address; you can put any text you want here, such as THIS END UP or FRAGILE or HAVE A NICE DAY.)

   You can also select an address from your Address Book; see "Storing and Retrieving Addresses" earlier in this chapter.

CAUTION

To use the address that's currently stored as your default return address, mark the Use Return Address check box.

3. In the Print area, choose Full Page of the Same Label.
4. (Optional) Change the label size or type if needed. To do so:
   a. Click the sample in the Label area. The Label Options dialog box opens.
   b. In the Printer Information area, select Continuous Feed Printers or Page Printers.

NOTE

A continuous feed printer uses a tractor-feed style of label, usually one label per row. Most continuous feed printers are dot matrix. The model numbers are different for this type of label than for page printers. Most page printers are inkjet or laser.

   c. Select the label manufacturer from the Label Vendors list. This sets up the model numbers.

    d. Select the model number from the Product Number list. In the Label Information area, confirm that the height and page size matches up with the label sheet's actual content.

       If you can't find the right number, see "Creating a Custom Label Specification" below.

    e. Click OK.

5. Click Print to send the print job directly to the printer (make sure your label sheet is loaded) or click New Document to create a new document containing the label sheet (which you can then edit as needed before printing).

PRINTING A SINGLE LABEL

Printing a single label is similar to printing a full sheet, except for one thing: When you're printing a single label, you're probably reusing a label sheet that is already missing one or more labels. So follow the steps in the preceding section, but in step 3, choose Single Label. Then enter the Row and Column numbers that describe the first available label on the sheet.

CAUTION

> Some label sheets don't feed through the printer very well when some of the labels are missing. If you find that paper jams occur frequently when reusing a label sheet, try using a different printer. Inkjet printers are often more forgiving of paper feed issues than laser printers are, for example.

CREATING A CUSTOM LABEL SPECIFICATION

If you're using a generic label brand and you don't know the equivalent model number for a well-known brand, you have a choice: You can browse through the product numbers for a well-known brand such as Avery until you find one that matches up with what you've got, or you can create a new custom label specification.

TIP

> Avery is the most popular manufacturer of labels; you will probably find what you want in the Avery Standard set.

To create a new label specification, follow these steps:

1. From the Labels tab of the Envelopes and Labels dialog box, click Options. The Label Options dialog box opens.

2. Select an existing label that closely matches the label you want to create. (It doesn't have to be exact.)

3. Click the New Label button. The New Custom dialog box opens.

4. Type a name for the new label in the Label Name box.

5. Change any of the label measurements or specifications as needed. Refer to the Preview area for what each measurement represents (see Figure 11.20).

6. Click OK to create the new label specification. The new label appears at the top of the Product Number list in the Label Options dialog box, and the Label Products box changes to Other/Custom.

Figure 11.20
Create a new custom label specification.

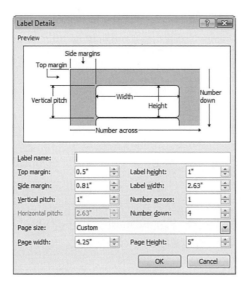

7. Click OK to accept the new custom label as the layout to use.

8. Continue printing normally.

FINE-TUNING THE LABEL APPEARANCE

Use the New Document button in the Envelopes and Labels dialog box to create a new document containing the sheet of labels for printing. You can then save it for later use like any other document.

A side benefit of creating a new document is that you can customize the labels before printing them. For example, you can change the font, size, color, or other attributes of the text.

The new document that holds the labels is laid out as a table. By default, the table gridlines are hidden, but you can display them by displaying the Layout tab and clicking Show Gridlines.

You can do anything with the labels that you can do with table cells, as covered in Chapter 12, "Creating and Formatting Tables." For example, you might add a colored background to the table cells. Here's how to do that:

1. Select the entire table by clicking the table selector box (the four-headed arrow box in the table's upper-left corner).

2. Right-click the table selector box and choose Borders and Shading.

3. Click the Shading tab.

4. Open the Fill list and choose a color.

5. Click OK. All the labels now have a shaded background.

That's just one example. Check out Chapter 12 to learn what else you can do with table formatting. Don't change the row heights or column widths, though, and don't add cell border lines, because those things can interfere with the appearance of the printed labels.

CREATING FOLDED NOTE CARDS

First, the bad news: Word is not the ideal program for creating special-paper projects like folded note cards. It doesn't have any of the friendly built-in helpers for such tasks like Microsoft Publisher does, so you have to either start with a template (if one is available that meets your needs) or set everything up manually. Nevertheless, sometimes Word is the only thing available and must be made to serve.

A folded note card is a printing challenge because certain fold types require some of the text to appear upside-down. For example, one of the most common layouts is a *quarter-fold* card, in which you fold a regular 8.5"×11" sheet of paper twice (see Figure 11.21).

Figure 11.21
A quarter-fold note card is printed with half the text upside-down so it will look right when folded.

Special note card paper is available that works in *half-fold* layout, meaning the sheet of paper is folded only once. This results in a card that is more like a store-bought greeting card. (The paper packs usually come with envelopes of the correct size for use with the cards.)

Custom paper size presents one challenge to this half-fold type of layout. There are various sizes of cards available, and most of them don't conform to any of the preset paper sizes in Word. (Their envelopes are often nonstandard sizes too.)

Depending on the fold location, other issues arise as well; for a top-fold card, half the content must be printed upside-down, and for both top- and side-fold cards, half the content must be printed on the opposite side of the paper.

The following sections explain how to address these challenges to create folded note cards in Word.

USING CARD TEMPLATES

Many greeting card templates are available in Word via Office Online, and these are great for helping you get started. Certain templates are designed for certain sizes of greeting card paper manufactured by Avery, and the Avery model numbers are indicated in the template names where applicable. Other templates are designated half-fold or quarter-fold for regular paper. Search for templates using the keywords *greeting card*, as you learned in Chapter 10, "Using and Creating Project Templates."

→ To review how to create a document by using a template, **see** "Starting a New Document Based on a Template," **p. 300**.

The templates are especially advantageous for quarter-fold cards because they already have placeholders for the upside-down parts. Rather than having to make upside-down text yourself, you edit what's there.

SPECIFYING THE PAPER SIZE AND TYPE

To specify the paper type and size, display the Page Layout tab and choose Size, More Paper Sizes. In the Paper Size list, select the paper size if it happens to appear there, or choose Custom Size from the bottom of the list and enter the exact size of the card sheet.

→ For more information about custom paper sizes, **see** "Setting Paper Size," **p. 269**.

Paper *type* cannot be controlled in Word itself, but some printers enable you to set a paper type in their driver. This can be useful on printers that treat paper with different coatings differently, such as printing in a higher resolution on glossy paper than on matte, or allowing for different feed roller positions for very thick cardstock paper. To explore the printer's paper settings, do the following:

1. Choose Office, Print to open the Print dialog box.
2. Select the desired printer and then click Properties.
3. Look for options for controlling the paper type, and set them to match the paper used for the card.
4. Click OK and continue printing normally.

CREATING UPSIDE-DOWN TEXT

Technically, Word cannot produce upside-down text. That is, nothing that Word considers to be "text" can be upside-down.

There are ways around every limitation, though, and in this case the solution is provided by WordArt. You can create a WordArt text object and then rotate the object 180 degrees. It's not really text—it's a graphic that looks just like text—but your audience will never know the difference.

WordArt is covered in detail in Chapter 15, "Working with Drawings and WordArt," but here's a quick preview of how to use it to create upside-down text for a card:

1. On the Insert tab, click WordArt and then click the first sample on the list (plain black outlined text). The Edit WordArt Text dialog box opens.

2. In the dialog box, type the desired text. Change the Font, Size, and Bold/Italic settings if desired (see Figure 11.22).

Figure 11.22
Enter the text that should appear upside-down on the card.

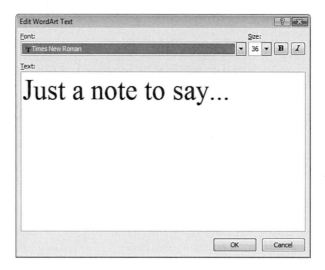

3. Click OK. The text appears on the page, and the Format tab appears.

4. Open the Shape Fill list and select a fill color.

5. Open the Shape Outline list and select a color for the outer line or choose No Outline.

6. Click the Text Wrapping button and choose Square, making the text floatable so you can drag it where you want it on the layout (see Figure 11.23).

Controls border color

Controls interior color   Controls text wrap

Figure 11.23
Edit the WordArt's fill
color, border color,
and text wrap setting
here.

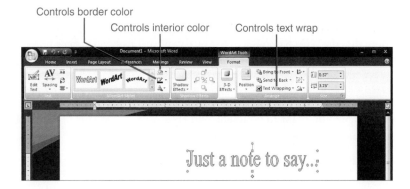

7. Click the Rotate button and then click Rotate Right 90° (see Figure 11.24). Do this twice so that the text is upside-down.

Figure 11.24
Rotate the WordArt
from the WordArt tab.

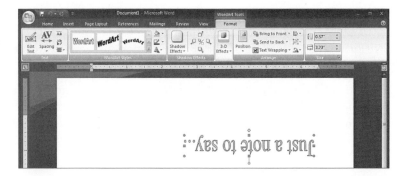

TIP

> To rotate the WordArt text some amount other than 90 degrees, make sure the Text Wrapping has been set to something other than In Line With Text, so that a green circle appears near the text when it is selected. Then drag that green circle to rotate the text a custom amount.

→ For more information about WordArt formatting, **see** "Creating and Modifying a WordArt Object," **p. 484**.

TROUBLESHOOTING

TEXT BOX COLORS DON'T CHANGE WITH THE THEME COLORS

When you use a formatting style to format a text box (from the Styles pane), you choose one of six fixed colors for the formatting. These are not tied to the color set in the theme. This is by design.

If you want to apply a theme color to the text box's line or fill, you can do so via the controls on the Format tab. In order to do so, though, you have to have a basic understanding of the effect that the style has applied, because you have to know where to look. For example, you have to be able to recognize a gradient versus a solid fill. (Chapter 15 can help with that if you're not sure.)

For example, if the text box is filled with a gradient applied by the style, on the Format Tab click Shape Fill, point to Gradient, and click More Gradients. Then click One Color and select one of the theme colors from the Color 1 list.

If it's a solid-color fill in the text box, the process is a lot easier: Click Shape Fill and select a theme color from the list that appears.

Next, do the same thing for the border, via the Shape Outline on the Text Format tab.

After making these changes, the colors of the text box will change when you change the color theme in the document.

Extra Line Spacing Appears in an Inserted Address from Outlook

Sometimes when you insert an address from Outlook using the Envelopes and Labels dialog box, the address appears with extra vertical space between each line.

To get rid of this extra space, you'll need to add the envelope to the document. Then select the paragraphs of the address and open the Paragraph dialog box (on the Home tab, click the dialog box launcher icon ⊡ in the Paragraph group) and set the Before and After spacing to 0".

Printing Is Off-Center on the Labels

Sometimes the small differences in the way various printers feed their paper can cause text to be offset on a label. To make an adjustment, follow these steps:

1. From the Labels tab of the Envelopes and Labels dialog box, click Options.
2. Confirm that the correct label product and product number are selected and then click Details. An information dialog box appears for the chosen label.
3. Change any of the measurements listed for the label. For example, to scoot everything over to the right, increase the Side Margin setting, or to start the labels slightly higher on the page, decrease the Top Margin setting (see Figure 11.25).
4. Click OK.

Figure 11.25
Offset the label positioning slightly to compensate for printer placement errors.

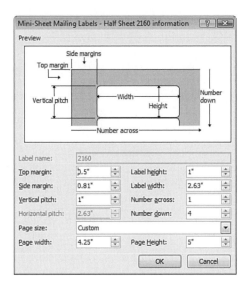

Rather than making a change to the overall specification for that product number, you might instead choose to create a new custom label specification that mirrors the label number but uses the different offset. Follow the steps in "Creating a Custom Label Specification" earlier in this chapter.

PART III

Tables and Graphics

CHAPTER 12

CREATING AND FORMATTING TABLES

In this chapter

CREATING A TABLE

A *table* is a grid of rows and columns that define *cells* at their intersections. Each cell is its own separate area, somewhat like a text box.

The most obvious use for a table is to organize multiple columns of data in tabular form, like in a spreadsheet. For example, in Figure 12.1, information about fish is displayed in a table. Some cells contain pictures; others contain text.

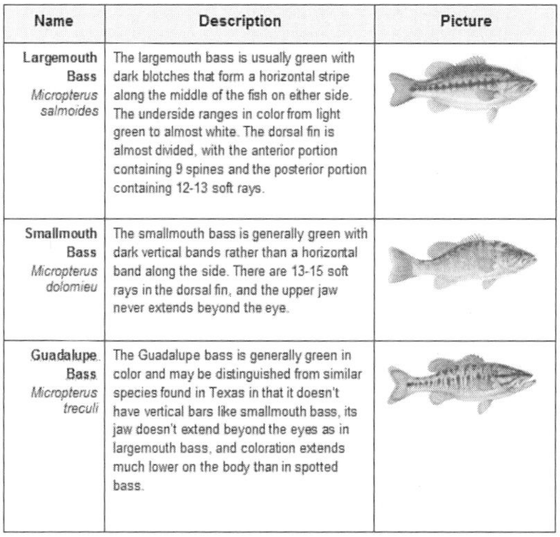

Figure 12.1
Tables are commonly used for organizing multicolumn data.

Name	Description	Picture
Largemouth Bass *Micropterus salmoides*	The largemouth bass is usually green with dark blotches that form a horizontal stripe along the middle of the fish on either side. The underside ranges in color from light green to almost white. The dorsal fin is almost divided, with the anterior portion containing 9 spines and the posterior portion containing 12-13 soft rays.	
Smallmouth Bass *Micropterus dolomieu*	The smallmouth bass is generally green with dark vertical bands rather than a horizontal band along the side. There are 13-15 soft rays in the dorsal fin, and the upper jaw never extends beyond the eye.	
Guadalupe. Bass *Micropterus treculi*	The Guadalupe bass is generally green in color and may be distinguished from similar species found in Texas in that it doesn't have vertical bars like smallmouth bass, its jaw doesn't extend beyond the eyes as in largemouth bass, and coloration extends much lower on the body than in spotted bass.	

Tables can also be used for page layout, a technique popular in web page design. In Figure 12.2, a table has been used to structure a newsletter layout, as an alternative to newspaper-style columns or text boxes. Word facilitates tabular layout by enabling you to merge and split certain cells, creating uneven numbers of rows and columns to accommodate nonstandard designs.

There are three ways to insert a table in a document: the Table menu, the Insert Table dialog box, and the Table Drawing tool. The following sections look at each of these methods.

Figure 12.2
Tables can be used to create multicolumn page layouts.

INSERTING A TABLE FROM THE TABLE MENU

To access the Table menu, click the Table button on the Insert tab. The main feature of the Table menu is a grid of squares, as shown in Figure 12.3. Drag across the grid to select the number of rows and columns desired; when you release the mouse button, Word places a new table in the document with those specifications.

Figure 12.3
Create a table by dragging across the squares on the Table menu's grid.

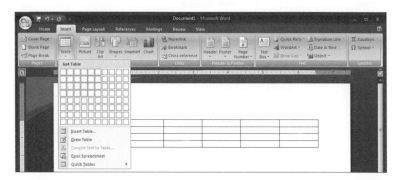

The tables inserted via this method have their cell widths set to Auto. The table itself occupies the full width of the page (between the margins), and the cells are equally sized to use that space. But when you start typing text into a cell, the cell begins expanding to hold that text, and all the other cells decrease in size to pick up the slack.

If you want some other type of cell-sizing behavior, use the following method of table creation instead.

INSERTING A TABLE VIA THE INSERT TABLE DIALOG BOX

The dialog box method of table creation takes longer, but enables you to specify how you want the text and the cell width to interact. Three AutoFit settings are available:

- **Fixed Column Width**—This can be set to Auto, which starts with a fixed column width such that the table fills the width of the page but enables a column to enlarge based on the text you enter. It can alternatively be set to a specific value in inches (at increments as small as 1/100th).

- **AutoFit to Contents**—This setting changes the cell widths so that whatever text you place in them fits on a single row. If a column contains nothing, it appears very narrow.

- **AutoFit to Window**—The table width changes depending on the size of the window in which it is being viewed. This setting is great for tables that will be displayed on web pages, because one never knows the size of the browser window a web page visitor will be using.

To use the dialog box method, follow these steps:

1. On the Insert tab, click Table and then choose Insert Table from the menu. The Insert Table dialog box opens (see Figure 12.4).

2. Enter the number of rows and columns desired in their respective boxes.

3. Select an AutoFit behavior setting.

4. (Optional) Mark the Remember Dimensions for New Tables check box to preserve these settings.

5. Click OK to create the table.

Figure 12.4
Use the Insert Table dialog box to create a new table.

DRAWING A TABLE

Drawing a table is useful when you want unequal-sized rows and columns, or a different number of rows in some columns than in others (or vice versa). This method turns your mouse pointer into a pencil, which you can use to create the table's overall borders and individual row and column dividers.

To draw the table, follow these steps:

1. On the Insert tab, click Table and then choose Draw Table. The mouse pointer turns into a pencil.

2. Drag to draw a box representing the outer borders of the table. When you release the mouse button, the cursor remains a pencil.

3. Drag to draw the rows and columns within the box you just drew (see Figure 12.5).

   To draw row and column dividers, draw straight lines. To draw a table within a table, draw a rectangle within a cell.

4. (Optional) If you need to erase a line you drew, click Eraser on the Design tab and then click the line to erase. To go back to drawing mode, click Draw Table on the Design tab.

5. When you are finished drawing lines, press Esc or click the Draw Table button on the Design tab.

NOTE

To draw additional lines later, click inside the table, then click the Draw Table button again to reenter drawing mode.

Figure 12.5
Use the mouse pointer as a "pencil" to draw the table.

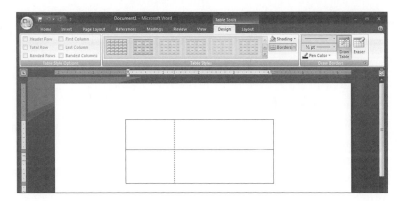

ENTERING DATA IN A TABLE

To type data into a cell, click in the cell and type. To move to the next cell, press Tab; to move to the previous cell, press Shift+Tab.

TIP

The Tab key doesn't work normally in a table cell because it's used to move around in the table, but there's a workaround. To create a tab character in a table cell, press Ctrl+Tab.

Depending on the AutoFit setting of the table, as you type text into a cell, one of two things will happen:

- The text will wrap to additional lines, and the cell will get taller.

■ The cell will try to widen itself as much as possible, taking space away from other cells as it is able, before it starts wrapping to additional lines.

→ To learn about column and row sizing, **see** "Sizing a Table," **p. 367**.

Table 12.1 summarizes the keyboard shortcuts available for moving around in a table.

TABLE 12.1 KEYBOARD SHORTCUTS FOR TABLE NAVIGATION	
To move to:	**Press this:**
Next cell (or to start a new row if already in the last cell)	Tab
Previous cell (in same row)	Shift+Tab
First cell in the row	Alt+Home
Last cell in the row	Alt+End
First cell in the column	Alt+Page Up
Last cell in the column	Alt+Page Down
Previous row	Up arrow
Next row	Down arrow

EDITING A TABLE

Tables are flexible; you can add and remove rows and columns, merge and split cells, move pieces around, and more.

SELECTING CELLS

As in most areas of Word, before you can format or modify a cell (or something within a cell), you must select it.

When a cell is selected, the entire cell appears highlighted, even if it is empty. To select a cell, position the mouse pointer at the bottom-left corner of the cell, so that the mouse pointer turns into a black diagonally pointing arrow, and then click (see Figure 12.6). Any formatting you apply when the entire cell is selected affects all the content within it.

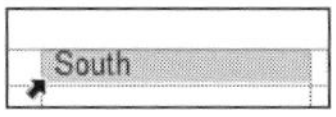

Figure 12.6
A selected cell.

There is also a keyboard method for selecting the entire cell: Position the insertion point at the end of any content within the cell and then press Shift+right arrow.

One other method for selecting a cell is found on the Layout tab. Open the Select menu and choose Select Cell (see Figure 12.7).

Figure 12.7
The Select menu enables you to quickly select various portions of the table.

Holding down the Shift key and pressing an arrow key extends the selection area by one character or line in the arrow direction, so why is it that pressing Shift+right arrow at the end of a cell selects the entire cell?

It happens because of a hidden end-of-cell marker that appears at the end of each cell's content. To see these markers, toggle on the Show/Hide ¶ feature on the Home tab (see Figure 12.8). When the insertion point is at the end of the cell content, and you extend the selection one character to the right, you select the end-of-cell marker, which in turn selects the entire cell.

Toggle non-printing characters on/off

Figure 12.8
Nonprinting end-of-cell markers appear in each cell.

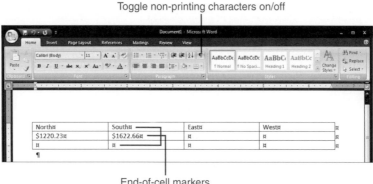

End-of-cell markers

On the other hand, when the *content* of the text is selected, only the content is highlighted; a portion of the cell background appears behind it in an unhighlighted state. You do not have to select all the content in the cell; this makes it possible to apply different formatting to certain characters or objects within the cell, but not others. To select text in a cell, drag across the text. To select a graphic or other object in a cell, click that object.

Dragging across cell content selects only the content, not the cell—until you drag to include more than one cell. When you drag across multiple cells, the cells themselves become selected.

To select noncontiguous cells, hold down the Ctrl key as you select each of the cells or ranges to include.

SELECTING ROWS, COLUMNS, OR TABLES

To select a row (or multiple rows), do one of the following:

- Click anywhere in the row. On the Layout tab, open the Select menu and choose Select Row.

- Drag across all the cells in the row, including the end-of-row marker to the far right of the row. This marker is another nonprinting character; it looks just like the end-of-cell markers (refer to Figure 12.8) but it is outside of the rightmost cell in the row. Drag up or down to select additional rows.

- Position the mouse pointer to the left of the row, so that the mouse pointer changes to a white arrow, and then click to select the entire row. Drag up or down to select additional rows (see Figure 12.9).

- Click in the first (leftmost) cell in the row and hold down the Shift key as you press the right-arrow key repeatedly until the entire row is selected. Press the up- or down-arrow key to select additional rows.

Figure 12.9
Select a row by clicking to its left or dragging across all its cells.

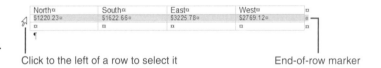

Click to the left of a row to select it   End-of-row marker

To select a column (or multiple columns), do one of these:

- Click anywhere in the column. On the Layout tab, open the Select menu and choose Select Column.

- Drag across all the cells in the column. There is no end-of-column marker to worry about. Drag to the right or left to select additional columns.

- Position the mouse pointer above the column, so that the mouse pointer changes to a black down-pointing arrow, and then click to select the entire column (see Figure 12.10). Drag right or left to select additional columns.

- Click in the first (topmost) cell in the column and hold down the Shift key as you press the down arrow repeatedly until the entire column is selected. Use the left- or right-arrow key to select additional columns.

Click above the row to select it
Table selector

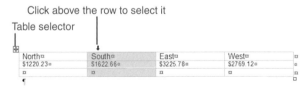

Figure 12.10
Select a column by clicking above it or dragging across its cells.

To select the entire table, click the table selector icon, shown in Figure 12.10, or press Alt+5 (using the 5 on the numeric keypad with Num Lock turned off). As another alternative, you can open the Select menu on the Layout tab and choose Select Table.

TIP

Another way to select is by turning on the Extend Selection feature (Ctrl+Shift+F8). When it is on, you can then use the arrow keys to extend a selection in any direction. (You don't have to hold down Shift with the arrows.) To turn off Extend Selection, press Esc.

INSERTING ROWS, COLUMNS, OR CELLS

To insert a single row or column, right-click a cell within a row or column adjacent to where you want the insertion to appear, and then point to Insert and click the option that best describes what you want. There are also buttons on the Layout tab for inserting rows and columns (see Figure 12.11).

Buttons for inserting rows and columns

Figure 12.11
Insert a row or column by right-clicking and selecting from the Insert submenu.

Right-click a cell and select from the Insert submenu

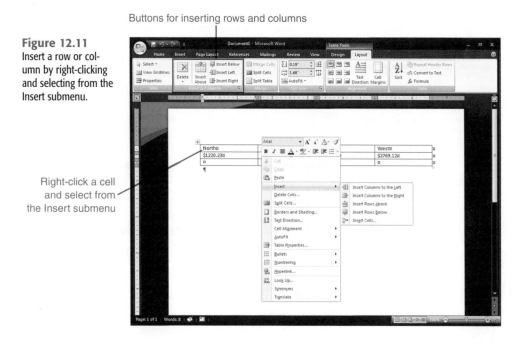

You can also insert individual cells, shifting the existing cells down or to the right. To do this, follow these steps:

1. Right-click the cell where you want to insert a new cell and choose Insert, Insert Cells.

   Alternatively, move the insertion point into the cell where you want to insert a new cell and click the dialog box launcher for the Rows & Columns group on the Layout tab.

2. In the Insert Cells dialog box, shown in Figure 12.12, click the insertion type you want. You can choose to shift the existing cells either down or to the right. (You can also use this dialog box to insert an entire row or column, although it's somewhat of a long way around for that.)

3. Click OK.

Figure 12.12
Choose what should happen to the existing cells to make room for the new cell.

Inserting a new cell adds another row or column to the table if needed to hold the shifted content; if there is already an extra row at the bottom or column at the right, the content simply shifts into it and no new rows or columns are created.

DELETING ROWS, COLUMNS, OR CELLS

A lot of people are surprised that the Delete key on the keyboard does not work to delete rows, columns, and cells. That's because Delete is not really a removal tool—it's a clearing tool. It clears whatever content is there, but it leaves the structure in place. Therefore, if you select a cell and press Delete, all the cell's content is deleted, but the cell remains.

The Layout tab's Delete button opens a menu of deletion choices. Move the insertion point into the row, column, or cell to affect and then select the deletion command from the menu, as shown in Figure 12.13.

Figure 12.13
Choose the portion of the table to delete.

If you choose Delete Cells, a Delete Cells dialog box opens, in which you can choose whether the remaining cells should be shifted to the left or up. (It's just like the Insert Cells dialog box from Figure 12.12, except it's deleting instead of inserting.)

The Cut feature of the Clipboard can also be used to remove entire rows or columns. (It doesn't work for individual cells; it just clears them.) To delete an entire row or column, select it and then press Ctrl+X or click the Cut button on the Home tab.

NOTE

Cutting isn't really deleting, but if you cut something and then never paste it, the effect is the same.

DELETING AN ENTIRE TABLE

To delete an entire table, display the Layout tab, click the Delete button, and choose Delete Table (see Figure 12.13).

There are also some less-direct methods. Just like with individual rows, columns, and cells, you can't delete an entire table with the Delete key; selecting the entire table and pressing Delete simply clears all the content out of the table. There's an exception to that, however. If you select a larger block of the document than just the table—for example, the table plus the end-of-paragraph marker before or after it—and then press Delete, Word will delete the entire block, including the table structure.

The Cut feature of the Clipboard also works on entire tables. Select the entire table and press Ctrl+X or click the Cut button on the Home tab. (You can also right-click the table selector icon and choose Cut to cut the entire table.) You can then paste the entire table from the Clipboard to another location in the document, if you want.

MOVING AND COPYING ROWS AND COLUMNS

To move or copy a row or column, you have a choice of two techniques: using a drag-and-drop operation or using the Clipboard (Cut/Copy/Paste).

Here's the drag-and-drop method:

1. Select the row(s) or column(s) to move or copy.
2. Position the mouse pointer over the selection, so that the pointer becomes a white arrow.

> **TIP**
> When moving a row, position the mouse pointer over the leftmost cell in the row.

3. (Optional) Hold down the Ctrl key if you want to copy (rather than move).
4. Drag to the left or right for columns, or drag up or down for rows, to move the selection to a new position.

Here's the Clipboard method:

1. Select the row(s) or column(s) to move or copy.
2. Cut or copy the selection to the Clipboard using one of these methods:
   - **Ribbon method**—Click Cut or Copy on the Home tab.
   - **Keyboard method**—Press Ctrl+X for Cut or Ctrl+C for Copy.
   - **Right-click method**—Right-click the selection and choose Cut or Copy.
3. Click where you want the selection to go. If you're moving/copying a row, click in the leftmost cell of the row that should appear below the selection; if you're moving/copying a column, click in the column that should appear to the right.

12

4. Paste the selection from the Clipboard using one of these methods:

- Ribbon method—Click Paste on the Home tab.
- Keyboard method—Press Ctrl+V.
- Right-click method—Right-click and choose Paste.

CAUTION

> Individual cells cannot be moved in the same sense as a row or column is moved, but you can move the cell content with either a drag-and-drop or cut-and-paste operation. Be careful, though, that you do not overwrite existing content. If the destination cells are not empty, the previous content is deleted—not moved over. (You're not working with cells here, but cell *content*.)

MERGING AND SPLITTING CELLS

Merging cells erases the dividers between them; *splitting* a cell adds a divider, creating two cells out of one. Using merging and/or splitting, you can create all sorts of interesting tables with unequal numbers of rows and columns, much like in the drawn tables you learned about at the beginning of the chapter. (In fact, the table-drawing tools provide one method of merging and splitting.)

To merge two or more cells, select the cells and click the Merge Cells button on the Layout tab (see Figure 12.14), or right-click the selection and choose Merge Cells.

Click here to merge the selected cells

Figure 12.14
Merge the selected cells.

When you're merging multiple nonempty cells, the resulting merged cell contains all the content from all the merged cells, separated by paragraph breaks.

When you're merging cells that contain different formatting settings, the resulting merged cell takes on the cell formatting from the leftmost or topmost cell in the merged range. This rule applies only to cell-wide formatting, though, not character formatting. For example, text that's bold will continue to be bold after the merge.

Another way to merge cells is to use the Eraser feature, found on the Design tab. Click Eraser, and the mouse pointer becomes an eraser. Then click the divider line between any two cells to merge them (see Figure 12.15).

Figure 12.15
Use the Eraser tool to merge cells.

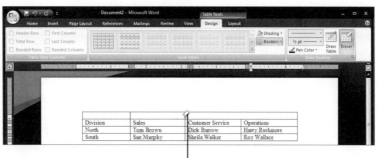

Mouse pointer becomes an eraser

Merging cells is simple because there aren't any options involved; cells are either merged or they are not. With splitting, however, you must specify how many pieces you want the cell split into vertically and/or horizontally.

To split a cell, follow these steps:

1. Click in the cell to be split and then click the Split Cells button on the Layout tab. Alternatively, you can right-click the cell and choose Split Cells.

2. Enter the number of columns and rows in which to split the selected cell. For example, to split it into four columns, enter **4** as the number of columns and **1** as the number of rows (see Figure 12.16).

3. Click OK to perform the split.

Figure 12.16
Enter information about the desired split.

You can also split using the table-drawing tools. This works just like it did when you were drawing the table initially (if you used that method to create the table). To split a table by drawing, follow these steps:

1. On the Design tab, click Draw Table. The mouse pointer turns into a pencil.

2. Drag to draw divider lines where you want splits to occur.

3. Click the Draw Table button again, or press Esc, to turn drawing mode off.

SPLITTING A TABLE

Splitting a table adds a blank paragraph (non-table) between two rows. To split a table, click in the row that should become the first row in the second table and then click the Split Table button on the Layout tab.

To rejoin a table that has been split, delete the paragraph marker between the tables.

CREATING A NESTED TABLE

A *nested table* is a table within a table. Nested tables can be useful when you are using a table for page layout and then want to use a table for data organization within the layout. For example, in Figure 12.17, a table-based newsletter contains a mini-calendar table within its right column.

Figure 12.17
A table can be nested within another table.

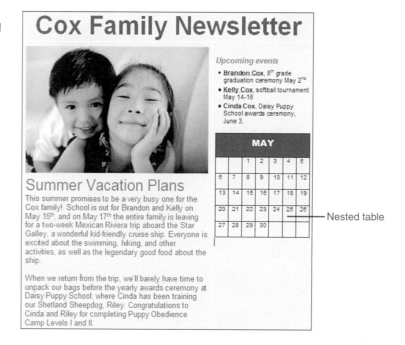

To create a nested table, click inside a cell and then insert a new table as you would normally, using any method you learned earlier in the chapter.

If the table to be nested already exists, you can paste it into a cell. Don't use a regular paste operation for this, though, because Word will assume you want to merge the two tables together. Instead, follow these steps to paste one table into another:

1. Cut or copy the table to be nested onto the Clipboard.
2. Place the insertion point in the cell in which you want to paste the table.
3. Right-click at the insertion point and choose Paste as Nested Table.

TIP

If you have a table such as the nested calendar in Figure 12.17 that you might want to reuse, consider saving it as a building block. To do so, select the table, display the Insert tab, and click Quick Parts. On the menu that appears, click Save Selection to Quick Part Gallery. Set up a building block entry for it in the Quick Parts gallery; you can then access it from the Quick Parts menu for reuse.

SIZING A TABLE

By default, a newly inserted table is as wide as possible, given the margin and indent settings at the location where it is placed. So, for example, if you place it on an 8.5"×11" page with 1" margins on each size, the table will be 6.5" wide. The columns are equal in size, so in an eight-column table that's 6.5" wide, for example, each cell is 0.83" (approximately 13/16") wide.

The default height of a table is determined by the number of rows, with a single-height line for text in each row. For example, if the default font size is 11-point, then each row's height will be such that one line of 11-point text can fit into it.

CHANGING THE AUTOFIT SETTING

The AutoFit setting determines how (or whether) the table's size will change as the content is added to it.

There are three possible AutoFit settings for a table, and you can switch among them from the AutoFit button on the Layout tab, as in Figure 12.18, or by right-clicking the table and choosing AutoFit:

Figure 12.18
Choose an AutoFit setting to govern the table's sizing.

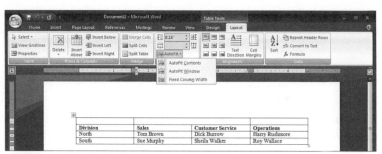

- **AutoFit Contents**—Each cell is as wide as it needs to be to hold its content. Empty columns are very small (one character wide). Text wraps to additional lines in a cell, but only after the cell has expanded as much as it can given the widths of the other columns and the overall table size.

- **AutoFit Window**—The table resizes itself depending on the size of the page on which it is displayed. This is useful for web pages and also for nested tables. For example, the calendar in Figure 12.17 would dynamically change its width as the column in which it resides changes width if you set it to AutoFit to Window.

- **Fixed Column Width**—Each cell stays at its current size until you manually change it.

The table's AutoFit setting forms the basis of its initial width settings, but there are numerous ways of manually adjusting those widths.

RESIZING BY DRAGGING

The easiest way to resize a row or column is simply by dragging; position the mouse pointer over the right border (for width) or bottom border (for height) and drag (see Figure 12.19). To change the width of the entire column or the height of the entire row, make sure that nothing is selected in the table when you begin dragging.

Figure 12.19
Resize a column by
dragging.

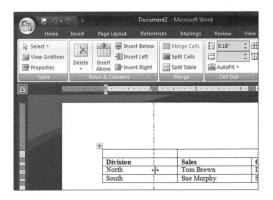

Dragging a column border changes the spacing between the cells it lies between, but no other cells are affected, nor is the overall size of the table. If you want all the other cells to stay the same size, and the overall size of the table to change with the resizing, hold down the Shift key as you drag.

If a cell is selected in the table when you drag, then the resizing affects only the row containing the selected cell. The adjustment affects only the two cells that the border lies between. To resize the whole row, hold down Shift.

SPECIFYING AN EXACT SIZE

If you need precise sizes for rows or columns, click in a cell and then use the Height and Width boxes on the Layout tab. The Height value affects the entire row; the Width value affects the entire column (see Figure 12.20).

Figure 12.20
Enter height and width
values for the row and
column of the current
cell.

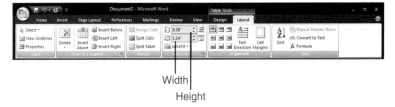

Width
Height

You can also change row and column sizes from the Table Properties dialog box. Follow these steps:

1. Right-click the row or column to affect and choose Table Properties.

   Alternatively, you can click in the row or column to affect and then either click the dialog box launcher for the Cell Size group on the Layout tab or click the Properties button in the Table group on the Layout tab.

2. In the Table Properties dialog box, click the Column tab. The width information for the selected column appears (see Figure 12.21).

3. Change the column width if needed.

4. To change another column, click the Next Column or Previous Column button and change the width for it. Do this for all the columns you need to change.

Figure 12.21
Set a specific size for
each column.

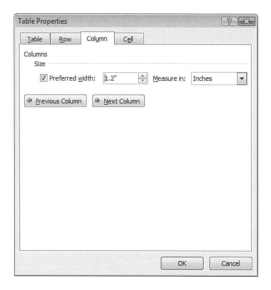

5. Click the Row tab. The height information for the current row appears. By default, the Specify Height check box is not marked, which enables the row to dynamically resize itself depending on its content.

6. If you want to specify an exact height for the row, mark the Specify Height check box and enter a value.

7. Set the Row Height Is value to either At Least or Exactly. At Least allows the height to grow larger than the specified value but not smaller. Exactly forces the row to be exactly the specified value, even if the text is truncated (see Figure 12.22).

8. Mark or clear the Allow Row to Break Across Pages check box as desired.

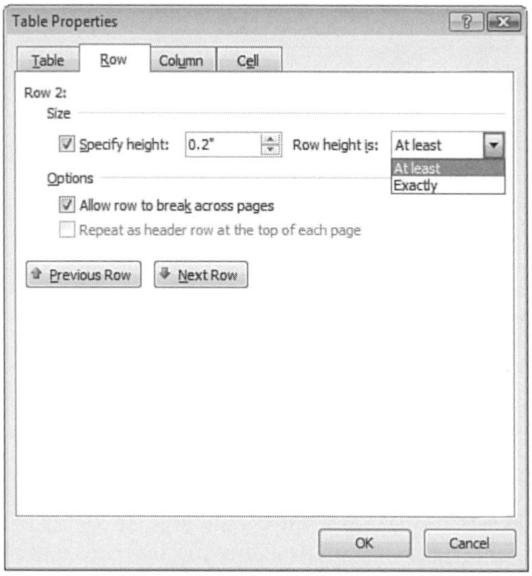

Figure 12.22
Set a specific size for
each row, or allow the
rows to auto-size.

12

9. To change another row, click the Next Row or Previous Row button and then change the height for it. Repeat until all rows have been set.

10. Click OK.

DISTRIBUTING COLUMN WIDTHS EVENLY

Tables start out with uniform-sized rows and columns, but as you have seen, you can make changes to those values. To go back to even spacing, click the Distribute Columns or Distribute Rows button on the Layout tab (see Figure 12.23). As an alternative method, you can select the entire table and then right-click the table and choose Distribute Rows Evenly or Distribute Columns Evenly from the shortcut menu.

Make rows equal height

Figure 12.23
Set row heights or column widths to use the available space equally.

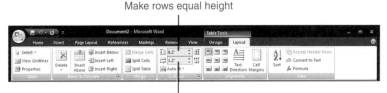

Make columns equal width

RESIZING THE ENTIRE TABLE

To resize the table as a whole, drag one of its outside borders. You'll get different results, though, depending on where you drag:

- **Left border**—Changes the width of the leftmost column.
- **Right border**—Changes the width of the rightmost column.
- **Bottom border**—Changes the height of the bottom row.
- **Bottom-right corner**—Changes the height and width of the table overall, with all rows and columns adjusted proportionally.

> **TIP**
>
> Holding down Shift while dragging the bottom-right corner constrains the resizing so that the table's aspect ratio (height-to-width ratio) is preserved.

FORMATTING A TABLE

Now that you've learned about the structural aspects of table creation and editing, let's look at some ways of making the table more attractive and readable.

APPLYING TABLE STYLES

Table styles are similar to the character and paragraph styles you learned about in Chapter 8, "Creating and Applying Styles and Themes." They quickly apply named sets of formatting. The main difference is that a table style contains table-specific features such as cell border formatting, cell shading, and special designations for the first and last row and column.

→ To learn more about styles, **see** "Understanding Styles," **p. 228**.

To apply a table style, click anywhere in the table and then select one of the table styles from the Design tab (see Figure 12.24). For more choices, click the down-arrow button to open a larger menu.

Table styles

Figure 12.24
Select a table style.

Specify special handling
for certain rows/columns

Click here for more styles

After applying a table style, use the check boxes in the Table Style Options group of the Design tab to turn on/off certain formatting extras. Each of these designates certain rows or columns to receive different formatting. For example, Header Row formats the first row differently; Total Row formats the last row differently. The Banded options make every other row or column different, for easier reading.

SETTING THE DEFAULT TABLE STYLE

To set a style as the default for new tables, right-click the desired style on the Styles list and choose Set As Default.

In the Default Table Style dialog box, choose either This Document Only or All Documents Based on the Normal.dotm Template to specify the scope of the setting. Then click OK to make the style the new default.

CREATING OR MODIFYING TABLE STYLES

To create a table style, you can either start with an existing one and give it a new name, or you can start from scratch with a new definition.

To create or modify a table style, follow these steps:

1. Open the Table Styles list on the Design tab and select the style that is closest to the one you want.

2. Open the Table Styles list again and choose Modify Table Style. The Modify Style dialog box opens.

3. In the Name box, type a new name. (It is better to create a new style rather than overwrite the definition of an existing one, and in some cases Word will not let you modify a built-in style.)

4. To make whole-table changes, set the Apply Formatting To value to Whole Table and then make formatting changes using the controls provided. You can choose a different font, size, and color, change the borders, change the cell shading and alignment, and more (see Figure 12.25). You will learn more about these formatting types in upcoming sections of this chapter.

5. To make changes to only certain rows or columns, select the desired scope from the Apply Formatting To list (for example, Header Row) and then make formatting changes.

12

Figure 12.25
Create your own table style definition.

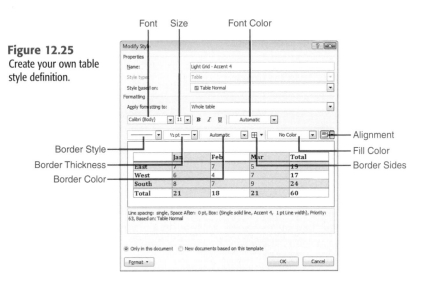

NOTE

If the formatting you want to apply does not appear in the dialog box, click the Format button to open a menu of more choices. For example, from the Format menu you can choose Stripes to fine-tune the bands to include more than one row or column per band.

6. (Optional) To store the style in the template (for reuse in other documents), click New Documents Based on This Template.

7. Click OK. The new custom table style is created.

Custom table styles, when they exist, appear at the top of the Styles list in the Custom section (see Figure 12.26).

Figure 12.26
Custom styles can be accessed from the Styles list on the Design tab.

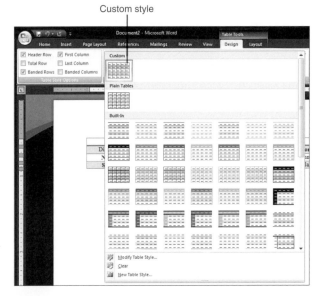

To better understand the formatting controls in the Modify Style dialog box, review the information in the following sections. The formatting can be applied manually, as explained in these sections, or integrated into the style.

CHANGING THE CELL BACKGROUND COLOR

To apply a solid-color background (fill color) to one or more cells, use the Shading drop-down list on the Design tab (see Figure 12.27). As in other areas of Word, you can choose between theme colors, tints of the theme colors, standard colors, or More Colors (to open a color selection dialog box).

→ To learn more about how Word uses colors, **see** "Changing Font Color," **p. 167**.

Figure 12.27
Select a solid-color shading.

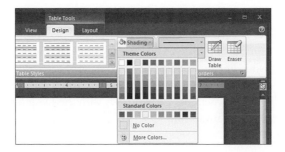

To apply a patterned background to a cell, you must use the Borders and Shading dialog box, as follows:

1. Select the cell(s) to affect.
2. Right-click the selection and choose Borders and Shading.
3. Click the Shading tab.
4. Open the Style list and select the pattern to apply to the background.
5. Open the Color list and select the basic color for the background.
6. Open the Fill list and select the color for the pattern (see Figure 12.28).

Figure 12.28
To apply a patterned background, use the Borders and Shading dialog box.

Pattern

Pattern foreground

Pattern background

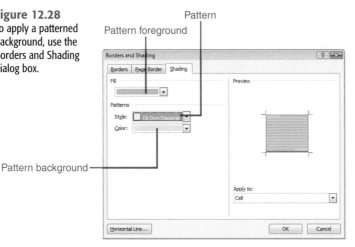

12

7. Click OK to apply the patterned background.

You can also use the Borders and Shading dialog box method to apply a solid-color background if you prefer it to the ribbon method. For a solid-color background, set the Style setting to Solid (100%).

CAUTION

> Avoid strongly contrasting patterns as backgrounds for cells containing text, because it makes the text difficult to read. A patterned background would be more appropriate for an empty row that separates two rows of text, for example, or as a background for a cell that contains a picture.

WORKING WITH CELL BORDERS

The term *border* in the context of a table has two subtly different meanings. In one definition, the border is the visible line around one or more sides of a cell. When you set a cell to "No Border," you are setting the lines around it to not be visible when printed. This is the definition generally adhered to when formatting tables with the Design tab, and in this section of the chapter, *border* has that meaning.

Another definition of *border* is the boundary around the four sides of the cell, whether or not it is visible. Using this definition, every cell has a border on every side. It's convenient to talk about cell borders this way when discussing resizing a cell by dragging, for example, because the ability to drag a border is not dependent on its having a visible line or not.

Nearly everything you learned about paragraph borders in Chapter 7, "Formatting Paragraphs and Lists," applies also to table cells. The same attributes apply to both paragraph and table borders: line style, line thickness, and line color.

→ To learn more about how borders work, **see** "Applying Paragraph Borders," **p. 217**.

One easy way to apply borders—that is, visible lines—to a table (or parts of a table) is to use the tools on the Design tab, as shown in Figure 12.29.

Figure 12.29
Tools for formatting table borders.

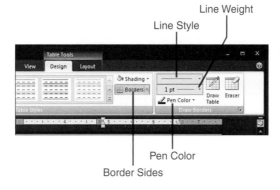

Line Weight

Line Style

Pen Color

Border Sides

Select the border style, width, and color first, and then apply the border sides. If you apply the sides first, the settings you later choose for style, width, and color will not be automatically applied; you will need to reapply the sides to put them into effect.

The Borders button opens a list of various border sides, shown in Figure 12.30. (Look back at Table 7.1 in Chapter 7 for a review of these.) Keep in mind that in a table, the borders refer to the selected cells as a group, not to the individual cells. For example, Outside Borders places the border around the selection, not around each individual cell, and Top Border places the border across the top of the selection, not at the top of each cell.

Figure 12.30
Select the border sides to apply to the table.

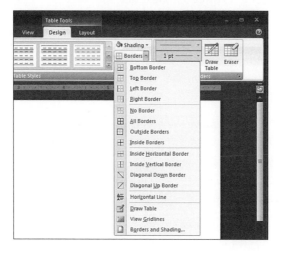

You can also use the Borders and Shading dialog box to apply borders, just as you did for paragraphs in Chapter 7. Follow these steps:

1. Select the cell(s) to affect.

2. On the Design tab, open the Borders list and choose Borders and Shading. The Borders and Shading dialog box opens.

3. Click the Borders tab if does not already appear (see Figure 12.31).

Figure 12.31
You can format cell borders from the Borders tab of the Borders and Shading dialog box.

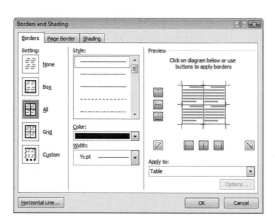

12

4. Select a border type from the Setting icons along the left side of the dialog box:
   - **None**—Turns off all borders.
   - **Box**—Places an outside border in which all sides are the same thickness.
   - **All**—Places the same border around all sides of all cells in the selected range.
   - **Grid**—Places a thicker outside border, and also a thinner inside border.
   - **Custom**—Enables you to select and format each side individually. (You can start with any of the other settings, and when you start to change individual sizes, the setting changes to Custom automatically.)

5. On the Style list, select a line style.

6. On the Color list, select a line color. (Color selection works the same here as with any other colored object.)

→ For an explanation of Word's color choices, **see** "Changing Font Color," **p. 167**.

7. On the Width list, select a line thickness.

8. (Optional) If you want to remove the border on certain sides, click the corresponding button in the Preview area. (There is a button for each of the four sides.)

9. Click OK to accept the new border.

SETTING CELL MARGINS

Each cell has internal margins—that is, an amount of space between the border on each side and the text you type into the cell. In this sense, a cell is very much like a text box.

→ For an explanation of text boxes and their internal margin settings, **see** "Creating Text Box Layouts," **p. 320**.

You can set the internal margins for all cells at once, or for individual cells.

SETTING OVERALL INTERNAL MARGINS FOR THE TABLE

The overall internal margins for the table provide a baseline; you can then make changes for individual cells later.

To set the overall internal margins for the table, follow these steps:

1. On the Layout tab, click Cell Margins. The Table Options dialog box opens.

2. Enter margin settings in the Default Cell Margins section for each side (see Figure 12.32).

3. (Optional) To place spacing between cells, mark the Allow Spacing Between Cells check box and enter an amount of space.

   This setting enables you to add extra space for the margins where two cells meet. The extra spacing is contextual; although it applies to the entire table, it applies to certain cells depending on their position. For example, with overall margin settings of 0.1" on all sides but an Allow Spacing Between Cells setting of 0.1", the topmost, leftmost cell in the table would have a top and left internal margin of 0.1" and a bottom and right internal margin of 0.2".

12

4. Mark or clear the Automatically Resize to Fit Contents check box.

When selected, the table cells can resize as you type to accommodate long text entries or large graphics.

5. Click OK.

Figure 12.32
You can format cell borders from the Borders tab of the Borders and Shading dialog box.

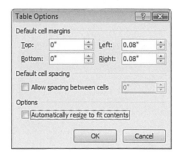

SETTING INTERNAL MARGINS FOR AN INDIVIDUAL CELL

Depending on a cell's content, you might need for it to have different internal margins than the rest of the table. To customize the internal margins for a certain cell, or a range of cells, follow these steps:

1. Select the cell(s) to affect.

2. On the Layout tab, click the Properties button. The Table Properties dialog box opens.

3. Click the Cell tab and then click the Options button. The Cell Options dialog box opens.

4. Clear the Same as the Whole Table check box. Individual internal margin settings become available for Top, Bottom, Left, and Right (see Figure 12.33).

Figure 12.33
Change the internal margins for individual cells.

5. Mark or clear the checkboxes as desired:

Wrap Text: Allows text to wrap to additional lines in the cell if needed.

Fit Text: Reduces the size of the font to fit the text in the cell if needed.

6. Click OK.

SETTING TEXT ALIGNMENT WITHIN A CELL

Regular paragraphs in a document have only one dimension in which they can be aligned: horizontally. Table cells, on the other hand, have both a vertical and horizontal alignment setting. There are nine combinations possible in all, and each is represented by a button in the Alignment group of the Layout tab. Select the cell(s) to affect and then click one of those buttons (see Figure 12.34).

Figure 12.34
Choose a vertical and horizontal alignment for selected cells.

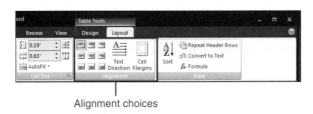

Alignment choices

You can also set alignment from the shortcut menu for any cell. Select the cell(s) to affect and then right-click the selection. Point to Cell Alignment and then select an alignment from the submenu.

CHANGING TEXT DIRECTION

Text in a table cell can be oriented in any of three directions: horizontal (left to right), vertical (top to bottom), or vertical (bottom to top), just like in a text box. To toggle between these orientations, click the Text Direction button on the Layout tab.

CAUTION

> Changing the text direction to a vertical one increases the height of the rows, and when you go back to horizontal orientation, the rows don't automatically go back to their earlier, smaller heights. To put the rows back to their original sizes, drag the bottom-right corner of the table frame up, or set the Height size to the original height. (With 11-point text, the original height is approximately 0.19".)

REPEATING HEADINGS ON EACH PAGE

When a table runs more than one page in a document, it can be a challenge to keep track of what each column represents when looking at the later pages. One solution to that is to repeat the heading row on each page by manually copying it, but then when you edit the table so that it contains more or fewer rows, that repeated heading row gets thrown out of place.

To solve this problem, Word enables you to set the header to be repeated on subsequent pages automatically whenever a table crosses a page break. To set this up, follow these steps:

1. Click in the header row.
2. On the Layout tab, click Properties. The Table Properties dialog box opens.
3. Click the Row tab and then mark the Repeat As Header Row at the Top of Each Page check box.
4. Click OK.

ORIENTING THE TABLE ON THE PAGE

So far in this chapter, we've been working *inside* a table, but now let's consider how the table interacts with the rest of the document. By default, a table takes up the full width of the page (or the full width of whatever you place it into), but it can be resized to a smaller width. When a table is less than full width, it can interact with the rest of the document as a graphic object would. It can be set for a certain horizontal alignment (like a paragraph), and text can be set to wrap around it in various ways.

SETTING TABLE ALIGNMENT

The paragraph's alignment does not have any effect unless the paragraph is narrower than the space available to it. Because by default it exactly fills the available space, and most people don't change that, table alignment is not that important for most users.

If you need to set the table alignment, however, it's fairly easy to do so. Follow these steps:

1. Click anywhere in the table.

2. On the Layout tab, click Properties. The Table Properties dialog box opens.

3. Click the Table tab, and in the Alignment section, click Left, Center, or Right (see Figure 12.35).

4. (Optional) If you chose Left as the alignment, enter an amount of indentation from the left. (This is like the left indent for a paragraph.)

5. Click OK.

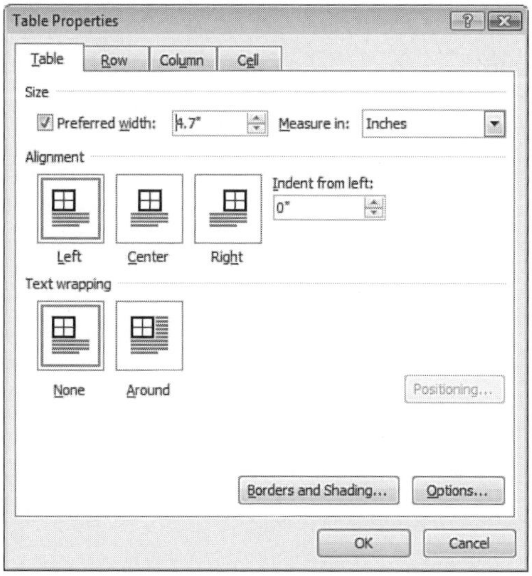

Figure 12.35
Set alignment for the table as a whole.

SETTING TABLE TEXT WRAP

Table text wrap allows the regular paragraphs of the document to wrap around the table if the table is narrower than the maximum document width. It is somewhat like the text wrapping around graphic objects or text boxes.

➔ For information about text wrapping for text boxes, **see** "Wrapping Text Around a Text Box," **p. 327**.

➔ To set text wrapping around a photo or other graphic, **see** "Setting Text Wrap," **p. 402**.

To set the text wrap for a table, follow these steps:

1. Click anywhere in the table.

2. On the Layout tab, click Properties. The Table Properties dialog box opens.

3. Click the Table tab, and in the Text Wrapping section, click Around (see Figure 12.35).

4. (Optional) Click Positioning, opening the Table Positioning dialog box (see Figure 12.36).

Figure 12.36
Fine-tune the position-
ing setting.

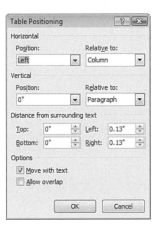

5. Set the horizontal position for the table. You can choose a setting from the drop-down list (Left, Right, Center, Inside, or Outside) or type a number representing an amount of offset in inches, in which case Left positioning is assumed.

> **NOTE**
>
> Inside and Outside are special settings that float the table to the left or right depending on whether the page is odd numbered or even numbered. It's designed to facilitate two-sided layouts. On an odd-numbered page, Inside aligns to the left and Outside to the right; on an even-numbered page, it's the opposite.

6. In the Horizontal section, set the Relative To setting to define what that setting is in relation to (Column, Margin, or Page).

NOTE

When working with a relative setting such as Left or Right, there is no real difference between Margin and Page, but when using specific numeric values, the difference is apparent; 1" from the margin is very different from 1" from the edge of the page.

7. In the Vertical section, set a Position and Relative To values. As with the Horizontal section, you can either choose a relative amount from the drop-down list or type a numeric value in inches. The measurement can be in relation to Paragraph, Margin, or Page.

8. In the Distance from Surrounding Text area, enter spacing amounts to separate the edge of the table from the text that wraps around it.

9. If the table should be anchored to the surrounding text, mark the Move with Text check box; if it should remain fixed on the page and the text should be able to move past it, clear that check box.

10. If the table should be allowed to overlap other content on the page, mark the Allow Overlap check box.

11. Click OK twice to close both dialog boxes.

CREATING A TABLE CAPTION

Long, complex reports often have multiple tables in them, numbered for reference. You can manually number the tables and create your own captions for them, but it is much easier to allow Word to manage the table-captioning process. That way, if you insert a new table earlier in the document, the tables that follow it are automatically renumbered.

To add a caption to a table, follow these steps:

1. Select the entire table, and then right-click the table and choose Insert Caption. The Caption dialog box opens (see Figure 12.37).

   Alternatively, you can click the Insert Caption button on the References tab.

Figure 12.37
Set up a caption for tables in the document.

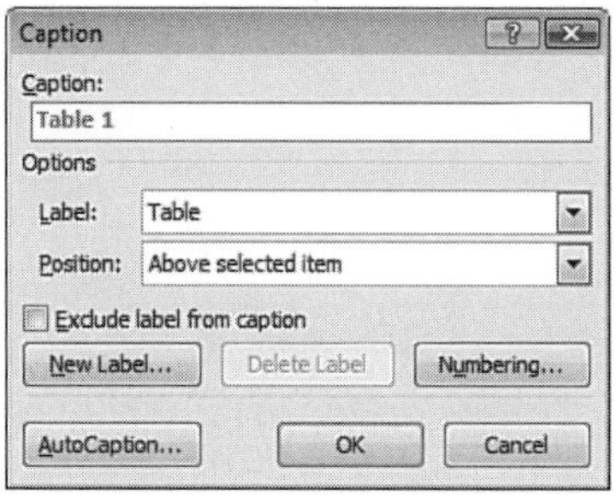

NOTE

> The Caption text box in the Caption dialog box shows you a sample of the caption that will appear based on the other settings in the dialog box.

   2. Leave the Label setting at Table.

   3. In the Position list, choose where you want the captions to appear for tables. (Usually tables have captions above them.)

   4. The caption will read *Table 1*. If you want some other word than *Table*, click New Label and specify some other word(s) instead.

      Alternatively, to omit using a word at all before the number, mark the Exclude Label from Caption check box.

   5. Click the Numbering button. The Caption Numbering dialog box opens (see Figure 12.38).

Figure 12.38
Control the number-ing style for table cap-tions.

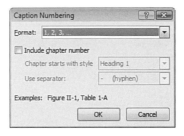

   6. Select a format from the Format list.

   7. (Optional) To include a chapter number with the caption, mark the Include Chapter Number check box and then choose what style designates a chapter and what separator character should be used.

   8. Click OK to return to the Caption dialog box.

   9. Click OK. The caption appears in the document, immediately above (or below) the table.

   10. Click to the right of the caption and type a text description if desired. For example, after *Table 1*, you might type a colon and then *Regional Management Team*, as in Figure 12.39.

This part is inserted automatically by captioning

Figure 12.39
A completed table caption with a manu-ally typed description.

This part was manually typed

SORTING TABULAR DATA

One reason people like to store data in table format is that it makes the data easier to search and sort. Word's Sort feature works with regular paragraphs too, but when it's used with a table or other delimited data it has some additional functionality, such as the ability to sort by multiple columns at once.

NOTE

Delimited data is text that is separated into columns. For example, comma-delimited data consists of regular paragraphs (one per row) in which the data for each column is separated by commas, like this: *data1,data2,data3*. Data can also be tab-delimited (as with the columns created via tab stops in Chapter 7), or it can be delimited using some other character.

→ For information about delimited data, **see** "Converting Text to a Table," **p. 389**.

Sorts can be either ascending (0 to 9, then A to Z) or descending (Z to A, then 9 to 0).

Sorts can be performed assuming a particular column contains text, numbers, or dates. This distinction helps you sort based on meaning rather than based purely on the first character:

- **Text sort**—No meaning assigned; sort is based purely on the first digit. For example, a list of 1, 5, and 10 would be listed in this order: 1, 10, 5.

- **Number sort**—Sort is alphabetical, except when numbers are involved; then it is based on the number chronology. For example, a list of 1, 5, 10 would be sorted in that same order.

- **Date sort**—Sort is alphabetical except when dates are involved; then it is based on date chronology. For example, a list of 10/1/06, 10/2/05, and 12/2/04 would be sorted from earliest to latest date.

To sort the data in a table, follow these steps:

1. Click anywhere in the table and then click the Sort button on the Layout tab. The Sort dialog box opens, as shown in Figure 12.40.

Figure 12.40
Set up a sort specification for the table.

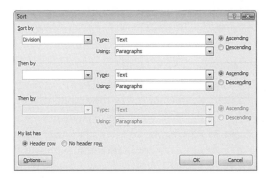

12

2. If the first row contains header labels, select the Header Row option button; otherwise, click No Header Row.

3. In the Sort By list, select the column by which to sort. If you chose Header Row in step 2, the text from that row appears as labels here; otherwise, generic names appear (Column 1, Column 2, and so on).

4. Open the Type list and select Text, Number, or Date.

5. Click Ascending or Descending.

6. (Optional) Set up a secondary sort in the Then By section. The secondary sort will take effect only in the event of a tie in the primary column. You can also enter a third level in the subsequent Then By section.

7. (Optional) To make the sort case-sensitive, click the Options button, mark the Case Sensitive check box, and click OK.

8. Click OK to perform the sort.

Sorting Delimited Data That's Not in a Table

What if your data is not in a table, but instead is delimited with commas, tabs, or some other character? You have a couple of options.

One option is to convert the delimited data into a table with the Convert Text to Table feature, covered later in this chapter.

Another is to perform the sort and specify the delimiter character. Select the paragraphs to sort and then go through the preceding steps. In step 7, clicking the Options button opens the Sort Options dialog box. One of the choices in this dialog box is Separate Fields At. You can specify Tabs, Commas, or Other as the delimiter character. Then click OK and perform the sort normally.

PERFORMING MATH CALCULATIONS IN A TABLE

Word is no substitute for a powerful spreadsheet program such as Excel, but it does have some basic math functions built into it. You can use these to perform operations such as sum, average, count, and round. You can also type your own math formulas for the cells, with or without functions.

One little hiccup in using math in a Word table is that the cells don't have names, at least not in the same sense as in Excel. There are no visible letters designating columns or numbers designating rows.

There's a secret to that, though; they actually *do* respond to those same names as in Excel. The columns have names starting with A at the left, and the rows have numbers starting with 1 at the top. So, for example, the second cell in the second row is B2. Those labels don't appear anywhere in Word, though, so you have to count across or down to determine how many positions away from A1 a particular cell lies, and then reference its name accordingly. You can also refer to all the cells in a certain direction with ABOVE, BELOW, LEFT, and RIGHT. For example, =AVERAGE(LEFT) averages everything to the left of the current cell.

Math formulas in a Word table begin with equal signs, just like in Excel. They can use the traditional math operators:

- Addition (+)
- Subtraction (–)
- Multiplication (*)
- Division (/)

Table 12.2 includes some examples.

TABLE 12.2   BASIC MATH FORMULAS FOR WORD TABLES

Formula	Description
=SUM(ABOVE)	Sums the contents of all the cells above the current one (same column)
=SUM(LEFT)	Sums the contents of all the cells to the left of the current one (same row)
=A1+A2+A3	Sums the contents of cells A1, A2, and A3
=SUM(A1:A3)	Same as above, but uses the SUM function
=A1*(A2+A3)	Multiplies A1 by the sum of A2 and A3

You can't just type a formula into a cell; you must use the Formula dialog box to set it up. Follow these steps to do so:

1. Position the insertion point in the cell where you want to place the formula.
2. Click Formula on the Layout tab to open the Formula dialog box (see Figure 12.41).
3. In the Formula box, a default function might appear, depending on the position of the cell within the table. Accept it, modify it, or delete it and type a different formula or function entirely. Table 12.3 lists the available functions and their syntax. Table 12.4 lists the valid comparison operators you can use for logical functions such as IF, NOT, and AND.

> **TIP**
>
> You can use the Paste Function list to select from among the available functions. The chosen function is added to the current content of the Formula text box.

4. (Optional) Choose a number format from the Number Format list. A number of currency, percentage, and other numeric formats are available.
5. Click OK.

Figure 12.41
Create a math formula.

TABLE 12.3   Math Functions for Word Tables

Function	Purpose	Examples
ABS()	Displays the absolute value of a number.	Absolute value of A1: =ABS(A1)
AND(x,y)	Displays 1 if both x and y are true, or 0 (zero) if either is false).	Check whether A1 and B1 are both greater than zero: =AND(A1>0,B1>0)
AVERAGE()	Averages the numbers in the named range.	Average the values in the cells above the current one: =AVERAGE(ABOVE)
COUNT()	Counts the number of numeric values in a list.	Count the number of numeric values in the cells to the left of the current one: =COUNT(LEFT) Count the number of numeric values in the range A1 through A6: =COUNT(A1:A6) or =COUNT(A1,A2,A3,A4,A5,A6)
DEFINED(x)	Displays 1 if x is a valid expression or 0 if it is not.	Check the formula in A1 for errors: =DEFINED(A1)
FALSE()	Displays a zero.	FALSE()
IF(x, y, z)	Evaluates the expression x, and executes the instructions in y if it is true or in z if it is false. The instructions in y and z can refer to a cell, a number, or TRUE or FALSE.	Display the content of A3 if A1>0; otherwise, display the content of A2: =IF(A1>0,A3,A2) Display TRUE if A1>0; otherwise, display FALSE: =IF(A1>0,TRUE,FALSE)
INT	Displays the numbers to the left of the decimal place only. (Does not round.)	Display only the integer portion of the number in cell A1: =INT(A1)

Function	Purpose	Examples
MAX()	Displays the largest number in the list range.	Display the maximum value in cells A2 through A4: =MAX(A2,A3,A4) or =MAX(A2:A4)
MIN()	Displays the smallest number in the list range.	Display the minimum value in cells A2 through A4: =MIN(A2,A3,A4) or =MIN(A2:A4)
MOD(x,y)	Displays the remainder after dividing x by y a whole number of times.	Display the remainder after dividing A1 by A2: =MOD(A1,A2) For example, if A1 contains 6 and A2 contains 4, the result would be 2 (because 4 goes into 6 one time with a remainder of 2).
NOT(x)	Displays 1 if x is false, or 0 if x is true.	Display 1 if A1 is not greater than or equal to 10: =NOT(A1>=10)
OR(x,y)	Displays 1 if either x or y is true; otherwise displays 0.	Display 1 if either A1 is less than 0 or A2 is greater than 6: =OR(A1<0,A2>6)
PRODUCT()	Multiplies a list of numbers.	Multiply the values in A1 and A2: =PRODUCT(A1,A2) Multiply the values in A1 through A3: =PRODUCT(A1:A3) Multiply the value in A1 by 7: =PRODUCT(A1,7)
ROUND(x,y)	Rounds the value of x to y number of decimal points.	Round the number in A1 to a whole integer (no decimal place): =ROUND(A1,0) Round the number in A1 to the number of decimal places specified in A2: =ROUND(A1,A2)
SIGN(x)	Displays 1 if x is a positive number or -1 if x is a negative number.	Check the positive/negative status of the number in A1: =SIGN(A1)

continues

12

TABLE 12.3 CONTINUED

Function	Purpose	Examples
SUM()	Adds numbers in the specified range.	Add the numbers above the current cell: =SUM(ABOVE) Add the numbers to the left of the current cell: =SUM(LEFT) Add the numbers in cells A1 through A4: =SUM(A1:A4) or =SUM(A1,A2,A3,A4)
TRUE	Displays a 1.	TRUE()

TABLE 12.4 COMPARISON OPERATORS

Operator	Meaning
>	Greater than
>=	Greater than or equal to
<	Less than
<=	Less than or equal to
=	Equal to
<>	Not equal to

12

Editing the Number Format

If none of the number formats are right, you can create your own by typing the codes into the Number Format text box. Here's a quick look at what you can do:

- **Literal symbols**—Type the actual symbols you want to use, in the spots where you want them. For example, precede the number with a currency symbol such as $ or follow it with a percentage symbol.

- **Commas and decimal points**—Add or remove these items as desired.

- **Required digits**—Represent these with 0. The numbers will have at least that many places, using leading zeros if needed. For example, 000 would produce 001.

- **Optional digits**—You don't have to specify these explicitly except when setting up commas between every three numbers, like this: #,##0.

- **Decimal places**—Set these up with 0s (required digits) after a decimal point. For example, 0.000 would ensure one digit before the decimal place and three after it.

- **Negative number handling**—After the main spec, add a semicolon and then indicate how you want negative numbers handled. For example, you could precede the negative number format with a minus sign or surround it in parentheses.

SETTING THE ORDER OF OPERATIONS

When including multiple math operators in a formula, keep in mind the default order of operation. Word processes multiplication and division first, followed by addition and subtraction. If you need to change that order, enclose the portions to be calculated first in parentheses.

For example, in the formula

=A1+A2*5

the A2*5 portion is calculated first, and then the result is added to A1. If you want the addition done first, write it this way:

=(A1+A2)*5

REFERENCING VALUES OUTSIDE THE TABLE

Formulas and functions can include references to numbers that exist elsewhere in the document, not just in cells within that table. To reference a number, set up that number as a bookmark and then reference the bookmark.

→ For more information about bookmarks, **see** "Working with Bookmarks," **p. 610**.

To create a bookmark and then reference it in a formula, follow these steps:

1. Select the number to be bookmarked in the document.
2. On the Insert tab, click Bookmark. The Bookmark dialog box opens.
3. In the Bookmark name box, type a name (keep it short, with no spaces) and click Add. The Bookmark dialog box closes.
4. In the table, begin creating the formula as you normally would. In the spot where you want the bookmark to be referenced, open the Paste Bookmark list and select the bookmark (refer to Figure 12.41).
5. Finish creating the formula as you normally would.

GETTING DATA INTO OR OUT OF TABULAR FORMAT

As you've seen so far in this chapter, one way of creating a table is to insert it from scratch and then type your data into it. But there are other ways to place tabular data into your document, as you'll learn in the next several sections.

CONVERTING TEXT TO A TABLE

Any text can be converted to a table in Word. The key question is, How many columns will it have?

When you convert regular paragraphs to a table, the table consists of a single column only, and each paragraph will be in its own row. If you want more columns, you must make sure that the text is properly delimited before the conversion.

Delimited text is text that is broken up into sections by some consistently used symbol. The most common delimiter characters are tabs and commas. For example, if you have set up a multicolumn layout with tab stops, those paragraphs are *tab-delimited*.

Data exported from a database program is usually in comma-delimited format. For example, the following is a comma-delimited data table consisting of four rows and three columns:

```
First Name,Last Name,City,State
Chuck,Perkins,Decatur,IL
Mildred,Perryman,Moweaqua,IL
Francis,Zindel,Moweaqua,IL
```

Word recognizes common delimiter characters, so when you convert delimited text to a table, Word is able to create the appropriate number of columns to hold it. If there are an inconsistent number of delimiters in the various rows you've selected for inclusion in the table, Word goes with the largest number. So, for example, if you accidentally type two commas between two values rather than the customary one comma, Word will take that as an invitation to insert two columns, and all the other rows will be off by one. That's the most common mistake people make when creating delimited text for table conversion, so pay sharp attention to the delimiter usage.

After preparing the data with delimiters, follow these steps to convert it to a table:

1. Select the text to include in the table.
2. On the Insert tab, click Table and then click Convert Text to Table. The Convert Text to Table dialog box opens (see Figure 12.42).
3. Confirm that the number of columns is what you expected. If it is not, your delimiters are off; click Cancel and fix them.
4. Set an AutoFit behavior for the new table. The options here are the same as when creating a table via Insert Table.

→ For more information about AutoFit options, **see** "Inserting a Table via the Insert Table Dialog Box," **p. 356**.

Figure 12.42
Convert the selected text to a table.

5. Select the delimiter character. Word has probably already made the correct choice, but just confirm that it is accurate.

6. Click OK. The text is converted to a Word table.

CONVERTING A TABLE TO REGULAR TEXT

You can also go the opposite direction: convert a table to regular text paragraphs. Again, you're faced with a delimiter character—what character will substitute for the column breaks? The traditional choice is tabs or commas, but you can use any character you wish.

To convert a table to text, follow these steps:

1. Select the entire table.

2. On the Layout tab, click Convert to Text. The Convert Table to Text dialog box opens (see Figure 12.43).

3. Select the delimiter character to be used.

4. If there are nested tables in the selected table, mark or clear the Convert Nested Tables check box to decide their disposition.

5. Click OK to convert the table to text.

Figure 12.43
Convert the table back to regular text.

PASTING TABLES FROM OTHER OFFICE APPLICATIONS

Several other Office applications utilize row-and-column data organization in various ways. For example, PowerPoint has its own custom table format (very similar to that of Word), and Excel has spreadsheets.

Using the Office Clipboard, you can copy and paste data between Office applications seamlessly, creating new Word tables on the fly to hold the new data.

To paste from Excel, follow these steps:

1. In Excel, select the cells to be copied and then press Ctrl+C (or click Copy on the Home tab) to copy them to the Clipboard.

2. Switch to Word, position the insertion point in the desired location, and press Ctrl+V (or click Paste on the Home tab) to paste the selection into Word.

3. A Paste Options icon appears next to the pasted selection; click it to open the Paste Options menu (see Figure 12.44).

Figure 12.44
Choose paste options after pasting the selection.

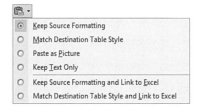

4. Click the desired paste option. You can choose to retain the original formatting, match the document's formatting, paste as a picture or text only, or create a dynamic link to the original data.

For even more pasting options, instead of step 2, click the down arrow on the Paste button and choose Paste Special. A Paste Special dialog box opens; from here you can choose to paste in a variety of formats. One of these options, Microsoft Office Excel Worksheet Object, keeps the data in actual Excel cells, so you can edit it later using Excel's own commands. This is called *embedding* (see Figure 12.45).

Figure 12.45
Pasting as an Excel Worksheet Object creates an embedded worksheet in Word.

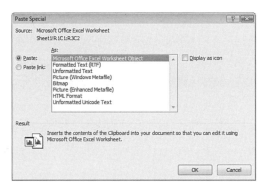

→ For more information about pasting and linking, **see** "Linking to Data in Other Files," **p. 620**.

The procedure is basically the same to paste from PowerPoint (and other applications); select the table in PowerPoint, copy it to the Clipboard, paste it into Word, and then set any paste options desired.

EMBEDDING EXCEL WORKSHEETS AS TABLES

Word's table feature enables you to perform some basic calculations with formulas and functions, as you saw earlier in this chapter. However, it isn't as robust as Excel in this regard. If you want the full Excel functionality, consider embedding an Excel worksheet into the document.

One way to embed an Excel worksheet is to copy data from an existing Excel file and then paste it with Paste Special, choosing Microsoft Office Excel Worksheet Object as the type. (See the preceding section for help with that.)

If the file does not already exist, however, you might find it easier to embed a new blank worksheet in the Word document. Follow these steps to do that:

1. Click in the Word document where you want the embedded worksheet to appear.
2. On the Insert tab, click Table and then click Excel Spreadsheet. A blank spreadsheet appears in the document, and Excel's commands and tabs appear.
3. Create the worksheet as you would in Excel; when you are done, click outside the worksheet's area to return to Word.

The resulting Excel object can be formatted, aligned, and otherwise handled like any other object. Right-click it and choose Format Object to open a dialog box with controls for size, layout, border, and other formatting options.

TROUBLESHOOTING

BANDED ROWS AND COLUMNS DON'T DISPLAY CORRECTLY

Not all styles support banded rows and columns. If nothing seems to be happening when you turn on Banded Rows or Banded Columns, try selecting a different table style.

If you're happy with the current table style except for wanting bands, modify the style. To do so, open the Styles list (from the Design tab) and choose Modify Table Style. Assign a new name in the Name box, and then open the Apply Formatting To menu and choose one of the band options (such as Banded Rows or Banded Columns). Change the formatting as desired and then click OK.

APPLYING A TABLE STYLE REMOVES MANUAL FORMATTING

When you apply a table style, any direct (manual) formatting applied to the table is wiped away. This is by design.

To change styles but keep the manual formatting, instead of clicking a style on the Table Styles list, right-click it to display a menu. Then on that menu, choose Apply and Maintain Formatting.

CHAPTER 13

WORKING WITH PHOTOS

In this chapter

UNDERSTANDING DIGITAL PHOTOGRAPHY

Word tends to treat all picture files more or less the same—it imports them and places them on the page where you specify. All digital images are not created equal, though. There are many types, and some of those types are radically different from others.

This chapter focuses on one specific type of image: the *digital photograph*. A digital photo is a computer representation of an analog source. It could be a photo of a person captured with a digital camera, or it could be a picture of a magazine clipping captured with a scanner. Digital photos can also be acquired from online sources or purchased on CDs.

A digital photograph is a type of *bitmap image*. The word *bitmap* comes from the fact that the picture consists of a grid (map) of tiny individual pixels of different colors, with the exact color for each pixel described as a string of binary digits (called *bits*). Figure 13.1 shows a zoomed-in example. (Another name for this type of image is *raster*.)

Figure 13.1
A photo consists of a grid of tiny colored pixels.

NOTE

There are actually two meanings for the term *bitmap*. One is generic, meaning any picture that is composed of a grid of colored dots. The other is a specific Microsoft-developed file format called Windows Bitmap, with a .bmp extension.

When a photo is taken on a digital camera, the camera uses a light-sensitive grid called a *charge-coupled device (CCD)* to measure the amount of red, green, and blue for each pixel. These values are then written to a file and stored inside the camera, and then eventually transferred to a computer or printer. When a hard-copy photo is scanned, a similar process takes place inside the scanner.

How large is the resulting file for that digital photo? It could be anywhere from less than 20KB to over 10MB. The exact size depends on these factors:

- **The color model**—The way the color of each pixel is described, such as CMYK or RGB.
- **The color depth**—The number of bits used to describe each color, such as 24-bit or 32-bit.
- **The file format**—The format in which the file is saved, such as JPEG or TIF.
- **The resolution**—The number of pixels that comprise the image horizontally and vertically.

The following sections look at each of these factors in greater detail.

UNDERSTANDING COLOR MODELS

A photo can use any of several color models. The most common of these are Red/Green/Blue (RGB) and Cyan/Magenta/Yellow/Black (CMYK).

RGB is the dominant color model used for onscreen display. Use RGB as the color model when creating web pages and other documents that will be distributed online. RGB works so well for onscreen use because it matches the way monitors display colors. RGB defines colors using a 24-bit system that uses 8 bits each for red, green, and blue. Each of the three colors has a value ranging from 0 to 255.

CMYK is the color model used for high-quality printouts. Use CMYK as the color model when creating brochures, newsletters, and other documents that will be printed. Cyan, magenta, yellow, and black are the four colors used in color printers. A CMYK image is a 32-bit image, with 8 bits each for cyan, magenta, yellow, and black. Only a few graphic file formats support CMYK; TIF is one of them.

Most digital cameras and scanners save their images as RGB by default, but there may be a setting you can adjust in the software that will change this mode if your camera will capture in TIF format. If not, you can open the picture in a graphics-editing program such as Photoshop or Paint Shop Pro and convert the image between models. You might need to save the file in a different file format to get CMYK color.

What happens if you don't convert the image? Not much, really, except a minor loss of color quality. You can certainly print RGB color images, and you can use CMYK images on web pages. The colors might not be quite as accurate, however, as if you had used the correct color model for the situation. CMYK and RGB have a slightly different *gamut*—that is, set of colors they include. If your image contains some colors that are out-of-gamut for the color model, the closest possible color is substituted.

UNDERSTANDING COLOR DEPTH

An image's color depth (also called *bit depth*) is the number of bits required to uniquely describe each possible color a pixel can be. In 1-bit color, each pixel is either black or white; in 4-bit color, there are 16 possible on/off combinations for bits, so there are 16 color choices. 8-bit color has 256 color choices (2 to the 8th power), and so on.

13

As noted in the preceding section, a color RGB image uses 24 bits to describe each pixel, and a CMYK image uses 32 bits. As you might guess, CMYK has more colors to choose from and is generally more accurate in expressing colors, but the file sizes are also larger.

Some scanners and digital cameras have a grayscale feature that takes the color depth down to 8-bit black-and-white. An 8-bit grayscale image captures 256 levels of gradation between white and black. A grayscale image usually has a much smaller file size than a color one because it requires fewer bits to describe each pixel.

Some scanners also have a black-and-white mode (separate from grayscale), which captures pictures in a 1-bit mode. Each pixel is either black or white and requires only 1 bit to describe it. The resulting files are extremely small (1/24th the size of a full-color RGB image), but not very attractive. Stand-alone fax machines often use this mode for sending and receiving faxes; that's why pictures tend to fax very poorly.

NOTE

> Scanners typically advertise higher bit depths than 24 or 32. The extra bits are for color correction. The scanner collects extra data and then throws out the bad bits to account for "noise" or error in the scanning process.

Depending on the file format, an RGB image might actually have more than 24 bits. For example, some file formats (such as Photoshop's native PSD format) support alpha channels, which are extra sets of 8 bits used for special purposes such as transparency or clipping. Such file formats tend to produce larger files than their strictly-24-bit counterparts like JPEG.

In some cases, the file format might specify *fewer* than 24 bits as the maximum. The Graphics Interchange Format (GIF) is like that, for example; it is limited to 8-bit color (256 colors in total).

UNDERSTANDING FILE FORMATS

The file format is the standard by which the information about each pixel is recorded. Different file formats can produce very different file sizes and quality levels. These differences are mainly due to two factors: the color depth supported (as described in the preceding section) and the type and amount of compression used.

Compression is an algorithm (a math formula) that decreases the amount of space a file takes up on disk by storing the pixel color data more compactly. Some file formats do not support compression at all; others support one of these types:

- **Lossless compression**—The image is compressed but no image quality is lost. The compression is performed via a completely reversible compression algorithm.
- **Lossy compression**—The image is compressed by recording less data. Either less information about each pixel is recorded, or some of the pixels are removed (and then resimulated when the image is displayed). The image is somewhat reduced in quality as a result.

Some file formats are always compressed; others give you a choice. The ones that give you a choice may also give you a sliding scale of compression level to choose from. You can set the compression level for a file when you resave it in a graphics-editing program.

The TIF format is interesting in a number of ways. It produces very large files, but it also supports a very high color depth (up to 48-bit), and it supports a number of lossless compression types, including LZW compression (the most common), Huffman encoding, Packbits, and FAX – CCITT 3. It is also one of the few file formats that Word supports that allows you to save in the CMYK color model. (Adobe Photoshop's .PSD format also does this, but Word does not accept that format.)

Table 13.1 lists some of the most popular file formats for photos as well as their support for compression and color depth.

TABLE 13.1 POPULAR PHOTO FORMATS SUPPORTED IN WORD 2007

Extension	Compression	Maximum Color Depth
JPEG or JPG	Lossy, adjustable (1 to 99)	24-bit
GIF	Lossless	8-bit
PNG	Lossless	48-bit
BMP	None	24-bit
TIF or TIFF	Lossless	48-bit

UNDERSTANDING IMAGE RESOLUTION

The final factor affecting an image's size is its *resolution*. Resolution has several different meanings, depending on whether or not the image is already stored in digital form and how the image is being captured.

For an image that is already a saved file, resolution is the number of pixels vertically and horizontally that comprise the image, such as 800 (wide) by 600 (high). You can change the resolution on a saved image by using a graphics-editing program to resample the image, either adding or removing pixels. When a graphics program adds pixels, it creates them by *interpolation*. It takes the numeric values of two adjacent pixels, averages them, and then inserts a pixel between them with the averaged values.

Digital cameras, because they tend to capture images of a consistent height-width ratio, often express the resolution as the total number of pixels (height times width). A million pixels is a *megapixel*, so a 3-megapixel camera captures images in which the number of pixels vertically times the number of pixels horizontally is somewhere around 3 million.

For an image that is being input into a computer via a scanner, you specify the resolution you want in dots per inch (dpi). The original size of the hard-copy image you are scanning, combined with the dpi setting you choose, determines the overall number of pixels that will comprise the image. For example, if you scan a 3"×5" photo at 200 dpi, it will have a resolution of 600×1000 when saved as a file.

13

HOW WORD 2007 HANDLES PICTURES

Pictures in Word 2007 get special treatment; they have their own set of controls on the Format tab (which appears when a picture is selected). You can apply many special effects such as picture styles, soft edges, reflection, and so on. You will learn about these special effects later in this chapter.

However, these new picture-formatting capabilities are available only in Word 2007's new file format, not in the older Word 97-2003 format. If you save your document in any document format other than the new Word 2007 format (.docx or .docm), commands for working with pictures are limited to those commands that were available in previous Word versions.

To determine if Word is considering your document to be a Word 2007 or a backward-compatible one, look at a picture's selection handles, and look at the Format tab. Figure 13.2 shows a picture in a Word 2007 document. It has round, pale blue selection handles, and the Format tab features a Picture Styles area.

Figure 13.3 shows a picture in a backward-compatible document. It has gray selection handles (although these could also be green circles, depending on the text-wrap setting for the picture), and the Format tab contains only controls for formatting features from earlier Word versions.

Figure 13.2
A picture in Word 2007 mode.

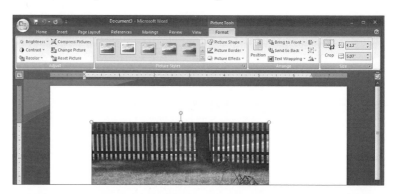

Figure 13.3
A picture in backward-compatible mode.

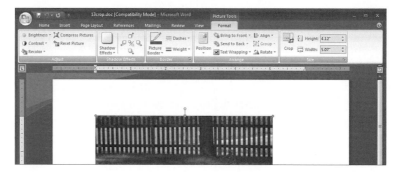

Images that you insert from files are placed in Word 2007 picture format, provided the document itself is a Word 2007 document (.docx or .docm). If you want to work with a picture using the backward-compatible version of the Format tab, use Office, Save As, Word

97-2003 Format to save the file; the picture's type changes automatically. To go the other direction—that is, to gain Word 2007 functionality for a picture in a backward-compatible document—choose Office, Convert to upgrade the file to Word 2007 format.

The tools and dialog boxes are somewhat different for Word 2007 pictures versus backward-compatible ones. In the following sections, I'll point out the differences where applicable.

INSERTING PICTURES FROM FILES

To insert a picture from a file stored on your hard disk (or other disk), follow these steps:

1. On the Insert tab, click Picture. The Insert Picture dialog box opens.

2. (Optional) By default, all supported file types are shown, as in Figure 13.4. To narrow down the files shown to a specific type, select the type.

   Under Windows Vista, type is set from the drop-down list button to the right of the filename. Under Windows XP, it's set from the Files of Type drop-down list.

   NOTE

   > If you are using Windows XP, to see thumbnail images, open the Views button's menu and choose Thumbnails. If you are using Windows Vista, thumbnails automatically appear for the picture icons.

3. Navigate to the folder containing the file and select it.

4. Click Insert.

Figure 13.4
Select a file to insert.

You can also create a dynamic link between the picture and the document, so the copy in the document stays up-to-date when the original changes. To do so, click the down arrow next to the Insert button in step 4 and choose either Link to File or Insert and Link. Link to File creates a link that is automatically updated each time the document is opened; if the picture file is not available, an error appears. Insert and Link creates a link but also retains a static copy of the picture, so that if the original is not available, the last available version appears.

→ To learn more about linking, **see** "Linking to Data in Other Files," **p. 620**.

Word accepts pictures in these formats:

- Windows Metafile (.wmf)
- Windows Enhanced Metafile (.emf)
- Compressed Windows Enhanced Metafile (.emz)
- Compressed Windows Metafile (.wmz)
- JPEG File Interchange Format (.jpg, .jpeg, .jfif, .jpe)

- Macintosh PICT (.pct, .pict)
- Compressed Macintosh PICT (.pcz)
- Portable Network Graphics (.png)
- Tag Image File Format (.tif, .tiff)
- Graphics Interchange Format (.gif, .gfa)

- Windows Bitmap (.bmp, .dib, .rle, .bmz)
- CorelDRAW (.cdr)
- Computer Graphics Metafile (.cgm)
- Encapsulated PostScript (.eps)
- WordPerfect Graphics (.wpg)

NOTE

Graphic import filters are registered in the Windows Registry in HKEY_LOCAL_MACHINE\Software\Microsoft\Shared Tools\Graphics Filters\Import. The actual filter files are stored in Program Files\Common Files\Microsoft Shared\GRPHFLT.

To use a picture that's in some other file format, open the file in a graphics-editing program and then do one of the following:

- Save it in one of the supported formats.
- Copy it to the Clipboard and paste it into Word.

SETTING TEXT WRAP

By default, a picture is placed into the document as an inline image at the insertion point. An *inline image* is a graphic that is treated as a character of text would be treated. As far as Word is concerned, the inline image is just a really big, funny-looking letter. When you edit the surrounding text, the picture scoots over to make room, just like text would scoot (see Figure 13.5).

Figure 13.5
A picture is an inline image by default.

Employee Fishing Trip
By Cynthia Hicks

On August 18, seventeen employees of ACME Industries traveled to Coldwater Dam to enjoy a day of sport fishing. While nobody came home with a record-setting catch, almost everyone caught a few fish and had a great time enjoying the sun and the outdoors.

You can drag an inline image to a different location, but it will continue to be treated as a text character, so you can drag it only into a spot where you could drag text; you can't drag it to the far left or right of the paragraph, for example. That's the nature of an inline image.

If you need more flexibility than that, you'll need to change the picture's Text Wrap setting so that it is no longer an inline image, but rather a free-floating object. You can then drag the picture anywhere on the page, regardless of the text. If there happens to be text in the spot where you drag the picture, the text and the picture interact according to the Text Wrap setting you chose. For example, if you chose Square, the text wraps around the picture's rectangular border, as in Figure 13.6.

Figure 13.6
Text now wraps around the picture.

To set text wrap for a picture, follow these steps:

1. Select the picture.
2. On the Format tab, click Text Wrapping, and then click the desired text-wrap setting.

   Alternatively, right-click the picture, point to Text Wrapping, and click the desired wrap setting (see Figure 13.7). This method does not work with backward-compatible pictures.

Figure 13.7
Set the picture's text-wrap setting.

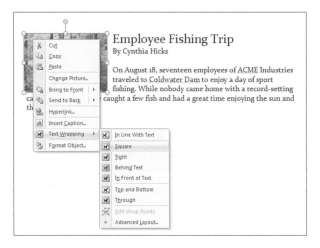

These are the same text-wrap options as for text boxes, which you learned about in Chapter 11, "Working with Nonstandard Document Layouts." All the wrap options allow the image to be free-floating except In Line With Text; that option takes the picture back to being an inline image.

For more control, choose More Layout Options from the menu in Figure 13.7, opening the Advanced Layout dialog box. From here, you can choose a basic wrapping style using buttons that correspond to the regular menu options, and you can then fine-tune the setting by specifying which sides to wrap around and what distance should be left between the text and the picture (see Figure 13.8). Depending on which wrapping style you choose, some of the options might not be available.

Figure 13.8
Specify advanced text-wrap settings.

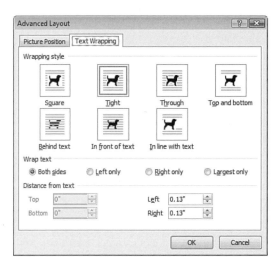

SETTING PICTURE POSITION

Often a picture's position within a document is significant because it needs to stay with certain text or stay in a certain location in relation to the margins. The following sections explain some methods of positioning a picture.

MANUALLY POSITIONING A PICTURE

A floating picture (that is, one with any text-wrap setting other than In Line With Text) can be positioned anywhere on the page simply by dragging it there. Position the mouse pointer over the center of the picture (or actually anywhere on it other than a selection handle) and drag.

WORKING WITH ANCHORS

Each floating picture has an anchor. An *anchor* is a marker that indicates how a floating paragraph relates to the document text. A picture anchors itself to whatever paragraph is nearest to its top edge. When you drag a picture around on a page, its anchor moves too, re-anchoring itself to whatever paragraph is nearest. You can view the anchor symbol by turning on the display of nonprinting characters (Show/Hide ¶ on the Home tab). Figure 13.9 shows an anchor.

Figure 13.9
Each picture has an anchor.

Anchor

The anchor is actually part of the paragraph. When the paragraph moves, the anchor moves too, and so does the picture connected with it. For example, if you select the paragraph containing the anchor and cut it to the Clipboard, the picture disappears with it. If you then paste that paragraph in a new location, the picture is pasted there too. If the paragraph floats to another page because of text additions or deletions, the picture floats with it.

CHANGING A PICTURE'S ANCHOR POINT

You can manually change which paragraph a picture is anchored to by dragging the anchor symbol to another paragraph. If you subsequently drag the picture to place it somewhere else, though, the picture re-anchors itself to the nearest paragraph, regardless of the anchor reassignment you made.

LOCKING AN ANCHOR

If you do not want a picture to re-anchor itself to the nearest paragraph when you drag the picture, lock the anchor point. That way the picture remains anchored to the current paragraph even if you move the picture.

To lock the anchor, follow these steps:

1. Select the picture and then display the Format tab.
2. Click the Position button, and click More Layout Options. The Advanced Layout dialog box opens.
3. Click the Picture Position tab.
4. Mark the Lock Anchor check box.
5. Click OK. The anchor now shows a lock symbol, indicating it has been locked.

To unlock the anchor, repeat these steps and clear the Lock Anchor check box.

CHOOSING A POSITION PRESET

Position presets are new in Word 2007. They are a combination of location settings and text-wrap settings, and determine where on a page the picture appears and how it interacts with surrounding text.

13

To select a position preset, follow these steps:

1. Select the picture.
2. If the Position button appears on the Format tab, click it; otherwise, click Arrange and then click Position.
3. Click one of the position presets.

The positions on the Position menu are grouped according to text-wrap type: Inline With Text or With Text Wrapping (see Figure 13.10). (If you want some other text-wrap setting than that, apply the position preset first and then change the text-wrap setting as in the preceding section.)

Figure 13.10
Select a picture position preset.

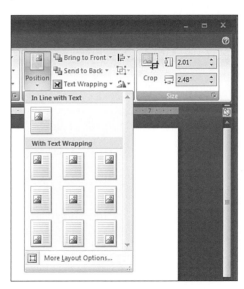

These picture presets set the horizontal and vertical alignment in relation to the document margins. The pictures will stay in place no matter how the text moves around them as a result of text editing you might do.

SPECIFYING A CUSTOM POSITION

For more alignment choices, choose More Layout Options from the menu shown in Figure 13.10, opening the Advanced Layout dialog box. Then click the Picture Position tab and use the controls there to fine-tune the picture's position (see Figure 13.11).

Figure 13.11
Set advanced picture position settings.

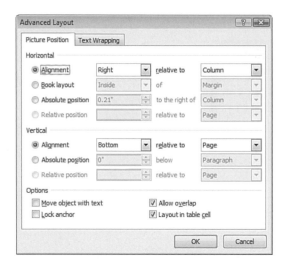

For horizontal positioning, choose one of these settings:

- **Alignment**—You can set a position (Right, Left, Centered) and what it should be in relation to (Margin, Page, Column, and so on). Most of the presets use this option. Using this setting ensures that if settings in the document change (such as margin settings), the picture will adjust itself accordingly.

- **Book Layout**—Use this setting for a two-sided layout in which you want the picture to float to the right or left depending on whether the page is an odd- or even-numbered one. The picture can be set to float either inside or outside of the margin or page.

- **Absolute Position**—Use this if the picture should be locked to a certain spot on the page and be unaffected by margins, columns, or any other document-layout settings.

- **Relative Position**—Use this setting to specify a percentage relative to some other element. For example, you could set a position of 25% relative to the page to position the object 25% of the way across the page.

For vertical positioning, the same settings are available, except there's no Book Layout and the alignments are Top, Centered, and Bottom instead of Right, Left, and Centered.

RESIZING PICTURES

To size a picture in a Word document, drag one of its selection handles.

In a Word 2007 document, you must hold down the Shift key as you drag a corner selection handle if you want to resize proportionally. In a backward-compatible document, resizing is automatically proportional when dragging a corner selection handle; to resize in only one dimension, drag a side selection handle.

If you need the image to be a specific size, use the Height and Width boxes on the Format tab (see Figure 13.12). These boxes are linked—changing one dimension also changes the other by a proportional amount.

13

Height

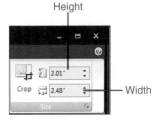

Figure 13.12
Set a height and width on the Format tab.

Width

NOTE

The Format tab becomes available when the picture is selected. Double-click the picture to bring the Format tab to the forefront.

For even more control over the size, click the dialog box launcher for the Size group on the Format tab. Depending on the picture type, this either opens the Size dialog box (for a Word 2007 document) or the Format Picture dialog box with the Size tab displayed (for a backward-compatible document).

If working in the Size dialog box, you can set a specific size in the Size and Rotate section, or you can increase or decrease the size by percentages in the Scale section (see Figure 13.13). If you're working in the Format Picture dialog box, the options are similar.

Figure 13.13
Set a precise size for an image.

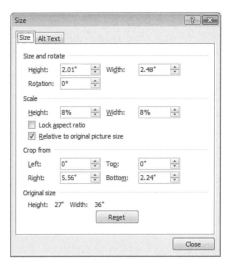

The Lock Aspect Ratio check box enables you to scale the picture proportionally. When it is marked, if you enter a certain value in the Height box, the Width setting will change by the same percentage.

The Relative to Original Picture Size check box makes the scaling occur in relation to the original size (listed at the bottom of the dialog box), rather than any interim sizing that has been done.

To go back to the picture's original size, click the Reset button, either in the Size dialog box or on the Format tab. (On the Format tab, it's called Reset Picture.)

CROPPING PICTURES

To *crop* a picture is to trim off one or more edges so your audience can focus in on what's most important in the image. For example, in Figure 13.14, all the extraneous background has been trimmed to show the dogs more clearly.

Figure 13.14
Cropping helps the reader focus on what's important in the image.

The easiest way to crop a picture is to use the Crop tool on the Format tab. Follow these steps:

1. Click the picture.
2. Click the Crop button. The selection handles on the picture change to black lines.
3. Drag a selection handle on the image inward to crop the image. Repeat on other sides as needed.
4. Press the Esc key or click the Crop button again to finish cropping.

You can uncrop a picture at any time by reentering cropping mode (steps 1–2) and then dragging the selection handle outward again. You cannot uncrop if you have compressed the picture, however, as discussed in the next section, because compression deletes the cropped areas of the picture.

Alternatively, you can crop by specifying an amount to crop from each side in inches. To crop by specifying values, follow these steps:

1. Click the dialog box launcher for the Size group on the Format tab, opening the Size dialog box (for a Word 2007 document) or the Format Picture dialog box (for a backward-compatible document).
2. If you're working in the Size dialog box, click the Size tab. If you're working in the Format Picture dialog box, click the Picture tab.
3. In the Crop From area, enter an amount in inches to crop off of each side of the image.
4. Click Close or OK.

13

To undo cropping using the dialog box method, set the cropping amounts to zero for each side. To undo cropping for the ribbon method, turn on cropping again and drag the corner(s) outward to remove the cropping.

COMPRESSING PICTURES

The larger the original image's file size, the larger the size will be of the Word file in which you insert it. Resizing or cropping the picture in Word does not decrease the file size; it stays the same as if the picture were being used at full 100% size. If file size is an issue (for example, if you plan to distribute the document via e-mail or the Web), consider taking some steps to decrease it as much as you can.

There are two ways of decreasing the file size. One is to resize or crop the image file in a third-party graphics-editing program *before* importing it into Word; another is to use the Compress Pictures feature in Word.

Compress Pictures combines a variety of techniques to decrease the file size, including removing cropped-out areas of pictures and resizing the image file to a particular number of pixels per inch based on the document's planned usage.

NOTE

> Pixels per inch (ppi) is a more common unit of measurement than dots per inch (dpi) when referring to onscreen resolution. Word 2007 uses ppi.

The dialog box appearance and options available vary depending on whether you are working in a Word 2007 or a backward-compatible document.

To compress pictures for a Word 2007 document, follow these steps:

1. Select one of the pictures to be compressed. If you do not want to compress all the pictures in the document, do one at a time, or select only the pictures you want to compress.

2. Click Compress Pictures on the Format tab. The Compress Pictures dialog box opens (see Figure 13.15).

Figure 13.15
Compress the pictures in the document to decrease the file size.

3. (Optional) If you want to compress only the selected picture(s), mark the Apply to Selected Pictures Only check box (see Figure 13.15).

4. Click the Options button. The Compression Settings dialog box opens (see Figure 13.16).

Figure 13.16
Configure compression settings for a Word 2007 document.

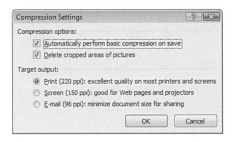

5. Set the compression options:

   ■ **Automatically Perform Basic Compression on Save**—When this is enabled, all pictures will be compressed when the file is saved, even if you do not use Compress Pictures specifically. This is turned on by default.

   ■ **Delete Cropped Areas of Pictures**—When this is enabled, your crops (if any) become permanent when compression is performed with Compress Pictures.

   ■ **Target Output**—Select an image quality, in pixels per inch, depending on the intended use. A lower ppi results in a smaller file size but poorer image quality. If the image is already at a low ppi, this setting will not increase its ppi; this setting only decreases ppi.

6. Click OK to return to the Compress Pictures dialog box.

7. Click OK to perform the compression now.

To compress pictures for a backward-compatible document, follow these steps:

1. Select one of the pictures to be compressed. If you do not want to compress all the pictures in the document, do one at a time, or select only the pictures you want to compress.

2. Click Compress Pictures on the Format tab. The Compress Pictures dialog box opens (see Figure 13.17).

Figure 13.17
Configure compression settings for a backward-compatible document.

3. Select the option button that indicates what you want to compress: Selected Pictures or All Pictures in Document.

4. Set the compression options. For a Word 2007 document, the options are:

- **Change Resolution**—This is equivalent to Target Output. Your only choices are Web/Screen (96 dpi), Print (200 dpi), or No Change.
- **Compress Pictures**—This enables the pictures to be compressed. If you turn off this option, no compression will take place (but cropping can still take place; see the next option).
- **Delete Cropped Areas of Pictures**—This is the same as for a Word 2007 document; when enabled, your crops (if any) become permanent.

5. Click OK to perform the compression now.

SETTING THE BRIGHTNESS, CONTRAST, AND COLOR MODE

You can adjust a picture's brightness, contrast, and image mode (color, grayscale, and so on) in a third-party graphics-editing program before importing the picture into Word, and usually that's how the professionals do it. Most photo-editing programs have great tools for applying such effects.

If you don't have access to an editing program, though, or you forgot to make the corrections before importing into Word, you can use Word's relatively modest tools to accomplish these effects.

ADJUSTING BRIGHTNESS AND CONTRAST

To adjust brightness, click the Brightness button on the Format tab and select an amount of change, from +40% to –40%. The same goes for contrast; use the Contrast button on the Format tab. Both of these go in increments of 10, as shown in Figure 13.18.

If you need an amount that's greater than 40%, or you need to specify the amount in a smaller increment than 10%, do the following.

For a Word 2007 picture:

1. Click the dialog box launcher for the Picture Styles group on the Format tab. The Format Picture dialog box opens.
2. Click Picture. Sliders for Brightness and Contrast appear.
3. Drag the sliders to adjust the amount (0% is in the center), or enter precise values in the text boxes provided.
4. Click Close.

For a backward-compatible document:

1. Click the dialog box launcher for the Border group on the Format tab. The Format Picture dialog box opens.

2. On the Picture tab, drag the Brightness and/or Contrast sliders to adjust the values (50% is in the center) or enter precise values in the text boxes provided.

3. Click OK.

Figure 13.18
Choose a Contrast or Brightness preset from the Format tab.

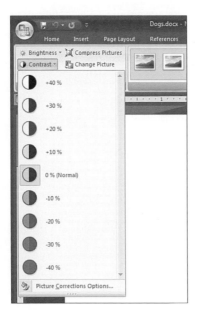

NOTE

Notice that in a Word 2007 document, 0% is the default value, whereas in a backward-compatible document, 50% is the default value.

CHANGING THE COLOR MODE

The image mode is controlled on the Recolor button's menu. The options available depend upon whether it is a Word 2007 or a backward-compatible document.

For a backward-compatible document, only four modes are available:

- **Automatic**—The default image.
- **Grayscale**—Color images are converted to grayscale; no change if the image is already grayscale or black-and-white.
- **Black & white**—Color and grayscale images are converted to black-and-white, with each pixel being converted to either black or white.
- **Washout**—The image remains in color, but all colors are lightened dramatically so the image looks like a watermark of itself.

13

For a Word 2007 document, there are these additional modes as well, as shown in Figure 13.19:

- **Dark Variations**—Dark-tinted color washes of various theme colors.

- **Light Variations**—Light-tinted color washes of various theme colors.

- **More Dark Variations**—A color palette from which you can choose a dark-tinted color wash using any color.

- **Set Transparent Color**—Turns the cursor into a color selector; click on any color in the image to make it transparent.

Figure 13.19
Recoloring options for pictures in Word 2007 documents.

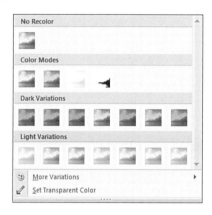

Image modes are useful when you want to see how a picture looks when distributed in a certain way. For example, Grayscale shows you how the image looks when printed on a monochrome printer, and Black and White shows you how the image looks when faxed. (Most pictures look like shapeless blobs in Black and White.)

Washout can be combined with a Behind Text text-wrap setting to create watermark-like effects on a page. (Word's own Watermark feature is more efficient for creating watermarks, though.)

→ To learn more about watermarks, **see** "Applying a Page Watermark," **p. 287**.

APPLYING PICTURE STYLES AND EFFECTS

New in Word 2007, you can apply a variety of picture styles to your pictures. These are presets that combine several types of formatting, including border style and shape, shadow, edge softening, glow effects, 3-D rotation, and reflection. Most of these effects are available only for Word 2007 pictures. However, rudimentary versions of some of the effects, such as shadows and borders, are also available for pictures in backward-compatible documents.

APPLYING A PICTURE STYLE

To apply a picture style, click the down arrow in the Picture Styles group of the Format tab and select one of the samples on the menu (see Figure 13.20).

Figure 13.20
Select a picture style.

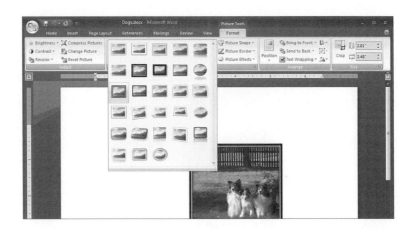

You cannot save your own picture styles (unfortunately), but you can modify a picture style by changing its effects.

To fine-tune the picture style, use the Picture Effects drop-down list in the Picture Styles group of the Format tab to specify various combinations of effects, such as Shadow, Reflection, Glow, Soft Edges, Preset, and 3-D Rotation.

APPLYING A SHADOW EFFECT

A *shadow* is a shaded background behind the image that makes it look like it is raised off the page.

A shadow has these adjustable attributes in Word 2007:

- **Color**—What color is the shadow?
- **Transparency**—How transparent or opaque is the shadow?
- **Size**—How far past the edges of the image does the shadow extend?
- **Blur**—How sharp or fuzzy are the edges of the shadow?
- **Angle**—Which sides of the image are shadowed?
- **Distance**—How far away from the image is the shadow?

Shadow effects are very different for Word 2007 versus in backward-compatible documents. For Word 2007 pictures, all of the previously listed attributes are fully adjustable. For backward-compatible documents, there are some limits. For example, for the angle, you must choose from among presets, and for transparency, there is only one option: semi-transparent. Blur is not available at all for backward-compatible documents.

Because the effects are applied differently, let's look at the shadows for the two picture types separately.

13

APPLYING A SHADOW IN A WORD 2007 DOCUMENT

For a Word 2007 picture, use the Shadow option on the Picture Effects drop-down list on the Format tab to select a shadow preset (see Figure 13.21).

Figure 13.21
Choose a shadow preset.

If none of the presets are exactly what you want, choose Shadow Options from the menu, opening the Format Picture dialog box. Then click Shadow to see the shadow options, as in Figure 13.22. Start with one of the presets if desired. Then change the shadow color, and drag each of the sliders to control the shadow's properties.

APPLYING A SHADOW IN A BACKWARD-COMPATIBLE DOCUMENT

The shadow effects available in backward-compatible documents are the same as the ones from earlier Word versions. Start by choosing a shadow style and direction from the Shadow Effects button on the Format tab. To select a different shadow color, or to toggle semi-transparency on/off for the shadow, open the Color submenu (see Figure 13.23).

To fine-tune the shadow positioning, click one of the Nudge Shadow buttons to the right of the Shadow Effects button. You can nudge the shadow in any of four directions. The center button toggles the shadow on or off entirely.

13

Figure 13.22
Fine-tune the shadow
settings here.

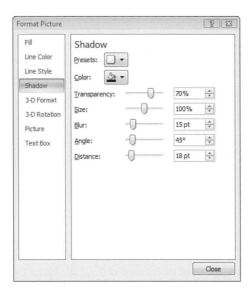

Figure 13.23
Choose a shadow
style and color.

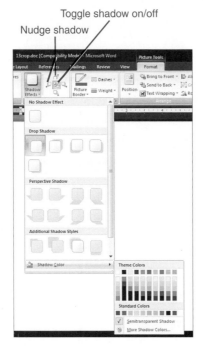

APPLYING REFLECTION

Reflection creates a reflected effect for the picture; a faint, flipped version of the picture
appears below it. Choose a reflection type from the Reflection menu, via the Picture Effects
menu on the Format tab.

APPLYING GLOW

Glow is an extra border around a picture with soft edges applied to it so that it looks like there is a colored light behind the picture. Choose a glow setting from the Glow list on the Picture Effects menu of the Format tab. To select a color that isn't on the menu, choose More Glow Colors and then click a color to use. To remove the glow, open the menu and choose No Glow.

APPLYING SOFT EDGES

The Soft Edges feature blurs the edges of the picture. The Soft Edges option appears on the Picture Effects menu on the Format tab. You can select a certain number of points to blur; a higher number blurs more of the picture. To remove the effect, open the menu and choose No Soft Edges.

CAUTION

> Soft Edges is incompatible with some of the Preset settings; when a preset is applied that specifies a certain treatment for the edges of the image, applying a Soft Edges setting will have no effect.

APPLYING A PICTURE PRESET

Word 2007 has a number of picture shapes and textures, known as *presets*. They add special effects to the picture, such as beveled edges, contours, and different surface textures and lighting. You can access these from the Preset option on the Picture Effects menu, shown in Figure 13.24.

Figure 13.24
Choose a picture preset.

For more options, choose 3-D Options from the menu and then click 3-D Format. You can then set amounts for top and bottom bevel, color depth, contour color, surface material, lighting, and angle.

→ 3-D Format effects are covered in greater detail later in the book. **See** "Formatting Drawn Objects," **p. 472**.

ROTATING A PICTURE

The procedures for rotation are different depending on the picture's type. If it's in a Word 2007 document, many more rotation options are available, including 3-D rotation; in a backward-compatible document, rotation is limited to two-dimensional spinning.

MANUALLY ROTATING A PICTURE

The basic manual type of rotation is the same for all picture types. When a picture is selected, a rotation handle (a circle) appears above it. Drag that handle to rotate the picture. This works for all images *except* backward-compatible images that have a Text Wrapping setting of In Line With Text (see Figure 13.25).

Rotation handle

Figure 13.25
Rotate a picture by dragging its rotation handle.

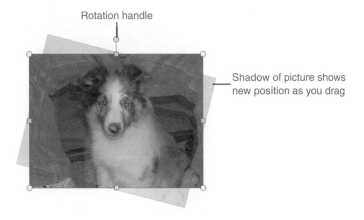

Shadow of picture shows new position as you drag

ROTATING A PICTURE BY A SPECIFIED AMOUNT

If eyeballing it isn't producing the desired results, consider rotating a picture by entering a specific rotation amount.

There are presets for rotating to the left or right 90 degrees; you can use one of these twice to rotate the picture 180 degrees (that is, to turn it upside-down). Here's how to use one of the presets:

1. Select the picture and display the Format tab.
2. Click the Rotate button on the Format tab.
3. To rotate 90 degrees left or right, select Rotate Left 90° or Rotate Right 90°.

If you need some other amount, follow these steps instead:

1. Select the picture and display the Format tab.

13

2. Click the Rotate button on the Format tab.

3. Click More Rotation Options. For a Word 2007 document, the Size dialog box opens; for a backward-compatible document, the Format Picture dialog box opens.

4. Type a number of degrees in the Rotation box, or use the up/down buttons to specify the value.

5. Click Close or OK.

APPLYING 3-D ROTATION

3-D rotation is new in Word 2007 and is available only with Word 2007 documents (not in backward-compatible documents). This is a far cry from ordinary rotation! With ordinary rotation, the image does not change; it's just rotated wholesale. With 3-D rotation, however, the image is actually distorted to simulate rotation along the X, Y, and Z axes. Figure 13.26 shows some examples.

Figure 13.26
3-D rotation examples.

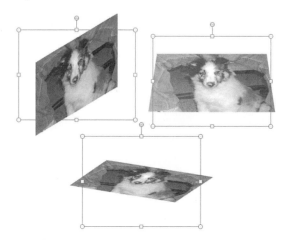

To apply a 3-D rotation preset, follow these steps:

1. Select the picture and display the Format tab.

2. Click the 3-D Rotation option on the Picture Effects menu.

3. Click one of the rotation presets (see Figure 13.27).

Here's how to create a custom 3-D effect:

1. Select the picture and display the Format tab.

2. Click the 3-D Rotation option on the Picture Effects menu.

3. Click 3-D Rotation Options. The Format Picture dialog box opens.

4. Click 3-D Rotation, displaying the rotation controls shown in Figure 13.28.

Figure 13.27
Select a 3-D rotation preset.

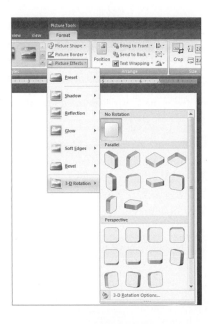

Figure 13.28
Create a custom 3-D effect.

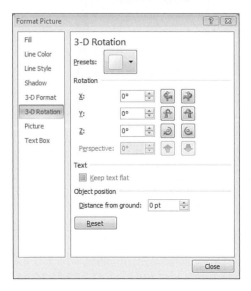

13

5. (Optional) To use one of the presets as a starting point, choose it from the Presets list.

6. Use the buttons in the Rotation section to enter amounts of rotation on the X, Y, and/or Z axes. The up/down arrow buttons increment/decrement the value by 10 degrees per click; you can also type specific values in the text boxes.

7. Click Close to accept the rotation settings.

APPLYING A PICTURE BORDER

A *border* is a line around the perimeter of the picture. Some of the picture styles include borders; others don't, but you can apply the border manually after applying the style; still others, especially the ones that involve 3-D, preclude the use of a border.

Three options can be set for a border from the Format tab: Picture Border (color), Dashes (style), and Weight (thickness).

The interface is somewhat different for Word 2007 versus backward-compatible documents. For a Word 2007 document, all the options are available from the Picture Border button's menu. Submenus appear for Weight and Dashes. In a backward-compatible document, there are separate buttons on the Format tab for Picture Border, Dashes, and Weight. Figure 13.29 shows the version for Word 2007 documents.

Figure 13.29
Set border options for the picture in a Word 2007 document.

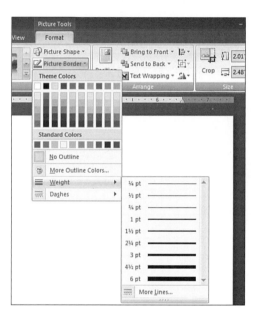

USING FIGURE CAPTIONS

In a document that contains multiple pictures, you might find it useful to number them using Word's Figure Captions feature. Using the Figure Captions feature is preferable to manually numbering the graphics because the numbers automatically change if you add or remove graphics as you edit the document. Figure captions work just like table captions (see Chapter 12, "Creating and Formatting Tables"), but it's a separate numbering set.

NOTE

You can add figure captions to other objects besides pictures; you can include charts, diagrams, and just about any other object as a figure.

To add a caption to a picture (or other object), follow these steps:

1. Right-click the picture and choose Insert Caption. The Caption dialog box opens (see Figure 13.30).

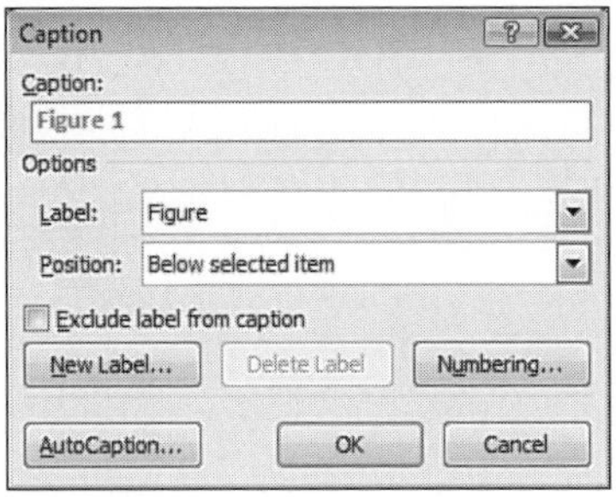

Figure 13.30
Set up a caption for figures in the document.

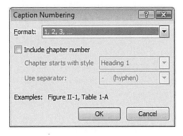

2. Leave the Label setting at Figure.

3. In the Position list, choose where you want the captions to appear for figures. (Usually figures have captions below them.)

4. The caption will read *Figure 1*. If you want some other word than *Figure*, click New Label and specify some other word(s) instead.

   Alternatively, to omit using a word at all before the number, mark the Exclude Label from Caption check box.

5. Click the Numbering button. The Caption Numbering dialog box opens (see Figure 13.31).

Figure 13.31
Control the numbering style for figure captions.

6. Select a format from the Format list.

7. (Optional) To include a chapter number with the caption, mark the Include Chapter Number check box and then choose what style designates a chapter and what separator character should be used.

8. Click OK to return to the Caption dialog box.

9. Click OK. The caption appears in the document, immediately above (or below) the picture.

10. Click to the right of the caption and type a text description if desired.

13

Automatically Captioning Certain Object Types

If you frequently insert certain graphic types and you always want to caption them, you can save some time by turning on AutoCaption.

From the Caption dialog box, click AutoCaption. Then in the AutoCaption dialog box, mark the check boxes for the file types that you want to automatically assign captions to. Use the Use Label and Position settings to fine-tune the labeling specs.

You might be surprised that many of the file types on the list are not graphics formats, but various other types of objects. This points to an important fact: All types of objects can have captions, not just pictures.

TROUBLESHOOTING

WORD 2007 PICTURE TOOLS ARE NOT AVAILABLE

When you're working with a document from an earlier Word format or are working with documents imported from other programs such as WordPerfect, Word's standard picture tools (on the Format tab) are not available; instead, a special version of the Format tab appears designed for backward compatibility. Check the title bar; if it reads "Compatibility Mode," it isn't in Word 2007 format.

To make the Word 2007 picture tools available, you must convert the document to Word 2007 format. To do so, open the Office menu and choose Convert.

CAN'T MANUALLY CHOOSE THE PICTURE SHAPE

In a Word 2007 document, you can indirectly apply various shapes to pictures by choosing a picture preset from the Picture Effects menu on the Format tab. However, you can't manually select a picture frame shape independently of the presets.

To get around this limitation, draw a shape using the Shapes button on the Insert tab, and then set the fill effect for the shape to Picture and choose the picture you want to insert into it.

→ **See** "Applying a Picture Fill," **p. 476** for more information about picture fills.

CHAPTER 14

WORKING WITH CLIP ART AND THE CLIP ORGANIZER

In this chapter

UNDERSTANDING CLIP ART AND VECTOR GRAPHICS

The term *clip art* comes from way back in the days before computers were common. People who needed line art for sales and marketing materials would buy enormous clip art books. These books consisted of nothing but page after page of line drawings of just about any business subject imaginable, all crammed together with dozens of images per page. When they found an image they liked, they would clip it out of the book with scissors and use it in their layout paste-up. (There was no desktop publishing back then, of course.) As computers and desktop publishing became popular, the term *clip art* stuck around, and began to refer to a line-art drawing saved in a file.

Usually clip art images are *vector graphics*, not bitmaps. Vector graphics are very different from the photos you worked with in Chapter 13, "Working with Photos." Whereas a bitmap image records a numeric color value for every pixel in the image, a vector drawing expresses the image as a set of mathematical equations, somewhat like what you learned in Geometry class in school. For example, a vector drawing of a circle consists of a math formula describing the circle (its shape and diameter) plus information about its border color and fill color. Because the graphic is constructed on the fly for each usage, its edges appear very smooth (see Figure 14.1).

Figure 14.1
A vector graphic has smooth edges that remain smooth even when resized.

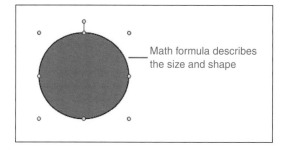

Math formula describes the size and shape

It doesn't take very much space to store that information, so vector drawings have very small file sizes compared to bitmap pictures. The benefits don't stop there, though. Vector drawings also have a huge advantage over bitmaps when they are resized. When a bitmap image is resized, it loses a certain amount of quality, especially when enlarged. Resized bitmap images tend to get the "jaggies"—that is, jagged edges on curves and lines—when they are used at different sizes (see Figure 14.2). Vector drawings are not subject to this problem because each time they are resized, their math formula is simply recalculated and they are redrawn.

14

Figure 14.2
A bitmap circle has jagged edges, which only get worse if the circle is resized.

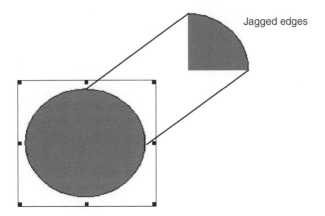

Jagged edges

Vector drawings will never replace photos because they are not realistic-looking. You can't save scanner or digital camera output in vector format. Vector graphics can't have complex shading, and it's very difficult to construct anything reasonably lifelike with them. Think about the people in 3D vector-based games such as *The Sims*, for example. They're fun to play with, but you would never mistake any of those images for photos of real humans. Vector drawings are best for cartoons, drawings, diagrams—and, of course, clip art.

Vector graphics are used for almost every object type that can be created using the tools contained within Word. You will learn more about vector graphics in upcoming chapters:

- WordArt and AutoShapes—Chapter 15, "Working with Drawings and WordArt"
- Charts—Chapter 16, "Working with Charts"
- SmartArt (diagrams)—Chapter 17, "Working with SmartArt and Math Formulas"

By purchasing Word (or Office), you gain access to a huge online repository of artwork from Microsoft. This artwork library consists of four types of files: clip art, bitmap photos, sounds, and movies (mostly animated GIF bitmaps). In this chapter, we are most concerned with the clip art, but you will also learn how to import the other types as well, through the Clip Art interface, and how to organize artwork of all file types using the Clip Organizer.

NOTE

> Most of the Microsoft-provided clip art is in one of two formats: Windows Metafile (.wmf) or Enhanced Metafile (.emf). These are both vector-based graphic formats that can be opened in almost any vector-based drawing program.

Most casual users will find that the Microsoft artwork library has more than enough clip art for their needs, but other clip art collections are also available, either online or on CD/DVD. You can integrate these clip collections with the Clip Organizer in Word so that all artwork is available from a single interface.

→ To learn more about integrating third-party clips with Word's Clip Organizer, **see** "Using the Clip Organizer," **p. 435**.

14

FINDING AND INSERTING CLIP ART

Clip art is organized by keyword, so you can search for a word and see all clips that contain that keyword. A clip can have multiple keywords assigned to it, so you might find the same clip by searching for *dog*, *animal*, *puppy*, and *pet*, for example.

NOTE

> Most of the clips are available via the Internet, so make sure the PC is online before beginning a clip art search; otherwise, the search results will be very meager.

➔ To learn more clip art keywords, **see** "Using the Clip Organizer," **p. 435**.

To find and insert a clip, follow these steps:

1. On the Insert tab, click Clip Art. The Clip Art task pane opens.
2. In the Search For box, type the keyword to search for.
3. In the Search In box, make sure All Collections appears. If it does not, open the drop-down list and click Everywhere.

NOTE

> The available collections are My Collections (your own custom ones), Office Collections (local collections that Office placed on your hard disk), and Web Collections (online collections). Usually searching all collections is desirable, but there might be some situations where you would want to exclude a collection. For example, if you have a very slow Internet connection and you know that the clip you want is on your hard disk, you might exclude Web Collections.

CAUTION

> When the check box for collection (other than Everywhere) is clear, clicking it once selects its top level only; click it again to select the entire collection.

4. Open the Results Should Be list and make sure only the Clip Art check box is marked. Clear any other check boxes. (see Figure 14.3).
5. Click Go. Word finds and displays clips that match the keyword you specified.

NOTE

> Clips with a globe icon in their bottom-left corner are from Web Collections. When you select one, there may be a momentary delay while the clip is downloaded to your PC.

6. Click a clip to place it into the document at the insertion point.

Figure 14.3
Search only for clip art.

Each found clip has its own menu. To see it, point at the clip and then click the down arrow that appears to its right (see Figure 14.4). The default command for a clip is Insert, so you can insert a clip either by clicking the clip or by opening the menu and choosing Insert.

Figure 14.4
Each clip has its own menu.

USING A CLIP IN ANOTHER APPLICATION

Clip art can be copied into other applications, even non-Microsoft programs. For example, suppose you are working with a desktop publishing program such as Adobe InDesign CS2, and you want to use a clip art image from Word in a document there. Copy the clip to the Windows Clipboard and then paste it into that application.

There are several ways to copy a clip to the Windows Clipboard:

- Insert the image in a Word document and then move or copy it to the Clipboard (with the Cut or Copy button on the Home tab).

- Find the image using Word's Clip Art task pane, but do not insert it. Instead, open the clip's menu and choose Copy (refer to Figure 14.4).

14

■ From outside of Word (Word doesn't even need to be open), open the Microsoft Clip Organizer. You'll find it in the All Programs, Microsoft Office, Microsoft Office Tools subfolder on the Start menu. From the Clip Organizer window, search or browse to find the desired clip and then open its menu and choose Copy.

→ To learn more about using the Clip Organizer, **see** "Using the Clip Organizer," **p. 435**.

NOTE
> If you paste a vector clip into a bitmap graphics program such as Paint Shop Pro or Paint, it is converted to a bitmap image, and its edges become less smooth.

Getting Clip Information

As you are browsing the found clips, you might have some questions about them. How large are the files? What format are they in? What keywords are associated with them? What are the filenames?

To get very basic information about a clip, such as a few keywords, the size, and the file format, simply point at the clip in the Clip Art task pane. A ScreenTip appears with that information (see Figure 14.5).

Figure 14.5
ScreenTips provide basic information about a clip.

For more complete information, open the clip's menu and choose Preview/Properties. The Preview/Properties dialog box appears, as shown in Figure 14.6. Its information includes the filename, path, image type, resolution, file size, and more. The left and right arrow buttons in the Preview/Properties dialog box move between found clips. You can use them to browse the properties of several clips without having to close and reopen the dialog box.

Figure 14.6
The Preview/
Properties dialog box
provides extended
information about
the clip.

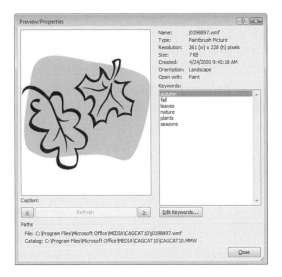

TIP

Knowing a clip's filename can be especially useful if the clip is stored on your hard disk (rather than being in an online collection only). The clips are just ordinary graphics, and you can use them in other programs or copy them to other computers, but you have to know their names—and the clip names are usually fairly cryptic. For example, in Figure 14.6, the clip name is j0298897.wmf.

→ To learn about editing clip keywords, **see** "Changing a Clip's Keywords and Caption," **p. 432**.

MAKING A CLIP AVAILABLE OFFLINE

Clips from the Web can be inserted into your documents, but you can't edit their keywords, and they aren't available as stand-alone files on your hard disk.

To make a Web clip fully your own, so you can edit its keywords and work with it offline, do the following:

1. Open the clip's menu and choose Make Available Offline. The Copy to Collection dialog box opens.

2. Click the desired category. (Use Favorites, or click the New button to create a new collection.)

3. Click OK. The dialog box closes, and nothing obvious seems to have happened, but the clip is now available offline.

14

To check to make sure the clip is available offline, re-run the same search as the one that originally found the clip. It will find two copies of the image—one near the top of the list (the local copy), and one later with the globe icon, which indicates an online clip.

If you decide you no longer want that clip to be available offline, select the clip (in the Clip Art task pane), open its menu, and choose Delete from Clip Organizer. This deletes only your offline copy; the Web-based copy from Microsoft will still reappear when you do searches for which the keyword is a match.

CHANGING A CLIP'S KEYWORDS AND CAPTION

After making a clip available offline, you can change its keywords. Adding keywords can be an effective way of narrowing down a search so that only the exact clip (or clips) you want appears. For example, if you have a few clips that a certain client likes you to use in his documents, you could add that client's name as a keyword.

A *caption* is descriptive text that appears with the clip. Captions can indicate what a clip is used for in your organization, for example. Suppose you have three versions of a particular clip, each for a different type of document; the caption could indicate which is which.

You can change keywords and captions only for clips stored on your own hard disk or network. The ones in the Web collection are shared with all other users of Office worldwide, so it makes sense that you could not modify the keywords for those clips. (If you want to modify the keywords for one of those Web collection clips, save it offline first, as described in the preceding section.)

To change a clip's keyword list and/or caption, follow these steps:

1. From the Clip Art task pane, open the clip's menu and choose Edit Keywords.

   Alternatively, from the Preview/Properties dialog box for the clip, click the Edit Keywords button (refer to Figure 14.6).

   The Keywords dialog box opens, as shown in Figure 14.7.

Figure 14.7
Modify the keywords and caption for a clip if desired.

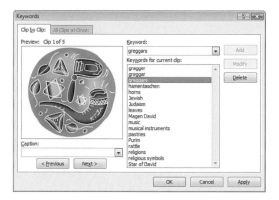

CAUTION

> The Keywords dialog box opens for any clip, but the buttons for adding and removing keywords are disabled except for clips in My Collections. Therefore, the only clips you can change keywords for are those that you have made available offline or saved to your own collections. This is so because other users on your local PC share the Office Collection and online users share the Web Collection, so any modifications you would make to clips there would affect other users. The My Collections group is all your own, though.

2. Do any of the following:
   - To add a keyword, type a word in the Keyword box and click Add.
   - To replace one keyword with another, select the word to replace and then type a replacement in the Keyword box and click Modify.
   - To delete a keyword, select the word and click Delete.
3. (Optional) Type a caption for the clip in the Caption box.
4. Click OK.

You can modify the keywords for more than one clip at a time, provided all the clips you select are keyword-editable (that is, local clips in My Collections). To edit keywords for multiple clips, follow these steps:

1. In the Clip Art task pane, select the clips to affect. Hold down the Ctrl key as you click each clip to select.
2. Right-click any of the selected clips and choose Edit Keywords.
3. Click the All Clips at Once tab.
   If the tab is unavailable, you have selected one or more clips that cannot be edited.
4. Any keywords that the selected clips have in common appear on the Keywords Shared by Selected Clips list. If desired, select one of these and click Delete.
5. (Optional) To add a keyword to all the selected clips, type it in the Keyword box and click Add.
6. Click OK.

You can also edit keywords from the Clip Organizer window, which you'll learn about later in this chapter.

→ To learn about the Clip Organizer, **see** "Using the Clip Organizer," **p. 435**.

BROWSING CLIPS VIA OFFICE ONLINE

14

Microsoft's clip art collection can be accessed from outside of Word, via a Web interface. Some people prefer to browse clips this way, picking the clips they like without having a particular document in mind for their immediate use. You can select as many clips as you want and have them transferred to your local hard disk, and then use them in Word later (or not).

NOTE

The clips available via Office Online include not just clip art, but also photos, sounds, and movies.

Here's how to reach the Office Online clip art collection and search for clips:

1. Click the Clip Art on Office Online hyperlink at the bottom of the Clip Art task pane. A separate Web window opens showing the Microsoft Office Clip Art and Media Home Page.

2. Type a keyword in the Clip Art box.

3. Click Search to see clips matching your search criteria. The search results appear momentarily, with a check box beneath each clip.

4. To select a clip, mark its check box. To see a larger version of a clip, click the magnifying glass icon beneath it. To view additional pages, click Next.

5. When you have selected all the clips you want, click the Download link in the Selection Basket section (see Figure 14.8).

   If you see a message about downloading an ActiveX control for Office Online, follow the prompts to do so.

Type the search keyword here

Click here to download the selected clips

Select the type of clip desired   Display additional pages

Figure 14.8
Use Office Online to transfer batches of clip art to your hard disk at once.

6. At the Download screen, click Download Now. A File Download dialog box appears asking whether you want to open the file.

The filename being downloaded will be ClipArt.mpf (MPF stands for Media Package File). This package contains all the clips you requested.

7. Click Open. The Microsoft Clip Organizer window opens.

   The clips you downloaded appear in the My Collections\Downloaded Clips collection. Depending on the clips you chose, they might appear in different subfolders. Subfolders are created on the fly for the chosen clips as needed.

8. Close the Clip Organizer window, or leave it open to explore in the next section.

9. Close the Web browser window.

USING THE CLIP ORGANIZER

The Microsoft Clip Organizer is a separate program you can access from outside of Word. It's very much like the Clip Art task pane, but with more features and flexibility.

To start the Clip Organizer, click the Organize Clips hyperlink at the bottom of the Clip Art task pane. Alternatively, from outside of Word, choose Start, All Programs, Microsoft Office, Microsoft Office Tools, Microsoft Clip Organizer.

The Clip Organizer has two panes. On the left is the Collection List, a series of folders and subfolders for managing clips. The main collections are listed here:

- **My Collections**—Collections you create yourself, or that have been created on your behalf (such as Favorites, Downloaded Clips, and Unclassified Clips).

- **Office Collections**—Collections for the clip art that Office 2007 installs on your local hard disk.

- **Web Collections**—Collections available online via Microsoft Office Online.

On the right, the clips in the selected collection appear in thumbnail form. For example, in Figure 14.9, the Abstract category is shown in the Web Collections/Microsoft Office Online folder.

Figure 14.9
Browse clips by category from the Clip Organizer window.

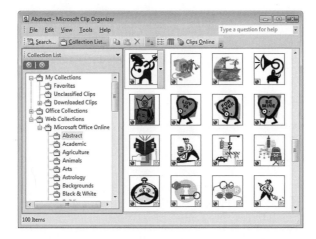

TIP

> As you use the Clip Organizer and its collections, errors and wasted space can accumulate and can cause clip art searches to be slower than normal. To correct any problems, use the Tools, Compact command in the Clip Organizer window. Do this periodically (every few months or so) as preventive maintenance.

BROWSING CLIPS BY CATEGORY

With the Clip Organizer, you can browse freely by category without having to enter a keyword. Click a plus sign to expand a category, and then click a folder to select it. When you've drilled down to the lowest-level folder, the clips within that folder appear (refer to Figure 14.9).

NOTE

> Notice that some of the clips in Figure 14.9 have a yellow star in the bottom-right corner. This indicates animation. These clips are animated GIFs rather than regular clip art. The animation runs when the clip is displayed on a Web page; when the clip is displayed in a regular document, it appears to be a normal graphic image. You can preview the animation from the clips's Preview/Properties dialog box.

SEARCHING BY KEYWORD IN THE CLIP ORGANIZER

You can also search by keyword using the Clip Organizer. Click the Search button in its toolbar to change the left side of the window to a Search pane. Then indicate the keyword you want to search for, the collection(s) in which to search, and file type(s), just like with the Clip Art task pane in Word (see Figure 14.10). To return to the Collection List, click the Collection List button in the toolbar.

Figure 14.10
Search for clips by keyword from the Clip Organizer window.

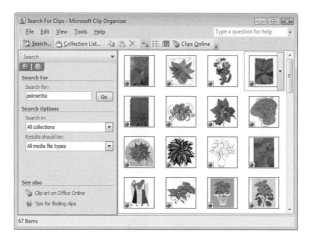

WORKING WITH FOUND CLIPS IN THE CLIP ORGANIZER

After locating a clip you want, open its menu to choose what to do with it. The menu is similar to the one for a clip in the Clip Art task pane in Word, but not identical. Here's what you can do:

- **Copy**—Copies the clip to the Clipboard; you can then paste it into any program that supports the Windows Clipboard.

- **Paste**—This command appears only if there is a compatible image currently on the Clipboard, and only when displaying a folder in My Collections. It pastes the image into the currently selected collection folder.

- **Delete from {folder name}**—This is available only for clips in My Collections. It deletes the clip from the current folder, but does not remove the clip from other collection folders in which it might appear.

- **Delete from Clip Organizer**—This is available only for offline clips. This command does not delete the clip itself from your hard disk, but removes it from being indexed by Clip Organizer. If the clip is listed in more than one collection folder, the command removes it from all of them.

- **Make Available Offline**—This is available only for online clips. It creates a copy of the clip in the My Collections group.

- **Copy to Collection**—This is available only for clips in My Collections. It enables you to copy the clip to another collection folder.

- **Move to Collection**—This is available only for clips in My Collections. It enables you to move the clip to a different collection folder. (See "Moving Pictures Between Collections" later in this chapter.)

- **Edit Keywords**—This command is available for all clips, but you can actually perform the edits only for offline clips. (See "Changing a Clip's Keywords and Caption" earlier in this chapter.)

- **Find Similar Style**—Some clip-art images are part of a collection designed in a particular artistic style. If the selected clip happens to be one of these, the Find Similar Style command finds additional clips of the same style. For the vast majority of clips, though, this command is unavailable.

- **Preview/Properties**—This opens the image's Preview/Properties dialog box, as you saw back in "Getting Clip Information" earlier in this chapter.

CREATING AND DELETING CLIP COLLECTION FOLDERS

The Clip Organizer can be used to organize all types of graphic files, not just clip art. If you want to use it extensively to manage your collections of artwork, consider creating extra collection folders to keep the clips neatly organized.

14

You can create collection folders only within the My Collections group. Follow these steps to create a new folder:

1. In the Collection List, click My Collections.

2. Choose File, New Collection. The New Collection dialog box opens.

3. In the Name box, type the desired name (see Figure 14.11).

4. (Optional) If you want the collection to be subordinate to one of the existing folders in My Collections, select the existing folder.

5. Click OK to create the new collection folder.

To delete a folder, right-click it and choose Delete {foldername}.

Figure 14.11
Create a new collection folder.

ADDING PICTURES TO THE CLIP ORGANIZER

There are several ways to add pictures to the Clip Organizer. You can have the Clip Organizer search your hard disk for eligible images or you can select the individual images you want.

ADDING ALL AVAILABLE PICTURES AUTOMATICALLY

The first time you open the Clip Organizer, you might be prompted to index the clips on your hard disk. If you choose to do this, your My Collections folder list is likely pretty long already, because the Clip Organizer will have created a separate collection folder for each folder on your hard disk that contained eligible images.

To initiate this indexing (if it didn't run initially, or if you want to re-run it), follow these steps:

1. Choose File, Add Clips to Organizer, Automatically. The Add Clips to Organizer dialog box opens.

2. Click the Options button. The Auto Import Settings dialog box loads and then initiates a drive scan, looking for folders that contain pictures.

3. Check marks appear next to the folders that contain pictures you can access from the Clip Organizer. Clear the check box next to any folder that you don't want to include (see Figure 14.12).

4. Click Catalog to add the clips to the My Collections group.

Figure 14.12
Choose which folders to include in the clip collections.

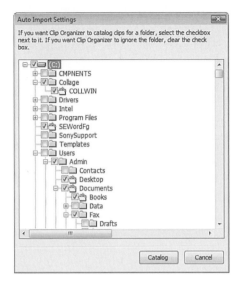

MANUALLY ADDING A PICTURE

If you need to add a certain clip but you don't want to have to completely reindex the drive, follow these steps:

1. (Optional) Select the collection folder in which you want to place the clip(s).

2. Choose File, Add Clips to Organizer, On My Own. The Add Clips to Organizer dialog box opens.

3. Browse to and select the desired file(s).

4. Click Add to add the clip(s) to the collection folder you chose in step 1.

   Alternatively, if you did not choose a collection folder in step 1, click Add To. Select the desired folder and then click OK.

MOVING PICTURES BETWEEN COLLECTIONS

After creating new collection folders and importing images into the Clip Organizer, you might find that the clips are not organized quite as you would like them to be.

You can either move or copy a clip between collection folders. (A clip can exist simultaneously in multiple collections.)

To copy a clip into another collection folder, drag the clip from the right pane and drop it on the desired folder at the left. Alternatively, display the clip's menu and choose Copy to Collection. In the Copy to Collection dialog box, select the new location and click OK.

To move a clip from one folder to another, hold down the Shift key and drag the clip from the right pane and drop it on the desired folder at the left. Alternatively, display the clip's menu and choose Move to Collection.

14

SETTING TEXT WRAP PROPERTIES

By default, a clip-art image is placed into the document as an inline image at the insertion point. An inline image is treated as a character of text; it moves when you edit the surrounding text, and it cannot be moved outside the text area. You can drag an inline image to a different location, but only within existing text paragraphs (see Figure 14.13).

Figure 14.13
By default, clip art is inserted inline.

Most people prefer to use clip art as floating images, which can be dragged anywhere on the page. Text interacts with a floating image according to its text wrap setting, such as Square, Tight, Top and Bottom, and so on (see Figure 14.14).

Figure 14.14
This clip art image is set to Square text wrapping.

TIP

> In Word 2007 documents, a clip art image has light blue selection handles regardless of its wrapping status. In backward-compatible documents, inline images have black square handles and floating images have round green handles.

Clip art uses the same Format tab as it does for photographic images. Select a clip's text wrap setting from the Text Wrapping button's menu on the Format tab, as shown in Figure 14.15.

14

Figure 14.15
Select a text wrap setting from the Format tab.

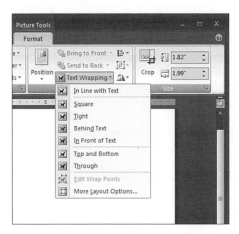

NOTE

As with photos, an Advanced Layout dialog box is available in which you can fine-tune the text wrap settings. Choose Text Wrapping, More Layout Options.

→ To review text wrap settings, including Advanced Layout, **see** "Setting Text Wrap," **p. 402**.

WRAPPING TEXT TIGHT AGAINST CLIP ART

There are some differences when working with clip art versus photographs, in that most clip art has a transparent background. This means that text can actually wrap around the image itself, and not just its frame. The Tight text wrap choice makes this possible, as shown in Figure 14.16.

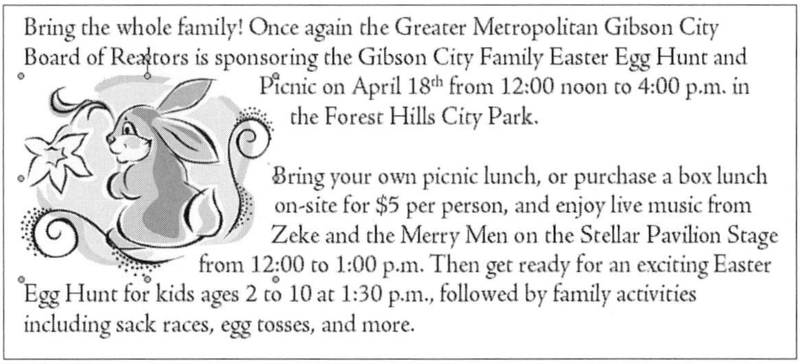

Figure 14.16
Tight text wrapping allows the text to wrap around the picture itself, not just its rectangular frame.

Bring the whole family! Once again the Greater Metropolitan Gibson City Board of Realtors is sponsoring the Gibson City Family Easter Egg Hunt and Picnic on April 18th from 12:00 noon to 4:00 p.m. in the Forest Hills City Park.

Bring your own picnic lunch, or purchase a box lunch on-site for $5 per person, and enjoy live music from Zeke and the Merry Men on the Stellar Pavilion Stage from 12:00 to 1:00 p.m. Then get ready for an exciting Easter Egg Hunt for kids ages 2 to 10 at 1:30 p.m., followed by family activities including sack races, egg tosses, and more.

14

EDITING TEXT WRAP POINTS

Sometimes the Tight text wrapping results in some odd-looking text wraps. When that happens, you can switch to Square wrapping (the easiest fix), but if the tight wrapping is important, you might instead choose to edit the wrap points. Wrap points are the markers that define the clip's wrap boundaries when Tight is used. These points are usually invisible, but you can display them and modify them.

To edit the wrap points for a clip, follow these steps:

1. Select the clip art image in the document.

2. Open the Text Wrapping menu on the Format tab and choose Edit Wrap Points. A dotted red line appears around the image, with black circles indicating the wrap points.

3. Drag a wrap point to change it. The red outline moves along with the wrap point to show the new boundary for the image (see Figure 14.17).

4. When you are finished editing the wrap points, press Esc.

Figure 14.17
Manually edit the image's wrap points by dragging.

Drag a wrap point away from the image to prevent text from wrapping into that area

MODIFYING A CLIP ART IMAGE

Now let's look at some ways you can change a piece of clip art. Many of these techniques are the same for clip art as for photographs, so to avoid duplication I'll reference the appropriate sections in Chapter 13 as needed. Some techniques, though, are unique to clip art.

SETTING CLIP SIZE AND POSITION

Clip art can be dragged to any position on the page. Just make sure the text-wrapping setting is something other than In Line with Text, and then drag the clip art where you want it.

To resize a clip, drag one of its selection handles. To resize the clip proportionally, hold down Shift and drag a corner handle.

The other techniques for changing size and position are the same for clip art as they are for backward-compatible photographs. See the following sections to review them:

■ To use and modify anchor points for positioning, **see** "Working with Anchors," **p. 404.**

- To specify a custom position with an exact measurement, **see** "Specifying a Custom Position," **p. 406**.
- To resize a picture using the Format tab or the Format Picture dialog box, **see** "Resizing Pictures," **p. 407**.

CROPPING AND COLOR-ADJUSTING CLIP ART

Clip art can be cropped the same as a photograph, using the Crop tool on the Format tab (see "Cropping Pictures" in Chapter 13). However, realistically speaking, you will probably not have much occasion to crop a piece of clip art. Clip art usually stands alone as a self-contained unit, without a lot of extraneous material in it. Cropped clip art can look like a mistake if not done strategically.

A clip-art image's brightness, contrast, and color mode can all also be set using the same procedures as for photographs (see "Setting the Brightness, Contrast, and Color Mode" in Chapter 13).

APPLYING CLIP ART BACKGROUND FILL

Most clip art has a transparent background. The frame around the clip art is rectangular, but within that frame, the image can be any shape. And as you saw earlier in the chapter, text can wrap around that image shape when you use the Tight style of text wrapping.

You can change that transparent background to a solid-color background, though, with a varying degree of transparency. That way, the clip appears to be a rectangular object, and text wrapping applies to the rectangle. Figure 14.18 shows some clip art with a solid background.

Figure 14.18
Apply a background to a piece of clip art.

Follow these steps to apply a background fill:

1. Select the clip art.
2. On the Home tab, open the Shading button's menu and select a color. You can choose a theme color, a tint of a theme color, or a standard color (see Figure 14.19). (Click More Colors to select a color from a wider palette.)

14

Figure 14.19
Choose a background
fill color for clip art.

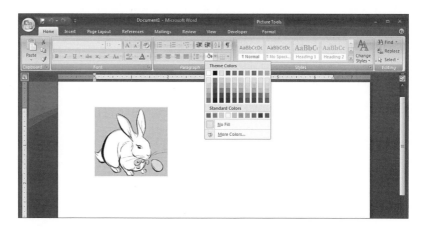

→ To review theme colors versus standard colors, **see** "Changing Font Color," **p. 167**.

Applying a Fill Effect to Clip Art

Word offers special fill effects such as gradients, textures, and patterns for some objects, but not for clip art. However, you can simulate background fill effects for clip art by layering transparent-background clip art over an AutoShape with the desired fill.

Here's how to do it:

1. Create a rectangle using the Shapes button on the Insert tab (see "Drawing an AutoShape" in Chapter 15).

2. Apply the desired fill effect to it (see "Formatting Drawn Objects" in Chapter 15).

3. Select the rectangle, and on the Format tab, choose Send to Back, Send Behind Text.

4. Insert the clip art into the document and make sure the clip's wrap setting is set to something other than In Line with Text.

5. Place the clip art on top of the rectangle.

6. Select both the rectangle and the clip art (holding down Ctrl as you click each one).

7. Right-click the selection and choose Grouping, Group. The clip art and the rectangle are now a single object.

8. If needed, reapply the text-wrapping setting to the object (see "Setting Text Wrap" in Chapter 13).

SETTING THE TRANSPARENT COLOR

When you are working with true clip art (WMF or EMF format), the background is usually transparent, as you just saw. This makes it easy to set up tight text wrapping around the image.

However, not every picture that the Clip Art task pane finds is real clip art. If you set the Results Should Be setting to All Media File Types, you'll also get an assortment of other files as well, including photos in JPG format and animated bitmaps in GIF format. And these usually do not have transparent backgrounds. Therefore, when you set text to wrap around them, the text wraps around the outer frame rather than around the image.

For example, consider the bunny in Figure 14.20. This is a JPG image provided by Microsoft Office Online, and inserted via the Clip Art task pane. It has a white background, which would be great if we were using it on a white page, but in this example the page happens to be shaded. Because this is a bitmap image, setting the background fill to No Fill has no effect.

Figure 14.20
This JPG file has a white background that Word can't take away with its background fill setting.

Bring the whole family! Once again the Greater Metropolitan Gibson City Board of Realtors is sponsoring the Gibson City Family Easter Egg Hunt and Picnic on April 18th from 12:00 noon to 4:00 p.m. in the Forest Hills City Park.

Bring your own picnic lunch, or purchase a box lunch on-site for $5 per person, and enjoy live music from Zeke and the Merry Men on the Stellar Pavilion Stage from 12:00 to 1:00 p.m. Then get ready for an exciting Easter Egg Hunt for kids ages 2 to 10 at 1:30 p.m., followed by family activities including sack races, egg tosses, and more.

To solve this problem, use the Set Transparent Color feature in Word. Word enables you to select one color of a bitmap image to "hide," and if you choose the image's background color, the background becomes transparent. Follow these steps:

1. Select the picture.
2. On the Format tab, click Recolor and then choose Set Transparent Color. The mouse pointer turns to a pen.
3. Click the background of the picture. All instances of that color in the picture become transparent.

Figure 14.21 shows our bunny with its background set to transparent. Only one color can be transparent in an image at once; if you set a different transparent color, the first one goes back to normal.

Figure 14.21
The JPG image's white background has been made transparent.

Bring the whole family! Once again the Greater Metropolitan Gibson City Board of Realtors is sponsoring the Gibson City Family Easter Egg Hunt and Picnic on April 18th from 12:00 noon to 4:00 p.m. in the Forest Hills City Park.

Bring your own picnic lunch, or purchase a box lunch on-site for $5 per person, and enjoy live music from Zeke and the Merry Men on the Stellar Pavilion Stage from 12:00 to 1:00 p.m. Then get ready for an exciting Easter Egg Hunt for kids ages 2 to 10 at 1:30 p.m., followed by family activities including sack races, egg tosses, and more.

CAUTION

All instances of that color in the image become transparent, not just the ones around the outer edges of the image. If you were to look very closely at the rabbit in Figure 14.21, you would see that the little white dot in his eye is now transparent too.

Setting the transparent color has no effect on text wrap. A Tight text wrap will still not wrap around the image in Figure 14.21, even though the white background is no longer visible. You can modify this behavior somewhat by editing the wrap points (Text Wrapping, Edit Wrap Points), but a rectangular image has only four wrap points, so there's only so much you can do with it. For example, in Figure 14.22, the wrap points have been moved a bit to make the text wrap as tightly as possible around the picture, but it's nowhere near as accurate as with real clip art.

Figure 14.22
Adjust wrap points to make text wrap around the JPG image.

e Greater
ealtors is
ster
n 12:00
ity Park.

ase a box
joy live
on the Stellar Pavilion Stage from

APPLYING A BORDER

Usually a border around clip art is unnecessary, and even undesirable. A border runs around the rectangular frame of the image rather than the image itself, so applying a border draws attention to the rectangular frame and disables the ability to wrap text tightly around the image. In some cases, however, a visible border on a clip art image might be useful. For example, if you have applied a fill color to the clip art background that is similar to the page background, a border might help call attention to the image.

Applying a border to clip art is the same as applying one to a photo. Use the Picture Border button on the Format tab.

→ To review applying borders to photos, **see** "Applying a Picture Border," **p. 422**.

For more line choices, choose More Lines from either the Dashes or the Weight submenu (from the Picture Border menu). This opens the Format Picture dialog box. From here you can use the Line Style controls to select a line type, thickness, color, and so on. The combinations and choices here are more extensive than on the tab's menus (see Figure 14.23).

Figure 14.23
Select properties for the border around the clip art.

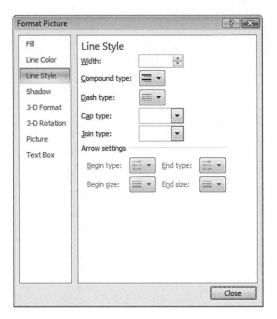

TIP

A border clings tightly to the rectangular frame of the clip art, and it touches the clip on each side. If you want a little more spacing than that between the clip art image and its border, combine a bordered AutoShape with a borderless clip art image, similar to what's described in "Applying a Fill Effect to Clip Art," earlier in this chapter.

14

APPLYING SHADOW EFFECTS

To apply shadow effects, open the Picture Effects button's menu on the Format tab and then select a shadow effect from the Shadow submenu. See "Applying a Shadow Effect" in Chapter 13 for details.

The main difference is that when you're applying a shadow effect to a clip art image with a transparent background, the shadow clings to the image, not to the rectangular frame. If the image has a border around it, the shadow also clings to the border. For example, in Figure 14.24, a shadow has been applied to a clip with a visible border and a transparent background.

Figure 14.24
Shadows cling to the image and to the border.

If you want the shadow to cling to the rectangular frame rather than to the image itself, apply a background fill to the image. (Make it the same color as the page background if you don't want it to be obvious.)

ROTATING CLIP ART

Clip art can be rotated in either 2D or 3D. A 2D rotation simply spins the clip around a center point; a 3D rotation alters its proportions so it appears to be shown at an angle. See "Rotating a Picture" in Chapter 13 to learn about 2D rotation and "Applying 3D Rotation" (also in Chapter 13) to learn about the 3D type.

FLIPPING CLIP ART

Flipping creates a mirror image of a clip. From the Format tab, click Rotate and then click Flip Horizontal or Flip Vertical.

One of the most common reasons to flip is to create a mirror-image pair of clips, such as for a masthead or logo. For example, Figure 14.25 shows two copies of a clip—one flipped and one regular.

14

Figure 14.25
Flipping an image mirrors it.

Flipped copy

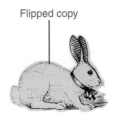

Hop on down to the
Gibson City
Family Easter
Egg Hunt
and Picnic

Original

EDITING CLIP ART

Because clip art is vector-based, it can be edited on a shape-by-shape basis. Even the most complex clip art can be reduced to a series of simple shapes, and each of those shapes can be moved, resized, deleted, recolored, or otherwise modified.

However, a clip cannot be modified in its native format; it must be converted to a Microsoft Drawing object. This is simple to do: Right-click the clip and choose Edit Picture. (If a warning appears, asking you to confirm the action, click Yes.)

When in Edit Picture mode, the Format tab changes to show drawing tools, and each part of the clip art image becomes a separately selectable and editable object. For example, in Figure 14.26, a carrot has been removed from the picture.

Selection handles around each individual shape

Figure 14.26
A clip art image consists of many individual shapes, all of which can be moved and modified.

 If a picture's Edit Picture command is not available, see "I Can't Edit a Clip" in the Troubleshooting section at the end of this chapter.

SELECTING AND MOVING SHAPES

To select a shape, click it. Selection handles appear around it. To select more than one shape at once, hold down Ctrl as you click additional shapes. This can be tricky; if you click a background shape, all the others may be deselected. Watch the mouse pointer for a plus sign, indicating that the item being pointed at will be added to the selection group. Another way is to drag a lasso around the shapes to be selected. To do this, start with the mouse

14

pointer *inside* the drawing canvas and then drag an imaginary box that encompasses the pieces you want to select.

To move a shape, position the mouse pointer over it so the pointer turns into a four-headed arrow, and then drag. To delete a shape, select it and press the Delete key on the keyboard.

RECOLORING SHAPES

To recolor a shape, select it and use the Shape Fill button on the Format tab (see Figure 14.27). You can choose any solid color or any fill effect (gradient, texture, pattern, and so on).

→ For more information about fill effects, **see** "Formatting Drawn Objects," **p. 472**.

Figure 14.27
Recolor individual pieces of a clip art image with the Shape Fill button's menu.

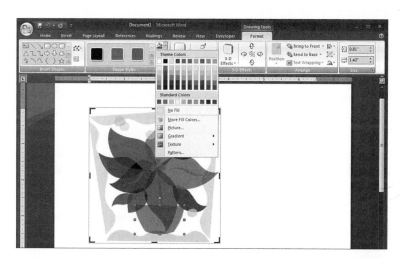

EDITING SHAPES

To edit a shape, right-click the shape and choose Edit Points. Black handles appear around the shape. (Zooming in will help you see them better.) Drag these handles to change the shape's contours and dimensions. This is very much like editing the wrap points for an image, as you did earlier in this chapter (see Figure 14.28). When you are finished changing the shape, press Esc to return to normal editing mode.

Figure 14.28
Change a shape by dragging the shape handles that form it.

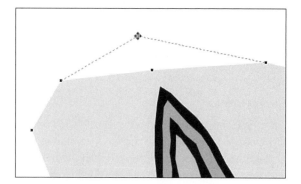

MOVING AND RESIZING A MODIFIED CLIP

After you've broken down a piece of clip art into individual pieces, it stays that way; there's no putting it back together again as a real piece of clip art. It's a drawing now, not a clip art image, technically speaking.

You can still move and resize the drawing, but the techniques for doing so are a little different.

Notice that when you click anywhere within the drawing, black lines appear around the corners. These mark the edges of the *drawing canvas*, which is the rectangular frame around the picture.

To enlarge the drawing canvas, position the mouse pointer over the bottom-right corner of the canvas, so the mouse pointer becomes a corner symbol, and then drag outward. This does not resize the drawing; it only resizes the canvas. You can also right-click the drawing canvas and choose Fit to resize the canvas to exactly fit the drawing, or right-click and choose Expand to enlarge the drawing canvas slightly.

To change the size of the drawing itself, click the drawing canvas frame, so that the frame's handles appear but no individual shape is selected. Then right-click inside the drawing canvas and choose Scale Drawing. The selection handles around the canvas temporarily change to circles; drag one of these selection handles to resize the drawing. An outline shows the new size as you drag (see Figure 14.29).

Figure 14.29
Resize the drawing by right-clicking and choosing Scale Drawing.

To move the drawing canvas, position the mouse pointer just barely outside one of the drawing canvas's selection handles, so the mouse pointer turns into a four-headed arrow, and then drag. (This works only if the text wrap is not set to In Line with Text.)

To move pieces of the drawing around within the drawing canvas, simply drag and drop them. If you want to work with multiple shapes at once, you might find it useful to group them. To do so, first select the pieces to group; then right-click the selection and choose Grouping, Group.

Life Outside the Drawing Canvas

A piece of clip art is never quite the same after you convert it to a Microsoft Drawing object, but you can almost get it back to normal by grouping all the pieces together and then dragging the item outside the drawing canvas. Follow these steps:

1. In the drawing canvas, drag a lasso around all the pieces of the drawing, selecting them all. Then right-click and choose Grouping, Group.

2. Drag the grouped object outside of the drawing canvas.

3. Select the drawing canvas and press Delete, deleting it from the document.

There is some weirdness associated with the resulting clip, though. For example, it doesn't have any text-wrapping capability anymore. You can either place it in front of the text (Bring to Front, Bring in Front of Text) or in back of it (Send to Back, Send Behind Text), but the Text Wrapping tools are disabled for it. If you need text to wrap around it, leave it in the drawing canvas. (The drawing canvas can support text-wrapping settings.)

If you decide you want the drawing canvas back after all, here's how to get it:

1. Select the drawing and use Cut to cut it to the Clipboard.

2. On the Insert tab, open the drop-down list for the Shapes button and choose New Drawing Canvas. A new drawing canvas appears.

3. Use Paste to paste the drawing into the new canvas.

TROUBLESHOOTING

THE FORMAT TAB DOESN'T LOOK LIKE WHAT'S SHOWN IN THIS CHAPTER

The clip is probably not a real piece of clip art (.emf or .wmf format), but rather a bitmap image. Microsoft Office Online provides clips in a variety of formats, not just traditional clip art. See Chapter 13 for an explanation of the controls on the Format tab when a bitmap image is selected. If you want to restrict the Clip Art task pane's search to only real clip art, open the Results Should Be list and make sure that all types are cleared except Clip Art.

Another possibility is that you are working in a backward-compatible document instead of a Word 2007 document. In backward-compatible documents, the commands on the Format tab are somewhat different and arranged differently to match the features that were available in the previous versions.

I CAN'T LASSO MULTIPLE SHAPES IN THE DRAWING CANVAS

The individual shapes in the drawing canvas can be lassoed, but the lasso must start *inside* the drawing canvas. If there are shapes tight against the edges of the canvas, making it hard to position the mouse pointer, expand the canvas temporarily. To do so, right-click it and choose Expand. When you're done, you can shrink it again; right-click and choose Fit.

I CAN'T EDIT A CLIP

In a Word 2007 document, when you right-click a clip, the Edit Picture command might not be available. If this happens, delete the clip and reinsert it.

If that doesn't work, try saving the document as a backward-compatible Word 97-2003 document (File, Save As). The clip should then be editable. You can then re-save the document in Word 2007 format (Office, Convert) when you're finished editing clips.

WORKING WITH DRAWINGS AND WORDART

In this chapter

15

DRAWING LINES AND SHAPES

The drawing tools in Word create simple vector graphics. Although Word is probably not going to end up being your all-time favorite drawing tool for professional illustrations, it will do nicely for basic lines and shapes. And by combining and layering lines and shapes, you can even create some surprisingly complex drawings. (For example, take a look at the dissected clip art at the end of Chapter 14, "Working with Clip Art and the Clip Organizer.")

Word's drawing tools are vector-based. As you learned in Chapter 14, a *vector* graphic is a line-based drawing that's created via a math formula, like in geometry. Unlike a bitmap image, a vector graphic can easily be modified and resized without any loss of quality. Each line and shape in a vector-based drawing has its own selection handles, so you can move, resize, and reshape it as needed.

DRAWING AN AUTOSHAPE

In Office programs, the lines and shapes you draw are known as *AutoShapes*. The "Auto" is a reference to the fact that Word provides dozens of predrawn shapes from which you can choose, including stars, arrows, circles, and polygons.

To draw a shape in a document, follow these steps:

1. On the Insert tab, click the Shapes button and then click the desired shape (see Figure 15.1). The mouse pointer changes to a crosshair.

Figure 15.1
Draw a shape using Word's drawing tools.

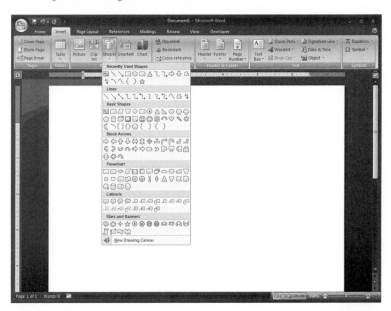

2. (Optional) Hold down Shift to constrain the dimensions of the shape, such as to force a rectangle to be a square or to force an oval to be a circle.

3. Drag to draw the shape. An outline shows the shape; release the mouse button when the shape is as you want it.

Finding More AutoShapes

There's a fine line between a Microsoft Drawing object (a collection of AutoShapes) and a piece of clip art. You saw this in Chapter 14 when you learned how to convert a clip art image to a set of shapes.

Microsoft's Clip Art collection includes some clips that are, technically speaking, AutoShapes. They include shapes that look like various types of office furniture and computers (useful in space planning drawings), simple conceptual pictures such as light bulbs and padlocks, and more.

From the Insert tab, click the Clip Art button. Then in the Search For box in the Clip Art task pane, type **AutoShape** as the keyword and click Go. Click the AutoShape you want to insert into the document.

Is it clip art, or is it an AutoShape? Check out the Format tab. It's the same as for drawings. Right-click the object and notice the Format AutoShape command. Yep, it's a real AutoShape, all right. And true to AutoShape behavior, you can't break it apart and edit it the way you can clip art.

DRAWING A FREEFORM POLYGON

A *polygon* is a shape that consists of line segments. A rectangle is a polygon, as is a star, a triangle, an octagon, and so on. The line segments do not need to be the same length or at any particular angle.

Word's drawing tools include a Freeform tool that creates custom polygons. Here's how to use it:

1. Open the Shapes menu on the Insert tab and click the Freeform button.
2. Click to place the start point. (Don't hold the mouse button down.)
3. Click somewhere else to place the next point. A straight line appears between the two points.
4. Repeat step 3 to create more points. Then do one of the following:
   - To end the shape and leave it open (that is, not joining the start and end points together), double-click instead of clicking for the final point.
   - To end the shape and close it, click on the start point. You don't have to be precise; if you click reasonably near the start point, the shape closes itself.

DRAWING A STRAIGHT OR CURVED LINE

Word's palette of shapes includes several types of lines:

Straight lines—Click the beginning point and then click the end point. After the second click the line is complete. A straight line can be plain or have arrows at one or both ends.

Straight (elbow) connectors—Click the beginning point and then click the end point.

15

NOTE

Connectors can be used by themselves but are traditionally used to join other shapes such as in a flow chart.

Curved connectors—Click the beginning point and then click the end point. After the second click the line is complete. You can adjust the shape of the curve by dragging the yellow diamond in the center.

Curve—This freeform curve is drawn differently from the others, as shown in Figure 15.2. Click the beginning point, then click to create a second point, then click again to create additional points. Between points, drag the mouse pointer to adjust the curvature of the line. When you are finished, double-click to end the shape.

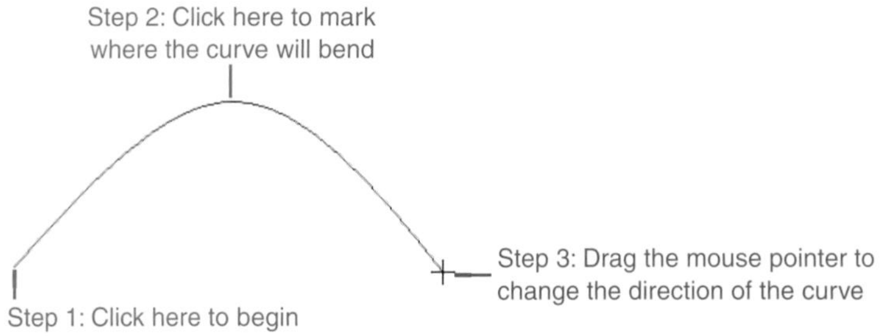

Figure 15.2
Draw a curve by clicking.

Step 2: Click here to mark where the curve will bend

Step 1: Click here to begin

Step 3: Drag the mouse pointer to change the direction of the curve

Scribble—This line is completely freeform. You can draw straight or curved segments, or a combination of them. Hold down the mouse button and drag to draw the line; when you release the mouse button, the line is completed.

WORKING WITH THE DRAWING CANVAS

A *drawing canvas* is a defined rectangular area in which you can place the lines and shapes. Using a drawing canvas is optional. If you use one, the drawing canvas functions as the backdrop on which all the lines and shapes sit. If you choose not to use one, the lines and shapes sit directly on the document page. Figure 15.3 shows a blank drawing canvas.

One advantage of using a drawing canvas is that you can apply a background fill (solid or a special effect) to the canvas, so your drawing will have a colored background separate from the document background. Another is that you can assign an automatically numbered caption to a drawing canvas, so a group of lines and shapes together can be considered a single figure for numbering purposes. (To do that, right-click the canvas and choose Insert Caption.)

Figure 15.3
A blank drawing canvas, ready for a drawing.

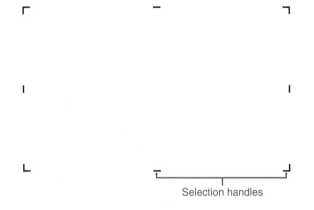

Selection handles

15

To create a new drawing canvas, follow these steps:

1. On the Insert tab, click the Shapes down arrow, opening the menu of shapes.
2. At the bottom of the menu, click New Drawing Canvas.
3. Use the Shapes menu to create lines and shapes within the drawing canvas as desired.

To delete a drawing canvas, select the outer border of the canvas (not any particular drawn item within it) and press the Delete key on the keyboard.

If you forget to create a drawing canvas and then later wish you had, it's not too late. Create a new drawing canvas and then drag any existing drawings onto it.

TIP

If you always (or nearly always) want to use a drawing canvas whenever you use the drawing tools, you can set up Word to make canvas-insertion the default whenever you draw. To do this, choose Office, Word Options, click Advanced, and then mark the Automatically Create Drawing Canvas When Inserting AutoShapes check box in the Editing Options area.

RESIZING THE CANVAS

The drawing canvas occupies the entire space between the margins horizontally by default, and is about 3.5" high. To resize it, drag one of its selection handles.

To size the drawing canvas so that it is exactly the size needed to hold the current content, right-click it and choose Fit (see Figure 15.4).

CAUTION

The Fit command is available only if the drawing canvas contains at least two drawn objects (lines or shapes).

Figure 15.4
Right-click the drawing canvas to access sizing options.

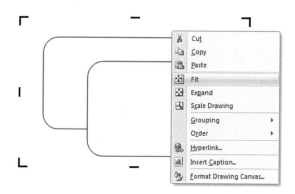

To expand the drawing canvas slightly (by about 1/2") so that the content has a little more space around the edges, right-click it and choose Expand.

The size of the canvas is constrained by the size of the content within it. You can't make the canvas smaller than its content. However, you can resize the canvas and its content together using the Scale feature:

1. Right-click the canvas and choose Scale Drawing. The selection handles for the drawing canvas turn to green circles.
2. Drag a selection handle to resize the canvas and the drawing together.

FORMATTING THE CANVAS

In terms of formatting, the drawing canvas is a lot like an AutoShape or other object. You can place a border around it, and you can apply a background fill. See "Formatting Drawn Objects" later in this chapter to review the techniques for applying borders and fills to objects.

You can also right-click the canvas and choose Format Drawing Canvas to open the Format Drawing Canvas dialog box. This is basically the same dialog box as Format Picture or Format Object. Here's what's available:

- **Colors and Lines**—Set the fill and line color and style here, as covered later in the chapter.
- **Size**—Specify an exact size for the canvas.
- **Layout**—Specify text-wrap settings for the canvas.
- **Alt Text**—Specify alternative text to appear if the drawing canvas cannot appear when displayed on a web page.

ADDING TEXT TO A SHAPE

AutoShapes can function as text boxes, and you can create some very interesting effects by adding text to unusual-shaped AutoShapes such as starbursts and arrows.

To add text to a shape, right-click the shape and choose Add Text, or click the Edit Text button on the Format tab. An insertion point appears in the shape; just type your text as you would in a text box and then click outside the shape when you are done.

Formatting text in an AutoShape is the same as formatting text in a text box. You can set all the usual paragraph and character formatting, and you can adjust the vertical and horizontal alignment and internal margins.

→ To review the procedures for formatting text in a text box, **see** "Creating Text Box Layouts," **p. 320**.

MODIFYING DRAWN OBJECTS

There are lots of ways you can modify drawing objects (lines and shapes). Some of these involve formatting, such as applying fill colors and border styles, and that type of modification is covered later in the chapter. This section, however, looks at modification from a structural standpoint—changing the contours and angles of the shapes and lines.

MODIFYING A STRAIGHT LINE

A straight line has only two selection handles—one at each end. Drag one of those selection handles to change the line's length or to point it in a different direction.

ADDING AND REMOVING ARROW HEADS

Each end of a line can be modified to include an arrow or not. Further, you can choose between different arrowhead styles. Follow these steps:

1. Right-click the line and choose Format AutoShape. The Format AutoShape dialog box opens, with the Colors and Lines tab displayed.
2. In the Arrows section, choose a Begin Style and an End Style setting.
3. For each end for which you've chosen an arrow, choose a Begin Size and an End Size setting (see Figure 15.5).
4. Click OK.

Figure 15.5
Select arrow styles and sizes for each end of the line.

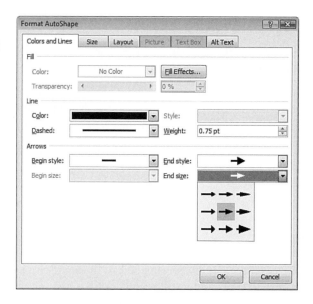

MODIFYING AN ELBOW OR CURVED CONNECTOR

An elbow connector is a line that turns at a 90-degree angle at some point, and then turns again the opposite way so it ends up going the same direction again. A curved connector is a two-segment curve.

You can drag either end to change the position and size, just like with any other line. The angled parts or the joint where the two segments meet remain centered.

An elbow connector has a yellow diamond in the center; you can drag the diamond to move the angles (see Figure 15.6). If you drag the diamond all the way in one direction or the other, one of the angles disappears and the line becomes a simple two-segmented right angle line.

Figure 15.6
Modify an elbow connector by dragging the yellow diamond.

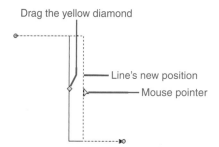

A curved connector also has a yellow diamond, but dragging it does something different—it changes the position of the point where the two curves join, and one or both curves change their shape in proportion (see Figure 15.7).

Figure 15.7
Modify a curved connector by dragging the yellow diamond.

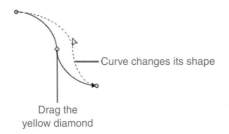

Curve changes its shape

Drag the
yellow diamond

Modifying Curves and Scribbles

A true curve—as opposed to a curved connector—has a variable number of bends in it. The same goes for a scribble. It may be a mixture of curves and straight lines, and it has a variable number of segments. Such lines do not have a yellow diamond for changing their shape; instead you must edit their points.

To edit a curve or scribble, follow these steps:

1. Select the line.

2. On the Format tab, click Edit Shape and then click Edit Points. Small black squares appear on the curve for each point.

3. Drag a point to reposition it. As you drag, the curve of the adjacent segments changes (see Figure 15.8).

4. Drag other points as needed; press Esc when you're finished.

Drag any black square

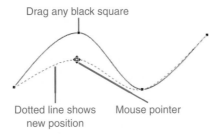

Figure 15.8
Modify a curve by editing its points.

Dotted line shows   Mouse pointer
new position

Scribbles, being freeform, have more flexibility. When you click a point on a scribble, notice that two small white squares appear near it. These squares represent the ends of directional lines that can control the contours of the segment without moving it. Drag one of these squares to reshape the segment while keeping the points at both ends of the segment stationary (see Figure 15.9).

15

Figure 15.9
Drag the directional lines for a point to change the segment's curve without moving the start or end point of the segment.

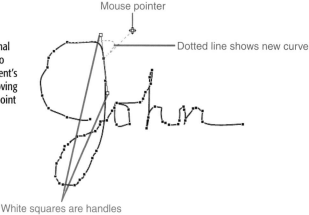

Mouse pointer

Dotted line shows new curve

White squares are handles for changing the curve

MODIFYING SHAPES

Some AutoShapes have one or more yellow diamonds on them when selected. You can drag these diamonds to modify the shape. Dragging the diamond does not change the shape's basic self—an arrow is still an arrow—but rather changes the proportions. For example, in Figure 15.10, the yellow diamond on an arrow AutoShape is used to change the thickness of the line and the size of the arrowhead.

Figure 15.10
Modify an AutoShape by dragging its yellow diamond.

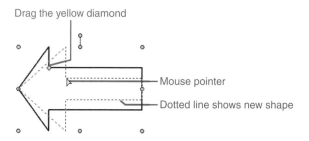

Drag the yellow diamond

Mouse pointer

Dotted line shows new shape

NOTE

Some shapes, such as the curved ribbon-style arrows, have multiple diamonds, each one controlling a different dimension of the shape.

ROTATING AND FLIPPING OBJECTS

You can rotate drawn objects just like you did clip art in Chapter 14. The easiest way is to drag the rotation handle (the circle at the top of the shape), as shown in Figure 15.11.

Rotation handle

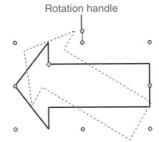

Figure 15.11
Rotate a shape by dragging its rotation handle.

You can also rotate a shape with the Rotate menu on the Format tab. Choose one of the presets there or choose More Rotation Options to open the Format AutoShape dialog box's Size tab. Then enter a rotation amount in degrees in the Rotation box. These skills were covered in detail in "Rotating a Picture" in Chapter 13, "Working with Photos."

Flipping creates a mirror image of the object. From the Format tab, click Rotate and then click Flip Horizontal or Flip Vertical.

SIZING AND POSITIONING OBJECTS

Now that you know how to create the lines and shapes you need for your drawings, let's look at ways to size and position those objects.

SIZING OBJECTS

Drawn objects (lines and shapes) can be sized in the same way as the other object types you've seen so far in this book. The quickest way is to drag a selection handle. Lines have only two selection handles—one at each end—but shapes have multiple handles. To keep the shape proportional as you drag, hold down the Shift key.

To specify an exact size for a drawn object, enter precise values in the Height and Width boxes on the Format tab (see Figure 15.12).

Height

Figure 15.12
Resize an object with the Height and Width controls.

Width

For other size-adjustment options, right-click the object and choose Format AutoShape. Then on the Size tab, enter absolute or relative heights and widths, or in the Scale section, enter a percentage by which to resize (see Figure 15.13).

Figure 15.13
More resizing options are available in the Format AutoShape dialog box.

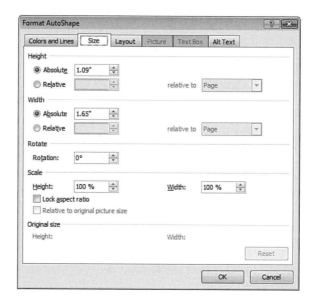

SETTING POSITION AND TEXT WRAPPING

The same position presets are available for AutoShapes as for pictures. Use the Position drop-down list on the Format tab to select a position if desired.

→ To review the available position presets, **see** "Choosing a Position Preset," **p. 405**.

The text-wrapping options are the same as for clip art. Drawn shapes are more like clip art than pictures in this regard because they sometimes have irregular edges around which text can tightly wrap. Choose text-wrap options from the Text Wrapping button on the Format tab. You can edit the wrap points the same as with clip art, or stick with standard text wrap styles.

→ To review text-wrapping options, **see** "Setting Text Wrap Properties," **p. 440**.

ANCHORING LINES TO SHAPES

When you are creating drawings that illustrate connections, such as flow charts, you might want certain lines and shapes to remain connected. Figure 15.14 shows an example of a flow chart. Suppose you wanted to move the shapes around, perhaps to compress the spacing between them. Wouldn't it be nice if the connecting lines stayed connected?

Figure 15.14
A flow chart uses connectors to join shapes.

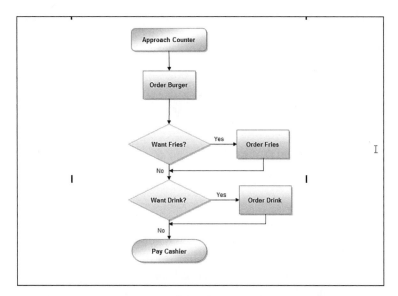

NOTE

You can create a flow chart like the one in Figure 15.14 using any shapes you like, but certain shapes are traditionally used in specific situations. For example, a rectangle usually indicates an action, and a diamond usually denotes a decision point. Many good tutorials are available online for flow charting; a quick search for "flow chart tutorial" using any search engine will turn them up. For starters, check out http://deming.eng. clemson.edu/pub/tutorials/qctools/flowm.htm.

To create connections between lines and shapes, anchor the line to a shape at one or both ends. Follow these steps:

1. Using a drawing canvas, draw the two shapes that you want to connect. For best results use the shapes in the Flowchart group.

2. Choose one of the line tools on the Insert Shapes menu: Straight Connector (line), Elbow Connector, or Curved Connector.

3. Hover the mouse pointer over the first shape. If the shape is already selected, the selection handles show the available connection points. If the shape is not already selected, small blue squares appear at the available connection points.

4. Click one of the connection points to anchor the beginning of the line to the shape.

5. Hover the mouse pointer over the second shape. Small blue squares appear around it (see Figure 15.15).

Figure 15.15
Small blue squares indicate points where a line can be anchored.

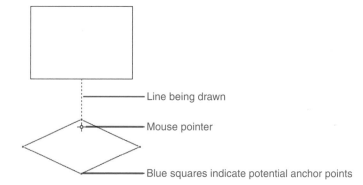

6. Click one of the blue squares to anchor the end of the line to the shape.

When both ends of a line are successfully anchored to shapes, red circles appear at each end of the line. When an end is not anchored, a green circle appears at that end instead (see Figure 15.16).

Figure 15.16
Line selection handles appear in red when the line is anchored at both ends.

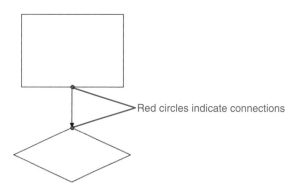

TIP

> Lines are not required to be anchored to shapes; you can have lines anywhere on your drawing that are not connected to anything.

Here are a few tips for working with flow chart layouts:

- **Adding text to a shape**—Usually a flow chart contains text in each shape. To add text, see the section "Adding Text to a Shape," earlier in the chapter.
- **Changing an anchor point**—To change the point to which an end of a line is anchored, drag its end point. You can re-anchor a line to a different point on the same shape or to a different shape entirely, or you can drag it away from any shape to make it free-floating.

- **Toggling connection points**—To toggle between the other possible connection points for a connector line, right-click the line and choose Reroute Connectors.

- **Changing the connector type**—If you decide you want a different connector type, right-click the line and pick a different type from the menu: Straight Connector, Elbow Connector, or Curved Connector. Then drag one end of the line or the other as needed. You might not see the effect of the change until you reposition one end or the other of the line.

- **Aligning shapes**—Your flow chart will look nicer if all the shapes are uniformly aligned. See "Aligning and Distributing Objects" later in the chapter to learn how to make that happen.

LAYERING OBJECTS AND TEXT

A Word document has two main layers. On the *text layer* is the regular document text and any inline images. (And remember, by default pictures are inserted as inline images.) The *graphics layer* contains everything else: text boxes, drawings, pictures, and anything else that's set for a text wrapping other than inline.

Within that graphics layer, it is possible to stack objects one on top of another. For example, you could create a drawing that consists of overlapping shapes and lines, and you could then use that drawing as a backdrop matte for a photo. Figure 15.17 shows an example.

Figure 15.17
Several overlapping drawn shapes form a background for this picture.

> **NOTE**
> Layering drawn shapes works only if you are *not* using a drawing canvas. Drag the shapes outside the drawing canvas if the layering tools do not work.

Word's layering options enable you to move objects in stacking order within the upper layer, but that's not all. They also enable you to move graphic objects behind the text layer itself, effectively creating an extra graphics layer behind the text layer. (The original graphics layer stays on top of the text layer, so you can have graphics both on top of and behind the text.)

15

When you overlap one graphic object with another, by default they are stacked according to the order in which they were originally drawn, with the oldest one on the bottom.

To bring an item all the way forward or back in the stack of objects (but still within the graphics layer), click the Bring to Front or Send to Back button on the Format tab.

To move an item one position within the graphics layer, open the drop-down list associated with the Bring to Front or Send to Back button and then click either Bring Forward or Send Backward, respectively. Figure 15.18 shows the Send to Back button's menu.

Figure 15.18
The Bring to Front button and Send to Back button each has its own menu.

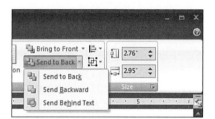

To move an object behind the text layer, open the Send to Back button's menu and choose Send Behind Text. To move it back above the text layer again, open the Bring to Front button's menu and choose Bring in Front of Text.

N O T E

> Depending on the object's text-wrapping setting, you might not see any immediate difference in using Send Behind Text or Bring in Front of Text. To see the difference most obviously, set Text Wrapping to Through.

GROUPING SHAPES

When creating complex drawings that have multiple shapes and lines in them, it can be a challenge to select, move, and resize all the pieces at once. To make it easier, consider grouping the pieces into a single unit. The grouped object can then be moved, sized, cut, copied, pasted, and so on.

To create a grouping, select all the pieces (lassoing them by dragging a box around them works well) and then right-click the group and choose Grouping, Group. The individual selection handles disappear, and a single set of selection handles appears for the entire group.

N O T E

> The lasso works only within the drawing canvas.

If you find you need to work with one of the pieces separately, right-click the group and choose Grouping, Ungroup.

After making changes, you can reestablish the group by right-clicking and choosing Grouping, Regroup.

ALIGNING AND DISTRIBUTING OBJECTS

Drag-and-drop can be a frustrating, inexact way of positioning objects in relation to one another. When creating stacked groupings of objects, you might instead prefer to use the Align and Distribute commands for more precision.

Two or more objects can be *aligned* with one another at the top, bottom, middle, right edge, left edge, or horizontal center.

Single objects can be aligned, but only in relation to some portion of the page. For example, you can align an object with any of the margins, or with the edge of the page.

To align objects, follow these steps:

1. Select the objects to align. (Hold down Ctrl and click on each object.) For Align to Page or Align to Margin, you need only select one object. For Align Selected Objects, you must select at least two.

2. On the Format tab, click Align and then choose the desired alignment relationship: Align to Page, Align to Margin, or Align Selected Objects (see Figure 15.19).

CAUTION

You can't select a bitmap picture and a drawn object at the same time, so you can't align and distribute them with each other. In addition, you can't use any type of Distribute command on Word 2007 format bitmaps.

This step doesn't perform any alignment; it just sets the stage.

Figure 15.19
Choose the type of alignment you want to do.

3. Click Align again and then select one of the alignments, such as Align Center or Align Left.

15

Distributing means spacing objects out equally. You can distribute three or more objects in relation to one another, or you can distribute two or more objects in relation to the margins or page.

Objects can be distributed either vertically or horizontally. Distribution is based on the amount of white space between the objects, not the centers of the objects, so objects of unequal size are still distributed with equal amounts of white space between them.

To distribute objects, follow these steps:

1. Select the objects to be distributed. (Hold down Ctrl and click on multiple objects.) For Align Selected Objects, you must select at least three.

2. On the Format tab, click Align and then choose the desired distribution relationship: Align to Page, Align to Margin, or Align Selected Objects.

   If you choose the latter, the objects are distributed between the rightmost and leftmost objects, or topmost and bottommost ones, but the overall space occupied by the group of objects will not change. If you choose Align to Page or Align to Margin, the distribution spreads out the objects to fill the available space on the page or between the margins.

3. Click Align again and then select one of the distributions: Distribute Horizontally or Distribute Vertically.

FORMATTING DRAWN OBJECTS

Once you get the objects sized, shaped, and placed where you want them, the next step is to think about their formatting. In the following sections, you'll learn how to change the colors, borders, shadows, and other effects associated with drawn objects.

APPLYING QUICK STYLES

Quick Styles are new in Word 2007, and they offer a way to quickly apply a complete set of formatting to a drawn object: color, border, and shadow. You can choose among ten designs from each of seven colors from the Shape Styles drop-down list on the Format tab. Select a shape and point to a Quick Style to see a preview of the Quick Style applied to the shape (see Figure 15.20).

The only problem with Quick Styles is that they're limited to the choices provided. If you want something other than what's provided, see the following sections to fine-tune.

Figure 15.20
Apply a Quick Style to an AutoShape.

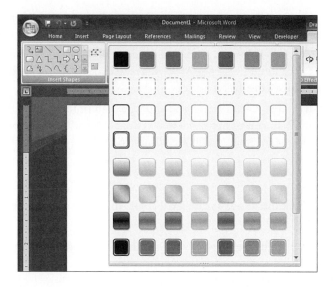

FORMATTING BORDERS

Most of what you've learned earlier in the book about borders also applies to drawn objects. You can apply a border with any style, thickness, and color desired.

Shape borders are called *outlines* in Word 2007 terminology. To format a shape border, open the Shape Outline menu from the Format tab, as shown in Figure 15.21, and select one or more of the following:

Figure 15.21
Apply border formatting to a drawn object.

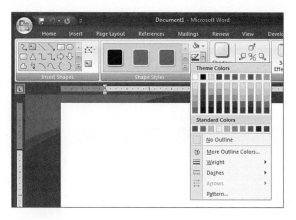

- **Color**—Choose a theme color, a tint of a theme color, or a standard color, or click More Outline Colors to select from a dialog box. This works the same as for font color (see "Changing Font Color" in Chapter 6, "Applying Character Formatting") and for text boxes (see "Applying Text Box Borders and Fills" in Chapter 11, "Working with Nonstandard Document Layouts").

- **Weight**—Choose a line thickness, from 1/4 pt to 6 pts, or click More Lines to specify some other weight in the Format AutoShape dialog box.

- **Dashes**—Choose a line style. Choices include solid lines and various types of dotted and dashed lines. If desired, click More Lines to choose from a wider variety of styles in the Format AutoShape dialog box.

- **Pattern**—If desired, click Pattern and choose a pattern for the line. Unless it's a really thick line, the pattern will not be viewable; the border will simply look like it's broken or fuzzy. Patterns are more useful for fills, as you will see in the next section.

APPLYING SOLID FILLS

You've learned about theme colors and fixed colors in several other places in this book, but let's quickly review.

A fixed color does not change, regardless of the theme applied. A few basic fixed colors are provided on the menu, but you can also choose More Colors to open a dialog box containing a wide variety of fixed color choices.

Theme colors are colors provided by the formatting theme you have applied (on the Page Layout tab). Choosing a theme color does not actually apply a color to the selection, but creates a link to one of the theme's color placeholders. Then whatever color happens to be assigned to that placeholder trickles down to the selection. That way, you can have elements in your document that change color automatically when you switch themes.

→ To change themes, **see** "Applying a Theme," **p. 256**.

Each theme color can be applied at full-strength or as a tint. A *tint* is a scaled-back version of a color, derived by blending the color with white. Tints are described in percentages, such as a 25% tint, a 50% tint, and so on.

To apply a solid color fill to a drawn object, follow these steps:

1. Double-click the object to select it and to display the Format tab.
2. Open the Shape Fill drop-down list (see Figure 15.22).

Figure 15.22
Select a font color, either a fixed color or one from the current theme.

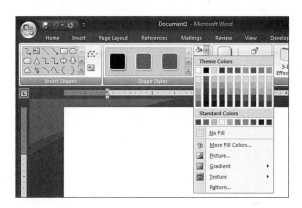

3. Do one of the following:

- Click No Fill to remove any color, making the shape transparent.
- Click a theme color (top row).
- Click a tint of a theme color.
- Click a standard (fixed) color (bottom row).
- Click More Fill Colors to select a different fixed color.

If you go with the latter choice, you can select a color from the Colors dialog box. On the Standard tab, you can click any of the colored hexagons, as in Figure 15.23.

Figure 15.23
Select one of the standard colors from the Standard tab.

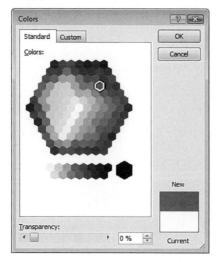

On the Custom tab, you can define a color precisely using its numeric value from either the RGB or the HSL color model (see Figure 15.24). These numeric color models can be useful when you are trying to match a color exactly; for example, many corporations have official colors to be used in all company correspondence and publications.

RGB stands for Red/Green/Blue; colors are defined with values ranging from 0 to 255 for each of those three colors. Equal amounts of each color result in varying shades of black-gray-white.

HSL stands for Hue/Saturation/Luminosity. These are also 0-to-255 values, but H is for all hues (0 and 255 are both red; the numbers in between are the other colors of the rainbow), S is for saturation (the intensity of the color, as opposed to neutral gray), and L is for the lightness/darkness (white to black). You can click any spot on the color grid to select that color, or you can drag the vertical slider up/down.

15

Figure 15.24
Define a color numerically on the Custom tab.

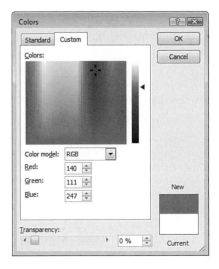

APPLYING A PICTURE FILL

A picture fill places a bitmap image inside a shape. It enables you to use any shape as a picture frame, as in Figure 15.25.

Figure 15.25
Picture fills allow any shape to be used as a picture frame.

There are several ways of setting up a picture inside a shape. One is to apply a picture preset, as you learned in Chapter 13. This works only with Word 2007 pictures, though, so it's somewhat limited. You can't do it in a backward-compatible document, for example, and it doesn't work with all pictures. You are also limited to the shapes provided in the Picture Presets list.

A more flexible way is to insert a shape in the document and then fill the shape with the picture. This works in all types of documents, both 2007 and backward-compatible, and you can use any AutoShape or draw your own custom shape.

To apply a picture fill to a shape, follow these steps:

1. Select the shape. Double-click it to display the Format tab if needed.

2. Click Shape Fill and then click Picture. The Select Picture dialog box opens.

3. Navigate to the folder containing the picture to use, select it, and click Insert. The picture is inserted into the shape.

The drawback to the preceding method is that the aspect ratio is not locked, so the picture might appear distorted. You can fix this somewhat by changing the dimensions of the shape, but it's guesswork.

If keeping the aspect ratio locked is important to you, use the following alternate method, which drops off portions of the image that don't fit into the shape but keeps the picture proportions static:

1. Select the shape. Double-click it to display the Format tab if needed.

2. Click Shape Fill, then click Pattern.

> **NOTE**
>
> In step 2, you don't really want a pattern, but it's a way of opening the Fill Effects dialog box.

3. In the Fill Effects dialog box, click the Picture tab.

4. Click Select Picture. The Select Picture dialog box opens.

5. Navigate to the folder containing the picture to use, select it, and click Insert. The picture appears on the Picture tab.

6. Mark the Lock Picture Aspect Ratio check box (see Figure 15.26).

7. Click OK. The picture is inserted into the shape with its proportions maintained.

Figure 15.26
Use the Picture tab of the Fill Effects dialog box if you want to lock the aspect ratio.

15

APPLYING A GRADIENT FILL

A *gradient* is a gradual blending of colors. A gradient can be single-color (one color plus either black or white), two-color (one color blending into another color), or preset (special combinations such as rainbow or gold).

Several common one-color gradients are available from the Shape Fill menu. Here's how to use one of these:

1. Apply a solid color fill to the shape.

2. Click Shape Fill, then point to Gradient. The Gradient menu appears (see Figure 15.27).

3. Click one of the gradient presets. (Never mind that they're all blue on the menu; the actual color used will be the color you selected in step 1.)

Figure 15.27
Select a gradient effect from the menu.

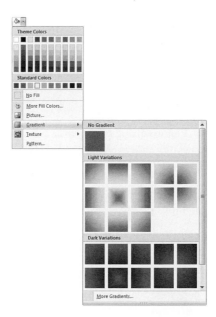

If you would like a different one-color effect, or if you want a two-color effect or a preset, follow these steps instead:

1. Double-click the object to display the Format tab.

2. On the Format tab, click Shape Fill, point to Gradient, and click More Gradients. The Fill Effects dialog box opens with the Gradient tab displayed.

3. Select the desired gradient type: One Color, Two Colors, or Preset.

4. Select the color(s) to use, or select a preset gradient. Figure 15.28 shows a single-color gradient; for a two-color gradient, there are two boxes for selecting color, and for a preset gradient, there's a list of presets.

5. If you're creating a one-color gradient, drag the slider to adjust the amount of white or black in the gradient. (This step is not applicable for two-color or preset gradients.)

Figure 15.28
Set up a custom gradient effect.

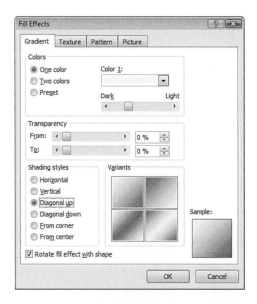

6. (Optional) To add transparency to the gradient, drag the From and To sliders in the Transparency area. This enables you to transition not only from one color to another in the gradient, but between differing amounts of transparency. (It's a cool effect, rather special-purpose.)

7. Select a shading style from the list provided and then click one of the samples in the Variants area to fine-tune it.

8. Mark or clear the Rotate Fill Effect with Shape check box as desired. This setting determines whether the fill effect will rotate if you rotate the shape later.

9. Click OK to apply the gradient to the shape.

APPLYING A TEXTURE FILL

A *texture* is a small bitmap image with edges that blend cleanly so that it can be tiled to occupy any size object. Textures come with Office 2007 (and earlier versions too) and have effects such as wood, cloth, paper, and marble. Figure 15.29 shows an example of a wood texture.

Figure 15.29
A texture fill makes the object appear to be made of a material such as wood or cloth.

15

NOTE

The difference between a texture and a picture fill is that the texture fill tiles the image to fill the shape, whereas the picture fill crops or stretches a single copy of the image to fill the shape.

To apply a texture fill to an object, follow these steps:

1. Double-click the object to display the Format tab.

2. On the Format tab, click Shape Fill, point to Texture, and click the desired texture (see Figure 15.30).

Figure 15.30
Apply a texture from the Texture submenu.

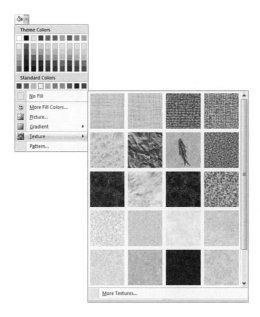

Any bitmap graphic can be used as a texture, but not all will produce good results. A texture is much like any other small graphic; the main difference is that it is created with tiling in mind, so the right and left edges blend in with each other, as do the top and bottom edges.

It is possible to create your own textures, but it's much easier to download already-made textures from online sources. Microsoft Office Online has some textures available in its clip art collection, for example, and there are many websites devoted to providing free and low-cost backgrounds and textures.

CAUTION

If you search for the keyword "texture" in the Clip Art task pane or the Clip Organizer, the results will include many graphics that are not true textures, in that they do not have the matched edges for tiling.

To use a texture graphic you have acquired, follow these steps:

1. Double-click the object to display the Format tab.

2. On the Format tab, click Shape Fill, point to Texture, and click More Textures. The Fill Effects dialog box opens with the Texture tab displayed.

3. Click the Other Texture button. The Select Texture dialog box opens.

4. Navigate to the folder containing the texture file. Select it and click Insert.

5. Back in the Fill Effects dialog box, click OK to apply the texture to the object.

Applying a Pattern Fill

A *pattern* is a simple, repeating overlay of a one-color design over a background of another color. For example, Figure 15.31 shows one that looks like bricks. There are also patterns with dots, dashes, lines, and so on.

Figure 15.31
An example of a pattern fill.

To set up a pattern fill, follow these steps:

1. Double-click the object to display the Format tab.

2. On the Format tab, click Shape Fill and then click Pattern. The Fill Effects dialog box opens with the Pattern tab displayed (see Figure 15.32).

Figure 15.32
Apply a pattern fill from the Fill Effects dialog box.

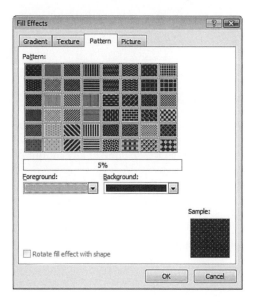

3. Click the desired pattern.

4. Open the Foreground menu and select the foreground color. As with other color selectors, you can select a theme color, a tint, or a standard color.

15

5. Open the Background menu and select the background color.

6. Click OK to apply the pattern.

APPLYING SHADOWS

The shadow effect for a drawn object is the same as for clip art and backward-compatible pictures. Start by choosing a shadow style and direction from the Shadow Effects button on the Format tab. To select a different shadow color, or to toggle semi-transparency on/off for the shadow, open the Color submenu (see Figure 15.33).

Figure 15.33
Choose a shadow
style and color.

To fine-tune the shadow positioning, click one of the Nudge Shadow buttons to the right of the Shadow Effects button. You can nudge the shadow in any of four directions. The center button toggles the shadow on or off entirely.

APPLYING 3-D EFFECTS

A 3-D effect adds depth to a drawn object, turning your flat drawings into something with perspective. Figure 15.34 shows an example.

Figure 15.34
An example of a 3-D effect.

A 3-D effect has these properties:

- **Color**—The color of the 3-D effect. This choice does not affect the color of the shape's front surface.

- **Depth**—The size of the 3-D effect, and the distance it extends from the front surface. It's not precision-customizable, but you can choose from among these values: 0, 36pt, 72pt, 144pt, 288pt, and Infinity.

- **Direction**—The direction from which the 3-D effect extends from the front surface. You can choose from nine directions. There are also separate selectors for two different views: Perspective and Parallel. These are two subtly different methods of calculating the trajectory of the 3-D effect. You won't notice much difference on a simple shape such as square, so try it on a wave or some other complex shape to compare.

- **Lighting**—You can choose Bright, Normal, or Dim, and you can also choose the direction of the "lighting" to change the shading of the 3-D effect.

- **Surface**—Choose Matte, Plastic, Metal, or Wireframe to affect the shading on the shape and its 3-D sides.

- **Tilt**—You can tilt the 3-D effect up or down, or to the right or left.

CAUTION

3-D effects can be combined with fill color settings, but are mutually exclusive with border colors and shadow effects; when you apply a 3-D setting, both of those are removed. The border returns when you remove the 3-D effect, but a shadow must be reapplied after removing 3-D.

To apply a simple 3-D effect, follow these steps:

1. Double-click the shape to display the Format tab.
2. Click 3-D Effects to open a menu of samples (see Figure 15.35). (Depending on the Window size, there might be a second 3-D Effects button to click on before the menu appears.)
3. Click the desired effect.

To turn the 3-D effect off, click the 3-D Effects button and then click No 3-D Effect.

If the window is large enough, a separate 3-D On/Off button appears in the 3-D Effects group so you don't have to open the button's menu.

15

Figure 15.35
Select a basic 3-D effect.

Tilt buttons   3D on/off

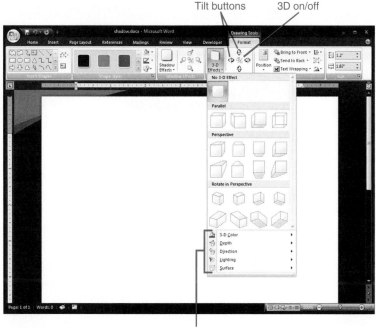

Submenus for fine tuning

To fine-tune the 3-D effect, use the submenus at the bottom of the 3-D Effects menu (as shown here) for color, depth, and so on. Use the tilt buttons to control the tilt of the 3-D effect.

CREATING AND MODIFYING A WORDART OBJECT

WordArt is a unique combination of a drawn object and text. You can make any words you like appear in it, but Word treats it more like a drawn object than like text. WordArt is great for company logos, headings, decorative graphics on flyers and advertisements, and so on. Figure 15.36 shows some WordArt examples.

Figure 15.36
Some WordArt examples.

To create WordArt, start with one of the preset designs and then modify it. Follow these steps to create WordArt with a preset:

1. On the Insert tab, click WordArt. A menu of presets appears (see Figure 15.37).

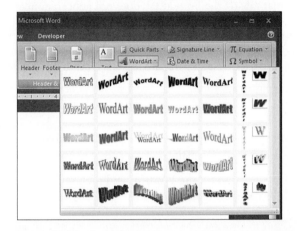

2. Click one of the presets. The Edit WordArt Text dialog box opens.
3. Type the text you want. Keep it short and simple for best results.

> TIP
>
> To create line breaks in the WordArt text, press Shift+Enter. To create paragraph breaks, press Enter.

4. (Optional) Choose a different font from the Font list, and a different size from the Size list.
5. (Optional) Click the Bold and/or Italic buttons to apply those formatting options.
6. Click OK. The WordArt appears in the document at the insertion point.

CHANGING WORDART TEXT WRAP AND POSITION

WordArt is placed inline with text by default (black square selection handles). To move it around on the page, set its Text Wrapping setting to Square, Tight, or one of the other non-inline options. (Use the Text Wrapping menu on the Format tab.) The position presets are active for WordArt, like for text boxes and clip art, and you can drag and drop a WordArt object anywhere in the document, like any other object.

→ To review the procedures for changing text wrapping, **see** "Setting Text Wrap," **p. 402**.
→ To review how to use position presets, **see** "Setting Picture Position," **p. 404**.

EDITING WORDART TEXT

After the WordArt has been created, you might decide the text needs to change. You cannot edit the text normally, but you can reopen the Edit WordArt Text dialog box by clicking Edit Text on the Format tab. (If the Format tab does not appear, double-click the WordArt.)

CAUTION

One of the most common mistakes beginners make with WordArt is to use too much text, which ends up looking crowded. WordArt is best with a simple word or two.

CHANGING THE SHAPE

The *shape* of the WordArt is the form into which the text is poured. Some of the presets use nonrectangular shapes, and there are many more shapes you can choose from as well.

To change the WordArt shape, select the WordArt and then select a shape from the Change Shape menu on the Format tab (see Figure 15.38).

Figure 15.38
Change the WordArt shape.

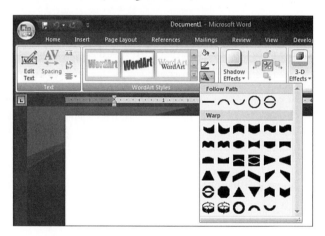

TIP

Sometimes it is hard to tell whether a shape is appropriate for the text until you see it in action. If you hover over a shape on the Change Shape menu, the selected WordArt will appear previewed with that shape.

You can also change the shape by selecting a different preset. The same presets that were available when you created the WordArt initially are also available from the WordArt Styles group on the Format tab. Click the down arrow to open the list and select again.

CHANGING THE SPACING

The *spacing* of the WordArt is the amount of blank space between the letters. Select a spacing option from the Spacing list on the Format tab, as shown in Figure 15.39. Choose from Very Tight, Tight, Normal, Loose, and Very Loose.

Figure 15.39
Adjust the between-letter spacing.

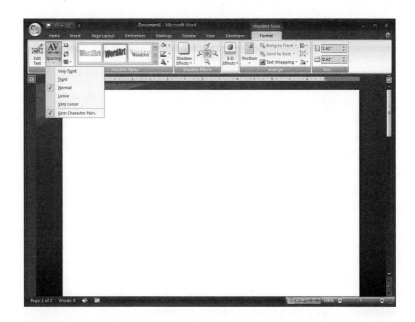

You can also choose whether or not to kern pairs from the Spacing menu. Recall from Chapter 6 that kerning involves adjusting the spacing between two letters based on their shapes. For example, a capital *A* and a capital *V* can fit more tightly together because their shapes dovetail with each other. Usually kerning is desirable for WordArt, but try it both ways to see for yourself.

→ For more information about kerning, **see** "Adjusting Character Spacing," **p. 176**.

CHANGING THE FILL

Fill for WordArt is just like it is for drawn objects. Use the Shape Fill drop-down list on the Format tab, and choose either a solid color or one of the fill effects you learned about earlier in this chapter.

→ For more information about the various types of fills, **see** "Formatting Drawn Objects," **p. 472**.

ADJUSTING LETTER HEIGHT

By default, the letter heights in WordArt mimic those of normal text—capital letters are larger than lowercase letters. When creating special effects, though, you might want to even them out. To do so, click the Even Height button on the Format tab. Figure 15.40 shows the difference between normal heights and even heights. Note that this option does not make the letters capitalized; it just increases their heights. Click the button again to toggle the feature off.

Figure 15.40
Normal heights (left) and even heights (right)

SWITCHING BETWEEN VERTICAL AND HORIZONTAL TEXT

 Some of the WordArt presets have vertical text, but you can make any WordArt vertical with a click of the Vertical Text button. Click the button again to toggle the vertical presentation off.

Note that Vertical Text makes the letters run vertically on the page, but it does not rotate the letters. Each letter appears oriented normally, one beneath the next. If you want vertical text with the text rotated 90 degrees, create regular WordArt and then rotate it using its rotation handle.

→ For more information about rotating, **see** "Rotating and Flipping Objects," **p. 464**.

SETTING WORDART ALIGNMENT

WordArt alignment is not an issue when the WordArt text consists of a single line, because the WordArt's outer frame is always exactly the size it needs to be to hold that text. To use a text box metaphor, suppose that you have some text that exactly fits across the width of a text box. Therefore, the Align Right, Center, and Align Left settings would have no effect on it because it has nowhere to go. That's what it's like for most WordArt. You can apply an alignment setting, but it won't make any difference.

When you start getting into multiparagraph and multiline WordArt, however, it does make a difference. For example, Figure 15.41 shows left alignment versus center alignment. (To make a line break, press Shift+Enter as you are entering or editing the text in the Edit WordArt Text dialog box.)

Figure 15.41
Left alignment (left) and center alignment (right).

Today Only! Announcing the Reynolds Mart 25th Anniversary sales event with savings of up to 50%

Today Only! Announcing the Reynolds Mart 25th Anniversary sales event with savings of up to 50%

To set alignment, use the Alignment menu from the Format tab (see Figure 15.42).

Figure 15.42
Select alignment for the WordArt.

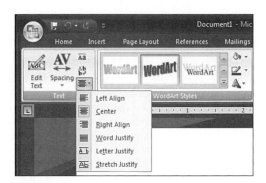

15

Three Justify options appear on the Alignment menu: Word Justify, Letter Justify, and Stretch Justify. Each of these specifies a different treatment for lines that contain less text than the longest line. Figure 15.43 shows the difference between these three.

- Word Justify keeps the words normal but adds space between them.
- Letter Justify keeps the letters normal but adds space between them and between words.
- Stretch Justify makes the letters larger and thicker to fill the available space.

Figure 15.43
Word Justify, Letter Justify, and Stretch Justify alignments.

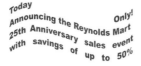
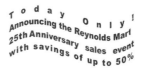

TROUBLESHOOTING

I CAN'T APPLY BOTH A 3-D EFFECT AND A SHADOW

This is by design; you can't simultaneously use both 3-D and shadows for WordArt and drawing objects.

However, there are ways to simulate a shadow by making a duplicate copy of the object and coloring it gray (or whatever color you want the shadow to be). Follow these steps to try it out on a simple shape:

1. Draw a shape.
2. Select the shape, press Ctrl+C to copy it, and then press Ctrl+V to paste the copy. (Alternatively, hold down Ctrl and drag the shape to create a copy.)
3. Select the top copy of the shape and apply the desired formatting to it, including a 3-D effect.
4. Select the bottom copy, and apply a plain gray fill. Remove its border.
5. Drag the bottom copy to position it in relation to the top copy so it looks like its shadow.

SOME DRAWING COMMANDS AREN'T AVAILABLE

Some of the commands for formatting drawn objects work only when the drawing canvas is used—or isn't used. For example, object stacking commands work only outside the drawing canvas, and lassoing to select works only inside the drawing canvas.

If you're having trouble with certain buttons or commands being unavailable, try moving the drawings into or out of the drawing canvas to see if that makes any difference.

CHAPTER 16

WORKING WITH CHARTS

UNDERSTANDING CHARTS

A *chart* is a graphical representation of numeric data. Charts can summarize data and help people make sense out of it. (Some people call them *graphs*, and in fact, so did Microsoft up until this version of Word; the program that was used to create charts was called Microsoft Graph.)

To work with charts in Word, you should have a general grasp of Word's charting vocabulary. Here are some of the key terms to know, many of which are pointed out in Figures 16.1 and 16.2:

- **Data point**—An individual numeric value, represented by a bar, point, column, or pie slice.
- **Data series**—A group of related data points. For example, in Figure 16.1, all the bars of a certain color are a series.
- **Category axis (X axis)**—The horizontal axis of a two-dimensional or three-dimensional chart.
- **Value axis (Y axis)**—The vertical axis of a two-dimensional or three-dimensional chart.
- **Depth axis (Z axis)**—The front-to-back axis of a three-dimensional chart.
- **Legend**—A key that explains which data series each color or pattern represents.
- **Floor**—The bottom of a three-dimensional chart.
- **Walls**—The background of a chart. Three-dimensional charts have back walls and side walls, which you can format separately.

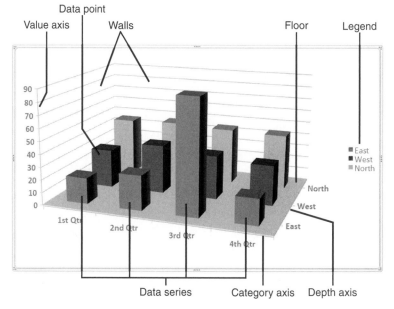

Figure 16.1
Key elements found in many charts (part I).

- **Data labels**—Numeric labels on each data point. A data label can represent the actual value or a percentage.
- **Axis titles**—Explanatory text labels associated with the axes.

- **Data table**—A table containing the values on which the chart is based.
- **Chart title**—A label explaining the overall purpose of the chart.

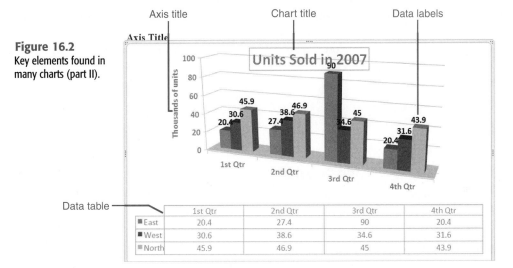

Figure 16.2
Key elements found in many charts (part II).

	1st Qtr	2nd Qtr	3rd Qtr	4th Qtr
■ East	20.4	27.4	90	20.4
■ West	30.6	38.6	34.6	31.6
■ North	45.9	46.9	45	43.9

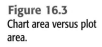

It is also important to understand the various areas of a chart. Each chart's complete package, including all its auxiliary pieces such as legends and titles, is the *chart area*. Within the chart area is the *plot area*, which contains only the chart and its data table. (Sometimes the chart title is overlaid on top of the plot area, but the chart title is not part of the plot area itself.) Figure 16.3 shows the chart area and plot area.

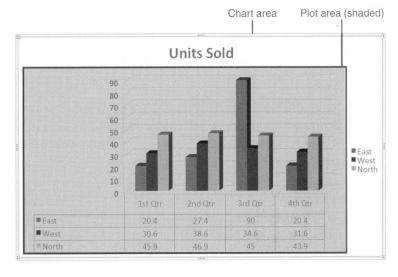

Figure 16.3
Chart area versus plot area.

CREATING A NEW CHART

If you have been frustrated with the charting tool—Microsoft Graph—in earlier versions of Word, you're in for a pleasant surprise in Word 2007. Charts are now much more powerful across all Office applications, and the tools in Word and PowerPoint are similar to those in Excel. Therefore, people who previously created charts in Excel and then linked or embedded them into Word will find that they don't need to do that anymore to get full charting capabilities.

Microsoft Graph has not gone away entirely, though. If you create or use an existing backward-compatible document in Word, the Microsoft Graph tools still appear, integrated with the new Word interface.

CREATING A CHART IN A WORD 2007 DOCUMENT

For maximum power and flexibility, create charts in Word 2007 documents rather than Word 97-2003 ones. This way you can take advantage of the powerful new charting features Word 2007 offers.

Follow these steps to create a new chart:

1. On the Insert tab, click Chart. The Insert Chart dialog box opens.
2. In the left pane, click the desired chart type (such as Column or Pie). Then in the right pane, click the desired chart subtype (see Figure 16.4).

Figure 16.4
Create a new chart.

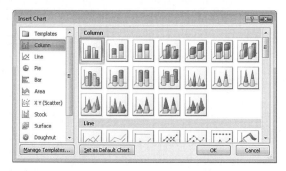

→ For detailed descriptions of the chart types and subtypes, **see** "Changing the Chart Type," **p. 501**.

3. Click OK. Microsoft Excel opens, displaying a sheet containing dummy data for the chart. (Word remains open in its own window.)
4. Change the data in Excel as needed. Edit both the numbers and the labels.

   You can add or delete rows and columns as needed, and the chart automatically reflects them.

→ For more information about changing the data range, **see** "Modifying Chart Data," **p. 497**.

5. Switch to the Word window to view the chart. (Minimize or close the Excel window if desired, or leave it open for later editing.)

Obviously there's a lot more to charting than the simple creation process. You'll probably want to change chart types, format charts, add optional elements such as labels, and so on. You will learn all these things in the rest of this chapter.

CREATING A LEGACY CHART

In a Word 97-2003 document, the charting tool used in Word 2007 is Microsoft Graph, the same charting tool as in earlier versions. The interface has been slightly updated, but the options and features are the same.

In a Word 97-2003 document, follow these steps to create a new chart:

1. On the Insert tab, click Chart. A sample chart appears, with a floating datasheet. The toolbars and menus for the previous version of Excel appear too (see Figure 16.5).

Figure 16.5
Create a new backward-compatible chart.

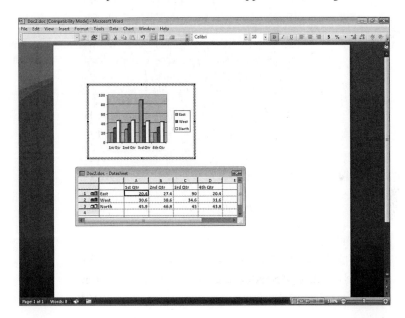

2. Change the data in the datasheet as needed. Edit both the numbers and the labels. Add or delete rows and columns as needed. (To delete a row or column, right-click the row or column heading and press Delete.)

> **TIP**
>
> To import data from an Excel worksheet for use in your chart, choose Edit, Import File and browse for an Excel file.

3. When you are finished, click away from the chart or the datasheet to return to Word.

To use Microsoft Graph charts in a Word 2007 document, see "How Can I Insert a Microsoft Graph Style–Chart in a Word 2007 Document?" in the "Troubleshooting" section near the end of this chapter.

WORKING WITH CHART TEMPLATES

Each of the chart types and subtypes you can select from the Create Chart dialog box (refer to Figure 16.4) represents a chart template. These templates are built-in and cannot be modified.

However, you can create your own chart templates, and start new charts based upon them. This feature is available only for Word 2007 charting, not backward-compatible charting.

CREATING A CHART TEMPLATE

To create a chart template, set the chart type, layout, and formatting as desired (as explained in the remainder of this chapter), and then follow these steps:

1. On the Design tab, click Save As Template. The Save Chart Template dialog box opens.

> **NOTE**
>
> The default location for storing user-created chart templates if you have Windows XP is Documents and Settings\username\Application Data\Microsoft\Templates\Charts. Under Windows Vista, it is \Users\username\Application Data\Microsoft\Templates. Chart templates have a .crtx extension.

2. Type a name for the template in the File Name box.
3. Click Save.

STARTING A NEW CHART BASED ON A USER TEMPLATE

You can use any of your saved templates as the basis for a new chart, rather than starting with one of the built-in templates.

To start a new chart based on one of your saved templates, follow these steps:

1. On the Insert tab, click Chart. The Create Chart dialog box opens (refer to Figure 16.4).
2. Click Templates. The My Templates list appears.
3. Click the desired template (see Figure 16.6).

> **TIP**
>
> To see a template's name, hover the mouse pointer over it.

Figure 16.6
Select a stored user template.

4. Click OK to start a new chart based on the chosen template.

MANAGING STORED CHART TEMPLATES

User-created chart templates can be modified or deleted at any time. To work with them, from the Insert tab, click Chart. Then from the Create Chart dialog box, click Manage Templates.

A file management window opens showing the folder containing the user-created charts. From here you can:

- **Rename a template**—Right-click it and choose Rename. Type the new name and press Enter.

- **Delete a template**—Click it and press Delete, or right-click it and choose Delete.

- **Back up your user templates**—Drag and drop the templates to another location or disk. To ensure that you are copying, rather than moving, hold down Ctrl as you drag.

MODIFYING CHART DATA

The whole point of a chart is to present data, so obviously the most important thing to get right in a chart is to show the correct numeric values. If your numbers aren't right, all the formatting in the world can't save you.

EDITING THE DATA

When you create a chart, an Excel window opens in which you can enter the data. That Excel data is an embedded datasheet in your Word document, and it's known as the *data source*.

To change the numbers or labels in the chart, select the chart, and then on the Design tab, click Edit Data. The datasheet opens in an Excel window (see Figure 16.7).

Click a column letter
to select that column

Insert or delete selected
rows or columns

Figure 16.7
Edit the datasheet.

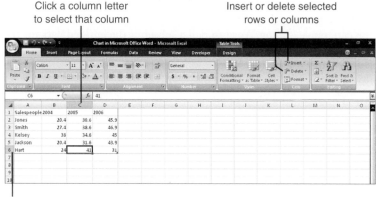

Click a row number to select that row

16

To make a change, click a cell and then type a replacement value and press Enter, just like you would in any spreadsheet.

You can also add and delete rows and columns from the sheet:

- To add a row at the bottom of the list or a column at the right, click in the first blank row or column and type new entries.

- To add a row or column between existing rows or columns, select the row where the new row should appear, or the column where the new column should appear, and then click Insert on the Home tab.

- To delete a row or column, select it by clicking its letter or number, and then on the Home tab, click Delete.

- To hide a row or column, select it, and then right-click it and choose Hide.

In the next section, you will learn how to use the Hidden and Empty Cell Settings dialog box to control what happens to a hidden row or column. It can be made to be included in the chart or not, as you prefer. Hiding a row or column is a good alternative to deleting it entirely if you think you might want to display it in the chart later. Another way to keep data in a datasheet but exclude it from the chart is to change the data range, as you'll learn next.

CHANGING THE CHARTED DATA RANGE

Notice on the datasheet that a blue box surrounds the data range, and a blue triangle appears in the bottom right corner of the last cell in the range. You can drag that triangle to expand or constrict the range to be included, as long as the range is a contiguous block on the spreadsheet.

Sometimes, however, you might want to change a chart so that it does not show all the data you have entered in the datasheet. For example, suppose you want to exclude a certain series from the chart temporarily, print a copy, and then include that series again. You don't want to delete the data altogether because you'll need it again later. In cases like this, you adjust the data range, telling Word to pull a subset of the entered data for the chart.

If you just want to redefine a smaller contiguous range, drag the blue triangle so that the range excludes some of the rows at the bottom or some of the columns at the right.

If you need more sophisticated range editing, follow these steps:

1. Click the chart to select it.
2. Display the Design tab, and click Select Data. The Excel window appears, along with the Select Data Source dialog box (see Figure 16.8).
3. Adjust the series (columns) as needed:
   - To redefine the overall range for the chart (provided that the desired range is in one contiguous block in the sheet), click in the Chart Data Range box, and then drag across the range and press Enter.
   - To remove a certain series from the chart, click its name in the Legend Entries (Series) box and click Remove.

- To re-add a series that you've removed, click the Add button in the dialog box. Then click on the column heading in the worksheet and press Enter.

- To reorder the series, click a series name in the dialog box and then click the Up or Down arrow button.

Figure 16.8
Change the range
included in the chart.

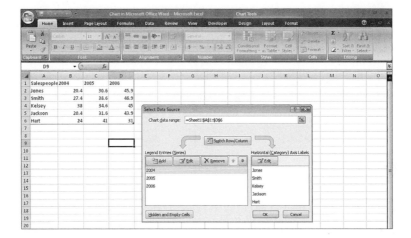

4. If needed, change the range from which the category labels are being pulled by doing the following:

a. In the Horizontal (Category) Axis Labels section, click Edit. The Axis Labels dialog box opens.

b. On the worksheet, drag across the range containing the labels.

c. Click OK in the dialog box, or press Enter.

5. Specify how to deal with hidden and empty cells by doing the following:

a. Click the Hidden and Empty Cells button. The Hidden and Empty Cell Settings dialog box opens.

b. Choose how to show empty cells: as gaps, as zero, or spanned with a line.

c. Mark or clear the Show Data in Hidden Rows and Columns check box.

d. Click OK.

6. Click OK. The datasheet becomes available for manual edits. Make any additional changes to it desired, and then close it and return to the chart in Word.

SWITCHING BETWEEN ROWS AND COLUMNS

By default, a chart displays datasheet rows as series and datasheet columns as categories. You can flip this rather easily, though, by clicking the Switch Row/Column button on the Design tab.

CONTROLLING HOW THE CHART AND DOCUMENT INTERACT

A chart is an object, in the same way that a photo, clip art image, or diagram is an object. Therefore, you can make it interact with the document text in all the standard ways, such as setting its positioning and text wrap. These settings were covered in detail in Chapter 13, "Working with Photos," but the basics are briefly repeated here for convenience.

SETTING TEXT WRAPPING

Text wrapping controls how the document text interacts with the chart. Text wrapping for a chart is identical to that for a picture:

1. Select the chart.
2. On the Format tab, click Text Wrapping. A menu of text wrap choices appears.
3. Click the desired text wrap setting.

→ For detailed descriptions of text wrapping choices and their effects on the surrounding text, **see** "Setting Text Wrap," **p. 402**.

POSITIONING A CHART

Position presets are available for charts, the same as for other graphic objects. These presets set the chart frame to precise relative or absolute positioning within the document page.

To apply a position preset to a chart, follow these steps:

1. Select the chart.
2. On the Format tab, click the Position button, and click one of the position presets (see Figure 16.9).

Figure 16.9
Select a position preset.

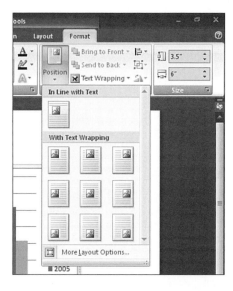

To set an exact position for the chart, follow these steps:

1. Select the chart.

2. On the Format tab, click the Position button and then click More Layout Options. The Advanced Layout dialog box opens.

3. On the Picture Position tab, set the desired layout. You can choose layout by Alignment, by Book Layout, or by Absolute Position.

> **NOTE**
>
> If no options are available on the Picture Position tab, set the text wrapping to something other than In Line with Text.

4. Set any options desired, such as Move Object with Text or Lock Anchor.

5. Click OK to accept the new position setting.

→ For more detailed descriptions of the position choices, **see** "Setting Picture Position," **p. 404**.

CHANGING THE CHART TYPE

The chart's type is the single most important design setting you can apply to it. The same data can convey very different messages when presented using different chart types. For example, if you want to show how each person's work contributed to the whole, a pie chart is ideal. If you would rather concentrate on the numeric value of each contribution, you might prefer a bar or column chart.

> **CAUTION**
>
> Each chart type and subtype is designed to serve a specific purpose. Choosing an inappropriate chart type can prevent your message from getting across to your audience, and in some cases can actually make the data misleading or incomprehensible. For example, if you change a multiseries bar chart to a pie chart, you lose all the data except the first series because pie charts are single-series charts by definition.

To change the chart type, follow these steps:

1. Select the chart.

2. On the Design tab, click Change Chart Type. The Change Chart Type dialog box opens. It is just like the Insert Chart dialog box shown in Figure 16.4, except for the name.

3. Select the desired category in the left pane, or scroll through the list in the right pane to browse the types. You'll find more details in Table 16.1.

4. Select the desired chart type in the right pane.

5. Click OK to change to the new chart type.

Word 2007 offers 11 chart categories, and several types within each category. The categories are listed in Table 16.1.

TABLE 16.1 CHART CATEGORIES

Category	Sample	Notes
Column		The default chart type, useful for measuring one numeric value against another. Multiple data series are handled via different bar colors. There are several types of column charts, and each presents a different look at the data. For example, a stacked column chart makes each bar into a mini pie chart, showing how each series contributes to the total height of the bar.
Line		Represents each numeric value as a point, and connects the points within a series with a line. Multiple series are handled via different line colors and styles.
Pie		Shows how the parts contribute to the whole without focusing on the actual numeric values. Most types of pie charts are single-series only.
Bar		Identical to the column chart type, except it's horizontal.
Area		Similar to a column chart, except the space between each column is filled in. When multiple series are shown, a larger area in front can potentially obscure a smaller area behind it, so care must be taken in arranging the series and applying 3-D effects.
X Y (Scatter)		Represents each numeric value as a data point, but does not necessarily connect them (although some types do draw lines). This enables you to spot trends in the data, such as clusters of points in a certain area. For example, suppose you are plotting hours studied (X axis) and test scores (Y axis). Each data point represents a student's score, and you can observe whether, generally speaking, there is a correlation between higher scores and more hours of study.
Stock		Represents financial information such as stock prices. This type of chart is useful primarily for showing high-low-close-open data for a stock or other tradable commodity.
Surface		A 3-D sheet, such as what might be created if you stretched a canvas over the tops of a 3-D column chart. It is useful for finding the highest and lowest points among intersecting sets of data. For example, if your data represents the profit made on certain sizes of certain products, you could see which product/size combination resulted in the greatest profit.
Doughnut		Very much like a pie chart, except it can hold multiple series, each in a concentric ring of the doughnut. For example, you could show how each member of a sales team contributed to the total sales in each of several months.

Category	Sample	Notes
Bubble		Similar to a scatter chart, except it adds an additional element: bubble size. You might use a bubble chart to show how many users bought certain products on certain days, for example. Days might be the horizontal axis (category), products the vertical axis, and the bubble size might represent the number of users.
Radar		Shows changes in data of frequency relative to a center point. Lines connect the values in the same data series.

Each chart type has at least two subtypes to choose from, and some have up to 19 subtypes. Don't let them overwhelm you, though; even though there are many subtypes, they fall into predictable categories.

Here are some of the major ways in which the chart subtypes can be differentiated:

- **2-D vs. 3-D style**—Some types show the shapes as flat 2-D objects; others show them as 3-D with sides and tops. The chart categories with available 3-D types are Column, Line, Pie, Bar, Area, Surface, and Bubble.

- **Clustered, Stacked, or 3-D**—When there are multiple series in a bar, column, or area chart, some types cluster the series, some stack them on a single bar (or other shape), and some add a third axis to the chart (front-to-back) and place each series on a separate axis.

- **Different shapes**—For bar and column charts, you can choose rectangular bars, cylinders, cones, or pyramids.

- **Regular or 100%**—For bar and column charts, a stacked bar can be regular (that is, the bar height represents the sum of the values), or each bar can be the same height (100%). A 100% bar is essentially a rectangular pie chart; it does not represent actual values, but rather the contribution of each series toward the whole.

- **Regular or exploded**—Pie and doughnut charts can optionally have one or more pieces set apart from the rest of the chart (exploded) to emphasize it.

- **Points, lines, or both**—A scatter chart can show data points without lines, lines without data points, or both.

- **Curved or straight lines**—When a scatter chart has lines, the line segments can be either curved or straight.

■ **Wireframe or filled**—Radar and Surface charts can appear with each series as a different color fill, or can appear in wireframe view (with transparency set for each series).

WORKING WITH CHART ELEMENTS

After choosing an appropriate chart type and subtype, the next task is to decide which additional elements to include in the chart. In other words, besides the data points, what do you want your chart to include? Possibilities include legends, walls, floors, gridlines, titles, data labels, and so on. Each of these can be displayed/hidden, positioned, and formatted.

APPLYING A CHART LAYOUT

Chart layouts are preset combinations of chart elements that serve as shortcuts to adding and formatting these elements. For example, one of the chart layouts places the legend across the top, adds data labels, removes the walls and floors, removes the gridlines, and adds a chart title.

> **NOTE**
>
> The main problem with chart layouts is that there aren't very many of them and you can't create your own. So take them for what they're worth, but you'll probably need to do some additional tweaking after applying one.

To apply a chart layout, select the chart and then select a layout from the Chart Layouts group on the Design tab (see Figure 16.10).

Click a layout...

Figure 16.10
Apply a chart layout to the chart.

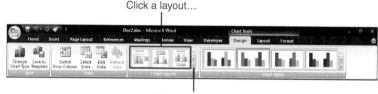

...or click here for more choices

ADDING A CHART TITLE

A *chart title* is a text box that floats above the chart and describes its purpose. The chart title can be placed in either of two locations: Centered Overlay (which places the title within the chart's plot area) or Above Chart (which places the title above the plot area). Figure 16.11 shows the difference.

Figure 16.11
Centered Overlay (left) versus Above Chart (right) for chart title placement.

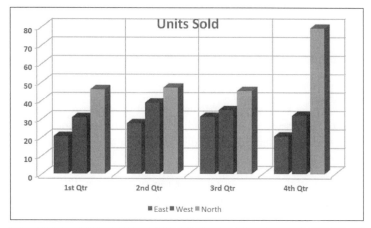

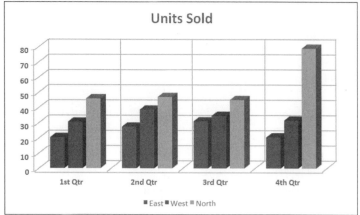

To create a chart title, first place the box, and then edit the placeholder text within it:

1. Select the chart.
2. On the Layout tab, click Chart Title. A menu appears.
3. Click Centered Overlay Title or Above Chart. The title appears in the chosen location.
4. Click in the chart title's text box, delete the placeholder text, and type your own text.
5. To format the chart title's frame, choose More Title Options from the menu and use the Format Chart Title dialog box to apply your selections. Click Close when you're finished.

NOTE

You cannot change the chart title box's size, but if you increase or decrease the font size, the box will grow or shrink automatically.

→ For detailed descriptions of the options in the Format Chart Title dialog box, **see** "Formatting Individual Chart Elements," **p. 522**.

6. To format the text in the chart title, select the text and then use the Home tab's controls in the Font group.

→ For more information about text formatting with the Home tab, **see** "Changing the Font and Size," **p. 158**.

WORKING WITH LEGENDS

The *legend* is the key that explains what each of the colors or patterns represents in a multi-series chart. It's critical to understanding the chart unless some other means of explanation is provided (as in a data table, or in individual labels for each pie slice or bar).

The legend can be placed either outside or inside of the chart's plot area, and it can be placed on any of the four sides or in the top-right corner. The Legend menu offers some presets, but you can also choose to display the Format Legend dialog box for additional options.

To turn the legend off, or select one of the presets:

1. Select the chart.
2. On the Layout tab, click Legend. A menu appears.
3. Select one of the presets on the menu, or select None.

Not all of the possible combinations of legend position are represented by the presets. To specify the desired position and choose whether it should overlap the chart, follow these steps:

1. Select the chart.
2. On the Layout tab, click Legend. A menu appears.
3. Click More Legend Options. The Format Legend dialog box opens (see Figure 16.12).
4. Select a legend position.
5. If you want the legend outside the plot area, mark the Show the Legend Without Overlapping the Chart check box. Otherwise, clear the check box to make the legend overlap the chart.
6. To format the legend box's frame, use the Format Legend dialog box to apply your selections for fill, line, shadow, and so on.

→ For detailed descriptions of the options in the Format Legend dialog box, **see** "Formatting Individual Chart Elements," **p. 522**.

7. Click Close.
8. To format the text in the legend, select the text and then use the Home tab's controls in the Font group.

→ For more information about text formatting with the Home tab, **see** "Changing the Font and Size," **p. 158**.

Figure 16.12
Select the legend position.

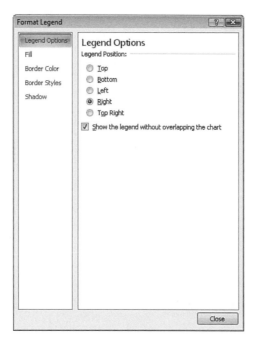

USING DATA LABELS

Data labels can be made to appear on (or near) each data point. A data label can contain any combination of these:

- The series name (duplicated from the legend, if present)
- The category name (duplicated from the category axis labels, if present)
- The numeric value represented by the data point
- The percentage of the whole that the data point represents (only on pies, doughnuts, and 100% bars)

Data labels can be applied to any chart type, but they're especially useful on pies, and in fact are often used as an alternative to a legend, as in Figure 16.13. This works especially well when presenting charts in black and white because then the audience does not have to match up the colors or patterns of the slices to the legend key. It makes the meaning of each slice or point more obvious.

Figure 16.13
Data labels can substitute for a legend.

To apply data labels, you can choose from one of the presets or define your own labels.

The preset data labels use the data point values only, and place them in your choice of locations. To use one of the presets:

1. Select the chart. (Optional: To affect only a certain data series or data point, select it.)

→ To learn how to select only a certain data series or data point, **see** "Selecting Chart Elements," **p. 522**.

2. On the Layout tab, click Data Labels.
3. Select one of the presets from the menu. (The menu varies somewhat depending on the chart type.)

To use other data in the labels, such as the series name, category name, or percentage, you must use the Format Data Labels dialog box. Follow these steps:

1. Select the chart. (Optional: To affect only a certain data series or data point, select it.)
2. On the Layout tab, click Data Labels.
3. On the menu, select More Data Label Options. The Format Data Labels dialog box opens (see Figure 16.14).
4. In the Label Contains section, mark or clear check boxes for the types of information to appear.
5. In the Label Position section, select a position for the label.
6. (Optional) Mark the Include Legend Key in Label check box, and then choose a separator character for it. The legend key indicates which series a value belongs to.
7. Click Close to apply the new settings.

Figure 16.14
Customize the data
labels for the chart.

APPLYING AXIS TITLES

Axis titles are text labels that appear on the axes to indicate what they represent. For example, a chart might have a value axis of 0 to 100, but what does that represent? Dollars? Millions of dollars? Units sold? Errors recorded? An axis title can help clarify what's being measured. Figure 16.15 shows a 3-D chart with three axes, all with titles.

Figure 16.15
Add axis titles where
needed to clarify the
meaning of the data.

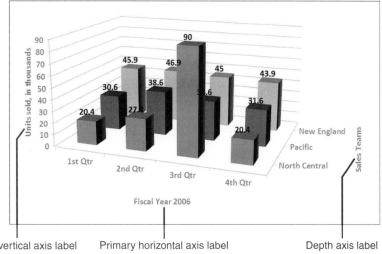

Each of the three dimensions of a chart (or two dimensions, depending on the chart) has its own separate setting for axis titles. On the Layout tab, click Axis Titles to open a menu, and then select from the submenu for the desired axis, choosing either a preset or custom settings. For example, in Figure 16.16, the choices for the primary vertical axis appear.

Figure 16.16
Different presets are available for each of the axes.

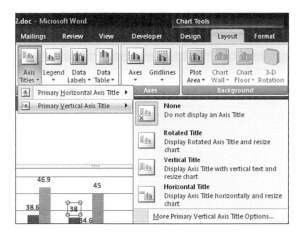

As you can see in Figure 16.16, for vertical axes you can choose whether you want the text to appear Rotated, Vertical, or Horizontal. Rotated text actually rotates each letter 90 degrees, whereas Vertical text makes the letters appear normally oriented but runs them vertically (stacked). In Figure 16.15, the primary vertical axis label and the depth axis label are both rotated.

MODIFYING AXIS PROPERTIES

Several types of modifications are available for the various axes in a chart. For example, you can make the axis scale run in a different direction (for example, right-to-left instead of the default left-to-right on a horizontal axis), and you can turn off the text on an axis. For numeric axes, you can also add automatic "thousands" or "millions" labels.

APPLYING AN AXIS PRESET

For some of the most popular changes, presets are available. To change an axis's properties using presets, follow these steps:

1. Select the chart.

2. From the Layout tab, click Axes. A menu opens listing the various axes available in the current chart.

3. Point to an axis on the menu to display its submenu (see Figure 16.17) and choose a setting.

Figure 16.17
Select a preset for the desired axis.

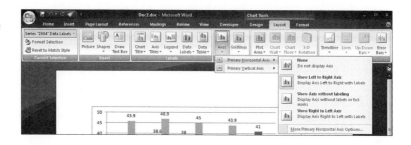

ADJUSTING THE AXIS SCALE

One of the most dramatic ways you can change how an audience interprets a chart is to adjust the axis scale. For example, in Figure 16.18, these two charts both use the same data, but different vertical axis scales. In the left chart, the difference between bars appears minimal, but in the right chart, it's dramatic.

Figure 16.18
Set the desired values for an axis's scale to modify the chart's appearance.

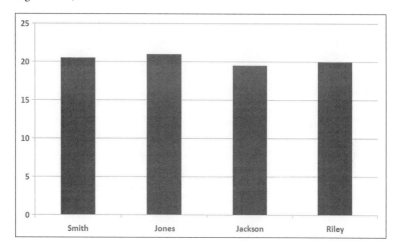

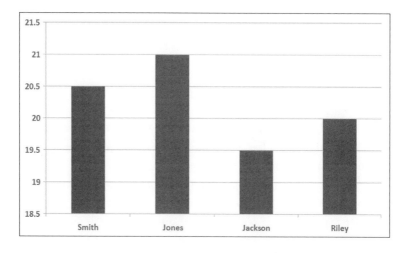

Word is actually pretty smart about adjusting the axis scale automatically; the chart on the right in Figure 16.18 shows the default for this data in Word. In cases where Word does not correctly deduce what you want, however, you can make manual changes.

To adjust the axis scale, follow these steps:

1. Select the chart.

2. From the Layout tab, click Axes. A menu opens listing the various axes available in the current chart.

3. Point to the desired axis, and then choose the More command for it. For example, for the primary vertical axis, choose More Primary Vertical Axis Options. The Format Axis dialog box opens.

4. To change the range of numbers represented on the axis, click Fixed for Minimum, Maximum, or both, and then enter the desired value(s). For example, in Figure 16.19, the minimum value on the axis is set to 10.0 and the maximum to 25.0.

5. To change the unit of measure shown on the axis (with numbers and gridlines), click Fixed next to Major Unit, Minor Unit, or both, and then enter the desired value(s). For example, in Figure 16.19, Major Unit is set to 1.0 and Minor Unit is left at the default.

Figure 16.19
Adjust the axis scale's minimum and maximum values, as well as major and minor units.

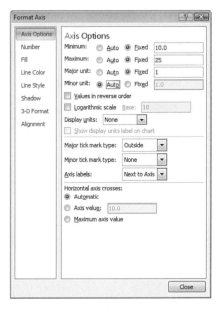

6. (Optional) To reverse the scale, mark the Values in Reverse Order check box.

7. (Optional) To use a logarithmic scale, mark the Logarithmic Scale check box and then enter a Base setting.

8. (Optional) To change the unit of display on the axis, open the Display Units list and choose a unit (for example, Thousands or Millions).

NOTE

Specifying a unit is somewhat like adding an axis label, except that in addition to adding the label for the unit, it also converts the numbers on the scale. For example, if your scale is currently 0, 1000, 2000, 3000, and so on, and you set the Display Units to Thousands, the scale will change to 0, 1, 2, 3.

9. (Optional) Use the Major Tick Mark Type and Minor Tick Mark Type settings to change how tick marks appear on the chart for the major and minor units. This does not affect the gridlines, only the small marks that appear on the axis line itself.

10. (Optional) In the Floor Crosses At section, choose Axis Value and then specify where the vertical and horizontal axes will meet. This setting makes it possible to have a chart that has data on both sides of the horizontal axis, as in Figure 16.20.

11. Click Close when you are finished.

Figure 16.20
When the Floor Crosses At value is set to 20, values that are less than 20 hang down below the horizontal axis.

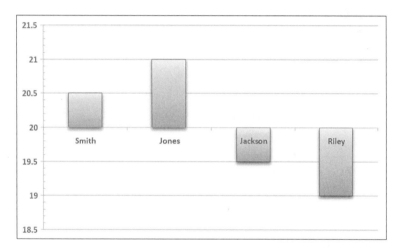

CHANGING THE AXIS NUMBER TYPE

On axes that contain numeric values, you can indicate what type of number formatting to use. For example, the numbers can appear as currency (with dollar signs), as percentages, or as any of several other number types.

To set the number type, follow these steps:

1. Select the axis.

2. On the Format tab, in the Current Selection group, click Format Selection. (Alternatively, right-click the axis and choose Format Axis.) The Format Axis dialog box opens.

   If you have selected the wrong chart area, you can select the correct area from the drop-down list in the Current Selection group.

3. Click Number. The Number options appear.

4. On the Category list, select the type of number formatting you want.

5. Adjust the settings that appear for the chosen category. For example, for currency you can set the number of decimal places and the currency symbol.

6. Click Close.

USING GRIDLINES

Gridlines are horizontal and/or vertical lines that appear on the chart's walls to help the audience's eyes track across from the values on the axes to the data points.

Word uses major horizontal gridlines by default in most chart types. The positioning of these gridlines is determined by the Major Units measurement set in the preceding section, in the Format Axis dialog box. The gridlines can be turned on/off, and you can also optionally turn on/off minor horizontal gridlines and/or vertical gridlines.

To toggle gridlines on or off, use the presets from the Gridlines button on the Layout tab. As you can see in Figure 16.21, vertical and horizontal gridlines have separate submenus, on which you can toggle major and minor lines.

Figure 16.21
Toggle major or minor gridlines on/off for vertical and horizontal axes.

To control the type of gridlines, choose the "More" option from the menu. (For example, in Figure 16.21, choose More Primary Horizontal Gridlines Options.) Then in the Format Gridlines dialog box (see Figure 16.22), set the properties for the line.

Figure 16.22
Format the gridlines by specifying a line thickness here.

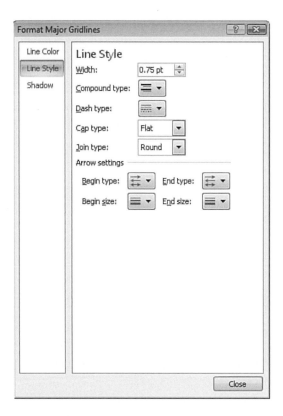

TIP

> There are other ways to format gridlines, and you will learn about these in "Formatting Individual Chart Elements" later in this chapter. On the Format tab, you can use the Shape Styles group to apply shape outlines and effects that change the gridline color, thickness, shadow, and more.

ADDING TRENDLINES

A *trendline* is a line superimposed over a two-dimensional chart (usually a scatter chart) that helps express the relationship between a pair of values. Trendlines are often used in statistics and scientific research to show overall trends of relationship between cause and effect.

To understand the value of a trendline, let's look at an example. Suppose a coach has asked his basketball players to practice shooting free-throws as many hours a day as they can for a one-week period. Different students approached this assignment with varying degrees of dedication; some players did not practice at all, whereas others practiced as much as 3 1/2 hours a day. At the end of the week, each player makes 100 free-throw attempts and records his or her number of successes.

To prove a positive relationship between practicing and success, the coach plots this data in a Word chart. The relationship is not mathematically perfect because we're dealing with humans, not machines. However, an overall trend is apparent (see Figure 16.23).

Figure 16.23
This scatter chart shows the relationship between two variables.

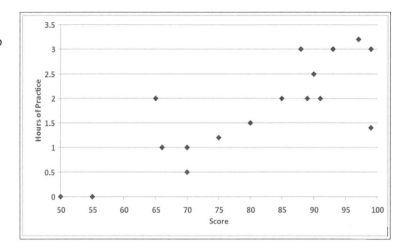

To quantify this trend, add a trendline to the chart. The simplest and most straightforward type of trendline is a linear one (a straight line). In Figure 16.24, a linear trendline has been applied. The trendline helps the data analysis in two ways. First, the line itself shows where the expected score will be for any number of hours of practice (or fractions thereof). Second, it shows a statistical equation that represents the relationship. In the formula shown in Figure 16.24, for example, you could plug in a number of practice hours for "Y" and then solve for "X" to determine the expected score.

Figure 16.24
Adding a linear trendline to the chart helps quantify the relationship.

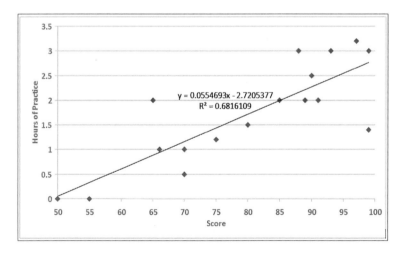

To add a trendline, follow these steps:

1. Select the chart.

2. On the Layout tab, click Trendline.

3. On the Trendline menu, select the desired trendline type. (If you are not sure what type you want, choose Linear Trendline.)

For more trendline options, choose More Trendline Options in step 3, and select the series to which they apply if prompted. Then in the Format Trendline dialog box, shown in Figure 16.25, change any of these options:

Figure 16.25
Set trendline options.

- **Trend/Regression Type**—Select a type here. More types are available in this box than were on the Trendline menu. Table 16.2 lists the trendline types.

TABLE 16.2   TRENDLINE TYPES

Trend/Regression Type	Useful For...
Exponential	Data that is increasing or decreasing at an accelerating or decelerating rate. Cannot be used with zero or negative data.
Linear	Data that is increasing or decreasing at a relatively steady rate.
Logarithmic	Data that rapidly increases or decreases and then levels out.
Polynomial	Data that fluctuates between high and low values.
Power	Data that increases or decreases at a constant rate. Cannot be used with zero or negative data.
Moving Average	Data that contains interim fluctuations that should be discounted when determining the trend overall.

■ **Trendline name**—This is useful when you have more than one trendline per chart. Automatic makes the trendline name the same as the data series name; Custom lets you enter a new name of your choosing.

■ **Forecast**—This lets you extend the trendline forward or backward to predict values that are outside of the data range.

■ **Set Intercept**—This changes the tilt of the trendline so that its left end points to a different number on the vertical axis.

■ **Display equation on chart**—This toggles on/off the equation.

■ **Display R-squared value on chart**—The R-squared value is a measurement of the reliability of the equation in predicting the outcome. Statisticians appreciate it, but most people don't know what it is. Toggle it on/off here.

ADDING ERROR BARS

When sampling a population for research purposes, how can you be certain that you didn't get unusual data? For example, what about the basketball player who is naturally so good at free throws that he can shoot 90% without any practice? With a small sample, you can't be sure that your data isn't being skewed by unusual cases, but as the sample size grows, so does your confidence in your results.

Even though the formula from the trendline in the preceding section can provide a prediction of a value, in reality that value may be off. The actual value might turn out to be higher or lower than that. For example, what if someone practices free throws for 1.5 hours? The chart in Figure 16.24 indicates that the expected score would be somewhere around 77, but that's just a guess. The amount by which a guess could be off—in either direction—is its *margin of error*. That margin of error is shown on a chart by using *error bars*.

For example, in Figure 16.26, the margin of error for each data point appears to be about 3 points horizontally and 1 hour vertically. In other words, given a player's number of hours practicing, his score could have been 3 points higher or lower, and given a player's score, his practice time could have been 1 hour more or less.

NOTE

Error bars can be used on area, bar, column, line, scatter, and bubble charts.

The amount of certainty in the results is described as the *amount of error*. In other words, how confident are we that, given a player's practice time, we can predict his score within a certain margin of error? Are we 90% confident? 95%? As the desired confidence level goes up, so does the margin of error required to achieve it, and the point spread grows.

CAUTION

> Don't confuse margin of error with amount of error; they're two different things. The margin of error is the point spread. The amount of error is the confidence level that the point spread is accurate.

Figure 16.26
Error lines show the range of statistically probable values if the data were resampled.

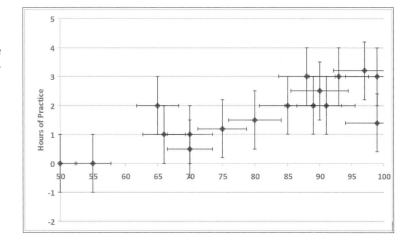

Amount of error can be measured in several ways: by standard error, standard deviation, or a specific percentage. We won't get into the differences between these calculation methods here—that's something for a college-level Statistics course to delve into—but let's assume you know which method you want to use. If you don't, go with a fixed percentage, because that's the easiest to understand.

To apply error lines to a chart:

1. Select the chart.
2. On the Layout tab, click Error Bars. A menu appears.
3. On the menu, select the calculation type for amount of error:
   - Error Bars with Standard Error
   - Error Bars with Percentage (by default 5% error, or 95% confidence)
   - Error Bars with Standard Deviation (by default 1 standard deviation)

To fine-tune the error bars, click Error Bars again and choose More Error Bars Options. Then in the Format Error Bars dialog box, set the error amount desired. You can enter a certain percentage, fixed value, or number of standard deviations (see Figure 16.27).

Figure 16.27
Fine-tune the amount of error to be expressed in the error bars and the method by which it will be calculated.

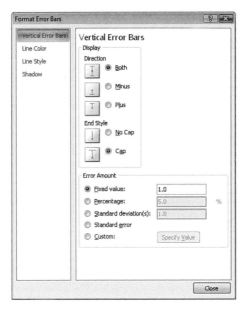

ADDING UP/DOWN BARS

Up/down bars are specific to the Stock type of chart. They are filled rectangles that run between the open and close value, as in Figure 16.28. When the open value is higher, the bar is dark; when the close value is higher, the bar is light. Up/down bars let you see at a glance the overall change in the stock that day, disregarding the fluctuations that occurred throughout the trading day. For example, you can see in Figure 16.28 that on 1/8/2007, the stock's price fluctuated a great deal (by nearly $5), but the next loss was only about 50 cents from opening to closing.

Figure 16.28
Up/down bars make the fluctuation between the high and the close values more obvious.

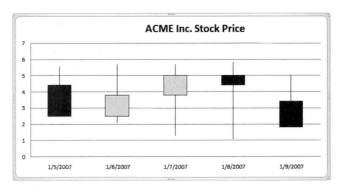

To turn up/down bars on or off, click Up/Down Bars on the Layout tab and choose Up/Down Bars from the menu that appears.

ADDING AND FORMATTING A DATA TABLE

A chart does a nice job of summarizing data, but sometimes it's useful to see the original data in addition to the chart. You can copy and paste the data from the Excel sheet into the document as a table below the chart, but it's much easier to simply turn on the display of a *data table*. A data table repeats the data on which the chart is based, as in Figure 16.29.

Figure 16.29
A data table provides the numbers with which the chart was constructed.

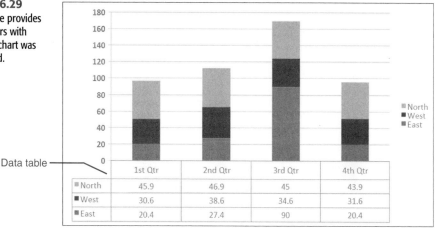

Data table

	1st Qtr	2nd Qtr	3rd Qtr	4th Qtr
North	45.9	46.9	45	43.9
West	30.6	38.6	34.6	31.6
East	20.4	27.4	90	20.4

A data table can optionally be set to show legend keys, as in Figure 16.28, or to simply show the data. If you display the legend keys, the legend itself becomes superfluous and can be removed if desired.

To turn on/off the data table, follow these steps:

1. Select the chart.
2. On the Layout tab, click Data Table.
3. On the Data Table menu, choose one of the following options:
   - None
   - Show Data Table
   - Show Data Table with Legend Keys

In the data table's options, you can choose which borders should be visible in the data table. From the Data Table menu, choose More Data Table Options, and then clear the check boxes for the borders to hide: Horizontal, Vertical, and/or Outline.

APPLYING CHART STYLES

The Chart Styles list on the Design tab applies colors from the current color theme to the chart in various combinations and with various effects (see Figure 16.30).

Figure 16.30
Apply the theme's colors to the chart in different ways with Chart Styles.

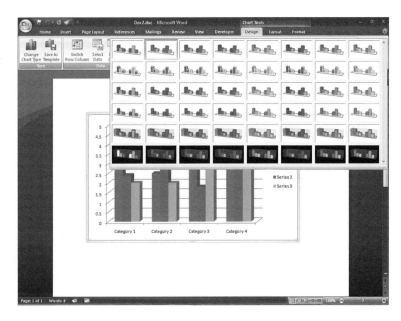

Chart Styles do *not* change the color set (color theme). The colors for the entire document are set on the Page Layout tab, as you learned in Chapter 8, "Creating and Applying Styles and Themes." Chart Styles simply combine the color placeholders defined by the theme in different ways. For example, some Chart Styles use the same theme color for all the bars, lines, or slices in a chart, but in different tints, whereas others use different colors from the theme for each item.

→ To change the theme colors, **see** "Working with Themes," **p. 256**.

FORMATTING INDIVIDUAL CHART ELEMENTS

Now let's look at the formatting options available for individual pieces of the chart—data series, data points, legends, titles, and so on. Each of these has its own Format dialog box. Some of the options in this dialog box do not change no matter what type of element; others are unique to a particular element.

SELECTING CHART ELEMENTS

Each chart element can be separately formatted, and many of them have special options you can set depending on the element type. We'll look at some of these in the remainder of this chapter. However, before you can format a chart element, you must select it.

Clicking on an element is one way to select it. Hover the mouse pointer over an element, and wait for a ScreenTip to appear to make sure you are in the right spot (see Figure 16.31). Then click to select the element.

Some elements can be selected either individually or as part of a group. For example, a group of bars in the same series in a bar chart can be selected together or separately. When you click once on such items, the entire group becomes selected; click again on the same item to select only that one object. You can tell when an element is selected because a rectangular box appears around it. When a data series is selected, a separate rectangular box appears around each bar (or other shape).

Figure 16.31
To select a chart element, position the mouse over it and click.

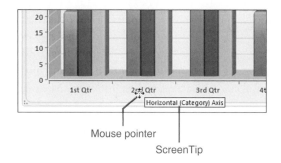

Mouse pointer

ScreenTip

It can sometimes be difficult to tell what you are clicking when several elements are adjacent or overlapping, so Word provides an alternate method of selection. On the Format or Layout tab, in the Current Selection group, a drop-down list is available. Choose the desired element from that list to select it (see Figure 16.32).

Figure 16.32
Select chart elements from the Current Selection group's list.

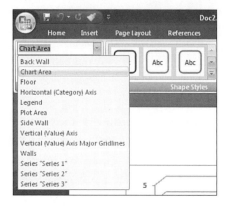

CLEARING MANUALLY APPLIED FORMATTING

Word's charting dialog boxes are *nonmodal*, which means they can stay open indefinitely; their changes are applied immediately, and you don't have to close the dialog box to continue working on the document. Although this is handy, it's all too easy to make an unintended formatting change.

To clear the formatting applied to a chart element, select it and then, on the Format tab, click Reset to Match Style. This strips off the manually applied formatting from that element, returning it to whatever appearance is specified by the chart style that has been applied.

APPLYING A SHAPE STYLE

Shape Styles are presets that can be applied to individual elements of the chart, such as data series, data points, legends, the plot area, the chart area, and so on. A Shape Style applies a combination of fill color, outline color, and effects (such as bevels, shadows, or reflection).

To apply a Shape Style:

1. Select an element of the chart, as you learned in a preceding section.

2. Open the drop-down list in the Shape Styles group of the Format tab and click the desired style (see Figure 16.33).

NOTE

Like the overall Chart Styles on the Design tab, the Shape Styles use the theme colors in various combinations. If you need to change the theme colors, do so from the Page Layout tab, as described in "Working with Themes" in Chapter 8.

Figure 16.33
Apply Shape Styles to individual elements of a chart.

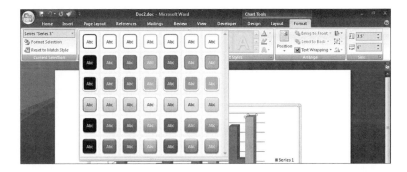

APPLYING SHAPE OUTLINES AND FILLS

The Shape Styles group on the Format tab contains Shape Fill and Shape Outline drop-down lists, from which you can apply manual formatting to the selected chart element. These work exactly the same as with drawn lines and shapes, which Chapter 15, "Working with Drawings and WordArt," covered in detail.

→ To learn about applying fill and outline formatting, **see** "Formatting Drawn Objects," **p. XXX** (Chapter 15).

APPLYING SHAPE EFFECTS

The Shape Effects menu (Format tab, Shape Styles group) enables you to apply various special effects to a chart's elements that make them look shiny, 3-D, textured, metallic, and so on. As shown in Figure 16.34, there are a number of presets available for 3-D effects that make the element look like it is raised, indented, shiny, rounded, and so on.

You can also create your own effects by combining the individual effects on the Shape Effects menu. The available submenus and effects depend upon the element selected; for data series and points, there are fewer options than for the chart area as a whole, for example.

Each effect on the Shape Effects menu also has a "More" command that opens the Format Shape dialog box for the selected element. The following sections look at these in more detail.

Figure 16.34
Shape Effects can be manually applied to individual chart elements.

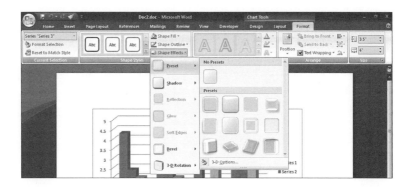

APPLYING SHADOW EFFECTS

Shadow effect presets are available from the Shape Effects, Shadow submenu. Choose outer or inner shadows, or shadows with perspective (see Figure 16.35).

Figure 16.35
Apply preset shadow effects here.

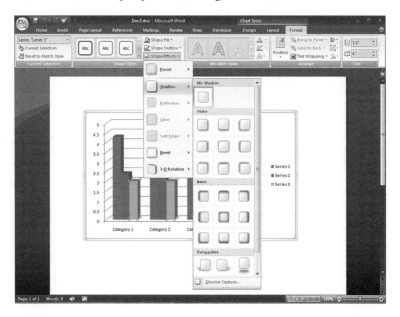

For additional shadow fine-tuning, choose Shadow Options from the menu to open the Shadow settings in the Format dialog box. (The exact name of the dialog box depends on the chart element chosen.) From here you can change the shadow color and adjust its transparency, size, blur, angle, and distance (see Figure 16.36).

Figure 16.36
Fine-tune shadow
effects.

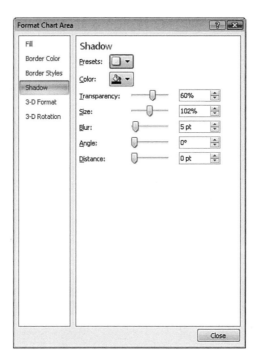

16

APPLYING REFLECTION EFFECTS

Reflection is unavailable on the Shape Effects menu when you're working with chart elements. Reflection is not totally off-limits for charts, though; you can make text reflected via the Text Effects list in the WordArt Styles group, as you will see later in this chapter.

APPLYING GLOW EFFECTS

A glow effect places a fuzzy "halo" of a specified color around the object. The samples on the Glow submenu show each of the theme colors in a variety of glow sizes. To change these colors, change to a different color theme for the entire document (on the Page Layout tab).

You can also specify a fixed color; from the Glow submenu, choose More Glow Colors and then pick a standard color, a theme color, or a custom color, as you would with any other object.

→ To review the color choices that Word provides, **see** "Changing Font Color," **p. 167**.

APPLYING SOFT EDGE EFFECTS

Soft Edges is just what it sounds like. It makes the edges of the selected element fuzzy. You can choose a variety of degrees of softness from the Soft Edges submenu: 1 pt, 2.5 pt, 5 pt, 10 pt, 25 pt, and 50 pt. (Sorry, there's no way to enter a custom number of points.)

APPLYING BEVEL EFFECTS

Beveling changes the shapes of the edges of the object. Beveling can make the object appear to have rounded corners, for example. Another name for beveling is 3-D Format.

Apply one of the preset bevel effects from the Bevel submenu, or select 3-D Options to open the 3-D Format options, shown in Figure 16.37. From here you can change the height and width of the effect at the top and bottom of the object, change the color of the depth and contours, and change the surface material, lighting, and lighting angle.

Figure 16.37
Fine-tune the bevel on the chart element from the 3-D Format settings.

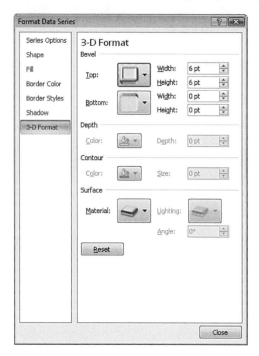

CHANGING THE SHAPE OF A SERIES

When specifying the chart's type and subtype for a bar or column chart, you choose the shape of the data bars for the entire chart. These can be bars, cylinders, cones, or pyramids.

You can also change the shape used on a series-by-series basis if desired. When you do this, a couple of extra shape types are available that you can't get with the Change Chart Type method: partial cones and partial pyramids. Instead of showing a full cone or pyramid of the size that the data point represents, the bar displays as a full-height cone or pyramid "sawed off" so that its top marks the data point position (see Figure 16.38).

Figure 16.38
The partial pyramid setting makes all pyramids the same size and then cuts off the tops of lower values.

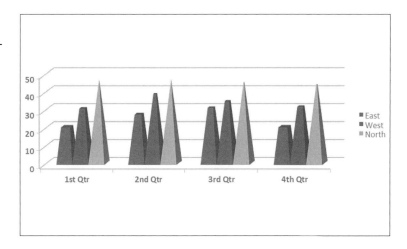

→ To change the bar shape for the entire chart, **see** "Changing the Chart Type," **p. 501**.

You can also change the shapes of an individual series by doing the following:

1. Select a data series.

2. Right-click any bar in the data series and choose Format Data Series to open the Format Data Series dialog box.

3. Click Shape to display the Shape options.

4. Select the desired shape.

5. Click Close. The change is applied to only the selected series.

ADJUSTING DATA SPACING

When working with chart types that involve multiple series of data in a bar, column, or similar style of chart, you can adjust the amount of blank space between the series. To do this, change the data spacing for any series, and all the others will fall into line:

1. Select any data series, and then right-click any data point within it and choose Format Data Series.

2. In the Format Data Series dialog box, click Series Options.

3. Drag the slider to adjust the Gap Depth setting. This is the amount of white space between bars from front to back in a 3-D chart. Figure 16.39 shows this setting at its minimum No Gap setting.

4. Drag the slider to adjust the Gap Width setting. This is the amount of white space from side to side between bars or series. Figure 16.39 shows this setting at its maximum Large Gap setting.

5. Click Close to close the dialog box.

Figure 16.39
Adjusting the spacing between the bars by changing the gap settings.

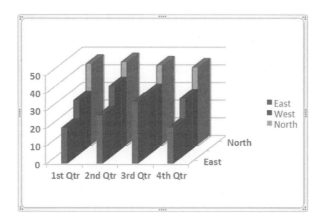

FORMATTING CHART TEXT

Text in a chart is an odd hybrid of regular text and WordArt, and its formatting options reflect that. There are two ways to format text in a chart: use regular formatting techniques from the Home tab, or apply a WordArt Style to the entire chart (preset or custom).

CHANGING THE FONT, SIZE, AND TEXT ATTRIBUTES

Most of the text formatting that applies to regular text also applies to chart text. On the Home tab, you can choose a different font, size, and color, just like with any other text.

> **NOTE**
>
> The Font Color button on the Home tab's Font group is the same as the Text Fill button on the Format tab's WordArt Styles group. You can set the font color in either place; making a change to one also makes the change to the other.

You can also format the text in the selected element using a special version of the Font dialog box, enabling you to specify less-common font formatting such as character spacing. To do this:

1. Select the desired chart element.
2. On the Home tab, click the dialog box launcher icon in the Font group. The Font dialog box opens. It's a different version than for regular text, as shown in Figure 16.40.
3. Choose the font, style, size, color, and effects desired from the Font tab.

   In addition to the regular font-formatting options, the following special options are available:

   • Equalize Character Height—When enabled, this option forces all the characters to the same height.

16

Figure 16.40
Format chart text
using a special version
of the Font dialog box.

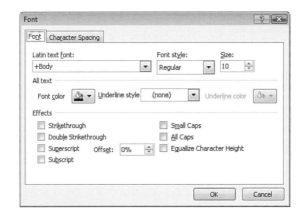

4. (Optional) Adjust the character spacing on the Character Spacing tab if desired. Normal spacing is the default, but you can set it to Expanded or Condensed and specify a number of points by which to adjust. You can also indicate that you want kerning for text at or above a certain size.

5. Click OK.

→ To review font formatting and character spacing, **see** "Changing the Font and Size," **p. 158** and "Adjusting Character Spacing," **p. 176**.

APPLYING A WORDART STYLE

WordArt Styles enable you to change the fill and outline for chart text, and to apply special effects to it such as Glow and Reflection.

You can affect all the text in the entire chart at once by selecting the Chart Area before applying a WordArt Style, or affect only certain text by selecting that element first.

From the Format tab, open the WordArt Styles gallery to see the available presets; point at a preset to see a preview of its application in the chart (see Figure 16.41).

Figure 16.41
Apply WordArt Styles
presets to quickly for-
mat all the text in the
chart at once.

If none of the presets meets your needs, use the Text Fill, Text Outline, and Text Effects lists to create your own custom WordArt effect:

- **Text Fill**—Works just like Shape Fill. You can apply any color (theme or fixed) or any type of fill effect, such as gradient or picture.

- **Text Outline**—Works just like Shape Outline. If you do not want an outline around your text, choose No Outline.

- **Text Effects**—Similar to Shape Effects. You can apply a Shadow, Reflection, or Glow effect to the text in the chart.

→ To review the Shape Fill and Shape Outline settings, **see** "Applying Shape Outlines and Fills," **p. 524** and "Formatting Drawn Objects," **p. 472**.

→ To review the Shape Effects, **see** "Applying Shape Effects," **p. 524**.

TROUBLESHOOTING

I WANT TO RETURN A CHART ELEMENT TO ITS ORIGINAL COLOR

Try this: Select the element and on the Format tab, click Reset to Match Style. This clears any custom formatting from that element so that the style's formatting can appear.

If that doesn't work, reapply the Chart Styles selection for the entire chart from the Design tab.

I WANT TO USE DATA FROM EXCEL IN MY CHART

Don't bring the data from Excel to Word; that's awkward, and the charting feature does not accept that very gracefully. Instead make the chart in Excel, using Excel's charting tools, and then copy and paste the chart from Excel into Word. The charting tools are nearly identical between Word and Excel, so you should have no difficulty with them.

HOW CAN I INSERT A MICROSOFT GRAPH–STYLE CHART IN A WORD 2007 DOCUMENT?

If you prefer the charting tools offered by Microsoft Graph, you are free to continue using them in Word 2007. Here's how:

1. On the Insert tab, click Object, Object. The Object dialog box opens.
2. On the Create New tab, select Microsoft Graph Chart.
3. Click OK.

I CAN'T EDIT THE SOURCE DATA WHILE IN THE EDIT DATA SOURCE DIALOG BOX

When you click Edit Data Source on the Design tab, the data source opens in Excel with the Edit Data Source dialog box open. The "editing" being referred to here means changing what cells the chart is based on, not changing what is actually *in* those cells.

To make changes to the data within the cells, close the Edit Data Source dialog box, or use the Show Data button on the Design tab in Word to open the data source without displaying the Edit Data Source dialog box in the first place.

CHAPTER 17

WORKING WITH SMARTART AND MATH FORMULAS

In this chapter

WHAT IS SMARTART?

SmartArt replaces and improves upon the Diagrams feature in earlier versions of Word. Using SmartArt, you can create a wide variety of graphical conceptual diagrams.

There are seven main categories:

- **List diagrams**—These diagrams show a list of items in a graphical format that helps to emphasize their importance.

- **Process diagrams**—These diagrams show the progress made toward a goal, and are useful for step-by-step procedures (see Figure 17.1).

Figure 17.1
A process diagram.

17

- **Hierarchy diagrams**—These diagrams show an organization's structure, or when run horizontally, can be used for tournament brackets. Figure 17.2 shows a simple organization chart, which is a type of hierarchy.

Figure 17.2
A hierarchy diagram.

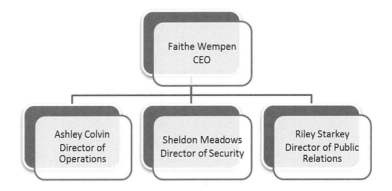

- **Cycle diagrams**—These diagrams show a repeating process. They are like process diagrams except the beginning and the end connect (see Figure 17.3).

- **Relationship diagrams**—These diagrams show how one item relates to another. For example, a relationship diagram can show that one group is a subset of a larger group, or how one process depends upon another. Figure 17.4 shows a Venn diagram relationship, which indicates overlap between groups.

- **Matrix diagrams**—These diagrams show relationships of components to a whole, such as how the various departments make up a business unit (see Figure 17.5).

Figure 17.3
A cycle diagram.

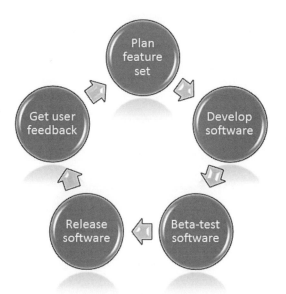

Figure 17.4
A relationship diagram.

Figure 17.5
A matrix diagram.

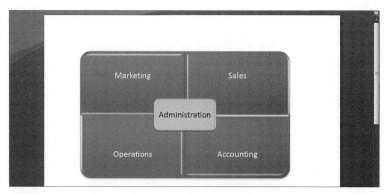

- **Pyramid diagrams**—These diagrams show the progression of items from largest quantity to smallest quantity, such as the relationship of the number of workers to the number of executives in a company (see Figure 17.6).

Figure 17.6
A pyramid diagram.

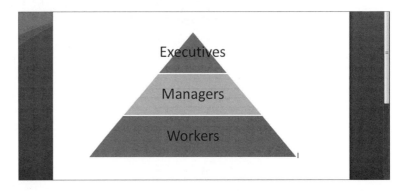

SmartArt diagrams represent one of the most dramatic improvements in Word 2007 over earlier versions, in both the variety of diagram types available and the automatic and manual formatting possibilities.

In some ways, SmartArt diagrams are similar to the charts that you learned about in Chapter 16, "Working with Charts." Both use a complex system of interrelated lines and shapes to create meaning out of data, and both can be formatted either with Quick Styles or with shape and WordArt formatting. The main difference is that whereas charts present numeric data, SmartArt presents text-based data.

NOTE

> Charts and SmartArt, as well as drawn objects (from Chapter 15, "Working with Drawings and WordArt"), are all based on a new drawing engine called Escher 2.0, which is incorporated into all Office 2007 products. Therefore, no matter which Office product you are working with, the drawing, charting, and SmartArt tools are consistent in interface and capability.

INSERTING A SMARTART DIAGRAM

SmartArt diagrams are considered illustrations, and they are inserted from the Illustrations group of the Insert tab. Follow these steps:

1. On the Insert tab, click the SmartArt button. The Choose a SmartArt Graphic dialog box opens.

2. Click the desired category of diagram, or click All to see all the diagrams at once (see Figure 17.7).

Figure 17.7
Create a new diagram by selecting the layout type you want.

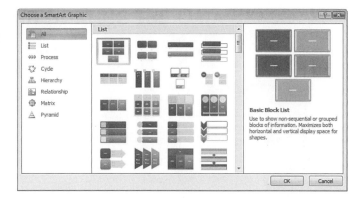

3. Click the desired diagram layout and then click OK. A text pane appears to the left of the empty diagram layout.

4. Click in a [Text] placeholder and type the desired text. Repeat for each [Text] placeholder.

CAUTION

> Spell check does not work on the text in a SmartArt diagram in Word. However, full spell-check features are available for SmartArt in PowerPoint (both dialog box and red underlines), and the dialog box–based spell check is available for SmartArt in Excel.

The basic layout and options might be okay, but the real power of SmartArt comes from its customization features. In the next several sections of the chapter, you'll learn how to make the SmartArt diagram your own by changing its layout, formatting, and text in various ways.

CHANGING THE DIAGRAM'S LAYOUT

The *layout* is what you selected in Figure 17.5 when you created the chart; it determines the size, shape, and arrangement of the shapes that comprise the diagram. Before you spend a lot of time on the formatting and appearance of a diagram, it's wise to make sure that you have the right layout for your needs. Preset layouts are available on the Design tab, and you can also customize the layout by adding or removing shapes, changing the diagram flow direction, and more.

CHOOSING A DIFFERENT LAYOUT

To change the layout of a diagram, use the Layouts group controls on the Design tab.

To change to a different layout within the same major category (for example, to change from one Process diagram style to another), open the list of Layouts and click the desired style, as in Figure 17.8.

Figure 17.8
Choose a different layout type from within the same major category.

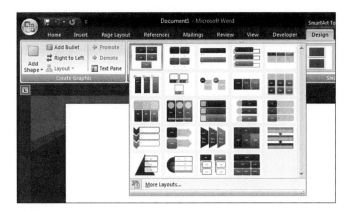

To change to a different layout in a different major category, choose More Layouts from the bottom of the menu shown in Figure 17.8. This reopens the Choose a SmartArt Graphic dialog box (refer to Figure 17.7), from which you can choose any layout, even one that is radically different from the existing one. (You might need to move some text around after changing to a very different layout.)

CHANGING THE FLOW DIRECTION

Most diagram types can be reversed so that they flow from right to left instead of left to right—or in the case of a cycle diagram, counterclockwise instead of clockwise.

To reverse the flow, click the Right to Left button in the Create Graphic group of the Design tab. Click it again to return to the original flow direction.

ADDING SHAPES

Each diagram type starts out with a default number of shapes in it, but you can easily add more shapes to it.

When inserting new shapes, you insert them in relation to an existing shape. The new shape can either be of the same level of importance (that is, the same outline level) as the existing shape, or be superior or subordinate to it. On most diagram types, there is only one level of shape, but on hierarchy charts many levels are possible.

To add a shape:

1. Select the existing shape to which the new shape should be related.
2. To insert a new shape at the default level, click the upper (graphical) portion of the Add Shape button on the Design tab.

   The default level for a single-level chart is a shape of the same level as the others. The default level for a hierarchy chart is the level subordinate to the topmost level.

   Alternatively, to specify the level at which to insert the new shape, click the arrow near the bottom of the Add Shape button and then select the desired relationship, as in Figure 17.9:

Figure 17.9
Select a level and
position at which to
insert the new shape.

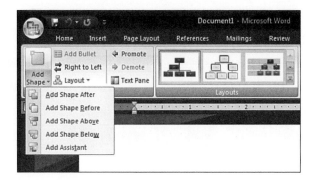

- **Add Shape After**—Inserts a shape of the same outline level either below or to the right of the selected shape.

- **Add Shape Before**—Inserts a shape of the same outline level either above or to the left of the selected shape, depending on the layout flow.

- **Add Shape Above**—Inserts a shape of a superior level to the selected shape, either above it or to its left. If no superior level is available, this option is unavailable.

- **Add Shape Below**—Inserts a shape of a subordinate level to the selected shape, either below it or to its right. If no subordinate level is available, this option is unavailable.

- **Add Assistant**—Available only for hierarchy charts, this option adds a shape that is subordinate to the selected shape but not part of the regular layout.

> **NOTE**
> Here's an alternate way of displaying the list of available shape insertion types: Right-click an existing shape and point to Add Shape.

REMOVING SHAPES

To remove a shape from the diagram, select the shape and press the Delete key on the keyboard, or right-click the shape and choose Cut. No warning appears; the shape is simply deleted. You can use Undo (Ctrl+Z) to reverse a deletion immediately afterwards, however.

> **NOTE**
> In a hierarchy chart, if you delete a shape that has subordinate shapes, the first (leftmost or topmost) subordinate that formerly reported to it moves up into its vacated position.

PROMOTING OR DEMOTING A SHAPE

Promoting or demoting individual shapes helps fine-tune a multilevel diagram. It is most obviously useful in a hierarchy chart such as an organization chart, but can be useful for adding detail to other chart types as well.

Each time you select a shape and click Demote, it moves down one level in significance. If there is no subordinate level, a bullet point is created beneath the preceding shape (that is, the shape that was formerly to its left or above it) at its former level. Figure 17.10 shows an example of a demoted item that has become a bullet point. You can click in the bullet point's text box and type more bullet points there if desired.

Figure 17.10
Items demoted past the lowest level of a shape in a diagram become bullet points.

Each time you select a shape and click Promote, it moves up one level. You can do this for bullet points too; select some bulleted text and click Promote to move it into its own shape in the diagram.

ADDING BULLETED LISTS

Demoting an item that is already at the lowest level of significance in a chart turns the item into a bulleted list, as you just learned. However, you can also create bulleted lists subordinate to any level in the diagram, without having to do any demotion.

To create a bulleted list subordinate to a shape, select the shape and then on the Design tab, click Add Bullet. A text box is created below the shape, and a bullet character is applied to it. Type the desired text. Press Enter to type another bullet item if desired.

To create a multilevel bulleted list, press the Tab key at the beginning of the bulleted paragraph to indent it one level in outline significance. Press Shift+Tab to promote a bullet level within the outline.

TIP

> Sometimes it can be easier to see the outline levels if you have a text-based outline to work with. The text pane appears by default; you can click the Text Pane button on the Design tab to toggle it on/off. In the text pane, you can type, edit, and promote/demote outline levels without having to worry about the graphical aspect of the diagram. For more information, see "Using the Text Pane" later in this chapter.

POSITIONING ORGANIZATION CHART BRANCHES

One of the drawbacks to a large organization chart is the space it takes up. When there are many levels and each level has many items, the chart can spread out horizontally to the point where it's not very readable.

The SmartArt organization chart layout has several positioning alternatives available, and you can apply them on a branch-by-branch basis on an org chart. For example, you can stack all the subordinate boxes vertically, or make them branch off from one or both sides of a center pillar.

To change the positioning of subordinate items on a branch of an organization chart, follow these steps:

1. Select the shape for which you want to change the subordinates.

2. On the Design tab, click Layout and then click the desired layout (see Figure 17.11).

Figure 17.11
Choose the desired positioning for the selected branch of the organization chart.

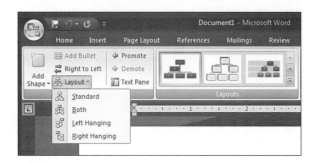

WORKING WITH DIAGRAM TEXT

Diagrams exist in order to convey text messages in graphical ways. The text in the diagram is the star of the show; the boxes, arrows, and other flourishes are just supporting players. In this section, you'll learn how to add, edit, and format a diagram's text.

ADDING AND EDITING TEXT

Each shape in the diagram starts out with a plain [Text] placeholder. That placeholder does not print, so you're free to leave some shapes without any text in them if that's appropriate for your message.

To replace the [Text] placeholder with some real text, click the placeholder (it immediately disappears when you do) and type the desired text. You can do this in the shape itself or in the text pane.

To edit text, click to move the insertion point inside the shape and then edit as you would any other text—use Backspace or Delete to remove characters, or select the text and press Delete to remove blocks of characters.

FORMATTING DIAGRAM TEXT

As with chart text (covered in Chapter 16), diagram text is a blend of regular text and WordArt text. As a result, the formatting you can apply to diagram text includes both standard text formatting and WordArt formatting.

CHANGING THE FONT BY APPLYING A FONT SET

The default font in a SmartArt diagram comes from the font theme, which is chosen on the Page Layout tab. SmartArt diagrams use whatever font is specified as the secondary font (the one for body text).

To change the fonts globally throughout the entire document, including on the diagrams, select a different font set from the Theme Fonts drop-down list on the Page Layout tab (see Figure 17.12).

Figure 17.12
Select different font sets to change the appearance of the chart.

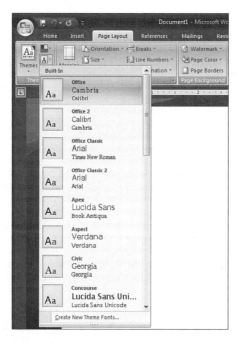

If you want to change the font only on the one individual SmartArt diagram, see the following section instead.

CHANGING THE FONT, SIZE, AND TEXT ATTRIBUTES MANUALLY

Most of the standard text-formatting controls are available for diagram text. Use the Font group on the Home tab, or right-click the text and use the Mini Toolbar, as in Figure 17.13.

Figure 17.13
Text in a diagram can be formatted via the Mini toolbar that appears when you right-click it.

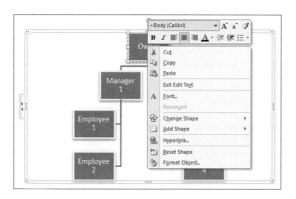

NOTE

The Font Color button on the Home tab's Font group is the same as the Text Fill button on the Format tab's WordArt Styles group. You can set the font color in either place.

You can also format diagram text via a special version of the Font dialog box that includes most of the usual text attributes (with the exception of Emboss, Engrave, and Hidden) plus Equalize Character Height, which sets all the characters to the same height. To access the Font dialog box, right-click the selected text and choose Font, or click the Home tab and then click the Font group's dialog box launcher icon. This is the same dialog box as for charts, and it works the same way (see Figure 17.14).

Figure 17.14
Fine-tune the diagram text's formatting using the Font dialog box.

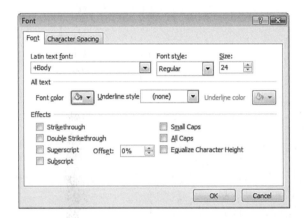

The Character Spacing tab in the Font dialog box works just like it does for regular text. Normal spacing is the default, but you can set it to Expanded or Condensed and specify a number of points by which to adjust. You can also indicate that you want kerning for text at or above a certain size.

→ To review font formatting and character spacing, **see** "Changing Text Font, Size, and Color," **p. 156** and "Adjusting Character Spacing," **p. 176**.

APPLYING WORDART QUICK STYLES TO TEXT

WordArt Styles enable you to change the fill and outline for diagram text, and to apply special effects to it such as Glow and Reflection. They work similarly in SmartArt and in charts, so if you mastered their use in Chapter 16, you're ahead of the game.

From the Format tab, open the WordArt Styles list to see the available presets; point at a preset to see a preview of its application in the diagram.

If none of the presets meets your needs, use the Text Fill, Text Outline, and Text Effects lists to create your own custom WordArt effect:

- **Text Fill**—Applies the selected color to the text. You can apply any color (theme or fixed) or any type of fill effect, such as gradient or picture.

- **Text Outline**—Applies a colored outline to the text. If you do not want an outline around your text, choose No Line.

- **Text Effects**—Applies a special effect to the text, such as Shadow, Reflection, Glow, or Bevel. These are the same as the Shape Effects you learned about in Chapter 16.

→ To review fill and outline settings, **see** "Applying Shape Outlines and Fills," **p. 524** and "Formatting Drawn Objects," **p. 472**.

→ To review Shape Effects, **see** "Applying Shape Effects," **p. 524**.

USING THE TEXT PANE

Each diagram has a text pane. It appears by default, and can be displayed or hidden in either of these ways:

- On the Design tab, click the Text Pane button.
- Click the left/right arrow button at the left edge of the diagram frame (see Figure 17.15).

To close the text pane, you can also click its Close button (the X in the upper-right corner).

Figure 17.15
Use the text pane to more easily edit the diagram's text.

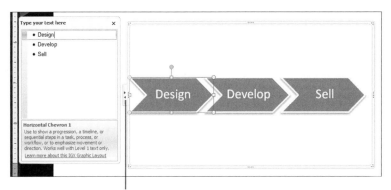

Click here to display/hide the text pane

In the text pane, you can create an outline for the diagram, much like you do with Outline view in Word or PowerPoint

Here are some things you can do in the text pane to modify the diagram's text:

- **Add a shape**—Click at the end of the text in a bullet and press Enter, and then type the text for the new shape.
- **Demote a shape**—Click anywhere within a bulleted list item and press Tab or click the Demote button on the Design tab.
- **Promote a shape**—Click anywhere within a bulleted list item and press Shift+Tab or click the Promote button on the Design tab.
- **Format text**—Right-click the text in the text pane and use the Mini toolbar that appears. Alternatively, you can select the text in the text pane and use the Home tab's Font group controls, or you can right-click the text and choose Font.

SETTING TEXT POSITIONING WITHIN A SHAPE

Within each shape is a *text area*, which is a rectangular area in which the text appears. The text area varies depending on the shape, but generally it lies completely within the shape, so that text will not hang outside of the shape's outline.

This text area functions much like a text box does. (See "Creating Text Box Layouts" in Chapter 11, "Working with Nonstandard Document Layouts," for a full description of text box formatting.) To access the text box controls for a text area, follow these steps:

1. Select the shape.
2. Right-click the shape and choose Format Shape. The Format Shape dialog box opens.
3. Click Text Box. The text layout options appear (see Figure 17.16).
4. In the Text Layout section, set the vertical alignment and text direction.
5. In the Internal Margin section, specify the amount of blank space that should be maintained between the edge of the shape and the text.
6. Click Close.

Figure 17.16
Adjust the internal margins and vertical alignment of the text within the shape.

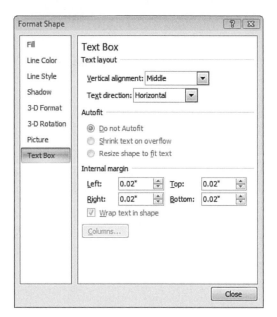

FORMATTING A DIAGRAM

Now comes the fun part—formatting the diagram. You can apply any of the many Quick Styles to the diagram as a starting point, and then fine-tune the settings by applying fills, outlines, and effects to individual diagram elements.

APPLYING DIAGRAM QUICK STYLES

To quickly apply formatting presets to the entire diagram, select it, and then open the WordArt Styles list from the Design tab and choose the desired style.

As you can see in Figure 17.17, the drop-down list has two sections: Best Match for Document and 3-D. The Best Match for Document styles format uses non-3-D features such as gradients, lines, fills, spacing; the 3-D styles add 3-D rotation and depth to that mix, to create fancier effects.

Figure 17.17
Select a Quick Style for the diagram.

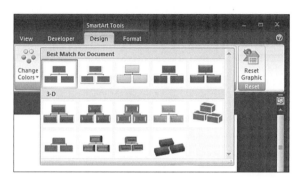

 If system performance suffers when you are working with 3-D diagrams, see "Applying a 3-D Style to a Diagram Slows Down Word's Performance" in the "Troubleshooting" section at the end of this chapter.

CHANGING THE THEME EFFECTS FOR THE ENTIRE DOCUMENT

When you insert a new SmartArt diagram, its default settings (colors and effects) depend on the theme applied to the document.

To format all the SmartArt in the entire document the same way, leave them all at their defaults and then select a different theme from the Page Layout tab, as you learned in Chapter 8, "Creating and Applying Styles and Themes."

The theme provides different settings in three areas: colors, fonts, and effects. If you like the current colors and fonts, but just want to apply different effects to graphical objects such as SmartArt, choose a different effect set from the Theme Effects list (also on the Page Layout tab). These effects apply not only to the selected SmartArt, but to every graphical object in the document that does not have manual formatting applied to it—SmartArt, charts, drawn shapes, and so on (see Figure 17.18).

→ To review how to apply themes, **see** "Working with Themes," **p. 256**.

CAUTION

If you have applied manual formatting to a diagram, or to one or more shapes within it, changing to a different theme or set of effects will have no effect on it. Right-click the frame of the graphic and choose Reset Graphic to reset the whole diagram, so that the theme can affect it, or right-click an individual shape and choose Reset Shape to reset a particular shape.

Figure 17.18
Apply effects to all the SmartArt, charts, and drawings in the document at once from the Theme Effects menu on the Page Layout tab.

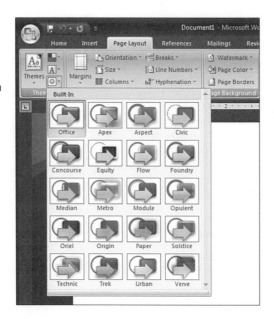

CHANGING DIAGRAM COLORS

To change a diagram's colors overall, use the Change Colors list in the Quick Styles group of the Design tab. As shown in Figure 17.19, you can select various combinations of the theme colors here. The entire document can use a single color, or you can choose one of the Colorful options to make each piece of the diagram a different theme-supplied color.

Figure 17.19
Select a SmartArt Style for the diagram.

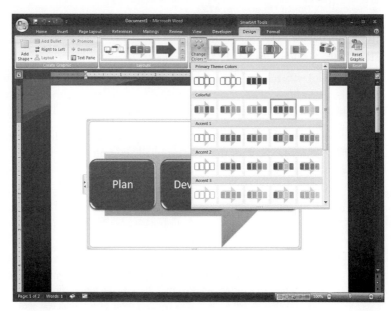

→ To review how to change the theme colors for the document, **see** "Working with Themes," **p. 256**.

FORMATTING AN INDIVIDUAL SHAPE

Each individual shape in the diagram can be formatted separately from the diagram as a whole. For example, if you don't like the color assigned to a certain shape, you can change it to a different theme color or to a fixed color of your choosing. You can also apply various fill effects separately to each shape, such as 3-D rotation, beveled edges, shadows, and glows.

APPLYING A SHAPE STYLE

The easiest way to reformat an individual shape is with a Shape Style. As you learned in Chapter 16 in "Applying a Shape Style," these are presets that can be applied to individual elements. A Shape Style applies a combination of fill color, outline color, and effects.

To apply a Shape Style:

1. Click a shape to select it. To select multiple shapes to affect, hold down Ctrl as you click on each one.
2. Open the drop-down list in the Shape Styles group of the Format tab and click the desired style.

APPLYING SHAPE OUTLINES, FILLS, AND EFFECTS

For maximum control over a shape's formatting, use the Shape Fill, Shape Outline, and Shape Effects drop-down lists in the Shape Styles group of the Format tab. These work the same way for SmartArt diagrams as they do for drawings, covered in Chapter 15, and charts, covered in Chapter 16. You can use solid colors, tints, gradients, or even picture fills for each shape.

→ To learn about applying fill and outline formatting, including special fills such as pictures and gradients, **see** "Formatting Drawn Objects," **p. 472**.

→ To learn about applying shape effects, **see** "Applying Shape Effects," **p. 524**.

CHANGING THE SHAPE GEOMETRY

Not happy with the type of shape used in the diagram? For example, would you rather have rectangles than chevrons, or stars rather than circles? It's easy to change to any shape you like. (Microsoft calls the shape's "shape" its *geometry.*)

All the same shapes that you worked with in Chapter 15 are available for use in a diagram. Figure 17.20 shows a diagram that was originally composed of chevrons, but now uses four different shapes instead.

Figure 17.20
Each shape in the diagram can be different.

CAUTION

When selecting the shape geometry for pieces of a diagram, keep in mind that the more similar to a rectangle the chosen shape is, the more efficiently text will fit inside it. Oddly pointed shapes such as stars typically have a very small text area.

To change a shape, follow these steps:

1. Select the shape.

2. On the Format tab, click Change Shape in the Shapes group. A menu of shapes appears (see Figure 17.21).

3. Click the desired shape.

Figure 17.21
Each shape in the diagram can be different.

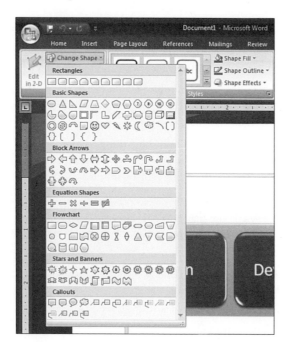

To go back to the default shape, right-click the shape and choose Reset Shape.

SIZING, POSITIONING, AND ROTATING A SHAPE

If a shape does not have any 3-D rotation applied to it, it has normal selection handles, like any other drawn object (see Figure 17.22).

Figure 17.22
A shape without 3-D rotation applied can be sized, positioned, and rotated freely like any other drawn object.

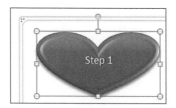

When 3-D rotation is applied, the object does not have normal selection handles when selected; instead a thin plain box appears around it, as in Figure 17.23.

Figure 17.23
A shape with 3-D rotation has a plain selection box around it, and it is more difficult to directly format it.

You can do all these things to a shape regardless of its 3-D rotation status:

- **Enlarge**—Click the Larger button on the Format tab to enlarge the shape and shrink the other shapes to make room for it. The positioning between them remains constant.

- **Shrink**—Click the Smaller button on the Format tab to shrink the shape and enlarge the other shapes so that the overall diagram continues to be the same size. Again, the positioning between them remains constant.

- **Rotate or Flip**—On the Format tab, in the Arrange group, click Rotate, and choose a flipping or rotation option. (The Arrange group might be collapsed into an Arrange button, depending on the width of the Word window.)

> **N O T E**
>
> To rotate by a precise amount, choose More Rotation Options from the Rotate menu. In the Size dialog box that appears, set a Rotation amount in degrees.

→ To learn more about rotating and flipping, **see** "Rotating and Flipping Objects," **p. 464**.

For non-3D-rotation shapes only, you can also do the following:

- Drag a selection handle to resize the shape.

- Drag its border (but not on a selection handle) to move it. A shape cannot be moved outside the diagram frame.

> **T I P**
>
> To move a shape with 3-D rotation, first remove the 3-D rotation and then move the shape. Then reapply the 3-D rotation.

- Drag its rotation handle (green circle) to rotate it.

→ To learn more about sizing and positioning drawn objects, **see** "Sizing and Positioning Objects," **p. 465**.

CONTROLLING DIAGRAM SIZE AND POSITIONING

Diagrams are objects, just like charts and graphics, and have the same sizing and positioning options. Here's a quick review; full details for object sizing and positioning can be found in Chapter 13, "Working with Photos."

RESIZING A DIAGRAM

When a SmartArt diagram is selected, a light blue border appears around it. This border has dotted tabs in the corners and on three sides; you can drag any of these to resize the diagram's frame (see Figure 17.24). (The left side doesn't have resizing dots; instead it has the two arrows for opening/closing the text pane.)

Figure 17.24
Resize a diagram by dragging the dotted areas on its frame.

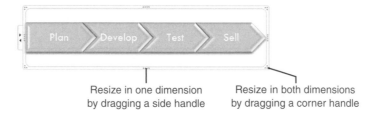

Resize in one dimension by dragging a side handle

Resize in both dimensions by dragging a corner handle

NOTE

Resizing the frame also resizes the diagram within it proportionally, but only if the resizing forces a change in the content. For example, suppose you have a short, wide diagram with lots of extra blank space above and below it. Decreasing the height of the SmartArt frame will not change the diagram; it simply tightens up the excess space. However, decreasing the width of the frame does shrink the diagram, and increasing the width enlarges the diagram. The reverse would be true for a tall, thin diagram that has extra blank space on the sides.

For more precise sizing of the diagram, use the Size controls on the Format tab. Enter precise values in the Height and Width boxes of the Size group.

POSITIONING A DIAGRAM

Position presets are available for diagrams, the same as for other graphic objects. These presets set the diagram frame to precise relative or absolute positioning within the document page.

To apply a position preset to a diagram, follow these steps:

1. Select the SmartArt diagram.
2. On the Format tab, in the Arrange group, click Position. Then click one of the position presets.

To set an exact position for the diagram, you must set Text Wrapping to something other than In Line with Text. So first do this:

1. On the Format tab, in the Arrange group, click Text Wrapping.
2. Click any of the text wrap settings other than In Line with Text.

→ For detailed descriptions of text wrapping choices and their effects on the surrounding text, **see** "Setting Text Wrap," **p. 402**.

Next, open the Advanced Layout dialog box and choose specific positioning as follows:

1. On the Format tab, in the Arrange group, click Position, More Layout Options. The Advanced Layout dialog box opens.

2. On the Picture Position tab, set the desired layout. You can choose layout by Alignment, by Book Layout, by Absolute Position, or by Relative Position.

3. Set any options desired, such as Move Object with Text or Lock Anchor.

4. Click OK to accept the new position setting.

→ For more detailed descriptions of the position choices, **see** "Setting Picture Position," **p. 404**.

CREATING MATH FORMULAS WITH THE EQUATION EDITOR

Mathematics has its own language, complete with special symbols and syntax, and even special types of line breaks, dividers, and superscript/subscript requirements. It's no wonder, then, that most word processing programs are inadequate for expressing complex mathematical equations.

Here are some of the reasons it's difficult to express math concepts in a word processing program:

- Special symbols are often required that are not found on a standard keyboard, such as sigma (Σ) and pi (π).

- Math formulas often involve complex combinations of superscript and subscript, sometimes with multiple levels.

- The proper size for certain symbols and characters can depend on the usage. For example, parentheses or brackets that span a complex, multiple-line equation must be very tall.

- Fractions need to be expressed with the numerator above the denominator—on separate lines, but part of a single unit. This can be nearly impossible to simulate with regular paragraphs or tables.

Figure 17.25 illustrates some of these issues. Notice that the symbols π and ∞ are used, along with some subscript characters and a fractional expression. Notice also that the two sets of parentheses are different sizes, and that fractions are represented with their numerators and denominators on split lines.

Figure 17.25
Math formulas like this one can be a challenge to create as regular text.

$$f(x) = a_0 + \sum_{n=1}^{\infty} \left(a_n \cos \frac{n\pi x}{L} + b_n \sin \frac{n\pi x}{L} \right)$$

Fortunately, the Equation Editor feature in Word makes creating complex equations like the one in Figure 17.25 a snap. By using a combination of regular typing, symbols, and placeholder boxes, the Equation Editor can build virtually any mathematical expression you would ever need.

INSERTING A PRESET EQUATION

In algebra and trigonometry, certain key equations seem to come up repeatedly, such as the Pythagorean theorem and the quadratic formula. There's no need to re-create them each time you need them; Word provides them as equation presets.

To insert an equation preset:

1. On the Insert tab, open the Equation button's drop-down list.
2. Click one of the presets.

The equation appears in its own object frame in the document. You can edit it if desired, as explained later in the chapter.

CREATING A NEW BLANK EQUATION OBJECT

If none of the presets matches your needs, create a new, blank equation object instead by clicking the Equation button (click its face, not its down arrow) or by pressing Alt+=. An equation frame appears, along with a text placeholder (see Figure 17.26).

Figure 17.26
A new blank equation
frame.

CREATING A BASIC EQUATION

To create a simple equation, just start typing it in the equation frame. You can use any number, letter, or symbol from the keyboard, plus you have access to a wide variety of math symbols from the Symbols group on the Design tab.

Basic math symbols are shown by default on the Symbols group's menu system, as shown in Figure 17.27.

Figure 17.27
The Basic Math collection of symbols
appears on the
Symbols group menu
by default.

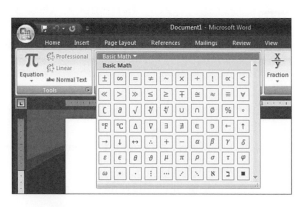

For access to other symbols, open the drop-down list at the top of the Basic Math collection's menu and choose the desired category. Some of the categories are very small and basic; others have dozens of choices and their own subsections, as in Figure 17.28.

Figure 17.28
Additional collections of symbols are available by selecting another category.

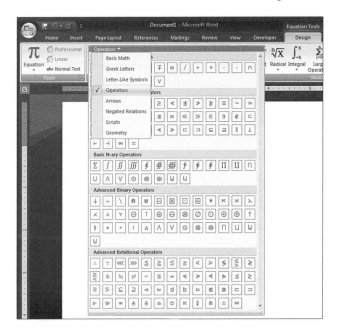

INSERTING AND FILLING STRUCTURES

Structures are symbols and/or combinations of text placeholder boxes that help you create math expressions that could not be easily expressed on a single line of text.

A *stacked fraction* is one of the simplest and most common examples. It consists of two placeholder boxes, one on top of the other, with a horizontal line between them (see Figure 17.29).

Figure 17.29
Structures contain one or more placeholder boxes.

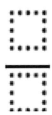

To insert and fill a structure:

1. In the equation, position the insertion point where you want the structure to be inserted.
2. On the Design tab, click one of the buttons in the Structures group to open its menu.
3. Click on the desired structure to insert it.
4. Click in a placeholder and type or insert the content. Repeat this for each placeholder.

NOTE

Structures can be nested. You can place one structure inside the placeholder box for another structure, creating complex nests of structures and equations.

For example, here are the steps for a simple superscript:

1. In the equation, position the insertion point where you want the structure to be inserted.

2. On the Design tab, click Script.

3. In the Subscripts and Superscripts section of the menu, click Superscript. Two place-holder boxes appear: one regular-sized and one smaller and slightly raised.

4. Click in the first placeholder box and type or insert the content that should precede the characters in superscript.

5. Click in the second placeholder box and type or insert the content that should appear *in* superscript.

All the other structures work exactly the same way, although some of them might appear intimidating and complex. Just click in the placeholders and fill in the content.

SWITCHING BETWEEN PROFESSIONAL AND LINEAR LAYOUT

The default type of equation layout is Professional, which shows structures spread out on multiple lines wherever appropriate. Professional layout makes math formulas that are easy to read and understand.

When space is an issue in a document, however, you might be loathe to give up two or more lines of a page in order to show an equation. For situations like that, it's helpful to switch the equation's view to Linear. Using a Linear view runs the equation on a single line, changing the symbols where needed to alternatives that can be expressed in a linear fashion (see Figure 17.30).

Figure 17.30
The same equation in Professional versus Linear view.

$$(x + a)^n = \sum_{k=0}^{n} \binom{n}{k} x^k a^{n-k}$$

$$(x + a)\verb|^|n = \Sigma\_(k = 0)\verb|^|n \quad [(n\vdots k) \; x\verb|^|k \; a\verb|^|(n - k)]$$

To switch between Linear and Professional views, use the corresponding buttons in the Tools group on the Design tab. Alternatively, click the down arrow at the bottom-right corner of the equation's frame and choose the desired view from the menu that appears.

FORMATTING AN EQUATION

In some ways, formatting an equation is like formatting the text in a text box. There are a few quirks, though. Here's a quick summary:

- **Font**—Cambria Math is used for formulas by default. While you can change this (right-click the equation and choose Font, or select the font from the Home tab), note that font changes will not take effect unless the font you choose supports mathematical symbols. Since Cambria Math is the only font that ships with Word 2007 that fully supports all math symbols used in the new Equation Editor, it is in effect your only choice.

- **Size**—By default, the baseline font for an equation is 11 point. Some characters can be larger or smaller than that depending on their context. You can select the equation's frame and then choose a different font size from the Home tab to adjust the overall size of the equation up or down proportionally from there.

- **Color**—Use the Font Color button on the Home tab to change the color of the text used for the equation if desired. Keep in mind, however, that equations are nearly always utilitarian objects, not decorative.

- **Bold**—You can apply boldface to individual characters or to the entire equation.

- **Strikethrough**—You can apply strikethrough to individual characters or to the entire equation.

- **Italics**—Letters in an equation are italicized by default, as are some symbols. It is usually best to leave these at their default, because people expect to see those items italicized, and the italics help them make sense of the equation.

- **Underline**—Underline cannot be applied to individual characters; it can be applied only to the equation as a whole.

- **Horizontal justification**—The equation frame is an inline object and cannot be floated freely in the document. However, you can set its horizontal justification—but not with the Paragraph controls. Instead, click the down arrow at the bottom-right corner of the equation frame, and on the menu that appears, point to Justification and choose a justification option (see Figure 17.31).

Figure 17.31
Set horizontal justification for the equation.

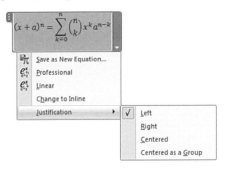

SWITCHING BETWEEN INLINE AND DISPLAY MODE

An equation is a graphic object—sort of. It's not a completely free-floating object, like a drawn shape or a photo, but it does have some independence from the surrounding text.

An equation can interact with the text in the document in either of two ways:

- **Inline**—The equation is treated as an inline image, and runs in with the text like any other character. Most of the font-formatting options available for a regular paragraph apply to it.
- **Display**—The equation is its own separate object, with positioning controlled by the Justification setting on the equation's menu. It appears on a separate line from the surrounding text.

To switch back and forth between these, click the down arrow at the bottom-right corner of the equation to open the equation's menu, and then choose Change to Display or Change to Inline. (The wording changes depending on the mode currently in use.)

Need More Text Wrap and Position Control Over an Equation?
Because an equation is not a truly independent object, it does not have Position and Text Wrapping settings the way a piece of SmartArt does. If you want to wrap text around an equation, you must place it in a container, such as a text box, that allows text wrapping.

To place an equation in a text box:

1. Draw the text box.
2. Select the equation and press Ctrl+X to cut it to the Clipboard.
3. Click inside the text box and press Ctrl+V to paste the equation there. Now the equation is part of the text box, and can be moved around with it.
4. Resize the text box to match the size of the equation, and move it where you want it.
5. Set the Text Wrapping for the text box to whatever you want it to be for the equation.
6. Remove the text box's visible border to make it blend into the background so the equation gets the attention.

SAVING AN EQUATION TO THE EQUATION GALLERY

After spending the time to create an equation, you can save it for later reuse by creating a building block for it in the Equation Gallery. The Equation Gallery is a section of the Building Blocks template that you've worked with in other chapters; it serves as a repository for custom user equations.

To save the current equation, follow these steps:

1. Select the equation.
2. On the Design tab, click the Equation button and then choose Save Selection to Equation Gallery.
3. In the Create New Building Block dialog box, a linear version of the equation appears in the Name box. Change this to a friendly text name that will help you remember the equation's purpose.

TIP

The equations appear on the list in alphabetical order, so to force one to the top of the list (above the Word-supplied presets), begin it with a number rather than a letter. To take this one step further, you can create a set of custom equations and specify the order in which they appear on the menu by preceding each one's name with a number representing the desired position.

4. Leave all the other options in the dialog box set at their defaults, as in Figure 17.32, or change them if desired.

5. Click OK.

Figure 17.32
Set equation options.

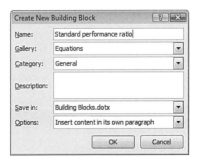

→ To review the options available in the Create New Building Block dialog box, **see** "Working with Building Blocks," **p. 90**.

The custom equation will now appear on the Equation menu, along with all the preset equations that come with Word.

TROUBLESHOOTING

Applying a 3-D Style to a Diagram Slows Down Word's Performance

On a PC with less RAM and CPU speed than average, editing a chart in a 3-D style can cause frustrating delays as the chart redraws itself. To avoid this problem, on the Format tab click the Edit in 2-D button. The chart appears temporarily without its 3-D effects. Then when you are finished editing it, click Edit in 2-D again to toggle it back to 3-D view.

Some Shape Effects Don't Show Up on a 3-D Diagram

When 3-D rotation is applied, some of the other shape effects don't show up properly. For example, you can't have both a shadow and a 3-D rotation applied to the same diagram. Removing the 3-D rotation will cause the other effects you've applied to appear.

How to Convert SmartArt to Regular Drawing Objects

If you're having trouble positioning, sizing, or formatting a shape in your SmartArt in a certain way, here's a workaround: Take the shapes out of the SmartArt frame and make them regular drawing objects instead. You lose the automation of the SmartArt feature, but you gain in formatting flexibility.

In PowerPoint, you can simply select a shape in a SmartArt diagram, cut or copy it to the Clipboard, and then paste it outside the diagram frame. However, if you try that in Word, instead of the shapes, you get a plain bulleted list containing the text that was in the pasted shapes. This happens because in PowerPoint, the default paste format is graphical, but in Word, the default paste format is HTML text.

To get around this problem, use Paste Special to paste the cut or copied shapes. Follow these steps:

1. Select the shape(s) in the diagram.
2. Press Ctrl+C to copy or Ctrl+X to cut the shape(s).
3. Click outside the diagram frame.
4. On the Home tab, open the Paste button's menu and click Paste Special. The Paste Special dialog box opens.
5. In the As list, select Microsoft Office Graphic Object.
6. Click OK.

COLLECTING AND MANAGING DATA

CHAPTER 18

PERFORMING MAIL AND DATA MERGES

In this chapter

UNDERSTANDING MAIL MERGES

Mail merge combines a main document with a list of database records to create customized copies of the main document for each record. The most common type of mail merge, of course, is a mailing. Mail merging was originally developed to create form letters, like the kind you probably get in your mailbox every day that address you by name and suggest that you buy some can't-live-without product.

Word's mail merge feature can actually do much more than generate form letters, however. You can use it to generate envelopes, labels, personalized copies of business reports or children's stories, auction catalogs—just about anything that combines fixed text with variable text.

Let's start by looking at the files involved in a mail merge. A mail merge uses two files:

- The **main document** is a Word document. It contains all the text that should remain the same from copy to copy.

- The **data file** contains the variable data to be merged. It can be a Word document (with the data in a table), an Excel worksheet, an Outlook contact list, a Windows Mail address book, a delimited text file, or any of several other data types.

→ To learn more about delimited text files, **see** the sidebar "Understanding Delimited Data" on **p. 571**.

To set up a mail merge, you insert merge fields that reference the data file into the main document. For example, if the data file has a FirstName field, you might have a line in the main document that looks like this:

Dear <<FirstName>>:

When you perform the merge, you can send the results either to a new file or directly to the printer. The result is a separate copy of the main document for each of the database records, with that record's information inserted:

Dear Joe:

You can set up a mail merge main document manually, but Word provides several features that partially automate the process. The features Word provides are different depending on the document type you wish to produce:

- **Letters**—Create a personalized form letter for each recipient. Each letter will print on a separate sheet of paper.

- **E-mail messages**—Create an email message for each recipient with customized information inserted from the recipient's contact information.

- **Envelopes**—Create an envelope for mailing a letter to each recipient. This is similar to Letters except for the paper size and type.

- **Labels**—Create sheets of mailing labels in which each label contains the mailing address of a different recipient. This is similar to Envelopes except instead of each recipient being on a separate sheet, they are combined.

- **Directory**—Create a listing of database entries, such as a product catalog. This is like Labels except there is not a defined area in which each record's data appears; instead you can set up the layout any way you like.

- **Normal Word Document**—This is a new option in Word 2007. It enables you to use mail merge features in an ordinary Word document—that is, one that is not one of the listed special types.

Word provides the tools you need for setting up merges on the Mailings tab, shown in Figure 18.1. You can go your own way with them, or you can use a step-by-step Mail Merge Wizard to guide you.

The Mailings tab has five groups to it. The first one, Create, has buttons for creating individual envelopes and labels, which you learned about in Chapter 11, "Working with Nonstandard Document Layouts." The Create group has no role in mail merging.

The other four groups on the Mailings tab, shown in Figure 18.1, correspond to the stages of setting up a mail merge. They appear from left to right in chronological order:

Figure 18.1
The Mailings tab contains buttons and lists for setting up mail merges.

- **Start Mail Merge**—In this group, you choose the type of document and select the data source.

- **Write & Insert Fields**—In this group, you insert field codes and set up rules that sort and filter the records to be included.

- **Preview Results**—In this group, you view and proofread the merge, so you can make any changes needed to it.

- **Finish**—In this group, you save the results to a file, print them, or email them.

This chapter covers all the controls in each of these groups in detail. Because many beginners find mail merges intimidating to set up, though, Word also offers a Mail Merge Wizard utility. The following section shows how to use this wizard to do a simple mail-merged letter.

PERFORMING A LETTER MERGE WITH THE MAIL MERGE WIZARD

The Mail Merge Wizard is a carryover from Word 2003. It guides you through the process of setting up a mail merge for letters, email messages, envelopes, labels, or a directory. Mail merge beginners find it useful because it prompts you for each step of the process; mail merge experts seldom use it because it is a bit clunky and because creating your own merges on-the-fly is faster.

Because the rest of this chapter covers each step of the mail merge process in much greater detail, I won't go into detail for each step here. Instead, the following steps take you through a very simple Letters type of merge using the Mail Merge Wizard and your Microsoft Outlook contact list. After you've completed the rest of this chapter, you can come back to the Mail Merge Wizard with a more complete understanding of its options.

To use the Mail Merge Wizard to create a set of mail-merged letters based on the addresses in your Microsoft Outlook contact list, follow these steps:

1. Start a new blank document. Then on the Mailings tab, in the Start Mail Merge group, click Start Mail Merge, and then click Step by Step Mail Merge Wizard. The Mail Merge task pane appears.

2. In the Mail Merge task pane, click Letters (see Figure 18.2, left). Then at the bottom of the task pane, click Next: Starting Document.

3. In the Select Starting Document section of the task pane, leave Use the Current Document selected (see Figure 18.2, center). Then click Next: Select Recipients.

4. Click Select from Outlook Contacts (see Figure 18.2, right).

Figure 18.2
The first three screens of the Mail Merge Wizard.

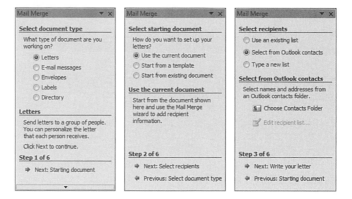

5. Make sure the correct one is selected by doing the following:
   a. Click Choose Contacts Folder.
   b. In the Select Contacts dialog box, click the desired contact folder. The name of the folder depends on your mail setup, and on whether you are using Outlook or Windows Mail.
   c. Click OK.

→ For more information about selecting a data source, **see** "Choosing an Existing Data Source," **p. 572**.

6. (Optional) If you don't want to send the letter to every contact in the data source, do the following:
   a. Click Edit Recipient List.
   b. In the Mail Merge Recipients dialog box, clear the check box next to each entry you want to exclude.
   c. Click OK.

→ For more information about excluding certain records, **see** "Filtering and Sorting the Data," **p. 585**.

7. At the bottom of the task pane, click Next: Write Your Letter.

8. Position the insertion point at the top of the document and then click Address Block (see Figure 18.3, left).

9. In the Insert Address Block dialog box, select any options to fine-tune the formatting of the recipient address, and then click OK. An <<AddressBlock>> code appears in the document.

NOTE

> To save you some time, Word has some built-in merge blocks that combine the data from multiple fields. To make up a standard postal mailing address, Word combines fields such as first name, last name, address, city, state, and ZIP into a single field called <<AddressBlock>>. Similarly, it combines fixed text such as "Dear" with first and/or last name fields to create the <<GreetingLine>> field.
>
> You are free to use individual fields in the mail merge if you prefer, or if the address and greeting blocks aren't delivering the results you want. To access the full list of available fields in the Mail Merge Wizard, choose More Items instead of Address Block or Greeting Line.

→ For more information about address blocks, **see** "Inserting Address Blocks," **p. 580**.

18

10. Press Enter a few times after the <<AddressBlock>> code and then click Greeting Line.

11. In the Insert Greeting Line dialog box, choose a greeting style and then click OK. A <<GreetingLine>> code appears in the document.

→ For more information about greeting lines, **see** "Inserting Greeting Lines," **p. 582**.

12. Finish composing the letter as you would any other letter. When you are finished, at the bottom of the task pane, click Next: Preview Your Letters.

13. In the Preview Your Letters section of the task pane, use the << and >> buttons to move between previews of the letters. To exclude a recipient, click Exclude This Recipient when that person's preview appears (see Figure 18.3, center).

 If it seems like there is too much space between the lines in the recipient's address block, see "The <<AddressBlock>> Puts Too Much Space Between the Lines" in the "Troubleshooting" section at the end of this chapter.

14. At the bottom of the task pane, click Next: Complete the Merge.

15. To send the letters to the printer, click Print (see Figure 18.3, right). A Print dialog box appears; print the letters from there.

   Or, to open the letters in a new document for further editing, follow these steps:

   a. Click Edit Individual Letters. The Merge to New Document dialog box appears.

   b. Click OK. The letters open in a new document.

Figure 18.3
The second three screens of the Mail Merge Wizard.

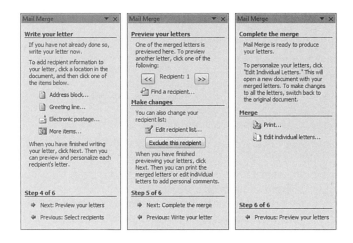

16. Save the main document if you think you will want to perform this same merge again. Otherwise, close the main document without saving.

Now that you've seen a bit of what mail merge can do via the semi-automated wizard process, let's take a closer look at each step of the process.

SELECTING A MAIN DOCUMENT TYPE

A mail merge starts by selecting the type of main document. To do this, click the Start Mail Merge button on the Mailings tab and select a type from the menu (see Figure 18.4).

Figure 18.4
Select the type of main document.

As listed at the beginning of this chapter, there are several main document types to choose from. The type you select changes the paper size and view that Word uses for the main document:

- **Letters**—Regular 8.5"×11" page size, Print Layout view.
- **E-mail messages**—Regular 8.5"×11" page size, Web Layout view.
- **Envelopes**—Opens an Envelope Options dialog box in which you set the size.

- **Labels**—Opens a Label Options dialog box in which you set the size.
- **Directory**—Same page size and view as Letters.

Let's take a closer look at the Envelopes and Labels choices, since they have additional options you can set.

SETTING ENVELOPE OPTIONS

When you select Envelopes from the Start Mail Merge button's menu, the Envelope Options dialog box appears, shown in Figure 18.5. From here you can select the envelope size from the Envelope Size list. Many standard sizes are provided; you can also choose the Custom Size option and enter your own dimensions for it.

Figure 18.5
Select the envelope options.

You can also set the font to be used for the delivery and return addresses on the envelopes. Click the Font button in either the Delivery Address or the Return Address area to set its font size, typeface, and color.

→ For details about setting the envelope font, **see** "Changing the Envelope Font," **p. 336**.

The From Left and From Top settings in the Delivery Address and Return Address sections enable you to fine-tune the positioning of those addresses on the envelope. The default setting of Auto places the return address ½" from the top-left corner, and places the delivery address in the horizontal center of the envelope, slightly lower than the vertical center. In most cases, the Auto setting is appropriate, provided you have correctly identified the envelope size.

Finally, you can choose how the envelopes feed into the printer—or rather, how Word perceives that they do. This was covered in Chapter 11, where you learned about printing individual envelopes. Refer to the section "Controlling How Envelopes Feed Into Your Printer," in Chapter 11.

SETTING LABEL OPTIONS

When you select Labels from the Start Mail Merge button's menu, the Label Options dialog box appears, shown in Figure 18.6. From here you can select the label type, which in turn tells Word the size of each label and how many rows and columns of labels appear on each sheet.

Figure 18.6
Select the label options.

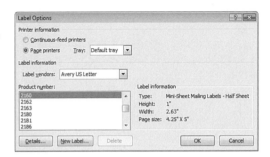

To print labels, you will need special label paper. There are many brands and sizes of labels; most come in full 8.5"×11" sheets, with perforated peel-off labels. Word recognizes the model numbers for many popular brands and sizes, and you can also set up custom labels in situations where none of Word's presets are appropriate.

CAUTION

> Make sure you buy the type of label sheets designed for your printer type. Labels designed for inkjet printers cannot withstand the heat generated by the laser printing process, and might become curled or wrinkled—or worse yet, peel off or melt inside the printer—if used with a laser.

From the Label Options dialog box, first select the type of printer you have: continuous-feed or page printer. This makes a difference because the label products available are different for each type. A *page printer* accepts individual sheets of paper. A *continuous-feed* printer uses a tractor feed to pull connected sheets through the printer. Most inkjet and laser printers are page printers, and most dot matrix printers are continuous feed. There are special labels-only printers, however, that use inkjet technology to print on continuous-feed labels.

After selecting the printer type, choose a label brand. The most common brand is Avery, but Word supports many other brands as well. Selecting a label brand filters the Product Number list to show only the product numbers for that brand. Select the product number that matches what you have.

If you're using a generic label brand and you don't know the equivalent model number for a well-known brand, you have a choice: You can browse through the product numbers for a well-known brand such as Avery until you find one that matches up with what you've got, or you can create a new custom label specification by clicking New Label and creating a new definition in the Label Details dialog box.

→ For complete steps for creating a new label specification, **see** "Creating a Custom Label Specification," **p. 342**.

SELECTING A DATA SOURCE

Word can pull data for a mail merge from a variety of data source types. Because Word is part of the Office suite, it's only natural that mail merge readily accepts data from Outlook, Excel, Access, Microsoft Works Database, and even other Word files (provided the data is in a table). It also accepts data from a wide variety of other non-Microsoft sources too, including dBASE, Paradox, and Lotus 1-2-3, as well as from delimited data files. Or, if the data source you need does not already exist, you can create a new data source via Word's own interface.

Understanding Delimited Data

A *delimited* data file is one that represents multiple columns without actually having any column lines. The break between columns is represented by a consistent character between entries, such as a comma or tab. Rows are represented by paragraph breaks.

For example, here's a plain-text delimited version of a table with three rows and three columns, with names in each cell:

Tom,Dick,Harry
Barbie,Ken,Skipper
Mary Ann,Ginger,Gilligan

Delimiters enable plain-text files to serve as databases. Almost all database programs can import and export delimited text files, which makes it possible to exchange data between almost any database program.

Delimited files also make it possible to do a Word mail merge based on virtually any data from any database program. If Word does not directly support mail merging from that database program, export the data to a delimited text file, and then use the delimited text file for your Word merge.

18

CHOOSING AN OUTLOOK CONTACT LIST AS A DATA SOURCE

Because Outlook 2007 is the default email and contact management program for Office 2007, Word makes it very easy to use it as the data source for a mail merge. The fields are already mapped between the two programs so that Outlook's address fields fit perfectly into the <<AddressBlock>> field, for example. There's very little you need to do in the way of setup if you're planning on using an Outlook file for the merge.

You saw earlier in the chapter, in "Performing a Letter Merge with the Mail Merge Wizard," how to choose Outlook as a data source from the wizard. To do it without the wizard, follow these steps:

1. From the Mailings tab, click Select Recipients.

2. On the Select Recipients menu, click Select from Outlook Contacts. The Select Contacts dialog box opens.

3. Click the desired Outlook contact file. If you are using Outlook on a home system, and you have set up only one contact list, there will be only one choice here, as in Figure 18.7. Otherwise, click the contact file you want to use.

4. Click OK to accept the chosen Outlook contact file.

Figure 18.7
Select the Outlook data file.

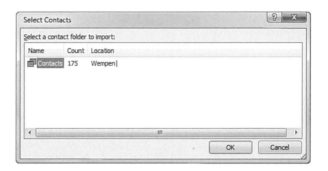

> **NOTE**
>
> When a valid Outlook contact file has been selected, the Edit Recipient List button becomes available on the Mailings tab. If the Edit Recipient List button remains unavailable, try again to select the Outlook contact list.

CHOOSING AN EXISTING DATA SOURCE

Outlook is only one possible program from which you can draw data. Word can accept data from a variety of data sources, including Excel worksheets, Word tables, plain-text files, and files from various database programs including Paradox and dBASE. You can also pull data from server-based SQL and Oracle databases.

CHOOSING AN EXCEL DATA SOURCE

An Excel worksheet works well as a data source for a mail merge, provided you set it up according to these guidelines:

- The first row of the file should contain the field names.
- The records should appear, one per row, immediately below the field names.

Some people set up an Excel worksheet with a sheet title in cell A1, a few blank rows, and then the data after that. Word cannot interpret such a layout as a valid data file for a merge, though, so you will need to edit the Excel file beforehand to omit any rows at the top that are extraneous to the data. Figure 18.8 shows an Excel file that is correctly set up.

Figure 18.8
This Excel file is properly configured to be used in a Word mail merge.

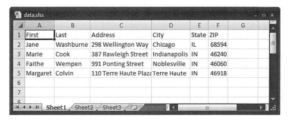

In addition, if you are planning on using the <<AddressBlock>> field to create an address block in the main document, rather than inserting individual fields, the field names in the first row of the worksheet should be similar to the field names used in Outlook: First Name, Last Name, Address, City, State/Province, ZIP/Postal Code, and Country/Region. The closer you get to that naming convention, the more flawlessly the data will map to Word's <<AddressBlock>> field.

To select an Excel file as a data source, follow these steps:

1. From the Mailings tab, choose Select Recipients, Use Existing List. The Select Data Source dialog box opens.

2. Select the Excel file to use as a data source and click Open. The Select Table dialog box opens.

3. Select the worksheet that contains the data. If you are not sure, try Sheet1$ (see Figure 18.9).

TIP

> You can rename the tabs in an Excel workbook by double-clicking a tab and typing a new name (in Excel). The names you assign appear in the Select Table dialog box if you have assigned any; otherwise, the sheet names appear generic, as in Figure 18.9.

Figure 18.9
Select the sheet that contains the data to be used in the mail merge.

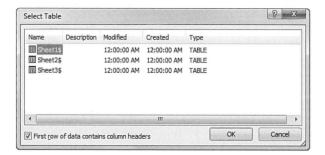

4. Click OK. The Excel file is now connected as the data source for the mail merge.

5. (Optional) To confirm that the field names have been set up properly, click the Insert Merge Field button on the Mailings tab. The field names should appear here.

   If generic names appear there instead, check the file in Excel to make sure the field names appear in row 1.

CHOOSING A WORD DATA SOURCE

A Word file can serve as a data source, provided that one of these conditions is true:

■ The Word document begins with a table, and that table contains the records, one per row, with the field names in the first row. In this case, the Word file is treated like an Excel worksheet.

■ The Word document contains the records, one per paragraph, with the fields delimited by a consistent character such as a tab or comma. In this case, the Word file is treated like a delimited text file (discussed later in the chapter).

To choose a Word document, follow these steps:

1. From the Mailings tab, choose Select Recipients, Use Existing List. The Select Data Source dialog box opens.

2. Select the Word document file to use as a data source and click Open.

3. If the records are delimited, rather than in a table, a dialog box might appear prompting you to specify the delimiter character. This happens only if Word cannot figure out the delimiters on its own. Enter the information required if needed and click OK.

CHOOSING A DELIMITED TEXT DATA SOURCE

In a data source file in which the fields are delimited, you might need to specify which character is used as the delimiter. Word will prompt you if needed. Other than that, it's pretty straightforward:

1. From the Mailings tab, choose Select Recipients, Use Existing List. The Select Data Source dialog box opens.

2. Select the text file to use as a data source and click Open.

3. If a Header Record Delimiters dialog box appears prompting you to specify the delimiter characters, specify the characters used for field and row delimiters, as in Figure 18.10, and then click OK.

This happens only if Word cannot figure them out on its own.

Figure 18.10
If prompted, specify the delimiter characters.

CAUTION

If there are a lot of extra spaces between the fields in the data file, as in the sample area in Figure 18.10, the file is probably set up as a fixed-width database rather than a delimited one. In other words, extra blank spaces have been inserted to create even columns. See "How Can I Use a Fixed-Width Data File?" in the "Troubleshooting" section at the end of this chapter.

SETTING UP AN ORACLE OR SQL DATABASE AS A DATA SOURCE

Word can connect to a variety of database server types, including SQL and Oracle. You set up a data source once, and then you can reuse it without having to go through its configuration again.

To set up a SQL or Oracle database, follow these steps:

1. From the Mailings tab, choose Select Recipients, Use Existing List. The Select Data Source dialog box opens.

2. Click the New Source button. The Data Connection Wizard dialog box opens (see Figure 18.11).

Figure 18.11
Choose the type of data source you want to set up.

3. Select the type of server to which you want to connect (Microsoft SQL Server or Microsoft Data Access – OLE DB Provider for Oracle) and click Next.

4. Type the server name in the Server Name box.

5. If the server is on your own network, you might be able to connect to it using Windows Authentication (the default Log On Credentials setting). If not, choose Use the Following User Name and Password and then enter the user name and password required to log into the server.

6. Click Next to continue. Word logs into the server.

7. When prompted, select the data table or query from which you want to pull records and then click Next.

8. At the Save Data Connection File and Finish screen, enter a filename in the File Name box for the shortcut that will be created to the database.

   You can optionally also enter a description and a friendly name.

9. Click Finish to connect to the data source and close the dialog box.

In the future, you can select the shortcut you just created from the Select Data Source dialog box (step 1) and bypass the other steps.

USING AN ODBC DATA SOURCE

ODBC (Open Database Connectivity) is a widely used standard for connecting to databases. Data sources that use ODBC use SQL to connect, but they go through an ODBC driver installed in Windows. Using ODBC you can access Excel workbooks, Access databases, dBASE databases, and other types of sources too if you have ODBC drivers for them, stored either on a server or on a local or network client. For example, if your company's customer database is stored in Access on the main server, you could access it via ODBC for your mail merge.

NOTE

You can also specify Excel and Access files as data sources by choosing them directly from the Select Data Source dialog box, as you would any file. In fact, that's what you did earlier in the chapter, in the section "Choosing an Excel Data Source." It's basically the same process except the method described in the following steps sets up an .odb shortcut to the file for easier access.

Follow these steps to connect to an ODBC data source:

1. From the Mailings tab, choose Select Recipients, Use Existing List. The Select Data Source dialog box opens.

2. Click the New Source button. Choose ODBC DSN from the list of server types (Figure 18.11) and click Next.

3. Select the type of ODBC data source to which to connect. The items on the list depend on the ODBC drivers set up on your PC; by default Windows Vista and Office 2007 provide dBASE, Excel, and Access. Then click Next.

4. As prompted, specify the data file you want to use and the specific data table within it.

5. At the Save Data Connection File and Finish dialog box, enter a filename in the File Name box for a shortcut to be created for this data source (see Figure 18.12).

   You can optionally also enter a description and a friendly name.

6. Click Finish to connect to the data source and close the dialog box.

Figure 18.12
Name the shortcut to the database so you can reuse it in the future.

In the future, you can select the shortcut you just created from the Select Data Source dialog box (step 1) and bypass the other steps.

CREATING A NEW DATA SOURCE IN WORD

If the data source does not already exist, you might find it easier to create it from within Word than to fire up some outside program to create it. Word makes it very easy to create a simple Access database to hold mail merge data for a personal contacts mailing list, even if you do not have Access installed on your PC and don't know anything about that program. It's all just fill-in-the-blanks.

To create a new data source, follow these steps:

1. From the Mailings tab, choose Select Recipients, Type New List. The New Address List dialog box appears.

2. If desired, customize the field names that appear in the columns. To do so, see "Customizing Fields" later in this chapter.

3. Enter the first record into the top row of the grid provided. To omit a field, simply leave it blank.

4. To start a new record, click New Entry. Another blank row appears (see Figure 18.13).

Figure 18.13
Create a new data source by entering records in the rows and columns provided.

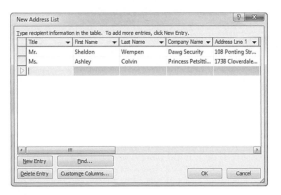

5. Continue adding records until you are finished; then click OK. The Save Data Source dialog box appears.

6. Type a filename to use, and change the location if needed.

7. Click Save. Word creates a new Access database containing a single table with the data you just entered.

CAUTION

You can open this database in Access if you have Access installed. Do not change the table name or structure, though, or the connection to your main document in Word will no longer work.

The new database can be used in future mail merge projects by choosing it as an existing data source, as you learned in "Using an ODBC Data Source" earlier in this chapter.

CUSTOMIZING FIELDS

The fields provided for a new data source are typical for a personal mailing list, including name, address, and phone number. Perhaps you do not need or want all those fields, or maybe you need some different fields instead or in addition. For example, if you are creating a new data source to store inventory or events, the default fields will need to be almost totally changed.

Here's how to customize the fields in the New Address List dialog box:

1. From the New Address List dialog box (from step 1 in the preceding section), click Customize Columns. The Customize Address List dialog box opens (see Figure 18.14).

Figure 18.14
Change the columns (fields) that appear in the Customize Address List dialog box.

2. Delete any fields you don't want. To delete a field, select it, click Delete, and click Yes to confirm.

3. Rename any fields as desired. To rename a field, select it, click Rename, type the new name, and click OK.

4. Add any new fields as desired. To add a field, click Add, type the new field name, and click OK.

5. Reorder any fields as desired. To move a field, select it and then click Move Up or Move Down.

6. Click OK to return to the New Address List dialog box. (If you're done, you can click the OK button for that dialog box, too.)

EDITING THE DATA SOURCE

Normally when you pick database records for your mail merge, you are not editing the data source; you're simply changing your usage of it. For example, if you exclude a certain person from a mailing, that person's record still exists in the database. To edit the database itself, you would normally go through the database program's own interface.

However, if you created the database from within Word, as in the preceding sections, then Word might be the only means you have of accessing that database, particularly if you do not have Access installed. If so, you might need to delete or add records to the database from Word.

To edit the data source from within Word, follow these steps:

1. From the Mailings tab, click Edit Recipient List. The Mail Merge Recipients dialog box opens.

2. In the Data Source box (bottom-left corner), select the data source (probably an .mdb file) and then click Edit. The Edit Data Source dialog box opens. It is just like the New Address List dialog box (refer to Figure 18.13) except for the name.

3. Do any of the following:

   - To create a new entry, click New Entry and fill in the fields.

   - To delete a record, click the gray box to its left to select it and then click Delete Entry and click Yes to confirm.

   - To change the columns, follow the steps in the section "Customizing Fields" earlier in this chapter.

4. Click OK to accept the changes to the data source.

5. Click OK to close the Mail Merge Recipients dialog box.

PREPARING THE MAIN DOCUMENT

The main document is the file in which you place all the boilerplate text and the merge codes that will personalize each copy. Depending on the type of merge you are doing, the main document can be an envelope, a label sheet, a letter, an email message, or just about anything else. It's just an ordinary Word document except for the presence of the merge fields.

To prepare the main document, do the following:

- Confirm that the margins, page size, and page orientation are correct for the document you want. These were set automatically when you chose the document type from the Start Mail Merge button's menu, but it's worth checking.

- If needed, apply a template and/or change the paragraph styles to suit the needs of the project. Choose a different formatting theme if desired.

- Type the boilerplate text, leaving blank spots or reminders for the fields that you'll insert. To avoid forgetting to insert a merge field later, you might want to type something like FIELD HERE in the spot where it will go and then apply a bright-colored highlight to it (from the Home tab or the mini toolbar).

TIP

> Some of the templates that Microsoft provides for Word 2007 have "merge" in their names, meaning they are special versions designed for mail merging. For example, try starting a new document with Median Merge Letter, one of the templates installed locally on your hard disk. It contains placeholders with suggestions for inserting merge fields. Those placeholders are "dead." In other words, they do not reference actual merge fields. You must delete them and replace them with real merge fields, as you'll learn in the next section.

INSERTING MERGE FIELDS

Now that the two essential pieces are in place—the main document and the data source—it's time to join them. To do this, you'll insert merge fields that reference the data source into the main document.

INSERTING SINGLE FIELDS

The most straightforward way to go is to insert individual fields, one at a time. When you insert a field, Word places a code with double angle brackets into the document, like this: <<City>>.

> **NOTE**
>
> The field names come from the data source, so they will change depending on the data source you've selected and might not be the same as shown in the examples in this chapter.

To insert fields into the main document one at a time, follow these steps:

1. Position the insertion point where you want the field to be placed.
2. On the Mailings tab, click Insert Merge Field. A list of available fields from the data source appears (see Figure 18.15).
3. Click the desired field. A code appears for it in the document.
4. Repeat these steps to insert additional fields in the document as needed.

Figure 18.15
Insert a merge field from the Mailings tab.

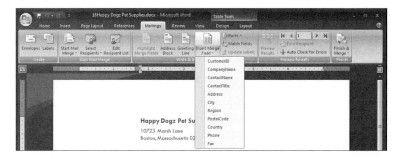

Make sure as you insert fields that you leave the appropriate spaces and punctuation between them. For example, press the spacebar once between a <<First_Name>> and a <<Last_Name>> field.

INSERTING ADDRESS BLOCKS

One of the most common uses for mail merge is to enter a mailing address block, like this:

Joe Smith
120 Main Street
Any Town, IN 46822

You can set up a mailing address block by inserting fields one at a time, as you learned in the preceding section, but it takes a long time to do so. Assuming the first and last name are in separate fields, and so are the city, state, and ZIP code, you end up having to insert six separate fields, just to create a simple address block.

Word offers a shortcut for setting up address blocks in the <<AddressBlock>> field. This field pulls the needed data from each of the applicable fields and creates a nicely formatted address block in a single step.

To insert an <<AddressBlock>> field, follow these steps:

1. Position the insertion point where you want the block to appear.

2. On the Mailings tab, click Address Block. The Insert Address Block dialog box opens (see Figure 18.16).

Figure 18.16
Specify options for the address block to be inserted.

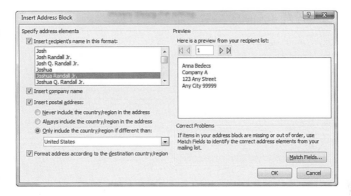

3. In the Insert Recipient's Name in This Format box, select the sample that best represents how you want the name to appear.

4. If you do not want the company name, clear the Insert Company Name check box.

5. In the Insert Postal Address area, specify how you want the country/region to be inserted (or not). The default setting is to include the country only if it is different from the value set in the drop-down list (United States in Figure 18.16).

6. Preview the addresses in the Preview area by clicking the right and left arrow buttons.

7. Click OK to insert the address block.

How does Word know what fields to use in the address block? It attempts to match up the fields in your data source with the various placeholders in an address block. If the data source uses common naming conventions, it usually does a pretty good job. If it makes any mistakes, click the Match Fields button in the dialog box to make adjustments. For more help with this, see "The <<AddressBlock>> Isn't Using the Correct Fields" in the "Troubleshooting" section at the end of this chapter.

INSERTING GREETING LINES

A *greeting line* is the line at the beginning of a letter that usually starts with "Dear." It's similar to an address block in that Word builds it automatically by drawing from multiple fields in the database.

To insert a greeting line, follow these steps:

1. Position the insertion point where you want the block to appear.

2. On the Mailings tab, click Greeting Line. The Insert Greeting Line dialog box opens (see Figure 18.17).

Figure 18.17
Specify options for the greeting line to be inserted.

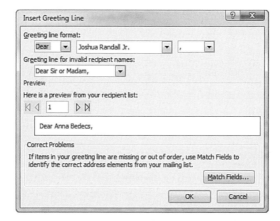

3. Set up the greeting the way you want it by selecting from the drop-down lists provided.

> **TIP**
>
> For business letters, it is customary to start with Dear, to use the person's title and last name, as in Mr. Jones, and to finish with a colon (not a comma). For personal letters, it is customary to start with Dear, use the person's first name, and finish with a comma.

4. Specify a greeting line for invalid recipient names. Word will use this setting if the field from which it is drawing the name is blank or unreadable.

5. Click OK to insert the field code.

As with address blocks, you can remap the fields that Word uses from the data source. To do so, click the Match Fields button in the Insert Greeting Line dialog box. For more help with this, see "The <<AddressBlock>> Isn't Using the Correct Fields" in the "Troubleshooting" section at the end of this chapter.

SETTING UP FIELDS ON LABELS

If you set up your mail merge using the Letters, E-mail Messages, or Envelopes document type (from the Start Mail Merge button's menu), then each record in the data source is used for a separate copy of the document. For example, you create a single letter in the master document, and then the merge process generates as many customized copies as needed for the data in the data source.

However, if you set up your mail merge for Labels, there will be more than one record per page of the document. A label layout consists of a table, and each record is in its own cell.

If you use the Mail Merge Wizard, the cells of the table are populated with the <<AddressBlock>> field automatically. However, if you are setting up labels manually, you will need to enter them yourself. This is not difficult; you simply create one label's layout and then update all the other fields.

Follow these steps to set up the fields in a label layout:

1. Begin the mail merge by choosing the document type (Labels) from the Start Mail Merge button and then setting up the type of labels you want, as you learned earlier in this chapter.

2. Select or create the data source, as you learned earlier in this chapter.

   After you've selected a data source, a <<Next Record>> field appears automatically in each cell of the table (except the first cell).

3. (Optional) To make the table cells easier to see, do the following:

   • On the Home tab, click the Show/Hide ¶ button to toggle on the display of hidden characters.

   • On the Layout tab, click View Gridlines.

4. Click in the top-left cell in the table and insert the field(s) you want. It is easiest to simply insert the <<AddressBlock>> field but you can manually create the address block if you prefer.

5. Click the Update Labels button. The <<AddressBlock>> field, or whatever fields you entered in step 4, are copied to the remaining cells (see Figure 18.18).

6. Continue with the merge, as described in the rest of this chapter.

Figure 18.18
Enter the field(s) in the top-left cell and then click Update Labels to populate the change in the rest of the cells.

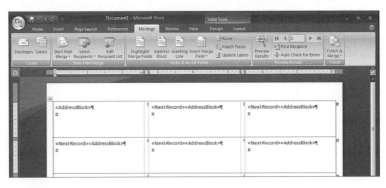

SETTING UP FIELDS IN DIRECTORIES

A directory is a free-form type of mail merge document, in which you can place many records on a page if you like. It's somewhat like a set of labels except there are no table cells to tell Word where to break things off. Instead, you must insert a <<Next Record>> field manually where you want one record to stop and the next one to begin.

For example, suppose you want a listing of people's names and phone numbers, as in Figure 18.19. This merge consists of three fields: first name, last name, and phone number.

Figure 18.19
A directory merge places information from multiple records on a single page.

Anna Bedecs	(317)555-3432
Thomas Axen	(317)555-7890
Martin O'Donnell	(217)555-5289
Ming-Yang Xie	(765)555-0098
Sven Mortensen	(765)555-7890
Peter Krschne	(765)555-4431
Andre Ludick	(317)555-7890
Helena Kupkova	(317)555-8799
Jean Philippe Bagel	(342)555-3421
Alexander Eggerer	(211)555-8754
Bernard Tham	(317)555-4533
Michael Entin	(765)555-3251
John Rodman	(504)555-1551
Karen Toh	(342)555-3241
Soo Jung Lee	(149)555-2521

NOTE

The merge shown in Figure 18.19 was created by inserting the name fields, pressing Tab, and inserting the phone number field. Then the tab stop was changed to a right-aligned stop and placed at the right margin, and a dot leader was added.

→ For information about setting tab stops and dot leaders, **see** "Working with Tab Stops," **p. 201**.

To create a directory merge, you need only to enter the desired fields once in the document, and then enter a <<Next Record>> field. Follow these steps:

1. Insert the fields to be displayed for each record.
2. On the Mailings tab, click Rules. Then click Next Record on the menu that appears. A <<Next Record>> field is inserted. Figure 18.20 shows the fields that were used for Figure 18.19, for example.

Figure 18.20
The merge fields used for the listing shown in Figure 18.19.

«First_Name» «Last_Name»...«Business_Phone»«Next Record»

3. Continue with the merge, as described in the rest of this chapter.

NOTE

If you preview the merge results before performing the actual merge, you will not see the directory as it will actually be; instead you'll see one record only. This is the normal behavior for a directory type of merge. The only way to see the full directory is to perform the merge to a new file or to the printer.

FILTERING AND SORTING THE DATA

If the data source was created specifically for this mail merge project, it might contain exactly the records you want and no others. If that's your situation, you can skip this whole section on filtering. (Stick around, though, if you want the records sorted in a certain way.)

Most of the time, however, people do mail merges using generic databases that are designed for more than just a single mail merge. For example, you might draw recipients from your Outlook contact list or a SQL database containing the personnel listings for your entire company. To avoid wasting paper and generating a lot of unneeded copies of the merge, you'll want to apply a filter to the data set so that it contains only the records you want.

EXCLUDING INDIVIDUAL RECORDS

If your data source does not contain a lot of records, you might find it easier to manually mark the records to exclude than to set up a formal filter that defines exclusion criteria.

To exclude records, follow these steps:

1. On the Mailings tab, click Edit Recipient List. The Mail Merge Recipients dialog box opens.
2. Clear the check box for the records you want to exclude (see Figure 18.21).
3. Click OK.

Figure 18.21
Exclude any records you do not want to use.

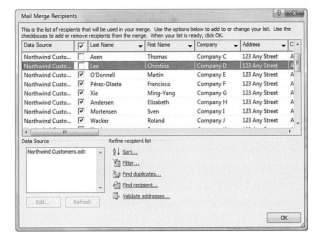

APPLYING A FILTER

Applying a filter is useful when the records that you want to include have something quantifiable in common. For example, perhaps you want only addresses in a certain range of ZIP Codes, or only people whose last names begin with a certain letter, or perhaps you want only the records that have complete mailing addresses. The following sections explain some techniques for filtering.

FILTERING FOR BLANK OR NON-BLANK ENTRIES

One of the most basic filters is to include only records in which a certain field is blank or non-blank. For example, for an e-mail merge, you might include only records for which the E-mail field is non-blank, or for a merge that prints labels to send cards to only your friends, not your business contacts, you might include only records for which the Company field is blank.

To filter for blank or non-blank entries, follow these steps:

1. From the Mailings tab, click Edit Recipient List. The Mail Merge Recipients dialog box opens.

2. Click the down arrow to the right of a field name to open a menu, and then click either (Blanks) or (Non-Blanks) from the menu (see Figure 18.22).

CAUTION

Be careful to click the arrow, not the field name itself. If you click the field name, the list becomes sorted by that field and the menu does not open.

Figure 18.22
Filter a particular field based on its blank or non-blank status.

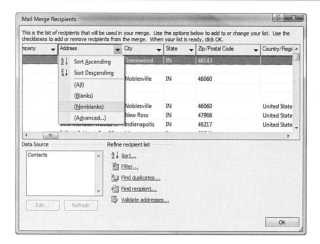

3. Repeat step 2 for each field you want to filter by. You can filter by multiple fields this way. For example, you could include only records that have non-blank Address, City, State, and ZIP fields.

To turn a filter off, reopen the menu for that field and choose (All).

CREATING AN ADVANCED FILTER

An advanced filter is one in which you actually specify criteria for inclusion based on certain values or ranges. It consists of one or more *criteria*. A criterion consists of a field name, a comparison operator, and a value. For example, in **ZIP equals 46240**, *ZIP* is the field name, *equals* is the comparison operator, and *46240* is the value.

Advanced filters can have multiple criteria, joined with either And or Or. If you use And, both of the rules must be true in order for a record to be included; if you use Or, at least one of the rules must be true.

To set up an advanced filter, follow these steps:

1. From the Mailings tab, click Edit Recipient List. The Mail Merge Recipients dialog box opens.

2. Click the Filter hyperlink. The Filter and Sort dialog box appears.

3. On the Filter tab, open the Field drop-down list and select the field for the first rule.

4. Open the Comparison drop-down list and choose the comparison operator.

5. In the Compare To box, type the value to which to compare. Figure 18.23 shows an example in which the ZIP Code must equal 46240.

Figure 18.23
Create filtering criteria in the Filter and Sort dialog box.

6. (Optional) Set the And/Or indicator for the second line and enter an additional rule. Keep entering additional rules as needed.

7. Click OK to apply the filter. The list in the Mail Merge Recipients dialog box changes to show only the records selected by the filter.

8. Click OK to accept the filtered list.

SORTING THE RECORDS

Usually when you create a mailing, the order in which the items print is not an issue because you're just going to drop them in the mailbox and they'll get all mixed up there anyway. However, with very large bulk mailings, the mail processing services ask that clients provide the items for mailing in a certain order, usually by ZIP Code. To have the items print in a certain order, you can set up a sort.

To perform a simple sort, click a field's column heading in the Mail Merge Recipients dialog box. Each time you click, it toggles between an ascending and descending sort. Alternatively, you can open the field's menu (by clicking its arrow) and choosing Sort Ascending or Sort Descending.

Advanced sorting is done in the Filter and Sort dialog box. You can set up a sort as part of creating the filter, as in the preceding section's steps; just click the Sort Records tab and enter the sort criteria before closing the Filter and Sort dialog box.

18

If you just want to sort (no filtering), or if you have already closed the dialog box, follow these steps:

1. From the Mailings tab, click Edit Recipient List. The Mail Merge Recipients dialog box opens.

2. Click the Sort hyperlink. The Filter and Sort dialog box appears with the Sort Records tab displayed (see Figure 18.24).

Figure 18.24
Set up one or more fields by which to sort.

3. Open the Sort By drop-down list and select the field by which you want to sort.

4. Click Ascending or Descending to set the sort order. Ascending is 0 to 9, then A to Z; Descending is Z to A, then 9 to 0.

5. (Optional) Specify additional sorts in the subsequent rows. The additional sorts will take effect only in the event of a tie for the first sort. For example, if two records have the same ZIP Code, perhaps you want the tiebreaker to be last name.

6. Click OK to accept the sort condition(s).

FINDING A RECIPIENT

In a large database, it can be a challenge to find a particular record by scrolling through and browsing. To access the Find feature within the Mail Merge Recipients dialog box, and use it to locate a certain record, follow these steps:

1. From the Mailings tab, click Edit Recipient List. The Mail Merge Recipients dialog box opens.

2. Click the Find Recipient hyperlink. The Find Entry dialog box opens.

3. Type the text string you want to find.

4. Choose one of the option buttons: All Fields or This Field. If you choose This Field, open the drop-down list and select the field to search.

5. Click Find Next. The list jumps to the first occurrence of that string.

6. Click Find Next again to find the next instance, and so on until you have found the record you are seeking.

FINDING DUPLICATE ENTRIES

Large databases can sometimes contain duplicate entries due to data entry errors and lack of synchronization between sources. To ensure that none of these duplicates get into your mail merge, you can use the Find Duplicates feature:

1. From the Mailings tab, click Edit Recipient List. The Mail Merge Recipients dialog box opens.

2. Click the Find Duplicates hyperlink. The Find Duplicates dialog box opens, showing groups of records that appear to be very similar or identical (if any).

3. Clear the check box for the items you do not want to be included in the mail merge (see Figure 18.25).

> **NOTE**
>
> In Figure 18.25, even though the first entry has been deselected for example purposes, it is not really a duplicate of its pair; the first names are different. This illustrates why you have to be careful in accepting Word's recommendations; it finds records that are similar, but not necessarily the same.

4. Click OK to return to the Mail Merge Recipients dialog box and continue the merge.

Figure 18.25
Evaluate entries that Word finds to be very similar, and deselect any that appear to be duplicates of another.

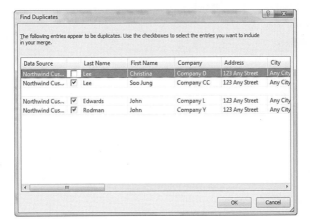

VALIDATING ADDRESSES

Address validation looks up addresses in an actual postal mailing database online and determines whether each one is deliverable. This feature is not included with Word, but Word does provide a link for accessing a third-party data validation service, such as Stamps.com.

If you have subscribed to such a service, you can access it from the Mail Merge Recipients dialog box by clicking Validate Addresses. If you have not signed up for a service, a message appears offering to take you to the Microsoft Office website, from which you can browse for available third-party services.

PREVIEWING AND PRINTING THE MERGE

After setting up the main document and performing any needed sorting or filtering on the data set, the next step is to preview the merge. Previewing is optional, but it can save you from printing stacks of documents that contain merge errors. With paper and ink costs as high as they are these days, that can be a real benefit.

To preview the merge results, click the Preview Results button on the Mailings tab. This button is an on/off toggle between the field codes and the merge results.

NOTE

> As noted earlier, if you are previewing a directory merge, or other merge type in which you have inserted the <<Next Record>> code yourself to separate records that will appear on a page together, you might see only one record at a time with Preview Results, not the entire page as it will actually be. To preview the page more accurately, merge to a new document (Finish & Merge, Edit Individual Documents).

While you're looking at the preview results, you can use the arrow buttons in the Preview Results group on the Mailings tab to scroll from one record to another (see Figure 18.26).

18

Figure 18.26
Preview merge results.

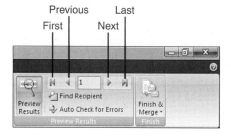

CHECKING FOR ERRORS

To save on paper, it's important to check the merge for errors before you print. But if you have thousands of records, it can be a chore to sort through them manually.

To automate the process of checking for common errors, such as empty fields or invalid field names, follow these steps:

1. On the Mailings tab, click Auto Check for Errors. The Checking and Reporting Errors dialog box opens.

2. Click Simulate the Merge and Report Errors in a New Document.

   You can use the other options in this dialog box to go ahead and complete the merge if you prefer.

3. Click OK. If there are any errors, they appear in a report in a new document. Otherwise, a dialog box appears, telling you there are no errors; click OK to clear it.

4. If any errors are found, correct them.

MERGING TO A NEW DOCUMENT

To save paper, I always merge to a new document rather than directly to a printer. That way if there are any errors that the Error Check did not catch, such as a missing ZIP Code or improper spacing between fields, I'll notice them before printing.

Merging to a new document also has the side benefit of enabling you to edit individual copies before printing. For example, perhaps for one certain person you want to add a personal note in an extra paragraph at the end of the letter.

To merge to a new document, follow these steps:

1. From the Mailings tab, click Finish & Merge, Edit Individual Documents. The Merge to New Document dialog box appears (see Figure 18.27).

2. Click All to merge all records, or specify a range of records if you don't want to do them all at once. (For example, perhaps you want only the first 100 records in the new file, and then you'll perform the merge again to put the next 100 in another new file, and so on.)

3. Click OK. The merge is performed and placed in a new document.

Figure 18.27
Merge all records or enter a range.

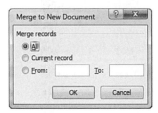

> **NOTE**
>
> The numbers you enter in the range in Figure 18.27 refer to the record numbers—that is, the records in the order you specified in the sort, or the default order from the data source if you did not specify a sort.

MERGING TO A PRINTER

If you're feeling very confident about your merge, you can send it directly to the printer, without creating a new document. You might do this for a merge that you've already completed successfully before, such as a merge you perform every month to send letters to the same group of people.

To merge directly to the printer, follow these steps:

1. From the Mailings tab, click Finish & Merge, Print Documents. The Merge to Printer dialog box appears. It is identical to the Merge to New Document dialog box in Figure 18.27 except for its name.

2. Click All to merge all records, or specify a range of records if you don't want to do them all at once.

3. Click OK. The Print dialog box opens.

4. Set any print options as desired (including selecting the printer to use), as you learned to do in Chapter 5, "Printing and Faxing Documents."

5. Click OK to print.

MERGING TO EMAIL

Merging to email sends the messages using your default email program, using the email address in whatever field from the data source you specify. (You must make sure, therefore, that your data source has an email address for every record you select.)

Follow these steps to merge to email:

1. From the Mailings tab, click Finish & Merge, Send E-mail Messages. The Merge to E-Mail dialog box appears (see Figure 18.28).

Figure 18.28
Merge to email by specifying the field containing the email addresses and the subject line and mail format.

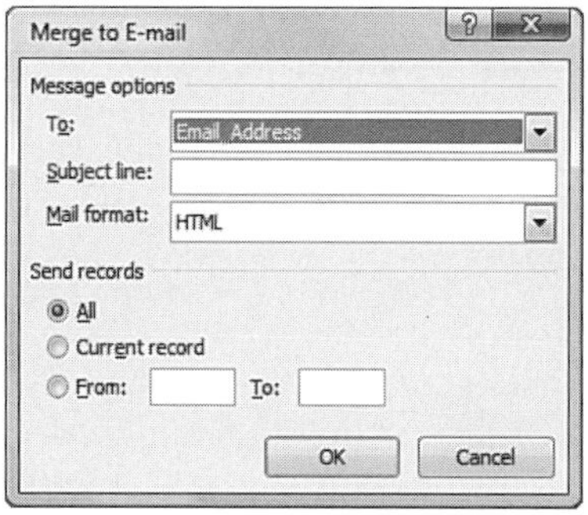

2. Make sure the field containing the email addresses is selected from the To drop-down list.

3. Enter the subject line to use in the Subject Line box.

4. Select a mail format from the Mail Format list.

   If your document includes formatting, such as colors, different font sizes, and so on, make sure you choose HTML as the mail format.

5. In the Send Records section, choose All, or choose the current record or a range of records.

CAUTION

> Before performing the next step, make sure your emails are just the way you want them. They will be sent immediately after the next step, with no opportunity to check them.

6. Click OK. Your email program opens, the emails are created, and they are placed in your Outbox folder for sending.

7. In your email program, perform a Send/Receive operation to send the messages if they are not sent automatically.

CREATING CUSTOM MERGES WITH WORD FIELDS

The simple mail merges you've learned about so far in this chapter insert data by referencing fields in the specified data source. Nine times out of ten, that's all you'll need for a mail merge. But wouldn't it be nice for that tenth time to be able to do something a little more complex?

Suppose you are creating a letter to all your customers, but you want the letter to say different things depending on the values in certain fields of your database. For example, perhaps you want customers who have not ordered from you in more than 6 months to receive a special promotional offer. Or perhaps you want to be able to enter a different promotional offer each time you run the merge, and be prompted to enter the offer in a dialog box. All that and more is possible by using fields.

There are two types of fields: merge fields and Word fields. Throughout this chapter, you've been using merge fields—that is, fields that come from the data source you specify for a mail merge. These fields exist only because of the data source connection. Word fields, on the other hand, are preprogrammed into Word itself, and can be used in any type of document, not just merge documents.

You will learn about fields in Chapter 20, "Working with Fields," including how to insert and modify them and how to control their syntax. For now, though, let's look at a few specific fields that are useful when doing merges. They're so useful for merges, in fact, that they appear on a special menu on the Mailings tab. Click Rules to see the list, as shown in Figure 18.29.

Figure 18.29
Certain Word fields that are especially useful in mail merges appear on the Rules menu on the Mailings tab.

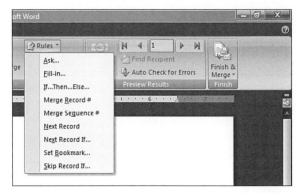

COLLECTING INFORMATION WITH A FILL-IN FIELD

A {FillIn} field prompts the user for an entry and then places it in the document. You can set it up to ask you only once per merge, or to ask you separately for each copy.

For example, suppose you have a standard form letter in which you offer customers a certain percentage of discount if they bring the letter with them into your store on certain dates. You can reuse the same main document time after time, and set it up to ask you each time how much discount you want to offer and what the date range should be.

To insert a {FillIn} field, follow these steps:

1. Position the insertion point where you want the field to appear.
2. On the Mailings tab, click Rules, and then choose Fill-In. The Insert Word Field: Fill-In dialog box opens.
3. In the top part of the dialog box, enter the prompt that will appear to the user.
4. (Optional) In the bottom part of the dialog box, shown in Figure 18.30, enter a default value that will be used if the user does not fill in the dialog box (for example, if he clicks Cancel or closes the dialog box without typing anything).

Figure 18.30
Create a {FillIn} field.

5. (Optional) If the value should be the same for every record in the merge, mark the Ask Once check box. Otherwise, Word will ask you repeatedly, once for each record.
6. Click OK to insert the field.

Whenever the document is opened or the merge is initiated, the field will be updated and will prompt the user for the entry.

{FillIn} fields are useful in situations where the value that the user enters does not need to be stored for reuse. In the aforementioned example, the user enters a discount amount to offer to the customers, but that discount amount does not need to be stored for calculations; it is simply placed in the document. If you need to store the user's entry as a variable and then perform a calculation on it or reprint it later in the document, use an {Ask} field instead, as described in the following section.

COLLECTING AND STORING INFORMATION WITH AN ASK FIELD

An {Ask} field is like a {FillIn} field, except the value that the user enters is stored in a bookmark for later reuse. So, for example, you could prompt for a certain value, such as a discount percentage, and then have that value be repeated in several places in the document.

You will learn about bookmarks in Chapter 19, "Copying, Linking, and Embedding Data." A *bookmark* is a named location or text entry in the document. Bookmarks have a variety of uses. You can create bookmarks to mark certain paragraphs, and then set up hyperlinks that jump directly to those paragraphs, for example.

→ To learn about bookmarks, **see** "Working with Bookmarks," **p. 610**.

When you use an {Ask} field to prompt the user for an entry, that entry is stored in a book-mark. The bookmark in this case is like a variable you might set in computer programming. You can then insert that bookmark's content in various places in the document by using a {Ref} field.

For example, at the beginning of the mail merge, you might use an {Ask} field to prompt the user for a salesperson's name and to store that name in a bookmark called *Employee*. Then that person's name can be set to appear in the body of the letter and also on the signature line.

To insert an {Ask} field and then reference its bookmark in the document, follow these steps:

1. Move the insertion point to the beginning of the document. Do not select any text.
2. Create the bookmark. To do so:
    a. On the Insert tab, click Bookmark.
    b. In the Bookmark dialog box, type the name you want to use.
    c. Click Add.
3. Create references to the bookmark as needed in the document. To do this:
    a. Move the insertion point to the location where the bookmark's content should be inserted.
    b. On the Insert tab, click Quick Parts, then click Field.
    c. On the Field Names list, click Ref.
    d. In the Bookmark Name list, click the bookmark name (see Figure 18.31).
    e. Click OK.

Figure 18.31
Reference a bookmark with the {Ref} field.

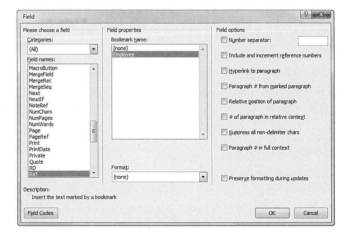

4. Move the insertion point to the beginning of the document.
5. On the Mailings tab, click Rules and then click Ask. The Insert Word Field: Ask dialog box opens.
6. On the Bookmark list, select the bookmark you created earlier.
7. In the Prompt box, type the text that should appear in the user prompt.

8. In the Default Bookmark Text box, type the default text to use if the user does not enter any text. Figure 18.32 shows the completed dialog box.

9. Click OK.

10. To test the field(s) in the document, select the entire document (Ctrl+A) and press F9 to update all the fields.

Figure 18.32
Create an {Ask} field that prompts the user to fill in the value for a bookmark.

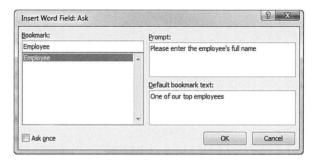

→ To learn more about updating fields, **see** "Updating Fields," **p. XXX** (Chapter 20).

SETTING UP CONDITIONS WITH AN IF...THEN...ELSE FIELD

The {If} field (a.k.a. the If...Then...Else field) can be used to insert different text in each copy of the merge depending on the value of a certain field. For example, suppose the mail merge letter is going to be sent to customers in several different countries, and depending on the country, you would like to offer a different promotion. In the spot where the sentences will appear with the promotional offer, you can insert an {If} field, and specify the value of the Country field as the condition in choosing one block of text or another to be inserted.

To create an {If} field that displays different text based on a condition, follow these steps:

1. Position the insertion point where you want the conditional text to appear.

2. On the Mailings tab, click Rules and then click If...Then...Else. The Insert Word Field: IF dialog box opens.

3. In the Field Name list, select the field that will provide the criterion.

4. In the Comparison list, select the comparison operator, such as Equal To or Greater Than.

5. In the Compare To box, type the value to which to compare the field.

6. In the Insert This Text box, type the text string to display if the comparison is true. (Leave it blank if you want nothing to display if true.)

7. In the Otherwise Insert This Text box, type the text string to display if the comparison is false. (Leave it blank if you want nothing to display if false.) Figure 18.33 shows a completed example.

8. Click OK to insert the field.

CAUTION

> Make sure you preview the merge before sending it to a printer after inserting an {If} field to make sure the results are as you intended.

Figure 18.33
Use an {If} field to set up different scenarios based on the entry in one of the fields.

USING A FIELD TO SET BOOKMARK TEXT

Earlier in the chapter, you saw how to use {Ask} to set a bookmark's value based on input from the user. A related field, {Set}, is used to set a bookmark without user input. You could use this to set an initial value for a bookmark, for example. (Then later in the merge, you could allow the user to change that value with a Fill-In or Ask.)

To insert a {Set} field into a document:

1. From the Mailings tab, click Rules and then click Set Bookmark. The Insert Word Field: Set dialog box opens.
2. On the Bookmark list, click the bookmark name for which you want to set a value.
3. In the Value box, type the value to which to set the bookmark.
4. Click OK.

One important usage for the {Set} field is within an {If} field. You might want a bookmark to be set one way if an {If} statement is true and another way if it is false. For example, if a letter recipient is female, you might want the pronouns in the document to be feminine (her/hers); otherwise, the pronouns should be masculine (him/his).

However, to nest a {Set} within an {If}, you must manually edit the field code, and you must manually create the {If} statement. (You can't use the Rules button's If...Then...Else insertion method.) Therefore, this might be a topic you want to postpone until after you've read Chapter 20. Then read the section "Nesting Fields" to learn how to nest one field inside another.

ASSIGNING NUMBERS TO MERGE RECORDS

Sometimes when creating a large number of merged copies, you need to sequentially number the copies as they are generated, so that each copy has a unique identifying number. There are two ways of doing this in Word: Merge Record # {MergeRec} and Merge Sequence # {MergeSeq}.

18

The {MergeRec} field assigns a number to each copy based on the actual number of the record within the data source. If you skipped over any records in the data source, the numbering skips too. For example, if a filter excluded the first 100 records, {MergeRec} would begin with 101.

The {MergeSeq} field assigns a number to each copy based on the records that were included in the merge, not the records in the original data source. So even if you skipped over 100 records, {MergeSeq} would always begin with 1.

To insert either of these, select it from the Rules menu on the Mailings tab: Merge Record # or Merge Sequence #. There are no options for either of these; they simply insert a code.

ADVANCING TO THE NEXT RECORD (OR NOT)

As you saw earlier in the chapter, in the section "Setting Up Fields in Directories," you can insert a {NextRecord} field to force the merge to continue to the next record without starting a new copy of the main document. To do this, on the Mailings tab, choose Rules, Next Record.

Two related fields, {NextRecordIf} and {SkipRecordIf}, enable you to set up conditions whereby you either process or skip the next record in the merge according to certain conditions you specify. Each of these has its own command for insertion on the Rules menu, and each opens a dialog box in which you can set up a criterion based on the contents of a field in the data source. Neither of these are very commonly used; if you want to skip certain records based on the content of a certain merge field, it's easier to simply set up a filter for the data source that excludes certain values for that field.

TROUBLESHOOTING

THE <<ADDRESSBLOCK>> PUTS TOO MUCH SPACE BETWEEN THE LINES

The <<AddressBlock>> field actually inserts three or more paragraphs, one for each line of the address. Each of these paragraphs has the default setting of having 10 points of space after it. That's where that extra space is coming from.

To fix it, follow these steps:

1. Right-click the <<AddressBlock>> code and choose Paragraph.
2. In the Paragraph dialog box, mark the Don't Add Space Between Paragraphs of the Same Style check box.
3. Click OK.

Another way is to insert the fields manually that comprise the address rather than relying on the <<AddressBlock>> field. You can do this from the Insert Merge Field button on the Mailings tab. Then instead of pressing Enter to create paragraph breaks between the lines of the address, use Shift+Enter to create line breaks instead.

If there's still too much space between lines, it's probably because the between-line spacing in the paragraph is set to 1.15 instead of 1. Select the paragraph(s) and on the Home tab, open the Line Spacing button's menu, and click 1.0.

HOW CAN I USE A FIXED-WIDTH DATA FILE?

Word cannot use a fixed-width data file in a mail merge; it accepts only delimited or tabular data files.

However, Excel can import fixed width data. In Excel, on the Data tab, click From Text and then select the file containing the data. Excel will walk you through a wizard that will enable you to select the column widths and import the data. Save your work in Excel, and then use that new Excel file as your data source for the mail merge in Word.

THE <<ADDRESSBLOCK>> ISN'T USING THE CORRECT FIELDS

Word does a pretty good job of figuring out which fields in the data source should be used for the <<AddressBlock>>, the <<GreetingLine>>, and other special fields, but it's not perfect, especially if the field names in the data source are cryptically named.

Remapping the data source's field names to the placeholders in Word will solve such problems. To do this, follow these steps:

1. From the Mailings tab, click Match Fields. The Match Fields dialog box opens. Word's internal names appear on the left, and the fields in the current data source to which they are mapped appear on the right (see Figure 18.34).

Figure 18.34
Use an {If} field to set up different scenarios based on the entry in one of the fields.

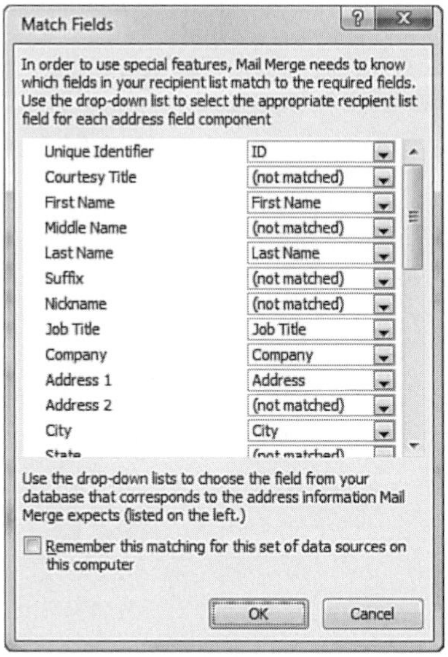

2. For any mappings that do not seem correct, open the drop-down list and select the proper field to map to that placeholder.

3. Click OK to accept the changes.

4. Update all fields in the document by selecting the entire document (Ctrl+A) and pressing F9.

If the <<AddressBlock>> field does not change, delete it and reinsert it.

CHAPTER **19**

COPYING, LINKING, AND EMBEDDING DATA

In this chapter

UNDERSTANDING TYPES OF DATA SHARING

Windows and Office both have some great data-sharing features that make it possible to move data easily from one application to another. You can embed Excel charts in Word, store PowerPoint slides in Access databases, insert web bookmarks and hyperlinks into email messages, and much more. There are so many data-sharing possibilities, however, that it can sometimes get confusing. In this chapter, you'll learn about the various ways of sharing data and their advantages and drawbacks.

For very basic data sharing, most people use the Clipboard, along with its associated commands (Cut, Copy, Paste), or drag-and-drop. These methods move or copy the content from one location to another without creating a connection between the locations.

→ To review data sharing via the Clipboard or drag-and-drop, **see** "Moving and Copying Text and Objects," **p. 72**.

The ordinary copy-and-paste operation has its limitations, however. For example, suppose you have a chart in Excel that you want to use in Word. If you copy and paste that chart into Word, and then the data changes in the Excel worksheet on which it was originally based, the copy of the chart in Word does not update automatically. Copy-and-paste creates a one-time snapshot of the chart.

For more active connectivity between a source and destination, a variety of sharing techniques are available:

- **Hyperlinking**—You can create a text-based link to the original source document. When you click the link, the original document opens for viewing.

- **Bookmarking**—You can create an invisible marker in a document, and then hyperlink to that marker rather than to the document as a whole.

- **Object linking**—You can create a link between the pasted copy and the file containing the original object, so that the pasted copy changes when the original does.

- **Object embedding**—You can insert various types of content into a document without converting that content to Word format. This makes it possible to edit the embedded object in its native program later.

- **Inserting with field codes**—You can use the InsertText and InsertPicture field codes to link external files to a Word document. This special-purpose technique has some benefits but also some drawbacks compared to object linking.

This chapter looks at each of these techniques with an eye toward better and more convenient content integration.

WORKING WITH HYPERLINKS

A *hyperlink* is a pointer to another file or to an email address. The hyperlink can be assigned to either text or a graphic. When you click the text or the graphic, the referenced file opens or a new message is started to that email address. That's called *following* the hyperlink.

Hyperlinks are most common on web pages, but any Word document can have hyperlinks in it. In fact, you might find that the easiest way to join a set of related documents is to place hyperlinks in each document that connect to the other documents in the set.

NOTE

> Hyperlinks are actually {Hyperlink} fields; you can see this by selecting the hyperlink and pressing Shift+F9 to toggle field codes on/off. Chapter 20, "Working with Fields," covers fields in detail.

AUTOMATICALLY CREATING HYPERLINKS BY TYPING

Because Word 2007 is able to identify web and email addresses as such, it automatically turns them into hyperlinks as you type them. This works with any text strings that start with http:// or www., or that are structured as an email address.

If you do not want certain instances to be hyperlinks, here are some ways to circumvent the process on a case-by-case basis:

- Immediately after the automatic conversion, press Ctrl+Z to undo the last action.
- At any time, right-click the hyperlink and choose Remove Hyperlink.

*To turn off the automatic conversion of text to hyperlinks, **see** "Turning Off Automatic Hyperlink Creation" in the Troubleshooting section at the end of this chapter.*

FOLLOWING A HYPERLINK

To *follow* a hyperlink is to activate it, so that the document, web page, or other referenced item opens.

In Word, clicking a hyperlink does not follow it. This is by design, because you might need to click in the hyperlink's text to edit it. Hold down Ctrl as you click on a hyperlink to follow it in Word.

If you like, you can turn off the Ctrl requirement for following a hyperlink, but there's a drawback to that: You can no longer click inside a hyperlink to edit its text. Instead, you must right-click the hyperlink and choose Edit Hyperlink and edit its text in the Edit Hyperlink dialog box.

NOTE

> If a security notice appears when you follow a hyperlink, click OK to continue. This notice appears when the location being referred to is not on Windows' list of trusted sites. If you know the site you're going to is valid, then it's perfectly safe to ignore this warning. To prevent the notice from appearing in the future for hyperlinks to that location, add that location to the Trusted Locations list, as you'll learn to do in Chapter 28, "Protecting and Securing Documents."

→ To set up a new trusted location, **see** "Specifying Trusted Locations," **p. 816**.

19

To set up Word to use a regular click (not Ctrl+click) to activate hyperlinks in Word, **see** *"Disabling Ctrl+Click to Follow Hyperlinks" in the Troubleshooting section at the end of this chapter.*

CREATING A TEXT HYPERLINK

The most common type of hyperlink is flagged in Word as a bit of underlined text. You've seen this hundreds of times on web pages, but you can also create this same type of hyperlink in any Word document. That hyperlink can point to another Word document, to a web page, to an executable file, or virtually anywhere else.

You can either turn some existing text into a hyperlink or insert brand-new text as you are creating the hyperlink itself. Either way, follow these steps:

1. (Optional) If the text that you want to use already exists in the document, select it.
2. On the Insert tab, click Hyperlink. The Insert Hyperlink dialog box opens (Figure 19.1).

   You can also reach the Insert Hyperlink dialog box by using the keyboard shortcut Ctrl+K or by right-clicking on the selected text and choosing Hyperlink from the shortcut menu.

Figure 19.1
Create a hyperlink to a file, web page, bookmark, or email address.

3. If you selected any text in step 1, it appears in the Text to Display box. Add or change text here if desired.
4. Do one of the following:
   - **Create a hyperlink to a web address**—Enter the web URL for the site to which you want the text to link in the Address text box.
   - **Create a hyperlink to a file on your hard disk**—Use the folder list under the Look In box to browse to the desired location and select the file.
5. (Optional) To add a ScreenTip to the hyperlink, click the ScreenTip button, type the text, and click OK.

NOTE

A ScreenTip is text that appears in a box when the user points at the hyperlink in a web browser. If you do not specify a ScreenTip, the hyperlink's address is the ScreenTip.

6. Click OK. When you return to your document, the text you highlighted is now a different color (blue, by default) and underlined, indicating that it is now an active hyperlink. The exact color of the hyperlinks depends on the theme colors.

Hyperlinking to an Executable File

Hyperlinks can also be used to run applications. This is a fairly uncommon usage, but it can come in handy. For example, in training materials, you might include a hyperlink as a shortcut to opening the application on which you want to train the users.

To create a hyperlink to run an application, specify the application's executable file instead of a web page or data file in step 4 of the preceding steps. An executable file usually has an .exe extension, or less frequently a .com or .bat extension.

To determine the correct name and location for an application's executable file, right-click its shortcut on the Start menu and choose Properties. Then look in the Target field on the General tab of the Properties dialog box. If you know the executable file's name, you can easily find it in Vista by typing the name into the Start menu's search field. If the executable file appears in the results, you can create a shortcut from it, rather than traversing through the rest of the Start menu, looking for it.

ADDING A HYPERLINK TO AN IMAGE

A graphic can function as a hyperlink, such that when the user clicks the image, the specified web page or document opens. The process for building a graphical hyperlink is similar to that for building a text hyperlink:

1. Select any clip art, picture, drawing object, or WordArt in the document.
2. On the Insert tab, click Hyperlink to display the Insert Hyperlink dialog box. (Or use the Ctrl+K or right-click method if you prefer.)
3. Type the address for the link in the Address box, or browse for and select the file to which to hyperlink.
4. (Optional) If you want a custom ScreenTip, click ScreenTip, type the text, and click OK. Otherwise, the ScreenTip will show the complete path to the chosen file.
5. Click OK to complete the hyperlink.

The picture will not look any different. If you hover the mouse pointer over the picture, however, the ScreenTip you specified will appear. To test the hyperlink, Ctrl+click the image.

CREATING AN EMAIL HYPERLINK

Besides referencing other files and web pages, hyperlinks can start the user's email editor and begin a blank email message with the recipient name filled in automatically. This is useful for providing a hyperlink through which someone can email you to comment on your web page.

Follow these steps to create an email hyperlink:

1. Select the text or choose an image for the hyperlink.

2. On the Insert tab, click Hyperlink to display the Insert Hyperlink dialog box. (Or use the Ctrl+K or right-click method if you prefer.)

3. In the lower-left corner of the Insert Hyperlink dialog box, click E-mail Address.

4. Enter the email address to which the hyperlink should send a message, as shown in Figure 19.2.

Figure 19.2
Hyperlinking to an email address.

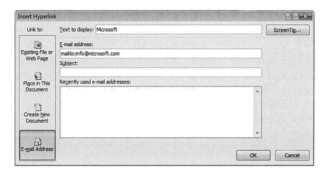

Notice how the phrase `mailto:` is automatically added to the beginning of your email address.

5. (Optional) To pre-enter the subject line for the message, type the text in the Subject box.

6. (Optional) If you want a custom ScreenTip, click ScreenTip, type the text, and click OK. Otherwise, the ScreenTip will show the email address.

7. Click OK to complete the link.

CREATING AND HYPERLINKING TO A NEW DOCUMENT

When creating groups of hyperlinked documents, it's best to create all the documents first, and then create the hyperlinks. If you forget to create one of the documents, though, it's easy to create it on the fly as you create the hyperlink. The Create New Document option in the Insert Hyperlink dialog box does just that.

Follow these steps to create a new document and a hyperlink to it:

1. Select the text or choose an image for the hyperlink.

2. On the Insert tab, click Hyperlink to display the Insert Hyperlink dialog box. (Or use the Ctrl+K or right-click method if you prefer.)

3. Click Create New Document.

4. In the Name of New Document text box, type the name to be used for the new document. Do not type the path—just the name.

5. If the path listed under Full Path is not correct, click the Change button, browse to a different path, and click OK.

6. (Optional) If you want a custom ScreenTip for the hyperlink, click ScreenTip, type the text, and click OK. Otherwise, the ScreenTip shows the complete path to the new document.

7. Click Edit the New Document Now if you want the document to open for editing in Word now, or click Edit the New Document Later if you want it not to open.

8. Click OK to complete the link.

EDITING A HYPERLINK

You can change a hyperlink's text, its address, its ScreenTip, or any other aspect of it. However, changing the underlined text in a hyperlink does not change its underlying address; they are two separate settings.

The easiest way to change a hyperlink's displayed text is simply to move the insertion point into the hyperlink text and edit it with Backspace, Delete, or any of the other editing techniques you use with regular text. Or, if you prefer, you can use the dialog box method described in the following steps.

TIP

> There's one minor way in which editing hyperlink text is different from editing regular text: You can't delete individual characters from the beginning of the hyperlink text by using the Delete key. Clicking in front of the hyperlink text and pressing Delete once selects the entire hyperlink; pressing Delete again deletes the entire hyperlink. If you want to delete characters at the beginning of the hyperlink text, click *after* them and then use the Backspace key, or select only the characters to delete and then press Delete or Backspace.

19

Here's how to edit a hyperlink:

1. Right-click the hyperlink and choose Edit Hyperlink. The Edit Hyperlink dialog box opens (see Figure 19.3).

2. Make any changes desired:
   - Change the text to display.
   - Click the ScreenTip button and change the ScreenTip text.
   - In the Address (or E-mail Address) box, change the address to which the hyperlink refers.
   - If it's an email address hyperlink, change the subject.

3. Click OK to accept the changes.

Figure 19.3
Edit the hyperlink's
properties.

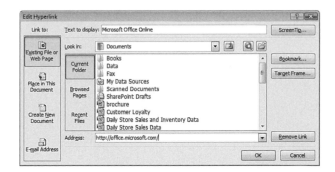

REMOVING A HYPERLINK

Removing a hyperlink doesn't remove the text; it just converts it to regular text. To remove a hyperlink, right-click the hyperlink and choose Remove Hyperlink from the menu. Simple, eh? If you already have the Edit Hyperlink dialog box open (refer to Figure 19.3), you can also click the Remove Link button there to remove a hyperlink.

CHANGING HYPERLINK UNDERLINING AND COLOR

Hyperlink text appears underlined, and it appears in whatever color the theme has assigned for hyperlinks (or visited hyperlinks).

> **NOTE**
>
> A *visited hyperlink* is one that you have clicked on (opened). Visited hyperlinks appear in a different color to help you keep track of which links you have used. This is perhaps not all that helpful in a Word document with a couple of stray hyperlinks in it, but on a page with a huge listing of links, it's invaluable.

You can remove the underlining from the hyperlink by selecting it and clicking the Underline button on the Home tab to toggle underlining off. However, be cautious when stripping off the underline from a hyperlink, because that makes it difficult for your readers to discern that a hyperlink is present.

The one quirk in hyperlink formatting is color. If you select a hyperlink and then try to change its font color, you'll discover that it won't work. The color remains whatever the theme has assigned for hyperlinks of its type.

> **NOTE**
>
> Your color choice actually *is* applied, but it's not visible because the hyperlink formatting sits on top of it. If you were to remove the hyperlink, the text would take on the color formatting you selected.

There are two ways to change the hyperlink's color. One is to manually strip off all existing formatting from it and apply your own. Do the following for each individual hyperlink:

1. Select the hyperlink and press Ctrl+spacebar. All formatting is removed, but the hyperlink itself remains.

2. Click the Underline button on the Home tab to re-underline the hyperlink text. (This is optional but recommended, because un-underlined hyperlinks are difficult to discern in a document.)

3. Apply the desired color.

The other way is to change the color that the theme assigns to hyperlinks. This method affects all the hyperlinks in the entire document at once:

1. On the Page Layout tab, open the Theme Colors list and choose Create New Theme Colors.

2. In the Create New Theme Colors dialog box, open the Hyperlink list and select a different color for (unvisited) hyperlinks.

3. Repeat step 2 for Followed Hyperlink. You can choose the same color as in step 2 or a different color (see Figure 19.4).

Figure 19.4
Change the colors assigned to hyperlinks.

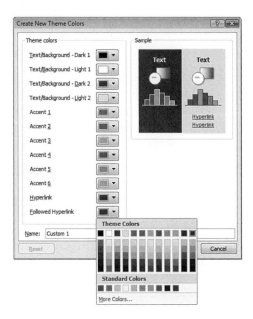

4. In the Name box, replace the default name with a name of your choosing.

5. Click Save.

WORKING WITH BOOKMARKS

Hyperlinks are great all by themselves, but they point to entire files, not specific parts of the file. If the referenced document is long, your audience will wonder what specific part of its contents you wanted them to view within it.

A *bookmark* provides a more specific way of referring to document content. You can create a named bookmark to indicate a certain spot in the document, and then reference that bookmark's name in a variety of referencing activities, including cross-references and hyperlinks. You can also quickly jump to a bookmark using the Go To feature, as you learned in Chapter 3, "Typing and Editing Text."

→ To review the Go To command and how bookmarks can be used with it, **see** "Using Go To," **p. 87**

NOTE

Bookmarks are actually {Bookmark} fields; you can see this by selecting the bookmark and pressing Shift+F9 to toggle field codes on/off. Chapter 20 covers fields in detail.

CREATING A BOOKMARK

You can create a bookmark to any portion of a document—a heading, a body paragraph, a specific word or phrase, or a graphic object of any type. The bookmark can be a single spot in the document (that is, a single character marker), or it can encompass multiple paragraphs and objects.

Does it matter how large the selection is that you bookmark? It depends on how you plan on using the bookmark. If you are going to use it only for navigation, such as with a Go To operation or a cross-reference, it makes no difference because it will always jump to the beginning of the bookmarked area regardless of the area's size. However, if you plan on using the bookmark for text insertion operations, such as with the {IncludeText} field covered later in this chapter, make sure you include everything within the bookmark that you want to be included in the insertion.

→ For information about the {IncludeText} field, **see** "Inserting Text with {IncludeText}," **p. 625**.

TIP

Many of the uses for a bookmark, such as a Go To operation or a cross-reference, work with all the headings in the document automatically, so you do not usually have to create bookmarks for the headings in your document in order to reference them.

To create a bookmark, follow these steps:

1. Position the insertion point in the spot where you want the bookmark to be inserted.

   To bookmark a paragraph, position the insertion point at the beginning of that paragraph. To bookmark a graphic object, select the object.

2. On the Insert tab, click Bookmark. The Bookmark dialog box opens.

3. In the Bookmark Name box, type a name for the bookmark (see Figure 19.5).

   The name can be up to 40 characters and can include letters, numbers, or a combination of the two, but no spaces and no symbols.

Figure 19.5
Create a bookmark.

4. Click the Add button. The bookmark is now created.

JUMPING TO A BOOKMARK

One use for a bookmark is to quickly locate it in the document. To jump to the bookmarked location in the document, follow these steps:

1. On the Insert tab, click Bookmark.
2. In the Bookmark dialog box, click the desired bookmark and click Go To.
3. Click Close.

Here's an alternative method:

1. Click the Select Browse Object button in the Word window, or press Ctrl+Alt+Home.
2. On the palette of icons that appears, click Go To. The Find and Replace dialog box opens with the Go To tab displayed.
3. In the Go to What list, select Bookmark.
4. Open the Enter Bookmark Name list and click the desired bookmark.
5. Click the Go To button to jump to that bookmark in the document.
6. Click Close.

INSERTING A HYPERLINK TO A BOOKMARK

A hyperlink to a bookmark is like a saved Go To operation. Rather than having to go through the Go To process each time, you can simply Ctrl+click the hyperlink to that bookmark.

19

HYPERLINKING TO A BOOKMARK IN THE SAME DOCUMENT

Most of the time, the bookmarks to which you will want to refer will be in the same document as the reference. This is considered a "Place in This Document" type of hyperlink, and there is a special button for it in the Insert Hyperlink dialog box.

To create a hyperlink to a bookmark that's in the same document, follow these steps:

1. Position the insertion point where you want the hyperlink to be inserted, or select the text that should be used as the hyperlink.
2. On the Insert tab, click Hyperlink. The Insert Hyperlink dialog box opens.
3. Click Place in This Document. A list of all the headings and bookmarks in the document appears.
4. Click the desired bookmark (see Figure 19.6).

TIP

You can also use this same procedure to create a hyperlink to the top of the document, or to any of the headings, by selecting one of those items instead in step 4.

Figure 19.6
Create a hyperlink to a bookmark in the same document.

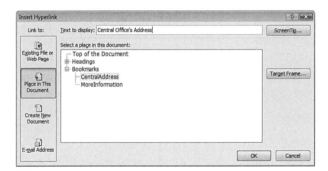

5. Check the text in the Text to Display box, and edit it if needed.
6. Click OK to insert the hyperlink.

NOTE

One obvious usage that might occur to you for hyperlinks to bookmarks is to create a table of contents at the beginning of a long document; each bookmark hyperlink could then jump the reader to a specified section of the document. And in fact, that's exactly how Word's Table of Contents feature does work, with one exception: Rather than keying on bookmarks, it works with headings (that is, paragraphs formatted with heading styles). It also does the setup automatically, so you don't have to manually create each hyperlink for each heading. Table of contents creation is the subject of Chapter 25, "Creating Tables of Contents and Other Listings."

HYPERLINKING TO A BOOKMARK IN ANOTHER DOCUMENT

Hyperlinks can also be created to bookmarks in other documents. When the hyperlink is followed, not only does the referenced document open, but the display jumps to the referenced bookmark.

Follow these steps to create a hyperlink to a bookmark in another document:

1. Start creating a new hyperlink as you normally would:
   a. Select text or position the insertion point.
   b. On the Insert tab, click Hyperlink.
   c. Change the text in the Text to Display box if needed.
   d. Set up a ScreenTip if needed.
2. Click Existing File or Web Page, and then browse for and select the desired document. (You must have already saved the document containing the bookmark for it to appear on this list.)
3. Click the Bookmark button. The Select Place in Document dialog box opens, listing all the bookmarks in the selected document (see Figure 19.7).

Figure 19.7
Create a hyperlink to a bookmark in another document.

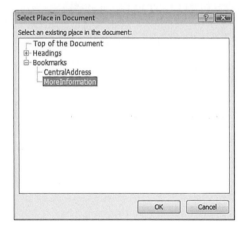

4. Click the desired bookmark.
5. Click OK to return to the Insert Hyperlink dialog box.
6. Click OK to insert the hyperlink.

> **TIP**
>
> Word uses standard HTML syntax to reference bookmarks, so if you happen to know the bookmark name, you don't have to do steps 3–5. Instead you can click at the end of the filename in the Address text box and then type a # sign followed by the bookmark name.

INSERTING A CROSS-REFERENCE TO A BOOKMARK

A *cross-reference* is a dynamic reference to a location. For example, suppose that on page 10 of your document, you want to refer to a certain definition in a paragraph that is currently on page 4 of your document. You could say "Refer to the definition on page 4," but then what if you add more text to the document later, or delete some text, such that the definition is no longer on page 4? With a cross-reference, rather than a manual reference, you don't have to worry about the reference becoming out-of-synch. Create a bookmark at the definition's location and then create a cross-reference to that bookmark.

> **NOTE**
>
> Cross-references are actually {Ref} or {Pageref} fields; you can see this by selecting the cross-reference and pressing Shift+F9 to toggle field codes on/off. Chapter 20 covers fields in detail.

Cross-references can be created to many different types of content, not just bookmarks. In Chapter 24, "Citing Sources and References," you'll learn more uses for a cross-reference, but for now let's take a quick look at how to cross-reference a bookmark:

1. Create the bookmark, as described earlier in this chapter.

2. Position the insertion point where you want to insert the cross-reference and then type any supporting text that should go along with it. For example, you might type something like:

   For more information, see Creating Special Effects on page

3. On the Insert tab, click Cross-Reference. The Cross-Reference dialog box opens.

4. Open the Reference Type list and select Bookmark.

5. Open the Insert Reference To list and select the type of information you want to appear as the reference. For the example given in step 2, you would want Page Number, for instance. Or for a bookmark, you could choose Bookmark Text to insert the literal text that the bookmark marks.

6. (Optional) If you want the cross-reference to function as a live hyperlink to the bookmark, make sure the Insert as Hyperlink check box is marked.

7. Select the bookmark from the For Which Bookmark list (see Figure 19.8).

8. Click Insert. The designated information is inserted as a code in the document.

9. Click Close.

Figure 19.8
Create a cross-refer-
ence to a bookmark.

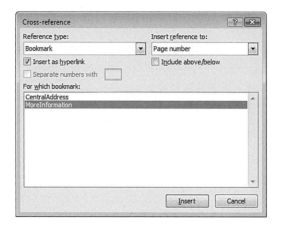

NOTE

If you marked the check box in step 6, the cross-reference is a hyperlink, but it's not underlined or a different color. The only way to know it's a hyperlink is to point at it; the ScreenTip appears and displays the name of the bookmark. If you think your readers need a more obvious cue, format the cross-reference by adding underlining and/or a different color.

→ For more information about cross-referencing, **see** "Creating Cross-References," **p. 742**.

EMBEDDING DATA

19

With a simple cut-and-paste operation that moves content between applications, the cut-and-pasted data retains no memory of the application from which it came. The receiving application converts the incoming data into the best possible format it can, given its capabilities. For example, Excel cells are converted to a table grid in Word. There's no going back; you must edit the inserted content in Word or not at all.

Sometimes, however, you might want the data to retain its connection to the source application. For example, you might want to be able to edit the inserted Excel cells in Excel in the future, because Excel has superior calculating features and can do things that can't be done in a Word table.

For situations such as this, what you want is *embedded data*. Embedded data remembers its roots, and it can be reopened in that same application later. You can embed existing data from another program, or you can create a new embedded object in Word using the tools from almost any other application installed on your PC.

CAUTION

Embedded data does not retain a connection to the original data file from which it came, so changes made later to the original data file are not reflected in the Word copy and vice-versa. If you need a connection like that, what you want is *linked data*, covered later in this chapter.

There are two different ways to embed existing data, depending on whether you want to embed an entire file or just a snippet of data.

EMBEDDING AN ENTIRE EXISTING FILE

When you embed an entire existing file in a Word document, you are in effect storing a complete copy of that file within the Word file, so the file size grows dramatically. There are advantages, however, to make up for the larger file size. When embedding an entire file, you do not necessarily have to *show* the entire file in Word, but the entire file remains available. So, for example, if you embed an Excel workbook that has multiple sheets, you can choose which sheet (or which portion of a sheet) you want to display in Word, and you can change your mind at any time later. You might want to display one sheet, print your work, and then display a different sheet, for example.

To embed an entire file in Word, insert it as an object by following these steps:

1. Position the insertion point where you want the object to appear.
2. On the Insert tab, click Object and then click Object from the resulting menu. The Object dialog box opens.
3. On the Create from File tab, click Browse.
4. Locate and select the desired file and click Insert. The complete path to the file appears in the File Name box (see Figure 19.9).
5. Click OK to insert the file.

Figure 19.9
Create an embedded object from an entire existing file.

The embedded object appears in the document. When you select the object, small black square selection handles appear around it, the same way a backward-compatible graphic would appear.

When you double-click the embedded object, the object opens in its native application for editing. If the native application is a Microsoft Office product, or other supported product, the ribbon or the toolbars for that product appear within the Word 2007 window, as in Figure 19.10. If the native application is not fully supported, the object opens in a separate window for that application.

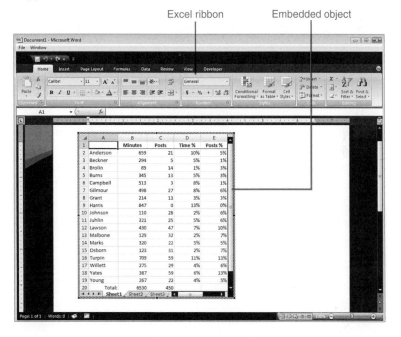

Figure 19.10
An embedded Excel worksheet opened for editing in Word.

To return to Word if you're working with a supported Microsoft Office product's content, click the Word document in an area away from the object. Word's ribbon reappears, and the object goes back to being a "picture."

To return to Word if you're working with an unsupported product's content, open the File (or Office) menu in that application and look for a command that includes *Return to* in it, such as Exit and Return to Document 1 (where "Document 1" reflects the Word document's filename).

Changing the View of the Embedded File

When an embedded file is selected, it can be resized like any other object. Drag a selection handle, and the content will enlarge or shrink to fit the new frame size. So, for example, suppose you have an embedded Excel worksheet that shows a 10×10 cell block. If you click once on the embedded object and then drag its bottom-right selection handle inward, the 10×10 block will shrink proportionally, but will still show 100 cells.

However, when an embedded file is activated (by double-clicking it), as in Figure 19.10, resizing its frame has a very different effect—it makes less or more of the file appear in the window. For the earlier 10×10 cell block example, you might double-click the object and then drag the bottom-right selection handle inward so only an 8×8 block of cells is visible. Then click away from the object to return to Word.

For Excel workbooks that contain multiple sheets, only one sheet can be shown at once, but you can switch freely among them with the worksheet tabs when the object is activated. If you need to show multiple sheets at once, copy the object and set a different sheet to display in each copy.

19

EMBEDDING A DATA SELECTION

Sometimes embedding an entire data file is overkill. Why embed a huge file, and grow your Word document's file size dramatically, when all you really want is a few worksheet cells or a single chart or graphic?

To embed a portion of a file, use the Paste Special command rather than Insert Object. As you learned in Chapter 3, Paste Special provides a means of setting options for a Paste operation, and that's exactly what is needed here.

Follow these steps to embed some data from another program into Word:

1. Open the other program and then open or create the data.

2. Copy the desired data to the Clipboard.

3. Switch to Word and position the insertion point where you want the pasted selection to appear.

4. On the Home tab, open the Paste button's menu and choose Paste Special. The Paste Special dialog box opens.

5. On the As list, select a document type that ends with the word *Object*. (There will probably be only one choice.) For example, in Figure 19.11, it's Microsoft Office Excel 2003 Worksheet Object.

> **NOTE**
> If there is no data type on the As list that ends in *Object*, you cannot create an embedded object using Paste Special for this data.

Figure 19.11
To embed, use Paste Special and make sure you choose an "Object" data type.

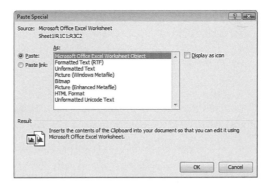

6. Click OK. The selection is pasted as an embedded object.

EMBEDDING A NEW OBJECT

When you want to embed a new object of some other type than Word, you can do so from within Word itself, so that the object is saved within the Word document rather than in a separate file. This can save some time and effort, as you don't have to open the other application separately.

You can create a new embedded object using almost any application installed on your PC. The only requirement is that the application must conform to the Windows Object Linking and Embedding (OLE) standards, and most productivity applications do.

To create a new embedded object, follow these steps:

1. In Word, position the insertion point where you want the new object to appear.

2. On the Insert tab, click Object and then click Object from the resulting menu. The Object dialog box opens.

3. On the Create New tab, scroll through the Object Type list and select the desired object type. The object types listed depend on the applications installed on your PC. For example, Figure 19.12 shows the creation of a new bitmap image.

Figure 19.12
Choose the type of new embedded object you want to insert.

4. Click OK to insert the new object. The tools and menus for the selected object type appear.

5. Create the object and then return to Word.

To re-edit the object at any time later, double-click it.

LINKING TO DATA IN OTHER FILES

The terms *linking* and *embedding* are sometimes thrown around loosely as if they were a single action, as in Object Linking and Embedding, but they are actually quite different.

As you just learned in the preceding section, *embedding* creates a static copy of an object within Word, retaining its memory of the application from which it came. Embedding can be done with whole files, snippets of existing files, or brand-new content that is not related to any existing file.

Linking, on the other hand, can be done only with existing saved files. Linking inserts a dynamic link to the original data file. That way, if the original data file changes, the version in Word also changes, and vice-versa. Linking is quite handy when you need to create connections between files that are not finalized yet, because you are always assured of having the most recent data.

However, linking is not always appropriate or even helpful. It has some definite drawbacks. The biggest one is that files containing links are slower to open and save. Whenever a file that contains a link is opened or saved, the linked data is updated, and this takes time. You can minimize this impact by setting the links to be manually updated, but then you run into the potential problem of forgetting to update them and losing the benefit of dynamic updates.

→ To learn how to set a link to be manually updated, **see** "Managing Link Update Settings," **p. 622**.

You must also take care not to move the linked files, or the Word document will not be able to find them. This causes an error when the document is opened. Before you distribute a file that contains links via email or on a network where not everyone has access to the folders containing all the files, you should disable or remove the links in it, because the recipients will not have access to the linked file.

→ To learn how to remove a link, **see** "Breaking a Link," **p. 624**.

> **NOTE**
>
> Links are actually {Link} fields; you can see this by selecting the linked content and pressing Shift+F9 to toggle field codes on/off. Chapter 20 covers fields in detail.

CREATING A LINK

As with embedding, there are two different procedures for creating a link, depending on whether you want to link to an entire file or only a portion of it.

LINKING TO AN ENTIRE FILE

The procedure for linking an entire file is very similar to that of embedding an entire file, except you indicate that you want the file to be linked. Follow these steps:

1. Position the insertion point where you want the object to appear.

2. On the Insert tab, click Object and then click Object from the resulting menu. The Object dialog box opens.

3. On the Create from File tab, click Browse.

4. Locate and select the desired file and click Insert. The complete path to the file appears in the File Name box (see Figure 19.13).

5. Mark the Link to File check box. This step is important; if you don't do it, you'll get an embedded file, not a linked one.

6. Click OK to insert the linked file.

Figure 19.13
Create a link with Insert Object.

A linked file functions very much like an embedded file in a Word document; when selected, it appears with square black selection handles and can be formatted as a graphic. The main difference is in the editing; when you double-click it to activate it, the original data file opens for editing in its own window, rather than using embedded tabs and menus within Word.

LINKING TO A PORTION OF A FILE

The procedure for linking a portion of a file is similar to embedding a portion of a file. One difference is that with linking, the data you are copying must be saved in another file, so you must make sure you've saved your work in the other application before linking it into Word.

To link to a portion of a file, follow these steps:

1. Open the other program and then open or create the data.

   If you're creating a new data file, make sure you save it before proceeding; otherwise, there will be no file name to link into Word.

2. Copy the desired data to the Clipboard.

3. Switch to Word and position the insertion point where you want the pasted selection to appear.

4. On the Home tab, open the Paste button's menu and choose Paste Special. The Paste Special dialog box opens.

5. Click Paste Link. The As list changes to show only the formats in which a link is possible (see Figure 19.14).

6. On the As list, select the desired content type.

NOTE

> You have a wider choice of content types here than with embedding. The content can be based in a variety of formats, any of which will maintain the link to the original data. For example, Formatted Text (RTF) pastes Excel data cells in as a Word table. Pay attention to the explanation in the Result area of the dialog box to find out what each available option does.

Figure 19.14
Create a link with
Paste Special.

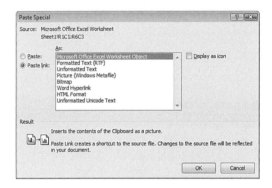

7. (Optional) If you would prefer that the link be an icon in the Word document, rather than a full display of the data, mark the Display as Icon check box. (Or, if you would prefer it be a text hyperlink, do not mark the check box, but choose Word Hyperlink as the As type.)

8. Click OK to create the link.

The linked file need not be edited from within Word. If you chose its native application as the content type (in step 6), you can open it separately in its native application, or if Word happens to be open already, you can double-click the linked file in Word to open it in its native application in a separate window.

MANAGING LINK UPDATE SETTINGS

Whenever you open or save a Word document containing a link, the link is updated automatically. Linked data is also updated automatically on the fly whenever both files happen to be open at the same time.

As mentioned earlier, updating links takes time, especially in a document with multiple links. To minimize the performance impact, you might choose to set the links for manual updating.

To change a link's update settings, follow these steps:

1. Right-click the object in Word and point to Linked Object to open a submenu. Then click Links. The Links dialog box opens.

The exact name of the command to open the submenu varies depending on the object. For example, for Excel data, it would be Linked Worksheet Object.

2. Select the link from the list of links (if there is more than one link in the document).

3. In the Update Method for Selected Link section, click Manual Update (see Figure 19.15).

4. Click OK.

Figure 19.15
Specify manual updating for one or more links.

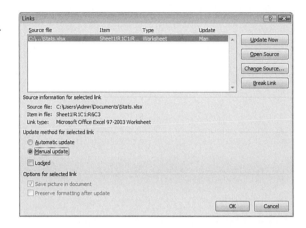

N O T E

The Locked check box locks the link so that it cannot be updated, either manually or automatically. You might use this to prevent an error from occurring if the linked data is taken offline, for example, or to preserve a certain version of the data in the document. (Of course, another way to preserve the current version would simply be to break the link entirely. See "Breaking a Link" later in this chapter.)

MANUALLY UPDATING A LINK

After setting a link to manual updates, you must update it yourself. To do so, right-click the linked content and choose Update Link. An alternative method: Display the Links dialog box (shown in Figure 19.15), click the link, and click Update Now.

CHANGING THE LINKED FILE'S LOCATION OR RANGE

If the linked file changes its location or name, or if you need to refer to a different portion of it (for example, a different range of cells from a worksheet), use the Links dialog box shown in Figure 19.15 to make that change. Follow these steps:

1. Right-click the object in Word and point to Linked Object to open a submenu. Then click Links. The Links dialog box opens.

   The exact name of the command to open the submenu varies depending on the object. For example, for Excel data, it would be Linked Worksheet Object.

2. Select the link from the list of links (if there is more than one link in the document).

3. Do any of the following:

- To check that the link's source file is still available, click Open Source. If it opens, the link is functional. Close the source file.

- To change the path or name of the source file (for example, if it has been moved or renamed), click Change Source and then browse for the new filename and location and click Open.

- To change what portion of the source file is linked, click Change Source, and then after selecting the file and location, click the Item button and specify the portion of the file to be linked. For Excel data, for example, you can specify a cell range or a bookmark name.

4. Click OK to close the Links dialog box.

BREAKING A LINK

When you no longer need the dynamic link between the source and the Word document, you should break the link for better performance. (Remember, links slow down the file's saving and opening.)

To break a link, follow these steps:

1. Right-click the object in Word and point to Linked Object to open a submenu. Then click Links. The Links dialog box opens.

   The exact name of the command to open the submenu varies depending on the object. For example, for Excel data, it would be Linked Worksheet Object.

2. Select the link from the list of links (if there is more than one link in the document).

3. Click Break Link. At the confirmation box, click Yes.

4. If there are no more links, the Links dialog box closes automatically. If other links remain, break them too if desired, or click OK to close the Links dialog box.

INSERTING CONTENT WITH {INCLUDETEXT} AND {INCLUDEPICTURE}

In Chapter 20, you'll learn a lot about *fields*, which are codes that insert objects, values, or data into a Word document. You've already seen several types of fields in this chapter: {Hyperlink}, {Ref}, {Pageref}, {Link}, and {Bookmark}. Each inserts or marks content in a certain way.

Now let's look at two more fields that are useful for inserting external content: {IncludeText} and {IncludePicture}. These are non-OLE alternatives, and the links do not automatically update. Use them for situations where the data is unlikely to change very often but you still would like to maintain a link.

INSERTING TEXT WITH {INCLUDETEXT}

The {IncludeText} field inserts a linked copy of external text into the document. It is not intended to replace OLE linking; instead, it's used for special-purpose insertions involving field codes. It is designed to provide a flexible block of text that you can combine with other fields. For example, if you have defined a certain number in one document as a bookmark, you could then use it in a field calculation in another document by using {IncludeText} to bring in that bookmark's content.

There are two ways of inserting an {IncludeText} field. You can use the Insert Text from File command, or you can use Insert Field. Each has its advantages and drawbacks.

CREATING AN {INCLUDETEXT} FIELD WITH INSERT TEXT FROM FILE

This first method inserts entire files rather easily, and it enables you to browse for the file you want to insert. However, it does not allow you to browse for bookmark names, so you must know the exact name of the bookmark you want (if you don't want the entire file). It also does not enable you to use any special switches in the field code. Here are the steps to follow:

1. Position the insertion point where you want the inserted text to appear.
2. On the Insert tab, click Object and then click Text from File. The Insert File dialog box opens.
3. Navigate to and select the file you want to include.
4. (Optional) To include only a bookmarked range, click the Range button, type the bookmark name, and click OK.
5. Open the drop-down list on the Insert button and choose Insert as Link (see Figure 19.16).

Figure 19.16
Insert a link to a text file to create an {IncludeText} field automatically.

CREATING AN {INCLUDETEXT} FIELD BY INSERTING A FIELD CODE

An alternative method provides dialog box options for including any of several switches, such as for XSL transformation or namespace mappings, but it does not enable you to browse for the path and name of the file. To use this method, follow these steps:

1. Position the insertion point where you want the inserted text to appear.
2. On the Insert tab, click Quick Parts and then click Field. The Field dialog box opens.
3. In the Categories list, choose Links and References (or choose All).
4. On the Field Names list, click IncludeText.
5. In the Filename or URL text box, type the complete path and name of the file (see Figure 19.17). If the path includes spaces, enclose it in quotation marks. Replace single backslashes with double ones.

Figure 19.17
Use IncludeText to insert text from a file.

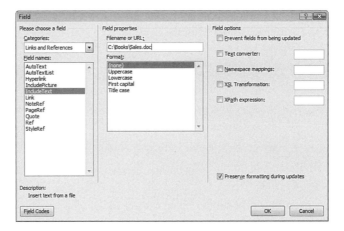

6. (Optional) If you want to enter a bookmark name, do the following:
   a. Click the Field Codes button. A Field Codes text box appears, showing the syntax that will be used for the field code.
   b. Click at the end of the existing code string and type a space. Then type the bookmark name.
   c. Click Hide Codes to return to the regular view of the dialog box.
7. (Optional) For any of the special-purpose field options, mark the check box and enter the desired value. Or, if you are more comfortable working directly with the switches, click Field Codes and enter the syntax manually. Table 19.1 explains the available switches.
8. Mark or clear the Preserve Formatting During Updates check box to indicate how you want formatting handled when the field is updated. When the check box is marked, the main document's formatting will prevail; when it's cleared, the formatting will be brought in with the text being inserted.
9. Click OK. The text is inserted.

TABLE 19.1 SWITCHES FOR THE {INCLUDETEXT} FIELD

Switch	Purpose	Arguments
\!	Prevents Word from updating fields in the inserted text unless the field results have changed in the original location.	None
\c className	Specifies a converter to use; necessary only for WordPerfect 5.x for Windows or 6.x files.	WrdPrfctWin or WordPerfect6x
\n mapping	Specifies a namespace for XPath queries.	The namespace
\t file	Specifies an XSLT file for formatting XML data.	The .xsl filename
\x path	Specifies the XPath for returning a fragment of data in an XML file.	An element of an XML file

UPDATING AN {INCLUDETEXT} FIELD

After inserting the field, you can update it by right-clicking it and choosing Update Field, or by selecting it and pressing F9.

To view the code on which the field is based, right-click it and choose Toggle Field Codes, or select it and press Shift+F9.

Text that has been inserted using {IncludeText} is directly editable in Word—unlike text brought in with Insert Object. However, the next time you update the field, any changes made to the text are wiped away as a fresh copy is loaded from the original source. To save your changes to the original source, press Ctrl+Shift+F7.

INSERTING A PICTURE WITH {INCLUDEPICTURE}

The {IncludePicture} field links to a picture from an outside source. Like {IncludeText}, it's not meant as a replacement for an OLE link, but rather has some special-purpose uses. For example, you might set up a field with a logical condition and then use two different {IncludePicture} operations to insert one picture or the other based on the condition.

CAUTION

A linked picture inserted with {IncludePicture} is updatable, but there's no way of updating it via Word's user interface. You have to use the shortcut key F9 in order to do it. Why? Well, an object must have a "context" that determines which right-click menu command set appears for it. A linked picture is a field-inserted object, but it is also an inline image. The designers of Word had to pick which context menu would be the most useful for you to have, and they went with the one for inline images. That's why there's no Update Field command on the right-click menu for a picture linked with {IncludePicture}.

19

There are two methods of creating an {IncludePicture} field: the Insert Picture command and the Insert Field command.

CREATING AN {INCLUDEPICTURE} FIELD WITH INSERT PICTURE

In Chapter 13, "Working with Photos," you learned how to insert a picture from a file. The resulting picture is a static image; it is not linked to the original.

→ To review the procedure for inserting a picture from a file, **see** "Inserting Pictures from Files," **p. 401**.

To use an {IncludePicture} link for it instead of inserting a static copy, there's just one little change: Instead of clicking the Insert button in the Insert Picture dialog box, open the Insert button's drop-down list and choose Insert and Link (see Figure 19.18). This method is simple and lets you browse for the file easily, but it does not allow any options to be set for the import and linkage.

Figure 19.18
Use the Insert Picture dialog box's Insert button menu to choose to insert and link the picture rather than simply inserting it.

CREATING AN {INCLUDEPICTURE} FIELD BY INSERTING A FIELD CODE

By using the field code insertion method, you can specify various options and switches for the {IncludePicture} field. However, it's not quite as easy a method as Insert Picture.

Before starting an {IncludePicture} insertion, make sure you know the full path and name of the file you want to insert, because you will not be able to browse for it when inserting the field. The full path includes the drive letter and folder, like this: C:\Books\Xfer.tif.

To insert a graphic by inserting an {IncludePicture} field code, follow these steps:

1. Position the insertion point where you want the inserted picture to appear.
2. On the Insert tab, click Quick Parts and then click Field. The Field dialog box opens.

3. On the Field Names list, click IncludePicture.

4. In the Filename or URL text box, type the complete path and name of the file. If the path includes spaces, enclose it in quotation marks. Replace single backslashes with double ones.

5. (Optional) Mark any of the Field Options check boxes for any special options desired:

   - **Graphic Filter**—You can specify a certain filter file to use (.flt file), but Word can usually determine this automatically for you. Marking this check box includes the \c switch with the filter you specify as the argument.

   - **Data Not Stored with Document**—Marking this check box includes the \d switch, which creates a link only; it does not insert the graphic data into the document. This reduces the document file size, but if the original file is not available, the graphic will not display.

   - **Resize Horizontally from Source**—Marking this check box includes the \x switch, which resizes the graphic horizontally based on the source image.

   - **Resize Vertically from Source**—Marking this check box includes the \y switch, which resizes the graphic vertically based on the source image.

6. Click OK. The picture is inserted.

The resulting inserted picture does not obviously appear to be a field, unlike the inserted text with IncludeText. It is not shaded gray, and if you right-click it, no special field-related commands appear. However, the picture *is* a field, and it *is* updatable; select it and press F9 to update it.

> **TIP**
>
> To update all the field codes in the document at once, press Ctrl+F9.

TROUBLESHOOTING

TURNING OFF AUTOMATIC HYPERLINK CREATION

By default, Word converts all web and email addresses to live hyperlinks. If you find yourself frequently undoing an automatic hyperlink conversion, you might want to turn that feature off.

Follow these steps to disable automatic hyperlink creation:

1. Choose Office, Word Options. The Word Options dialog box opens.

2. Click Proofing and then click AutoCorrect Options. The AutoCorrect dialog box opens.

3. On the AutoFormat As You Type tab, clear the Internet and Network Paths with Hyperlinks check box.

4. Click OK.

5. Click OK to close the Word Options dialog box.

Disabling Ctrl+Click to Follow Hyperlinks

In Word, you must Ctrl+click to activate a hyperlink; regular clicking will not work. This is by design because you might need to click in a hyperlink and edit its text, and you couldn't do that if clicking were set up to activate the hyperlink. (You could still right-click it and choose Edit Hyperlink, however, to edit the text.)

If you would rather have regular clicking activate hyperlinks in Word anyway, follow these steps:

1. Choose Office, Word Options. The Word Options dialog box opens.
2. Click Advanced.
3. In the Edit section, clear the Use CTRL+Click to Follow Hyperlink check box.
4. Click OK.

CHAPTER **20**

WORKING WITH FIELDS

In this chapter

UNDERSTANDING FIELDS

Fields are the often-underappreciated placeholders that work behind the scenes in a document. They help perform the magic involved with many of the most powerful features in Word, such as mail merging, indexing, automatic generation of tables of contents, automatic figure numbering, cross-referencing, page numbering, and more.

There are many different types of fields, each with a specific purpose, but they break down into three main categories. Fields can be used to do the following:

- Insert text or graphics into the document, such as page numbering, dates and times, text from other documents, graphics from external files, document properties, or calculated values.

- Mark a location for later use, such as with a bookmark, table of contents marker, or indexing code.

- Perform an action, such as running a macro or opening a hyperlink in a web browser.

Many people use fields in Word without even realizing it because so many of Word's features automatically insert and modify fields. For example, when you insert a date or time and set it to be automatically updated, Word inserts a {Date} or {Time} code. And when you create an OLE link to an object, Word inserts a {Link} code.

Throughout this book, you've been learning about fields in an indirect way. Whenever a feature has been discussed that used a field, you've learned to insert that field via a button or dialog box, but you haven't looked too deeply yet at what's really going on behind the curtain. Table 20.1 lists some of the Word features that employ fields and cross-references them to where those skills are covered in the book.

TABLE 20.1   WORD FEATURES THAT USE FIELDS

Field	Purpose	Covered in
{AutoText}	Inserts an AutoText entry	"Working with Building Blocks," p. 90
{Bookmark}	Creates a bookmark marker	"Working with Bookmarks," p. 610
{Date}	Inserts an automatically updated date	"Inserting a Date or Time Code," p. 281
{Hyperlink}	Inserts a hyperlink	"Working with Hyperlinks," p. 602
{IncludePicture}	Inserts a non-OLE linked picture from an external file	"Inserting a Picture with {IncludePicture}," p. 627
{IncludeText}	Inserts non-OLE linked text from an external file	"Inserting Text with {IncludeText}," p. 625

20

Field	Purpose	Covered in
{Index}	Generates an index	"Generating the Index," p. 772
{Link}	Inserts an OLE-linked object	"Creating a Link," p. 620
{NoteRef}	Inserts the number for a footnote	"Working with Footnotes and Endnotes," p. 733
{Page}	Inserts an automatically updated page number	"Inserting a Page-Numbering Code," p. 279
{PageRef}	Inserts the number of the page containing the specified bookmark	"Inserting a Cross-Reference to a Bookmark," p. 614
{Ref}	Inserts the text marked by a bookmark	"Inserting a Cross-Reference to a Bookmark," p. 614
{Seq}	Inserts an automatically numbered caption	"Using Figure Captions," p. 482
{Symbol}	Inserts a symbol from a specified font	"Inserting Symbols and Special Characters," p. 63
{Time}	Inserts an automatically updated time	"Inserting a Date or Time Code," p. 281
{TA}	Marks a table of authorities entry	"Creating Citations and Tables of Authorities," p. 761
{TC}	Marks a table of contents entry	"Creating a Table of Contents," p. 748
{TOA}	Inserts a table of authorities	"Creating Citations and Tables of Authorities," p. 761
{TOC}	Inserts a table of contents	"Creating a Table of Contents," p. 748
{XE}	Inserts a marker for an index entry	"Marking Index Entries," p. 767
{=}	Inserts a formula or calculated field	"Performing Math Calculations in a Table," p. 384

This chapter delves into the technical nitty-gritty details that govern fields, and shows you how you can select, insert, modify, and format fields to accomplish a wide variety of document-creation and formatting tasks. Even if you don't end up working manually with fields very often, this is not wasted study! The more you understand about how fields really work, the better you will be able to troubleshoot problems that may occur or to tweak an individual field's options to fit an unusual formatting need.

20

INSERTING FIELDS

Many fields can be inserted via the regular Word user interface, as listed in Table 20.1. However, you can also insert a field using the Insert Field command, a more direct route that provides access to more of the field's optional switches and parameters.

To insert a field, follow these steps:

1. Position the insertion point where you want the field to be inserted.
2. On the Insert tab, click Quick Parts and then click Field. The Field dialog box opens.
3. (Optional) On the Categories list, select a category to narrow down the list of field names.
4. On the Field Names list, click the desired field name. Lists and check boxes appear for the available options for that field. For example, in Figure 20.1, the options for the Date field are shown.
5. Select any options as needed and then click OK.

Figure 20.1
Insert a field from the Field dialog box.

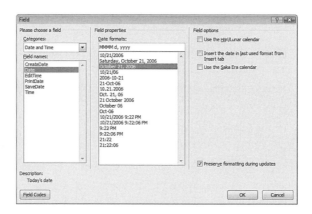

SPECIFYING FIELD PROPERTIES AND OPTIONS

As you insert a field (as in the preceding section), the Field dialog box prompts you to select the properties and options you want. *Field properties* are settings from which you must make a selection (or accept the default). For example, in Figure 20.1, the date format is a property. If you do not choose one, Word uses a default property. *Field options* are optional parameters; to omit them, simply leave their check boxes blank.

If you are interested in the codes behind these user-friendly dialog box controls, click the Field Codes button to display the Field Codes text box. It shows the code that Word will insert for the properties and options you have selected so far (see Figure 20.2).

Figure 20.2
View the codes behind the properties and options you have selected.

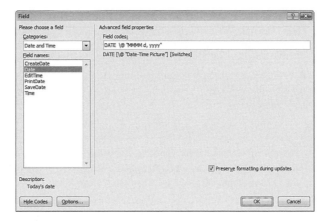

To delve even further into the field's coding, click the Options button to display the Field Options dialog box. Each available switch and option for the field is listed and described on the Field Specific Switches tab. To add one of them, select it and click Add to Field (see Figure 20.3).

NOTE

> The Field Options dialog box doesn't do anything that the check boxes and lists in the Field dialog box don't do, but the description of each option in the Description area of the Field Options dialog box can help you figure out what a particular option does.

Figure 20.3
Work directly with the field's optional switches and properties in the Field Options dialog box.

20

MANUALLY TYPING FIELD CODES

If you know exactly what you want in terms of field codes, you might find it easier and quicker to simply type them into your document.

Field codes are bracketed with curly braces, like this: {Date}. However, you can't manually type the curly braces, because Word won't recognize the code as a field. Instead you must press Ctrl+F9 to get the ball rolling.

Ctrl+F9 inserts a blank set of curly braces in a shaded field box. From there you can type the desired field name and any switches or other syntax needed. (If you don't know the exact syntax you need, it's better to go with the dialog box method of field insertion.)

TIP

> You can add a button to the Quick Access toolbar that starts a new blank set of field braces. Choose Office, Word Options, and click Customize. Select All Commands from the Choose Commands From list. Then select Insert Field Chars and click Add>>.

Here are some tips for getting the syntax right:

- Field names are not case-sensitive.
- If a property or argument contains spaces, you must enclose it in quotation marks. For example, {Username "John Doe"} would be correct. {Username John} would also work because John does not have any spaces in it, but {Username John Doe} would be incorrect.
- If you need a real quotation mark, use "\".
- If you're specifying a path, use double backslashes rather than single—for example, {IncludeText C:\\Docs\\Myfile.doc}. This is necessary because single backslashes indicate switches and special codes.
- Leave one space between the field name and each property or switch.
- Leave one space between the backslash (\) in the switch and its parameters.
- Leave one blank space to the right of the left bracket and to the left of the right bracket.

 To troubleshoot problems with field code syntax, see "Common Syntax Errors in Field Codes" in the Troubleshooting section at the end of this chapter.

TOGGLING BETWEEN DATA AND FIELD CODE VIEWS

By default, a field displays its result in the document rather than its code. (Exception: Fields that do not generate results, such as bookmarks and index markers, do not display at all by default.)

To toggle between displaying the field result and the field code, do either of the following:

- Select the field and press Shift+F9.
- Right-click the field and choose Toggle Field Codes.

Note that this toggles only the selected field. To toggle more than one field at once, select a contiguous area of the document that includes multiple fields and press Shift+F9. To toggle all the field codes in the entire document at once, press Alt+F9, or select the entire document (Ctrl+A) before pressing Shift+F9.

Field codes in the document appear just like they do in the Field dialog box (refer to Figure 20.2). They appear with a gray background, which helps you remember they are fields, but that gray background does not print and does not appear in Print Preview or Full Screen Reading view.

NOTE

> There is one minor difference between what appears in the Field dialog box and what appears with codes displayed inline in the document. If the Preserve Formatting During Updates check box was marked in the Field dialog box, the * MERGEFORMAT switch appears inline. It does not appear in the Field dialog box's version of the code string.

EDITING FIELD CODE STRINGS

When a field code string is displayed in the document (Shift+F9), it can be edited manually just like any other text. The trick is knowing what to type. Many fields have fairly complex code strings with various properties and options.

Most people aren't able to remember all the syntax rules for each field type, of course, so Word provides an easier way to edit a field code string: Right-click the field code and choose Edit Field. The Field dialog box reappears, as in Figure 20.1, and you can make any changes needed via a friendly dialog box interface.

TIP

> After creating a custom field code string, save it to the Quick Parts gallery for easy reuse. To do so, on the Insert tab click Quick Parts, and then click Save Selection to Quick Part Gallery. Store it in any gallery you like. (You might want to create a new category called Custom Fields, for example.)

UPDATING FIELDS

Most fields are not automatically updated each time you open or save the document. (In this way, they differ from OLE linked objects, which are automatically updated by default.)

To update a single field, select it (or click anywhere in it) and press F9, or right-click the field and choose Update Field. If you have toggled the display of the field code string on, updating the field toggles it back to displaying the results.

To update multiple fields at once, select them as part of a contiguous selection range and press F9. To update all the fields in the entire document, select the entire document (Ctrl+A) and press F9. If the update takes too long, you can abort it by pressing Esc.

Not all fields can be updated. Certain fields are not affected by performing an update because they do not pull information from a source that can be changed. For example, the Print, MacroButton, GoToButton, and Eq fields are like that.

In addition, certain fields are not affected by performing a manual update because they automatically update themselves. Examples include Date, Time, Page, and Seq. Date and Time update each time you open or print the document (or open it in Print Preview), and item-numbering fields such as Page and Seq update whenever there is a change in pagination or item sequencing, respectively.

Before we get into specifics, it's worth noting that a lot of keyboard shortcuts are involved in working with fields, and some of them are the only way to accomplish a particular action. Table 20.2 includes a quick summary of these shortcuts.

TABLE 20.2 SUMMARY OF KEYBOARD SHORTCUTS FOR FIELDS

Description	Shortcut
Save changes to the source file (only for {IncludeText}).	Ctrl+Shift+F7
Update the selected field(s).	F9
Toggle field code display.	Shift+F9
Insert a blank set of field braces.	Ctrl+F9
Run macro (only for {MacroButton}).	Alt+Shift+F9
Unlink a field.	Ctrl+Shift+F9
Go to the next field.	F11
Go to the previous field.	Shift+F11
Lock a field from changes.	Ctrl+F11
Unlock a locked field.	Ctrl+Shift+F11

LOCKING FIELDS AGAINST UPDATES

Some fields can be *locked*, so they are never updated even when someone issues an Update Field command on them. For example, if you use a field to enter the current date on the day the document was created, you would not want that field to update every time you open the document.

Some fields have a Prevent Fields from Being Updated check box in the Field dialog box. Marking this check box adds a \ ! switch in the code string for that field. You can type the switch into the code string manually if you find that easier than going back to the Field dialog box.

If the field you want to lock does not have that \ ! switch as part of its syntax, here's another way: Click in the field and press Ctrl+F11. To confirm that the field has been locked, right-click it; the Update Field command will be unavailable on the menu that appears.

To unlock a field that has been locked this way, click in it and press Ctrl+Shift+F11.

UPDATING FIELDS FOR PRINTING

By default, Word does not automatically update fields before printing. This is intentional, because it gives you more control over your data. If you would like to change this behavior so that all links are updated before printing, open the Word Options dialog box (Office, Word Options), click Display, and mark the Update Fields Before Printing check box.

> **TIP**
>
> You do not have to turn on Update Fields Before Printing in order for dates and times to update; they update automatically when you view the document in Print Preview or when you print.

FINDING AND MOVING BETWEEN FIELDS

Sometimes it can be difficult to know where the fields are actually located in a document, especially when some of the fields do not contain any visible content, such as a bookmark or index marker.

There are several ways to surmount this obstacle. One way is to select the entire document and toggle the field codes (Shift+F9). It doesn't take you to the codes, but it makes them easy to see.

Another way, which can actually be combined with the preceding one, is to go to the next field code by pressing F11 or to the previous one by pressing Shift+F11. Word jumps to the beginning of the next or previous field. You might not see anything there (if the field is hidden), but after jumping to that spot, right-click the spot and choose Toggle Field Codes or press Shift+F9 and the field will appear.

A third way is to use the Select Browse Object feature, covered in Chapter 3, "Typing and Editing Text," to move from one field to the next. Click the Select Browse Object button (or press Ctrl+Alt+Home) and choose Browse by Field to go to the next field.

→ To review Select Browse Object as a method of finding objects, **see** "Using Select Browse Object," **p. 86**.

CONVERTING FIELDS TO PLAIN TEXT

If you decide at some point that you will never want to update a particular field again, you can convert it to regular text (that is, *unlink* it). Doing so copies its current value into the document and then deletes the field placeholder.

Before unlinking a field, update it one last time (F9) if needed. Then select it (or select multiple fields to operate on at once) and press Ctrl+Shift+F9. Unlinking can be reversed with an Undo operation, but is otherwise a one-way route. To restore the field, you would need to reinsert it from scratch.

> **NOTE**
>
> Unlinking has no effect on a marker type of field, such as a bookmark or index entry.

SELECTING THE RIGHT FIELD

A big part of using fields in Word is knowing what fields are available and which ones are most applicable to a particular situation. The following sections explain the types of fields available.

DATE AND TIME FIELDS

In Chapter 9, "Formatting Documents and Sections," you learned that you can click Date & Time on the Insert tab to insert a date or time code via a dialog box interface. If you mark the Update Automatically check box in this dialog box, Word inserts a {Date} field rather than the actual date or time. If you toggle the field code on an inserted date, it might look something like this:

```
{ Date \@ "M/d/yyyy" }
```

The main switch for the {Date} field is \@, which is followed by the syntax for the date or time format you want.

> **TIP**
>
> When inserting a date or time via the Field dialog box, the examples that appear in the Date Formats list show today's date. If you are more comfortable choosing based on the generic syntax, such as M/d/yyyy, click the Field Codes button and then click the Options button; the list of formats that appears in the Field Options dialog box shows the generic codes.

The {Date} field has a few other switches, but you'll probably never use them:

- \h is for the Hijri/Lunar calendar.
- \l is used to insert the date with the last format chosen using the Date and Time dialog box.
- \s is used for the Saka Era calendar.

You might be surprised to find that inserting a time with the Date and Time dialog box does *not* insert a {Time} field. Instead it inserts a date field with time-based formatting. For example:

```
{ Date \@ "HH:mm" }
```

So what's the {Time} field for? It's basically the same as {Date}, except with fewer options. You can't specify a certain alternative calendar via switches, for example. Strictly speaking, the {Time} field is redundant. It need not exist, except that people expect it to exist and might not think to use a {Date} field to express a time.

→ To learn how to create custom date and time formats, **see** "Constructing a Custom Date or Time Format," **p. 650**.

Besides the {Date} and {Time} fields, there are several other date/time-related fields from which you can choose. All of them pull their information from the file's properties, not from the PC's clock/calendar.

- {CreateDate} displays the file creation date. It never changes, because the document's creation date never changes.

- {PrintDate} displays the date on which the document was last printed. It updates itself automatically when you print the document.

- {SaveDate} displays the date on which the document was last saved. It updates itself automatically when you save the document.

- {EditTime} displays the total amount of time spent editing the document. It does not update automatically.

Document Information Fields

As you learned in "Inserting a Document Property" in Chapter 9, each document has a set of properties. Some of those properties are editable, such as Author; others are automatically calculated by Word, such as FileSize. These document properties can be inserted into the document using the document information fields.

Most of these fields have an obvious one-to-one correlation with a certain property. For example, the {Author} field inserts the author's name, the {Comments} field inserts any comments that have been placed in the document properties, and so on. The field properties vary depending on the nature of the information being inserted. Fields that insert text have properties for setting text case; fields that insert numbers have properties for choosing a number format. Some fields also have additional options. For example, in Figure 20.4, the {FileSize} field's result can be expressed in either kilobytes or megabytes.

Figure 20.4
Document information fields insert various document properties.

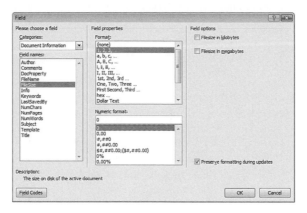

If you do an item-by-item check of fields versus properties, you will find that not every document property has a corresponding field. The {DocProperty} field helps overcome this problem. It is a generic inserter for whatever document property you specify. Its list of available properties includes every property available for the document (except custom properties).

For example, suppose you want to insert the company name from the Company property. There is no Company field, so you would use {DocProperty} like so:

```
{ DocProperty Company }
```

Document Information Content Controls

There is another way of inserting document properties into the document text—content controls. A content control is an XML-based tag that pulls information from a data source—in this case, your document file's properties.

To insert document information via a content control, on the Insert tab click Quick Parts, Document Property and then click the desired piece of information, such as Author.

Content controls are not fields; they are a new type of link in Word 2007. Content controls automatically update when their data changes; for example, if you change the author name of the file, an Author content control will update immediately in the document; in contrast, an {Author} field will not.

USER INFORMATION FIELDS

These three simple fields pull user information from Word. They are somewhat like the document information fields, but this data is not stored with the document, but rather with the logged-in user on the PC:

- {UserAddress} inserts the user's address, if set up in the program. To set up an address, choose Office, Word Options, click Advanced. In the General section, enter the address in the Mailing Address box.

- {UserInitials} inserts the user's initials, if set up in the program. To set up initials, choose Office, Word Options, click Popular, and enter the initials in the Initials box.

- {UserName} enters the user's name, if set up in the program. To set up the name, choose Office, Word Options, click Popular, and enter the name in the User Name box.

NUMBERING FIELDS

The numbering fields all have one thing in common: They help you automatically number various types of items in your document. Each is automatically updated whenever you add more numbering fields or rearrange existing fields. For example, if you switch the positions of two figure captions, they also switch numbering.

Most of the numbering fields are inserted via Word's user interface in various contexts, but a few are available only via the Field dialog box. The numbering fields are listed here:

- {AutoNum} inserts an automatic number. You can specify the formatting you want for it (Arabic, Roman, letters, and so on). Use this to number anything you like. Each {AutoNum} code in the document shows an incremented value.

- {AutoNumLgl} inserts an automatic number in legal format, with or without a trailing period.

- {AutoNumOut} inserts an automatic number in outline format.

The {AutoNum}, {AutoNumLgl}, and {AutoNumOut} fields are all sequenced together, so the same list continues regardless of which of the three field codes you use. There are no switches or properties; the list is completely automatic.

- {BarCode} inserts a delivery point bar code based on the text found in a bookmark. Generally the bookmark would point to a ZIP Code field and would change for each mail merge record with the {Set} field.

- {ListNum} inserts numbering for a list. This is somewhat like {AutoNum}, but rather than there being three separate fields for regular numbers, legal numbers, and outlines, instead there are field properties that define which type of list to use. The valid values for this property are LegalDefault, NumberDefault, and OutlineDefault. Another difference is that you can set the level in the list, and you can set a start-at value, so you can have some control over the list.

- {Page} inserts the number of the current page. This is most commonly used in headers and footers, but can be used anywhere in the document.

- {RevNum} counts the number of times the document has been saved. Each time it is saved, the {RevNum} counter is incremented.

- {Section} displays the section number in which the field is placed.

- {SectionPages} displays the total number of pages in the section in which the field is placed.

- {Seq} inserts an automatic sequence number. This is the field used for figure captions and other automatically numbered items. A bookmark is created to indicate what type of item is being sequenced. For example, to automatically number figures, each figure would have a caption like this: Figure {Seq Figure}. Optional switches can be added for formatting—for example, {Seq Figure \? ARABIC}.

EQUATION AND FORMULA FIELDS

These math-related fields are mostly covered elsewhere in Word; you will seldom have reason to insert them manually via the Field dialog box. Here's a quick round-up of them:

- {=} is a formula field. Do not try to construct its syntax manually; instead, click the Formula button in the Field dialog box and construct the formula via the Formula dialog box.

- {Advance} offsets the position of the subsequent text by a specified number of points in a specified direction. You might use this to fine-tune the positioning of text on a page when trying to make printed text line up correctly on a preprinted form, for example.

For the {Advance} field, the expected entries for the field options are not obvious in the Field dialog box. For more information, click Field Codes, and then click Options to see a complete list of the switches and get information about each one.

- {Eq} inserts an equation using the legacy-style Equation Editor (that is, the version from Word 97-2003). Word does not recommend that you construct the syntax manually; click the Equation Editor button in the Field dialog box to open the legacy Equation Editor.

- {Symbol} inserts a symbol, by character number, from a specified font. If no font is specified, the font assigned to the paragraph in which the field resides takes precedence. Usually it is preferable to use the Symbol insertion controls on the Insert tab to insert a symbol because you can browse for the desired symbol more easily (that is, you don't have to know its number).

INDEX AND TABLE FIELDS

These fields mark entries for tables of contents, indexes, and tables of authorities, and then generate those items. (The "Table" in this category's name refers to tables of contents, tables of authorities, and tables of figures, not to ordinary Word tables.)

These codes are hardly ever inserted manually. A user would use the Table of Contents, Table of Authorities, or Index feature in Word to insert the markers and generate the listings. However, it is useful to know what the various codes mean, in case you see them in documents and need to decide whether to keep or delete them.

These are the codes for indexes:

- {XE} marks index entries. Various properties and options are available for defining an entry, but these are best created with the Mark Index Entry dialog box (covered in Chapter 26, "Building Effective Indexes").

- {Index} generates the index.

For tables of contents, these codes apply:

- {TC} marks table of contents entries. Usually tables of contents are generated automatically based on heading levels, but you can use this field to manually mark some text to be included.

- {TOC} generates the table of contents.

For tables of authorities:

- {TA} marks the table of authorities entries.

- {TOA} generates the table of authorities.

→ To create an index, **see** "Marking Index Entries," **p. 767** and "Generating the Index," **p. 772**.
→ To create a table of contents, **see** "Creating a Table of Contents," **p. 748**.
→ To create a table of authorities, **see** "Creating Citations and Tables of Authorities," **p. 761**.

LINK AND REFERENCE FIELDS

This category contains fields that insert linked content from other locations, as well as fields that do automatic numbering of pages and footnotes. (Automatic numbering of other items, such as list numbering or figure caption numbering, is handled by fields in the Numbering category, covered previously in this chapter.)

Several of the linking-type fields were covered in Chapter 19, "Copying, Linking, and Embedding Data." Here's a quick review of those:

- {Hyperlink} inserts a hyperlink. Hyperlinks are more commonly inserted via the Hyperlink command on the Insert tab.

- {Link} inserts an OLE link to an object. OLE links are more commonly inserted via Paste Special or the Insert Object command.

- {IncludePicture} inserts a non-OLE link to an external picture. Picture links are more commonly inserted via the Insert Picture dialog box, by selecting Insert and Link from the Insert button's drop-down list.

- {IncludeText} inserts a non-OLE link to an external text file. Text links are more commonly inserted via the Insert Text from File command, by selecting Insert as Link from the Insert button's drop-down list.

The following fields insert numbering codes:

- {NoteRef} inserts the number of a footnote or endnote. These numbers are automatically updated as content changes in the document. These are normally placed via footnote and endnote insertion.

- {PageRef} inserts the page number on which the specified bookmark appears. This code is inserted when you create a cross-reference that refers to a page number.

And these fields insert text strings of various types:

- {Quote} inserts a literal text string that you specify. For example, {Quote "Hello world"} displays the text Hello world.

- {Ref} inserts text marked by a bookmark. You learned about this one in Chapter 19, in the section "Inserting a Cross-Reference to a Bookmark."

- {StyleRef} inserts the text from a paragraph that has the specified style applied. For example, if you have the title of your document set up with a style called DocTitle, the field {StyleRef DocTitle} would insert that title later in the document.

There are also two AutoText-related fields:

- {AutoText} inserts the specified AutoText entry as an updatable link. This is different from inserting AutoText items from the Building Blocks feature, as in "Working with Building Blocks" in Chapter 3, because the latter inserts an unlinked, non-updatable copy.

- {AutoTextList} creates a shortcut menu based on AutoText entries in the active template. You specify some placeholder text to appear in the field. When the user right-clicks the field, a pop-up list appears of AutoText entries to choose from to fill in that field.

20

Creating a Pop-up List

The {AutoTextList} field generates a pop-up list based on the style applied to the field and the items in the AutoText gallery that share that same style. Here's a quick exercise to see how it works:

1. Create a new paragraph style called Popup (or anything else you want to call it).

2. Type the text for the first entry you want on your pop-up list into the document and then apply the Popup style to it.

3. Select the entire entry, and on the Insert tab, click Quick Parts and click Save Selection to Quick Part Gallery.

4. In the Create New Building Block dialog box, set the Gallery to AutoText and save it there.

5. Repeat steps 2–4 for each item you want to appear on the pop-up menu.

6. Position the insertion point where you want the field and then press Ctrl+F9 to start a new, blank field. Within the field's curly braces, type the following:

   ```
   AutoTextList "Right-click here" \s Popup
   ```

7. Press Shift+F9 to toggle the field codes off.

8. Right-click the field, and a menu appears showing your AutoText choices.

9. Click one of the choices on the menu to fill in the field.

DOCUMENT AUTOMATION FIELDS

The document automation fields are used for setting up code strings that automate processes in the document. Some programmers prefer to use document automation fields rather than Visual Basic for Applications for some basic automation tasks like filling in a form with user information or determining whether one value equals another. Here are a few simple examples.

The {Compare} field compares two values and returns a 1 if the comparison is true or 0 if it is false. It is a programming construct, useful for setting up logical conditions. For example, you might count the number of words in the document with the {NumWords} field and then compare that value to 1000:

```
{ Compare {NumWords} >= 1000 }
```

This {Compare} field returns a 1 if the word count is 1000 or above; otherwise, it returns a 0.

The 1 and 0 are all well and good, but it might be nicer to show some meaningful text based on the condition. For that, we need an {If} field. An {If} field's syntax is:

```
Expression1 Operator Expression2 TextTrue TextFalse
```

Suppose, for example, that if {NumWords} is at least 1000, we want to print "OK" in the document; otherwise, we want to print "Need More Words". Here's the {If} field that would do the job:

```
{ IF {NumWords} >= 1000 "OK" "Need More Words" }
```

20

Here are the other available document automation fields:

- {DocVariable} inserts the value of a VBA Word document variable. (This is not the same as the document's properties, which you can insert with document information fields covered previously in this chapter.)

- {GoToButton} inserts a button that, when clicked, jumps the insertion point to a specified bookmarked location.

- {MacroButton} inserts a button that, when clicked, runs a specified macro.

- {Print} sends a print instruction to the printer; it could be used to automatically print a document, for example. It is usually combined with some other field, such as {If}, rather than standing alone.

> **NOTE**
>
> If you want to learn more about working with Visual Basic, Sams Publishing has an excellent resource: *Sams Teach Yourself Microsoft Visual Basic .NET 2003 in 21 Days*, 2nd Edition, by Steve Holzner (ISBN# 0-6723-2531-4).

MAIL MERGE FIELDS

Chapter 18, "Performing Mail and Data Merges," covers the Mail Merge feature in Word, which is a very robust tool for merging the data from one file or database with a document in another file. Most of the fields involved in mail merging are automatically inserted when you work through the mail merge, or they can be inserted using the Rules list on the Mailings tab.

- {AddressBlock} inserts data pulled from multiple fields in order to form a standard postal mailing address.

- {Ask} prompts the user to enter a value to be stored in a bookmark. The content of that bookmark can then be inserted anywhere in the document via the {Ref} field.

- {Compare} compares two values and shows a 1 or 0, depending on whether they match or not. You learned about this field earlier in the chapter in the "Document Automation Fields" section.

- {Database} inserts the results of a database query in a Word table.

- {Fill-in} prompts the user to enter a value and then displays it in the field. This is different from {Ask} in that it does not store the value in a bookmark for later reuse.

- {GreetingLine} inserts a greeting line in a mail merge document. You can optionally use the \e switch to specify what name to use if the name is blank. For example, you might want something like *Dear Valued Customer*.

- {If} prescribes two different actions to take based on the outcome of a logical test. This is like {Compare} except you can specify the output in each situation rather than accepting the default 1 and 0 outputs.

- {MergeField} inserts a mail merge field. It requires a field name property, like this: {MergeField FirstName}.

20

- {MergeRec} numbers each merged record in a mail merge. If any records are excluded by a filter, they will still be numbered and the numbered records will have gaps in the numbering.

- {MergeSeq} also numbers each merged record in a mail merge, but does not number any records excluded by a filter.

- {Next} goes to the next record.

- {NextIf} goes to the next record in a mail merge only if a condition is met.

- {Set} assigns new text to a bookmark.

- {SkipIf} skips the next record in a mail merge only if a condition is met. It is the opposite of {NextIf}.

FORMATTING FIELDS

When a field inserts data from another source, such as from a bookmark or an external text file, the formatting of the original is inserted too. For example, suppose you bookmark the text *The New Deal* in one section of your document, and you create a bookmark for it called NewDeal. Now when you insert that bookmarked text elsewhere in the document with the {Ref NewDeal} field, the inserted text will appear bold and in italics too.

That's the basic default for the formatting, but there are some ways to circumvent that, as you'll learn in the next several sections.

PREVENTING THE FORMATTING FROM CHANGING

What happens if you change the formatting of the original and then update the field? That depends on a switch. Ordinarily the formatting would change, but you can prevent it from changing by using the * MERGEFORMAT switch. For example:

```
{ Ref NewDeal \* MERGEFORMAT }
```

MERGEFORMAT can also be employed to lock in any manual formatting you have applied to the field.

SPECIFYING FONT FORMATTING FOR A FIELD

To apply specific font formatting to the text displayed in a field, toggle the field code display on and then format the first character in the field name the way you want the field result to be. (Font formatting in this context includes font, size, color, and attributes such as bold, italic, and underline.)

For example, with the {Ref} example from the preceding section, suppose you want to format that field's result as italic. Select the "R" in "Ref" and click the Italic button mini toolbar that appears. Then add * charformat to the end of the code string (this part is not required if the field has no arguments):

```
{ Ref NewDeal \* charformat }
```

Then update the field (F9) to see the change.

SPECIFYING A NUMBERING TYPE

Numeric fields can use any of several types of characters to represent the numbers, such as Arabic (1, 2, 3), Roman (I, II, III), and so on. To specify the type of numbering, use the * switch followed by the appropriate code. The easiest way to set a numbering type is in the Field dialog box; it provides a list of the available types. Alternatively, you can use switches in the field code, as in Table 20.3. (Note that the codes are case-sensitive; alphabetic is different from ALPHABETIC, for example.)

TABLE 20.3   CODES FOR NUMBERING TYPES

Numbering	Switch	Example	Notes
1, 2, 3	* Arabic	23	
a, b, c	* alphabetic	w	After the 26th letter, the letters start repeating: 27 would be aa, 28 would be ab, and so on.
A, B, C	* ALPHABETIC	W	Same as above except uppercase.
i, ii, iii	* roman	xxiii	
I, II, III	* ROMAN	XXIII	
1st, 2nd, 3rd	* Ordinal	23rd	
First, Second, Third	* Ordtext	twenty-third	
One, Two, Three	* Cardtext	twenty-three	
Hex	* Hex	17	Hexadecimal numbering. Each place is 16, so 23 would be ×161 plus ×17.
Dollar Text	* DollarText	Twenty-three and 00/100	Format traditionally used for writing checks.

CONSTRUCTING A CUSTOM NUMERIC FORMAT

A numeric field's number format (a.k.a. the *numeric picture*) controls the appearance of the number in cosmetic ways, such as its number of decimal places, the presence of currency symbols or percent signs, and so on.

The easiest way to set the number format is in the Field dialog box; a list of available types is provided. It is much easier to construct the codes this way than to build them manually. Alternatively, you can use the \# switch, followed by the numbering format in quotation marks. For example:

```
{ FileSize \# "#,##0" }
```

If you want to build the numbering format code manually, consult Table 20.4 for the symbols to use.

20

TABLE 20.4 CODES FOR NUMERIC PICTURES

Character	Purpose	Notes
#	A number if present; otherwise, a blank space. Rounds off extra fractional digits.	Use this to limit a number to a maximum number of decimal places, like this: #.##. Any places not needed do not appear.
0	A number if present; otherwise, a zero.	Use this to force a number to a minimum number of decimal places, like this: 0.00. Any places not needed appear as zeros.
$	Places a literal dollar sign in the field result.	
+	Places a plus or minus sign in front of any field result other than zero.	This is not a literal plus sign; it will change to a minus sign for a negative number.
-	Places a minus sign in front of negative numbers.	This is not a literal minus sign; it will not appear for a positive number.
.	Places a literal decimal point in the field result.	Use this to separate # or 0 codes to show where in the number those codes are referring to. For example, 0.0# indicates a required digit before and after the decimal point in the number, and an optional second decimal place if needed.
,	Places a literal comma in the field result.	Use this to separate hundreds from thousands to the left of the decimal point: #,###.##. It does not necessarily conform to common usage that dictates a comma every third place; you could just as easily set up one like #,0 that would place a comma between the first and second digits.
;	Separates multiple options for a number.	You can have separate formatting sections for positive, negative, and zero numbers, in that order. For example, $###.00;($###.00),$0.00.
text	Adds literal text to the format.	Enclose in single quotes. For example, use this to include the word *Dollars* after the number: ###.00 'Dollars'

CONSTRUCTING A CUSTOM DATE OR TIME FORMAT

When you select a date or time from the Date and Time dialog box, or from the Field dialog box, a list of sample formats appears. Choosing a format from one of those locations relieves you of the need to manually construct a date/time picture with switches.

However, in some cases, the format you want might not be available on the list. In such situations, you must manually construct the needed code for the switch yourself.

For date and time fields, a \@ switch is used, followed by the desired formatting codes in quotation marks. For example:

```
{ Date \@ "MMMM d yyyy" }
{ Time \@ "hh:mm AM/PM" }
```

The code is a combination of placeholders and literal characters. The valid literal characters are colon (:), dash (-), and slash (\). They are used to separate the parts of the date or time. Typically colons are used to separate hours, minutes, and seconds in times, and dashes or slashes are used to separate months, days, and years in dates.

The valid characters for placeholders are shown in Table 20.5.

TABLE 20.5   CODES FOR DATE OR TIME FORMATS

Characters	Purpose	Sample Code	Sample Result
M	Month number, 1 through 12	{ Date \@ "M" }	8
MM	Month number, 01 through 12	{ Date \@ "MM" }	08
MMM	Three-letter month abbreviation	{ Date \@ "MMM" }	Aug
MMMM	Full month name	{ Date \@ "MMMM" }	August
d	Day number, 1 through 31	{ Date \@ "d" }	5
dd	Day number, 01 through 31	{ Date \@ "dd" }	05
ddd	Three-letter day of the week abbreviation	{ Date \@ "ddd" }	Tue
dddd	Full day of the week	{ Date \@ "dddd" }	Tuesday
y	Two-digit year	{ Date \@ "y" }	07
yy	Four-digit year	{ Date \@ "yy" }	2007
h	Hour on 12-hour clock, 1 through 12	{ Time \@ "h" }	3
hh	Hour on 12-hour clock, 01 through 12	{ Time \@ "hh" }	03
H	Hour on 24-hour clock, 0 to 23	{ Time \@ "H" }	3 or 17
HH	Hour on 24-hour clock, 00 to 23	{ Time \@ "HH" }	03 or 17
m	Minutes, 0 to 59	{ Time \@ "m" }	4
mm	Minutes, 00 to 59	{ Time \@ "mm" }	04
AM/PM	AM or PM, uppercase	{ Time \@ "hh:mm AM/PM }	03:04 AM
am/pm	am or pm, lowercase	{ Time \@ "hh:mm am/pm }	03:04 am

20

NESTING FIELDS

When using fields that require input, such as the logical condition ones like {Compare} and {If}, you might sometimes want that input to come from other fields. To manage this, you can nest one field inside of another.

For example, you might want to test whether today is a certain day of the week. If it is Friday, this message should appear: "Time cards are due today by 5:00 p.m." Otherwise, this message should appear: "Time cards are due on Fridays by 5:00 p.m." Here's the complete syntax for that:

```
{ If { Date \@ "dddd" } = "Friday" "Time cards are due today by 5:00 p.m." "Time
cards are due on Fridays by 5:00 p.m." }
```

The main thing to remember when nesting fields is that you can't type the braces for the nested fields; you must insert the braces with Ctrl+F9. Let's go over the general process.

First, you would start the outer field:

1. Press Ctrl+F9 to insert a new blank set of braces.
2. Type the desired field name and then any portion of the field's properties or switches that should come before the nested field.
3. Press Ctrl+F9 to insert another new blank set of braces, and in the new set, type the field to be nested.
4. Click to move the insertion point to the right of the closing bracket for the nested field, and continue typing the outer field.
5. Press F9 to update the field and display its result.

Here's another example. The {Set} field is used to create a bookmark. It requires two pieces of information: the bookmark name and the text that should be placed within it. So, for example, if you want to create a bookmark called CompanyName and set its value to Microsoft, the field should read as follows:

```
{ Set CompanyName "Microsoft" }
```

That's fine, but what if the company name changes? You can instead use the {FillIn} field to ask the user to specify the company name:

```
{ Set CompanyName { FillIn "Enter the company name" } }
```

Now suppose you want to enter that company's name in the Title field of the document's properties. Create another nested set of fields like this:

```
{ Title { Ref CompanyName } }
```

TROUBLESHOOTING

FIELD DOESN'T UPDATE

Remember, most fields do not update automatically. To manually update a field, right-click it and choose Update Field, or select it and press F9.

If neither of these methods works, check to make sure the field is not locked. Try unlocking it by selecting the field and pressing Ctrl+Shift+F11. Also examine the field's code and make sure that the \! switch is not present. (That switch locks the field against changes.)

Check to make sure that it's actually a field. When you right-click it, does the Update Field command appear on the shortcut menu? If not, perhaps it's not a field; it might have gotten unlinked (perhaps you accidentally pressed Ctrl+Shift+F9 on it to unlink it), or it might not have been a correctly constructed field in the first place.

If all else fails, delete the field and re-create it.

COMMON SYNTAX ERRORS IN FIELD CODES

When manually typing the code for a field, it is easy to make a mistake. Word fields have different syntax than you might be used to in Excel functions or VBA, for example.

Here are some of the most commonly broken syntax rules. If you're having a problem with a field code, check to make sure you are following all of these rules:

- Spaces are required between the outer braces and the codes inside them.

  Right: `{ Date }`

  Wrong: `{Date}`

- Spaces are required between each argument and switch in the code, and between the switch and its parameter.

  Right: `{ Date \@ "hh:mm" }`

  Wrong: `{ Date\@"hh:mm" }`

- Text strings must be in quotation marks if they contain any spaces.

  Right: `{ Set CompanyName "ACME Corporation" }`

  Wrong: `{ Set CompanyName ACME Corporation }`

- Do not use colons, semicolons, commas, or any other characters to separate arguments or parameters. (This is not an Excel function!)

  Right: `{ If { Date \n "MM/dd" } = 12/25 "Merry Christmas!" "Have a nice day!" }`

  Wrong `{ If { Date \n "MM/dd" } = 12/25; "Merry Christmas!"; "Have a nice day!" }`

- When nesting fields, do not manually type the curly braces for the inner field; insert them with Ctrl+F9.

CHAPTER **21**

CREATING FORMS

In this chapter

UNDERSTANDING FORMS

Forms enable you to collect information from people via a fill-in-the-blanks interface. The forms you create in Word can be printed and completed on paper or filled out from within Word. With a little extra programming know-how, they can also be connected to an XML data system or an Access database.

Word 2007 introduces a whole new class of form fields called *content controls*, which are used throughout Office 2007 applications as a means of interfacing with external data sources. These content controls have some great new capabilities that were not present in earlier versions of Word, but they also have a few drawbacks to them. Therefore, Word 2007 also provides access to—and support for—legacy form controls that will work in backward-compatible documents. In this chapter, you'll learn about both.

DESIGNING THE FORM

The first step in creating a form is to create an ordinary Word document that contains all the "fixed" text used on the form. For example, before creating a Name field that the user fills in, first type **Name** in the document and leave some space after it for the field to come later. To ensure that there is enough space for the fields, you might enter dummy characters where they will go, like this:

Name: &&&&&&&&&&&&&&&&&&&&&&&
Address: &&&&&&&&&&&&&&&&&&&&&&&
City: &&&&&&&&&&&&& State: && ZIP: &&&&-&&&&

If you simply type the text and placeholders into a document, though, the form might not be as tidy as you would like. Notice in the preceding example how the Name and Address text, having different numbers of characters, start the field at different spots. Adding a Tab character after the colon for each label might help with that:

Name: &&&&&&&&&&&&&&&&&&&&&&&
Address: &&&&&&&&&&&&&&&&&&&&&&&
City: &&&&&&&&&&&&& State: && ZIP: &&&&-&&&&

There's still an alignment issue with the State and ZIP, though. They aren't aligned with anything in particular; they're just hanging out there after City. So what if you put the whole thing into a table, like this?

Name:					
Address:					
City:		State:		ZIP:	

As you can see, a table can be a great help in creating a form on which the fields and labels align in an orderly way, and if you define separate cells for each label and entry, you don't need the placeholders to define where the fields will go. Tables are not appropriate for every form project, but they're a good addition to your toolbox of techniques.

The form does not necessarily have to be in a single table; you could divide it up into several tables, or you could use a combination of regular text and tables. Figure 21.1 shows an example. This is pure text and table at the moment—it contains no form fields.

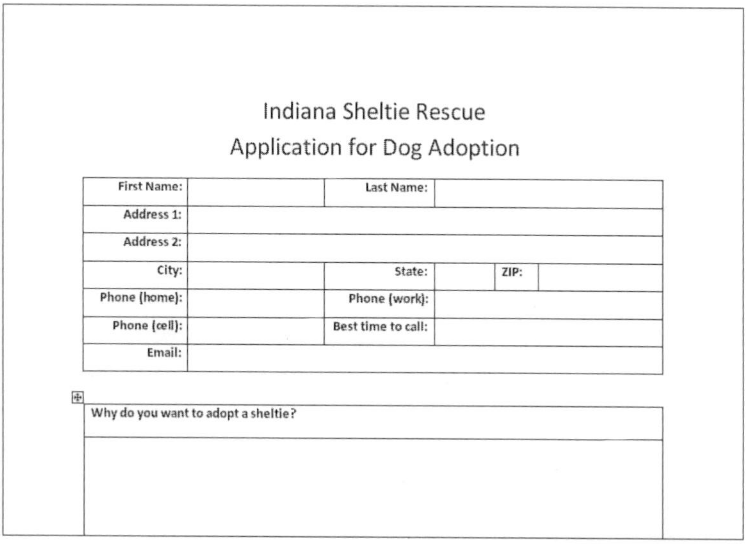

Figure 21.1
Create the skeleton of a form, to be populated with form fields later.

Indiana Sheltie Rescue
Application for Dog Adoption

First Name:		Last Name:	
Address 1:			
Address 2:			
City:		State:	ZIP:
Phone (home):		Phone (work):	
Phone (cell):		Best time to call:	
Email:			

Why do you want to adopt a sheltie?

Using whatever layout you find the most expedient for your situation, design the form and lay out all its pieces with placeholders, as in the preceding examples. Here are some tips:

- **Arrange fields in logical groups**—Group the information into sections based on the type of information being gathered. For example, in Figure 21.1, the contact information is in one group, and each question being asked of the applicant is in a separate group. Each group is in its own table in this example, but you don't necessarily have to use tables for yours.

- **Place fields in the expected order**—People expect certain fields to be in a standard order. For example, they expect City to come before State. If you mix them up, users may have problems filling out the form.

- **Plan for different types of fields**—When you actually insert the fields, you will be able to use not only text boxes, but drop-down lists, option buttons, and check boxes. If you think any of those will be useful, insert placeholders for them—and leave enough space for them. For example, a set of option buttons takes up more space than a drop-down list.

- **Leave enough space for user input**—Users will be frustrated if their information won't fit on the form. Leave plenty of space for names, addresses, and so on. Theophilus Maximillian Kreutzcampf will thank you for it.

21

■ **Be clear with your labels**—Make sure it's obvious what users should put in each field. For example, suppose you have a City of Birth field, followed by a field labeled Date. Do you want the date of birth there, or the current date? Fifty percent of your users will probably guess wrong.

SAVING THE FORM AS A TEMPLATE

The form isn't finished yet, of course, but now is a good time to save your work as a template. You'll want a template file, not a regular document file, because users will be creating new documents based upon it.

To save the form as a template, follow these steps:

1. Choose Office, Save As. The Save As dialog box opens.
2. Open the Save as Type list and choose Word Macro-Enabled Template (.dotm).

   If you aren't planning on storing any macros in the template, you could go with Word Template (.dotx) instead.
3. In the File Name box, type the name for the template file (see Figure 21.2).

TIP

> If you want the template to be easily accessible when starting a new document, store it in the default location for user templates:
> C:\Users*username*\AppData\Roaming\Microsoft\Templates.

4. Click Save. The template is saved.

Figure 21.2
Save the document as a template. (You'll resave it after inserting the form fields later.)

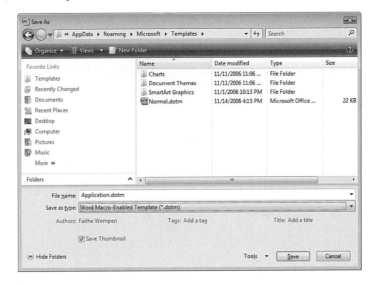

CAUTION

> Make sure you choose Word Template or Word Macro-Enabled Template and not Word 97-2003 Template. If you go with a legacy format, you will not be able to access the Word 2007 content controls. See the next section for a discussion of the types of form fields.

WORD 2007 OR LEGACY FIELDS?

Now you're ready to start inserting the form fields. There are two kinds, though—the Word 2007 form fields (a.k.a. content controls) and the legacy form fields that are a carryover from earlier Word versions.

The Word 2007 form fields are a natural choice if all the users of your form will be using Word 2007. Here are some of the advantages:

- There are more types of controls, including rich text, pictures, and a calendar/date picker.
- The document doesn't have to be protected for forms, so you won't have troubles with disabled commands such as spell-checking that plague protected forms.
- You can set a content control so that it can't be deleted, or so that it unlinks itself immediately after it's filled in.
- Their XML format makes form fields ideal for connecting with XML data sources.

There are a few things you can't do with Word 2007 content controls that the legacy forms could do, however:

- You can't save the data only in a separate Word document.
- You can't easily link a macro to a control.
- You can't automatically format input in a predefined number format (such as currency, for example).
- You can't set up a form field that performs a calculation.
- You can't limit the length of an entry.
- You can't fill out a Word 2007 form in an earlier version of Word.

This chapter focuses mostly on the new content controls, but also provides information about the legacy form fields in case you need their capabilities or their backward compatibility.

It is possible to combine the two types of fields in a single form. For example, you could use Word 2007–style controls for all the text boxes, and then if you have any check boxes to include (which Word 2007 controls do not provide), you could use legacy check box fields.

However, beware when combining the two field types, because they work very differently behind the scenes. Here are some reasons to stick to one field type or the other:

- **Saving data only**—If you want to save the data only from the form into a plain-text file (covered later in this chapter), use legacy fields only. This won't work with Word 2007 fields.

21

- **Supporting Word 97-2003 users**—If the form will be filled out by people who use earlier versions of Word, use legacy fields only, and make sure you save the template as a Word 97-2003 template (.dot), not a Word 2007 .dotx or .dotm file.

CAUTION

> If you create a form using content controls and then use Save As to save the form in a Word 97-2003 format, a warning appears telling you that the fields will be converted to static text. That's right—static text, not legacy form fields. You lose all your form fields with that backward-saving, so make sure you construct the form using legacy fields if you think you will be saving in an older format later.

- **Preparing a database front end**—If you are creating the form as a user interface for entering data into a database, check with the database developer to find out what type of fields you should use—Word 2007 or legacy. Stick only with that type. Don't mix and match because that will make the programming of the connection difficult or impossible.

On the other hand, if you are creating a form to be printed, or to be filled out in Word 2007 only and saved as a new Word 2007 document, both field types can be used freely.

DISPLAYING THE DEVELOPER TAB

To work with forms, you need to work with the Developer tab. It does not appear by default. Here's how to display it:

1. Choose Office, Word Options.
2. Click Popular.
3. Click Show Developer tab in the ribbon.
4. Click OK.

The Developer tab appears just to the right of the View tab. On the Developer tab is a Controls group that contains the buttons you will need to build your form.

The Controls group contains seven buttons for Word 2007 content controls, plus one button for legacy and ActiveX controls. That latter button opens a palette of the legacy controls, as shown in Figure 21.3.

Figure 21.3
The Controls group on the Developer tab is used to insert form fields.

The Design Mode button in the Controls group toggles the form between Design Mode (where fields can be added and edited) and regular mode (where fields can be used to collect information).

CREATING A FORM WITH CONTENT CONTROLS

Content controls work only in Word 2007 documents and templates. They look nice (friendly pale-blue frames with names, as opposed to the plain drab gray boxes in legacy forms), and they are easy for users to understand and use. You can apply formatting styles to them, and you can prevent them from being edited or deleted.

INSERTING A CONTENT CONTROL

To insert a content control, follow these steps:

1. Position the insertion point where you want the new control.
2. On the Developer tab, make sure Design Mode is selected.
3. Click one of the content control buttons on the Controls group to insert it into the document.

There are seven content controls you can insert, summarized in Table 21.1.

TABLE 21.1   CONTENT CONTROL TYPES

Control	Purpose
Aa Rich Text	Holds text that can optionally be formatted by the user (bold, italic, and so on).
Aa Plain Text	Holds plain text that the user cannot format.
Picture	Holds a picture that the user inserts.
Combo Box	Displays a list of values from which the user can select, and also allows the user to enter other values.
List Box	Displays a list of values from which the user can select. Other values are not permitted.
Date Picker	Displays a calendar from which the user can click a date.
Building Block Gallery	Inserts a placeholder from which the user can select a building block from a gallery you specify.

CONFIGURING A CONTROL

A content control is generic after insertion; you must provide its context via its Properties box. To view the Properties for a control, right-click it and choose Properties, or select it and then click the Properties button in the Controls group on the Developer tab.

NOTE

If you insert the content control into a table, right-clicking shows the Table Properties option. To get to the properties for the control in that case, use the Properties button on the Developer tab.

21

SETTINGS COMMON TO ALL CONTROL TYPES

The options available in the Properties dialog box depend on the control type, but all controls have a Title box, in which you specify the text that should appear in the thin blue bar across the top of the control. Figure 21.4 shows a photo with a title of January, for example.

The Locking settings shown in Figure 21.4 are also available for all types of controls:

- **Content control cannot be deleted**—This prevents users from deleting the control itself.
- **Contents cannot be edited**—This prevents users from changing what they enter in the control after the initial entry.

Figure 21.4
These content control options are common to all types of controls.

STYLE OPTIONS

By default, a field takes on the paragraph formatting of whatever paragraph you place it in. For some field types, though, you can override this formatting by applying a different style to the field entry.

For Rich Text, Plain Text, Combo Box, and List Box, you can mark Use a Style to Format Contents and then select a style from the Style list (see Figure 21.5). You can also click New Style to create a new style on the fly for it.

Figure 21.5
For text fields you can specify a style to apply.

MULTIPARAGRAPH TEXT OPTIONS

For a plain-text field only, you can choose Allow Carriage Returns (Multiple Paragraphs). This option enables users to press Enter to start a new paragraph within the field. This option is not available for rich-text fields because they always allow this.

FIELD-REMOVAL OPTIONS

For both rich text and plain text, you can choose Remove Content Control When Contents Are Edited. This option deletes the field placeholder after the user enters text into it, leaving only the text as a regular part of the document.

LIST OPTIONS

Combo boxes and list boxes enable you to set up the list that appears when the user activates the control. In the Drop Down List Properties area of the Content Control Properties dialog box, follow these steps:

1. Click Add. The Add Choice dialog box opens.
2. Enter the Display Name. This is the text that will appear on the screen.
3. Enter the Value. This is what will be entered into the database if one is connected to the form; otherwise, this just gets stored with the field (see Figure 21.6).

Figure 21.6
Set up a list from which users can select.

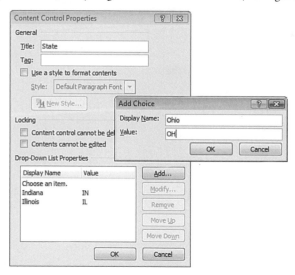

4. Click OK.
5. Repeat steps 1–4 to add more choices to the menu.
6. (Optional) Modify the list by doing any of the following:
   - To modify an entry, select it, click Modify, make changes, and click OK.
   - To delete an entry, select it and click Remove.
   - To reorder the list, select an item and click Move Up or Move Down.
7. Click OK.

21

Date Options

For a date field, you can control these four settings, as shown in Figure 21.7:

- **Display the Date Like This**—Select a format from the list provided.
- **Locale**—Select a country and language.
- **Calendar Type**—Select a type based on your country. In the United States and most of Europe, the calendar is Western.
- **Store XML Contents in the Following Format When Mapped**—This setting is important only if you will be connecting to an XML data source. Select from the list of formats provided.

Figure 21.7
Set date options for a Date content control.

Building Block Options

The same versatile building blocks that you have learned about in other chapters are available for use in forms. For example, you can access any built-in or custom galleries such as Equations, AutoText, and Quick Parts.

The implications of this capability are significant. For example, suppose you have a set of boilerplate paragraphs that you want to be able to select among when composing letters. You could place a Building Blocks field in your template and then have easy access to those paragraphs by clicking that field whenever you are creating a new letter.

The default building block content control doesn't do anything at first; you have to set it up to be associated with a certain gallery and category. To set that up, choose a gallery and category from the Document Building Block Properties.

CAUTION

Building block insertion works only if the PC on which the form is being completed has the same Building Blocks available.

→ To learn more about building blocks, including how to create your own categories, **see** "Working with Building Blocks, **p. 90**.

EDITING PLACEHOLDER TEXT

The placeholder text for a content control is the text that appears inside the box by default, with instructions such as *Click here to enter text.* You can customize the wording of that instruction so that it is different for each field if you like. For example, for a control that holds first names, you could change it to *Click here and type your first name.*

To edit a placeholder, follow these steps:

1. Make sure Design Mode is selected on the Developer tab.
2. Click the content control. An arrow appears above it.
3. Click the arrow to open a menu, and choose Edit Placeholder Text.
4. Type the desired text. You won't see an insertion point until you start typing.
5. Click away from the placeholder to save your changes to it.

CREATING A FORM WITH LEGACY FORM FIELDS

Legacy form fields are the field types that were available in earlier versions of Word. You can continue to use them in Word 2007, and you *must* use them for forms to be saved in Word 97-2003 format.

Legacy form fields are accessible from the Legacy Tools button's menu in the Controls group on the Developer tab, as you saw in Figure 21.3. Table 21.2 explains each of them.

TABLE 21.2   LEGACY FORM FIELD TYPES

Form Field Type	Purpose
ab Text Form Field	Holds text. Unlike with content controls, the text cannot be formatted within the field; however, the field itself can be formatted.
☑ Checkbox Form Field	Creates an on/off check box.
Drop-down Form Field	Displays a list containing values you specify. Users cannot add their own entries.

21

Yes, there are only three types of legacy form fields. The other three buttons in the Legacy Forms section of the list have other purposes. Table 21.3 describes them.

TABLE 21.3   OTHER LEGACY FORM TOOLS

Tool	Purpose
Insert Frame	Creates a frame. Frames are similar to text boxes; they hold static content.
Form Field Shading	Toggles form field shading on/off.
Reset Form Fields	Clears all entries in fields.

→ For more information about the differences, and about when to use a frame versus a text box, **see** "Working with Frames," **p. 331**.

INSERTING A LEGACY FIELD

To insert any legacy field, follow these steps:

1. Position the insertion point where you want the field.

2. On the Developer tab, make sure Design Mode is selected.

3. In the Controls group, click the Legacy Tools button. Its palette of tools appears.

4. Click the desired field type.

The field appears in the document as either a shaded gray box (for drop-down lists and text boxes) or as a check box (for check boxes).

Inserting a field is simple, but you will probably want to configure it after insertion. One advantage of legacy form fields is that they have some different formatting and configuration options available than content controls; depending on what you want to do with the form, the legacy form fields might have just the option that will make your life easier.

To view the properties for a form field, right-click it and choose Properties. If there is no Properties command, make sure Design Mode is marked in the Controls group and click the Properties button. Figure 21.8 shows the Properties box for a text field.

Figure 21.8
Set properties for a legacy form field.

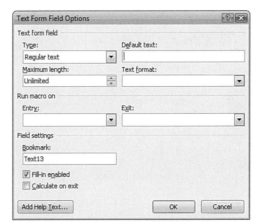

CONFIGURING LEGACY TEXT FIELD OPTIONS

There are three basic field types: Regular Text, Number, and Date. Depending on which of these types you select, different formatting options and length restrictions will become available in the Options dialog box. The other three choices on the Type menu are special-purpose types, discussed later in this chapter.

If you choose Regular Text, the options shown in Figure 21.8 are available:

- **Default Text**—You can optionally specify default text to appear in the field before the user enters his or her own value.
- **Maximum Length**—This is measured in number of text characters. The default is Unlimited.
- **Text Format**—Choose among Uppercase, Lowercase, First capital, or Title case.

→ To learn about First capital and Title case as formatting options, **see** "Changing Text Case," **p. 173**.

If you select Number, you can choose among these options:

- **Default Number**—This is just like Default Text; enter a default if desired.
- **Maximum Length**—This is measured in number of digits.
- **Number Format**—This drop-down list lets you specify a numeric format, some of which include currency symbols or percentage signs.

→ For information about number format codes, **see** "Constructing a Custom Numeric Format," **p. 649**. You cannot construct a custom format here, but that section will help you understand the available choices.

And finally, if you choose Date, you can choose among these options:

- **Default Number**—This is just like Default Text; enter a default if desired.
- **Maximum Length**—This is measured in number of digits. It is not typically limited for dates, as dates take up only as much space as they need.
- **Date Format**—This drop-down list lets you specify a date format, including various combinations of month, day, and year.

→ For information about date format codes, **see** "Constructing a Custom Date or Time Format," **p. 650**. You cannot construct a custom format here, but that section will help you understand the available choices.

INSERTING THE CURRENT DATE OR TIME

If you choose Current Date or Current Time from the Type list in the field's Options dialog box, the field changes to show the current date or time, as determined by the PC's clock. The field no longer accepts user input. It does not automatically update, but you can update it manually by selecting it and pressing F9.

21

SETTING UP A CALCULATION

If you choose Calculation as the type for the field, an Expression text box appears in the Field Options dialog box. In it, enter the formula for the calculation. You can then use any of the calculation methods that Word supports.

TIP

> For best results, set up the data to be calculated in a table, and place the calculated field in that same table. That way, you can refer to various cells by their row and column designators.

→   For more information about the calculations that can be performed in Word, **see** "Performing Math Calculations in a Table," **p. 384**.

AUTOMATICALLY RECALCULATING AN EXPRESSION

After setting up a calculation, you can specify whether or not the expression will be recalculated when the user exits the field. Beware, though—the process for setting it up is not what you think.

In viewing the Field Options box for the calculated field, you might have noticed a Calculate on Exit check box and figured that it would make that field recalculate automatically. Wrong! That check box makes a field re-report its value to other fields that depend upon it. It doesn't go out and poll any dependent fields for their values. Therefore, if you want a field to automatically recalculate, you must set the *other* fields, the ones that its expression refers to, to automatically calculate on exit.

An example will make this clearer. In Figure 21.9, each of the first four fields is set up with the properties shown in the Field Options dialog box. Each one is a number with a currency number format, and each one is set to Calculate on Exit. Each of these resupplies its value to the Total field when you tab away from it. The Total field is simply a passive receptacle for the changes; it does not need Calculate on Exit set for it.

Figure 21.9
All these fields *except* the last one are set for Calculate on Exit.

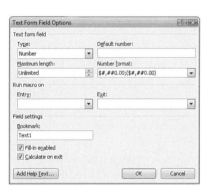

NOTE

> To properly test a calculated field, you must protect the form. Otherwise, you won't be able to enter values in the fields. See "Protecting a Form" later in this chapter for more information.

CONFIGURING LEGACY CHECK BOX OPTIONS

Check boxes are useful when you have a list of items and the user can select as many of them as he or she wants.

Check boxes have two unique options you can set for them, shown in Figure 21.10:

- **Check Box Size**—The default is Auto, which makes the check box the same size as the text that follows it. If you prefer, you can choose Exactly and enter a size in points.
- **Default Value**—This is set to Not Checked unless you specify otherwise. It determines the check box's starting state.

Figure 21.10
Set the options for a check box.

Using Option Buttons on a Form

Technically, Word has no capability for option buttons on form fields. However, Word does offer an ActiveX option button. It won't work seamlessly with your other fields if you have big plans for connectivity with a database, and it won't be included if you save or print the data only in a form. However, if you are designing the form to be filled out and saved in ordinary Word documents or on paper, you are probably more concerned with the look of the form than its back-end functionality.

Option buttons are sets of mutually exclusive options, such as Yes/No/Maybe. When the user selects one of them, the others in the group become deselected.

To create an option button set, follow these steps:

1. Position the insertion point where you want the first option button.
2. On the Developer tab, in the Controls group, click Legacy Tools, and in the ActiveX section, click Option Button (the round button, fourth from the left on the top row). A new option button and placeholder label appear.
3. Right-click the option button and choose Properties. The Properties pane opens.
4. In the Caption box, type the text that should appear next to the button.
5. In the GroupName box, type any name you like. (It must be the same for all buttons in the group, though.)
6. Repeat steps 2–5 to insert more option buttons, and make sure they all have the same GroupName.
7. Close the Properties pane.
8. Turn off Design Mode on the Developer tab and try out the buttons.

21

If you are interested in doing some VBA programming behind an ActiveX control, so that it actually does something other than sit there and look good, right-click the control while in Design Mode and choose View Code, and then work in the Microsoft Visual Basic window that appears. (You have to know how to program in VBA for this to be much help to you.)

CONFIGURING LEGACY LIST OPTIONS

A legacy list box, also called a Drop-Down Form Field, is like the list box in the 2007 content controls. It does not allow the user to input his or her own entries like a combo box does.

The main thing to set up for a list box is the list itself. Follow these steps to create the list:

1. From the Options dialog box for the field, type the first list item in the Drop-Down Item text box.
2. Click the Add>> button.
3. Repeat steps 1–2 to enter the other values (see Figure 21.11).
4. (Optional) If you need to remove an item, select it and click Remove.
5. (Optional) To reorder the items, select an item and click the Move up and down arrows.
6. Click OK.

Figure 21.11
Create the drop-down list options.

SETTING A MACRO TO RUN ON ENTRY OR EXIT

If you have any macros stored in the template or document, you can run one of them when the user enters or exits a particular field. For example, you might want to set up a macro that saves the file and associates it with exiting the final field on your form.

To set a macro to run on entry or exit, select the macro from the Entry or Exit drop-down list in the field's Options dialog box (see Figure 21.12).

21

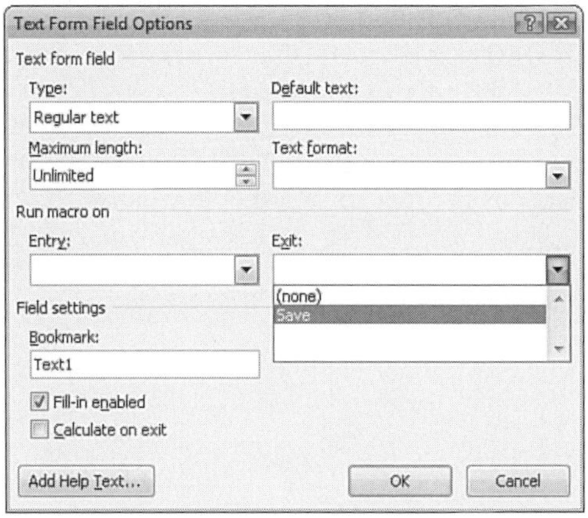

Figure 21.12
Set a macro to run at
entry or exit for that
field.

CAUTION

> Macro-enabled fields are possible only with legacy form fields. They work in legacy documents and templates (.dot or .doc), and in Word 2007 macro-enabled templates and documents (.dotm and .docm), but not in the regular "x" file formats (.dotx and .docx). It's not that you can't associate a macro with a field in those file formats, but that macros cannot exist in those files, so there are no macros to be referenced.

ENABLING OR DISABLING A FIELD

In some cases you might want to prevent users from changing the content of a field. Some would argue, "Why use a field at all if the user can't change it?" But there are reasons for that. For example, if you save the form data only to a text file, only what's in the fields will be saved, so you might want some fixed values to travel along with the user-entered data.

To set up a field so that users cannot input anything into it, or change its content, open up its Options dialog box (right-click and select Properties) and clear the Fill-in Enabled check box.

ASSIGNING A BOOKMARK TO A FIELD

Each field has a default bookmark name so you can refer to that field whenever you reference a bookmark. See the section titled "Using a Field to Set Bookmark Text" in Chapter 18, "Performing Mail and Data Merges," and the section "Working with Bookmarks" in Chapter 19, "Copying, Linking, and Embedding Data," to learn about the various uses for a bookmark.

To change a field's default bookmark name, open its Options dialog box (right-click and select Properties) and change the text in the Bookmark text box.

ADDING HELP TEXT

For legacy form fields, you can create help text that tells the user what to put in the field. With Word 2007 fields, this isn't necessary because you can customize the placeholder text

21

in the field, as you saw earlier in the chapter. But the unfriendly gray boxes of the legacy fields need the extra help.

Help can be set up to appear in either or both of two ways: in the status bar, or in a pop-up window that appears when the user presses F1 while the insertion point is inside the field. (Pressing F1 any other time opens the regular Word help window.)

To set up help messages, follow these steps:

1. Right-click the field and choose Properties.
2. Click Add Help Text. The Form Field Help Text dialog box opens.
3. To set up F1 help:
    a. Click the Help Key (F1) tab.
    b. Select the option Type Your Own.
    c. Type the text to appear in the help message (see Figure 21.13).
    d. Click OK.
4. To set up status bar help:
    a. Click the Status Bar tab.
    b. Select the option Type Your Own.
    c. Type the text to appear in the help message.
    d. Click OK.
5. Click OK.

Figure 21.13
Set up help text.

Creating Consistent Help Messages Across Multiple Forms

For simple forms that aren't part of an extensive form library, you'll probably want to use Type Your Own, as in the preceding steps. However, if you need to reuse the same messages over and over across many forms, consider setting up the help messages as AutoText entries, and then choosing AutoText Entry in step b. That way, if you change the help message later, all the forms that use it will draw from the same updated version.

To create an AutoText entry that will serve as a help message, follow these steps:

1. Type the message text in any document.
2. On the Insert tab, choose Quick Parts, Save Selection to Quick Part Gallery.
3. Type a name for the entry in the Name box.

4. Open the Gallery menu and choose AutoText.

5. Click OK to create the entry.

Now when you choose AutoText Entry from the field's Form Field Help Text dialog box, the entry you created will be on the list of available entries.

PROTECTING A FORM

With a legacy form, you must protect it in order to use the fields. With content controls, protecting the form is optional but recommended.

There are several types of document protection, but the type we're interested in here makes the document uneditable except in the form fields.

To protect a form, follow these steps:

1. On the Developer tab, click Protect Document. The Restrict Formating and Editing task pane opens.

2. In the Editing Restrictions section, mark the Allow Only This Type of Editing in the Document check box.

3. Open the drop-down list below the check box and choose Filling In Forms (see Figure 21.14).

Figure 21.14
Set up protection for the form so that only the fields will be editable.

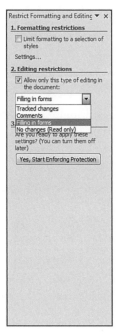

21

4. Click Yes, Start Enforcing Protection. The Start Enforcing Protection dialog box opens.

   If this button is not available, make sure you are not still in Design Mode. Click Design Mode on the Developer tab to turn it off if needed.

5. To put a password on the protection (recommended), type the desired password in the Enter New Password (Optional) box, and then retype it in the Reenter Password to Confirm box (see Figure 21.15).

6. Click OK.

Figure 21.15
Assign a password for the protection if desired.

The Restrict Formatting and Editing task pane remains open; close it if desired by clicking the X in its upper-right corner.

To remove the protection so you can further edit the form, follow these steps:

1. If the Restrict Formatting and Editing task pane is not already displayed, click Protect Document on the Developer tab.

2. Click Stop Protection.

3. If you put a password on the protection, a dialog box appears prompting you for the password; enter it and click OK.

FILLING OUT A FORM

You will probably want to test your forms as you build them to make sure they are user-friendly. Filling out a form is a little different depending on the field type, so the following sections look at the processes separately.

CAUTION

The form can be tested either in the template file or in a document file based upon it. If you test the form in the template, though, make sure you do not save your changes with the fields filled in.

FILLING OUT A WORD 2007 FORM

To enter text in a Word 2007 content control, click inside the content control and then type the entry for it (see Figure 21.16).

Figure 21.16
Type in a content control.

If the form is protected, the insertion point flashes at the beginning of the document, and clicking anywhere in a protected region will not move the insertion point; it jumps back to the beginning. The only areas you can successfully move the insertion point into are the content controls. With Word 2007 content controls, however, it is not mandatory that the document be protected in order to test a field. If the document is not protected, you can click anywhere and edit anything, not just the field entries. That's by design; it allows you to put content controls into any document.

Depending on the options set up for the content control, the content control might go away after you enter something into it, or it might become locked against further editing after the initial entry. If either of those conditions are unsatisfactory, you can turn off their options in the content control's Properties.

Preventing Accidental Content Control Deletion

Because the form is not necessarily protected, the possibility exists that a user will accidentally delete the content control. To prevent that from happening, you can protect each individual control from deletion by turning on the Content Control Cannot Be Deleted option in the control's Properties dialog box. Follow these steps:

1. Unprotect the form if it is protected, and make sure Design Mode is selected on the Developer tab.
2. Right-click the content control and choose Properties. The Content Control Properties dialog box opens.
3. Mark the Content Control Cannot Be Deleted check box.
4. Click OK.

FILLING OUT A LEGACY FORM

A legacy form won't work properly unless it is protected. When unprotected, the form treats the fields as foreign objects, and you can't enter anything into them.

On a protected form, you can click in a field and then type the text into it, or you can press Tab to move from field to field.

If help has been set up for a field, you can press the F1 key to see the help information when the insertion point is within that field. (Pressing F1 any other time opens the general Word 2007 help window, not the specific help for that field.)

21

SAVING ONLY THE FORM DATA

In Word 2003, you could set a save option in the Save As dialog box to save only the form data in a plain-text file. You can't do that from the Save As dialog box anymore in Word 2007, but there's an alternative method you can use.

To save only the form data in a text file, follow these steps:

1. Choose Office, Word Options. The Word Options dialog box opens.
2. Click Advanced.
3. Scroll down to the Preserve Fidelity When Sharing This Document section, and make sure the correct document is selected on the list.
4. Mark the Save Form Data as Delimited Text File check box and click OK.

CAUTION

> If your form contains only Word 2007 content controls, the check box in step 4 is grayed out. If the form contains a mixture of content controls and legacy form fields, the check box is available, but the resulting save will capture only the data from the legacy fields.

5. Choose Office, Save Copy As. (Notice the command name has changed from the usual Save As.) The Save As dialog box opens with Plain Text set as the file type.
6. Type a name for the file and click Save to save the text file.

In the resulting text file, the data is comma-delimited with quotation marks around text entries. For example, an address block might look like this:

"Sheri Harris","10783 Westwood Place","Anderson","IN","46282"

PRINTING ONLY THE FORM DATA

Printing form data is similar to saving form data, in that it works only with legacy form fields, not content controls. When you choose to print only the form data, none of the other text from the form prints. However, if the form was constructed within a table, and that table had visible borders or shading, the table will print along with the data. (If you don't want the table to print, set its borders to None before printing.)

To print only the form data, follow these steps:

1. Choose Office, Word Options. The Word Options dialog box opens.
2. Click Advanced.
3. Scroll down to the When Printing This Document section, and make sure the correct document is selected on the list.
4. Mark the Print Only the Data from a Form check box.
5. Click OK.
6. Print the document as you normally would. None of the text prints except the text in the form fields.

TIPS FOR CREATING PRINTED FORMS

Some forms end up being used for both onscreen and on-paper data entry. That's fine, but what constitutes an effective online form might not always be the same as what constitutes an effective printed form.

Here are some things to think about when moving between printed and electronic formats:

- In an onscreen field, users can enter a lot of data in a small field because the text scrolls within the field (at least it does on a legacy form field). When that field is printed, however, there will be a limited amount of space for it. Will your users be able to adequately record their entries in the space provided?

- Drop-down fields do not work on a printed form, so you must replace them with check boxes or option buttons. (See the sidebar "Using Option Buttons on a Form" earlier in this chapter for details.)

- Check boxes might need to be larger on printed forms than on electronic ones. To change the size of a check box, right-click it and choose Properties and make the change in its Options dialog box.

- Calculated fields and fields that insert the current date/time will not work on printed forms, so remove them or change them to user-editable fields.

- Instead of using a legacy check box field, you might prefer to use a bullet character that looks like a check box. If the form will not be submitted electronically, it doesn't matter that it's not a real field, and more formatting options are available with a bullet character.

TROUBLESHOOTING

THE PROPERTIES COMMAND DOESN'T APPEAR ON A CONTENT CONTROL'S RIGHT-CLICK MENU.

You must be in Design Mode to get access to this command. Make sure the Design Mode button is selected on the Developer tab.

HOW CAN I USE CALCULATED FIELDS WITH CONTENT CONTROLS?

You can't. That's one of their unfortunate drawbacks. However, you can still use legacy form fields for calculations, as described in this chapter.

CAN I CREATE FORMS WITHIN EMAIL MESSAGES?

Yes, but you can also send Word forms as email attachments in any email program, which actually might be a better way to go because of the limitations of some of the email clients that the recipients might be using.

When people receive an email with form fields (use legacy fields for this, by the way), they'll see the fields embedded in it. Then when they reply to the email, those fields will be editable. See Chapter 30, "Working with Blogs and Email," for more information about how Word works with email.

How Can I Program ActiveX Controls?

Along with the legacy form fields, you also have access to a set of ActiveX controls on the Legacy Tools button's menu. You saw the option button type in the "Using Options Buttons on a Form" sidebar earlier in this chapter, but we really didn't do much with it there other than place it on the form and make it look okay for printing.

If you want to actually do some programming for an ActiveX field, you must know Visual Basic for Applications (VBA). To access the Visual Basic editor for a control, right-click the control while in Design Mode and choose View Code. Then work in the Microsoft Visual Basic window that opens.

Long Documents

OUTLINING AND SUMMARIZING DOCUMENTS

In this chapter

22

OUTLINE BASICS

Almost everyone has, at one time or another, stared at a blank page trying to get started on a long or complex writing project. Where to begin? What to include? It can be hard to wrap your thoughts around the project without a grasp of the big picture.

That's where outlining comes in. By starting with an outline, you create a structure or map that helps guide your writing each step of the journey and forces you to think through the entire writing process. Once the document's headings are in place, you can start filling in the body text beneath them. Suddenly the project doesn't seem so overwhelming when you're tackling it one section at a time with a clear vision of what you want to accomplish.

Word's Outline view makes it easy to create complex, multilevel outlines. (Word was the tool used to outline and write this book, in fact!) Word enables you to view the outline at various levels of detail and to easily move topics around. It even can automatically number the headings for you and update the numbering when topics are moved.

Outlines are based on heading styles. The default heading styles are automatically applied as you promote and demote items in an outline. For example, Figure 22.1 shows part of the outline for Chapter 3 of this book. The top-level heading (Heading 1) is the chapter title; the second-level headings (Heading 2) are the major sections, and so on.

Figure 22.1
A multilevel outline based on heading styles.

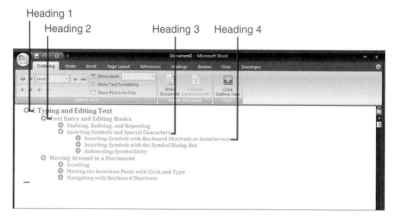

In addition to the default heading styles, outlining can also be set up to work with any custom styles you might have created. In "Setting a Style's Outline Level" later in this chapter, you will learn how to define which outline level is associated with which style(s).

TIP

> The Document Map feature is very similar to an outline, except it's not editable. If you want to browse the full document and its outline at the same time, turn on the Document Map pane by marking the Document Map check box on the View tab. The document map appears in a separate pane to the left of the main document window. Note that because any outline level you click in the Document Map takes you to that section of the document, the Document Map is also a handy bookmarking tool that doesn't actually require you to use bookmark field codes. You can customize the levels that appear in the outline pane by right-clicking the outline pane and choosing a level.

TYPING AN OUTLINE IN OUTLINE VIEW

To type or edit an outline, switch to Outline view. To do this, click Outline on the View tab, or click the Outline View button in the status bar of the Word window.

Then type the first item for the outline (see Figure 22.2).

Figure 22.2
Begin typing the headings for the outline in Outline view.

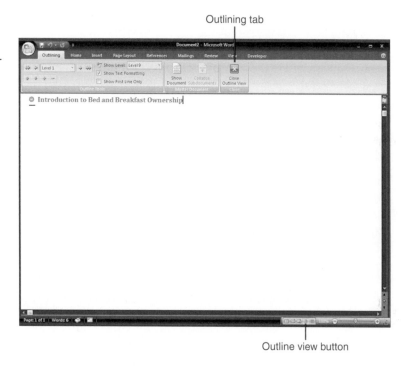

Outlining tab

Outline view button

Press Enter after each entry. Another line of the same outline level appears. At this point, you can type more lines at the same level, or you can *demote* the new line so that it is subordinate to the one above it. See the following section for information about promoting and demoting.

Once you're satisfied with the outline, you can start using it as a starting point for writing the rest of the document. You will probably want to switch to Print Layout or Draft view before adding body text. (Use the View tab or buttons to switch views or click the Close Outline View button on the Outlining tab.) Each outline item appears as a heading in the document, with Word's default heading styles applied. Under each heading, type the appropriate body text, using Normal style or whatever style you have designated for body text in the document.

TIP

> It seems only natural to make a document's title the highest level item in the outline (Heading 1). But do you really want to waste the Heading 1 style on an item that appears only once in the document? It might be better to make all the major content headings in the document Heading 1 style, and either style the document title also as Heading 1 or create a special style just for the title (and set its outline level to 1).

DEMOTING AND PROMOTING OUTLINE ITEMS

To demote the line, press Tab or press Alt+Shift+right arrow. It appears indented, and the line above it acquires a plus sign, indicating that it now has subordinates.

To *promote* a line so that it moves up a level in importance, click it and press Shift+Tab or Alt+Shift+left arrow.

NOTE

> In Outline view, the insertion point does not have to be at the beginning of the line to use Tab or Shift+Tab to demote or promote. That's because the Tab key does not move the insertion point to tab stops in Outline view. Switch back to Draft or Print Layout view if you want to work with tab stops.

If you prefer to use a mouse to promote and demote, click an item's plus sign (or minus sign) and then drag it to the left or right. As you drag, the item is promoted or demoted.

You can also click the buttons on the Outlining tab or use keyboard shortcuts, as in Table 22.1.

TABLE 22.1 OUTLINING BUTTONS AND SHORTCUTS FOR PROMOTING AND DEMOTING

Button	Purpose	Keyboard Shortcut
	Promote to Heading 1	n/a
	Promote (one level)	Shift+Tab or Alt+Shift+Left arrow
Level 2	Outline level (select from list)	n/a
	Demote (one level)	Tab or Alt+Shift+Right arrow
	Demote to body text	Ctrl+Shift+N

If you demote an item as completely as possible, it becomes *body text*. In this context, "body text" refers to an outline level, not to a particular style. You can have many different styles that all have body text set as their outline level.

→ To change a style's outline level, **see** "Setting a Style's Outline Level," **p. 688**.

CHECKING THE STYLES USED IN THE OUTLINE

In Outline view, there is no obvious indicator of what styles are in use. To find out, press Ctrl+Shift+S to display the Apply Styles pane and then click a line in the outline. The style is reported in the Style Name box (see Figure 22.3).

Figure 22.3
Demote (indent) a line by pressing Tab. Style usage can be checked from the Apply Styles pane.

Outline level   Insertion point in this line   Style name

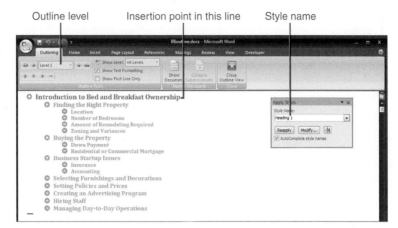

The Outline Level box on the Outlining tab lists the outline level at which the selected line is set, and if you are using the default heading styles for outlining, this corresponds to the heading level. For example, if the Outline Level box reports Level 3, the paragraph is using Heading 3 style. However, if you are using nonstandard styles for your outline, this correlation does not hold.

NOTE

> Perhaps an easier way to see styles at a glance in an outline is to turn on the display of the Style area. To do so, choose Office, Word Options. Click Advanced, and then in the Display section, set a positive number in inches in the Style Area Pane Width box (for example, 1").

CREATING AN OUTLINE FROM AN EXISTING DOCUMENT

Outlines aren't just for prewriting planning; you might also want to see an outline of a document you have already written.

To make sure the outline is accurate, first check that you have applied the appropriate heading styles to the headings. The first-level headings should be styled as Heading 1, the second-level as Heading 2, and so on. You can have up to nine levels of headings.

TIP

> If you would rather use other styles than the default Heading ones in your outline, see "Setting a Style's Outline Level" later in this chapter. Keep in mind, however, that you can redefine the formatting for all the default Heading styles, and you can apply different style sets from the Change Styles list on the Home tab. You don't have to apply different styles to achieve a different look.

22

After confirming the styles on the headings, switch to Outline view. By default, the Outline view shows not only the headings, but also the body text. Body text paragraphs appear with gray circles beside them. These are not bullets; they are there to help you remember you are in Outline view, and to serve as selectors for the paragraphs. You can select a paragraph by clicking its gray circle, or you can move it by dragging its circle (see Figure 22.4).

Body text

Figure 22.4
Body text appears in an outline with a gray circle to its left.

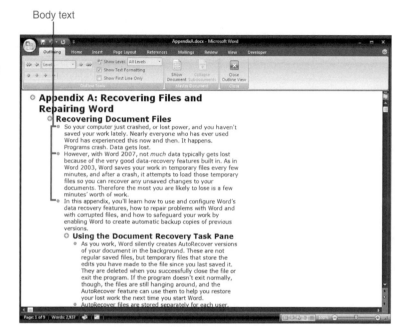

Outline view makes it easy to catch any style errors you might have made, such as applying the wrong style to a particular heading or accidentally styling one of the body paragraphs as a heading. If you find any style application errors, correct them by clicking that line and then choosing the desired style from the Apply Styles pane. (Press Ctrl+Shift+S to display this pane if needed.) Alternatively, you can promote or demote the items with Shift+Tab or Tab, respectively, or you can apply the built-in heading styles with shortcut keys: Ctrl+Alt plus the number of the heading level desired (Ctrl+Alt+1 for Heading 1, and so on). To demote to body text, press Ctrl+Shift+N.

If you do not want to see the body text in the outline, and/or if you want to see only certain heading levels, collapse the Outline view, as explained in the following section.

VIEWING AND ORGANIZING THE OUTLINE

When the outline is fully expanded, as it is in Figure 22.4, even body text appears in it. That's useful for checking the content of a section, but it takes away the main benefit of the outline, which is to provide a high-level summary. Therefore, most of the time, you will probably want to view the outline at some level of compression.

You can collapse or expand the entire outline so that it shows only headings of a certain level and higher. For example, if you set the outline to show Level 3, anything that is not styled with a Level 3 heading or higher is hidden. To collapse the outline to a specific level, choose a level from the Show Level list on the Outlining tab (see Figure 22.5).

Figure 22.5
Choose a level to collapse or expand the entire outline.

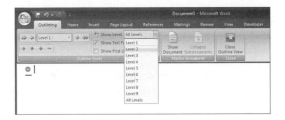

You can also collapse or expand individual branches of the outline.

To toggle a branch between being expanded or collapsed, double-click the plus sign to its left.

Other expansion and collapse methods operate on individual branches:

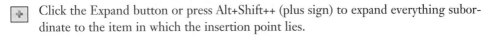 Click the Expand button or press Alt+Shift++ (plus sign) to expand everything subordinate to the item in which the insertion point lies.

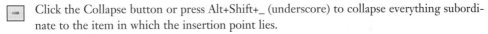 Click the Collapse button or press Alt+Shift+_ (underscore) to collapse everything subordinate to the item in which the insertion point lies.

Expanding and collapsing is not the only way of changing the view of the outline, although it's the most dramatic way. Here are a couple additional settings on the Outlining tab that control outline appearance:

- **Show Text Formatting**—This on/off toggle shows or hides the different fonts and sizes used for the various heading levels.

- **Show First Line Only**—This on/off toggle makes multiple-line items (such as body paragraphs and very long headings) show up as single-line items on the outline.

REARRANGING OUTLINE TOPICS

If you have ever tried to rearrange sections of a large document, you know how cumbersome cut-and-paste operations can be in that situation. You have to cut some text and then scroll to the section where you want to paste it, perhaps many pages away.

It is much easier to rearrange a document in Outline view because you can collapse all the body text beneath the headings and work with the document in a bird's-eye view. When you move a heading in Outline view, all the collapsed content beneath it moves automatically with it, so there's no need to scroll through pages and pages of body text to find the spot in which you want to paste.

One way to move a heading in the outline is to drag and drop it. This method works well when you need to move a heading and all its subordinate headings:

1. Click the plus sign (or minus sign) next to a heading to select it and all its subordinates. The mouse pointer becomes a four-headed arrow.

2. Drag up or down to move the heading and its subordinates to a new location.

Another way is to use the buttons on the Outlining tab. This method works well when you need to move one individual heading but not its subordinates, or when you need to move a block of headings (not necessarily in a neat subordinate structure):

1. Select the content to be moved up or down. You can select any number of headings or body text at any level.

2. Click one of these buttons to move the selection up or down one position in the outline:

   ⬆ Move Up

   ⬇ Move Down

3. Repeat step 2 as needed until the content is at the desired position.

SETTING A STYLE'S OUTLINE LEVEL

As mentioned earlier, Word uses its built-in heading styles for outlines (Heading 1, Heading 2, and so on) by default. When you create an outline by typing directly into Outline view and pressing Tab and Shift+Tab to demote and promote, those heading styles are automatically applied to the outline levels. There are 10 outline levels: Level 1 through Level 9 headings, plus body text.

→ To review how to modify a style, **see** "Modifying Styles," **p. 248**.

If you would rather use your own custom styles than the built-in ones for headings, you must set the custom styles' outline levels so Word knows how to treat them.

To specify the outline level for a style, follow these steps:

1. Display the Styles pane. To do so, on the Home tab, click the dialog box launcher icon in the Styles group. The Styles pane opens.

2. In the Styles pane, right-click the style and choose Modify (see Figure 22.6).

   Make sure it's a user-created style you're modifying; you cannot change the outline level for one of the built-in heading styles.

3. In the Modify Style dialog box, click the Format button and then choose Paragraph from its menu. The Paragraph dialog box opens.

4. Open the Outline Level drop-down list and choose the desired outline level for this style (see Figure 22.7).

5. Click OK to accept the new outline level.

6. Click OK to close the Modify Style dialog box.

Click here to open the styles pane

Right-click the style and choose modify

Figure 22.6
Modify the style to set its outline level.

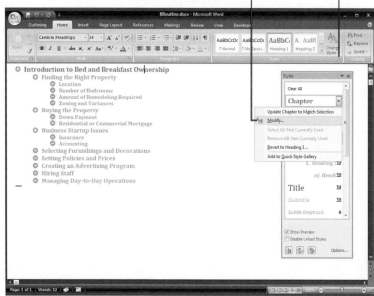

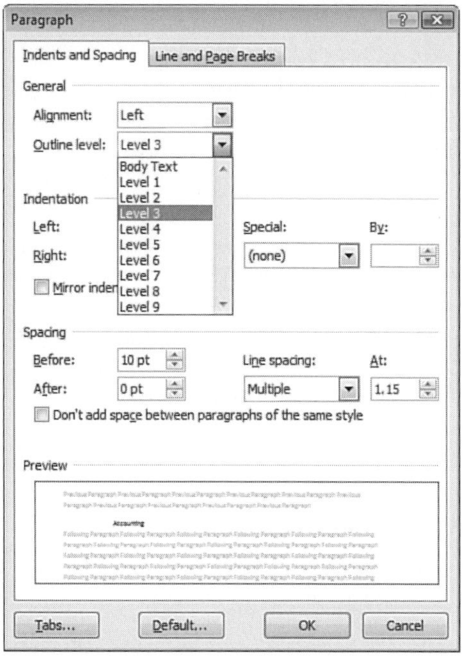

Figure 22.7
Change a style's outline level from its Paragraph properties.

TIP

> Here's another way of changing a custom style's outline level: In the Modify Style dialog box, choose a different style from the Style Based On list. The custom style will take on whatever outline level is assigned to the style on which it is based unless you set a specific outline level for it. However, with that method, all the unspecified attributes of the custom style change to match the new basis, so additional unwanted formatting changes might occur to the style's formatting.

SETTING AN INDIVIDUAL PARAGRAPH'S OUTLINE LEVEL

You can also change the outline level on an individual paragraph-by-paragraph basis, without affecting the style. For example, you could force a certain body paragraph to appear in the outline by setting its outline level to one of the levels currently being shown in the outline. Here's how to set the outline level for a paragraph without changing its style:

1. Right-click the paragraph and choose Paragraph.
2. In the Paragraph dialog box, open the Outline Level list and select an outline level.
3. Click OK.

This works on paragraphs formatted with all styles except the built-in heading styles (Heading 1 through Heading 9).

Using Outline Levels to Change How Theme Fonts Are Applied

Now that you know about outline levels, let's revisit a topic from Chapter 8: font themes.

As you learned in Chapter 8, "Creating and Applying Styles and Themes," there are two fonts in a theme: one for headings and one for body text. Word decides which of those two fonts to apply to a paragraph based on the outline level assigned to its style. Anything with a style that has an outline level of Level 1 through Level 9 receives the font specified for headings; anything with a style that has an outline level of Body Text receives the font specified for body text.

Knowing this, you can rig a style to show one font or the other regardless of a paragraph's actual status as heading or body text. Suppose, for example, that you want a certain body paragraph to look different from the others. Apply an unused heading style to it, such as Heading 9, and then modify that style so that it looks the way you want it. Or better yet, create a custom style, do not base it on any other style, and then apply an outline level to it (Level 1 through Level 9). As long as a heading style is the paragraph's basis, it will use whatever heading font has been specified in the theme (unless, of course, you override the font choice manually).

NUMBERING OUTLINE ITEMS

When creating an outline that includes consecutively numbered items, you can save yourself some time by allowing Word to manage the numbering for you.

The time savings is not so much in the initial creation of the outline, but rather in its later editing. For example, when writing a book, the first task is to create an outline of the chapters to include: Chapter 1, Chapter 2, Chapter 3, and so on. If you manually type that text as

22

part of each chapter title, and then you rearrange the chapters, you're in for a tedious job of manually editing each title. However, if you allow Word to handle the numbering for you, you never have to deal with the numbering again; Word renumbers items automatically as you rearrange them.

To number an outline, you apply list formatting to it. List formatting can be set up in either of two ways:

- You can apply multilevel lists and create your own list definitions, via the Multilevel List button on the Home tab. This feature was called Outline Numbered List in earlier versions of Word; the name change was made to reflect the fact that you can apply multilevel list formatting to more than just outlines.

- You can create and apply a list style in which to store the outline numbering format. A list style can do everything a multilevel list can do, plus it can have a name and can have a shortcut key combination assigned to it. It can also be saved with a particular template.

Applying a Multilevel List

You can apply a multilevel list or list style to individual portions of an outline, but usually it's best for the entire outline to be formatted the same way for consistency.

Select the entire outline (Ctrl+A) or the portion you want to format, and then on the Home tab, open the Multilevel List button's drop-down list and click a list or list style. Each item receives the numbering format specified for its outline level.

The Multilevel List button's menu presents a gallery of list-formatting choices, including both lists and list styles (if any have been created in the current document or template). The gallery has several sections:

- **Current List**—Appears at the top of the list and shows the currently applied list type, or the default list type if none is currently applied. (You can click the Multilevel List button, rather than opening its menu, to apply the current list.)

- **List Library**—This collection of list presets always appears. Word provides several, and you can also add your own lists.

- **List Styles**—If you have defined any list styles (using the Styles feature, covered later in this chapter), they appear here; otherwise, this section does not appear.

- **Lists in Current Documents**—If you have applied any multilevel numbering already, the types you have applied appear here for easy reapplication. Otherwise, this section does not appear.

As shown in Figure 22.8, you can filter the Multilevel List button's menu to show only one of these four categories. Click All to open a menu and then click the category you want to show. To return to showing all the categories, reopen that menu and click All.

22

Click here to open the menu

Choose a category to filter the list

Figure 22.8
Apply a list style pre-set from the Multilevel List button. Filter the list if desired.

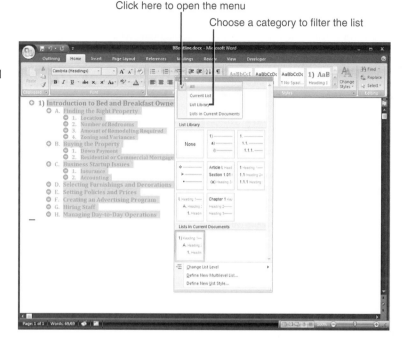

CREATING YOUR OWN MULTILEVEL LISTS AND LIST STYLES

You can create a multilevel list definition as either an ordinary multilevel list or as a list style. The main difference between them is where they are stored:

- A multilevel list exists only in the current document. However, if desired, you can easily add it to the List Library gallery, and after you do that, it is available globally, no matter what template you are using. It can't be modified, but it can be deleted and re-created.

- A list style can be set up to exist either in the current document only or in the currently applied template. If you save it in the template, it is available whenever you are working with a document based on that template. A list style can be modified.

The dialog boxes for creating a new multilevel list versus a list style appear to be quite different, but if you compare them feature by feature, they come out almost identical. And in fact, when you are defining a list style, you can access a duplicate of the Define New Multilevel List dialog box, so anything you can do with a multilevel list can be saved as a list style.

CREATING A MULTILEVEL LIST

To create your own multilevel list, follow these steps:

1. (Optional) To apply the new list to an outline or list, or a portion thereof, select the text to which to apply it. (You can apply it later if you prefer.)

2. (Optional) If you want to base the new multilevel list on an existing one, open the Multilevel List button's menu (on the Home tab) and click the desired list to apply it to the selected text.

3. Open the Multilevel List button's menu and choose Define New Multilevel List. The Define New Multilevel List dialog box opens (see Figure 22.9).

Figure 22.9
Define the formatting for a new multilevel list.

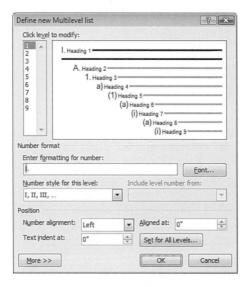

4. Click the number representing the level you want to modify.

5. In the Number Style for This Level list, select the numbering style desired. The place-holder (shaded gray) in the Enter Formatting for Number box changes to represent the new style.

6. In the Enter Formatting for Number box, type any additional text that should surround the number placeholder.

For example, you could type **Chapter** in front of the placeholder, or add punctuation after it, such as a period, colon, or parenthesis.

7. (Optional) To change the font formatting, click the Font button, make any changes desired, and click OK.

All font attributes are available to apply to outline numbering except Outline and Small Caps.

8. (Optional) To change the position (alignment, indentation, and so on), make changes to the values in the Position section of the dialog box.

You can control every aspect of the positioning here, including the amount of indentation before and after the numbering or bullet, whether a tab character appears after the number, and whether there should be a tab stop to go with that tab character.

9. (Optional) To change the position settings for all levels at once, click the Set for All Levels button. In the Set for All Levels dialog box shown in Figure 22.10, choose an indentation and text position for the first level and then specify the amount of additional indent for each level beneath it. This creates an orderly cascade effect between levels. Click OK to return to the Define New Multilevel List dialog box when finished.

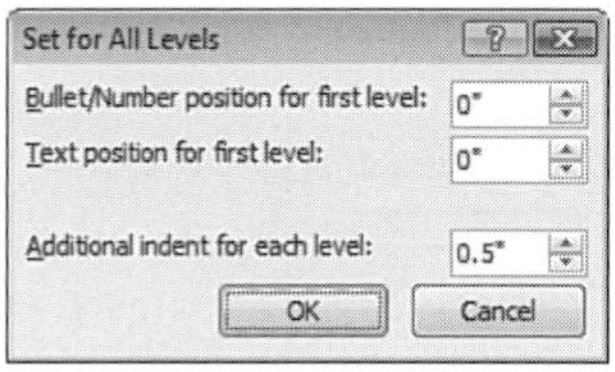

Figure 22.10
Define the formatting for all levels of outlining at once.

10. (Optional) For more options, click the More button in the bottom-left corner of the dialog box. This displays the additional options, as in Figure 22.11.

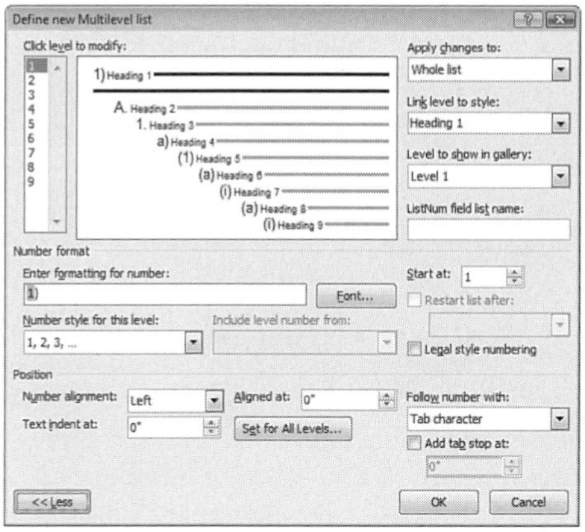

Figure 22.11
Set additional options that will affect all levels of outlining.

11. Set any of the additional options as needed:

- To link a particular level to a certain style, select a style from the Link Level to Style list. This enables you to create a special outline level that pertains only to a certain style, and anytime you apply that style in the document, the numbering appears with it.

- To define which levels appear when this list appears in the Gallery, choose a level from the Level to Show in Gallery list.

- To use the specified list formatting with a ListNum field list, specify a name in the ListNum Field List Name box. (Make up a unique name.) Then when you create a numbered list with the { ListNum } field, you can use the name as a parameter to specify the list's formatting.

→ To learn more about the { ListNum } field, **see** "Numbering Fields," **p. 642**.

- To start the numbering for a level at a number other than 1, specify a number in the Start At box.

- To use legal-style numbering, mark the Legal Style Numbering check box. This forces all the numbering to Arabic (1, 2, 3), regardless of its setting otherwise in the style or list definition.

- To specify a character to appear after the number, set the Follow Number With setting. You can use a tab, a space, or nothing.

  If you want some other character to follow the number, type that character following the number code in the Enter Formatting for Number box.

- If you include a tab character after the number, you might want to set a tab stop for it. To include a tab stop in the formatting, mark the Add Tab Stop At check box and then enter a position in inches.

12. When you are finished with the specification for the selected level, select another level from the Click Level to Modify list and then repeat steps 5–11. Repeat for each level.

13. Click OK to create the new list format.

The new list format is applied to the portion of the list that was selected when you began the creation process. You can also apply it from the Multilevel List button's menu, from the Lists in Current Documents section of the menu.

INCLUDING NUMBERS FROM HIGHER OUTLINE LEVELS

Suppose you want each outline item to be double-numbered, including both the higher level item's number and its own, like this:

> Chapter 1, Section A
>
> Chapter 1, Section B
>
> Chapter 1, Section C

To set this up, use the Include Level Number From drop-down list in the Define New Multilevel List dialog box. For example, here's how to set up the preceding example for Level 2:

1. In the Define New Multilevel List dialog box, click 2 on the Click Level to Modify list.

2. Open the Number Style for This Level list and choose A, B, C. An A appears (shaded) in the Enter Formatting for Number box.

3. Click to move the insertion point to the left of the shaded A code, and type **Chapter** and press the spacebar once.

4. Open the Include Level Number From drop-down list and choose Level 1. The 1 code appears in the Enter Formatting for Number box, after the word *Chapter*.

5. Press the spacebar twice after the 1 code, and then type **Section** and press the spacebar once. Now the entry in the Enter Formatting for Number box looks like this: Chapter 1 Section A.

6. Open the Follow Number With list and choose Space.

7. Continue creating the list definition as usual.

ADDING A CUSTOM MULTILEVEL LIST TO THE GALLERY

A custom multilevel list, like the one you created in the preceding section, is saved with the current document only. It does not have a name (like a style would have), and it cannot be transferred between documents.

To add the list formatting specification to the Gallery (that is, the List Library area of the menu) so that it is available in all documents, do the following:

1. Open the Multilevel List button's menu.

2. In the Lists in Current Documents section, locate and right-click the list to be added.

3. Choose Save in List Library. The list formatting now appears in the List Library portion of the menu. It is also saved to the Normal.dotm template, so it will be available in future documents you create.

CREATING A LIST STYLE

A list style defines a multilevel list in a slightly different way; it contains all the specifications for a regular multilevel list, but it saves them in a named style that you can then apply as you would any other style. You can also store it with a specific template.

To create your own list style, follow these steps:

1. (Optional) To apply the new list to an outline or list, or a portion thereof, select the text to which to apply it. (You can apply it later if you prefer.)

2. (Optional) If you want to save the style to a particular template, apply that template to the current document.

→ To apply a different template to a document, **see** "Changing a Document's Template", **p. 312**.

3. (Optional) If you want to base the new style on an existing multilevel list, open the Multilevel List button's menu (on the Home tab) and click the desired list to apply it to the selected text.

4. On the Home tab, open the Multilevel List button's menu and choose Define New List Style. The Define New List Style dialog box opens (see Figure 22.12).

5. Type a name for the style in the Name box.

6. (Optional) To start the numbering at a number other than 1, change the value in the Start At box.

7. Select an outline level from the Apply Formatting To list.

8. Choose text formatting for that list level: Font, Size, Bold, Italic, Underline, and Color.

9. For the selected level, click either the Numbering or Bullets button.

10. Select a number type or bullet character. You can do the following:

    • Select a bullet or number type from the list of presets to the right of the Numbering and Bullets buttons.

- Click the Insert Symbol button and select any character from any font to use as a bullet character.
- Click the Insert Picture button and select a picture bullet.

Figure 22.12
Define the formatting
for a new list style.

Bullets
Numbers
Font
Size
Insert symbol
Insert picture
Increase indent

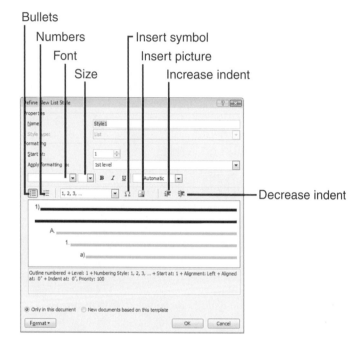

Decrease indent

TIP

> If you want to set other text formatting than what appears in the dialog box (for example, strikethrough or superscript), click the Format button and choose Font to open the Font dialog box.

11. (Optional) Click the Decrease Indent or Increase Indent button to change the amount of indent for the chosen outline level.

12. Choose where to save the style: Only in This Document or New Documents Based on This Template.

13. Choose a different outline level from the Apply Formatting To list and then repeat steps 8–12.

14. (Optional) To further fine-tune the numbering of the list levels, click the Format button and choose Numbering. Then select additional options from the Modify Multilevel List dialog box.

This dialog box is identical to the one shown in Figure 22.11, except for its name. Refer to step 11 in the section "Creating a Multilevel List" earlier in this chapter for specifics about this dialog box. When you are finished working with it, click OK to return to the Define New List Style dialog box.

15. Click OK to define the new style and apply it to the selected text.

Order of Style Application Revisited

Remember from Chapter 8's sidebar "Order of Style Application" that when multiple styles are applied to the same text and one layer contradicts another, the formatting is determined according to a hierarchy. Character takes top priority, followed by Paragraph, then List, and finally Table.

So how does that affect outline numbering? Well, suppose you have an outline consisting of a bunch of Heading 1 and Heading 2 style headings, and you apply a list style to the entire list. (It doesn't even need to be in Outline view necessarily.) The paragraphs still retain their Heading 1 and Heading 2 style designations; if you check them out in the Styles pane, you'll see that the paragraph styles are intact and unmodified. The list styles are applied *on top of* the paragraph styles, as separate elements. If the list style specifies anything that contradicts the paragraph style, the list style prevails, but the paragraph style controls anything that the list style does not specify.

DELETING A MULTILEVEL LIST OR LIST STYLE

Once you add a multilevel list to the List Library gallery, it's there until you remove it, in all documents regardless of their template. To remove a list from the My Lists gallery, right-click it on the Multilevel List button's menu and choose Remove from My Lists.

A list style theoretically could be deleted like any other style (by right-clicking it in the Styles task pane and choosing Delete), except for one thing: List styles don't show up in the Styles task pane. So instead you must go through the Manage Styles dialog box to delete a list style. Follow these steps:

1. On the Home tab, click the dialog box launcher icon in the Styles group to open the Styles task pane.

2. Click the Manage Styles button at the bottom of the task pane. The Manage Styles dialog box opens.

3. Click the name of the style to delete.

4. Click the Delete button.

5. At the confirmation box, click Yes.

6. Click OK to close the Manage Styles dialog box.

PRINTING OR COPYING AN OUTLINE

Unfortunately, printing an outline leaves something to be desired in Word 2007, as with earlier versions. The Help system tells you that you can print the outline at any level of detail desired by collapsing the outline to the view you want and then clicking the Quick Print button to print it. However, this is not the case; the entire document prints.

So how, then, can you print an actual outline, with indented levels, just like what you see on the screen? Your best bet is to generate a table of contents, as you will learn in Chapter 25, "Creating Tables of Contents and Other Listings," and then print the table of contents.

22

The same goes for copying an outline. When you select a collapsed outline and then copy it and paste it, the pasted copy is the full document, not just the outline, and you can't change that. The only way to get a copy of just the outline headings is to generate a table of contents.

USING AUTOSUMMARIZE

The AutoSummarize feature has been removed from Word 2007, but the old Word 2003 version of it is still available, if you know where to look for it.

AutoSummarize attempts to summarize a document based on the frequency of certain words and phrases used. It's a flawed process, to be sure, and sometimes the results are nonsensical. (That's probably why Microsoft decided to remove the feature in Word 2007.) However, when you're faced with a huge document and not much time to review it, AutoSummarize can be a useful tool in getting a grasp on the main points. AutoSummarize works best on scientific papers, theses, articles, and reports. It does not work very well on fiction, correspondence, or how-to instructions.

To use AutoSummarize, you'll first need to add it to the Quick Access toolbar:

1. Choose Office, Word Options and then click Customize.
2. Open the Choose Commands From list and select Commands Not in the Ribbon.
3. Click AutoSummary Tools and then click Add>>.
4. Click OK.

Now an AutoSummary Tools drop-down list appears on the Quick Access toolbar, and you can use it to select summary commands (see Figure 22.13).

Figure 22.13
Add the AutoSummary tools to the Quick Access toolbar.

Then follow these steps to summarize a document:

1. On the Quick Access toolbar, choose AutoSummary Tools, Auto Summarize. The AutoSummarize dialog box opens.
2. Click the type of summary you want:
   - **Highlight Key Points**—This marks the key points in yellow highlighting. You can then review them in the document, without taking anything out of context.
   - **Create a New Document and Put the Summary There**—Word takes the content that it thinks is important and creates a new document. This new document remains when you turn AutoSummarize off.

- **Insert an Executive Summary or Abstract at the Top of the Document—**
  This copies the content that Word thinks is important to the beginning of the
  document, where it can be edited and saved. This new text remains when you turn
  AutoSummarize off.

- **Hide Everything But the Summary Without Leaving the Original
  Document—**This option hides everything but the parts it thinks are important. It
  does not actually delete the rest of the document; it just hides it for as long as
  AutoSummarize is enabled.

3. In the Length of Summary box, enter the percentage of the original that the summary
   should be. A common percentage for a summary is 25%.

4. Click OK. The summary is created, in whatever form you specified in step 2.

5. If you specified highlighting or hiding, get the original document back by choosing
   Close from the AutoSummary Tools menu on the Quick Access toolbar.

   Alternatively, if you created a new document or inserted an executive summary, examine
   and edit it; then keep or discard it.

> **TIP**
>
> If you want to remove the AutoSummarize button from the Quick Access toolbar, right-
> click the button and choose Remove from Quick Access Toolbar.

TROUBLESHOOTING

ALL LEVELS CONTINUE THE SAME NUMBERS ON MY OUTLINE

One common problem in a document that uses custom styles is that Word numbers every
paragraph equally when you apply a multilevel list, so you end up with something like this:

    1) Major Heading

       2) Minor Heading

       3) Minor Heading

    4) Major Heading

First, check to make sure the appropriate outline level has been assigned to each style. To
modify a paragraph style to appear at a certain outline level, see "Setting a Style's Outline
Level" earlier in this chapter.

If that doesn't work, try manually assigning a particular list level to all the paragraphs that
use that style. From the Styles pane, right-click the style and choose Select All *xx* Instances.
Then open the Multilevel List button's menu on the Home tab, point to Change List Level,
and click the desired list level.

SUBORDINATE ITEMS DON'T RESTART NUMBERING UNDER A NEW MAJOR HEADING

Another potential problem with outline numbering is that the subordinate items don't restart the numbering after an intervening major heading, like this:

1) Major Heading
      A. Minor Heading
      B. Minor Heading
2) Major Heading
      C. Minor Heading
      D. Minor Heading

To correct this problem, modify the list style definition (or create a new multilevel list definition) and make sure that the Restart List After check box is marked and the appropriate upper level is selected (see Figure 22.14).

Figure 22.14
The subordinate levels should be set to restart their numbering.

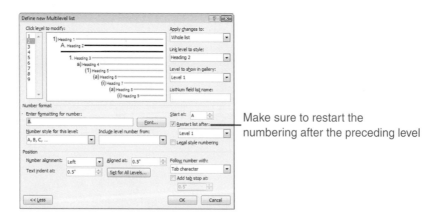

Make sure to restart the numbering after the preceding level

I CAN'T EDIT A MULTILEVEL LIST DEFINITION

This is one of the inherent drawbacks of using a multilevel list definition instead of a list style. You can't edit it. You have to create a new multilevel list.

Fortunately, it's not difficult to recreate the list. Select the outline (or text that has the existing list applied to it) and then start a new multilevel list definition. It will take its default settings from the selected text; just make the changes necessary and click OK to save the new definition.

If you want to save the multilevel list definition as a list style, select the text to which it is applied. Then from the Multilevel List button's menu, choose Define New List Style. The new list style's default settings will be based on the selected text.

To modify the definition of a list style, right-click the style on the Multilevel List button's menu and choose Modify. (This command is not available on the right-click menu for non–style list definitions.)

USING MASTER DOCUMENTS

In this chapter

23

UNDERSTANDING MASTER DOCUMENTS

When a Word document grows to be more than a certain size—usually around 100 pages or so—it starts becoming unwieldy to work with. It takes longer to save and open than normal, and sometimes there are delays in scrolling, pagination, and picture display. And the larger it gets, the more pronounced the problems become. To get around this, many people create large documents in chunks, with each chunk residing in a separate Word file. For example, as I was writing this book, I put each chapter in a separate document.

Dividing a large writing project into separate files has disadvantages, though, especially if you are doing your own desktop publishing from within Word. Each document has its own page numbering and styles, and it can be a challenge to generate a master table of contents or index that encompasses all the files.

The Master Documents feature in Word offers a compromise between the two approaches. A master document is a regular Word document that contains active links to multiple other document files, inserted as *subdocuments*. When the links to the subdocuments expanded, the master document appears to contain all their content, so you can view your entire project as if it were a single document.

A master document does not just help with viewing, however. You can also perform the following tasks:

- Do a single spell-check for all subdocuments.
- Number pages consecutively across all subdocuments.
- Number captions and footnotes consecutively.
- Generate a single index for all subdocuments.
- Generate a single table of contents.

In some instances, a master document offers the best of both worlds when working with large documents—you retain the flexibility and performance of individual document files for each section, while still gaining the benefits of having a combined document.

CAUTION

> The use of master and subdocuments in Word has always been somewhat flaky, dating back to its first implementation. For whatever reason, Microsoft has not seen fit to give this feature the overhaul it very much needs. While you can successfully make use of master and subdocuments, treat the files and folders in which these documents reside with caution. It's very easy to gum up the works if you move or rename a master or subdocument file from its original location.

MASTER DOCUMENTS AND STYLES

Master documents enforce a consistent set of formatting across multiple subdocuments, some of which might have very different formatting from the others. Toward this end, the master document imposes its own definition of each style on all the subdocuments.

Subdocuments retain their own style definitions when they are opened up for editing separately from the master document. If you open a subdocument using the Office, Open command, it shows its own styles. If you open a subdocument from its link in a master document, on the other hand, it shows the styles from the master document.

For example, suppose that your master document defines Heading 1 as Arial Bold, and you import another document into it as a subdocument that defines Heading 1 as Times New Roman. When viewed as part of the master document, the headings in the subdocument appear as Arial Bold, but when the subdocument is viewed as a standalone document, its headings appear as Times New Roman.

The master document redefines the definitions for any styles that it has in common with the subdocuments, but if a subdocument contains a style that the master does not contain, that custom style carries over to the master document. For example, suppose in the subdocument you have a style called MyHead1, and it's applied to all the headings in the subdocument. The master document does not have this style. When the subdocument is imported into the master document, those headings will remain MyHead1, and they will not change.

There's an exception to this rule, though. If MyHead1 is based on another style, and that style is differently defined in the master document, then you might see a trickle-down change. For example, if MyHead1 is based on Heading 1, then any facet of MyHead1 that is not explicitly defined will carry over from the master document's definition of Heading 1.

→ For more information about styles, **see** "Understanding Styles," **p. 228**.

MASTER DOCUMENTS AND HEADERS/FOOTERS

The master document applies its headers and footers to all the subdocuments. If a subdocument has its own header or footer that is different, it will be suppressed when the subdocument is viewed within the master document. (However, the subdocument's own header and footer will continue to be available when the subdocument is opened outside of the master document.)

That doesn't mean, however, that you can't have different headers and footers for each subdocument. When Word inserts subdocuments, it separates them with continuous section breaks. (You can see this by switching to Draft view.) And as you learned in Chapter 9, "Formatting Documents and Sections," each section can have its own header and footer definition. Therefore, you can set up different headers and footers for each subdocument from within the master document.

→ For information about creating headers and footers that are different for each section of a document, **see** "Working with Multiple Headers/Footers," **p. 285**.

MASTER DOCUMENTS AND TOCS AND INDEXES

Tables of contents and indexes work the same way in a master document as in any other document. You position the insertion point where you want the TOC or index to appear, and then you generate it using the commands on the References tab.

23

The main thing to watch out for when generating a TOC or index for a master document is to make sure you create it within the master document itself, and not in one of the subdocuments. To ensure you get the insertion point positioned correctly, display the document in Outline view and then click outside of any of the subdocument borders. Then switch back to Print Layout view (or whatever view you prefer to work in) and create the table of contents or index.

→ For information about creating a table of contents, **see** "Creating a Table of Contents," **p. 748**.

→ To learn how to create an index, **see** "Marking Index Entries," **p. 767** and "Generating the Index," **p. 772**.

Master Documents and Numbered Notes or Captions

Elements such as footnotes, endnotes, figure captions, and other automatically numbered elements are automatically numbered across all subdocuments. The numbering codes continue from one subdocument to the next automatically.

→ To create automatically numbered figure captions, **see** "Using Figure Captions," **p. 422**.

→ To create footnotes and endnotes, **see** "Working with Footnotes and Endnotes," **p. 733**.

Creating a Master Document

There are two ways to go about creating a master document, depending on what raw material you have already created:

- If the subdocuments already exist and you need to combine them into a master document, start with a blank document to be the master document and insert the documents as subdocuments.

- If the entire text exists as a single document and you want to break sections of it into subdocuments, start with the existing document as the master document and then create subdocuments from pieces of it.

The following sections explain each of these procedures in detail.

Inserting Existing Documents into a Master Document

If parts of the document already exist in separate files, a master document can be useful in joining them together without them losing their identities as separate files. After you insert them into the master document, the subdocuments can be edited within the master document or they can be edited as individual files—whatever works best for you.

> **TIP**
>
> To reduce the number of style conflicts between the master document and its subdocuments, apply the same template to all the subdocuments and to the master document before inserting the subdocuments.

To insert a subdocument, follow these steps:

1. Create a new document to function as the master document.

2. (Optional) Type any text into the master document that should exist outside of any subdocuments. For example, perhaps you want a cover page for the project as a whole.

> **TIP**
>
> You don't have to do step 2 now; you can do it anytime. However, sometimes it is easier to find your place in a master document's structure when there is text in it that lies outside of a subdocument, especially when the subdocuments are collapsed. It can also be easier to move the insertion point before the first subdocument later if there is already text there. Therefore, I usually type a few lines of text before the first subdocument, if for no other reason than as a placeholder.

3. If the master document is not already in Outline view, switch to it. This is necessary because the Master Document controls are on the Outlining tab.

4. On the Outlining tab, in the Master Document group, click Show Document.

5. Click the Insert button. The Insert Subdocument dialog box opens.

6. Select the document to be used as a subdocument and then click Open.

The document appears embedded in the main document, surrounded by a nonprinting border (see Figure 23.1). The icon in its top-left corner is a selector; you can click it to select all the text in the subdocument at once.

At this point, the display is still in Outline view, but you can switch to any view you like to work with the document. Repeat the steps to insert additional subdocuments where needed.

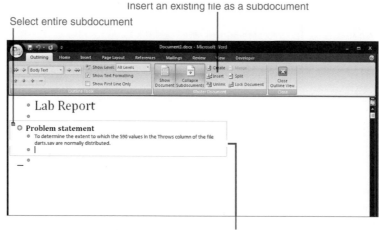

Figure 23.1
The document is inserted as a subdocument.

Insert an existing file as a subdocument

Select entire subdocument

Non-printing border shows boundary of subdocument

SEPARATING AN EXISTING DOCUMENT INTO SUBDOCUMENTS

Now let's look at the other side of the coin—what if the document is *already* in one big file and you want to split out pieces of it into subdocuments? Splitting a large document into subdocuments can dramatically improve Word's performance because it does not have to manage so many pages at once. And by using a master document to keep the pieces joined, you can retain all the benefits of having a single document, such as combined pagination and indexing.

Subdocuments can be especially useful in situations where multiple people are collaborating on a project; by breaking up a document into subdocuments, each person can then take their part and work separately, and then recombine their work into the single master document when finished. For example, in Figure 23.2, a lab report has been broken into subdocuments.

Each heading and its content is in a separate subdocument

Figure 23.2
The document has had its content separated into individual subdocuments.

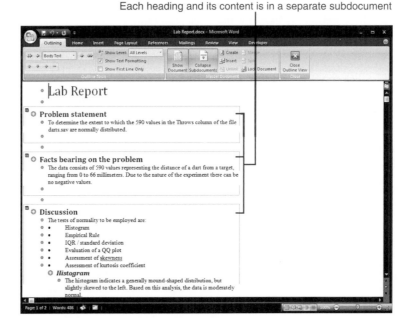

To break text out into a subdocument, it must begin with a heading (preferably a Heading 1 style one, but others will work too). Word uses the text of that heading as the filename for the subdocument.

You can break out individual subdocuments, or you can break up a document into multiple subdocuments all at the same time. If you want to simultaneously create multiple subdocuments, the document must conform to some rules:

- The use of heading styles must be consistent. In other words, for two headings of the same importance in the document, the same style must be applied.

- The heading style that should delineate the subdocument breaks must be the highest level heading used in the selection. It does not *have* to be Heading 1, but a lower level heading will work only if there are no Heading 1 paragraphs in the selection.

To create subdocuments, follow these steps:

1. Switch to Outline view, if not already there, and click the Show Document button on the Outlining tab if needed to make the Create button available.
2. Click the plus sign next to a heading to select it and all the subordinate text beneath it.

   (Optional) To create multiple subdocuments at once, select other headings of the same level as the one you selected above. (Hold down Shift and click on the plus signs to their left.)
3. Click the Create button. Each of the headings in the selection (and all its subordinate text) becomes its own subdocument.

Word assigns subdocument filenames automatically based on the text in the leading heading in the subdocument. It can use up to 229 characters, including spaces in the name, but does not use any symbols or punctuation marks. If it finds one of those, it truncates the name at that point. So, for example, the heading *Don't Panic* would generate a subdocument called Don.docx. If you want to change a subdocument's filename, see "Renaming a Subdocument" later in this chapter.

TIP

> To avoid having to rename files, write the headings with the names you want for the subdocument files. Then after the subdocuments have been created, you can rewrite the headings, if you like.

VIEWING AND COLLAPSING SUBDOCUMENTS

By default, the master document shows all the subdocuments expanded after their insertion. You can collapse them to show only their hyperlinks by clicking Collapse Subdocuments on the Outlining tab (see Figure 23.3).

When you close and reopen a master document, all the subdocuments appear collapsed. To expand them, click Expand Subdocuments on the Outlining tab.

CAUTION

> You cannot expand or collapse individual subdocuments; it's an all-or-none proposition. However, you can open individual subdocuments in their own windows, as you'll learn in the next section.

Once you've inserted or created the subdocuments you need, there's no reason you have to stay in Outline view. Switch to any view you like for editing.

Double-click Subdocument icon to open document

Expand/Collapse Subdocuments toggle

Figure 23.3
When collapsed, sub-documents appear as hyperlinks to the files.

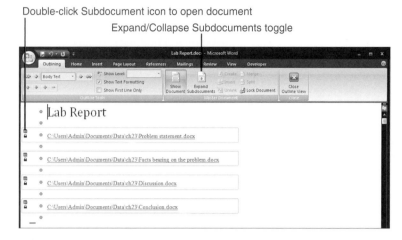

If you switch to Draft view, you'll notice that Word has inserted continuous section breaks between the subdocuments. You must leave these in place; they're necessary for the proper functioning of the master document. These section breaks can also be viewed from Outline view if you toggle off the Show Document feature on the Outlining tab. If you accidentally delete a section break, press Ctrl+Z to undo the deletion, or reinsert the section break.

EDITING SUBDOCUMENTS

You can edit subdocuments within the master document, just as you would any other document content, using any view you like. When you switch to some other view, such as Print Layout, the borders disappear that delineate the subdocuments, so the master document appears to be one big seamless piece. Content can be moved and copied between subdocuments as easily as between different sections in a single document.

To edit a subdocument within the master, follow these steps:

1. Expand the subdocuments, as you learned in the preceding section.
2. Switch to Print Layout view, or your favorite view for text editing.
3. Make changes to the subdocument(s).
4. Save your work (Office, Save). Changes are automatically saved to the subdocuments as well as to the master document.

If you prefer, you can open an individual subdocument for editing in its own window. This is faster and more efficient because Word does not have to keep track of the other subdocuments, and it's the best way to go when you need to make changes that affect only that one subdocument.

There are several ways to open a subdocument in its own Word window:

■ Open the document file as you would any other (Office, Open).

- When subdocuments are collapsed in the master document, Ctrl+click the subdocument's hyperlink.

- Double-click the Subdocument icon to the left of the subdocument in the master document, as shown in Figure 23.3.

When a subdocument is open in its own window, it behaves exactly like any other regular document. There's no indication that it is a subdocument. That's because subdocuments are really just ordinary documents; they are considered subdocuments only in relationship to the master document that references them.

Changes you make to a subdocument from outside the master document are reflected in the master document when you save your work on the subdocument. The copy in the master document cannot be edited while the subdocument is open in a separate window; it is locked there until the separate-window copy is closed.

> **TIP**
>
> You can set up a header and footer for a subdocument, as described in Chapter 9, to be used when the subdocument is printed by itself. When the subdocument is printed as part of the master document, however, it takes on the header and footer of the master document, and any header/footer that it has on its own is ignored.

MODIFYING THE MASTER DOCUMENT'S STRUCTURE

In addition to editing the individual subdocuments, you can also change the way the master document organizes them. The following sections explain some of the changes you can make.

MOVING A SUBDOCUMENT

It's easiest to rearrange subdocuments from Outline view because you can clearly see where each subdocument starts and ends because of the gray outline around each subdocument.

To move a subdocument within the master document, use one of these methods:

- Select the entire subdocument (by clicking its Subdocument icon) and drag and drop it up or down. This can be done when subdocuments are either expanded or collapsed.

- If subdocuments are expanded, select the entire subdocument (by clicking its Subdocument icon) and then cut it to the Clipboard (Ctrl+X). Position the insertion point where you want it to go and then paste it (Ctrl+V).

> **CAUTION**
>
> To maintain the separateness of each subdocument, make sure you drop or paste the subdocument in an empty spot, not within another subdocument. (Combining subdocuments is a separate topic, covered later in this chapter.) If you have a hard time finding an empty spot, click where you want to place the subdocument and press Enter a few times to create some extra space in the master document; then paste the subdocument.

REMOVING A SUBDOCUMENT

To remove a subdocument from the master document completely, select its hyperlink and press Delete on the keyboard. Removing the subdocument from the master document does not delete the subdocument file; it still exists and can be inserted into any other master document or used as a standalone document.

UNLINKING A SUBDOCUMENT

Unlinking a subdocument converts it to regular text within the master document and removes the link to the subdocument file. The subdocument file still exists outside the master document, but it is no longer linked to the master document, so that changes made in one place are no longer reflected in the other.

Here's how to unlink a subdocument:

1. Display the document in Outline view and expand subdocuments.
2. Click anywhere within the subdocument you want to unlink.
3. Click Unlink on the Outlining tab (see Figure 23.4).

Figure 23.4
Select a subdocument and then click Unlink.

Click Unlink to convert the subdocument to regular text within the master document

If you do not want the subdocument anymore after it has been unlinked, delete it from any file management window (Computer, Windows Explorer, and so on).

RENAMING A SUBDOCUMENT

Word automatically assigns subdocument names when you use Create to create new subdocuments out of existing text. These names are derived from the heading text, so usually they are appropriate, but sometimes you might end up with filenames that are too long to be practical or too short to be understandable.

To rename a subdocument's file, follow these steps:

1. Display the master document in Outline view and collapse all subdocuments.
 2. Double-click the Subdocument icon to open the subdocument in a separate Word window.
3. Choose Office, Save As, and save the subdocument under a different name.
4. Close the subdocument's window. The hyperlink in the master document reflects the new name for the subdocument.

The old subdocument file still exists, but it is no longer linked to the master document; instead, the copy with the new name is linked. You can delete the old copy if you like; deleting unused subdocuments keeps your file organization tidy and prevents you from accidentally working with outdated copies.

CAUTION

> Do not rename a subdocument file from Windows Explorer or any other file management window because the master document will lose its connection to it. Rename a subdocument *only* using the procedure described in the preceding steps.

MERGING SUBDOCUMENTS

As you work on your master document, you might find that you have been overzealous creating subdocuments. If it makes more sense to have fewer subdocuments, you can easily combine them.

To combine two subdocuments into a single one, follow these steps:

1. View the master document in Outline view and then expand subdocuments.
2. Make sure the two subdocuments to be merged are adjacent to one another. Move one of them if needed.
3. Select the first subdocument, and then hold down Shift and select the other one, so that both are selected plus any space between them is selected.
4. Click the Merge button on the Outlining tab. The two subdocuments are combined into a single one that has the name of the subdocument that was above the other.

   The old file for the orphaned subdocument still exists on your hard disk; you might want to delete it to avoid later confusion.

Here's an alternative method for merging two subdocuments. This one doesn't involve the Merge button; instead it uses the Outline Tools on the Outlining tab:

1. View the master document in Outline view and then expand subdocuments.
2. Select the text of the subdocument that should move into the other one.
3. Click the Move Up or Move Down arrow button in the Outline Tools group of the Outlining tab to move the selected subdocument up or down one position in the outline. Keep clicking the button until the subdocument has moved completely into the other subdocument's border.
4. Save the master document to save the new content into the combined subdocument.

NESTING SUBDOCUMENTS

Nesting a subdocument is slightly different from merging two subdocuments. When you merge subdocuments, two are combined into one file. When you nest one subdocument inside another, the two separate files continue to exist, but one is referenced within the other. Most people don't use nested subdocuments because most projects are not so long and complex as to need that level of organization. However, when you do have an extremely complex project that needs to be divided up at multiple levels, having the feature available can be a godsend.

When you nest one subdocument inside another, you are in effect creating nested masters. For example, if A is your master document and B and C are your subdocuments, and you choose to nest D and E inside of B, then B is both a subdocument (of A) and a master document (of D and E). Figure 23.5 illustrates this concept.

Figure 23.5
You can nest subdocuments within other subdocuments, creating a virtual document "tree."

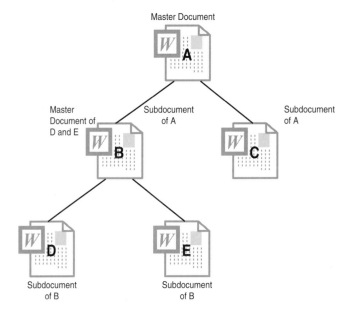

To nest one subdocument into another, follow these steps:

1. View the master document in Outline view and then expand subdocuments.
2. Select the subdocument that is to be nested within another.

3. Drag and drop the Subdocument icon for the selected subdocument inside the border of another subdocument.

The subdocument appears indented, with a gray box inside the gray box of its master.

SPLITTING A SUBDOCUMENT

Splitting a subdocument leaves the first heading and its subordinate text under the original subdocument name, and creates a new subdocument for each of the additional headings. (All the headings must be the same level.)

To split a subdocument, follow these steps:

1. Display the master document in Outline view and expand subdocuments.
2. Ensure that the subdocument begins with a heading of the highest level. (That is, there should be no headings of a higher level later in the subdocument than that one.)
3. Add more headings of the same level as the first one in the spots where you want splits to occur.
4. Select the entire subdocument by clicking the Subdocument icon to its left.
5. Click the Split button on the Outlining tab.
6. Save the master document.

> **NOTE**
>
> Splits and merges appear to happen immediately onscreen, but they do not actually take effect in the data files until you save the master document. That's why if you collapse the subdocuments, Word will ask if you want to save your changes—it can't display accurate filenames until it updates the files.

LOCKING AND UNLOCKING A SUBDOCUMENT

When a subdocument is locked, the copy in the master document cannot be modified, and it does not update when the subdocument is modified outside of the master. It might be useful to lock a subdocument when its content is in flux and you want to preserve the most recent "official" version of it until you are ready to update the entire project.

To lock a subdocument, click anywhere within the subdocument in the master document and then click the Lock Document button on the Outlining tab. A lock icon appears to the left of the subdocument, indicating that it is locked (see Figure 23.6).

Figure 23.6
A locked subdocument shows a lock icon to its left.

Lock a subdocument

Lock icon

If a document appears to be locked even though the Lock Document button is not selected on the Outlining tab, see "The Subdocument Won't Unlock" in the Troubleshooting section at the end of this chapter.

PAGINATING AND PRINTING A MASTER DOCUMENT

A master document's header and footer override those of the individual subdocuments, so pagination is a simple matter. Just place a page-numbering code in the master document's header or footer, and let Word take care of the rest.

→ For information about using page-numbering codes in headers and footers, **see** "Adding and Formatting a Page-Numbering Code," **p. 278**.

The print results are different depending on which view you print from:

- In Outline view, what you see is what will print. Expand or collapse the subdocuments and outline levels and then print. Word prints whatever was showing.

→ To learn about expanding and collapsing outline levels, **see** "Outline Basics," **p. 682**.

- In any other view, the entire master document prints, including all subdocuments, with the page numbering, styles, and headers/footers defined in the master document. (Any of those settings in individual subdocuments that conflict are ignored.)

TROUBLESHOOTING

THE SUBDOCUMENT WON'T UNLOCK

If you can't edit a subdocument within a master document, first make sure that the Lock Document button is not selected on the Outlining tab. Toggle it off there if needed.

If that's not the problem, next check to see if the subdocument is open for editing in a separate Word window. If it is, you won't be able to edit the copy in the master document until you close that separate window.

Finally, check to make sure that the subdocument's file properties have not been set for read-only. Usually you would remember if you set that, but sometimes the read-only property gets set automatically, like when you copy files from a CD-R to your hard disk. It's worth a check.

When multiple users work on subdocuments, local and network file permissions become an issue. For example, if a subdocument is stored in a shared folder to which you have only Read-Only access, the subdocument will appear locked in the master document and you won't be able to unlock it. To fix a situation like that, you must modify the network permissions (or have your administrator do it). It can't be resolved from within Word.

HOW CAN I PREVENT OTHERS FROM EDITING A SUBDOCUMENT?

If you are contributing a subdocument to someone else's master document, perhaps you might want to lock your subdocument so that the person compiling the master document will not be able to make changes to it.

There are several ways to lock the subdocument, some more secure than others:

- Store the subdocument in a folder to which other users have only Read-Only access, but to which you yourself have full access. Instead of providing the document file via email or on disk, point them to the network location where it is stored.

- Set the Read-Only attribute in the file's properties. (Right-click the file and choose Properties to access them.) The users can turn Read-Only off for the file, but they have to know how to do it, so it slows them down.

- When saving the file in the Save As dialog box, click Tools, choose General Options, and mark the Read-Only Recommended check box. This opens the subdocument as Read-Only by default. The user can resave it without Read-Only enabled, but it's an extra step.

- Set a password for the file. To do so, from the Save As dialog box, click Tools, choose General Options, and enter a password in the Password to Modify box. The person assembling the master document will need to know the password to make changes to your subdocument.

And of course, there's also the low-tech method of simply asking your coworker to show you any changes he or she makes.

Master Documents Make Word Crash

Since its inception, the Master Documents feature has always been a bit quirky and buggy, and that fact hasn't changed with Word 2007, unfortunately. The reason is somewhat technical; it has to do with the fact that a master document's hyperlink is not a simple hyperlink but a complex set of hooks that tie the content to the master document. It's this complexity that enables master documents to do all the unique things they can do, such as integrate a single set of styles, but it's also the complexity that makes them crash-prone. There's an interesting article about this at http://word.mvps.org/faqs/general/WhyMasterDocsCorrupt.htm.

If you find yourself with a master document that makes Word crash whenever you open it, there's no good way of repairing it. Instead, convert it to a regular document (by unlinking each subdocument) and then copy and paste its content into a new blank document. Then re-create the subdocuments from that new document.

You might also think about finding an alternative to using master documents for your project. You might insert the files with the Insert Object, Text from File command on the Insert tab, for example. This method does not maintain a dynamic link between the file and its source, but it does let you combine several documents into one.

If you need a dynamic link but don't need the tight integration of numbering, headers/footers, styles, and so on that a master document provides, consider using an OLE link to insert the content, as you learned in Chapter 19, "Copying, Linking, and Embedding Data."

CHAPTER **24**

CITING SOURCES AND REFERENCES

In this chapter

UNDERSTANDING SOURCES AND CITATIONS

A *bibliography* is a list of works cited in a report. Students in most high school and college classes routinely have to write research papers that contain bibliographies, and so do professional researchers and scholars.

Even if you haven't written a research paper lately, you probably have some vivid memories of your last experience in doing so. Citing sources in the proper format (that is, the format your school teaches, or the format customary in your profession) has always been one of those "tear your hair out" tasks because there are so many rules—and exceptions to the rules—regarding the proper capitalization, spacing, and indentation of listings. Entire reference manuals have been published (and have sold very well!) that do nothing but demonstrate how to format various types of entries. And with the rise of Internet research, the potential for confusion over bibliography formatting has only gotten worse because there are even more types of sources from which to draw.

One of the most valuable new features in Word 2007, at least from the perspective of students and researchers, is its ability to automatically generate bibliographies or lists of works cited in any of a variety of well-known formats, including MLA and APA (the big two for academia). I sure could have used this when I was in school!

Citing sources in Word 2007 involves four steps:

1. **Select a citation style.** You can change your mind later about this, but selecting the style you think you are most likely to use will help Word present the applicable fields in which to enter information about your sources.

2. **Enter sources.** You enter each source into an internal database of sources stored in the document. You can do these all upfront, or you can enter them individually as you write the document. Even if a source is referenced multiple times in the document, it needs to be entered only once.

3. **Insert in-text references.** Each time you want to refer to one of the sources in the document, you insert a code that places either a parenthetical reference to the source or a footnote or endnote, depending upon the dictates of the citation style you are using.

4. **Generate a bibliography.** When you are finished with the document, you generate a Bibliography page that presents all the sources from the internal database in a specified format. (In some citation styles, this is called a Works Cited page.)

In the following sections, you will learn how to accomplish each of these steps.

SELECTING A CITATION STYLE

A *citation style* is a set of rules for formatting various types of sources. The most significant difference between them is their handling of citations. Some styles use inline citations, wherein a source is referenced in parentheses after its first usage. The complete information about the source is then presented either in a Bibliography or a Works Cited page. Other styles use numbered footnotes or endnotes. There are also formatting and alphabetization differences between styles.

Select the citation style from the Style drop-down list on the References tab (see Figure 24.1).

Figure 24.1
Select a citation style.

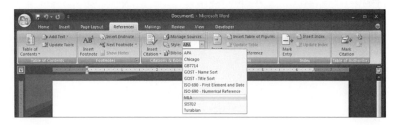

Table 24.1 provides a list of the citation styles that Word 2007 supports. It is not critical for you to understand the differences and subtleties of each format; the main thing is to know which style is required for your school or business.

TIP

> The Citations and Bibliography tools in Word work best if you set the citation style before you begin entering sources. This is because some citation styles require more information about the source than others, and Word needs to make sure that it prompts you appropriately. However, if you change your mind later and choose a different citation style, you do not have to reenter all your source information. In most cases, Word can make the transition seamlessly without reprompting you for additional source information.

TABLE 24.1 CITATION STYLES IN WORD 2007

Word Calls It...	Stands For...	Used In...	Notes
APA	American Psychological Association	Academic research, scientific research, professional journals	Uses inline citations and a Bibliography page
Chicago	Chicago Manual of Style	Journalism, publishing	Uses footnotes or endnotes
GB7714	N/A	China	
GOST	*gosudarstvennyy standart*, which is Russian for "State Standard"	Russia and many former Soviet-bloc countries	Can be sorted by either name or title
ISO 690 First Element and Date	International Standards Organization	Patents, industry, manufacturing	Uses inline citations
ISO 690 Numerical Reference	International Standards Organization	Patents, industry, manufacturing	Uses footnotes or endnotes

continues

TABLE 24.1 CONTINUED			
Word Calls It...	**Stands For...**	**Used In...**	**Notes**
MLA	Modern Language Association	English studies, comparative literature, literary criticism, humanities	Uses inline citations and a Works Cited page
SIST02	N/A	Japan	Used only in Asia
Turabian	Named for its developer, Kate Turabian	Academic research, especially musicology, history, and theology	A simplified version of Chicago Manual of Style format

CAUTION

> As mentioned in Table 24.1, some citation styles use footnotes or endnotes instead of in-text citations. However, Word does not enforce that particular convention; if you use Insert Citation, Word always inserts an inline citation, even if your chosen citation style does not use inline citations. Therefore, be aware of the rules regarding inline or footnote citations in your chosen style at least at a basic level.

ENTERING SOURCES

Word 2007 stores the sources you enter in a database inside the document, so that the source list is always available whenever that document is open. Sources can also be saved to a master database called Sources.xml, located in Users\username\Roaming\Microsoft\Bibliography, so you can reuse sources in multiple documents.

As you enter the data for a source, Word displays the field text boxes to fill in based upon the type of source being used. For example, if you are entering information about a book, it prompts you for fields including Author, Title, and Publisher, whereas for a piece of artwork, it prompts for fields such as Artist, Title, and Institution.

To add a source, follow these steps:

1. Check to make sure you have chosen the appropriate style from the Style list. See the preceding section for details.
2. On the References tab, in the Citations & Bibliography group, choose Manage Sources. The Source Manager dialog box opens.
3. Click the New button. The Create Source dialog box opens.
4. Open the Type of Source list and choose the type (for example, Book, Journal Article, or Web site). The fields change to reflect what's needed for that type of source. For example, Figure 24.2 shows the fields for a book.

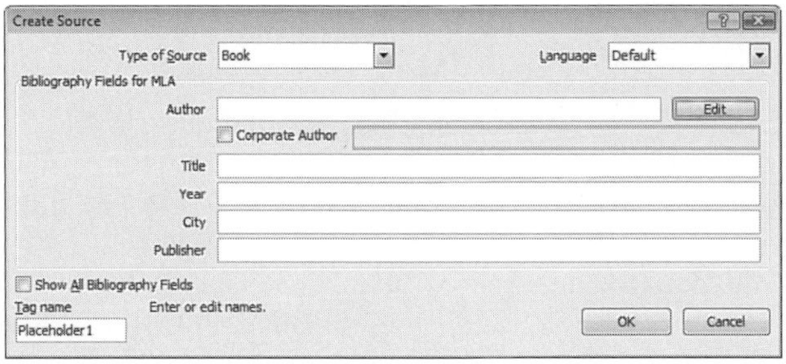

Figure 24.2
Fill in the fields provided for the selected source type.

5. Enter the author or artist's name in one of these ways:

- Type the author's full name directly into the Author or Artist box. You can type it either as *First Middle Last* or as *Last, First Middle*. (Word can figure it out based on your usage of a comma or not.) If there is more than one author, separate them with semicolons.

- If the author is an organization, mark the Author as Organization check box and then enter the organization's name.

- Click the Edit button and enter each part of the name in the boxes provided in the Edit Name dialog box (see Figure 24.3). If there is only one author, click OK; if there are multiple authors, click Add after each one, and click OK when finished.

Figure 24.3
Specify the parts of the name explicitly in the Last, First, and Middle boxes.

TIP

> Multiple authors are usually ordered alphabetically by last name. If one author is more significant than the others, use the Up and Down buttons in the Edit Name dialog box to reorder them.

NOTE

> If you want access to the other fields in the database that Word does not consider applicable to this source type, mark the Show All Bibliography Fields check box.

6. Fill in the other fields for the selected source type.

7. Click OK to return to the Source Manager dialog box.

8. Create more sources, or click Close when you are finished.

EDITING A SOURCE

It is uncommon to need to edit a source (unless you make a mistake when initially entering it) because a source represents a fixed point in time. A book is published, and its author, date, and title never change. However, online sources are changing this rule a bit because their content can change on a daily basis, so the information you retrieve depends on the date on which you accessed it.

To edit the information for a source, follow these steps:

1. On the References tab, click Manage Sources. The Source Manager dialog box opens.

2. Click the desired source, either from the Master List or the Current List, depending on which location you want to change. If you want to change both the copy in the document and the master copy, it does not matter which you select (see Figure 24.4).

Figure 24.4
Select the source to be changed.

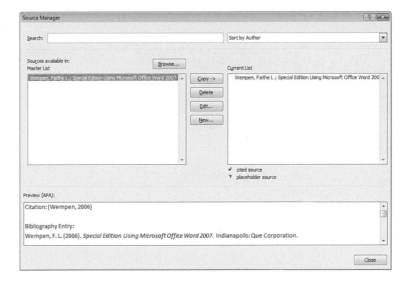

3. Click Edit. The Edit Source dialog box opens. It's the same as the Create Source dialog box from Figure 24.2.

4. Make any changes needed to the source information.

5. Click OK.

6. Change another source, or click Close.

DELETING A SOURCE

You can delete a source from the Master List, from the Current List, or from both places. However, if the source is cited in the current document, you must delete the citation before you can delete the source to which it refers from the Current List. (You can still remove it from the Master List without deleting the citation.)

To delete a citation, follow these steps:

1. On the References tab, click Manage Sources. The Source Manager dialog box opens.
2. Click the desired source, either from the Master List or the Current List, depending on which location you want to delete the source from (refer to Figure 24.4).
3. Click Delete. The source is removed from the list.
4. Delete other sources, or click Close.

TRANSFERRING SOURCES TO AND FROM THE MASTER LIST

The Master List is a source database maintained separately from the current document. You can use it to quickly retrieve previously used sources for use in other documents. By default, every source you create is entered into the Master List.

To transfer sources between the Current List and the Master List, follow these steps:

1. On the References tab, click Manage Sources. The Source Manager dialog box opens.
2. Click the desired source, either from the Master List or the Current List.
3. Click the Copy button to copy that source from its current list to the other one. The button face changes to show a → or ← arrow, depending on which side is selected (see Figure 24.4).

> **TIP**
>
> The most common copy direction is from the Master List to the Current List. Because the Master List's entries are automatically created, there is usually not much reason to copy a source to the Master List. However, if you accidentally delete a source from the Master List, you might want to copy that source back to it from the Current List.

INSERTING INLINE REFERENCES TO SOURCES

An inline reference to a source is inserted in parentheses in the text. Depending on the citation style you have chosen and the type of source you are citing, the parenthetical citation includes one or more of these items:

- Author's name (always included)
- Year
- Title
- Page number

The most common usage is the author name and date, like this:

A recent study has found that students who abstain from illegal drug use are 25% more likely to finish high school than students who do not (Smith, 2006).

Even if the citation style requires these elements, they may be omitted if the text includes them. For example:

A recent study by Sally Smith (2006) found that students who abstain from illegal drug use are 25% more likely to finish high school than students who do not.

→ To omit part of a citation, **see** "Editing a Citation," **p. 728**.

To insert a citation, follow these steps:

1. Position the insertion point where you want the citation.

   Depending on the context, the citation can go at the end of the sentence (as in the first of the preceding examples) or within the sentence (as in the second example).

2. On the References tab, click Insert Citation. A menu appears listing all the sources in the current document (see Figure 24.5).

3. Click the desired source. A reference to it is inserted as a field.

Figure 24.5
Select the source to cite.

→ If the desired source does not appear on the list but you have all the information you need to enter it now, **see** "Creating a New Source When Entering a Citation," **p. 726**.

→ If the desired source does not appear on the list and you do not have the needed information to enter it now, **see** "Inserting Temporary Placeholders for Later Entry of Sources," **p. 727**.

CREATING A NEW SOURCE WHEN ENTERING A CITATION

Sometimes it's hard to know what sources to enter until you get to the point in the document where you need to cite them. If you did not already enter the source you want to use, follow these steps to insert the citation and create its source entry at the same time:

1. Position the insertion point where you want the citation.

2. On the References tab, click Insert Citation. A menu appears (refer to Figure 24.5).

3. Click Add New Source. The Create Source dialog box appears.

4. Enter the information for the new source, as you did in the section "Entering Sources" earlier in this chapter.

5. Click OK in the Create Source dialog box. The source is created and a citation for it is inserted in the document.

INSERTING TEMPORARY PLACEHOLDERS FOR LATER ENTRY OF SOURCES

As you are writing the document, perhaps you realize there is a source you need to cite but you don't have all the details handy to formally enter it as a source. In situations like that, you can create a temporary placeholder for the source, so you can go ahead and insert its citations. Then later, when you have all the facts you need, you can update the source listing in the Source Manager.

To insert a citation and create a temporary placeholder for the source, follow these steps:

1. Position the insertion point where you want the citation.

2. On the References tab, click Insert Citation. A menu appears (refer to Figure 24.5).

3. Click Add New Placeholder. The Placeholder Name dialog box appears.

4. Type a name for the placeholder. A good name would be something that will help you remember the source you plan on citing, such as the author's last name or an abbreviated version of the article title.

5. Click OK. A citation is inserted into the document with the placeholder in parentheses.

To complete the information for a placeholder when you have the information available, follow these steps:

1. On the References tab, click Manage Sources.

2. On the Current List, click the placeholder. Placeholders are identified by question mark icons, as in Figure 24.6.

3. Click Edit. The Edit Source dialog box opens.

4. Enter the information needed for the source and click OK.

5. Complete other placeholders, or click Close.

Placeholder

Figure 24.6
Select and edit the
placeholder.

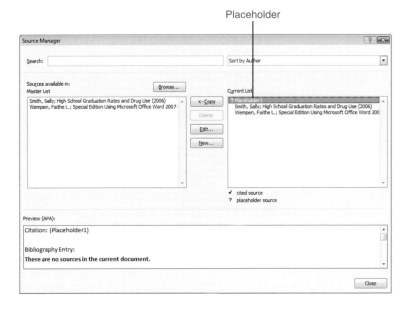

EDITING A CITATION

A citation is a field that pulls its information from the source on which it is based, so you cannot edit its text directly. You can, however, show or suppress certain pieces of information. For example, you can make a citation show a page range (useful when citing two or more articles in the same journal, for example), and you can suppress the usage of the author, date, and/or title.

To edit a citation, follow these steps:

1. Click the citation in the document. It appears in a blue box, indicating that it is a field.
2. Click the down arrow to the right of the field, opening a menu (see Figure 24.7).

Figure 24.7
Open the menu for
the citation field.

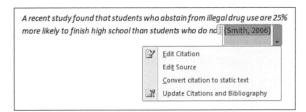

3. Click Edit Citation. The Edit Citation dialog box opens (see Figure 24.8).

Figure 24.8
Include a page range
or suppress one or
more of the standard
items.

4. (Optional) To add page numbers, type a range in the Pages box. Use a dash but no spaces to separate a range, like this: 12-24.

5. (Optional) In the Suppress area, click the check box for any elements to suppress.

TIP

> Even if a certain element does not appear in the current citation style, you can still suppress it, so that if you change to a different citation style that does include that element, it will be suppressed at that point.

CONVERTING A CITATION TO PLAIN TEXT

To edit a citation directly (that is, by changing its text), and not just add or suppress elements, you must convert it to plain text so that it is no longer a field linked to a source.

As you can imagine, converting a citation to plain text is not a good idea in most cases because it no longer updates when you change the source information or the citation style. However, sometimes it's the only way to achieve the desired effect.

To convert a citation to text, follow these steps:

1. Click the citation in the document. It appears in a blue box, indicating that it is a field.

2. Click the down arrow to the right of the field, opening a menu (refer to Figure 24.7).

3. Click Convert Citation to Static Text. The citation remains in place but is no longer a field.

GENERATING A BIBLIOGRAPHY

The bibliography appears at the end of the document, and lists all the sources cited. Usually sources are arranged alphabetically by the author's last name.

NOTE

> A couple of citation styles arrange bibliography entries differently. For example, GOST – Title Sort sorts by title, and ISO – 690 Numerical Reference sorts chronologically by position in the document. (That style also numbers inline references rather than using author and date.)

The formatting of the bibliography, and the facts that appear about each source, depend heavily on the citation style in use. For example, Table 24.2 shows the same entry in several different styles. As you can see, some styles use bold, italics, and/or underlining, some use the complete name of the author, some begin with the title rather than the author's name, and so on. Some separate items with commas, some use ellipses, and some use colons.

TABLE 24.2   COMPARISON OF BIBLIOGRAPHY FORMATTING AMONG CITATION STYLES

Citation Style	Example
APA	Smith, S. (2006). High School Graduation Rates and Drug Use. *Journal of Education Research*, 23-31.
Chicago and **Turabian**	Smith, Sally. "High School Graduation Rates and Drug Use." Journal of Education Research (2006): 23-31.
GB7714 and **ISO 690** **First Element and Date**	**High School Graduation Rates and Drug Use. Smith, Sally. . 2006.** , Journal of Education Research, 23-31.
MLA	Smith, Sally. "High School Graduation Rates and Drug Use." Journal of Education Research (2006): 23-31.
ISO 690 **Numerical Reference**	1. High School Graduation Rates and Drug Use. **Smith, Sally. .** , 2006, Journal of Education Research, 23-31.
SIST02	High School Graduation Rates and Drug Use. Smith, Sally. , 2006, Journal of Education Research, 23-31.

I've shown you the examples in Table 24.2 not to try to teach you the syntax of each style, but rather to illustrate how changing the citation style affects the bibliography. You can change to a different citation style either before or after the bibliography is generated, and Word will automatically keep the entire document's citations and bibliography consistent with the selected style.

Word 2007 comes with four built-in bibliography layouts in its Bibliography Gallery:

- **Bibliography**—Begins with a Heading 1 styled "Bibliography" paragraph, followed by the entries in a paragraph style called Bibliography. Does not start the bibliography on a new page.

- **Bibliography Page**—Same as Bibliography, except it does start on a new page.

- **Works Cited**—Same as Bibliography, except the text at the top is "Works Cited" instead. Does not start on a new page.

- **Works Cited Page**—Same as Works Cited, except it does start on a new page.

You can create additional bibliography-formatting specifications and save them to the Bibliography Gallery for later reuse if desired.

INSERTING A BIBLIOGRAPHY FROM THE BIBLIOGRAPHY GALLERY

The Bibliography Gallery is the list of bibliography layouts that appears when you open the Bibliography button's list on the References tab. Word calls the layouts "bibliographies," although of course they are not real bibliographies but codes that generate bibliographies using the sources in the current document. That's important because you can save and reuse bibliographies between documents.

TIP

These layouts are actually building blocks that can be renamed, deleted, and so on from the Building Blocks Organizer. See "Working with Building Blocks" in Chapter 3, "Typing and Editing Text," for details.

To create a bibliography using one of the layouts in the Gallery, follow these steps:

1. Position the insertion point where you want the bibliography to appear.

2. On the References tab, click Bibliography.

3. Click the gallery entry that best represents the bibliography you want to create (see Figure 24.9). It is inserted in the document at the current position.

Figure 24.9
Open the Bibliography Gallery.

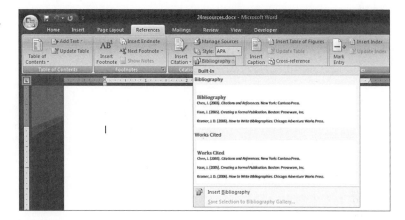

If you want to insert the bibliography at the beginning or end of the document or the current section, you do not have to move the insertion point to the desired spot beforehand (step 1). Instead you can right-click a gallery entry and select a location from the shortcut menu, as in Figure 24.10.

Figure 24.10
Select a position for the bibliography from its shortcut menu in the gallery if desired.

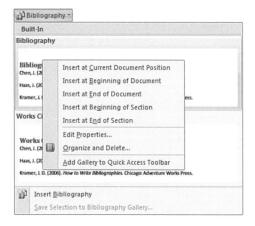

24

WORKING WITH A BIBLIOGRAPHY FIELD

The inserted bibliography appears in a field, with a light blue box around it like any other field.

You can click the Bibliographies button at the top to open a menu, as shown in Figure 24.11, from which you can do three things:

- You can convert the bibliography to static text, so that it no longer updates and can be edited freely like any other text.

- You can filter the entries to show only the ones in your native language.

- You can access the Bibliography Gallery to choose a different preset.

Figure 24.11
The button at the top of the bibliography provides commands for managing the field.

SAVING A BIBLIOGRAPHY AS A NEW GALLERY ENTRY

After inserting a bibliography, you can format its text. For example, you can apply a different heading style to its heading, or a different body style to its body, or you can add indentation or other special formatting.

Then you can save your changed version of the bibliography as a new Bibliography Gallery entry for later reuse. To create a new entry, follow these steps:

1. Format the bibliography as you want it.

2. Select the bibliography. On the References tab, click Bibliography and select Save Selection to Bibliography Gallery. The Create New Building Block dialog box opens.

3. Change the name in the Name box to something descriptive of the format you're creating.

CAUTION

> The default name is the text from the first entry in the bibliography at present, or is blank, and neither of those are a good name because you will potentially apply this bibliography format in other documents that do not have these same sources.

4. (Optional) Enter a brief description in the Description box (see Figure 24.12).

5. Click OK to create the new bibliography gallery entry.

Figure 24.12
Create a new building block entry for the bibliography.

Your gallery entries appear at the bottom of the Bibliography button's menu. (Scroll down the menu if you don't see them at first.) To access its building block properties later, right-click it and choose Edit Properties.

REMOVING A BIBLIOGRAPHY FROM THE GALLERY

To remove one of your custom bibliographies from the gallery, follow these steps:

1. On the References tab, click Bibliography, and scroll down the list to locate your custom entry.

2. Right-click the entry and choose Organize and Delete. The Building Blocks Organizer dialog box opens with the chosen entry already selected.

3. Click the Delete button.

4. Click Yes to confirm.

5. Click Close.

WORKING WITH FOOTNOTES AND ENDNOTES

Another way of citing a source is to create a footnote or endnote for it. Footnotes and endnotes are the same except for their position: *footnotes* appear at the bottom of the page on which the reference occurs, whereas *endnotes* appear at the end of the document or section.

Figure 24.13 shows a footnote and points out some of the key features involved in footnote usage:

- **Reference mark**—Appears within the body text. This is usually a number but can also be a symbol.

- **Separator line**—The line that separates the body text from the footnote area.

- **Footnote reference**—The corresponding number or symbol to the reference mark, appearing at the beginning of the footnote.

- **Footnote text**—The footnote itself. It is different from the footnote reference, and is formatted using a different style.

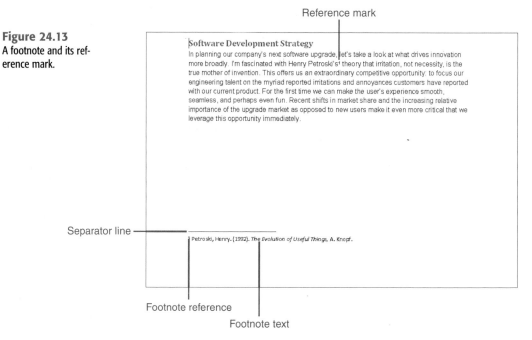

Figure 24.13
A footnote and its reference mark.

An endnote also has all those same pieces: reference mark, separator line, endnote reference, and endnote text. However, with an endnote, the separator line and the notes that follow it appear on the last page of the document, immediately after the last body text paragraph (not at the bottom of the page).

NOTE

> In this section of the chapter, I'll refer to footnotes and endnotes generically as "notes" for simplicity whenever there is no difference between them in functionality.

Where Should the Reference Mark Be Placed?

A reference mark is usually placed either immediately after the item being referenced or at the end of the sentence. There is no hard-and-fast rule for choosing between these, but logic usually dictates the best choice.

Often the placement of the reference mark sets up reader expectations of what the note will contain. For example:

The Kemmerly Hypothesis[1] has some merit in the Johnson case, in my opinion.

Readers will expect the footnote to explain the Kemmerly Hypothesis itself, unrelated to the Johnson case.

The Kemmerly Hypothesis has some merit in the Johnson case, in my opinion[1].

Readers will expect the footnote to elaborate on your assertion of the applicability of the Kemmerly Hypothesis to the case.

INSERTING A FOOTNOTE

To insert a standard footnote, do either of the following:

- Press Ctrl+Alt+F.
- On the References tab, click Insert Footnote.

Word inserts a reference mark at the insertion point, and then jumps to the bottom of the page and places a footnote reference. It then leaves the insertion point flashing there next to the footnote reference, so you can type the footnote text.

If you're working in Draft view, footnotes do not appear on the document page itself. Instead a separate Notes pane appears at the bottom of the Word window, as in Figure 24.14. If the pane does not appear, click the Show Notes button on the References tab. The divider between the panes can be dragged up or down to see more or less of the note area at once.

Figure 24.14
A new footnote in Draft view, ready for you to enter its text.

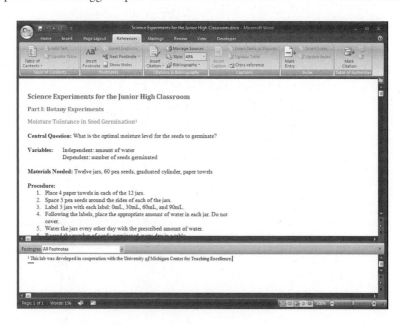

NOTE

To move a reference mark, select it and then cut and paste it or drag it to a new location. If the new location puts it out of sequence, Word automatically renumbers the notes. To copy a footnote, copy its reference mark (with a copy-and-paste or a Ctrl+drag-and-drop operation). Word creates a copy of the note too.

INSERTING AN ENDNOTE

To insert an endnote, do either of the following:

- Press Ctrl+Alt+D.
- On the References tab, click Insert Endnote.

Word inserts a reference mark at the insertion point, and then jumps to the end of the document and places a new endnote reference. It leaves the insertion point flashing there so you can type the endnote text.

In Draft view, endnotes appear just like footnotes, in the separate Notes pane at the bottom of the screen (refer to Figure 24.14).

DELETING A NOTE

To delete a note, delete its reference mark in the body text. The footnote or endnote goes away automatically.

You can delete all the text for a footnote or endnote, but its number or symbol remains in the Notes pane (or at the bottom of the page or end of the document) until you delete the reference mark from the body of the document.

JUMPING TO THE NOTE THAT CORRESPONDS TO A REFERENCE MARK

When working with footnotes, it's easy enough to find the note that corresponds to the number or symbol—just scroll down to the bottom of the page. However, with endnotes, it is not always so easy because the note might be on a page far removed from its reference.

To jump to the footnote or endnote, double-click the reference mark in the body text.

MOVING BETWEEN NOTES

There are several ways to jump from one footnote or endnote reference mark to another within the body text.

Perhaps the easiest method is to use the Next Footnote button on the References tab. Click it to go to the next footnote, or open its menu to go to the previous footnote or the next or previous endnote (see Figure 24.15).

Figure 24.15
Use the Next Footnote button to move between notes.

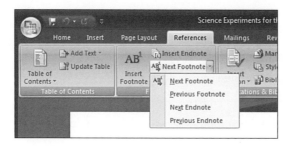

Another way to move between notes is with the Go To command on the Home tab. This method lets you specify a certain footnote or endnote number to find:

1. On the Home tab, click the arrow beside the Find button and click Go To. The Find and Replace dialog box opens with the Go To tab displayed.
2. On the Go To What list, click Footnote or Endnote.
3. Enter the footnote or endnote number you want to find (see Figure 24.16).

    You can either enter an exact number or enter a plus or minus sign and a number to move relative to the current position (-2, for example).
4. Click Go To.
5. Click Close.

Figure 24.16
Use Go To to jump to a specific footnote or endnote.

Finally, you can "page" through the footnotes or endnotes with the Select Browse Object controls below the vertical scroll bar:

1. Click the Select Browse Object button, and then click Browse by Footnote or Browse by Endnote (see Figure 24.17).
2. Click the Previous or Next button to jump to the next or previous instance of whichever you chose.

Figure 24.17
Use Select Browse Object and then browse by footnote or endnote.

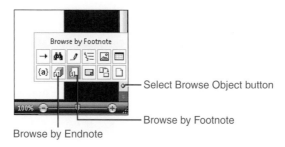

SWITCHING BETWEEN FOOTNOTES AND ENDNOTES

Perhaps you started out using footnotes and later decide you want endnotes instead—or vice versa. No matter; it's easy to change between them.

One way is to change each note individually:

- To change a footnote to an endnote, right-click it and choose Convert to Endnote.
- To change an endnote to a footnote, right-click the endnote text and choose Convert to Footnote.

Another way is to change all the notes in the document at once:

1. Right-click any note and choose Note Options, or click the dialog box launcher in the Footnotes group of the References tab. The Footnote and Endnote dialog box opens.

2. Click the Convert button. The Convert Notes dialog box appears. The options available depend on what type of notes you already have in the document. For example, in Figure 24.18, the only option is to convert footnotes to endnotes because the document does not currently contain any endnotes.

Figure 24.18
Convert all notes at once.

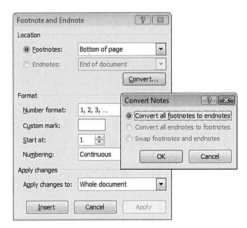

3. Click OK and then click Close.

CHANGING THE POSITIONING OF THE NOTES

Notes can appear either at the bottom of the page or immediately below the text on the page. By default, footnotes appear at the bottom and endnotes appear below the text, but this can be changed.

To change the text positioning, follow these steps:

1. Right-click any note and choose Note Options, or click the dialog box launcher in the Footnotes group of the References tab. The Footnote and Endnote dialog box opens.

2. In the Location section, open the drop-down list for Footnotes or Endnotes and choose the desired position (see Figure 24.19).

3. Click Apply.

Figure 24.19
Change where the footnotes or endnotes will be placed on the page(s).

CHANGING THE NOTE NUMBERING OR SYMBOLS

By default, footnotes use Arabic numbering (1, 2, 3) and endnotes use lowercase Roman numbering (i, ii, iii).

To change to a different style of numbering, or to a set of symbols, follow these steps:

1. Right-click any note and choose Note Options, or click the dialog box launcher in the Footnotes group of the References tab. The Footnote and Endnote dialog box opens.

2. Select a format from the Number Format list (see Figure 24.19).

This setting will apply to all the notes in the document or section.

Alternatively, you can enter a custom symbol to use, or browse for a symbol.

This setting will apply to only the current footnote or endnote; it enables you to enter your own symbols to use for each note on an individual basis. Your own symbols override the default ones.

3. (Optional) Set a different Start At value than 1 if desired.

4. (Optional) To restart numbering with each section or page, choose how you want restarts to occur from the Numbering list. The default is Continuous, which means no restarting of numbering.

5. In the Apply Changes To list, choose the scope for your changes. Unless you have multiple sections in your document, the only choice here is Whole Document.

6. Click Apply.

MODIFYING NOTE STYLES

You can format footnotes or endnotes manually, as you can any text, but it is much more efficient to modify their styles instead and let those changes populate automatically through the document.

Four styles are used for notes:

- **Footnote reference**—For the reference mark that appears in the footnote area.
- **Footnote text**—For the text of the footnote.
- **Endnote reference**—For the reference mark that appears in the endnote area.
- **Endnote text**—For the text of the endnote.

Here's a way to modify a style used in a footnote or endnote:

1. Display the Styles task pane by clicking the dialog box launcher in the Styles group of the Home tab.
2. Format the footnote or endnote reference or text the way you want the style to be.
3. Select the footnote or endnote reference or text.
4. On the Styles task pane, right-click the style and choose Update to Match Selection.

TIP

> If the footnote and/or endnote styles are not listed in the Styles task pane, access them via the Style Inspector.

And here's another way:

1. Right-click the footnote or endnote reference mark or text and choose Style. The Style dialog box appears.
2. Select the style you want to modify.
3. Click Modify. The Modify Style dialog box appears.
4. Make any changes to the style as needed.
5. Click OK, and then click Apply.

→ To learn more about modifying styles, **see** "Modifying Styles," **p. 248**.

CHANGING THE NOTE SEPARATOR LINE

The *note separator line* is the line between the body text and the footnotes or endnotes. By default, it is a plain 1-point black line that runs one-third of the way across the page.

Word treats this separator line as a single character of text. As such, you can format it only by doing the things you can do to text: You can increase its width and thickness slightly by increasing its "font size," and you can change its color and make it bold.

Here's how to access that line for the limited formatting just described:

1. View the document in Draft view (View tab, Draft).

2. If the Notes pane is not already displayed, click Show Notes on the References tab.

3. In the Footnotes (or Endnotes) drop-down list on the Notes pane, select Footnote Separator (or Endnote Separator). The line appears (see Figure 24.20).

Figure 24.20
To view the line, switch to Draft mode, display the Notes pane, and then choose Footnote Separator from the drop-down list.

4. Select the line.

5. Use the Font tools on the Home tab or on the Mini Toolbar to change the line's color and thickness as desired.

If you want a real AutoShape line as the separator, complete with all the formatting that's inherent in an AutoShape, you won't be able to have it appear automatically on each page that has footnotes. Instead you'll need to delete the line from the Footnote Separator in the Notes pane (refer to Figure 24.20) and then draw a line manually on each page on which a footnote occurs.

TIP

For a double separator line, apply Underline formatting to the separator line.

MANAGING FOOTNOTE CONTINUATIONS

When a footnote is too long to fit on one page and still be on the same page as its reference mark, Word splits the footnote and continues it on the next page. When that happens, a continuation separator and continuation notice appear. The continuation separator line is just like the regular separator line except it's longer. The continuation notice is blank by default; you can enter it in yourself—perhaps something like *(continues on next page)*.

NOTE

Continuation is an issue only for footnotes, not endnotes.

To format the continuation separator and continuation notice:

1. Switch to Draft view.

2. On the References tab, click Show Notes to display the Notes pane if needed.

3. Open the Footnotes drop-down list and choose Footnote Continuation Separator. The separator line appears.

4. Format the separator line as desired. See the preceding section for help with that.

5. Open the Footnotes drop-down list and choose Footnote Continuation Notice. By default, nothing appears.

6. Type the text you want to use as the separation notice into the Notes pane.

7. Close the Notes pane when finished. (Click Show Notes again on the References tab.)

CREATING CROSS-REFERENCES

Perhaps you've noticed that this book has a lot of cross-references. Whenever I'm talking about a topic that's covered in another section, a cross-reference note appears telling you which page to turn to for more information.

Unfortunately, due to the page layout process that this book has to go through, those cross-references are not automatically generated. Yes, believe it or not, there is a person with a four-year college degree whose job is to go through and manually insert the correct page numbers for each of those cross-references.

If only this book were laid out in Microsoft Word 2007, the cross-referencing process could be completely automated. (Of course, someone might be out of a job....) In Word, you can create cross-references to bookmarks, headings, sections, captions, or just about any other marker in a document. These cross-references update dynamically, so if the page on which a particular heading changes, all cross-references to that heading will change too.

You got a taste of cross-referencing in Chapter 19, "Copying, Linking, and Embedding Data," in the section "Inserting a Cross-Reference to a Bookmark," but now let's take a look at the full gamut of cross-referencing that's available.

First, here's how to insert a basic cross-reference:

1. On the References tab, click Cross-Reference. The Cross-Reference dialog box opens.

2. Select the type of item being referenced from the Reference Type list.

3. On the For Which list, select the instance of the reference type to be referenced. For example, if you chose Heading in step 2, select from a list of all the headings in the document (see Figure 24.21).

4. Select the way you want to refer to it from the Insert Reference To list.

5. (Optional) To make the cross-reference a live hyperlink, make sure the Insert as Hyperlink check box is marked.

6. (Optional) To includes the word "above" or "below" with the cross-reference, mark the Include Above/Below check box.

7. Click Insert to insert the cross-reference.

8. Click Close to close the dialog box.

Figure 24.21
Create a cross-reference.

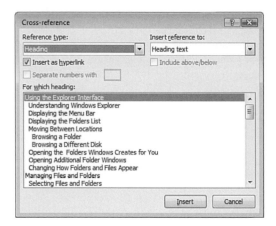

The resulting cross-reference is a field such as {REF}. You can check this out for yourself by right-clicking it and choosing Toggle Field Codes. You can work with it the same as any other field; see Chapter 20, "Working with Fields." (See, another cross-reference! They're everywhere once you start noticing them.)

CAUTION

Cross-references apply only within the current document; you cannot create a cross-reference from one document to another. If you are working with a master document, and there are cross-references between subdocuments, make sure you expand all the subdocuments before printing; otherwise, the cross-references will not work.

CROSS-REFERENCING OPTIONS

Now that you know the basics, let's delve a little further into the types of cross-references you can create. A cross-reference can refer to any of these elements:

Numbered item	Heading
Bookmark	Footnote
Endnote	Equation
Figure	Table

The cross-reference itself can consist of any of these:

- The actual text of the item being referenced.
- The page number on which the referenced item lies.
- The number of the referenced item in the chronology of the document (for example, 3 for the third paragraph).
- The caption of the item (if it has one), either with or without its numbering (for example, *Figure 3: Sales Revenue*).
- The word "Above" or the word "Below," depending on whether the cross-reference comes before or after the item being referenced in the document.

24

> Some editing purists object to the usage of "above" or "below" to refer to material that is actually on a previous or subsequent page. I'm not allowed to use those terms that way in this book, for example! Word does not enforce this rule, though; it will allow you to use Above/Below even when the cross-reference is separated from the item it is referring to by many pages.

CROSS-REFERENCE CONTEXT

Some of the cross-reference types give you a choice of various *contexts*. The context determines how much information will appear depending on where the cross-reference lies in relation to the referenced location.

For example, suppose you want to refer to heading 3(a)(iii). The full context for that reference would appear as 3(a)(iii). But if the cross-reference were also in section 3, you might not need to include the 3; you could simply use (a)(iii). Further, if the cross-reference were in section 3(a), you could simply use (iii).

Word provides three settings for cross-reference types that might have a context. The names are different depending on the type, but here are the ones for headings:

- **Heading Number**—Provides contextual numbering
- **Heading Number (No Context)**—Provides only the lowest level numbering
- **Heading Number (Full Context)**—Provides the complete numbering regardless of position

For numbered items and bookmarks, context is set by paragraph number. (Replace the word "heading" with "paragraph" in the preceding list.)

The other types of cross-references do not support contextual referencing.

FOOTNOTE AND ENDNOTE CROSS-REFERENCES

For footnotes and endnotes, you can choose to insert the note number (formatted or unformatted), the page number on which it appears, or the word "above" or "below." Often it is useful to combine more than one cross-reference in the body of the text, like this:

> *For more information on shellfish allergies, see note 1 on page 47.*

In that example, both the numbers 1 and 47 are separate cross-references. They both refer to the same footnote but they are set up to provide different information.

So what's the difference between a formatted and unformatted note number? An unformatted one takes on the formatting of the paragraph into which you place it; a formatted one retains the formatting applied to footnote reference numbers by the Footnote Reference style.

CAPTION CROSS-REFERENCES

Equations, figures, and tables can all have captions, and these captions can be cross-referenced. When you choose any of these three types of content, you get the following options for what to insert:

- Entire caption (Example: *Table 2: Quantities in Stock*)
- Only label and number (Example: *Table 2*)
- Only caption text (Example: *Quantities in Stock*)
- Page number
- Above/Below

TIP

You can create building blocks for cross-references you want to reuse. Just select the entire block of text, including the cross-reference within it, and on the Insert tab, click Quick Parts, Save Selection to Quick Part Gallery.

TROUBLESHOOTING

HOW CAN I TELL WHAT STYLE A FOOTNOTE OR ENDNOTE IS USING?

Unless you have applied other styles, footnotes always use Footnote Reference for the number and Footnote Text for the text. Endnotes always use Endnote Reference and Endnote Text.

If you're not sure whether the correct styles are applied, try displaying the Styles task pane (from the Styles dialog box launcher on the Home tab) and noting what style is highlighted on that list.

If that doesn't work, click the Style Inspector button on the Styles task pane to display the Style Inspector window. Then click in the footnote or endnote. The style in use will appear there (see Figure 24.22).

Click here to display Styles task pane

Figure 24.22
Use the Style Inspector to check out style usage in footnotes and endnotes.

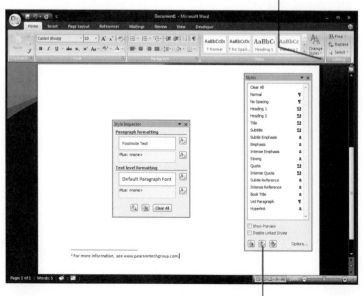

Style Inspector button

MY FOOTNOTES DISAPPEARED WHEN I SAVED IN WEB FORMAT

They didn't disappear; they just moved. When you save a document in Web format, footnotes are converted to endnotes, with hyperlinks that connect the footnote numbers in the body text to the notes at the end.

WHY DOES THE PAGE FOOTER OVERLAP THE FOOTNOTE AREA?

This can happen if the footnote area and the page footer area both are very large (more than five lines) and there's a section break on the same page. Either remove the section break or add some blank lines above the footnote text in the footnote area.

WHY CAN'T I DELETE A FOOTNOTE OR ENDNOTE?

The only way to delete a footnote or endnote is to delete the reference mark for it in the body text. You cannot delete one from the Notes pane or the footnote or endnote area of the document.

MY HEADINGS AREN'T SHOWING UP AS HEADINGS FOR CREATING A CROSS-REFERENCE

Make sure you have your custom heading styles set up to correspond to a heading outline level. To do this for a style:

1. Display the Styles task pane by clicking the dialog box launcher in the Styles group of the Home tab.
2. Right-click the style in the Styles task pane and choose Modify.
3. In the Modify Style dialog box, click Format and then click Paragraph.
4. In the Paragraph dialog box, set the Outline Level setting to a heading level (such as Heading 1).
5. Click OK twice.

WHY DOES MY CROSS-REFERENCE PRODUCE AN ERROR?

Check to make sure you have not deleted the item being cross-referenced. For example, if you cross-reference a heading and then delete that heading, an error message displays on the cross-reference field. If that doesn't help, try pressing F9 to update the field. Still no good? Delete the cross-reference and re-create it.

CHAPTER **25**

CREATING TABLES OF CONTENTS AND OTHER LISTINGS

In this chapter

CREATING A TABLE OF CONTENTS

A *table of contents* (TOC) is a listing at the beginning of a document (usually) that shows all the headings of a certain level and higher and their page numbers. This book has one, and so does almost every other technical book. Don't confuse a TOC with an *index*, covered in the next chapter; an index appears at the end of the document (again, usually) and shows an alphabetical list of topics and their page numbers. Figure 25.1 shows a typical TOC. It contains multiple levels and uses dot leaders to align the entries with the right-aligned page numbers.

Figure 25.1
A typical TOC.

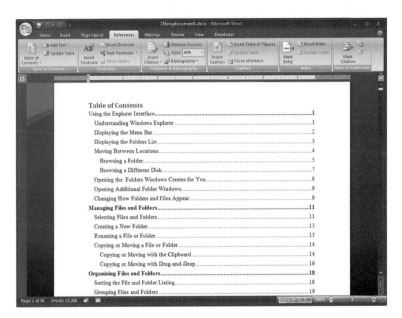

CHECKING STYLE OUTLINE LEVELS

The key to generating an accurate TOC is to make sure the document is properly formatted beforehand, with the correct styles in place.

As you learned in Chapter 22, "Outlining and Summarizing Documents," you can assign an outline level to each style (Level 1 through Level 9 or Body). Word uses each style's heading level to determine the level of the TOC to which it belongs. For example, all styles defined as Level 1 are at the top level of the TOC, and so on. So your first task is to check out the styles you've used for the document headings and make sure they are appropriately assigned to an outline level. (This is not an issue if you use Word's built-in heading styles because they are already appropriately assigned.)

To view and change the outline level for a heading style, follow these steps:

1. Click the dialog box launcher in the Styles group on the Home tab. The Styles task pane opens.

2. Right-click the style and choose Modify. The Modify Style dialog box opens.

3. Click the Format button and choose Paragraph. The Paragraph dialog box opens.

4. If needed, change the Outline Level to reflect the style's level of importance in the outline and click OK.

5. Click OK to close the Modify Style dialog box.

CREATING A TOC FROM A PRESET

After making sure your style usage is consistent, you are ready to generate the table of contents. It can be as easy or as difficult as you make it, depending on how picky you want to get with the options.

By far the easiest way to go is to choose one of the TOC presets, as shown in the following steps:

1. Position the insertion point in a new blank paragraph where you want the TOC. Typically it goes at the beginning of the document, but this is not mandatory.

2. On the References tab, click the Table of Contents button. A menu opens.

3. Click one of the TOC presets on the menu (see Figure 25.2).

Figure 25.2
Select a preset from the menu for a quick-and-easy TOC.

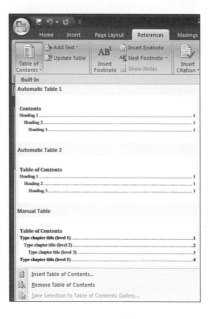

There are three presets on the Built-In section of the menu:

- **Automatic Table 1**—Places a default TOC at the insertion point, with the title "Contents."

- **Automatic Table 2**—Places a default TOC at the insertion point, with the title "Table of Contents."

■ **Manual Table**—Creates a TOC using content control placeholders that turn into regular text after you type in them. This is not an automatically updating TOC, and it does not use the TOC feature; it simply creates the look of a TOC for manual use.

→ For more information about content controls, **see** "Creating a Form with Content Controls," **p. 661**.

The TOC appears in a content control frame (yes, it's a content control, like the ones in Chapter 21, "Creating Forms"). When you click inside the TOC, two buttons become available, as shown in Figure 25.3. The left one opens the Table of Contents menu, the same as the one on the References tab. The right one updates the TOC (as described in the next section).

Display the Table of Contents menu
Update the TOC

Figure 25.3
A TOC is in a content control frame, with buttons at the top for controlling it.

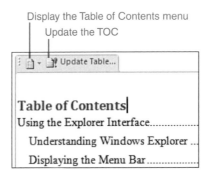

Table of Contents

Using the Explorer Interface.................
    Understanding Windows Explorer ...
    Displaying the Menu Bar.................

UPDATING A TOC

As the document changes, the table of contents might become out of date. A TOC does not update automatically by default, so you must issue a command to update it.

To update a table of contents, follow these steps:

1. Click the Update Table button at the top of the TOC's frame (refer to Figure 25.3). The Update Table of Contents dialog box opens.

   You can also click the Update Table button on the References tab.

2. Select the type of update you want (see Figure 25.4):

   • **Update Page Numbers Only**—This is the quickest, but it ignores any changes made to the headings or any new headings you might have added.

   • **Update Entire Table**—This takes a little longer; it completely regenerates the TOC. Except in very long documents, you will not notice much difference in the speed.

Figure 25.4
Select the type of update to perform.

REMOVING A TOC

To get rid of the TOC, you can just select it in the document and press Delete, the same as with any other content control. Here's an easier way, though:

1. On the References tab, click Table of Contents. (You can also display this same menu by clicking the Table of Contents button at the top of the TOC's frame.)
2. Click Remove Table of Contents.

MANUALLY MARKING ENTRIES FOR THE TOC

Besides the headings in your document, you might occasionally want some non-heading text to appear in the TOC. One way to do this would be to use a unique style for that text, and set that style's outline level to the desired TOC level. See "Checking Style Outline Levels" earlier in this chapter if you want to do that.

However, if you don't want to change the text's style in order to force its inclusion in the TOC, there are a couple of alternatives.

INCLUDING AN ENTIRE PARAGRAPH WITH ADD TEXT

If you want an entire paragraph to appear in the TOC that is styled such that it would not normally appear, here's a simple way to mark it for inclusion:

1. Click in the paragraph to be included in the TOC.

   You do not actually have to *select* the text; just move the insertion point into its paragraph. The entire paragraph will be included in the TOC regardless of what portion of it you select.
2. On the References tab, click Add Text. A menu opens.
3. Click the level at which that text should appear. A field code is inserted that marks the entry.
4. Repeat steps 1–3 for each additional entry to include.

> **NOTE**
>
> To reverse an inclusion, so that the paragraph no longer shows up in the TOC, repeat steps 1–3 for the paragraph, but instead of choosing a level in step 3, choose Not Shown in Table of Contents.

USING {TC} FIELDS TO MANUALLY MARK ENTRIES

You can also use {TC} fields to manually create TOC entries. There's a bit of extra work involved in setting them up, and you have to change the TOC options to make sure they are included, but these fields offer excellent flexibility. Options are available with a {TC} field that aren't available with the newfangled method described in the preceding section. For example,

25

you can specify the exact text that should appear in the TOC (not necessarily the whole paragraph), and you can specify that the page number should be suppressed for that entry.

→ To learn more about specifying what is included in the TOC, **see** "Choosing What Styles and Entries Are Included," **p. 754**.

To begin inserting a {TC} field, position the insertion point where you want the field and press Alt+Shift+O. This opens the Mark Table of Contents Entry dialog box shown in Figure 25.5.

Figure 25.5
Use the Mark Table of Contents Entry dialog box to insert a legacy-style {TC} code.

From here, enter the following information:

- **Entry**—This is the literal text that will appear in the table of contents.
- **Table Identifier**—If you have more than one TOC in the document, you can pick the one to which you want the entry to apply. Leave this set to the default for the main TOC.
- **Level**—Select the TOC level at which the entry should appear.

→ For more information about multiple TOCs in the same document, **see** "Working with Multiple TOCs," **p. 757**.

Another way to insert a {TC} field is to press Ctrl+F9 to create a new set of field brackets and then manually type the code. Here's the basic syntax:

{ TC "Text that should appear in the TOC" [*switches*] }

These are the switches you can use:

- \l—That's a lowercase L, not a 1. It specifies the outline level. Examples:
  { TC "Summary" \l 3 }
  { TC "Sales Plan" \l 2}
- \n—This suppresses the page number for the entry. Example:
  { TC "Main Office" \n }

CAUTION

When manually typing field codes, don't forget the syntax rules for fields, as described in the "Troubleshooting" section at the end of Chapter 20, "Working with Fields."

TIP

After creating a {TC} field with the correct syntax, you can copy that code and paste it in other spots, and then just change the text within the quotation marks.

CREATING CUSTOM TOCS

You can generate a TOC using your own custom settings, changing nearly every aspect of the table of contents from the text styles to the type of tab leader. Then you can save your custom TOC as a preset that will appear on the Table of Contents button's menu, so you can reuse those settings in other documents.

STARTING A CUSTOM TOC

To start a custom TOC, click Table of Contents on the References tab and choose Insert Table of Contents. The Table of Contents dialog box opens, as shown in Figure 25.6.

Figure 25.6
Start a custom TOC from the Table of Contents dialog box.

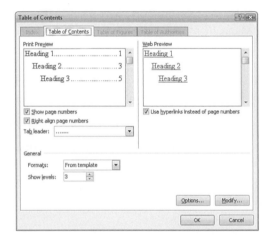

SETTING BASIC TOC OPTIONS

The most basic options for a TOC are found on the Table of Contents tab. Set any of these as desired:

- **Show Page Numbers**—This toggles on/off the page numbering. Each page number is generated based on the page on which the heading appears.

- **Right Align Page Numbers**—When this option is disabled, the page numbers appear immediately after the text; when it's enabled, they appear at the right margin.

- **Tab Leader**—By default, a dotted leader is used when Right Align Page Numbers is turned on (see previous). You can use other styles of leaders or not use a leader at all.

- **Use Hyperlinks Instead of Page Numbers**—This refers only to Web Preview versions of the document and versions saved to Web formats. Online it is more useful for the reader to have each heading be a hyperlink since page numbering is relative onscreen.

- **Formats**—This drop-down list contains alternative style sets, like the ones you find on the Home tab when you click Change Styles. The TOC can use a different style set than the rest of the document. (The default, From Template, matches the TOC with the document's style set.)

- **Show Levels**—This indicates the number of heading levels that will be included in the TOC. The default is 3, which includes outline levels 1–3.

→ For more information about style sets, **see** "Changing the Quick Style Set," **p. 231**.

CHOOSING WHAT STYLES AND ENTRIES ARE INCLUDED

By default, the following are included in a TOC:

- All headings using the built-in heading styles (Heading 1, Heading 2, and so on).
- All paragraph styles that have outline levels assigned to them, up to the level indicated in the Show Levels setting, covered in the preceding section.
- All paragraphs manually marked for the TOC with the Add Text button on the References tab. (See "Manually Marking Entries for the TOC" earlier in this chapter for details.)

If you want to include other styles in the TOC, or if you want to include entries you have manually marked with the {TC} field, you must make some adjustments.

To specify which styles and entries should be included, follow these steps:

1. From the Table of Contents dialog box (refer to Figure 25.6), click Options. The Table of Contents Options dialog box opens.

2. For each style that you want to include in the TOC, type a number in the TOC Level column indicating the desired level (see Figure 25.7).

Figure 25.7
Select the styles to be included in the TOC.

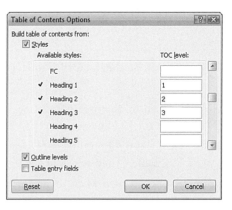

NOTE

If you do not want any styles to be included (only {TC} entries and outline levels, perhaps?), clear the Styles check box.

3. (Optional) To include outline styles or not (that is, custom styles based on their Outline Level setting), mark or clear the Outline Levels check box. It is marked by default.

4. (Optional) To include entries marked with {TC} field codes, mark the Table Entry Fields check box.

→ To use {TC} fields, **see** "Using {TC} Fields to Manually Mark Entries," **p. 751**.

5. Click OK.

DEFINING THE APPEARANCE OF THE TOC

The entries in the TOC are formatted according to special built-in paragraph styles with names that begin with "TOC". You can modify these styles as you would any other style, from the Styles pane, as you learned in Chapter 8, "Creating and Applying Styles and Themes."

CAUTION

Don't confuse the styles that go into the TOC with the styles that are used to display it. The TOC includes entries for various headings in the document, but when those entries are in the TOC, they are formatted with the corresponding TOC style, not their original style. So, for example, text that is Heading 1 in the document will be TOC 1 in the TOC.

There is also a TOC-specific interface for modifying TOC styles. Follow these steps to use it:

1. From the Table of Contents dialog box, click Modify. The Style dialog box appears. Only the TOC styles appear on the list (see Figure 25.8).

2. Click one of the TOC styles and review its specifications in the Preview area.

3. (Optional) If you need to change the definition of the style, click Modify.

4. Use the Modify Style dialog box to change the style definition, and then click OK.

5. Click OK to close the Style dialog box.

Figure 25.8
You can modify the TOC styles by selecting one and clicking Modify.

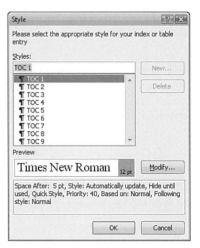

→ For information about using the Modify Style dialog box to change a style, **see** "Modifying a Style Definition," **p. 249**.

Understanding the {TOC} Field Code

When you insert a TOC, you are actually inserting a {TOC} field code. It has certain switches based on the settings you choose in the Table of Contents dialog box. You can view the field code by selecting the TOC, right-clicking it, and choosing Toggle Field Codes.

For example, here's a typical code:

{ TOC \o "1-3" \h \z \u }

Table 25.1 lists a few of the most common switches for the {TOC} field; for practice, decipher the preceding example from that table. You don't need to memorize these or be able to manually construct complex TOCs from them because the Table of Contents dialog box will handle this for you in almost all cases; this reference is handy mostly for when you need to make small tweaks to the TOC's behavior.

TABLE 25.1   COMMON FIELD CODE SWITCHES FOR {TOC}

Switch	Purpose
\b	Uses a bookmark to specify the area of the document from which to build the TOC. (This is the one you'll need for making a partial TOC.)
\f	Builds a TOC by using {TC} entries.
\h	Hyperlinks the entries and page numbers in the TOC.
\l	Defines the {TC} field level used. Follow this by the level range in quotation marks, such as "1-3".
\n	Builds the TOC without page numbers.
\o	Uses outline levels. Follow this by the level range in quotation marks, such as "1-3".
\p	Defines the separator between the table entry and its page number. Follow this by the separator in quotation marks.
\t	Builds the TOC using style names other than the standard outline styles. Follow this by the extra style names and their levels in quotation marks, with each one separated by commas. For example, you would use the following if the style named B1 is to be included at level 1 and the style named CX is to be included at level 2: "BL,1,CX,2".
\u	Builds the TOC using the applied paragraph outline levels.
\w	Preserves tab characters within table entries.
\x	Preserves line breaks within table entries.
\z	Hides page numbers when in Web Layout view.

TIP

You can manually construct a table of contents code. To do so, press Ctrl+F9 to place a blank field code bracket set at the insertion point, and then type **TOC** followed by the desired switches, as in Table 25.1.

WORKING WITH MULTIPLE TOCS

You can have multiple TOCs in a single document. This book has that—did you notice? There is a brief TOC at the beginning that lists just the chapter titles, and then a second, more detailed TOC following it.

If you have multiple TOCs, you might want them to both cover the same content, as the ones in this book do, but at different levels of detail. Alternatively, you might want each of them to cover different content—perhaps a separate TOC for Parts I and II of a book, for example.

ADDING A SECOND TOC FOR THE ENTIRE DOCUMENT

To add another TOC that covers the entire document, simply position the insertion point and repeat the TOC insertion as you normally would. A dialog box appears, asking whether you want to replace the current TOC; click No, and a second TOC appears.

ADDING A TOC THAT COVERS ONLY PART OF A DOCUMENT

Things get a little trickier if you don't want the TOC to cover the entire document. You must define a bookmark that includes all the text you want to include, and then manually edit the {TOC} field's code string to specify a bookmark with the \b switch.

Here are the specifics:

1. Select all the text to be included in the TOC, and define a bookmark for it. To do so, on the Insert tab, click Bookmark. Type a bookmark name and click Add.

→ To learn about bookmarks, **see** "Working with Bookmarks," **p. 610**.

2. To edit the code for an existing TOC, select the TOC, right-click it, and choose Toggle Field Codes. Or, to create a new TOC code, press Ctrl+F9 to insert new brackets and then type **TOC** followed by a space.

3. In the TOC field code, add the \b switch, followed by the bookmark name. (The bookmark name does not appear in quotation marks, since it is not literal text but an identifier.)

4. Generate (or regenerate) the TOC by right-clicking the field code and choosing Update Field.

→ For more information about field codes, including updating them and toggling their displays, **see** Chapter 20, "Working with Fields," **p. 631**.

BUILDING A TOC ACROSS MULTIPLE DOCUMENTS

To create a TOC that covers multiple documents, use the Master Documents feature to bring the documents together in a single container document, and then generate the TOC with all the subdocuments expanded.

→ To learn about master documents, **see** Chapter 23, "Using Master Documents," **p. 703**.

25

If you do not want to use master documents (and that's understandable, since the feature is a bit clumsy), there's an alternative: the {RD} field. RD stands for Referenced Document; it provides a way of inserting a reference to an external document within the current one.

You can either press Ctrl+F9 and type **RD**, or you can insert the field with the Insert, Quick Parts, Field command, as you learned in Chapter 20. Make sure you position the insertion point where you want the reference.

If you are referencing a file in the same location as the file receiving the field, you can simply place the filename in quotation marks, like this:

{ RD "extrainfo.docx" }

If you need to point to another location, use the complete path, like this:

{ RD "C:\\projectfiles\documents\extrainfo.docx" }

After inserting the {RD} field, generate the TOC as you normally would. The contents of the referenced document are included in the TOC using the same rules as applied to the TOC in the current document. For example, if you create a TOC that uses outline levels 1–2, then any headings in the referenced document at those outline levels will be included as well.

CREATING A CUSTOM TOC PRESET

After generating the TOC exactly as you want it, you can save its specifications for later reuse. To do so, follow these steps:

1. Select the TOC.
2. On the References tab, click Table of Contents, and then choose Save Selection to Table of Contents Gallery. The Create New Building Block dialog box opens.
3. In the Name box, type the name to assign to the preset (see Figure 25.9).
4. Leave the Gallery set to Table of Contents. Leave the Category assigned to General (or create/change the category if you prefer).
5. Leave Save In set to Building Blocks.dotx.
6. In the Options list, choose whether or not the new TOC should be on its own page:
   - **Insert Content in Its Own Paragraph**—Starts a new paragraph for the TOC but not a new page.
   - **Insert Content in Its Own Page**—Starts the TOC on a new page.
7. Click OK to create the new entry. It now appears on the Table of Contents button's menu.

To delete a custom preset, right-click it on the Table of Contents button's menu and choose Organize and Delete. Then in the Building Blocks Organizer dialog box, click Delete, click Yes to confirm, and click Close to close the dialog box.

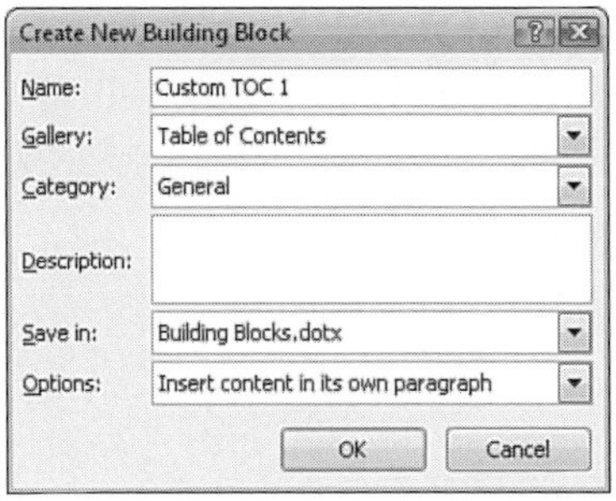

Figure 25.9
Create a building block
for the new TOC preset.

CREATING A TABLE OF FIGURES

A table of figures is just like a TOC except instead of headings, it lists figures and their captions. Many technical manuals provide a table of figures that is separate from the TOC so users can easily look up a particular diagram or schematic, for example.

CAPTIONING FIGURES

A table of figures is easiest to generate if you have used Word to insert captions for each figure. You learned how to do this in Chapter 13, "Working with Photos," but here is a quick review:

1. Right-click a graphic and choose Insert Caption, or select the graphic and click the Insert Caption button on the References tab. The Caption dialog box opens.

2. In the Caption box, the numbering is already filled in. Click after the numbering and type a descriptive caption if desired (see Figure 25.10).

→ For more information about the options available for captions, **see** "Using Figure Captions," **p. 422**.

3. Click OK. The caption appears adjacent to the graphic.

Figure 25.10
Create a caption for
the selected graphic.

The caption's paragraph style is Caption; you'll use that style to generate the table of figures in the next section.

TIP

You do not have to use the Insert Caption feature in order to create figure captions. You can simply type the desired text and then apply the Caption paragraph style to it. The captions will not be automatically numbered that way, however.

GENERATING THE TABLE OF FIGURES

After ensuring that all the figure captions use a common paragraph style (for example, Caption), you can generate the table of figures. Its options are virtually identical to those for a TOC except there are no presets.

Follow these steps to generate a table of figures:

1. Position the insertion point where you want the table of figures to appear.
2. On the References tab, in the Captions group, click Insert Table of Figures. The Table of Figures dialog box opens (see Figure 25.11).

Figure 25.11
Build a table of figures.

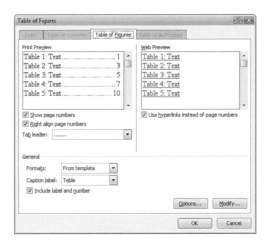

3. Click the Options button. The Table of Figures Options dialog box opens.
4. Open the Style drop-down list and select the style used for the captions (probably Caption), as shown in Figure 25.12.

Figure 25.12
Set the style to be used for the table of figures.

NOTE

If you want to include {TC} codes in the table of figures, as described in the following section, mark the Table Entry Fields check box.

5. Click OK.

6. Set up the other options for the table of figures. They are the same as the options available for a TOC. See "Creating Custom TOCs" earlier in this chapter for a full explanation.

7. Click OK. The table of figures appears in the document.

MANUALLY MARKING CAPTIONS

As you saw in the preceding steps, you must specify a single style that all the figure captions share, and the table of figures is based upon that style. (It is the Caption style if you use Word's captioning feature.)

But what if there is more than one style used for the figure captions? In that case, you must insert {TC} field codes to manually mark the entries. This is very similar to using the {TC} codes to mark TOC entries, covered earlier in this chapter.

The main difference is that you need to add an extra switch: \f. Then you follow the switch with a letter identifier to identify the table of figures. It can be any letter you want as long as you use the same letter for all entries that should share a common table of figures. For example:

{ TC "A typical network topography" \f a }

Then as you are compiling the TOC, make sure that in the Table of Figures Options dialog box, you mark the Table Entry Fields check box. This tells Word to include {TC} codes in the listing.

CREATING CITATIONS AND TABLES OF AUTHORITIES

"Citation" might sound like a generic term, but it actually has a very specific meaning in Word. A *citation* is a reference to a legal document, such as a case or statute. Citations are different from footnotes and bibliography entries, and are used almost exclusively in the legal profession. Word makes it easy to enter citations inline in the text and then compile them into a master reference called a *table of authorities*.

MARKING CITATIONS

When citing a source for the first time in a document, you typically enter a long (full) version of it, which includes the case numbers, dates, and other information. Then in later references within the same document, you usually enter a short version, which typically consists of only the case name.

To create a citation, follow these steps.

1. Select the long version (first usage) of the first in-text citation in the document.

2. Press Alt+Shift+I or click Mark Citation on the References tab. The Mark Citation dialog box opens with the citation already filled into the Selected Text box (see Figure 25.13).

Figure 25.13
Mark a citation.

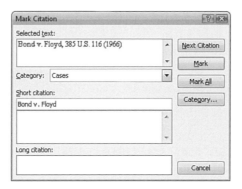

3. Edit the text as needed in the Selected Text box.

4. Open the Category list and choose the type of citation (cases, statutes, treatises, and so on).

> **TIP**
>
> You can create a custom category if needed. Click the Category button, and in the Edit Category dialog box, select one of the numbers at the bottom of the list and type a new name for it in the Replace With box. Click Replace and then click OK.

5. In the Short Citation box, enter a shortened version of the citation, to use for subsequent references. The default is for it to be the same as the selected text.

6. Click Mark. The selected text appears in the Long Citation box.

   Alternatively, if you want Word to search the whole document and mark all references to the same citation, long and short, click Mark All.

7. To do another citation, click Next Citation. Word jumps to the next citation.

> **NOTE**
>
> Word looks for the next citation by looking for telltale identifiers such as "v." or "In re."

8. Select the entire citation, and repeat steps 3–6 for it.

So what's actually happening behind the scenes here? Word is inserting a {TA} field code. You can see that code by clicking the Show/Hide ¶ button on the Home tab to toggle on the display of hidden text. For example, it might look something like this for a long citation:

> { TA \l "Bond v. Floyd, 385 U.S. 116 (1966)" \s "Bond v. Floyd" \c 1 }

For a short citation, the syntax is simpler:

> { TA \s "Bond v. Floyd" }

Table 25.2 explains the switches you can use with the {TA} field.

TABLE 25.2   SWITCHES FOR THE {TA} FIELD

Switch	Purpose
\b	Makes the page number bold.
\c	Defines the category number for the field. Follow this with a digit representing the position of the category chosen from the Mark Citation dialog box. Here's a quick reference: 1: Cases 2: Statutes 3: Other Authorities 4: Rules 5: Treatises 6: Regulations 7: Constitutional Provisions 8 and up: Undefined, but you can define them yourself
\i	Makes the page number italicized.
\l (lowercase L)	Defines the long citation. Follow it with the long citation in quotation marks.
\r	Includes the bookmark's range of pages in the page number for the field.
\s	Defines the short citation. Follow it with the short citation in quotation marks.

GENERATING THE TABLE OF AUTHORITIES

After you have marked all the citations, you are ready to compile the table of authorities. Follow these steps to do so:

1. Position the insertion point where you want the table of authorities to appear.

2. On the References tab, click Insert Table of Authorities. The Table of Authorities dialog box opens (see Figure 25.14).

Figure 25.14
Set the style to be used for the table of figures.

3. Set any of these options as needed:

- **Use Passim**—It is common when listing citations that appear repeatedly in the same document to substitute the word *passim* for the multiple page references. By default, Word uses *passim* whenever there are at least five references to the same citation. Clear this check box if you want to display the actual page numbers in each instance instead.

- **Keep Original Formatting**—Some citations contain character formatting such as bold, italic, and underlining. That formatting carries over to the table of authorities automatically by default. If you do not want it to, clear this check box.

- **Tab Leader**—This is the same as with a table of contents. Select the leader type or none at all.

- **Formats**—This is also the same as with a table of contents. Select one of the style sets, or use From Template to match the style set that the document uses.

- **Category**—The default here is All, which generates a table containing all categories. You can narrow that down to a certain category by selecting it here.

4. (Optional) Click Modify to modify the styles used for the table of authorities, as you did with the TOC styles earlier in the chapter. There are only two styles used here: Table of Authorities and TOA Heading.

5. Click OK to generate the table of authorities.

TROUBLESHOOTING

WHY CAN'T I ADD A NEW STYLE FOR TOC ENTRIES?

From the Table of Contents dialog box, if you click Modify, a Style dialog box appears that lists TOC styles 1 through 9. There is a New button, but it is grayed out. You can't add new TOC styles.

So why is the button there, if you can't use it? It's because this same dialog box is used for other parts of the program, such as indexing, and in some of those parts you can add new styles.

I SEE AN "ERROR! BOOKMARK NOT DEFINED" MESSAGE

This happens if you delete one or more of the headings or {TC} codes from the document and then update the TOC using the Update Page Numbers Only option. Do an update that re-creates the entire TOC instead to fix this.

THE PAGE NUMBERS ARE INCORRECT IN THE TOC

This can happen when headings shift onto other pages due to editing, displaying, or hiding hidden text, or changing the margins or indentations and you have not updated the TOC since those changes occurred. Update the TOC to fix this problem.

CHAPTER **26**

BUILDING EFFECTIVE INDEXES

In this chapter

ABOUT INDEXES

An *index* is an alphabetical listing of topics, usually at the back of a book or long document, that lists the page numbers on which the topics are covered. There's one in this book, for example, and you might have even used it already to look up a topic or two.

Creating a really good index is a skill that takes time to learn. It's not as simple as marking every instance of every word, because some words are not important to index (such as "the") and some words are used so frequently in the document that you must decide which are the most significant occurrences. There are people who make a full-time living creating indexes, and there are even international conventions and seminars for indexers. Word's indexing capabilities are adequate for most people, although professional indexers might use other tools.

Creating an index is a three-step process:

1. Decide on the conventions for the index.
2. Mark the entries for the index.
3. Generate the index.

The rest of this chapter elaborates on those three steps.

CAUTION

It's okay to mark index entries as you write, but there's no point in generating the index until the document is complete. If you make changes to the document that affect pagination, you will need to regenerate the index afterward.

NOTE

Each document is indexed separately in Word, so if you are writing a publication with different chapters in separate Word documents, you will need to tie them all together somehow before indexing. See "Indexing Across Multiple Documents" later in this chapter for some ideas.

DECIDING ON THE INDEXING CONVENTIONS

As you mark entries, you specify the wording of the entry and the formatting of the page numbers. Therefore, before you start marking entries, you should make some basic decisions about conventions. Here are some things to think about:

- **Page number format**—Will page numbers be bold, italic, or both?
- **Proper names**—Will proper names be listed by the person's last name, as in Smith, John? (That's usually the best way to go.)
- **Acronyms**—Will acronyms be listed by acronym or by the spelled-out version, or both? If both, will they both have the page number, or will one of them be a cross-reference to the other?

- **Verb forms**—Will you index verbs by the gerund form (Saving) or the infinitive form (Save)?

- **Verb vs. noun entries**—When there's an action being performed on an object, will it be listed under the noun or the verb? For example, when saving a file, will it be under File with a subentry of Save, or will be under Save with a subentry of File?

- **Adjectives**—Most professional indexers avoid entries that start with adjectives. For example, instead of listing Multiple Tables, you might want to list that under Tables with a subentry of Multiple.

- **Word form**—You'll want to avoid multiple forms of the same word as primary entries. For example, instead of having separate entries for Install, Installation, and Installing, combine them with a common usage.

Create your list of rules that you'll follow when indexing, and keep that list handy as you proceed through this chapter.

MARKING INDEX ENTRIES

When you mark an index entry, you specify that the selected word or phrase should be included in the index, along with the page number. You can mark entries manually or automatically.

When you mark entries manually, you maintain complete control over which instances of a term are marked. You might not want every mention of a word to be marked, for example— just the instances where the topic is discussed in detail. Marking entries manually takes a long time in a large document, but this results in a superior index because you can follow the conventions you set in the preceding section.

When you mark entries automatically, you create an Index AutoMark file that contains the words to include in the index. Then you use the AutoMark feature to apply that list to your document, and Word automatically inserts indexing codes for all instances it finds of the words contained in the AutoMark file. AutoMarking is fast, but you lose the ability to make little adjustments to the wording as you go. For example, if you wanted to combine several word forms into a single entry, AutoMarking would not be able to accomplish that.

MANUALLY MARKING INDEX CODES

When you manually mark an index entry, you insert an {XE} field. You don't have to manually create the field, though; you can use the Mark Index Entry dialog box. The dialog box interface helps you set up the field code, so you don't have to remember the syntax.

To mark an index entry, follow these steps:

1. Select the text to include in the index. This is typically a single word or phrase—something concise.

   Alternatively, if you want to create a single entry for a multiparagraph section, create a bookmark that marks the entire section and then position the insertion point at the beginning of the section.

26

NOTE

> Index entries are inserted immediately before the selected text. You do not have to select text in step 1; if you prefer, you can just position the insertion point where the index entry should be placed. If you don't select any text, though, you will need to type the entry in step 3; it will not be prefilled for you.

2. Press Alt+Shift+X, or on the References tab, click Mark Entry. The Mark Index Entry dialog box opens.

3. In the Main Entry text box, the text you selected in step 1 appears. Confirm that it appears as you would like it to appear in the index; change it if needed (see Figure 26.1).

Figure 26.1
Mark an index entry.

TIP

> If you selected text in step 1 that contains a colon or a quotation mark, Word adds a backslash (\) symbol before the character to indicate that it is a literal character, not a special code. If you manually type the text in step 3 for the entry, put the backslash symbol in yourself if including a colon or quotation mark.

4. (Optional) Apply any bold, italic, or underline formatting to the Main Entry text as desired. Select the text in the Main Entry text box, and then use these shortcut keys: Ctrl+B for bold, Ctrl+I for italic, or Ctrl+U for underline. To strip off existing formatting, press Ctrl+spacebar.

CAUTION

> Use manual formatting as in step 4 sparingly and strategically. In most cases, index entries should be plain text. If you selected some text in step 1 that was already marked as bold, italic, or underlined, that formatting carries over automatically; strip it off with Ctrl+spacebar if needed.

5. In the Options section, choose the option button that best represents what you want for this entry:

- **Cross-Reference**—Use this for a reference to another main entry. See "Creating Cross-References" later in this chapter if you want one of these.

- **Current Page**—This is the default setting. It prints the page number on which the index entry begins.

- **Page Range**—If you choose this, you must then select a bookmark from the Bookmark list. The page range shown will be the range on which the bookmarked range lies. You must have created the bookmark in step 1 (or prior to that).

6. (Optional) If you want the page number to be bold or italic, mark the Bold and/or Italic check boxes.

CAUTION

Be consistent with your use of bold and italic for page numbers. Professional indexers sometimes use bold and italic to give special meaning to entries. For example, if there are many entries for a particular topic, they might bold the page number for the most important entry.

7. Click Mark. The entry is marked with an {XE} code.

TIP

You can see the indexing codes by turning on the display of hidden characters; click the Show/Hide ¶ button on the Home tab.

8. If you have other entries to mark, leave the Mark Index Entry dialog box open, and select other text and repeat the process. The Mark Index Entry dialog box can remain open as you edit the document.

9. When you are finished marking entries, click Cancel to close the dialog box.

CREATING SUBENTRIES

Often it is useful to have a multilevel index, where one major topic is placed in the alphabetical main list and beneath it multiple subtopics form their own mini-list. For example:

```
Folders
        Attributes, 22
        Creating, 18
        Deleting, 19
        Renaming, 21
```

To create a subentry, follow the steps in the preceding section, but after step 4, enter the subentry text in the Subentry box. The resulting code will create an entry that is alphabetized according to the Main Entry text, but with a page number next to the Subentry text.

26

You can also enter a subentry in the Main Entry text box. To do this, separate the main entry and the subentry by a colon, like this: Folders:Creating. Don't put a space on either side of the colon. To save even more time, you can copy such an entry to the Clipboard and then paste it into the Main Entry text box for each entry you want to create, changing the subentry for each one.

Occasionally you might find that you need more than two levels of subentries. You can create that by entering multiple colon-separated items in the Main Entry text box. For example:

```
Folders:Creating:In Windows XP
```

CREATING CROSS-REFERENCES

Sometimes the same content goes by two or more different names, and you aren't sure which one the user will look up in your index. In a situation like that, if it's a single entry, you might just include both entries in both places. However, if it's a complex, multilevel series of entries, you can save space in your index by creating the entries in one place and then cross-referencing them with all the other possible synonyms the user might look up.

To create a cross-reference, follow the same steps as in "Manually Marking Index Codes" earlier in this chapter, except choose Cross-Reference in step 5, and then enter the cross-reference text in the Cross-Reference text box.

There are two subtly different types of indexing cross-references. The standard "See" type points to the alternate name of a topic where the index entries for it occur. For example, since a *folder* and a *directory* refer to the same thing in PC computing, under Directory you might have a listing such as *See* Folder. A "See also" type, on the other hand, points to a related but not synonymous entry. For example, if some of the information presented in a section on files is also applicable to folders, you might have an entry like this under Folders: *See Also* Files.

A cross-reference does not insert a page number; it just inserts the literal text you specify. Therefore, it does not really matter where you insert the cross-reference code. You can insert all the cross-reference codes at the beginning or end of the document if you find that more convenient, or you can insert them throughout the document wherever they occur to you.

NOTE

These cross-references for indexing are different from the cross-references you learned about in Chapter 19, "Copying, Linking, and Embedding Data." The cross-references covered there insert in-document references, and have nothing to do with indexing.

MARKING MULTIPLE INSTANCES OF THE SAME TEXT

To save some time, you can have Word mark all the instances of a specific text phrase in the document.

Follow the steps in "Manually Marking Index Codes" earlier in this chapter, but instead of clicking Mark in step 7, click Mark All.

Although this procedure marks every instance of a specific word or phrase, it does not mark multiple phrases at once; you have to repeat it for each individual index entry. If you want to automatically mark multiple entries at once, see the next section.

UNDERSTANDING {XE} FIELD CODES

The {XE} index marker codes are very simple. They do not have any options switches; all they have is the XE code plus the index entry in quotation marks, like this:

{ XE "Folders" }

AUTOMARKING INDEX ENTRIES

AutoMarking can possibly save you some time if you have a very large document to be indexed. Not only does it mark multiple instances of the same text, as in the earlier section, but it marks multiple words and phrases at once. There are two steps in this process: Create the AutoMark file, and then run it to create the entries in your main document.

CAUTION

> To prepare for AutoMarking, you must set up a list of words to be marked. Creating this list can take a significant amount of time, so you might find that AutoMarking does not save you all that much time after you've taken the trouble to compile the AutoMark file. AutoMarking also will probably not mark everything you want to include in the index, so you will likely need to go back though your document afterwards and add more entries manually. It's a trade-off, and its usefulness must be determined on a case-by-case basis.

CREATING THE AUTOMARK FILE

To create the AutoMark file, start a new blank document and insert a two-column table.

→ For information about creating tables, **see** "Creating a Table," **p. 354**.

In that table, in the left column, type words or phrases to be included in the index. In the right column, type the entry the way it should appear in the index. You can use colons to create subentries where needed, as you learned in "Creating Subentries" earlier in this chapter. Apply bold or italics as needed to the text in the right column. If you leave the right column blank for a row, Word will use the same text as in the left column.

Indexing is case-sensitive, so be sure that the left column includes all variations of words that might appear in your document in both uppercase and lowercase. However, make sure you standardize on either uppercase or lowercase in the right column so that your index contains only one main entry for that word. Further, make sure that you capture all the forms of a word in the left column, but place the same entry for each of them in the right column. For example, Figure 26.2 shows all the entries for words that will appear under a single heading of Training in an index.

26

Figure 26.2
A portion of an
AutoMark file.

Trainer	Training
trainer	Training
Trainers	Training
trainers	Training
Training	Training
training	Training
Train	Training
train	Training
classes	Training
learning	Training
teaching	Training

TIP

> You might want to view the AutoMark table side-by-side with the main document you are indexing to help you recall what words you want to include. You can manually arrange the windows or use the View tab's Arrange All button or View Side by Side button to auto-arrange the open windows.

After creating all the entries in the table, save and close the file. It does not matter what name you give it, as long as you remember what you chose.

AutoMarking the Main Document

Generating the AutoMark file is the time-consuming part; using it to mark the entries in the main document is quick and easy. Follow these steps:

1. Open the main document to be indexed.
2. On the References tab, click Insert Index. The Index dialog box opens.
3. Click the AutoMark button. The Open Index AutoMark File dialog box opens.
4. Select the AutoMark document you created in the preceding section and click Open. The entries are automatically marked with {XE} codes.

GENERATING THE INDEX

After marking the entries for the index, you are ready to compile it. If you accept all the default formatting options, it is very simple. Follow these steps:

1. Position the insertion point where you want the index to appear.
2. On the References tab, click Insert Index. The Index dialog box opens (see Figure 26.3).
3. Click OK. The index appears in the document.

Figure 26.3
Create an index from the Index dialog box.

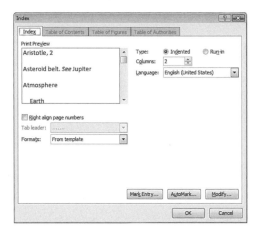

The index appears in its own section, and a section break is inserted between it and the rest of the document. Because it is in its own section, you can apply different page formatting to it, such as different margins, headers/footers, and page numbering.

If the index doesn't match what you want in content or appearance, see the next section to learn about the options available for it.

FORMATTING THE INDEX

Indexes, like TOCs, can be formatted in various ways. Some of those formatting options are layout-related and are controlled from the Index dialog box (refer to Figure 26.3); others are style-related and are controlled by modifying the Index styles. The following sections explain the details.

SETTING THE INDEX LAYOUT

In the Index dialog box (References tab, Insert Index), you can choose from among several options that control the way the index is laid out on the page.

TYPE

The Type setting controls how subentries appear. The default is Indented, which places each subentry on a separate line and indents it, like this:

```
Folders
        Attributes, 22
        Creating, 18
        Deleting, 19
        Renaming, 21
```

The alternative is Run-in, which runs subentries in with the main entry, separating each part with semicolons, like this:

```
Folders: Attributes, 22; Creating, 18; Deleting, 19; Renaming, 21
```

Indented layouts are much easier to read, but take up more space. If page count is an issue, using a run-in index layout can help fit the index onto fewer pages.

COLUMNS

The Columns setting determines the number of newspaper-style (snaking) columns that will be used for the index. Since most index lines are fairly short, using several columns can help fit the index on fewer pages. An average number of columns for a typical index is three. Fewer than that, and there is too much white space; more than that, and longer entries are broken into too many very short lines.

LANGUAGE

The Language setting determines the alphabetization rules. There is probably only one option on this menu—the one for the default language and country for your copy of Word.

RIGHT ALIGN PAGE NUMBERS

This setting places the page numbers at the right margin of the column, and optionally adds a tab leader (in your choice of styles) between the entry and the number, like this:

```
Folders
        Attributes........22
        Creating..........18
        Deleting..........19
        Renaming..........21
```

FORMATS

As with TOCs, this setting enables you to apply a different style set to the index than to the rest of the document. The default setting, From Template, uses the same style set as the main document.

→ For more information about style sets, **see** "Changing the Quick Style Set," **p. 231**.

DEFINING INDEX STYLES

As with TOCs and tables of authorities, the styles for index entries come from built-in styles Index 1 through Index 9. You can modify the definitions of these styles to control the various levels of the index. (An index can have up to nine levels of subentries, which is why there are nine index styles.)

To modify an index style, follow these steps:

1. On the References tab, click Insert Index. The Index dialog box opens.

2. Click Modify. The Style dialog box appears, listing only the index styles (see Figure 26.4).

Figure 26.4
Redefine one or more of the paragraph styles that govern index formatting.

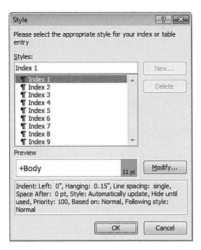

3. Click one of the styles, and then click Modify. The Modify Style dialog box opens.

4. Make changes to the style, as you learned to do in Chapter 8.

5. Click OK to accept the changes to the style.

6. Repeat steps 3–5 to modify other styles if needed, then click OK.

→ For information about using the Modify Style dialog box to change a style, **see** "Modifying a Style Definition," **p. 249**.

TIP

> If you want the new definitions of the index styles to be saved with the template so that new documents will use them too, in the Modify Style dialog box, mark the New Documents Based on This Template option button.

26

UPDATING THE INDEX

If you make changes to the document after creating the index, the index might become out of synch with the actual page numbers. To fix this, update the index.

The index is a field code, the same as a TOC or any other similar listing, so you can update it by selecting it, right-clicking it, and choosing Update Field. You can also click the Update Index button on the References tab, or click inside the index and press F9.

Spell-Checking an Index

The spell-checker does not check an index because the index is not "real" text in the document; it's a field.

To get around this, run a spell check with hidden text turned on (via the Show/Hide ¶ button on the Home tab), so that all the {XE} field codes appear. Word will check the spelling in them, and since they form the text in the index, the text will be indirectly checked.

Another way is to select the index and press Ctrl+Shift+F9 to unlink the index field. This changes the index field into plain text, but you can no longer update the index after doing that, because it is no longer an {Index} field. Therefore, you would want to do this as the very last step in the document-creation process.

WORKING DIRECTLY WITH {INDEX} FIELD CODES

The index is generated by an {Index} field code. You can see it by selecting the index, right-clicking it, and choosing Toggle Field Codes. Table 26.1 lists the switches for the {Index} field. You do not need to change these in most cases, as they are automatically generated based on your choices in the Index dialog box. They are provided here in case you might want to add one of the more obscure options that the dialog box does not control. Some of the sections later in this chapter use some of these codes for special functions.

Each of the switches is followed by a parameter, usually entered in quotation marks (except in the case of the \b switch, where the bookmark name is not in quotation marks).

TABLE 26.1 SWITCHES FOR THE {INDEX} FIELD

Switch	Purpose
\b	Uses a bookmark to specify the area of the document from which to build the index. Follow this by the bookmark name.
\c	Defines the number of columns if more than 1. Follow this by the number in quotation marks.
\d	Defines the separator between sequence and page numbers. Follow this by the separator character in quotation marks.
\e	Defines the separator character used between the index entry and the page number. Follow this by the separator character in quotation marks.
\f	Creates the index by using only the specified entry type. Follow this by a letter in quotation marks representing the entry type. It can be any letter except "i". (Using "i" places the entry in the main index, and is the same as omitting the \f switch entirely.) You'll learn more about this option later in the chapter, in "Indexing Only Selected Entries."
\g	Defines the separator character used in a page range. Follow this by the separator character in quotation marks.
\h	Defines the spacing or heading for each letter grouping. See "Controlling the Appearance of Index Headings" later in this chapter for details.
\k	Defines the separators between cross-references and other entries. Follow this by the separator character in quotation marks.
\l	Defines the separators between page numbers for multiple-page references. Follow this by the separator character in quotation marks.
\p	Limits the index to the specified letters. See "Indexing Only Selected Letters of the Alphabet" later in this chapter for details.
\r	Runs index subentries onto the same line as the main entry.
\s	Includes the referenced sequence number with the page number.
\y	Enables the use of yomi text for index entries.
\z	Defines the language ID Word used to generate the index. The default is "1033," which is the code for U.S. English.

26

CONTROLLING THE APPEARANCE OF INDEX HEADINGS

An index can have headings for each letter—an A heading followed by all the entries that begin with A, and so on. To include such a heading, add the \h switch to the {Index} field code.

To use capital letters, follow the switch with a capital A in quotation marks, like this:

> { Index \h "A" }

To add some other symbols to the heading, include them along with the capital A, like this:

> { Index \h "====A====" }

You can use any symbol character in a normal text font (such as * or $), but you cannot use letters of the alphabet. (You can't use an all-symbol font such as Symbol or Wingdings, however.)

To use lowercase letters, add *lower (*not* in quotation marks), like this:

> { Index \h *lower }

To omit the letter but include spacing, place a space in quotation marks, like this:

> { Index \h " " }

INDEXING ACROSS MULTIPLE DOCUMENTS

If you need to index multiple documents as a single unit, your best bet is to use a master document, as described in Chapter 23, "Using Master Documents." Expand all the subdocuments, and then make sure the insertion point is at the end of the master document (outside of any subdocument) and generate the index. You can mark the entries in the individual documents while they are open within the subdocument, or you can prepare each one individually ahead of time outside the master document.

Another alternative if you don't like master documents, or if you have problems with them crashing, is to use the {RD} field, which stands for Referenced Document. This was mentioned in Chapter 25, "Creating Tables of Contents and Other Listings," too, in the context of TOCs, but it works for indexes as well. An {RD} field tells Word to search another file and use its contents in any index or TOC you create in your current document. You could start a new blank document just for the index, and then refer to each of your individual Word files with a separate {RD} code within it. Then when you generate the index, the index will pull marked entries from all the referenced files.

You can either press Ctrl+F9 and type **RD**, or you can insert the field with the Insert, Quick Parts, Field command, as you learned in Chapter 20, "Working with Fields."

If you are referencing a file in the same location as the file receiving the field, you can simply place the filename in quotation marks, like this:

{ RD "Chapter1.docx" }

If you need to point to another location, use the complete path, like this:

{ RD "C:\\projectfiles\documents\Chapter1.docx" }

After inserting the {RD} field, generate the index as you normally would. The contents of the referenced documents are included in the index using the same rules as applied to the index in the current document.

CREATING MULTIPLE INDEXES IN A SINGLE DOCUMENT

Just like with TOCs, you can use bookmarks to define regions of the document to include in an index, and then index only those bookmarked regions. To do this, you must manually edit the index's field code to add the \b switch.

Follow these steps:

1. Select all the text to be included in the index, and define a bookmark for it. To do so, on the Insert tab, click Bookmark. Type a bookmark name and click Add.

→ To learn about bookmarks, **see** "Working with Bookmarks," **p. 610**.

2. To edit the code for an existing index, select the index, right-click it, and choose Toggle Field Codes. Or, to create a new index code, press Ctrl+F9 to insert new brackets and then type **Index** followed by a space.

3. In the Index field code, add the \b switch, followed by the bookmark name. (The bookmark name does not appear in quotation marks, since it is not literal text but an identifier.)

4. Generate (or regenerate) the index by right-clicking the field code and choosing Update Field.

→ For more information about field codes, including updating them and toggling their displays, **see** Chapter 20, "Working with Fields," **p. 631**.

INDEXING ONLY SELECTED ENTRIES

Not every entry marked with an {XE} code must necessarily appear in every index. By manually editing the field codes for your {XE} markers, you can define an entry as belonging to one index or another.

The switch you'll use for this is \f. Follow the switch by a letter, in quotation marks. It can be any letter except "i". Using "i" indicates it belongs in the master index, which is the same as omitting the \f switch entirely. Use the same letter for each entry that should be in the same index together. You can use any single character from the ANSI character set, including letters, numbers, and symbols.

Display the {XE} field codes by toggling Show/Hide ¶ on from the Home tab. Then in each {XE} field, add the \f switch and the chosen letter, like this:

{ XE "Tables:Creating" \f "k" }

Next, modify the {Index} field code by right-clicking it and selecting Toggle Field Codes, and then add the same switch and letter to it. Or, to create a new index, create a new {Index} field by pressing Ctrl+F9 and typing **Index**:

{ Index \f "k" }

TIP

> If you need a single {XE} field to appear in more than one custom index, or the custom index plus the main one, insert separate {XE} codes for each index it should appear in. Just copy and paste the existing {XE} code and then change the letter specified for the \f switch.

INDEXING ONLY SELECTED LETTERS OF THE ALPHABET

If you need to split up your index into multiple sections alphabetically, you might want to create a separate index for each letter, or for groups of letters. To do this, use the \p switch.

Modify the {Index} field code by right-clicking it and selecting Toggle Field Codes, and add the \p switch to it followed by the range of letters (no quotation marks). Place two hyphens between the first and last letters in the range, like this:

{ Index \p a--h }

CAUTION

> If AutoCorrect tries to convert the double hyphen into a dash, press Ctrl+Z to undo that. If you find yourself using double hyphens a lot, you might be better off disabling the dash conversion in AutoCorrect (covered in "Automating Corrections with AutoCorrect" in Chapter 4).

26

TROUBLESHOOTING

SOME OF MY MARKED ENTRIES DON'T APPEAR IN THE INDEX

Here are some things to check:

- Check the spelling of the entry and subentry to make sure there are no typos that are placing the entry in an unexpected location.
- If your index is in a master document, were all the subdocuments expanded when you generated the index?
- If you are using the \f switch to limit an entry to a certain index, are you using the correct letter with it, and is the letter in quotation marks?
- Make sure each subentry is separated from the other entries by a colon.

- If you manually added any switches, make sure you got the syntax right for those switches.

- If the index depends on a bookmark, make sure the bookmark exists and is spelled correctly in the reference to it in the {Index} field code's \b switch.

HOW CAN I USE A COLON OR QUOTATION MARK IN AN INDEX ENTRY?

Word interprets a colon in the main entry as a separator between it and a subentry; this enables you to enter the main entry and the subentry together in the Main Entry text box, saving some time. If you want a literal colon in the index entry, precede it with a \ symbol, like this: *10\:00 Appointment.*

The same goes for quotation marks. In an {XE} field code, the text is set in quotation marks, so you cannot use regular quotation marks within the code string. If you need a literal quotation mark in an entry, precede it with a \ symbol, like this: "\"WYSIWYG\"".

I CAN'T SEE THE INDEX MARKING CODES I CREATED

Index field codes show up only when hidden text is displayed. On the Home tab, click the Show/Hide ¶ button to toggle on the display of hidden text.

I MANUALLY CREATED AN {INDEX} FIELD CODE AND IT DOESN'T WORK

Make sure you are following the syntax prescribed for field codes in Word. One of the most common mistakes people make is to forget to leave a space after the opening bracket and before the closing bracket. See the "Troubleshooting" section at the end of Chapter 20 for more help with field syntax.

THE PAGE NUMBERING IN THE INDEX DOESN'T MATCH THE PRINTED COPY OF THE DOCUMENT

This can happen if your document contains hidden text (enough to throw off the page numbering) and the hidden text is displayed when you generate the index. The onscreen version will be tracked with the onscreen text (which contains the hidden text), but when you print the document, the hidden text won't print, so the page numbering will be different.

On the Home tab, click Show/Hide ¶ to hide the hidden text and then regenerate the index.

COLLABORATION AND ONLINE SHARING

CHAPTER 27

COLLABORATING WITH OTHERS

In this chapter

UNDERSTANDING AND CONFIGURING COLLABORATION TOOLS

When multiple people edit a document, it is often useful to have a clear trail of who changed what, or who made what change or remark. To facilitate this type of tracking, Word provides several tools that enable users to "mark up" a document without losing sight of the original. You can:

- Use the Comments feature to attach comments to various parts of the document, somewhat like sticky notes on a hard copy.

- Use the Tracking feature to track content and formatting changes by user, and to easily accept or reject the changes that others make.

- Use the Compare feature to look at two versions of a document side by side for a line-by-line comparison, or to see a merged version that incorporates the differences between them as tracked changes.

CAUTION

The collaboration features covered in this chapter all assume that everyone has unrestricted access to the document. In a close-knit team environment, that might be fine, but if you need to place restrictions on the editing allowed for the document, see Chapter 28, "Protecting and Securing Documents."

DISPLAYING OR HIDING THE REVIEWING PANE

The *Reviewing pane* is a separate pane that appears alongside the main window, listing the changes that have been made to the selected text. As you can see in Figure 27.1, it shows all the tracked revisions and comments, broken down by category (Main Document Changes and Comments, Header and Footer Changes, and so on).

To toggle the Reviewing pane on/off, click the arrow beside Reviewing Pane button on the Review tab. To choose a vertical or horizontal orientation for it, open the button's menu and select the desired orientation.

Figure 27.1 points out two buttons on the Reviewing pane's title bar:

- **Update Revision Count**—This re-polls the document for the number of revisions and updates the counter in the title bar of the Reviewing pane.

- **Show Detailed Summary**—This toggles on/off some extra information about the breakdown of the revision count (how many comments, how many deletions, and so on).

NOTE

Earlier versions of Word had only the horizontal reviewing pane, which was awkward to use because you could see only a few lines of it at a time. Most people will probably prefer the new vertical-style reviewing pane.

Figure 27.1
Display or hide the
Reviewing pane.

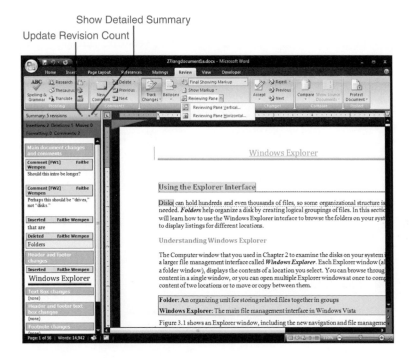

CONTROLLING THE USE OF BALLOONS

Tracked changes can appear as markup within the document text, or as colored balloons outside the text's right margin.

Figure 27.2 illustrates the difference with a comment. With a balloon, you can see the comment alongside the text; with an inline reference, you see only a comment number and the initials of the person making the comment. When you point to the comment with your mouse, a pop-up box appears showing the comment. You can also open the Reviewing pane and read the comments there.

Figure 27.2
Revisions with balloons
on (top) versus off
(bottom).

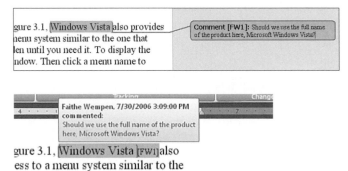

27

To control the appearance of balloons vs. inline revisions and comments, follow these steps:

1. On the Review tab, open the Track Changes button's menu and choose Change Tracking Options. The Track Changes Options dialog box opens (see Figure 27.3).

Figure 27.3
Set up balloon options at the bottom of the Track Changes Options dialog box.

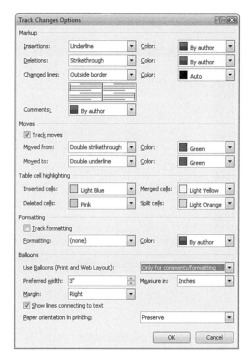

2. At the bottom of the dialog box, open the Use Balloons list and select Always, Never, or Only for Comments/Formatting.

3. If you chose Always or Only for Comments/Formatting, set up your preferred specs for the balloons:

   - **Preferred Width**—The width of the extra space that appears to the right of the page onscreen, in which the balloons appear.
   - **Measure In**—The unit of measurement for the preceding setting.
   - **Margin**—The side of the page on which balloons appear. The default is Right.
   - **Show Lines Connecting to Text**—Connects a balloon to the comment or change to which it refers.
   - **Paper Orientation in Printing**—Choose Auto (switches to Landscape if needed to make comments fit), Preserve (sticks with the page's established orientation), or Force Landscape (always prints in landscape when comments are present).

4. Click OK to accept the new balloon settings.

TIP

You can also adjust the balloon usage from the Balloons button on the Review tab.

CHANGING THE COLORS AND MARKINGS USED FOR REVISIONS

In the Track Changes Options dialog box (refer to Figure 27.3), not only can you control the balloon behavior, but you can change the colors used to mark the various types of revisions.

For each revision type, you can choose a type style (such as underline or strikethrough) and a color. You can choose a fixed color, choose Auto (which is the same as saying "don't change the color"), or choose By Author. The By Author option automatically colors each reviser's work differently, so you can see at a glance who changed what.

Here are the changes for which you can specify colors and markings:

- **Insertions**—New text, typically indicated in underlining and a different color. Your choices are Color Only, Bold, Italic, Underline, Double Underline, and Strikethrough.

- **Deletions**—Deleted text, typically indicated by strikethrough and a different color. The choices are the same as for Insertions, plus a few extras such as Hidden, ^, #, and double strikethrough.

- **Changed Lines**—Any line in which there is a change, typically indicated by a vertical line at the border. The settings here are Left Border, Right Border, Outside Border, and None. If you choose Outside Border, the border will appear at the left for left-hand (verso) pages and at the right for right-hand (recto) pages.

- **Comments**—Notes you insert with the New Comment feature, covered later in this chapter. Here, you can set the color of the comment balloon or indicator.

- **Moves**—New in Word 2007, you can track moves from one location to another. In earlier versions, moves were not treated specially; they were just combinations of deletions and insertions. For both Moved From and Moved To, you can choose all the same options as for Insertions. In addition, for Moved From, you can choose double-strikethrough, carets (^), hash marks (#), or Hidden.

- **Table Cell Highlighting**—New in Word 2007, changes you make to a table structure are marked by applying colors to the cells affected. In earlier versions, changes made to table structures were not tracked.

- **Formatting**—Formatting is not tracked by default, but you can enable its tracking and choose what marks and colors are used, with the same options as for insertions.

27

CHANGING THE USER NAME

If you specify any of the colors in the preceding section as By Author, Word will automatically assign a different color to each person's changes and comments. It determines whether a different person is editing the document by looking at the User Name that's set up in Word. If you want to simulate a different user, or if a different user sits down to make changes at the same PC, logged in as the original Windows user, you will want to change the user name in Word so the color used will be different.

To change the user name, follow these steps:

1. Choose Office, Word Options.

2. Click Popular.

3. In the User Name box, type a new name (see Figure 27.4).

4. In the Initials box, type the initials for the new name. Initials are optional to enter; the full user name will be used in place of initials if no initials are entered.

5. Click OK.

Figure 27.4
Change the user name here in order to trigger a different color for revisions set up to be colored By Author.

User name ——
Initials ——

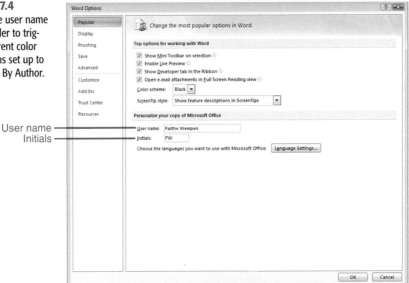

WORKING WITH COMMENTS

Comments are like little sticky notes you insert to make notes about the document. In book publishing, for example, an editor might use a comment to ask the author a question about a certain sentence or phrasing. The Comments feature in Word enables you to insert, edit, and delete comments, and to browse the document by jumping from comment to comment.

NOTE

Comments do not replace revision marks; each has its place in the editing process. Use comments when you have a question or remark to make about the document but you are not proposing a specific change; use revision marks when you want to demonstrate your idea for a change.

INSERTING COMMENTS

Comments can be inserted anywhere in a document, including in the body, the header or footer, footnotes or endnotes, and so on. Depending on whether or not you have enabled balloon usage, the comment will either appear in a balloon or in the Reviewing pane.

To create a comment, follow these steps:

1. Select the text to which the comment refers, or position the insertion point where you want the comment marker to appear.

   TIP

   > If the comment applies broadly to a large section, position the insertion point at the beginning of that section. If the comment refers to a specific word or phrase, though, it is better to select that in step 1.

2. On the Review tab, click New Comment. A new comment balloon appears (if balloon usage is turned on), or the Reviewing pane appears with the insertion point flashing within a new comment line (if balloon usage is turned off).

   The text you selected in step 1 also becomes highlighted with the color assigned to comments for the current user, and the current user's initials and a number appear there. For example, for the first comment from John Doe, it would show [JD1].

   NOTE

   > Comments appear in the Reviewing pane, not in balloons, when you are working in any view other than Print Layout, Web Layout, or Full Screen Reading.

3. Type the comment, and then click away from it to accept it.

VIEWING AND EDITING COMMENTS

When balloons are turned on, you can view and edit the comments directly in the balloons.

When balloons are turned off, you can view a comment by pointing at the comment indicator in the document, but to edit it, you must open the Reviewing pane.

Click Reviewing Pane on the Review tab to toggle it on or off, or right-click a comment and choose Edit Comment. Then just click in the desired comment in the Reviewing Pane and type your edits (see Figure 27.5).

To move between comments using the Reviewing pane, click the comment you want; the document view jumps to that comment. Alternatively, click the Next or Previous button in the Comments group of the Review tab to move between comments. (The Previous and Next buttons in the Changes section move between revisions, rather than comments.) You can also use Select Browse Object to browse between comments, although that is more work and does the same thing as the Previous and Next buttons do.

27

Move between comments
with Previous and Next

Click in a balloon
and edit the text

Figure 27.5
View and edit com-
ments from the
Reviewing pane or
from balloons.

Click in the
Reviewing pane
and edit the text

Jump to the
next comment
by clicking it

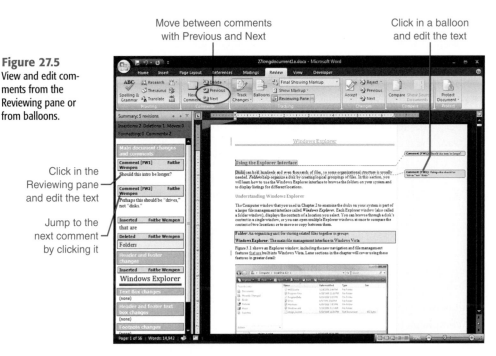

→ For information about Select Browse Object, **see** "Using Select Browse Object,"
p. 86.

CAUTION

If you want to comment on someone else's comment, it is usually best to insert a new
comment rather than typing your remarks within the original comment, so the tracking is
clearer; it can sometimes be difficult to tell where one comment starts and another
begins if they are in the same balloon together.

DELETING COMMENTS

To remove a comment, right-click the comment indicator in the text, or the comment body
in the Reviewing pane, and choose Delete Comment. You can also delete a comment by
deleting the text to which it is attached, or you can right-click the balloon in the margin and
choose Delete Comment.

To remove all comments, click the down arrow to the right of the Delete button in the
Comments group on the Review tab, and choose Delete All Comments in Document.

USING REVISION TRACKING

Revision tracking marks insertions, deletions, moves, and (optionally) formatting changes.
Earlier in this chapter, you learned how to configure the revision tracking feature to mark
what you want, and in the style and color that you prefer. Now let's look at how to actually
do revision tracking.

27

To turn revision tracking on or off, click the Track Changes button on the Review tab. When Track Changes is on, the revision markings you specified appear in the document as you edit.

The revisions appear differently depending on whether balloons are enabled. For example, suppose you change the word "provides" to "includes." This is actually two different revisions: deleting *provides* and inserting *includes.* When balloons are enabled, the insertion appears inline in the document (underlined and in color by default), and the deletion appears in a balloon (see Figure 27.6).

Insertion appears inline

Figure 27.6
When balloons are enabled, deletions appear in balloons.

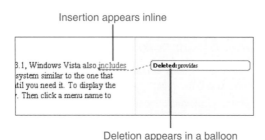

Deletion appears in a balloon

When balloons are disabled, or are set to show only comments and formatting, both the insertion and the deletion appears inline in the text, and a change bar appears alongside the paragraph, as in Figure 27.7.

Change bar   Insertion appears inline

Figure 27.7
When balloons are disabled, both insertions and deletions appear inline.

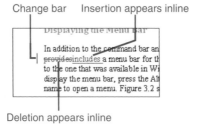

Deletion appears inline

REVIEWING REVISIONS

You can review your own revisions, but it is much more common to review someone else's revisions, or even revisions from multiple reviewers. You can then respond to the reviewing marks by accepting or rejecting each change individually or accepting or rejecting all changes as a whole (or all changes within a selected range).

DISPLAYING OR HIDING REVISION MARKS

Showing revision marks is not always necessary or appropriate. For example, as you are reviewing a document that someone else has written, you might want to make changes to it without being distracted by seeing the changes that other people have already made to it.

One way to avoid showing revision marks is to turn off the Track Changes feature and accept any existing revisions, of course, but then you lose the tracking benefits. Instead, to track changes but not show the changes onscreen, set the Display for Review list's setting to Final. To display the tracking marks again, set it to Final Showing Markup (see Figure 27.8).

27

Figure 27.8
Show or hide revision marks, and view the final or the original version.

As you can see in Figure 27.8, that Display for Review list also has two other options: Original and Original Showing Markup. These show the document as it was before tracked revisions were made.

DISPLAYING OR HIDING CERTAIN TYPES OF REVISIONS

Perhaps you want to see revisions, but only certain types. For example, maybe someone on your team has insisted that you track formatting changes, but it drives you crazy to see all those formatting change balloons and marks onscreen.

To choose which types of changes appear, open the Show Markup list on the Review tab and select or deselect the types of revisions you want to view (see Figure 27.9). Not only can you choose which types, but you can discriminate between reviewers if there have been more than one.

Figure 27.9
Choose which specific reviewers and revision types you want to see onscreen.

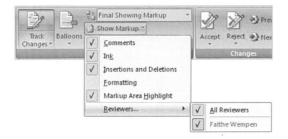

MOVING AMONG REVISIONS

To move between revisions, you can use the Next and Previous buttons in the Changes section of the Review tab. Don't confuse them with the buttons of the same names in the Comments group, which are just for comments. You can also use Select Browse Object to move between them. (Select Browse Object calls them "Edits" rather than revisions.)

→ For information about Select Browse Object, **see** "Using Select Browse Object," **p. 86.**

Simply moving between revisions does nothing to them; you're just viewing them. If you want to accept or reject them at the same time as you're moving to them, see the following section.

ACCEPTING OR REJECTING REVISIONS

To accept or reject an individual revision, move to it or select it and then click the Accept or Reject button on the Review tab. If you choose Accept, the revision is incorporated into the document and the revision marks are removed; if you choose Reject, the original text is restored and the revision marks are removed.

TIP

> Here's an even quicker way to accept or reject changes: Select the revised text, and then right-click it and choose Accept Change or Reject Change. This works for multiple changes; just select a range that includes multiple revisions, and they will all be accepted or rejected at once.

The behavior of these buttons is slightly different than it was in earlier versions of Word, because by default each of these jumps to the next revision automatically after it performs its action. That makes it convenient to quickly move through a series of revisions because you do not have to click Next to go to the next instance as a separate step. However, it does cause a problem if you want to look at the accepted/rejected revision after accepting or rejecting it, to make sure it looks right in context.

If you would prefer *not* to advance to the next revision after accepting or rejecting, open the drop-down list for the button and select the alternative version of the command that does not involve moving to the next revision. For example, in Figure 27.10, you would select the Accept button's Accept Change option. For the Reject button, the equivalent is Reject Change.

Figure 27.10
Select a type of acceptance or rejection from the button's menu.

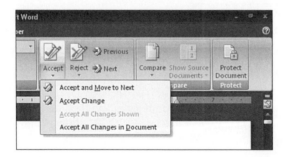

> **TIP**
>
> There is no way to make Accept Change and Reject Change the defaults on the Accept and Reject buttons. However, you can add those commands to the Quick Access toolbar if you like. Right-click the command and choose Add to Quick Access Toolbar. Once a command is on the Quick Access toolbar, it has an automatic shortcut key assigned to it based on its position on the toolbar. For example, if the new command is in position 6 (from left to right), press Alt+6.

To accept all revisions in the entire document, open the Accept button's menu and choose Accept All Changes in Document. If some of the revisions are not currently displayed (for example, if you selectively turned off some of them with the Show Markup button's menu), an additional command appears: Accept All Changes Shown. This accepts all the changes currently displayed but not the hidden ones.

The same thing goes for the Reject button. Choose Reject All Changes in Document or Reject All Changes Shown to do a mass rejection.

Preventing Others from Tampering with Revisions

You just saw how easy it is to accept or reject revisions, or to turn them off completely. That means that anyone revising your document can make changes that you aren't aware of, and can accept or reject other people's changes before you even get a chance to see them.

To prevent that from happening, you can lock down the document so that all changes are tracked and tracking cannot be disabled. You'll learn more about security lockdowns in Chapter 28, but here's a quick summary of how to do it:

1. On the Review tab, click Protect Document and click Restrict Formatting and Editing.
2. In the Protect Document task pane, mark Allow Only This Type of Editing in the Document.
3. Set the drop-down list to Tracked Changes.
4. Click Yes, Start Enforcing Protection.
5. Type a password, and then type it again to confirm it.
6. Click OK.

When the document is thus protected, the Track Changes, Accept, and Reject buttons are unavailable. To turn protection off, click Stop Protection in the Restrict Formatting and Editing task pane and enter your password.

COMPARING DOCUMENTS

Tracking changes works well when multiple people are working on a single copy of the document. Perhaps they are circulating it from one person to another, or accessing it at different times from a server, but there exists only one version of the document that everyone edits.

When one person saves his or her own separate copy and then makes changes to it, though, that system breaks down. Suddenly you have two versions of the document, each with some changes that the other one does not have. For situations like that, you must compare the two versions and integrate the changes from both into a single master copy.

VIEWING TWO DOCUMENTS SIDE BY SIDE

One way to compare two documents is to view them side by side in separate windows. You can choose to lock the scrolling together so that when you scroll one window, the other scrolls an equal amount, or you can allow the windows to scroll separately.

To view two documents side by side, follow these steps:

1. Open both documents. Display one of the two as the active document.
2. On the View tab, click View Side by Side. If only two documents are open, they immediately appear side by side. If three or more are open, the Compare Side by Side dialog box opens (see Figure 27.11).
3. Click the document to display side by side with the first one and click OK. The two documents appear side by side, each in its own copy of Word, as shown in Figure 27.12.

By default, the two windows are set for synchronized scrolling. To turn this off, on the View tab, click the Synchronous Scrolling button.

Figure 27.11
Select the document to compare with the active one.

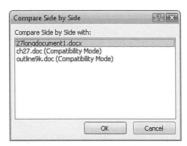

Figure 27.12
Two documents displayed side by side.

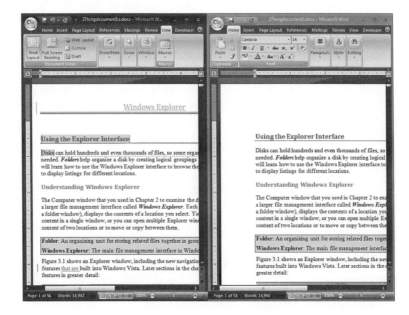

Don't see a Synchronous Scrolling button? That's probably because your screen is not wide enough to show complete tabs for two document windows side by side. Instead, some of the groups appear as buttons. Click the Window button to open a menu containing the Window group's options, and you'll find the Synchronous Scrolling button there (see Figure 27.13).

Figure 27.13
When the windows are narrow, each group is a button that displays a drop-down list.

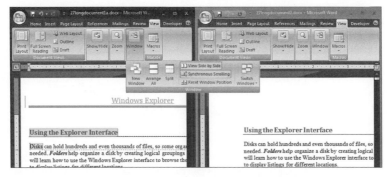

→ For more information about the Window group and its various options, **see** "Displaying Multiple Documents and Windows," **p. 22**.

COMPARING AND COMBINING DOCUMENTS

Instead of manually comparing the documents line by line, you might prefer to use the Compare feature in Word to automatically insert revision marks to show how one document differs from another.

There are actually two variants of the process:

- **Combine**—Merges the revisions from both copies into a single document, which can be either the original or the copy, as you specify, or a brand-new document. You can repeat the Combine operation to combine revisions from multiple copies. All revision marks are kept in both copies and remain attributed to the original reviewers.

- **Compare**—Generates a new copy that combines the two versions; this is also called *legal blacklining*. The major difference between this and Combine is that in situations where the original also has revision marks in it, those revision marks will be accepted in the resulting document, and the changes between it and the second document will appear as a single user set of revision marks. All differences are attributed to a single new reviewer.

COMBINING TWO OR MORE DOCUMENTS

To combine two or more documents, you combine them two at a time. In other words, you start with one, and compare another to it, taking on the revisions from the second one. Then you compare that resulting version to a third, and that result to a fourth, and so on until all versions have been combined.

To combine documents, follow these steps:

1. On the Review tab, click Compare, and then click Combine in the menu that appears. The Combine Documents dialog box opens.

2. Open the Original Document drop-down list and select one of the documents to combine.

3. Open the Revised Document drop-down list and select the other document to combine, or click Browse to browse for it (see Figure 27.14).

Figure 27.14
Choose the two documents to combine.

Browse buttons

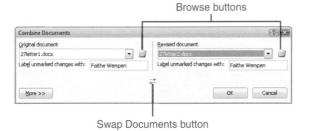

Swap Documents button

NOTE

It does not really matter which one is used in which spot since later in these steps, you are able to specify where the revisions will be placed. If you get them in the opposite order than you want, though, you can easily swap their places by clicking the Swap Documents button.

4. By default, the Label Unmarked Changes With setting is whatever user name is set up in Word as the current user. Change the name if desired in either of the text boxes.

NOTE

> Unmarked changes are differences between the two documents that are not currently marked with revision marks attributed to a particular reviewer.

5. (Optional) Click the More button and then set any of the following options, as shown in Figure 27.15:

- **Comparison Settings**—Clear the check boxes for any comparisons you want to omit. For example, you might not care about differences in white space or case changes.

- **Show Changes At**—By default, revisions are marked at the Word level, but you can set this to Character level if you prefer. (See the sidebar that follows for more information.)

- **Show Changes In**—Choose where the combined markup will appear. You can choose to place the revisions in the Original document, the Revised document, or a new document.

NOTE

> "Original" and "Revised" are defined as the documents you specified at the top of the dialog box; Word makes no evaluation of which one is actually newer.

6. Click OK to perform the combine operation.

7. Repeat the process if needed to combine additional documents with the newly combined one.

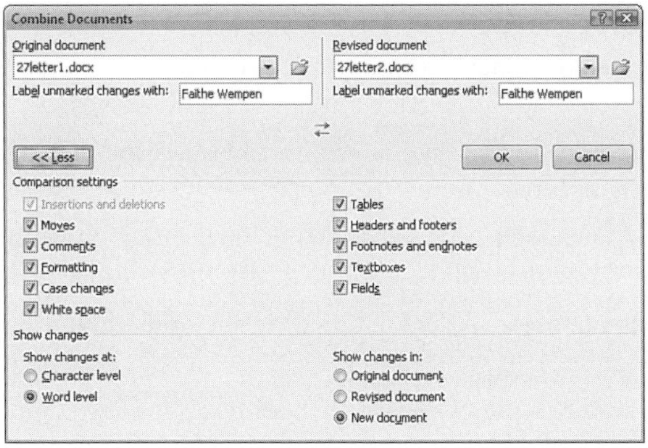

Figure 27.15
Advanced options for combining documents.

27

Understanding Character-Level vs. Word-Level Revisions

The default type of revision tracking operates at the word level. That means if a word is even one letter differ-ent from another word, the entire word gets struck-through and replaced, like this:

~~differing~~different

Word-level revisions are easier to browse because most people read entire words at a time.

Character-level revisions, on the other hand, show revisions within the individual words. If not all the letters of the word change, not all will be marked as changed:

Differ~~ing~~ent

COMPARING WITH LEGAL BLACKLINE

When you compare with legal blackline, all previous unresolved revision marks in the docu-ments are accepted, and only the differences between the two documents appear as markup. The new markup is attributed to whomever you specify in the Label Changes With text box. Other than those two things, the process is nearly identical to that of combining, covered in the preceding section.

Follow these steps to compare two documents:

1. On the Review tab, click Compare, and then click Compare in the menu that appears. The Compare Documents dialog box opens. It is identical to the Combine dialog box shown in Figure 27.14, except the Label Changes With box is not available for the Original Document. (Actually it starts out unavailable for the Revised Document too, but becomes available after you select the revised document.)

> **NOTE**
> The reason you cannot specify an author for changes in the original document is that during the process of comparing, all unaccepted changes in the original are accepted automatically.

2. Open the Original Document drop-down list and select one of the documents to com-bine, or click Browse and browse for it (refer to Figure 27.14).

3. Open the Revised Document drop-down list and select the other document to combine, or click Browse and browse for it.

4. For the Revised Document, if desired, change the name in the Label Changes With box. This is the name that will be associated with the revision marks that are inserted.

5. (Optional) Click the More button and then set any of the following options, as shown previously in Figure 27.15:

   - **Comparison Settings**—Clear the check boxes for any comparisons you want to omit. For example, you might not care about differences in white space or case changes.

   - **Show Changes At**—By default, revisions are marked at the Word level, but you can set this to Character level if you prefer. (See the preceding sidebar for more information.)

- **Show Changes In**—Choose where the combined markup will appear. You can choose to place the revisions in the Original document, the Revised document, or a new document.

6. Click OK to perform the combine operation.

7. Repeat the process if needed to combine additional documents with the newly combined one.

WORKING IN FULL SCREEN READING VIEW

When reading a document onscreen, you might prefer to work in Full Screen Reading view (also called Reading Layout view). This view changes the pagination and layout of the document in order to make its text larger and more easily readable onscreen.

Full Screen Reading is not a suitable view for reviewing documents in which you must check for proper pagination and overall page attractiveness, because it flows the text and graphics into a custom two-column layout that has no relationship to the document's actual print layout. It excels, however, in situations where you need to read, highlight, and comment on the document. Figure 27.16 points out a few of its features.

Figure 27.16
Full Screen Reading view works well when you're reviewing someone else's work.

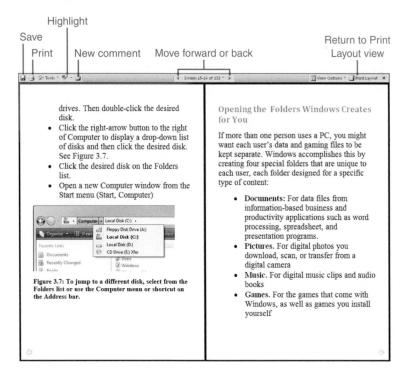

To enter Full Screen Reading view, click the Full Screen Reading button at the bottom-right corner of the Word window, or select it from the View tab, the same as with any other view.

To leave Full Screen Reading view, click the Print Layout button in the upper-right corner of the Full Screen Reading display.

NOTE

> The X button in the upper-right corner closes the document; it does not take you back to Print Layout view.

MOVING BETWEEN SCREENS

A *screen* in Full Screen Reading view is an onscreen page. By default, Word displays two pages at a time, side by side like in a book, as in Figure 27.16.

To move between screens, click the right and left arrow buttons at the top of the window, pointed out in Figure 27.16. Note that the left and right sides of the screen are considered different "screens," so in Figure 27.16, you are actually seeing screens 15 (left) and 16 (right).

To jump to a particular screen, heading, or other marker, click the screen number at the top of the window to display a Screen menu, as in Figure 27.17. You can also access the Go To and Find features from here.

Figure 27.17
Use the Screen menu to jump to a particular screen or heading in the document.

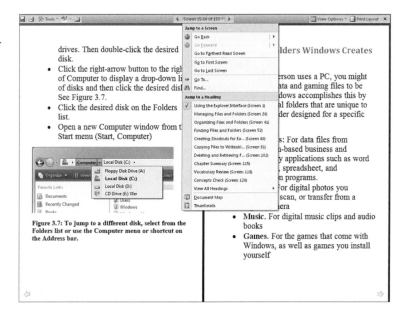

USING THE FULL SCREEN READING TOOLS

Click the Tools button to open a menu (see Figure 27.18) from which you can select several of the most common Word features that you might need while reading a document:

- **Research**—Opens the Research pane, and switches Full Screen Reading view to showing a single page at a time. From here you can use any of the research tools, covered in Chapter 4, "Using Spelling, Grammar, and Research Tools."

> If you like seeing a single page at a time, see "Setting Reading View Options" below to make that the default.

- **Translation ToolTip**—Opens a menu from which you can toggle on/off translation ToolTips. These were also covered in Chapter 4.

- **Text Highlight Color**—This is the same as the Highlighter button on the toolbar, to the right of the Tools button. You can turn highlighting on/off and change the highlight color. See Chapter 6, "Applying Character Formatting," for details about highlighting.

- **New Comment**—This is the same as the New Comment button on the toolbar. It starts a new comment in a balloon (if comments are configured to appear that way), and switches to showing a single page at a time.

- **Find**—Opens the Find and Replace dialog box, which you can use to locate specific text strings, as you learned in Chapter 3, "Typing and Editing Text."

Figure 27.18
The Tools menu provides quick access to popular tools for reading and revising documents.

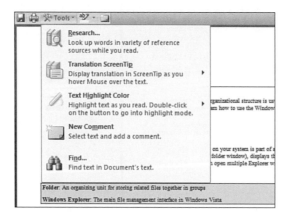

SETTING READING VIEW OPTIONS

The View Options button's menu in Full Screen Reading view, shown in Figure 27.19, is a rich source of viewing and editing options and features:

- **Open Attachments in Full Screen**—When this is enabled, Word documents that come to you as email attachments and documents from SharePoint Services sites open in Full Screen Reading view by default.

- **Increase Text Size and Decrease Text Size**—These commands make the text larger and smaller, respectively, to help with readability. Graphics are not affected.

- **Show One Page and Show Two Pages**—These commands toggle between one-page and two-page viewing. A "page" in this context is the same as a "screen."

- **Show Printed Page**—When this option is enabled, the page borders appear.

- **Margin Settings**—When this option is enabled, the text runs all the way to the edges of each screen, making more text visible at once.

- **Allow Typing**—When this option is enabled, you can position the insertion point and edit text from within this view.

- **Track Changes**—Opens a submenu from which you can control revision tracking, so the edits you make (see Allow Typing) can be tracked or not, as desired.

- **Show Comments and Changes**—Enables you to toggle on/off individual types of changes.

- **Show Original/Final Document**—Opens a submenu from which you can choose whether or not to show revisions onscreen and whether to show the original or the revised version.

Figure 27.19
The View Options menu enables you to control the appearance and functionality of Full Screen Reading view.

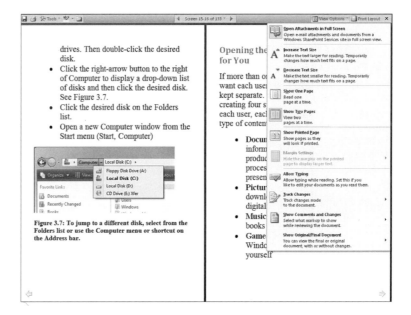

TROUBLESHOOTING

HOW CAN I TURN OFF LOCKED REVISION MARKS IF I DON'T KNOW THE PASSWORD?

There's not an easy way to do it. Saving as a different filename won't do it, nor will saving in Rich Text Format or HTML. If you just want to see the document without revision marks, set the Display for Review setting to Final on the Review tab.

You can, however, get rid of revision marks by saving in plain text format. Then close and reopen the file, and all the revision marks will have been accepted. You'll need to reapply all the formatting, of course; that's the disadvantage.

I DON'T LIKE THE TWO-COLUMN DISPLAY IN FULL SCREEN READING VIEW

Switch to a single-column display by opening the View Options button's menu and clicking Show One Page.

THE TEXT GETS TOO SMALL WHEN BALLOONS ARE ENABLED

The display has to shrink the zoom somewhat when you use balloons to track changes and comments to make room for the balloon area to the right (or left) of the main page. You can ameliorate this somewhat by making the balloon area narrower. To do so, follow these steps:

1. From the Review tab, open the Track Changes button's menu and choose Change Tracking Options.
2. In the Balloons area, decrease the Preferred Width setting.
3. Click OK.

CHAPTER 28

PROTECTING AND SECURING DOCUMENTS

In this chapter

UNDERSTANDING DOCUMENT PROTECTION IN OFFICE 2007

As you create, edit, and manage documents, you might not always want everyone who has access to the drive to be able to open and modify all documents. Word 2007 offers a variety of ways of protecting documents. They break down into these areas:

- **Restricting access to the document entirely**—This includes using Windows file encryption, setting network access permissions, and placing a password on the file in Word.

- **Restricting what users can do to a file**—This includes restricting style usage and editing, and preventing users from turning off revision marks, as well as setting a document to be read-only.

- **Marking a document as finalized**—You can mark a document as Final, and also add a digital signature to it to confirm that it has not been changed since being marked as such.

- **Preventing macro-based attacks**—To avoid macro viruses, you can choose to use macro-enabled file formats only when necessary, and you can set up trusted locations in which to store macro-enabled files. Files not in those trusted locations can then have higher macro security levels.

- **Protecting your privacy**—This includes removing personally identifying information from the file, such as the author name and keywords, controlling when Word does or does not go online to retrieve extra content, and participating (or not) in the Customer Experience Improvement program.

This chapter looks at each of these types of protection.

RESTRICTING ACCESS TO A DOCUMENT

The most basic type of protection for a document is to prevent others from accessing it entirely. There are several ways to do this. You can put a password on the file within Word itself, you can locally encrypt the location in which it is stored, or you can remove network access to the location.

PASSWORD-PROTECTING A DOCUMENT IN WORD

You can put two separate passwords on a file: one to open it and one to modify it. That way you can give one password to certain people and the other password to others, depending on what you want them to be able to do with it. (You can also set more complex editing permissions, as you'll learn later in this chapter.)

When you password-protect a document against being opened in Word, Word encrypts it internally, and the encryption can only be decrypted by entering the correct password. This is important because then someone using a text editor outside of Word cannot browse the protected file. Password protection does not simply prevent the file from opening in Word; it actually changes the file.

When you password-protect the file against changes being saved to it, the file is not encrypted. That password simply prevents it from being saved; someone could still go into the file with a text editor and look at it (or with Word itself for that matter).

SAVING WITH A PASSWORD

To password-protect a file, follow these steps:

1. Choose Office, Save As. The Save As dialog box opens.

2. In the Save As dialog box, click Tools and choose General Options. The General Options dialog box opens (see Figure 28.1).

3. (Optional) In the Password to Open box, type a password. Passwords can be up to 15 characters long.

> **TIP**
>
> For best security, use passwords that combine lowercase and uppercase letters, numbers, and symbols.

4. (Optional) In the Password to Modify box, type a different password. You can use one or both passwords, but if you use both, they must be different.

5. Click OK. A Confirm Password dialog box opens.

6. Retype the password and click OK.

7. In the Save As dialog box, click Save to save the file with the password.

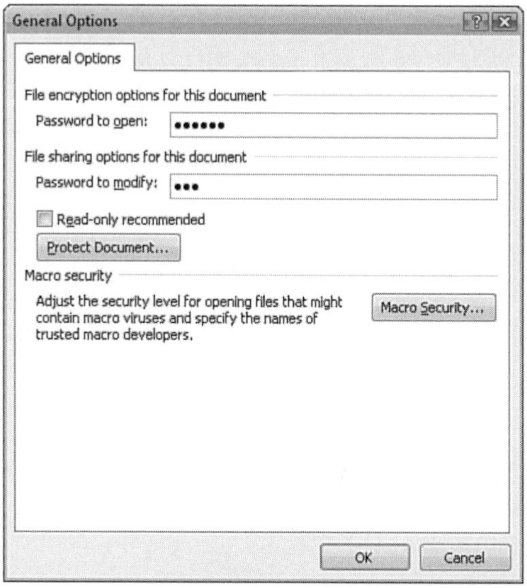

Figure 28.1
Set a password for the file in its General Options dialog box while saving.

> **NOTE**
>
> The Read-Only Recommended check box does not enforce anything; it simply opens the document by giving the user a choice of read-only or not. It is not related to password protection, even though it is in the same dialog box as the passwords.

28

REMOVING A PASSWORD FROM A FILE

To remove a password from a file, you must open the file, so you have to know the password. Assuming you do, here's how to remove it:

1. Choose Office, Save As. The Save As dialog box opens.
2. In the Save As dialog box, click Tools and choose General Options. The General Options dialog box opens (refer to Figure 28.1).
3. Clear the password boxes. (Select the current password and press Delete.)
4. Click OK.
5. Click Save to save the file without the password.

USING WINDOWS ENCRYPTION

If you have a drive that uses the NTFS file system under Windows 2000 or higher, you can encrypt folders so that anything you put in those folders is accessible only to the currently logged-in user.

Windows NTFS encryption is designed to prevent multiple people who share the same physical PC from accessing each other's private files. It does not prevent people accessing your PC via the network from accessing the files, as long as you are logged in as you and sharing them.

It is possible to encrypt individual files, but it is better to encrypt an entire folder, and then place the files into it that you want to protect. Any files in an encrypted folder are automatically encrypted; when you move or copy them outside that encrypted location, they become decrypted. As long as you are logged in as the user who encrypted the folder, the encryption is invisible and unobtrusive. Encrypted folders can hold any files, not just Word documents, of course.

ENCRYPTING A FOLDER

To encrypt a folder in Windows Vista, Windows XP, or Windows 2000, follow these steps:

1. In any file management window (such as Windows Explorer), right-click the folder and choose Properties. The Properties dialog box opens.
2. On the General tab, click Advanced. The Advanced Attributes dialog box opens (see Figure 28.2).
3. Mark the Encrypt Contents to Secure Data check box.
4. Click OK.
5. Click OK again. A Confirm Attribute Change dialog box opens.
6. Click how you want the encryption to apply:
   - Apply changes to this folder only.
   - Apply changes to this folder, subfolders, and files.
7. Click OK. The folder's name turns green in the file listing.

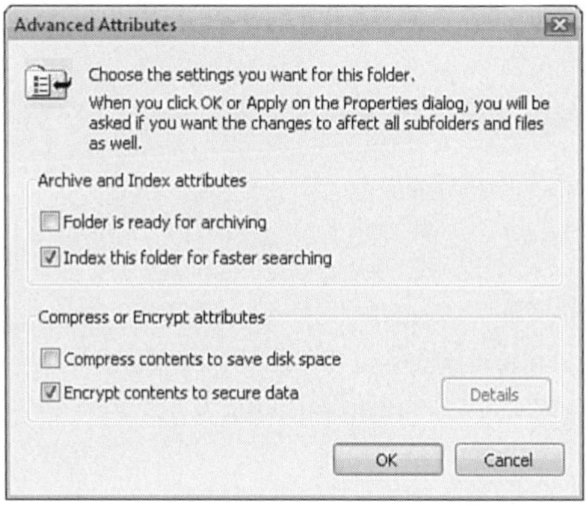

Figure 28.2
Encrypt a folder on
your hard disk in which
to store private files.

DECRYPTING A FOLDER

To decrypt a file within an encrypted folder, simply move or copy it somewhere else. You do not have to decrypt the entire folder just to decrypt the file.

If you do want to decrypt the entire folder, however, here's how:

1. In any file management window (such as Windows Explorer), right-click the folder and choose Properties. The Properties dialog box opens.

   You can tell an encrypted folder because its name appears in green.

2. On the General tab, click Advanced. The Advanced Attributes dialog box opens (refer to Figure 28.2).

3. Clear the Encrypt Contents to Secure Data check box.

4. Click OK.

5. Click OK again. A Confirm Attribute Change dialog box opens.

6. Click how you want the decryption to apply:
   - Apply changes to this folder only.
   - Apply changes to this folder, subfolders, and files.

7. Click OK. The folder's name turns from green back to black in the file listing.

REMOVING NETWORK SHARE PERMISSION FOR A LOCATION

If your PC is connected to a network, you can share certain folders with others on the network. One way to prevent someone from accessing a file is to remove the share permission for that folder, so that people can no longer browse that location.

To check to see if a location is shared, and remove sharing from it if needed, follow these steps from Windows Vista:

1. From a file management window (such as Windows Explorer), right-click the folder and choose Properties. The Properties dialog box opens.

28

2. Click the Sharing tab. If there is a path in the Network Path section, the folder is being shared.

3. To unshare it, click the Share button. A File Sharing dialog box opens.

4. Click Stop Sharing.

5. Click Done.

To do the same in Windows XP:

1. From a file management window (such as Windows Explorer), right-click the folder and choose Sharing and Security. The Properties dialog box opens with the Sharing tab displayed.

2. Clear the Share This Folder on the Network check box.

3. Click OK.

RESTRICTING WHAT USERS CAN DO TO A DOCUMENT

In addition to preventing access completely to a document, you can restrict what a user can do to it. As you saw earlier in the chapter, you can assign a password to modify the document, effectively making it read-only if the person does not know the password. There are other ways to restrict the document as well.

RECOMMENDING READ-ONLY

You can make the document read-only in general, unrelated to a password for modification, and you can either make this restriction optional or required.

Look back at Figure 28.1; notice the Read-Only Recommended check box. When this is marked, each time the document is opened, a message appears as in Figure 28.3. This gives the user the option of read-only, which prevents accidental changes from being saved to the original. If the users choose to allow the read-only attribute to be enabled, they can still modify the document onscreen, but they cannot save their changes to overwrite the original file.

Figure 28.3
You can set a document to recommend read-only.

MAKING THE DOCUMENT FILE READ-ONLY

You can also make a document read-only from outside of Word by setting the file's properties to Read-Only. There's no way to lock this on, so someone who is determined to make changes to the file can go into the properties and turn off the read-only attribute, but it does provide a layer of annoyance that will slow people down from making changes, and might prevent an inexperienced user from making them.

To make a document read-only from Windows, follow these steps:

1. From a file-management window, such as Windows Explorer, right-click the file and choose Properties. The Properties dialog box opens for that file.

2. On the General tab, mark the Read-Only check box (see Figure 28.4).

3. Click OK.

Figure 28.4
Set a file's properties to read-only from Windows.

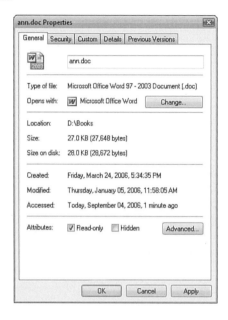

SETTING A READ-ONLY EDITING RESTRICTION

In addition to protecting the document at a file level, you can protect it from inside Word by applying editing restrictions.

When you set a document to be read-only via editing restrictions, not only can people not save changes to it, but they can't *make* changes to it. You can put a password on that protection if desired, or leave it open so that people who know how to manage document protection settings can override it.

Follow these steps to prevent document editing:

1. On the Review tab, click Restrict Formatting and Editing. The Restrict Formatting and Editing task pane appears.

2. In the Editing Restrictions section, mark the Allow Only This Type of Editing in the Document check box.

3. Open the drop-down list and choose No Changes (Read Only), as shown in Figure 28.5.

Figure 28.5
Set the document to be read-only.

4. Click Yes, Start Enforcing Protection. The Start Enforcing Protection dialog box opens.

5. (Optional) If you don't want users to be able to disable the read-only status, enter a password in the Enter New Password (Optional) box, and then repeat it in the Reenter Password to Confirm box (see Figure 28.6).

   If you omit the password, anyone can override the document's read-only status from the Protect Document task pane.

6. Click OK.

Figure 28.6
If desired, enforce the read-only status with a password.

Restricting a Document to Comments Only

You can set a document's editing restrictions so that users can enter comments (with the New Comment button on the Review tab) but otherwise cannot edit the document. To do this, follow the steps in "Setting a Read-Only Editing Restriction," but instead of choosing No Changes in step 3, choose Comments.

→ To learn more about comments, **see** "Working with Comments," **p. 788**.

28

RESTRICTING A DOCUMENT TO FORM FILL-IN ONLY

You can set a document's editing restrictions so that form fields can be filled in, but otherwise no changes can be made. Follow the steps in "Setting a Read-Only Editing Restriction," but in step 3 choose Filling In Forms.

→ To learn how to create forms to fill out onscreen, **see** Chapter 21, "Creating Forms," **p. 655**.

FORCING REVISION MARKS TO STAY ON

When you use revision marks to track changes, anyone editing the document can turn them off and thereby hide the changes they are making. To prevent this, you can set the editing restriction so that changes are permanently tracked on, and can't be turned off without knowing the password.

To force revisions to stay on, follow the steps in "Setting a Read-Only Editing Restriction," but in step 3 choose Tracked Changes.

→ To learn how to track changes and accept/reject revisions, **see** "Using Revision Tracking," **p. 790**.

RESTRICTING STYLE USAGE

If you are collaborating with others on a document, it might be important that only certain styles be used for formatting. For example, as I was writing this book, I used a template in which the editor had assigned certain styles for certain types of paragraphs, and I was not supposed to create any new styles. If you trust people not to create new styles, great, but if you don't, you might want to lock down the document so that styles are limited to a certain set you define.

To restrict style usage, follow these steps:

1. On the Review tab, click Restrict Formatting and Editing. The Restrict Formatting and Editing task pane displays.

2. Mark the Limit Formatting to a Selection of Styles check box.

3. Click the Settings hyperlink. The Formatting Restrictions dialog box opens (see Figure 28.7).

4. Ensure that the check boxes are marked for the styles you want to allow and cleared for the styles you do not.

   You can get a head start by clicking All or None, or Recommended Minimum to get a whittled-down list recommended by Microsoft.

5. (Optional) Mark any of these check boxes:

   - **Allow AutoFormat to Override Formatting Restrictions**—When this is enabled, AutoFormat will be able to apply styles that you have not selected on the list in step 4.

   - **Block Theme or Scheme Switching**—When this is enabled, users will not be able to apply different document themes (for example, from the Page Layout tab).

   - **Block Quick Style Set Switching**—When this is enabled, users will not be able to use the Change Styles feature on the Home tab to switch style sets.

28

Figure 28.7
Restrict style usage to
the styles you specify.

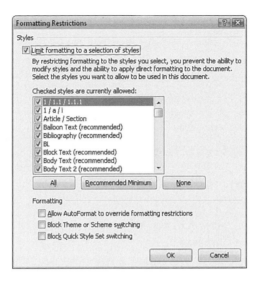

6. Click OK to accept the settings. A warning appears asking whether you want to remove unallowed style usage from the document. Click Yes or No.

7. Click Yes, Start Enforcing Protection in the Protect Document task pane to turn protection on.

SETTING UP PER-USER EXCEPTIONS TO RESTRICTIONS

You can set up the restrictions on a document so that they do not apply to certain users. To do this for groups (if groups are defined), mark the check box next to the desired group in the Exceptions section of the Restrict Formatting and Editing task pane.

If there is not a group set up that represents the users to be excluded from restrictions, you can manually set up the individual user names. To do this, click the More Users hyperlink in the Restrict Formatting and Editing task pane, opening the Add Users dialog box (see Figure 28.8).

Figure 28.8
Specify users to whom
the restrictions should
not apply.

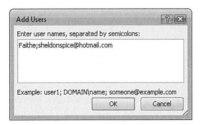

Then enter the users, separating the names with semicolons. You can use any of the following nomenclatures:

- **User name**—For local users on this PC, enter the names by which they log in.
- **Email addresses**—For email recipients, enter their email addresses.

■ **Domain user names**—For network domains, enter the domain name, a slash (\), and the user name, like this: *Domain\user*.

After you enter the names and click OK, Word attempts to verify the names and addresses. (It does not verify email addresses really; it just checks them for correct form.) Names that are verified appear in an Individuals section in the task pane; you can then mark their check boxes there to select them (see Figure 28.9). (They are not selected simply because you entered them in the Add Names dialog box; selecting their check box is a necessary separate step.)

Figure 28.9
Users you add appear in the Individuals section.

Exceptions (optional)

Select parts of the document and choose users who are allowed to freely edit them.

Groups:

☐ Everyone

Individuals:

☐ sheldonspice@hotmail.com

More users...

MARKING A DOCUMENT AS FINAL

A finalized document is read-only, and when it is being viewed, some features in Word are not available. When users try to edit it, they see a message in the status bar that the document is final.

To mark a document as final, follow these steps:

1. Click the Office button and point to Prepare.
2. Click Mark as Final.

This is not a security feature; anyone who receives an electronic copy of it can simply turn off the Mark as Final attribute by repeating the preceding steps. It is merely a way to designate a document so that no *inadvertent* changes are made to it.

PREVENTING MACRO-BASED ATTACKS

Macro viruses were prevalent back a decade or so ago, in Word 97. A macro virus would travel along with a document, and infect the Normal.dot template, causing various mischief in the program. One common result of macro virus infection, for example, was that any time you tried to save a file, it would save as a template (.dot) rather than a document (.doc). Macro viruses are no longer common, due mostly to the fact that Microsoft aggressively implemented macro virus protection in later versions of Word. (Excel was also vulnerable to some macro viruses.)

Word 2007 has very good protection against macro viruses, taking a multiprong approach to preventing them from doing damage.

28

CHOOSING NON-MACRO FILE FORMATS

The most basic way to protect against macro viruses is to use a file format that does not support viruses. Word 2007 offers two document formats: The regular .dotx does not support macros, and the macro-enabled .dotm does. When you do not need macro capability, use .dotx.

SPECIFYING TRUSTED LOCATIONS

In Word 2007, macros are allowed to run in a macro-enabled document or template—or not—based on the location of the file. You can set up certain locations to be trusted, and then whatever files you put in that location will automatically have full macro-running privileges.

The following folders are trusted by default:

Program Files\Microsoft Office\Document Themes 12

Program Files\Microsoft Office\Templates

Users\username\AppData\Roaming\Microsoft\Word\Startup

Users\username\AppData\Roaming\Microsoft\Templates

NOTE

In Windows XP, the last two folders in this list are:
- Documents and Settings\username\Application Data\Microsoft\Startup
- Documents and Settings\username\Application Data\Microsoft\Templates

To set up additional trusted locations, follow these steps:

1. Choose Office, Word Options. The Word Options dialog box appears.
2. Click Trust Center.
3. Click the Trust Center Settings button. A separate Trust Center dialog box appears.
4. Click Trusted Locations (see Figure 28.10).
5. Click Add New Location.
6. Click the Browse button and browse to the desired location; then click OK.
7. If desired, mark the Subfolders of This Location Are Also Trusted check box (see Figure 28.11).
8. Click OK.

Figure 28.10
View and add trusted
locations.

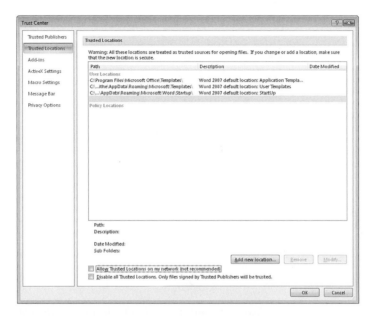

Figure 28.11
Create a new trusted
location.

Other settings that you can optionally use for trusted locations (refer to Figure 28.10) are:

- **Allow Trusted Locations on My Network**—Enables you to add trusted locations that exist other than on your local PC.

- **Disable All Trusted Locations. Only Files Signed by Trusted Publishers Will Be Trusted**—Just what the name says. (You'll learn about trusted publishers in the next section.)

- **Remove**—Removes a trusted location from the list.

- **Modify**—Opens the Microsoft Office Trusted Location dialog box.

28

WORKING WITH TRUSTED PUBLISHERS

Another way to trust a macro is to verify that it comes from a trusted publisher. Macro settings enable you to specify what should happen when a macro from a trusted publisher wants to run outside of a trusted location.

When you open a document that includes one or more signed macros, Word prompts you as to whether or not you want to trust macros from that signer. Information about the signer's certificate appears, including the name, the issuing authority, and the valid dates. If you choose Yes, that signer is added to your Trusted Publishers list. If this hasn't occurred yet, then your Trusted Publishers list will be blank in the Trust Center dialog box.

To view the Trusted Publishers list, follow these steps:

1. Choose Office, Word Options.
2. Click Trust Center.
3. Click the Trust Center Settings button.
4. Click Trusted Publishers.

If you have a trusted publisher on your list, you can select it and then click View to view its information or Remove to un-trust it.

ADJUSTING MACRO SETTINGS

Macro settings apply only to macros that are stored in presentations not in trusted locations. They determine whether or not the macro should run and whether you should receive notification.

Follow these steps to get to the macro settings, and to change them if desired:

1. Choose Office, Word Options.
2. Click Trust Center.
3. Click Trust Center Settings. The Trust Center dialog box opens.
4. Click Macro Settings (see Figure 28.12).
5. Select the macro setting that best describes what should happen when a macro tries to run outside of a trusted location.
6. Click OK on both open dialog boxes.

Figure 28.12
Adjust macro settings for locations other than trusted locations.

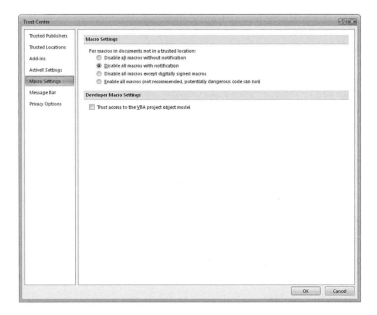

PROTECTING YOUR PRIVACY

When you distribute a Word document, or make it available to others, a certain amount of personal information about its author travels along with it. This can include properties, headers and footers that you might have neglected to remove, comments, revisions, and other items. You can see that information, and remove it, in Word 2007.

FINDING AND REMOVING PERSONAL INFORMATION

Inspecting a document shows you all the hidden and less-obvious pieces of personal information that might potentially travel along with a document, so that you can remove them if desired.

To inspect a document, follow these steps:

1. Choose Office, Prepare, Inspect Document. If prompted to save your document, click Yes. The Document Inspector dialog box opens (see Figure 28.13).

2. Clear the check boxes for any content you do not want to check for.

3. Click Inspect. Results appear, as in Figure 28.14. For each type of content found, a Remove All button appears.

4. Click Remove All to remove a type of content.

5. When finished, click Reinspect or click Close.

28

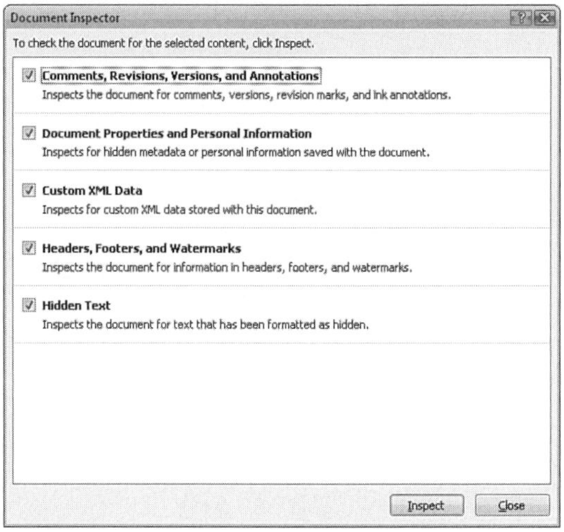

Figure 28.13
Select the items for which you want to inspect.

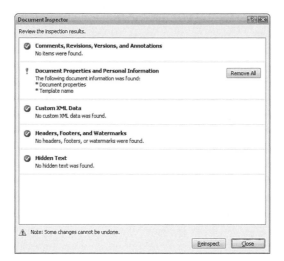

Figure 28.14
Select the items for which you want to inspect.

SETTING PRIVACY OPTIONS

In the Trust Center's Privacy Options section are a number of settings that control how much—or little—information is sent over the Internet and with documents. You can also access the Document Inspector from there, which you used in the preceding section.

To access the privacy options, follow these steps:

1. Choose Office, Word Options.

2. Click Trust Center.

3. Click the Trust Center Settings button. The Trust Center dialog box opens.

4. Click Privacy Options.

5. Mark or clear the check boxes for the desired options. See Figure 28.15.

6. Click OK on both open dialog boxes.

TIP

> Some of the options have i symbols next to them, indicating more information is available. Point to one of those symbols to get help on that option.

Figure 28.15
Set privacy options.

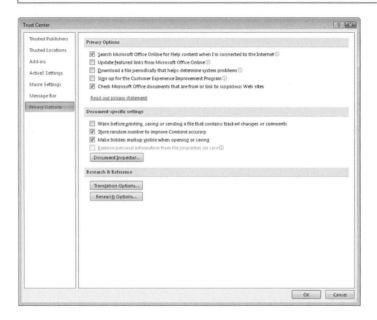

ADDING A DIGITAL SIGNATURE

Digital signatures are certifications of a document's authenticity. When sending legal documents online, or other important documents, a digital signature can provide some measure of certainty that a document has actually come from its purported source and that it has not been altered since it was sent.

You can get a certificate from a certificate authority, a third-party service online, but this is not free. (It costs around $370 for secure2trust, for example.)

To find out about third-party certificates, choose Office, Finish, Add a Digital Signature, and then click Signature Services from the Office Marketplace.

You can also self-certify a document, but this is not all that secure and carries no legal authority. If you want to practice using digital signatures, though, a self-certificate will work.

To add a digital signature to a document, follow these steps:

1. Choose Office, Prepare, Add a Digital Signature.

28

2. If you do not have a third-party signature file installed, a dialog box appears warning of that, and offering to either take you to the Office Marketplace or continue. Click OK to continue.

3. In the Sign dialog box, type a description of why you are signing the document. For example, if you are approving it, you might write that.

4. If your correct name does not appear in the Signing As box, click Change and change the name.

5. Click Sign. A message appears that your signature has been added.

6. Click OK.

A Signatures task pane appears with the signature name listed in it, and the document is no longer editable. (By definition, a signed document is uneditable.)

If you need to edit the document, you must remove the signature(s). To remove a signature:

1. Point to the signature in the Signatures task pane, so a down arrow appears next to it.

2. Click the arrow to open the menu and choose Remove Signature.

3. Click Yes.

4. Click OK.

TROUBLESHOOTING

I DON'T HAVE PERMISSION TO ENCRYPT OR DECRYPT A FOLDER

In Windows Vista, you must be logged in with administrative privileges to encrypt or decrypt folders. Even if you are, you might still see a warning box saying you do not have permission. Click Continue in that box and Windows will let you finish the operation. If that doesn't work, log out from the Start menu and log back in as a user with greater privileges.

ONLINE COLLABORATION WITH OFFICE LIVE AND SHAREPOINT TEAM SERVICES

In this chapter

29

COLLABORATING WITH ONLINE COLLABORATION TOOLS

In Chapter 27, "Collaborating with Others," you learned about Word's built-in collaboration tools, which allow you to mark up and comment on documents by passing documents back and forth between your teammates. This is called *offline collaboration*. In addition to the offline methods of collaboration discussed in Chapter 27, Word supports several kinds of online collaboration. Online collaboration allows you to store your documents in a controlled environment and work together with your teammates to update, comment, and correct your documents.

The process for collaborating with online documents is much the same, no matter which tools you use to share the documents. The two main mechanisms for sharing documents within the Office system are detailed in the following list:

- **Office Live workspaces**—Office Live workspaces are designed for smaller businesses to share information across an easy-to-set-up online system hosted by Microsoft. These workspaces include email, a website, several business tools, and document libraries. In this chapter, we will be looking at using document libraries to store and share your documents.

- **SharePoint Team Services workspaces**—SharePoint sites are designed for larger businesses. They are the model out of which Office Live grew. Your company hosts SharePoint sites on a machine you control. Just like the Office Live workspaces, these workspaces include a website, business tools, and document libraries. SharePoint sites can have a variety of styles of document libraries, targeted to the types of documents contained within them. In this chapter, we look at the document libraries that are used with Word documents.

This chapter looks at sharing your Word documents using basic document libraries in both types of sites.

USING OFFICE LIVE DOCUMENT WORKSPACES

Office Live sites are new with Office 2007. These sites allow the smaller business to access the features of a SharePoint document workspace, without needing to host the workspaces and libraries on a machine they control. The advantages to using Office Live are that smaller businesses can encourage collaboration between employees, present a unified front end to customers, and not need to maintain an IT department to keep the system up and running.

The Office Live workspaces are easy to set up, relatively inexpensive, and easy to use. You can access most Office Live features from Word 2000 or later. Some features may require you to have Word 2003 or Word 2007.

WHAT IS A DOCUMENT WORKSPACE?

A document workspace is an area where employees can store documents that others need to see and work on. In addition, document access can be controlled and tracked.

Controlling document access entails setting up permissions to the workspace's library so that users can only change documents in spaces they have been given permission to access. By controlling access, you limit unexpected document changes and deletions by those who shouldn't have access in the first place. At the same time, since you can set up read-only access to any area as well, those who need to see the documents can see them without changing them.

Tracking access to the documents helps ensure that everyone using a document is on the same page. Utilizing check-in and checkout procedures, you can ensure that when a document is changed, everyone who is using the document is notified when changes are made.

Another advantage to a document workspace is that all finalized documents are stored in a common, consistent place, which in turn minimizes downtime. If one employee's computer goes down, documents stored on that computer can't be accessed by anyone until that computer is fixed. On the other hand, if documents are stored in a common document workspace, access doesn't depend on a particular machine being down. Since the workspace is on a controlled computer, it is less likely to go down and cause problems. Since the data on the controlled computer is backed up more regularly, if it does go down, no data will be lost. Microsoft will restore your data when the system comes back up.

CREATING A DOCUMENT WORKSPACE

When you sign up for Office Live, you are automatically signed up for a set amount of online storage. Some of that storage is automatically set aside for a document workspace.

When you sign up for Office Live, you will be asked to complete information needed to create a site for your company, which includes information needed to register a domain name. Once you have successfully registered the domain name, it takes up to three days to gain access to the site from other machines. The person creating the site will be notified by email when the site registration is complete and access is available.

Once you have access to your site, you will need to invite people to join the site. After you log into Office Live and access your site, do the following to invite others to your site:

1. From the Shared Sites tab (page), click the Users and Accounts link. The list of current site users shows.
2. Click the Add User button to start the Add User – Webpage dialog box (see Figure 29.1).
3. Provide an email address and display name. Click Next.
4. Choose the roles for each area of the site for this user. Click Next.

   There are three possible roles:

   - **Administrator**—Full access to add and change site sections, users, and content.
   - **Editor**—Full access to add and change site sections and content, but not to add or change users.
   - **Reader**—Access only to read what is on the site, not to edit or change the site in any way.

Figure 29.1
Assigned roles for a new user with access to the Office Live site.

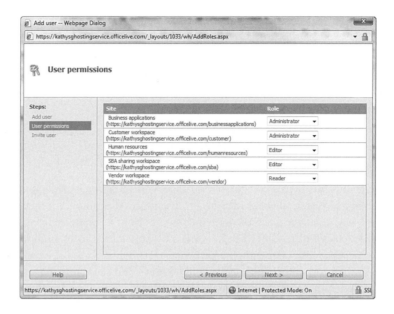

5. Create an invitation email to be sent to the new user. Click Next to send the email and then Finish to return to the user list.

> **NOTE**
>
> Make sure the email address is correct before you send the email. It will go as soon as you click Next and you can't retrieve it if the message is sent to the wrong address.

ACCESSING THE DOCUMENT WORKSPACE FROM THE BROWSER

Once someone has been invited to the site, they will be given access to the document work-space in the site. To access the document library, you need to navigate to it first:

1. Click the Business Applications tab from your Office Live site.

> **NOTE**
>
> The Office Live site is the site you get to by logging into Office Live; it is not the website you create when you register your domain.

2. Click the Dashboard link, then select Documents from the Company drop-down list.

This list shows any documents that have been stored in your library. If this is the first time you have accessed the library, there will be no documents there. From here, you can use the following command:

- **New Document**—This opens a new instance of Word with a blank document. You can use this to create documents directly on your Office Live site. When you are done creating the document, you can use File, Save to save the document directly to the work-space. You will be prompted to log in and provide a document name. Once you have logged in, you will see a list of available documents (see Figure 29.2).

Figure 29.2
Document list with
document created
from New Document.

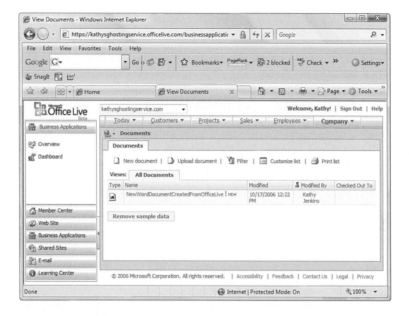

- **Upload Document**—Allows you to upload one or more files from your computer to the site using the browser. To use it, browse to the file(s) and click Save & Close.

- **Filter**—Turns on the filters for each column. Filters allow you to show only the documents within your library that meet your defined criteria. When the filters are showing for each column, this link changes to Hide Filter Choices.

- **Customize List**—Allows you to change what you see and how you see it for each document. Changes you make can be applied either to the default view or to a new view you create.

- **Print List**—Creates a printable list of your documents for you to send to the printer of your choice.

CHECKING OUT DOCUMENTS TO MAKE CHANGES

In Figure 29.2, you can see the columns in your default document view. The first four columns tell you information about your documents that you are used to seeing—the file type icon, the name of the document, when it was modified, and who modified it. The last column, Checked Out To, may be new to you.

When you add documents to the library, you put them under document control. Once they are under document control, you can't make changes to them on the fly. You need to check them out of the library in order to make changes.

To check out a document, click the drop-down arrow next to the document name. From the list, select Check Out. Your name will appear in the Checked Out column. You haven't made changes to the document, you have just told the document library that you are going to make changes and that no one else should be allowed to make changes until you check the document back in. To make changes, you need to download the document to your computer and edit it with Word.

WHEN WOULDN'T I CHECK OUT A DOCUMENT?

If you need to open a document for reference, not to work on it, you are best off to just open it, not to check it out. When you do this, Word keeps track of the fact that this is a document from the workspace and alerts you to any changes that have been made to the document, when someone has checked the document out to make changes, and when that person has checked the document back in.

By only checking out the document when you need to make changes, you ensure that it is available to those who need to make changes at any time. In addition, being diligent about not checking things out when you don't need to make changes makes it easier to get the new versions when they are available.

DOCUMENT ALERTS

When you know that you will be accessing a document with some regularity, you may want to set up an alert for that document. Alerts are set by selecting Alert Me on the right-click menu for the document name (see Figure 29.3).

Figure 29.3
Document alert options.

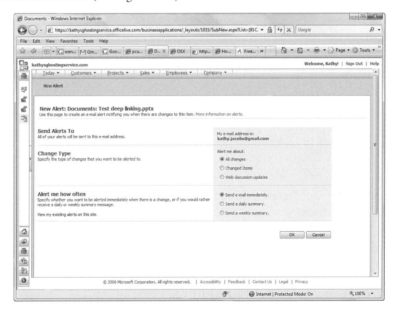

You have two decisions to make when you create an alert: What document changes do you want to be alerted of, and how frequently do you want to be told of changes?

For alert types, you have three options. You can choose just to be told about changes to the item itself, just to be told about changes to discussions about the item, or to be told about all changes.

For the frequency, you can choose emails for each change, or a daily or weekly summary of the changes.

Once you have decided which changes and how often you want to hear about them, click OK. From that point on, you will be notified by email when your alert is triggered.

EDITING FILES FROM A DOCUMENT WORKSPACE

You can edit a document in your library by either sending it to Word from your browser session or by navigating to the document from Word. The two processes are similar and have the same result; the difference is in how you get to the document to edit it.

SENDING A DOCUMENT TO WORD FROM THE DOCUMENT WORKSPACE

If you are already looking at your document workspace in your browser, you can use that interface to send the documents to your hard drive and work with the documents from Word. To do this, follow these steps:

1. From your document workspace on Office Live, click the document name.

2. You may be asked if you want to open or save the document. Opening the document saves it to your hard drive and opens the new copy in Word. Saving it just saves it to your hard drive.

> **N O T E**
>
> You might also get a security warning. You can trust the document, so go ahead and allow it to be opened.

3. Click Open. When prompted whether you want to save the document, click Save. A Save As window will appear.

4. Navigate to where you want to save the document, then click Save to save it with the same name.

5. (Optional) If you are prompted again to open the document, do so. Whether you see this prompt will depend on your browser settings.

The document is now opened in Word, and you can edit and change it in any manner you need to.

OPENING A DOCUMENT IN WORD FROM THE DOCUMENT WORKSPACE

On the other hand, if you have Word open, you will find it easier to access the library from Word and have Word do the work of grabbing and saving the document. To do this, follow these steps:

1. In your browser, select the path for your Office Live document workspace. Copy the beginning of the path to the Clipboard. You only want the part up to the word *business-applications*, like so:

   https://kathysghostingservice.officelive.com/businessapplications

2. From Word, open the Office menu and click Open.

29

3. Paste into the File Name box.

4. Complete the password when you are prompted. The document will open in Word, and you can edit it.

NOTE

> If instead of seeing a list of documents, you see a list of libraries. Navigate to the library, and then select the document.

SAVING FILES TO A DOCUMENT WORKSPACE

If you are saving a new document to a document library, you use the File, Publish, Document Management Server command. This brings up what looks like a normal Save As dialog box. However, because you are saving to a document workspace, you will need to add the document workspace URL to the beginning of the document name before clicking Save.

Once you have saved the document to the workspace, two new elements appear on your menu: Server and Workflows. Because workflows are not implemented in Office Live, information on them can be found later in this chapter in the section, "Working with the Workflow Tasks for Your Documents."

The options under Server allow you to work with the document information on the server. You can check out your document to make changes, you can view a version history for the document, you can view any workflow information that might exist for the document, and you can view the document management information for the document.

Checking in and checking out your document from Word changes the status of the document on the site. If you have previously checked the document out, you will see Check In instead of Check Out on the menu list.

When you check in a document, you will be prompted to provide a short piece of text that documents what changes were made to the document while you had it checked out. Being diligent about completing this information will help you keep track of how and when changes were made to a document during its life.

Use the View Version History option to see what notes have been made when this document has been previously checked into the document library. If you are careful to always provide versioning information when you check in a document, you will find that this is a good way to track what has been done.

Selecting Document Management Information brings up the task pane shown in Figure 29.4.

Figure 29.4
Default view of the Document Management task pane.

There are six tabs to this task pane:

- **Status**—Shows any changes or updates to the current document. If you are working with a document that you don't have checked out, this tab shows you who has the document checked out. If you have the document checked out, as shown in Figure 29.4, you can do a "one-button check-in" by clicking the Check In link to check the document back in.

- **Members**—Lists the status of all members with access to this document library.

- **Tasks**—Lists tasks to be done yet for this document. Since tasks and workflows are not supported in Office Live, this tab will be blank.

- **Documents** and **Links**—Related information for the document being edited. These features are not implemented in Office Live.

- **Information**—Shows who created the document, when it was last updated, and who did the updating.

When you are working with a document from a workspace, you can use the Get Updates button to quickly get the most recent version of the document from the library.

When you don't have the current document checked out for editing, you will see a warning note below the ribbon, as shown in Figure 29.5.

Figure 29.5
Server document warning.

29

This warning reminds you that you don't have the ability to save changes to this document under its current name. If you need to make changes to the document, you must click the Edit button to create a local copy. This doesn't check the document out to you; it only creates a local copy that you can edit for your own purposes.

NOTE

Making changes to a document you don't have checked out isn't something you should do very often. When you make changes to a document that you don't have checked out, you run the risk of "forking" the document. Forking is when you make changes at the same time someone else does. You run the risk of overwriting their changes with your changes. How? Simple. They check their changes in. You check the document out and check your version in. Since you didn't make your changes in their version, their changes are lost.

At the bottom of the Document Management task pane is a link to the task pane's options. These options help you control how you work with the server (see Figure 29.6). The first part controls when you see the Document Management task pane. The remainder helps you customize when you check for and get updates to documents in the library.

Figure 29.6
Document Management service options.

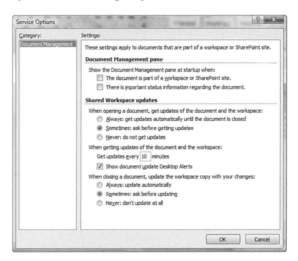

NOTE

Changes made to this task pane affect documents associated with both Office Live libraries and SharePoint libraries.

TASK PANE OPTIONS

These two check boxes allow you to customize when you want the task pane to appear automatically. You can set the task pane to show any time an open document comes from a library, any time important status information changes happen to the document, or any time either is true.

At first glance, you might think that the second option would be automatic if the first is selected. However, since you can close a task pane at any time, the second option is there. It allows Word to open the task pane if you don't have it open, but have chosen to see update notifications.

WORKSPACE UPDATE OPTIONS

The default settings are to not open the task pane automatically. You might select the other options if other users frequently change the document you are working on or referencing.

You have three decisions to make: whether to get the updates automatically, when to get updates, and when to update the workspace.

Figure 29.6 shows the default settings:

- Ask before getting any updates when a workspace document is opened.
- Check for document updates every 10 minutes and show any alerts that come from the server about this document.
- Ask before updating the server copy when changes are made to a document.

These settings are a good, middle-of-the-road solution. If you are referencing a document that is being changed frequently, you will want to check for updates more frequently. On the other hand, if you are referencing a stable document, you may want to check for updates only on open or close.

DELETING FILES IN A DOCUMENT WORKSPACE

Deleting documents from the Office Live site can only be done while logged into the Office Live site. You must have editor access to the library. Once you have this access, you can delete a document by selecting Delete from the drop-down list for the document name in the library view. (This menu is also accessible by right-clicking the document name.) When you delete a document, you will be prompted to verify that you want to delete the document prior to its deletion. Once a document has been deleted from the library, it can't be undeleted without re-uploading it.

When a document is deleted from the library, those who have an alert set for the document will be notified. Versions of the document that have been downloaded to an individual's computer but not checked out will not be deleted; only the copy on the server will be deleted.

CAUTION

> You can delete a document without having it checked out.

WORKING WITH SHAREPOINT TEAM SERVICES

Whereas an Office Live site is aimed at a smaller company, SharePoint Team Services allow larger companies to maintain their document controls, communications, and team services on a system they control. SharePoint servers are generally located in enterprise environments. These companies have a dedicated IT staff responsible for maintaining, backing up, and controlling access to the server containing the company information.

Unlike Office Live, SharePoint access is created and maintained by someone within your company. You may have been granted access to an existing library by the IT staff, or they may have granted you access to create the library yourself. However, the IT department manages the information stored in the site, not you.

SharePoint document libraries do everything that Office Live document libraries do, plus more. For example, documents in SharePoint document libraries can have tasks and workflows attached to them, where those in the Office Live libraries cannot.

NOTE

> The remainder of this chapter is based on a SharePoint site created with basic Team Site template and the default settings.

CREATING A SHAREPOINT DOCUMENT LIBRARY

Creating a document library on a SharePoint site is done from the main page of your team site. Toward the upper-right of that page is a Site Actions button. The drop-down menu for this button allows you to create your libraries and other site pieces, edit the current page, and manage the settings for the site. You are going to create a new library.

1. Using the information provided to you by your IT department, navigate to your team site.
2. From the Site Actions list, select Create.
3. Click Document Library. This should be the first entry in the first column.
4. Name and describe the library with descriptive text using the first two fields (see Figure 29.7).

Figure 29.7
Create a new document library.

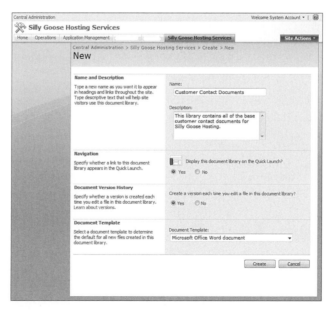

5. Decide whether to display this library in the quick launch list on the left side of site pages.

6. Turn on versioning for the library. Versioning allows you to keep each set of changes along with the history of the documents in the library. This allows you to refer back to the actual changes made at any given check in. While this doesn't replace the need for good check-in comments, it does make it a little easier to recover when the comments aren't as good.

7. Select a default document type for documents in the library. Other documents can be stored in the library, but choosing Word documents allows you to define that the majority of documents for this library will be Word documents created with Word 2007.

8. Click Create to create the workspace.

Once the workspace is created, it will be shown to you. It is empty at the moment, ready for you to add documents to it. The view shown is the default view. You can create other views that are targeted to your document content.

The default view allows you to create new documents and folders for them to reside in, upload documents one at a time or in bulk, work with the documents in bulk, or work with the views of the documents. You can also set alerts for the documents in the library using this view.

CREATING AND SAVING DOCUMENTS FOR A SHAREPOINT TEAM SITE

The first step in using your document library is to populate it with documents. You can add documents to the library by pulling them from Word while in SharePoint or by pushing them to SharePoint while in Word.

ADDING DOCUMENTS FROM SHAREPOINT

When you first create a document library, it is likely that you will need to populate it with documents that already exist on your computer. While you could do this from Word by opening each and saving it to the library, it is easier to upload the documents using SharePoint. Here are the steps to follow:

1. While viewing your document library, select Upload Document from the Upload menu.

2. Use Browse to navigate to the document you wish to add to the library.

3. (Optional) Leave the box Add as a New Version to Existing Files checked. If this is the first version of the document added to the library, versioning won't matter much. However, if this is any upload after the first, checking this box ensures you keep the previous version of the document instead of overwriting it.

4. Provide versioning information for this document (see Figure 29.8). Versioning information includes what was changed and why.

5. Click OK to upload the document to the library.

Figure 29.8
Upload individual documents to the library.

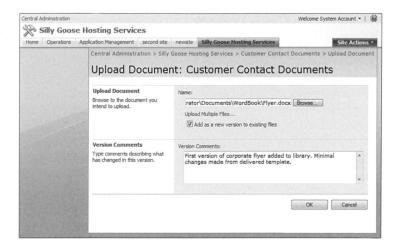

What about uploading multiple documents at the same time? The Upload Multiple Documents interface allows you to choose documents from your hard drive using a Windows Explorer–like interface. If you use this feature, be aware that setting the new version indicator when uploading multiple documents will set it the same for all the documents. This doesn't mean that all documents will be set to the same version, but that if you want a new version created for any of the documents, you will get it for all of the documents.

> **NOTE**
>
> Upload Multiple Documents only allows you to upload multiple documents from a single directory. If you select documents from a variety of directories, only the ones in the last directory selected will upload.

ADDING DOCUMENTS FROM WORD

After you have started using your SharePoint document library, you will need to add documents to it as you create them. When you have a document ready for storage in the library, you will publish it from Word.

Before you publish your documents to the library, you will need the URL for the library. You may have been provided this information by the IT department, but if you haven't, you can get it by navigating to your library using a browser and copying the part of the URL that you need directly from the browser.

When you are looking at a document library URL, it contains more information than you need to provide to Word. The full URL contains the information for SharePoint that tells it how you want to view the documents. Word doesn't need to know how to view the documents; it only needs to know where to put them. If you are looking at the default view of your library, the URL in your browser will end with "/Forms/AllItems.aspx". This is the part Word doesn't need. Copy everything up before that slash, and you will have the URL that Word needs.

Once your document is ready to share, do the following to publish it:

1. Use File, Publish, Document Management Server to save your document. In the Save As dialog box, paste in the path to your network over the existing folder name. Leave the name of document as it is and paste your library URL into the Location box.

2. Click Save. Word will create a copy of your document in the library and connect the two copies.

3. To see that the document is in the library, return to the browser window and refresh the view. Your document should now appear in the list (see Figure 29.9).

Figure 29.9
Document library
default view.

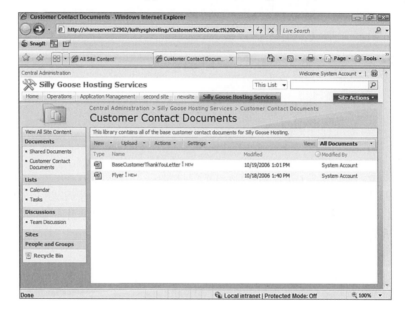

What if you need to create a new document library while you are working on a document in Word? Use the File, Publish, Create Document Workspace command and follow these steps:

1. Use File, Publish, Create Document Workspace to bring up the Document Management task pane.

2. Paste or type the path to the site in the Location box. This is the part of the URL up to the name of the site itself.

3. Leave the name of document as it is and paste your library URL into the Location box.

4. Click Save.

5. (Optional) When prompted, save the document locally if you haven't already.

6. Switch to the browser to view the new library. To find it, you will need to view all site content and then scroll down to sites and workspaces. Your new library will have a rather generic name.

7. Click the name of the new library, and you will be taken to the home page for this site. Notice that the view of the document library here is more like a web page view than a library list view (see Figure 29.10).

Figure 29.10
Document library in
web page view.

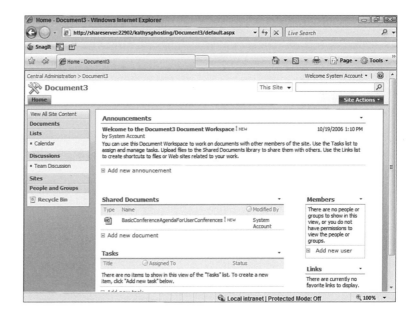

No matter whether you create a new workspace for your document or add your document to an existing workspace, you will work with it in the same manner. In fact, you will work with it in much the same manner as you did with documents saved to the Office Live document library. Because Office Live is based on SharePoint, the process of checking in and checking out documents is the same.

For the remainder of this chapter, the focus will be on the things that are available in SharePoint that aren't in Office Live.

WORKING WITH DOCUMENTS AND LINKS

When you have a document open that is connected to a SharePoint library, the Document Management task pane gives you the ability to see and work with other documents and links that have been shared in that library.

DOCUMENTS TAB

The Documents tab shows you which documents are available from the current library. To access any other documents in the library, click the name of the document. The document will open in Word. It will not be checked out; it will only be opened.

NOTE

If you open a document in this manner, it is opened in a somewhat unusual state. In order to save it locally, you need to use Save As to create a local copy.

29

In addition to opening other documents from this library, the Documents tab also lets you do some basic work with each of the documents. For documents other than the current document, you can also delete the document or set up alerts for the document. For the current document, you can do the following:

- Set up alerts for the document.
- Check the status of the document.
- Create a document workspace just for this document.

Each of these three elements is done using the processes described earlier in this chapter.

At the bottom of the Documents tab of the task pane, you will see three new links. These links are only available if you are using SharePoint for your document library:

- **Add a New Document**—Allows you to browse your computer for documents to add to the library. Any document added using this link must already exist on your local hard drive.
- **Add New Folder**—Allows you to name and create an empty folder on the document server. This folder will be created under the current library. Once it has been created, you can save documents to it from either Word or SharePoint. You can't move existing documents from one level to the other.
- **Alert Me About Documents**—Opens the Alert interface in SharePoint in a browser window.

Links Tab

The Links tab lets you work with website links in the same manner as the Documents tab lets you work with documents. These links are not stored in the document library; instead they are stored in the Links area of the SharePoint site.

Just as you can add alerts for documents in your document library using the Documents tab, you can add alerts for links using this tab.

Working with the Workflow Tasks for Your Documents

Unlike Office Live sites, SharePoint sites allow you to set up specific tasks your team needs to complete. You can create tasks either from Word or from SharePoint.

Tasks are things that need to be done to or with a document or other items related to the site. Examples of tasks are create, edit, get approval, review, print, and distribute documents.

Adding Tasks from Word

Adding tasks from Word is done via the Tasks tab of the Document Management task pane. Here, you can use the following commands:

- **Add New Task**—Allows you create a new task using the Task dialog box (see Figure 29.11).

29

Figure 29.11
Completed task
definition dialog box.

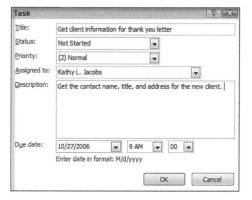

- **Alert Me About Tasks**—Opens the Alert interface in SharePoint in a browser window.
- **View Workflow Tasks**—In addition to creating generic tasks for your team, your SharePoint administrator may have defined specific tasks that need to be done for each document. These tasks are called Workflow tasks. They allow you to define the order of tasks and signatures needed to add documents to the library.

For some SharePoint systems, tasks have been predefined for your team and for the documents in the libraries. In these cases, when you add a document to the library the first time, the related tasks are created for you.

Once tasks have been added to your workspace, they will be listed in the task pane (see Figure 29.12). You can then edit them, create alerts for them, or delete them just as you can a document or a link. In addition, you can check the box to the left of the task to mark it completed. This will change the completion status to Completed with the current date and time as the completion time and date.

Figure 29.12
Task list for this docu-
ment library.

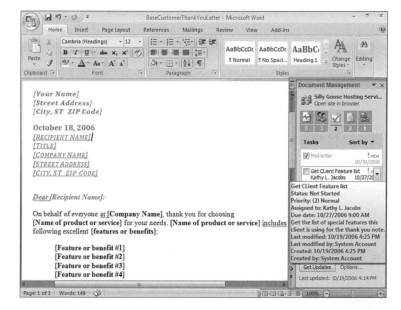

As you can see, the Mail letter task has been completed. It remains in the list of tasks but is dimmed out. When you have a task selected, the details about that task will show in a callout box underneath the task.

ADDING TASKS FROM SHAREPOINT

Adding tasks from SharePoint is done by going to your task list for the site. There should be a link to the task list either on the left side of your web page or from the home page of your site.

SEARCHING AND CATEGORIZING DOCUMENTS USING SHAREPOINT PORTAL SERVER

Part of the power of your SharePoint site is the added search functionality you get with the documents in your library. At the top of every page in your SharePoint site, you have a search box. From that box, you can search for the things you are used to looking for, such as a document name or text within the document, but you can also search for documents whose properties contain specific text or meet criteria you define. The search box works just as it does on any other site or computer.

CREATE A NEW VIEW

In addition, you can create specific views to show only those documents that meet the criteria you want to see. This is called *filtering* the documents. The easiest way to see this is to create a new view with more information about each document, and then filter the list based on the information in the view.

1. While viewing your document library, select Create View from the View menu.
2. Click Standard View as the type of view to create.
3. Create a public view named Documents with check-in information.
4. Check the boxes to add the following columns:
   - Check In Comment
   - Checked Out To
   - Created
   - Created By
   - Version
5. Scroll to the bottom of the page and click OK to create the view (see Figure 29.13).

When the view is created, it will be shown to you so that you can apply any filters you wish.

Figure 29.13
Definition of a new view.

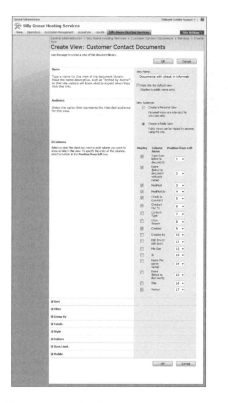

FILTER WHICH DOCUMENTS YOU SEE

You can filter your view based on any of the fields shown in the view with the exception of the Name field. To filter on any of the fields, click the drop-down arrow to the right of the field name and select the filter criteria from the list.

Some common sorts you may want to play around with include:

- Documents created on a certain date (created in this case meaning added to the library).
- Documents at versions higher than one.
- Documents of a certain type.

CREATE NEW PROPERTIES FOR THE DOCUMENTS

Once you have a document library created in SharePoint, you can add new properties to the library documents by adding columns using the Settings, Create Column menu option. You can add any of 11 different predefined types of columns to your documents. When you add a property to a document library, the property is not automatically populated for existing documents. If you specify it, the property can be automatically completed for new documents added to the library after the property was created.

> **NOTE**
>
> Once you have added a property, you will need to add it to a view in order to see the values for the property.

29

To easily fill in the new property for your existing documents, use the Edit in Datasheet action to view the documents. This will change from a document list type of view to one that looks like an Excel worksheet. While you won't be able to change the properties of any folders using this screen, you can change the values for individual documents. In addition, if you select the same property for a number of documents, you can change their properties at the same time using either autofill or fill down. Autofill gives each document the default value. Fill down fills the property for each selected document with the value for the first selected document.

NOTE

> When you are trying to change the values of a property you added, you may get a read-only error on the property. If you do, scan left and find out if you are trying to change the properties for a file or a folder. While you can change property values for a file, you can't for a folder.

Once you have added new properties for your documents, you can search or filter on these documents as well as on the document name or content. If you do filter your document view to show only those documents that meet your desired criteria, remember that you have done so. The only indications that you have set a filter will be that not all the documents show and that the filter you have applied will be checked in the drop-down list next to the property name.

Getting Alerted When Documents Change

Since you won't be the only one using the documents in the library, you are likely to find that you need to know when a document is changed, added to, or deleted from the library. To do this, you need to set up alerts for your library. You can set up the alerts from either Word or from SharePoint.

You can set up alerts from a document in Word or from SharePoint itself. In either case, you will end up at the same screen. To get there from Word, use the Document Management task pane for any document from the library. You don't have to have the document checked out to create an alert, you just have to have one open. Here are the steps to follow:

1. While viewing a document from your document library, bring up the Document Management task pane.
2. From the Documents tab, click the Alert Me About Documents link at the bottom of the task pane. You will see the New Alert page appear in your browser window.

If you want to set up alerts from SharePoint, view the document library in any view. Then, use the Alert me option from the Actions menu.

From this page, you define the following:

- **Who you want the alerts sent to**—By default, it will be you (the current user), but you can add other users by typing their name in the list or by selecting them from the contact list.

- **What type of alerts you want to see**—By default, you will be notified of all changes to the documents in the library, but you can restrict the alerts to any one of the following: addition of new items, modification of existing items, deletion of items, or updates to discussions about the items.

- **Whether you want the alerts filtered**—By default, you will get alerts anytime anyone makes changes. You can filter these down to when someone else makes a change to any document, to any document you created, or to any document that you were the last one to modify.

- **When you want to get the alerts**—By default, the alerts are sent when the changes are made. If you are working in an environment where you would prefer to see changes in a single email, you can set that email to come daily or weekly (see Figure 29.14). If you choose daily, you can then set the time of day you want to get the email. If you choose weekly, you can set the day of the week and the time of that day that you want to get the email.

Figure 29.14
Creating a new alert.

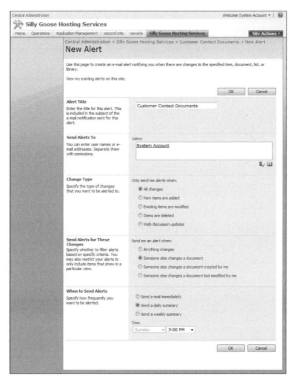

In addition to setting up alerts on documents, you can also set up alerts for both links and tasks. These alerts are done in the same way that the document alerts are done; only the starting point is different.

DOCUMENT DISCUSSIONS

When you work with the documents in your document library, you have the option to also create discussions about the documents. Discussions allow you to exchange information about a document with others accessing your site. They are conversations you hold with other users. You can use them to document decisions, to discuss changes, and a myriad of other things.

To start or add to a discussion, you must be viewing your SharePoint site in your browser. In the left column of the site, you will see a link to the discussion area of your site. You may also have a link to the discussions from the front page of your site.

To create a new discussion, use the Discussion option on the New menu. You will be prompted for a subject (which is required) and a message body (see Figure 29.15). Discussion text is much like the text you put into an email. You can format it as you desire, or you can leave the information plain text.

You also have the option to attach a file to your discussion. This is useful if you have a file on your local hard drive that is not ready to be added to the library, but about which you need informal comments or information.

Figure 29.15
Creating a new discussion item.

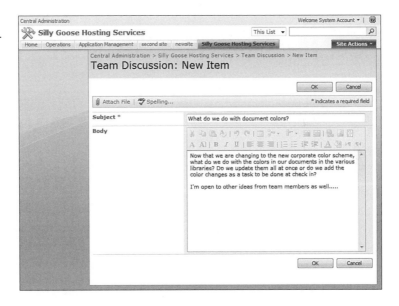

Once you have completed the subject and body, clicking OK will return you to the discussion list with your new discussion now showing. People can view your discussion item by clicking its name. They will be able to reply to the discussion by either clicking the Reply button when viewing the discussion or via Reply off the Name drop-down menu list.

By default, when you reply to a discussion, the original thread is attached. If you are going to leave it attached, be sure to crop outdated information from the reply. You will want to leave enough information so that others can understand what is discussed, without leaving so much that the replies become cluttered.

TROUBLESHOOTING

SOME OF MY DOCUMENTS DON'T HAVE VERSION COMMENTS, EVEN THOUGH I HAVE COMMENTS REQUIRED

When you use Upload Multiple Documents to add documents to a SharePoint library, you are not prompted for versioning comments. You can add the comments later, but you are not able to add them at upload.

WHEN I WORK WITH SHAREPOINT OR OFFICE LIVE, I AM PROMPTED FOR ACTIVE X CONTROLS

Most of the work of SharePoint and Office Live are actually done on the server. In order to get the results to your computer, the server must run some code on your machine. This code is contained within a series of Active X controls. You will need to accept these controls the first time you try to use the functionality they run.

CHAPTER 30

WORKING WITH BLOGS AND EMAIL

BLOGGING WITH WORD

If you've read a newspaper or news magazine lately, you probably already know what a blog is. A *blog* is an online journal of sorts, either business or personal, which can be read on the Web or via an RSS (Really Simple Syndication) feed to a feed reader program or email program. Outlook 2007 supports RSS feeds, for example, so you can read blog posts as if they were email messages from there. Many people are touting blogs as the next big thing in communications; they are easy and inexpensive to set up, and they enable almost anyone to broadcast their opinions to the world.

30

> **NOTE**
> What differentiates a blog from a web page? They do have some things in common, and blogs can be read from web interfaces. A blog is a series of dated postings and comments, with the newest listed first, whereas a web page can take any format. And a blog is typically hosted on a site that provides all the formatting and layout, so all the blogger has to do is type the text and click Send. In Chapter 31, "Developing Web Content," you will learn about the somewhat more complex task of creating complete web pages via Word.

Most blogging services provide web interfaces from which you can create new posts for your blog, and some email programs also enable you to generate new blog postings. So why use Word? It is primarily a matter of convenience. Word's spell-checking, research, and other proofing tools can come in handy when you are trying to make a good impression to the world, and Word's formatting features are more robust than those of most blogging services.

Perhaps you're wondering about compatibility. But remember, Word 2007 is XML-based, and XML is a cousin to HTML, the language of the Web. So, compatibility is not as much an issue as you might think. Word 2007 provides a blog template that you use to start a new document, and the template ensures that the entries you create conform to the strict HTML standards required for most blogging services. You don't have to worry about the coding or the server—you just focus on the writing!

UNDERSTANDING THE WORD BLOGGING INTERFACE

When you are composing a blog entry, the tabs on the ribbon change to show only the tools that are applicable to blog entries. The usual tabs are distilled down to just two: Blog Post and Insert.

On the Blog Post tab, shown in Figure 30.1, are the usual tools for editing and formatting text that you normally find on the Home tab. There are also a few proofreading tools that are normally on the References tab, and a Blog group that's unique to blogging, used for uploading your post to the blog service.

On the Insert tab, shown in Figure 30.2, are buttons for inserting a variety of types of graphical content, including charts, SmartArt, and equations. These lose their special Word 2007 functionality when you upload, though; they become regular static graphics.

Figure 30.1
The Blog Post tab for a blog posting.

Figure 30.2
The Insert tab for a blog posting.

REGISTERING YOUR BLOG SERVER IN WORD

Before you can post to your blog from within Word, you must register your blogging service with your copy of Word 2007 to set up the username and password required for posting.

The first time you start a new blog posting, you will be prompted to register your service, as in Figure 30.3. You can click Register Now to begin the process, or click Register Later to begin creating your blog entry without registering. You can save the blog entry to a Word file, but you cannot post it until you register at least one blogging service.

Figure 30.3
If you have no blog services set up yet, you are prompted to register one.

CAUTION

Registering a blog in Word 2007 is not the same as creating a new blog account. This chapter assumes you already have a blog account and just need to set up Word to work with it.

NOTE

After you have one service registered, you can register more services by clicking Manage Accounts on the Blog Post tab and then clicking New to set up a new service.

When you click Register Now, the New Blog Account dialog box opens. Select your blogging service and then follow the prompts to set it up.

The following sections provide a few notes for some of the most popular services. If you do not have a blog yet, click the I Don't Have a Blog Yet hyperlink in the New Blog Account dialog box. This displays a Web page explaining how to get a blog account at one of the supported services.

WINDOWS LIVE SPACES

Before you can post to your Windows Live Spaces account from Word, you must configure your Windows Live Spaces account for email posting, so you will need to get a secret word. A *secret word* is like a password, but different from the main password with which you log in to your page. From your Windows Live Spaces page, click Options, and click the Email Publishing tab. Then follow the prompts to set up your secret word.

Next, follow these steps to register the account in Word:

1. From the New Blog Account dialog box, open the Choose Your Blog Provider list and choose Windows Live Spaces. Then click Next.

2. In the New Windows Live Spaces Account dialog box, shown in Figure 30.4, set up your space name and secret word.

Figure 30.4
Set up your Windows Live Spaces blog in Word 2007.

3. (Optional) If you want to post pictures to your blog, click Picture Options, and then choose the picture provider. The default is None – Don't Upload Pictures, but you can also choose your own picture server. If you choose to use your own server, prompts appear for Upload URL and Source URL. Fill them in, and then click OK.

4. Click OK. A confirmation box appears after a few seconds.

5. Click OK again.

BLOGGER

For Blogger, all you need is your user account and password. Then just fill in the blanks. Here are the steps:

1. From the New Blog Account dialog box, open the Choose Your Blog Provider list and choose Blogger. Then click Next.

2. In the New Blogger Account dialog box, shown in Figure 30.5, enter the username and password.

3. (Optional) If you want to post pictures to your blog, click Picture Options, and then choose the picture provider. The default is None – Don't Upload Pictures, but you can also choose your own picture server. If you choose to use your own server, prompts appear for Upload URL and Source URL. Fill them in, and then click OK.

4. Click OK. A confirmation box appears after a few seconds.

5. Click OK again.

Figure 30.5
Set up your Blogger blog in Word 2007.

SHAREPOINT 2007

If your blog is hosted on a SharePoint 2007 server, you will need to enter two URLs in the setup: one for your blog and one for your pictures (if you want to include pictures). The blog URL is your main blog page address minus the filename. So, for example, if your blog is http://spserver/tomsblog/default.aspx, your blog URL for setup would be http://spserver/tomsblog.

Armed with that information, choose SharePoint as the Blog Provider in the New Blog Account dialog box, click Next, and then just fill in the blanks (see Figure 30.6).

Figure 30.6
Set up your SharePoint 2007 blog in Word 2007.

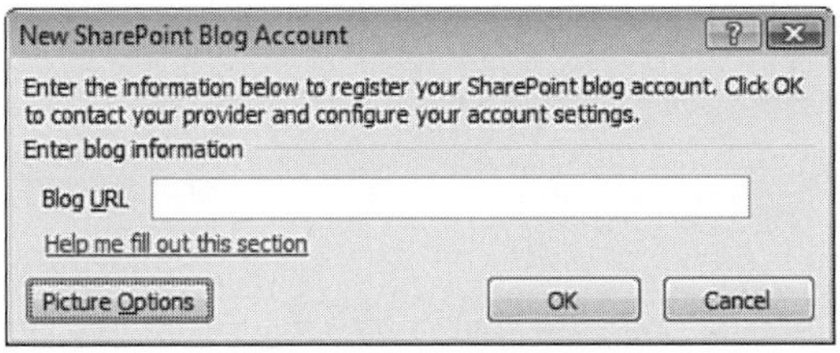

For picture hosting, click Picture Options and then choose None, your own picture server, or SharePoint blog. If you choose the latter, the pictures will be hosted on the SharePoint blog site if that capability is available for your server.

COMMUNITY SERVER

A community server is a server provided for a group of people to keep in contact with one another and share information, such as in a workgroup within an organization. If your blog is hosted on one, you'll need your username and password, plus your blog host URL. The Blog Post URL is your server name (minus your unique user info) with metablog.ashx added on the end. For example, if your blog is http://blogs.msdn.com/johndoe, your post URL would be http://blogs.msdn.com/metablog.ashx. (How does it know who you are? That's where the username and password come in.)

TYPEPAD

For a Typepad account, you enter your user name and password, and everything else is configured automatically for you. If you want pictures, click Picture Options and choose My Blog Provider. (Typepad allows images, and it accepts them automatically from Word with this option enabled.)

WORDPRESS

For a WordPress account, you enter your user name and password, just like with a Typepad account, but you also must fill in your Blog Post URL. Fill it in between the http:// and the /xmlrpc.php. Don't delete any of the / signs, but do delete the angle brackets and the placeholder text (see Figure 30.7).

Figure 30.7
Set up a WordPress blog by entering a blog post URL and your user name and password.

OTHER PROVIDERS

Word does not support all blog providers, but it does support most that use either the Atom or the Metaweblog protocol. For most of these, you must enter a username and password, as with a community server, and you use a generic URL for posting. When Word contacts the posting URL, it identifies you by sending your login information.

CREATING A NEW BLOG POST

After you've configured your blog service, creating a new post is almost as easy as creating an ordinary document.

To publish the current document as a blog, choose Office, Publish, Blog. Otherwise, to start a new document as a blog post, choose Office, New and then select from the New Document dialog box and click Create.

A new blank page opens with a placeholder for the title. The default blog name appears next to *Account*. If you have more than one blog service set up, you can switch among them by clicking the blog name and then selecting from its drop-down list (see Figure 30.8).

Figure 30.8
This blank blog post is ready for some text.

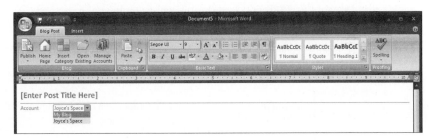

When you are ready to publish, click the Publish button on the Blog Post tab. Or, if you click the down arrow beneath the Publish button, you can then choose either of the following:

- **Publish**—To post your text immediately.
- **Publish as Draft**—To save your text to your blog server but not post it until you log in to that server via your regular web interface and approve it.

If a username and password prompt appears, enter the info requested and click OK. After the post has been successfully sent, a yellow bar appears across the top of the document showing that it has been posted, and showing the date and time.

ADDING PICTURES AND OTHER GRAPHICS TO A BLOG

You can include almost any type of picture in a blog entry that you can include in a Word document. When you save, however, every type of graphic is converted into a static image, regardless of its original type (chart, SmartArt, and so on).

Most blogging services cannot accept graphics directly from Word. Instead, you must specify a picture hosting service at which to store the pictures that will accompany your blog text. When you set up your blogging service, as you learned earlier in this chapter, you specify whether pictures are allowed, and if so, what picture service you want to use.

The most straightforward option is simply to use your own server to host your pictures—but you can also use an image provider service. To set up the picture hosting if you have not done so already, follow these steps:

1. Click Manage Accounts.
2. Click the desired blog and click Change.
3. In the dialog box for that service, click Picture Options.
4. Open the Picture Provider drop-down list and choose:
   - My Blog Provider—This option is available only if your blogging service permits pictures.
   - My Own Server—Use this option if you have server space of your own you want to use.
   - Some other service—Depending on your blogging service, there may be other options listed.

> **NOTE**
>
> If you don't have an image provider, click I Don't Have an Image Provider, and follow the steps on the Web page that appears to get one.

5. Fill in the URLs for the Upload URL and the Source URL.
6. Click OK.
7. Click OK.

CATEGORIZING BLOG ENTRIES

Many blogging systems enable you to categorize your entries. To add a category to an entry in Word, follow these steps:

1. Click Insert Category on the Blog Post tab. A Category line appears in the document.
2. Open the drop-down list for the Category line that was inserted and choose a category. This list comes from your blogging service.
3. Continue composing your entry as you normally would.

> **TIP**
>
> If you are editing an entry you started some time ago, you might want to refresh the categories to make sure the desired category is still available. To do this, click Category on the Blog Post tab and then click Refresh Categories.

MANAGING THE BLOG LIST

To add or delete blogs from Word, use the Blog Accounts dialog box. Display it by clicking the Manage Accounts button on the Blog Post tab (see Figure 30.9).

Figure 30.9
Manage your list of blogs here.

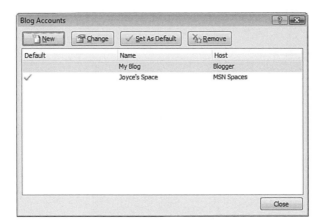

From here, you can:

- Click New to set up an additional site.
- Click a blog and click Change to change its settings. For example, you might need to go back and configure a URL for pictures if you did not do that initially.
- Click a blog and click Set as Default to mark the blog that should be used when you start a new blog entry.
- Click a blog and click Remove to stop using it in Word. (It does not do anything to your blogging service account or previous postings.)

SENDING EMAIL FROM WORD

If you use Outlook 2007 as your email program, you have probably noticed that its email-composition window has many of the same tools as Word 2007. Even users who don't have Word installed still have that basic set of Word-like capabilities in Outlook. This is a major departure from earlier versions of Office, in which Outlook could be set up to compose email either within Word or without it. Users with Word installed were expected to use Word; users without Word could fall back on Outlook's own composition window.

A side effect of this change is that Word no longer needs to function as a full-fledged email editor. Because Outlook handles its own composition now, it is no longer critical that users be able to compose email in Word. To reflect this change in priorities, Microsoft has removed most of the references to email composition from Word. It is no longer the power-house feature it used to be.

There are still situations, however, where you might want to compose and send email from Word. For example, perhaps you have a document with some pictures in it, and you want to send the document as a graphical email rather than attaching the picture files to a text email or attaching the Word document itself to an email.

The capability of sending a document as an attachment is still readily available in Word 2007. Here's how to access it:

1. Choose Office, Send, E-Mail. A new message opens in Outlook (or your default email program) with the current document attached.

2. Compose the email and click Send.

TROUBLESHOOTING

I CAN'T GET MY BLOG SET UP IN WORD

Not all blog services work with Word's blogging tool. Contact your blogging provider and find out if any help is available for configuring Word.

HOW CAN I MODIFY A POST I'VE ALREADY MADE TO MY BLOG?

On the Blog Post tab, click Open Existing. A list of posts you've made to your default blog appear. From there, select a post and click OK to open it for editing. Then republish it to save your changes.

I GET A MESSAGE THAT MY EMAIL CAN'T BE SENT

Many email systems have limitations on the size of messages they will process. Certain aspects of Word's operation can easily lead to files that are too large to be sent, and will be "bounced back" by your system's email server. To reduce file size, compress the pictures in the document.

→ To learn about picture compression, **see** "Compressing Pictures," **p. 410**.

CHAPTER 31

DEVELOPING WEB CONTENT

In this chapter

WEB PAGE DEVELOPMENT: WORD'S STRENGTHS AND WEAKNESSES

Word 2007 is a viable choice for the nonprofessional web designer who may be already familiar with Word and reluctant to learn a new application. Using Word, even people with no HTML programming language experience can create basic web pages with ease. However, Word lacks most of the high-end web design features of an application such as Microsoft FrontPage or Macromedia Dreamweaver, so someone who does web design for a living would likely not choose Word for that work.

Word makes web design easy by shielding the user from the raw coding, instead allowing the user to work in a familiar WYSIWYG (what you see is what you get) environment in which formatting can be applied with toolbar buttons and menu commands. Then when the document is saved, Word converts all that formatting to HTML coding that web browser applications can understand.

WEB TECHNOLOGIES SUPPORTED IN WORD

Word 2007 is similar to Word 2003 in its web design features. Word supports all the basic HTML codes that you would expect for formatting, plus several other technologies, scripting languages, and supplemental HTML code. Some of the features that were prominent in Word 2003's web design have been deprecated, meaning that they are still available to add to the Quick Access toolbar, but are not a part of the regular interface anymore. (Creating web-based frames is like that, for example.)

Word supports all these types of web content:

- **HTML**—Hypertext Markup Language is the *lingua franca* (medium of exchange) of the World Wide Web. Almost every web page is built with this language. HTML, a simple formatting and organizational language, is ideal for the display of text, simple graphics, and hyperlinks. It doesn't do anything fancy like search a database or display pop-up dialog boxes. The appeal of HTML lies in its ease of use and universal acceptance.

- **CSS**—Cascading style sheets are used to define the layout of a document precisely. Style sheets are more powerful than the styles found in Word because style sheets can also specify page layout. A style sheet can be a separate document, or it can be embedded in each HTML page. Because browsers have different capabilities in how they interpret these styles, they interpret what they can and ignore the rest; that is, they cascade down in their interpretation and display what they are able to.

- **XML**—eXtensible Markup Language is more robust and extensible (hence its name) than HTML. You can define new tags and their uses at any time and in any way by referencing them in an associated text document. The strength of XML is its capability to use these new tags to identify specific information. This technology vastly improves the users' abilities to find specific-subject web pages and opens up the Internet to even more data mining. Chapter 32, "Preparing XML Content," deals with XML in detail.

- **VML**—Vector Markup Language uses text to define geometric shapes, colors, line widths, and so forth. These words are then interpreted and displayed as graphical images in browsers that understand VML (Microsoft Internet Explorer 5 and higher). No matter what size circle you want to display, you use the same amount of text to define it. VML reduces the bandwidth required to send a graphical image from a web server to a browser. This improves the browser page load time, improves image quality, and helps reduce Internet or intranet network congestion.

- **JavaScript and VBScript**—Both of these script-style programming languages are in common everyday use on the Web right now. These languages handle simple programming tasks without having to load a separate application. JavaScript is supported by the vast majority of browsers; VBScript is supported by only Microsoft Internet Explorer browsers. These languages enable you to program interactivity into web pages.

You don't need to know how to use each or any of these technologies to build or edit web pages in Word 2007. However, if you are an experienced web page designer, it's nice to have these tools supported in Word so that you need not turn to some other editing program simply because you want to use one of them.

WEB PAGE FILE FORMATS

When Word saves in Web Page format, it creates a file that contains all the HTML coding needed for display in a web browser, *plus* all the Word coding needed for full-featured editing and display in Word. Therefore, you can switch freely between Word and a web browser and the file will look the same in both places. Microsoft calls this interchangeability of file formats *round-tripping*, and it works with Word 2000 and higher.

NOTE

> Round-tripping applies only to web pages created in Word. If any other web page is edited in Word, it may or may not look like it originally did after it has been saved in Word.

This beefed-up web page format that Word uses can display most Word features on a web page. These supplementary technologies increase the capability of HTML so that web pages can display Word-specific formatting and features that pure HTML does not support.

However, round-tripping comes at a cost: The file sizes of the HTML files generated by Word are larger than those for regular HTML because they contain all that extra code for Word support. Therefore, Word 2007 also offers an alternative mode called Web Page, Filtered that saves in pure HTML without round-trip support for Word. A filtered HTML file is nearly identical to one you would create in a pure HTML editing application such as Dreamweaver.

Word also offers support for MHTML (MIME HTML), a file format that creates a single file out of a web page that might ordinarily require support files. For example, suppose you have a Word document that contains a graphic. If you save it in either regular Web Page format or filtered format, Word will create an HTML file (.htm) and a support folder containing a separate picture file. This can be awkward to distribute to others via email. With the Single File Web Page (.mht) format, the web page file contains both the text and the graphics with no need for support folders or files. The only drawback is that some older browsers are not able to display MHTML files.

NOTE

MIME is an encoding scheme for sending graphics and formatted text via email. It's been around for a long time, and most email programs support it.

WORD FEATURES LOST WHEN SAVING IN WEB FORMAT

Some weaknesses in Word's capability to translate all its features to web pages still exist, even with the latest improvements. Here are a few Word features that do not transfer when you save in any of the Web Page formats:

- Passwords
- Word file headers/footers
- Newspaper-style column flow (though the text is unaffected)

The reason for the lack of support for passwords is that typically on a website, the web server controls passwords, rather than individual documents (or pages) doing so.

The lack of support for columns and headers/footers occurs because web browsers simply have no functionality (that is, there is no HTML equivalent) to display these formatted items. When the web page is reloaded into Word 2007, however, columns and headers and footers are restored. Because these "translation" problems are due to shortcomings in HTML or some other web technology, Microsoft simply cannot create a version of Word that is 100% compatible with web pages.

TIP

If you plan to edit your web pages in an HTML editor application, save them as filtered web pages. Many HTML applications have trouble dealing with Word's extra formatting codes that it places in a standard web page document.

WHY YOU MIGHT *NOT* WANT TO USE WORD

When you have a choice between an application designed for a certain purpose and one designed for a more generic one, you will usually find that the specific program does its task better and with less effort. That's true with most of the higher-end full-featured web design applications.

If you are designing a commercial website that will have a lot of pages and some complex linking requirements, you will find the job much easier in an application such as Expression or Dreamweaver. These programs have all kinds of great shortcuts and wizards for creating, formatting, and debugging HTML code and active web content. Although Word will serve as a vessel for many kinds of web objects, such as JavaScript and VBScript, it doesn't help you generate those items in an automated manner.

CREATING AND SAVING A WEB PAGE IN WORD

In Word 2007, creating a web page is much the same as creating a Word document. You do not need to open up a special environment or think differently about the contents of your page.

To begin building from a blank web page, start a new document and then switch to Web Layout view (from the View tab or the view buttons in the bottom-right corner of the screen).

NOTE

> In Word 2002, there were a Web Page Wizard and a group of web page templates you could choose from the New dialog box; however, these were cut from later versions.

Then what do you do? Just start creating your document. This is the beauty of Word: A web page is mostly the same thing as a regular document in terms of basic typing, formatting, and layout. We'll get into some specifics that are exceptions later in the chapter.

31

PREVIEWING A WEB PAGE

As you are building your web page, you can work in Web Layout view as your main editing mode and see the page very nearly as it will be when displayed on a web page.

If that's not enough and you need absolute realism, you can use Web Page Preview to examine the page (read-only) in an actual web browser.

Web Page Preview is not available as a command on any of the default tabs in Word 2007, but you can add it to the Quick Access toolbar:

1. Choose Office, Word Options. The Word Options dialog box opens.
2. Click Customize.
3. Open the Choose Commands From list and select Commands Not in the Ribbon.
4. Click Web Page Preview and click Add to place it on the Quick Access toolbar.
5. Click OK.

Once the button is on your Quick Access toolbar, you can click it anytime to open the current Word document in your default browser. You do not have to save it as a web page before doing this.

CAUTION

> Remember that just because your web page looks good in one browser doesn't mean that it will look good in all browsers. Unless you know that everyone will be accessing your web page with the same browser and version, it is a good idea to test your web pages with the latest versions of Microsoft, Firefox, and Netscape browsers as well as earlier versions, if possible. Note that if some things do not show up in one browser (the scrolling marquee, for instance, is not supported by Netscape browsers), you may need to remove those elements or build browser-specific pages.

SAVING A WEB PAGE

To save a web page, save normally, but set the file type to one of the web formats:

- Use Single File Web Page (.mht) when you are planning to send the web page via email or distribute it as a document that you want people to be able to easily download and work with. Do not use this format if you think your users may be using very old web browser software.

- Use the standard Web Page format (.htm) when you are planning to round-trip the page between Word and a web browser, and if you don't mind that a separate folder for graphics and support files is required for page viewing. Don't use this format if you are planning to email the page to others, or if compatibility with other HTML editing software such as Dreamweaver is important.

- Use the Web Page, Filtered format (.htm) when you need the resulting file to be plain HTML with no special Word tags in it. For example, use it when you are going to integrate the page into a larger website created with Dreamweaver or FrontPage (although FrontPage does do a decent job of accepting Word web content, because it's also by Microsoft). Don't use this format if you plan to edit the page in Word in the future.

You can choose any of the formats from the Save as Type drop-down list in the Save As dialog box (Office, Save As).

To save a Word document as a web page, follow these steps:

1. Choose Office, Save As. The Save As dialog box opens.
2. Open the Save as Type drop-down list and select the desired format.
3. Click the Change Title button. (This button becomes available after you have selected a web format.)
4. In the Set Page Title dialog box (shown in Figure 31.1), type the desired title for the page and click OK.
5. If needed, change the location. You can save directly to a web server, or save to a local hard disk and then upload to a web server later.
6. Click Save.

This procedure doesn't provide much in the way of flexibility, but there are many ways of setting specific options when you save. The following sections address these options.

Figure 31.1
Save a file as a web page by selecting a web-based file format.

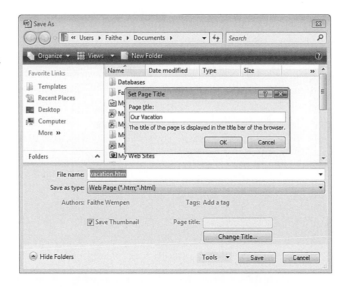

OPTIONS FOR WEB PAGE SAVING

Web options enable you to change the way Word saves web pages. These are more subtle options, not the big ones like filtered/unfiltered or single page/multipage. Most people won't find it necessary to change them, but you should know about them in case a situation ever arises in which they are useful.

There are two ways to open the Web Options dialog box:

- From the Save As dialog box, click Tools and select Web Options.
- Choose Office, Word Options, click Advanced, scroll down to the General section, and click Web Options.

The following sections look at each of the tabs in this dialog box individually.

SAVING FOR COMPATIBILITY WITH SPECIFIC BROWSERS

Under the Browsers tab for Web Options, you can set your target browser (see Figure 31.2). The target browser is based on version number and runs from Internet Explorer 3 and Netscape Navigator 3 up through Internet Explorer 6 and higher. Select your default target browser based on the audience viewing your web pages. To reach the widest audience on the Internet, use the lowest version numbers. You might choose Internet Explorer 6 as your target browser on a company intranet where everyone has standardized on Internet Explorer 6 or higher and you need these capabilities to support the content in your web pages.

Figure 31.2
Set browser-specific Save options here, balancing compatibility with feature richness.

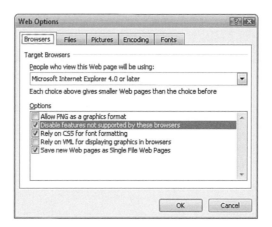

Each target browser setting enables or disables a set of supported features, including these:

- **Allow PNG as a Graphics Format**—This new format is not yet widely supported on the Internet but has advantages over GIF and JPEG files. See the following section for details.

- **Disable Features Not Supported by These Browsers**—For instance, no VML would be used in web pages designed for Internet Explorer 4 because version 4 browsers do not understand VML. If you clear this box, every web page feature built into Word 2007 is used without regard for whether any browser version can support it.

- **Rely on CSS for Font Formatting**—Only version 3 browsers cannot understand CSS. I recommend leaving this option on for the greatest flexibility in changing web page formatting.

- **Rely on VML for Displaying Graphics in Browsers**—VML reduces overall web page size, but browsers before version 5 do not understand it. See the following section for more on VML.

- **Save New Web Pages as Single File Web Pages**—This format has the advantage of storing all the files in a single file. You can, of course, override this option each time you save your web page.

MORE ABOUT PNG AND VML

The most common graphics file formats used in web pages are GIF (Graphics Interchange Format) and JPG (Joint Photographic Experts Group, also JPEG). Word automatically exports all images to these two formats when you save as a filtered web page.

Word also supports the display of two additional graphics file formats in web pages: VML (Vector Markup Language) and PNG (Portable Network Graphics).

VML GRAPHICS

Vector images are defined by equations. As such, they scale perfectly to any size. This is in contrast to bitmap images, in which each pixel has a defined position and color value. Bitmap images scale poorly because the graphics program must interpolate pixels as the image dimensions are changed. Items created in Word using the Drawing tools are drawn as vector objects. When you save as a web page or a single file web page (.mht) in Word, the graphical object is defined by the VML language. The primary advantage of using VML is economy of size, especially if you're using large images. But a significant disadvantage is that vector objects can be displayed only by Internet Explorer version 5.0 or later.

PNG GRAPHICS

PNG is basically an improved version of GIF. The idea behind this format is to solve the primary weaknesses of .gif and .jpg files: GIF can support only 256 colors, and JPG gains its small file size using a lossy compression scheme (that is, as you make your file smaller, you lose photo clarity and resolution as image data is discarded). Also, GIF supports transparency and animation, but JPG does not.

PNG supports 32-bit color, supports transparency, and uses a file compression scheme that does not reduce the file size at the expense of image clarity. The main reason that this format is not widely used now is that older browsers cannot read the PNG format.

SELECTING WEB PAGE FILE OPTIONS

From the Files tab of the Web Options dialog box, shown in Figure 31.3, you can change some filename options and make choices about Word 2007 being your default Web page editor.

Figure 31.3
Setting filenames, locations, and default editor options using Web Options in Word 2007.

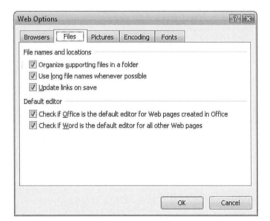

The first check box asks whether you want to organize supporting files in a folder. When Word saves a web page, it sends many (though not all) supporting files—such as graphics—to a separate folder. If you deselect this check box, it places the supporting files in the same folder as the HTML file.

The Use Long File Names Whenever Possible check box is marked by default. The only operating system that does not support long filenames is DOS (with or without Windows 3.x). Unless you have many people using this operating system (which is unlikely), leave this check box checked.

The final check box in the section, Update Links on Save, updates links to supporting graphics and components in your web page. It does not update or check hyperlinks.

The Default Editor portion of the Files tab under Web Options enables you to decide if you want Office to be the default editor for web pages created in Office (checked by default) and Word to be the default editor for all other web pages (checked by default).

CHANGING PAGE SIZE

The Pictures tab, shown in Figure 31.4, defines the target monitor you want for your web page.

Figure 31.4
Choosing your target monitor size and resolution for display of your web pages.

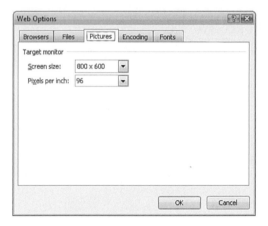

The target monitor refers to the screen resolution you want to optimize your web pages for. This determines the "size" (width) of the page. Screen resolution is expressed in pixels, usually as width × height. The most common screen resolutions in use today on PCs are:

- 800×600
- 1024×768
- 1280×1024

The larger the number, the more pixels (and thus more information) are displayed on the screen. If you choose a target monitor size of 800×600 for building your web pages in Word and view the resultant page at 1280×1024, much of the screen will be empty space with most of the information crowded to the left side of the screen. On the other hand, if you design your pages at 1280×1024 and view the resultant page at 800×600, you will have to keep scrolling to the right to see all the information. The default of 1024×768 is suitable for most uses, unless you're sure that most of your audience uses other screen resolutions.

You can also change the pixels per inch of your target monitor. Again, the default of 96 is suitable for most users. Using higher values greatly increases the size of your graphics and increases your web page load time. Using a value of 120 slightly increases the detail in your web page. A value of 72 gives you smaller web graphics, but your web page will have a slightly coarser appearance.

Changing Language Encoding

The Encoding tab in the Web Options dialog box (see Figure 31.5) enables you to choose the language code page from those installed on your machine. Choose the appropriate code page for the language you are using to build your web page.

Figure 31.5
Choosing the language code page using Web Options.

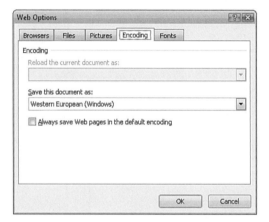

Changing the Default Fonts

You can set the default proportional and fixed-width fonts for your web page from the Fonts tab, as shown in Figure 31.6.

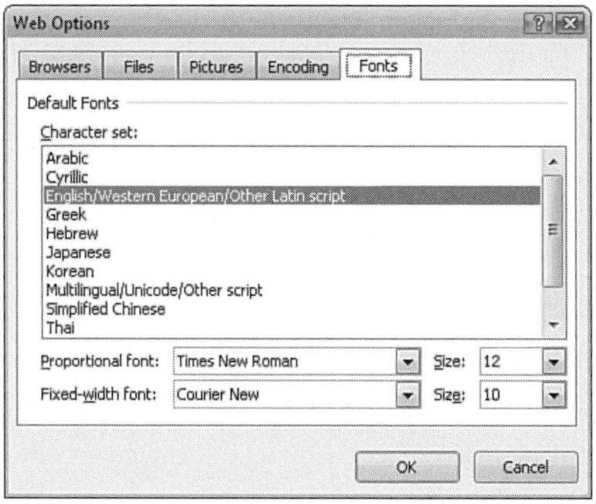

Figure 31.6
Changing the default font for your web page.

Use common fonts for your defaults. If you use fonts in your web pages that aren't installed on your viewers' PCs, their browsers can't render your fonts and will substitute their own default fonts.

WORKING WITH WEB PAGE PROPERTIES

When you build a web page with HTML coding, you place all the text for the web page itself in a section called <BODY>. There's also a <HEADER> section at the top of the file that contains some other information about the page, such as keywords that a search engine can use to index the page, and a page title.

The page title is important because it's what appears in the title bar of the web browser when the page is displayed. When you save a web page in Word, you have the option of changing the default page title by clicking the Change Title button, as you saw in Figure 31.1. But you can also change the page's title at any time, not just during the save operation, as well as specify other header information.

To work with the page's header information, do the following:

1. Choose Office, Prepare, Properties.
2. On the Summary tab, in the Title box, enter a title for the page (see Figure 31.7).
3. (Optional) Enter keywords that describe the document in the Keywords box.
4. Click OK to close the Properties dialog box.

Figure 31.7
The Properties dialog box controls the title and keywords reported to the web browsers that will display the web page.

CREATING HYPERLINKS

A *hyperlink* is the combination of some descriptive text or an image and the location (also called the *address*) of a web page or an object. Any text or image on a web page can hold a hyperlink. Hyperlinks most commonly point to the following:

- Web pages
- Media objects such as sounds, video, or pictures
- Email addresses

The easiest way to create a hyperlink is simply to type it and let Word make it into a live hyperlink automatically. Whenever you type a string of characters that appears to be a web or email address, Word automatically converts it for you. If it doesn't for some reason, or if you want to specify some options (such as ScreenTips), see the following sections.

CREATING A TEXT HYPERLINK

Any text phrase, word, or part of a word can be included in a hyperlink. To build a hyperlink, you need some text in a document and the exact location where you want the hyperlink to lead when it is clicked:

1. From a document in Word, highlight a text phrase. For instance, highlight "Microsoft" in the phrase "For more information, visit the Microsoft home page."

2. On the Insert tab, click Hyperlink. The Insert Hyperlink dialog box opens, as shown in Figure 31.8.

   You can also reach the Insert Hyperlink dialog box by using the keyboard shortcut Ctrl+K, or by right-clicking on the selected text and choosing Hyperlink from the shortcut menu.

Figure 31.8
Filling in the Insert
Hyperlink dialog box.

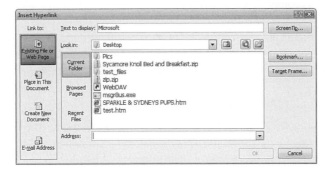

3. In the top box, labeled Text to Display, the text you highlighted is displayed. Change it if desired.

4. In the Address text box, enter the web URL for the site to which you want the text to link.

5. (Optional) To add a ScreenTip to the hyperlink, click the ScreenTip button, type the text, and click OK. A ScreenTip is text that appears in a box when the user points at the hyperlink in a web browser. If you do not specify a ScreenTip, the URL will be used as a ScreenTip.

6. Click OK. When you return to your document, the text you highlighted is now a blue color and underlined, indicating that it is now an active hyperlink.

NOTE

URL stands for *uniform resource locator*. It's the complete address to the web page or other location being referenced. Web page URLs usually begin with http:// and a great many of them (but not all) are then followed by www. Usually a company will place its web pages on a server with the www designation, but some companies with large web presences may have separate servers for support, sales, and so on. For example, to get support from Microsoft, the URL is http://support.microsoft.com.

ADDING A HYPERLINK TO AN IMAGE

A graphic can function as a hyperlink, such that when the user clicks on the image, a web page loads. The process for building a clickable or hot image is similar to that for building a text hyperlink:

1. Select any clip art, picture, drawing object, or WordArt within a web page.
2. Click Hyperlink on the Insert tab to display the Insert Hyperlink dialog box. (Alternatively, use any of the other previously described methods of opening the Hyperlink dialog box.) The Text to Display line will be dimmed because there is no text.
3. Type the address for the link in the Address box at the bottom.
4. (Optional) If you want a ScreenTip, click ScreenTip, type the text, and click OK.
5. Click OK to complete the hyperlink.

The picture will not look any different. If you view the web page using Web Page Preview, the default mouse pointer changes to a hand with a pointing finger when it hovers over the image to indicate that it is now clickable, and the ScreenTip appears.

CREATING AN EMAIL HYPERLINK

Besides referencing other pages, hyperlinks can start the user's email editor and begin a blank email message with the recipient name and subject filled in automatically. This is useful for providing a hyperlink through which someone can email you to comment on your web page.

Follow these steps to create an email hyperlink:

1. Select the text or choose an image for the hyperlink.
2. Click the Hyperlink button on the Insert tab to display the Insert Hyperlink dialog box.
3. In the lower-left corner of the Insert Hyperlink dialog box, click on Email Address.
4. Enter the email address, as shown in Figure 31.9.

   Notice how the phrase "mailto:" is automatically added to the beginning of your email address.

Figure 31.9
Hyperlinking to an email address.

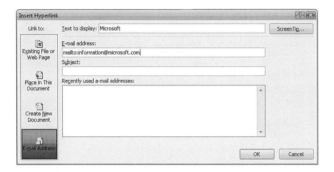

5. (Optional) Type a subject in the Subject box if you want one to be filled in each time.

6. Click OK to complete the link.

When the link is clicked, a blank, pre-addressed email is opened. The email hyperlink is a convenient means for letting visitors to your web page send you feedback or questions.

BUILDING MULTICOLUMN LAYOUTS WITH TABLES

Web pages very commonly use tables to create multicolumn layouts. The "traditional" organization of a web page is to place a navigation bar at the left or top and the main content to the right or below. Figure 31.10 shows an example of the left/right layout, and Figure 31.11 shows an example of the top/bottom one.

Figure 31.10
A web page that uses a table to create a left-right layout with links to other pages at the left.

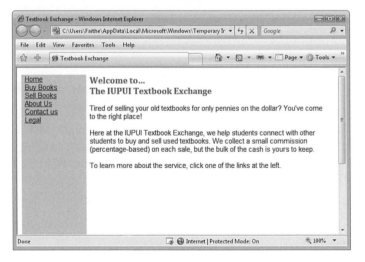

31

Figure 31.11
A web page that uses a table to create a top-bottom layout with links to other pages at the top.

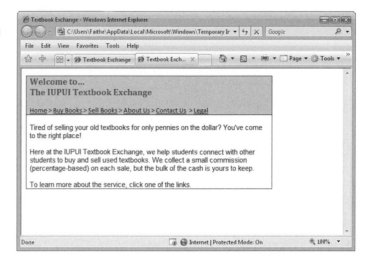

31

We won't go into table creation and usage here because Chapter 12, "Creating and Formatting Tables," covers the topic thoroughly. I will, however, explain in a big-picture way how to create a page like the ones in Figures 31.10 and Figure 31.11:

1. Start a new web page and create a table. Size the table rows and columns as appropriate. To make a row taller, click a cell inside it and press Enter a few times.

   For example, you might want a large column at the right and a thinner one to the left that will hold navigation hyperlinks.

2. If you want any of the cells to have a colored background, right-click the cell and choose Borders and Shading. On the Shading tab, select the desired color or shading, and then in the Apply To section, open the drop-down list and choose Cell (see Figure 31.12). Click OK when done.

Figure 31.12
Apply shading to an individual cell if desired.

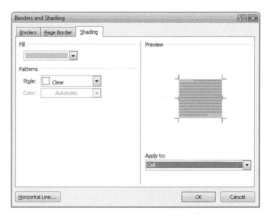

3. (Optional) Remove the borders from around all sides of the table. (With the table selected, open the Borders drop-down list on the Paragraph group of the Home tab and select No Border.)

4. Type or insert hyperlinks in the cell that you have decided will function as your navigation bar. If you want to hyperlink to other pages you have not created yet, decide what you will name them and then go ahead and create the hyperlinks for them.

> **TIP**
>
> In the navigation bar cell, include a hyperlink to the page that you are on. Clicking it will do nothing, so it's okay to have it. The reason: You will probably copy this page and then edit the copy when you create the other pages in the website, and having the link to this page already in place will prevent your having to create it on each page later.

5. Type or insert the text for the main body of the page in the cell that will function in that capacity.

6. Save the page.

7. Save it again under a different name—one of the names you chose for the hyperlinks in the navigation bar.

8. Delete the main body content and enter the content for the new page. The navigation links should be able to remain the same.

9. Repeat until you have created all the pages for your site.

CREATING YOUR OWN WEB PAGE TEMPLATES

If you will be creating a lot of web pages that share some similar elements, such as a navigation bar or a consistently sized table, creating a template can save you from having to re-create those elements each time, thus saving you a lot of time.

A template is a file you use to base new Word documents on. Can you just open a Word document and save it under a new name? Of course. But will you occasionally have a "duh" moment when you forget to save it under a new name and overwrite the original, causing yourself hours of rework? Undoubtedly. The beauty of a template is that it doesn't allow that kind of mistake to ruin your day.

To build a new web page template, do the following:

1. From the New Document dialog box, double-click Blank Document.

2. Switch to Web Layout view.

3. Create the elements the template should contain. You might include:
   - A company logo
   - One or more tables
   - A background texture or color
   - Font colors and styles
   - A basic text outline
   - Standard hyperlinks, such as one to your website home page

4. Save your document as a template by choosing Office, Save As, Word Template.

ATTACHING A CASCADING STYLE SHEET

A cascading style sheet (CSS) is a file that defines formatting for a web page. It works much like a set of styles in Word. For example, suppose you define the Paragraph tag <p> in the style sheet as using 12-point font. If you then apply that style sheet to a web page, all the paragraphs on that page that use that tag will appear in 12-point font.

NOTE

You can create cascading style sheets in any text editor, but the syntax is important, and is different from regular HTML. Consult an HTML reference book to develop your own CSS.

If you would like to use an existing cascading style sheet (CSS) to format your web document, you can attach it by following these steps:

1. Display the Developer tab. If it is not already displayed, choose Office, Word Options, click Personalize, click Show Developer Tab in the Ribbon, and click OK.
2. Click the Document Template button. The Templates and Add-Ins dialog box opens.
3. Click the Linked CSS tab.
4. Click the Add button.
5. Select the cascading style sheet (.css extension) and click Open to attach it.
6. Click OK to close the Templates and Add-Ins dialog box.

TROUBLESHOOTING

HOW CAN I SIMPLIFY THE HTML THAT WORD GENERATES?

A web page saved from Word contains many complicated scripts, XML, and several extra files. You want to simplify this file and eliminate the extra files so that you don't have to keep track of them anymore.

To eliminate the complicated scripting and XML, you need to save your document as a filtered web page:

1. With your document open in Word, choose Office, Save As.
2. From the Save as Type list, choose Web Page, Filtered.
3. Save your document.

To eliminate the extra files, save your document as a single file web page:

1. With your document open in Word, choose Office, Save As from the menu.
2. From the Save as Type list, choose Single File Web Page.
3. Save your document.

There is no single file format available to simplify the HTML and eliminate the extra files associated with web pages.

CHAPTER **32**

USING WORD TO DEVELOP XML CONTENT

In this chapter

AN OVERVIEW OF XML

A lot of attention has been given to the extensive support for XML in Microsoft Office 2007 and Microsoft Word 2007. In this chapter, we discuss what XML is and what Word's support of XML can do for you. It's important to keep in mind that this chapter is meant for users who are comfortable dealing with raw data and XML code as opposed to those simply interested in Word for conventional document creation.

NOTE

> XML features, other than saving documents as XML in the WordML schema format, are available only in Microsoft Office Professional and the standalone version of Microsoft Word.

WHAT XML IS AND WHAT IT DOES

HTML, the language of the World Wide Web, uses a structure of "tags" to identify data elements in a hierarchical manner. For example, you might have a page with content of:

```
<html>
<head><title>My Very Short Page</title></head>
<body>
    <p>This text is <b>bold</b>.</p>
</body>
</html>
```

The text with the angle brackets, such as `<body></body>` or `<p></p>`, makes up the tags. Each set of tags has a specific meaning. For example, the bold tag (`<b></b>`) tells the browser to render text in bold.

XML is similar to HTML in that it also uses tags to specify information; but distinct differences exist between HTML and XML. So what makes XML different from HTML? These are some of the distinguishing features:

- The rules for creating XML documents are well structured and more rigidly enforced than those for creating HTML documents. HTML browsers allow authors to leave out end tags (`<p>` instead of `<p></p>`, for example) or to improperly "nest" tags (`<b><i>very</b> important</i>` instead of `<i><b>very</b> important</i>`, for example). This flexibility makes it easier on web page authors, but much more difficult for browser creators, who must anticipate every variation.

- XML is designed to describe the data and its structure, whereas HTML describes the presentation of the data. For example, you won't find an XML tag to make text bold. Instead, you'll find tags that specify what information *is*, and let the application handle it accordingly. For example, you might find an XML tag such as `<companyName></companyName>`, with an application that knows that the information in this tag should be rendered in bold.

- XML establishes extensible rule sets (a set of XML rules is called a *schema*) that can be used to create a virtually infinite number of markup vocabularies for specialized purposes and environments. For example, LegalXML includes a number of subspecifications that make it possible to describe contracts, legislative documents, and other legal filings, whereas Health Level 7 Healthcare XML Format eases the exchange of clinical data. HTML is based on a specific and fixed set of rules for describing web presentation, which cannot be easily altered or extended.

XML's Advantages Over Previous Approaches

Because XML describes the content of data rather than its presentation, it enables applications to more easily analyze data in order to determine its meaning. As a result, XML is rapidly becoming the data exchange format of choice for an enormous range of business applications.

For example, a typical HTML page listing company contact information might have HTML that looks something like this:

```
<html>
<head><title>My Information</title></head>
<body>
    <h3>Microsoft</h3>
    <p>1 Microsoft Way<br />
        Redmond, WA 98052<br />
        (425) 882-8080</p>
</body>
</html>
```

The information is all there for the human brain, but a computer will have more difficulty interpreting it, because all of the tags provide presentation information (for example, the h3 tag means, among other things, to print this text large, and in bold) as opposed to structure information that indicates exactly what each piece of text means.

XML would represent that information differently, with a structure such as:

```
<?xml version="1.0" encoding="UTF-8" standalone="no"?>
<company>
    <companyName>Microsoft</companyName>
    <address locationType="main">
        <streetaddress>1 Microsoft Way</streetaddress>
        <city>Redmond</city><state>WA</state><zip>98052</zip>
    </address>
    <phone>(425) 882-8080</phone>
</company>
```

Now the tags provide information an application can use. This enables you to not only feed the data to an application that will process it, but also to automatically format the data using stylesheets, as you'll see later in this chapter.

XML consists of a hierarchical structure of "elements" such as

```
<companyName>Microsoft</companyName>
```

and an element's attributes, such as

```
locationType="main"
```

Elements are arranged in a parent-child structure; an element can have as its children other elements (such as the companyName child of company) or text (such as the 1 Microsoft Way child of streetaddress). That's actually a bit of a simplification, but in general, that's what you need to know.

32

Word's XML support gives you the ability to build your own XML data and validate it against a schema, or set of rules, and integrate that XML data into normal documents for users. It also enables you to generate data for use by other XML-based applications, and access data managed or produced by those applications.

Having a structure that describes the data instead of its presentation leaves you free to use the same source document for several different purposes without duplicating the information in various places. You simply attach a different style sheet or use a different transformation to provide new instructions for how to format and display each type of data contained in the document.

In the past several years, many applications have sprung up that use XML data, and many standard XML vocabularies have come into their own. For example, XBRL standardizes the communication of financial reporting data among corporations. VoiceXML provides a standard language for controlling voice applications such as automated voicemail or call center systems. The publishing industry has had the benefit of the DocBook XML vocabulary for years. We could spend an entire chapter just listing out XML vocabularies in common usage.

Finally, the fact that XML is plain text cannot be overlooked as a huge advantage. In the not-too-distant past, developers trying to exchange structured data were forced to contend with proprietary binary file formats that required multiple conversion steps to use the data, complex network and authentication scenarios to allow binary connections, and text files containing character-delimited data (that is, tab-delimited files) that varied from site to site with no good way to indicate structure or relationships.

With the advent of the World Wide Web and HTML, networks are already configured to allow text-based traffic to easily move in and out with ease. In fact, Microsoft Word 2007 itself uses XML to store its own data.

WORDML

Since its inception, Microsoft Word has stored its files in a binary format. This format provides storage and performance advantages, but it also makes the documents impossible to deal with if users are without an application specifically designed to understand them. In Microsoft Word 2007, that all changes.

WHAT IS WORDML?

Microsoft attempted to create a text-based file storage format with Rich Text Format, and to some extent, it was successful. But from the standpoint of someone writing an application to deal with the data, Rich Text Format is very difficult to work with and still requires specialized processing.

With Microsoft Office 2007, Microsoft Word uses its own XML vocabulary as the default method of storing data that defines documents. This language, WordML, includes all the information normally stored in a Word document, but because it is an XML vocabulary, it is possible to directly manipulate the data from outside the word processing application.

WHY SHOULD THIS MATTER TO ME?

While the move to the so called "paperless office" was supposed to result in a decrease in documents, it has in fact led to a virtual explosion of them. Business today involves the generation and processing of many thousands of documents, even by the smallest company or department.

Once these documents are generated, they are generally dead wood. You can read them, you can store them, and in most cases you can even search them, but reusing the data for another purpose—such as automatically posting an HTML version of reports and memos to the company intranet—is next to impossible in today's world.

By storing data in a standard XML format, you gain the ability to not only extract this information, but also to manipulate it. For example, you can easily change sales collateral materials after a product name change, or update all customer-facing documents to reflect a new logo.

And you don't even need to use the application that created the data; any XML-aware application can extract and manipulate this data.

CREATING WORDML

To help familiarize you with WordML and to give you an idea of how easy it is to get at this data, let's create a document in Word and change the data from outside of Word. Follow these steps:

1. Create a new document in Word. The actual content doesn't matter, but for the sake of the example, be sure to include a header by clicking the Insert tab and using the Header button (see Figure 32.1).

Figure 32.1
The original document.

2. Save the file as a standard Word document (*.docx) and close it.

3. A .docx file is actually a collection of XML files collected together as a zip file. Back in the operating system, find the file and change the .docx extension to .zip.

> **TIP**
>
> If you don't see the file extensions, you can turn them on in Microsoft Vista by opening Windows Explorer and choosing Organize, Folder and Search Options, View and unchecking Hide extensions for known file types. Click OK to close the dialog box.

4. Double-click the zip file to open it and see its contents.

5. Click the Extract All Files link.

6. Click Browse… and use the Make New Folder option to create a new folder called **alteredmemo**.

7. Click OK.

8. Click Extract.

9. Navigate to the alteredmemo folder and open the word subfolder.

10. Notice that this folder contains a number of different files, including document.xml and styles.xml. Open the document.xml file by right-clicking it and choosing Open With, Wordpad. You should see a mass of XML tags, but if you look closely, you'll also see your text:

```
<?xml version="1.0" encoding="UTF-8" standalone="yes"?>
<w:document ...>
  <w:body>
    <w:p><w:pPr><w:jc w:val="center"/><w:rPr><w:sz w:val="44"/><w:szCs
w:val="44"/></w:rPr></w:pPr></w:p>
    <w:p><w:pPr><w:jc w:val="center"/><w:rPr><w:sz w:val="44"/><w:szCs
w:val="44"/></w:rPr></w:pPr>
        <w:r w:rsidR="000C75D8" w:rsidRPr="000C75D8"><w:rPr><w:sz
w:val="44"/><w:szCs w:val="44"/>
        </w:rPr><w:t>MEMORANDUM</w:t></w:r></w:p>
    <w:p><w:pPr><w:rPr><w:sz w:val="28"/><w:szCs w:val="28"/></w:rPr>
</w:pPr></w:p>
    <w:p><w:pPr><w:rPr><w:sz w:val="28"/><w:szCs w:val="28"/></w:rPr>
</w:pPr><w:r w:rsidR="000C75D8">
        <w:rPr><w:sz w:val="28"/><w:szCs w:val="28"/></w:rPr>
<w:t>To: All staff</w:t></w:r></w:p>
    <w:p><w:pPr><w:rPr><w:sz w:val="28"/><w:szCs w:val="28"/></w:rPr>
</w:pPr><w:r w:rsidR="000C75D8">
        <w:rPr><w:sz w:val="28"/><w:szCs w:val="28"/></w:rPr>
<w:t>Regarding: Staff behavior</w:t>
        </w:r></w:p>
    <w:p><w:pPr><w:rPr><w:sz w:val="28"/><w:szCs w:val="28"/></w:rPr>
</w:pPr></w:p><w:p><w:pPr><w:rPr>
        <w:sz w:val="28"/><w:szCs w:val="28"/></w:rPr></w:pPr>
<w:r w:rsidR="000C75D8"><w:rPr>
        <w:sz w:val="28"/><w:szCs w:val="28"/></w:rPr>
<w:t>Staff members are advised that they are not to ride their motorcycles in the building.
The mud is getting ground into the carpets, and
housekeeping is threatening to quit.</w:t></w:r></w:p>
    ...
  </w:body></w:document>
```

I've cleaned this up a bit, so you can see that each paragraph you created in Word is part of a <w:p> element, which is how WordML represents a paragraph. The <w:p> element also includes lots of other information, but unless you're going to do hard-core processing, you don't need to worry about that right now.

Make Changes to WordML

Next, we'll make some changes to the actual XML data to see how it affects the final Word document.

1. Open the header1.xml file in Wordpad to see the header information. It should look something like this:

```
<?xml version="1.0" encoding="UTF-8" standalone="yes"?>
<w:hdr ...>
    <w:p><w:pPr><w:pStyle w:val="Header"/><w:jc w:val="center"/><w:rPr>
        <w:sz w:val="52"/><w:szCs w:val="52"/></w:rPr></w:pPr>
        <w:r w:rsidR="00437139" w:rsidRPr="00437139"><w:rPr>
        <w:sz w:val="52"/><w:szCs w:val="52"/></w:rPr>
        <w:t>From the desk of J. Mortimer Boss</w:t></w:r></w:p>
</w:hdr>
```

> **TIP**
>
> If you don't see your text in header1.xml, try header2.xml or header3.xml.

2. Change the text in the header:

```
<?xml version="1.0" encoding="UTF-8" standalone="yes"?>
<w:hdr ...>
    <w:p><w:pPr><w:pStyle w:val="Header"/><w:jc w:val="center"/><w:rPr>
        <w:sz w:val="52"/><w:szCs w:val="52"/></w:rPr></w:pPr>
        <w:r w:rsidR="00437139" w:rsidRPr="00437139"><w:rPr>
        <w:sz w:val="52"/><w:szCs w:val="52"/></w:rPr>
        <w:t>Important Information</w:t></w:r></w:p>
</w:hdr>
```

3. Save the file.

4. Go back to the alteredmemo directory and select all the folders and documents. Right-click one of the selected items and choose Send To, Compressed (zipped) Folder.

5. Call the document **alteredMemo.zip**.

6. Rename the document **alteredMemo.docx**. Click Yes to confirm the name change.

7. Double-click the new document to see the changes (see Figure 32.2).

32

Figure 32.2
The altered document.

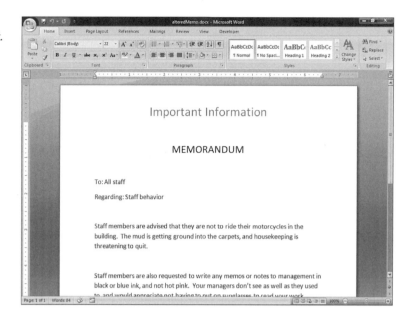

Now let's look at working with your own XML data.

XML SCHEMAS: KEEPING YOUR DATA IN LINE

Microsoft Word includes a fairly robust XML editor, as I discuss later in the chapter, but in order for it to work, it has to understand the structure of the document you're trying to create. In order to make that happen, you will need to use XML schemas.

WHAT ARE XML SCHEMAS?

XML schemas are documents that define the structure of an XML vocabulary. For example, consider this sample document, for which we will be defining rules:

```
<ContactList xmlns="http://tempuri.org/contactML.xsd">
  <Contact>
    <Fullname>
      <prefix>Mr.</prefix>
      <firstname>Nicholas</firstname>
      <middlename>Morgan</middlename>
      <lastname>Chase</lastname>
    </Fullname>
    <Address addressType="business">
      <company>Backstop Media</company>
      <streetaddress>555 Main Street</streetaddress>
      <city>Anywhere</city><state>CA</state><zip>90120</zip>
    </Address>
  </Contact>
  <Contact>
    <Fullname>
      <prefix></prefix>
      <firstname>June</firstname>
```

```
      <middlename></middlename>
      <lastname>Landis</lastname>
   </Fullname>
   <Address addressType="business">
      <company>Winter Spring Summer Fall Tree Service</company>
      <streetaddress>123 Spruce Street</streetaddress>
      <city>Boston</city><state>MA</state><zip>02134</zip>
   </Address>
  </Contact>
</ContactList>
```

Looking at it, we can see that the document starts with a base, or root, element of ContactList, and that the ContactList element can contain one or more Contact elements. We can also tell what sort of content—a FullName element and an Address element—belongs in the Contact element.

An XML schema defines these rules in such a way that an XML processor can understand it. This way, a processor like Word can offer you the option of adding a Fullname or Address element from within a Contact element.

What Does a Schema Look Like?

Microsoft Word supports the use of schemas based on the W3C's XML Schema Recommendation. A schema based on this specification would describe the preceding XML document as follows:

```
<?xml version="1.0" ?>
<xs:schema id="ContactML"
  targetNamespace="http://tempuri.org/contactML.xsd"
  xmlns="http://tempuri.org/contactML.xsd"
  xmlns:xs="http://www.w3.org/2001/XMLSchema"
  attributeFormDefault="qualified" elementFormDefault="qualified">

<xs:element name="ContactList">

    <xs:complexType>
      <xs:sequence>

        <xs:element name="Contact" maxOccurs="unbounded">
         <xs:complexType>
           <xs:sequence>

             <xs:element name="Fullname" minOccurs="1" maxOccurs="1">
                <xs:complexType>
                 <xs:sequence>
                   <xs:element name="prefix" type="xs:string"  />
                   <xs:element name="firstname" type="xs:string"
                                    minOccurs="1"  maxOccurs="1"/>
                   <xs:element name="middlename" type="xs:string" />
                   <xs:element name="lastname" type="xs:string" />
                 </xs:sequence>
                </xs:complexType>
             </xs:element>

             <xs:element name="Address"  minOccurs="0"
                                    maxOccurs="unbounded">
               <xs:complexType>
```

```
              <xs:sequence>
                <xs:element name="company" type="xs:string"  />
                <xs:element name="streetaddress" type="xs:string"
                                    minOccurs="0" maxOccurs="2" />
                <xs:element name="city" type="xs:string"  />
                <xs:element name="state" type="xs:string" />
                <xs:element name="zip" type="xs:string" />
              </xs:sequence>
              <xs:attribute name="addressType" type="xs:string" />
            </xs:complexType>
          </xs:element>

        </xs:sequence>
      </xs:complexType>
    </xs:element>

    </xs:sequence>
  </xs:complexType>
</xs:element>
</xs:schema>
```

A complete discussion of XML schemas is beyond the scope of this chapter, but here are the basics.

TIP

> You can find more information on the W3C's XML Schema language at http://www.w3.org/XML/Schema#dev. You can also find a tutorial on validating XML using schemas at http://www.nicholaschase.com/validation.php.

We have a definition of an element, ContactList. That element contains other elements, which makes it a complexType. It can contain any number of Contact elements. Each of those Contact elements contains a sequence of two elements: Fullname and Address.

A Contact must have a minimum of one Fullname and a maximum of one Fullname element. The schema then goes on to define the elements that make up the Fullname, and specifies that the text each element holds must represent a string.

The process is the same for the Address element, except that it is optional (minOccurs="0"). Also, if it is present, it may appear as many times as you like (maxOccurs="unbounded"). In addition, the address elements may also have an attribute, addressType.

All of these rules apply to XML that is in the target "namespace" of http://tempuri.org/contactML.xsd. A namespace is a way of separating sets of data. For example, we know our sample data belongs to this same namespace because we specified it, as in:

```
<ContactList xmlns="http://tempuri.org/contactML.xsd">
  <Contact>
...
```

XML schemas can be quite powerful, and enable you to specify complex patterns types. But this simple schema will do for our purposes.

CREATING A SCHEMA AS A PLAIN XML DOCUMENT IN WORD 2007

In order to use the XML schema, we need to have it as a plain XML file. You can type it into an application such as Wordpad, of course, but this is a book on Microsoft Word. Follow these steps to create the XML schema as a plain XML file in Word:

1. Type the preceding schema in Word 2007.
2. To save the XML only, open the Office menu and choose Save As.
3. Specify the name of the file as contactML.xsd.
4. In the Save as Type field, choose Microsoft Word 2003 XML document (.XML).
5. Enable the Save XML Data Only check box and click Save.
6. Close the file and open it again using Word 2007 in the XML editor interface, confirming that this is indeed an XML document (see Figure 32.3).

Figure 32.3
The schema, seen as XML by Word 2007.

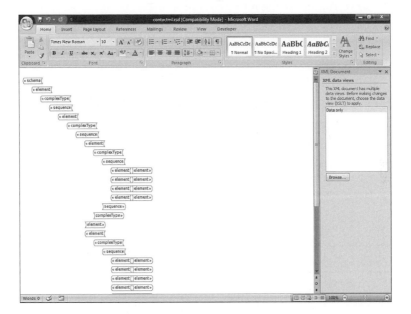

ADDING THE XML SCHEMA TO THE LIBRARY

Up until now, everything you've been doing has been to "use" Word and its functions. Now you're about to plunge into what Word considers a "developer" function. Does this mean that you need to be a programmer in order to perform these tasks? Certainly not.

All you need to continue from here is a willingness to dig a little deeper than you might normally do when using a word processor.

The next thing you're going to look at is the Word 2007 Schema Library. The library is a collection of XML schemas that Word knows about. These schemas are available to add to a document or documents.

In order for Word to be able to use the schema you created in the previous section, you will need to add it to the library. Follow these steps:

1. First add the Developer tab to the Ribbon if it's not already there. To do that, open the Office menu and click the Word Options button at the bottom of the menu.

2. Click the Popular tab in the left pane and check Show Developer tab in the Ribbon. Click OK.

3. Click the Developer tab.

4. Click Schema in the XML group of the Ribbon.

5. Click the Schema Library button.

6. Click Add Schema and navigate to the ContactML.xsd file. Select the file and click Open.

7. Add an alias and click OK. This is the name by which you will refer to the schema later, when you are adding it to a document.

8. Click OK, and then click OK again.

Now you have an available schema, so you can begin to create XML files using Word 2007.

USING WORD 2007 TO CREATE XML FILES

You can always create an XML file by typing raw XML and saving it as XML, as we did in the previous section. But the real power of Word's XML capabilities is your ability to create an XML file using the built-in editor.

CREATE THE NEW FILE

To prepare a new document for editing XML, follow these steps:

1. Create a new blank document in Word 2007.

2. On the Developer tab, click the Schema button.

3. In the dialog box that appears, check the box next to the schema you want.

4. Click the option Validate the Document Against Attached Schemas.

5. Click OK.

> **NOTE**
>
> You can also click the Allow Saving Even Though Document Is Invalid option to save XML files and come back to them later.

6. Click the Structure button in the Developer ribbon to open the Structure pane, if necessary.

7. Click the option Show XML Tags in the Document in the Structure pane.

Notice the Choose an Element to Apply to the Current Section option at the bottom of the Structure pane. This list shows you the elements you can add to the document at the position of the cursor. Check and uncheck the List Only Child Elements of the Current

Element check box to see the difference in your options. Keeping this option checked makes it easier to create valid documents.

For example, with the option checked, you have the option to add only a ContactList element, as you can see in Figure 32.4.

Figure 32.4
Limiting your options to only those that are valid.

This makes sense, because with no content in the document yet, the ContactList is the only element you can "legally" add to the document. If, on the other hand, you uncheck that option, you will see that you have a host of options (see Figure 32.5).

Figure 32.5
All of your options.

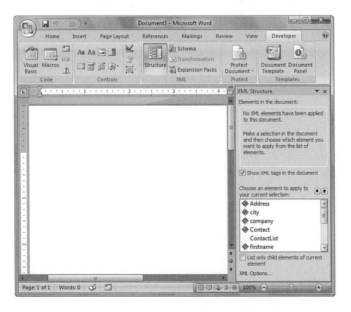

Having access to all of the elements is more convenient if you are creating the document "out of order," but this makes it possible to create a document that is invalid; in other words, it doesn't follow the rules set out in the schema.

XML OPTIONS

Before we go any further, it's important to understand some of the options you have when dealing with XML data. At the bottom of the Structure pane, you will see the XML Options button. Clicking it gives you access to the options listed in the following sections.

XML SAVE OPTIONS

- **Save data only**—All Word 2007 files are saved as XML. You can use this option to tell Word to save only your XML data, not the WordML that makes up a typical file.

- **Apply custom transform**—XML data can be easily transformed using XSLT stylesheets, as you will see in the next section. This option enables you to specify one of these style sheets.

SCHEMA VALIDATION OPTIONS

- **Validate document against attached schemas**—This is the typical situation, in which you specify a structure using a schema and Word 2007 enforces that structure.

- **Hide schema violations in this document**—Just as you can turn off notification of spelling and grammar errors, you can use this option to turn off notification of validation errors, which occur when the document doesn't follow all the rules in an XML schema.

- **Ignore mixed content**—This option enables you to tell Word to ignore text that appears between elements, in places in which it doesn't expect to find text.

- **Allow saving as XML even if not valid**—This option enables you to save the XML file and come back to it later. For example, you might need to save a document before you have all of the information required by a document's schema. Unless you choose this option, Word will not allow you to save an XML file that violates its attached schema.

XML VIEW OPTIONS

- **Hide namespace alias in XML Structure pane**—Namespaces can be vital to proper XML usage, but they can also make the document difficult to read. This option suppresses the display of namespace aliases to eliminate that problem.

- **Show advanced XML error messages**—This option makes it much easier to figure out what is wrong with your XML document when Word encounters an error in XML code. It displays much more informative error messages; I recommend you leave this turned on. (You'll see an example of this in the later section, "Validation Errors.")

- **Show placeholder text for all empty elements**—This option tells Word to add text (specifically, the element name) to any elements that have no content. This enables you to see elements that might otherwise be rendered invisible in some circumstances, such as when the XML is displayed without its tags.

ADDING ELEMENTS TO EXISTING DATA

Before we look at adding XML content to a page, let's look at turning existing text into XML data. To see this process in action, execute the following steps:

1. In the XML structure view, add the text to turn into XML, such as contact information.

2. Select the text you want to turn into an element. In this case, that would be the entire contact.

3. At the bottom of Structure pane, click the ContactList element (see Figure 32.6).

Figure 32.6
Create the
ContactList
element.

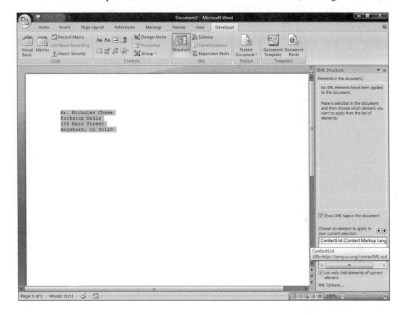

4. Click the Apply to Entire Document button to specify that this is the root element for the document.

5. With the contact information still selected, click Contact in the XML Structure pane.

6. Select the contact name and click Fullname in the XML Structure pane.

7. Follow step 6 to assign elements to the rest of the document. For example, select the contact's first name and click the firstname element, and so on. The result is shown in Figure 32.7.

TIP

> To remove an element designation from existing content, right-click the content in the XML Structure pane and choose Remove <tagname> tag.

Figure 32.7
The first complete
contact.

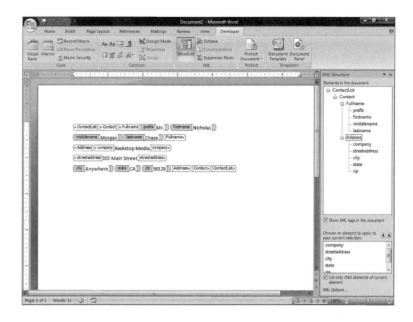

ADDING DATA TO EXISTING ELEMENTS

Adding data to existing elements follows virtually the same process:

1. Click within the ContactList element, either before or after the existing Contact element, and press the Enter key to add linefeeds to make room for more data.

2. Click Contact to add a new Contact element.

3. While the cursor is in the Contact element, notice that the Structure pane changes to offer Fullname and Address elements (see Figure 32.8). When you click Fullname to add a new Fullname element, the Structure pane changes to offer the child elements of that element.

4. Disable the List Only Child Elements of Current Element check box and notice that the XML Structure pane now shows additional elements (see Figure 32.9). Elements that are not allowed in the document in the cursor's location have a small "not allowed" icon next to them.

5. Enable the List Only Child Elements of Current Element check box.

6. If you look between the open and close tags (they look like purple bubbles) for the Fullname element, you will see the firstname element. Click between the start and the end of the firstname element. The cursor is in the firstname element; type the first name for the contact.

7. Now you want to put the cursor after the close tag for the firstname element so you can add the middlename element. You can do this by clicking after the firstname element, or by pressing the right-arrow key.

8. Click the middlename element in the Structure panel. Enter the contact's middle name.

Figure 32.8
The XML Structure pane is context sensitive.

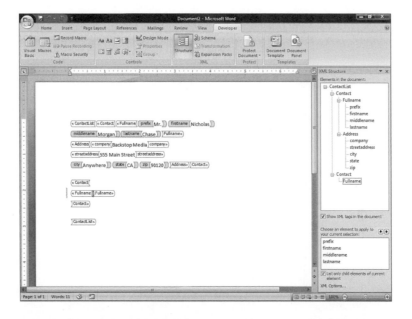

Figure 32.9
Showing all elements.

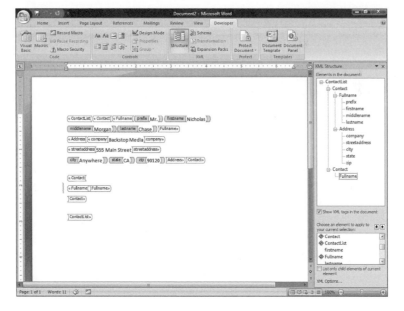

9. Press the right-arrow twice to place the cursor after the Fullname element and then the Enter key to position the cursor for the Address element.

10. Follow steps 6–8 to add the Address elements. You can see the finished document in Figure 32.10. The number and position of any blank lines will depend on how you added the line feeds in step 1.

Figure 32.10
The complete document.

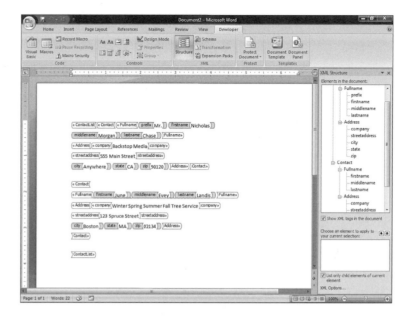

11. Click the Office button and choose Save As.

12. Choose a location and filename.

13. As shown in Figure 32.11, set the Save as Type field to Word XML Document (.xml).

14. Click Save.

Figure 32.11
Saving the file.

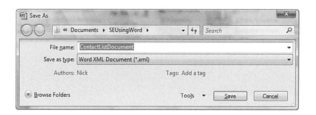

TIP

Although you might think so because of the description, this method does not save just the raw XML, but also the WordML describing it. The difference between this and a regular .docx file is that it is a single file, and not an archive.

ADDING ATTRIBUTES

No program designed to help you edit XML would be complete without the ability to add attributes to an element. The ContactML vocabulary includes an attribute on the Address element, specifying the type of address. Attributes appear in the start tag for the element, as in

```
...
  <Address addressType="business">
    <company>Backstop Media</company>
    <streetaddress>555 Main Street</streetaddress>
    <city>Anywhere</city><state>CA</state><zip>90120</zip>
  </Address>
...
```

You can add as many of these name-value pairs to an element as you like, as long as they are defined in the schema. Follow these steps to add the addressType attribute:

1. The Elements in the Document control shows all the content currently in the document. Right-click one of the Address elements and choose Attributes (see Figure 32.12).

Figure 32.12
Adding an attribute.

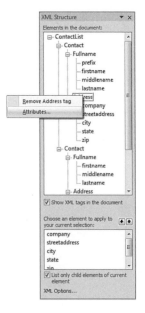

2. Select an available attribute—in this case, there is just one, called addressType—and then type a value into the value field (see Figure 32.13).

3. Click Add.

4. Click OK.

5. Save the file, either as regular Word XML or as data only using Word 2003 XML. In either case, you'll be able to edit the XML using Word. However, if you intend to take the file to another XML-enabled application, you'll want to go the data-only route.

Figure 32.13
Adding an attribute value.

VALIDATION ERRORS

The information I've provided up to this point is all well and good, but what happens if the XML document doesn't match the schema? In this situation, we say that the document is "invalid." Word has several ways to tell you that there's a problem. Follow these steps to see how Word 2007 handles invalid documents:

1. Delete the middle name and prefix from one of the names in your XML file and add text for the middle name, but don't add the `middlename` element itself.

2. If you look at the list of elements in the document, you will see an error symbol next to `firstname`. Placing your mouse over the error shows you what the problem is (see Figure 32.14).

3. Granted, this is a very vague message. "This is not allowed in this context" is not really helpful. To see a more informative message, click the XML Options button and check the Show Advanced XML Error Messages check box.

4. Click OK.

5. Now put your mouse over the error message and notice the difference (see Figure 32.15).

6. The error now specifies that Word is expecting the prefix, giving you more of the information you need to fix the problem. In this case, simply add the `prefix` element to the document.

7. The document used in this example still has a problem, however, because the `middle-name` element is missing. You can turn off notations by choosing XML Options, Hide Schema Violations in This Document.

8. Attempt to save the document as an XML file. Notice that even though you are not seeing any errors, you still can't save the file (see Figure 32.16).

Figure 32.14
Error in an invalid
document.

Figure 32.15
Advanced validation
errors.

32

Figure 32.16
Saving an invalid XML
document.

Fortunately, this doesn't mean that you can't save a document that's invalid. You have two choices. To save it as XML, choose XML Options, Allow Saving as XML Even If Not Valid.

You also have the option to simply save the file as a Word document. In either case, when you reopen the document in Word, the XML structure will still be visible so you can continue where you left off.

TRANSFORMING XML

XSLT enables you to programmatically transform XML from one form into another without having to actually write an application.

This provides you a way to easily repurpose your XML. In this chapter, you've been working with a contact list that was, for example, structured for a contact management appliction. You can take that XML and transform it into HTML or XML to be used with another system.

You do that by creating a stylesheet.

CREATING A STYLESHEET

The first step is to create a stylesheet, which is an XML document defining the steps necessary to transform the data:

```
<?xml version="1.0"?>
<xsl:stylesheet xmlns:xsl="http://www.w3.org/1999/XSL/Transform" version="1.0"
                          xmlns:cl="http://tempuri.org/contactML.xsd">

<xsl:template match="/">

<companies>
   <xsl:for-each select="cl:ContactList/cl:Contact">
      <contact>
          <organization>
           <xsl:value-of select="cl:company"/>
          </organization>
          <name>
           <xsl:value-of select="cl:Fullname/cl:lastname"/>,
           <xsl:value-of select="cl:Fullname/cl:firsttname"/>
          </name>
      </contact>
   </xsl:for-each>
</companies>

</xsl:template>

</xsl:stylesheet>
```

This is a fairly simple stylesheet intended to transform the data into another structure. A complete discussion of XSLT is well beyond the scope of this chapter, but let's take a quick look. This stylesheet takes the document and creates a companies element. Within that element, it loops through each of the Contact elements in the original document and for each one creates a contact element. Within that contact element, it creates an organization and a name element, each of which is populated with information from the original document.

> You can get more information on XSLT at http://www.w3.org/Style/XSL/, or you can read an introduction to XSLT transformations at http://www.nicholaschase.com/xslt.html.

Create this document and save it as an XML file.

ATTACH THE STYLESHEET

Microsoft Word 2007 enables you to use XSLT stylesheets in two ways. First, you can use the stylesheet to transform the document when you're viewing it in Word, which enables you to choose the appearance of the document from one or more attached stylesheets, or data views. (Once you do edit the document, you're locked into the data view you've chosen.)

You can also transform the document when you save it, which results in a document that uses the new structure. Here are the steps to follow to attach a stylesheet:

1. Make sure the XML has no errors (for example, make sure both contacts have a `prefix`) and open it in Word 2007 (see Figure 32.17).

Figure 32.17
Applying transformations.

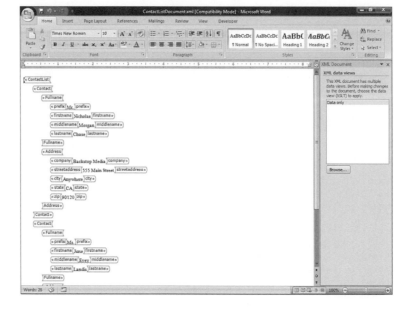

32

2. Click Browse.
3. Navigate to the style sheet and click Open.
4. You should now see the document in the new view (see Figure 32.18). You also have the option to change it back by clicking Data Only.

Figure 32.18
The transformed document.

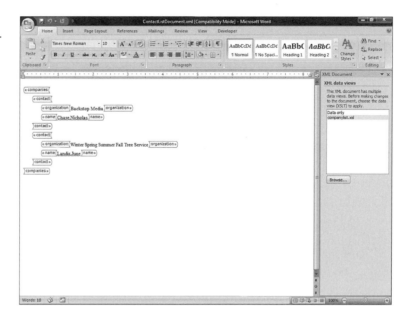

Note that if you save the document now, you will lose all the data excluded from the current document. In this case, the document would look like this:

```
<?xml version="1.0" encoding="UTF-8" standalone="no"?>
<companies><contact><organization>Backstop Media</organization><name>Chase,Nicho
las</name></contact><contact><organization>WinterSpring Summer Fall Tree Service
</organization><name>Landis,June</name></contact></companies>
```

AFFECTING APPEARANCE

You can also affect the appearance of an XML document in Word 2007 by transforming it into HTML. For example, consider this stylesheet:

```
<?xml version="1.0"?>
<xsl:stylesheet xmlns:xsl="http://www.w3.org/1999/XSL/Transform" version="1.0"
 xmlns:cl="http://tempuri.org/contactML.xsd">

<xsl:template match="/">

<html>
<head><title>Companies on the contact list</title></head>
<body>
    <h2>Companies on the contact list</h2>
    <ul>
    <xsl:for-each select="cl:ContactList/cl:Contact">
       <li>
           <xsl:value-of select="cl:Address/cl:company"/>
             (<xsl:value-of select="cl:Fullname/cl:firstname"/>
             <xsl:text> </xsl:text>
             <xsl:value-of select="cl:Fullname/cl:lastname"/>)
```

```
        </li>
      </xsl:for-each>
      </ul>
  </body>
  </html>

</xsl:template>

</xsl:stylesheet>
```

This stylesheet creates a simple bulleted list.

It can be useful to attach the stylesheet to the XML document by adding a directive to the XML file itself:

```
<?xml version="1.0" encoding="UTF-8" standalone="no"?>
<?xml-stylesheet type="text/xsl" href="webstylesheet.xsl" version="1.0" ?>
<ContactList xmlns="http://tempuri.org/contactML.xsd"><Contact><Fullname>
<prefix>Mr.</prefix><firstname>Nicholas</firstname>
```

This way, you can view the XML in the browser, and the browser will render it according to the stylesheet (see Figure 32.19).

Figure 32.19
Transformed to HTML.

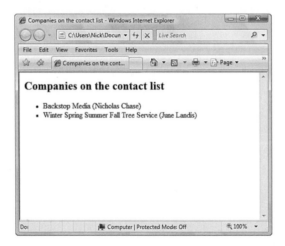

More importantly, adding the stylesheet to the document attaches it to the document as far as Word is concerned, so the stylesheet appears when Word is looking for data views (see Figure 32.20).

Figure 32.20
Choosing a data view.

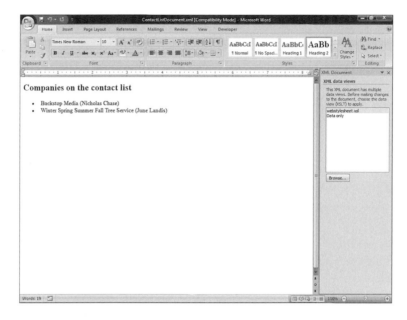

Using this method, you can attach multiple views to a document.

TROUBLESHOOTING

WORD CAN'T OPEN MY XML FILE

Several different problems can prevent Word from opening an XML file:

- An XML file must be well formed for Word to open it. If you see a message indicating that this situation exists, open the file in Notepad, fix the problem, and then try opening the file again.

> **TIP**
>
> If you have problems finding the specific location of an XML syntax error, try opening the file in Internet Explorer. It will attempt to validate the structure and provide more specific information about where the problem is.

- If you have created a document that does not have any XML structure elements in it and then choose to save data only, nothing will be saved. This is because the document text has no root node; therefore, a properly formed XML document cannot be created. When you try to open the file back up, it will be empty. If the content of your document does not contain valid XML, don't use the Save Data Only option.

- If you have specified an XSLT transformation and Word cannot use it, Word will try to apply any other transformation that is included in the document. If no others are available, Word will then try a default transformation to open the document. If all of these attempts fail, Word gives you a message indicating the problem. You must either use a different transformation file or open the XML file in Notepad and fix the source of the problem.

THE XML DOCUMENT TASK PANE DISAPPEARS

If you have selected a data view in the XML Document task pane and then open that file for editing, the data view is automatically activated. Because the data view is an XSLT transformation, you cannot reverse the process that results in removal of the XML Document task pane. To avoid this situation, make sure that you select the desired data view before you start editing.

INSERTING XML FROM ANOTHER FILE DOESN'T WORK

When using an XPATH expression to select data from another XML file, Word does not validate the syntax of the expression. If you enter an expression that is invalid or does not match anything in the XML file, nothing will be inserted and no error messages will be displayed. Keep these things in mind when using XPATH queries:

- Querying XML structures is a case-sensitive operation. Make sure you are specifying your element or attribute names with the correct case.
- If the XML file you are selecting data from was saved using Word's default WordML schema, your XPATH query must address that XML structure before it will work.

A DATA VIEW OR TRANSFORMATION DOES NOT FIND ANY DATA

Querying XML structures via XPATH or XSLT is not always a simple operation. If you enter an expression that is invalid or does not match anything in the XML file, nothing will be displayed and no error messages will be displayed. Keep these things in mind when working with data views and transformations:

- Querying XML structures is a case-sensitive operation. Make sure you are specifying your element or attribute names with the correct case.
- If the XML file you are selecting data from was saved using Word's default WordML schema, your XPATH query must address that XML structure before it will work.

YOU LOSE DATA AFTER SAVING YOUR XML FILE

If you save a file using an XSLT transformation, Word saves only the result of the transformation. The original data file is not saved. To prevent loss of data when using these transformations, keep a separate copy of the source XML file. Be sure to use the Save As menu when you apply your transformation.

The List of Elements Is Hard to Read

Sometimes you may find that the element names in the XML Structure task pane have long strings on the end that start with {urn:,. This string is the namespace that the element belongs to. Although this is useful when multiple namespaces are used in the same document, it can also make the element names hard to read. You can turn off the display of the namespace by clicking on the XML Options, and then selecting the Hide Namespace Alias in XML Structure Task Pane check box.

No Elements Are Available to Add When Editing an XML Document

Word requires access to a valid XML schema before it will allow any changes to be made to the structure itself. Make sure that the required schema has been added to the Schema Library.

PART VII

CUSTOMIZING AND EXTENDING WORD

CHAPTER 33

MACROS AND ADD-INS

In this chapter

UNDERSTANDING MACROS

A *macro* is a sequence of operations that Word can execute whenever you tell it to. Word's powerful macro facilities enable you to automate just about anything you would do manually in Word. You can assign a macro to a keyboard shortcut, run it from the Macros dialog box, or place a button for it on the Quick Access toolbar.

There are two general approaches to creating Word macros:

- Use Word's macro recorder to capture the steps in your macro as you perform them in Word. After you save the macro, you can play it back at any time using one of the options listed previously.

- Write the code of the macro yourself in the Visual Basic for Applications (VBA) programming language. Word comes with a complete programming environment, the Visual Basic Editor, that you can use to enter and edit your code, as well as powerful tools to help you debug and test your macros.

This chapter focuses mostly on recording and playing back a Word macro. To use the VBA method, you must have some background in Visual Basic programming.

WHAT TASKS SHOULD YOU AUTOMATE WITH A MACRO?

The most common purpose for macros is to speed your work, by taking a set of operations that you perform repeatedly and turning them into a one-step operation. Anytime you find yourself doing the same set of actions over and over again, you might have found a good candidate for a macro. Macros also make your work more reliable by ensuring that the steps of the macro are performed exactly the same way, each time the macro runs. Of course, that does mean it is essential to record the macro properly. Otherwise, it performs the same *wrong* set of steps each time it runs.

Before you take the step of creating a macro, however, you might want to consider some of the other timesaving features in Word that you can use instead of macros:

- If you often need to type the same text, such as your name or address, including formatting, you might want to use Word's Building Blocks feature, which lets you save named collections of text and formatting.

→ To learn about building blocks, **see** "Working with Building Blocks," **p. 90**.

- To quickly apply formatting in a consistent way throughout one or more documents, you can use styles and themes.

→ To learn how to create and apply styles and themes, **see** Chapter 8, "Creating and Applying Styles and Themes," **p. 227**.

- To create neatly formatted standard documents, such as letters, résumés, or fax cover sheets, you can use one of the document templates or wizards that come with Word, or create your own template.

→ To learn about working with templates in Word, **see** "Creating a Document Based on a Template, **p. 29**.

If none of Word's automated features alone will do the job for you, or if you want to use several of these features together, you can create a macro to carry out your commands. There is just about no end to the uses you might think of for macros. A few of the most common include the following:

- Applying complex formatting that you can't easily capture in a style, such as a mixture of different formatting types.

- Completing any task that takes several steps, such as creating a mail merge, applying complicated page setup settings, or requesting custom printing routines.

- Performing repetitive tasks in a long document. This is especially useful for documents that you have imported from other programs or that other users have created. You can record a macro that finds and replaces special characters, removes extra paragraph breaks, or applies formatting.

- Performing commands normally found in Word's built-in dialog boxes. You might want to turn a display feature—such as the display of field codes—on or off as needed. Or you might want to quickly apply a text attribute that is not on the Ribbon, such as double-strikethrough.

DECIDING TO USE THE MACRO RECORDER

When you need to create a new macro, you have a choice between recording the macro and typing the VBA code yourself. Of course, if you don't know the VBA programming language, your only option is to record the macro. You can even use the recorder as a teaching tool by recording the macro and then studying the resulting VBA code. As mentioned, this book focuses on using the macro recorder.

It's worthwhile to know a little about how the macro recorder works before recording a macro. After you turn on the macro recorder, it captures just about everything you do in Word, including typing text, applying formatting, and performing menu commands. The recorder is very literal: It picks up just about every detail during the recording session. Don't be surprised, if you look at the VBA code that results from recording a macro, if it seems that Word recorded a lot more than you had in mind.

If you are, or become, proficient with VBA, you'll probably find that it is often useful to record a macro and then edit the resulting code to get it to work exactly as you want. As your VBA skills improve, you might even find that it's sometimes quicker and more accurate to type the code yourself in the first place.

PLANNING TO RECORD YOUR MACRO

It's always a good idea to take some time to think about exactly what you want your macro to do before you begin recording. You might even want to take a few notes on paper that you can refer to while you record the macro. Think about several things before recording your macro:

33

■ Consider how your document should be set up before the recording begins. For example, if your macro is to apply font formatting to selected text, you need to have the appropriate text selected before you start recording the macro. On the other hand, you might want to record the actual selection of the text. In many cases, the first action you record will be moving to the beginning of your document. This can ensure that the steps that follow are applied to the entire document.

■ Make sure that you know your keyboard shortcuts, especially the ones for moving through the document and for selecting text. Word doesn't record text selections or navigation you perform with the mouse, but you *can* use keyboard shortcuts to perform the same tasks. (You can still use the mouse to select toolbar and menu commands while recording.)

TIP

If you want to record a macro that performs a series of actions to selected text, select some text before you begin recording the macro. Then record your macro as you normally would. For example, you could create a macro that makes selected text bold and italic. Select some text, begin recording the macro, click the Bold and Italic toolbar buttons, and stop recording. The resulting macro toggles the bold and italic setting for any selected text.

■ Think about the exact meaning of what you want to record. For example, to move to the beginning of the next paragraph while you are recording, press the shortcut key to move to the next paragraph (Ctrl+down arrow). If you simply use the arrow keys to move to the desired location, your macro records the arrow movements, not your intention to move to the following paragraph. When you run it in a different document, it replays the arrow movements, which may not have the same result in that document.

A good way to plan a macro is to take one or more "test runs" before turning on the recorder: Perform the commands and write down exactly what you did along the way. When you're satisfied that you've written down a workable list of steps, use it as a reference when recording the macro.

RECORDING A MACRO

Ready to record? Click the Record Macro button (the little red ball) on the status bar. The Record Macro dialog box opens (see Figure 33.1).

NOTE

Another way to start a new macro is to click Record Macro on the Developer tab. If the Developer tab does not appear, choose Office, Word Options, click Personalize, and click Show Developer Tab in the Ribbon.

The Record Macro button is also available on the Developer tab

Figure 33.1
Enter the name and description of your new macro in the Record Macro dialog box.

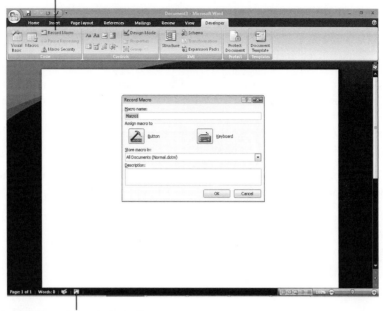

Record Macro button in status bar

Before you can begin recording the macro, you must give it a name and decide where you want to store it. You can also assign the macro to a keyboard shortcut or a custom toolbar button. Although you can change all these items later, it's far more convenient to make these decisions up front and enter them correctly now.

NAMING YOUR MACRO

As you can see from Figure 33.1, Word suggests a name for your macro: Macro1, Macro2, and so on. It's usually much more useful to give your macro a more descriptive name so that it will be easy to identify when you want to use it later. Your macro name should describe the purpose of the macro and must follow these rules:

- Macro names must begin with a letter but can include numbers.
- Names can contain up to 80 letters and numbers. Spaces and other characters are not allowed (except the underscore character).

For example, the following macro names are legal:

    ApplyMyCustomFormatting
    Insert5BlankParagraphs
    TwoB_Or_Not2B

33

The following names are not legal:

Create Letter

2Spaces

New?Document

Word does not give you any warning that your macro name is invalid until you click OK to start recording your macro. If your macro name contains invalid characters, Word will display a dialog box indicating Invalid Procedure Name. Simply click OK and launch the Record Macro dialog box again. Edit the name until it conforms to the naming rules. When it does, Word allows you to proceed.

At the time you name your macro, you can also enter a description for the macro. It's a good idea to enter a more specific description for your macros. For example:

This macro goes to the top of the document and then performs a find and replace to eliminate the second space between sentences.

DECIDING WHERE TO STORE YOUR MACRO

Macros can be stored in templates and in individual documents. A macro is available for you to run only if the document or template that contains the macro is open. Macros can be stored in the following locations:

- **Normal.dotm**—The simplest way to create a macro that you can run at any time, in any document, is to store the macro in your Normal template. As you can see in Figure 33.1, the Normal.dotm template is selected by default as the storage place for recorded macros.
- **Active Document**—If you prefer to store the macro in the active document, click the Store Macro In drop-down list to select the document. The macro will be available for you to run only when this document is the active document.
- **Other Templates**—If you store a macro in a template other than the Normal template, the macro is available only when that template is open or when a document based on that template is open. For example, suppose that you have created a template for writing sales proposals. If you want to record a macro that you will use only when you are working on these proposals, be sure to select the template name in the Store Macro In drop-down list. The template, or a document based on the template, must be the active document at the time you record the macro.

ASSIGNING A MACRO TO A KEYBOARD SHORTCUT OR TOOLBAR BUTTON

If you expect to use your macro often, and you want to save time when you run it, you can assign a shortcut key or Quick Access toolbar button for running the macro. Then you can run your macro quickly by pressing the shortcut key combination or clicking the button.

Word does not require you to assign your macro to anything: You can always run the macro using the Play Macro button (the green triangle on the status bar) or the Macros button on the Developer tab. Although adding some form of shortcut can make a macro more accessible, you might prefer not to use up a key assignment or space on a toolbar for macros you use only rarely.

For commonly used macros, however, you probably should assign a keyboard shortcut or Quick Access toolbar button.

Keyboard shortcuts are a great convenience for macros that you use often. If you use a macro only occasionally, however, you might find it difficult to remember the shortcut key. Also, if you're creating macros for other users, some users prefer shortcut keys, whereas others don't want to memorize anything.

A button on the Quick Access toolbar makes a macro readily available for use at any time. Many people prefer not to memorize shortcut keys but don't mind clicking a button.

TIP

You can print a list of the custom key assignments associated with any document or template. To do so, choose Office, Print; then choose Key Assignments from the Print What drop-down box and click OK. Word first prints all custom key assignments associated with the document itself, and then all custom key assignments associated with the template the document is based on.

ASSIGNING A MACRO TO A KEYBOARD SHORTCUT

To assign a keyboard shortcut to the macro you're about to record, follow these steps while the Record Macro dialog box is open:

1. Click Keyboard in the Assign Macro To group. The Customize Keyboard dialog box appears, as shown in Figure 33.2.

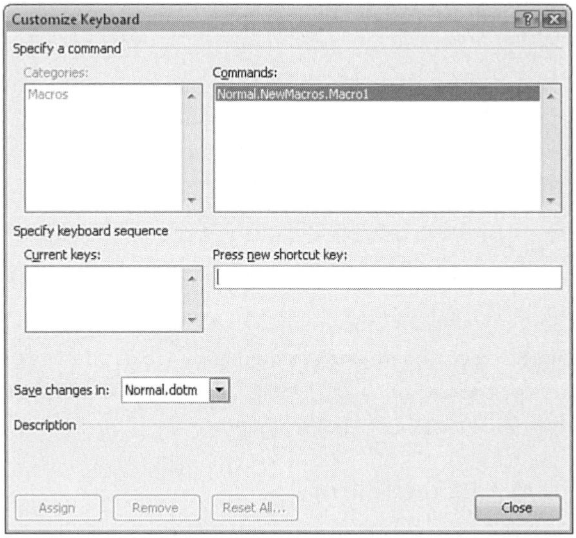

Figure 33.2
Use the Customize Keyboard dialog box to assign a key combination for your macro.

33

2. Make sure that the correct template or document is selected in the Save Changes In drop-down list. In nearly every case, you'll want to save the keyboard shortcut in the same template or document the macro will be stored in. (Word's default setting is to store the change in the Normal.dotm template, not the current document.)

3. Click in the Press New Shortcut Key box if the insertion point is not already there.

4. Press the shortcut key combination you want to use for the macro. You can create keyboard combinations that include function keys F1 through F12, the Ctrl key, the Alt key, and the Shift key (but not the Windows key). The key combination you choose is displayed in the Press New Shortcut Key text box. Under the text box, the current assignment for this key combination is displayed, or the combination is shown as *[unassigned]*.

CAUTION

> Word allows you to override default keyboard shortcut assignments. In fact, it doesn't even require you to confirm this with a confirming dialog box. As soon as you click Close to start recording your macro, the macro replaces the default key assignment.
>
> To reset the keyboard shortcuts, choose Office@@>Word Options, click Customize, click Customize, and click Reset All.
>
> You should be very reluctant to change default key assignments. For example, if you decide to assign Ctrl+P as the shortcut key for your macro, you can no longer use that keyboard combination to print. If you store your macro in a specific document or a template you've created, the change in keystrokes will affect only the document, or documents, created with that template. In other words, the same keystrokes will perform different tasks at different times, which can be terribly confusing—for you and especially for others who may use your macro.
>
> If you store the macro in Normal.dotm, the change will affect all documents—but now, Word will behave differently from the way its online documentation (and this book) says it will.

5. To accept the new keyboard assignment, click Assign. The new assignment appears in the Current Keys list. You can assign more than one key combination for each macro if you want to, but remember that a relatively limited number of key combinations is available for everything Word has to do. Use the Remove button to delete a previously assigned shortcut.

6. To complete the assignment and continue with the recording process, click Close to begin the recording.

You cannot set up both a keyboard shortcut and a button for a macro while initially recording it, because the macro recording begins immediately when you click Close in step 6, but you can add a button for the macro to the Quick Access toolbar after the recording is finished. You'll learn how to do that later in the chapter.

ASSIGNING A MACRO TO A TOOLBAR BUTTON

To assign a toolbar button to run your macro, follow these steps when the Record Macro dialog box is displayed:

1. Click Button in the Assign Macro To group. The Customize page appears in the Word Options dialog box.

2. Click the macro name in the left list, and then click the Add button to move it to the right list (see Figure 33.3).

3. Click OK. The macro recording begins.

As noted in the preceding section, you cannot set up both a button and a keyboard shortcut for a macro while initially recording it, because the macro recording begins immediately when you click OK in step 3, but you can add a shortcut key combination after the recording is finished. You'll learn how to do that later in the chapter.

Figure 33.3
Add a macro to the Quick Access toolbar.

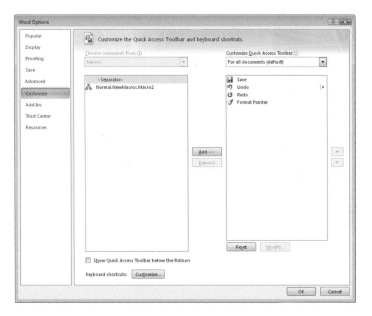

RECORDING THE STEPS FOR YOUR MACRO

If you chose to assign a keyboard shortcut or toolbar button to your macro, Word turns on the macro recorder after specifying one or the other. If you have not assigned either one, click OK in the Record Macro dialog box to get the recording started.

When recording is enabled, a Stop Recording button (blue square) appears in the status bar, and the mouse pointer turns into a cassette tape symbol. If the Developer tab is displayed, you also have access to a Pause Recording button that you can use to temporarily halt the recording while you set something up, then continue the recording (see Figure 33.4).

33

Pause Recording (Developer tab only)

Figure 33.4
When a macro is recording, the status bar shows a Stop Recording button.

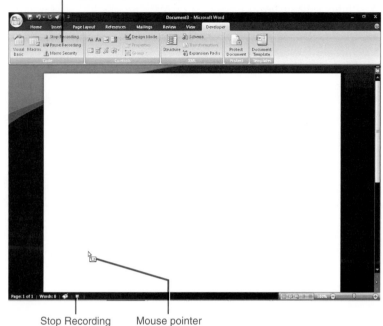

Stop Recording   Mouse pointer

When the macro recorder is active, you can perform most normal activities in Word, and those activities are recorded as part of your macro. Some examples of actions you can record in your macro include the following:

- You can type, edit, and delete text.
- You can select text and move through the document with keyboard shortcuts. You can't use the mouse to select text or scroll while you are recording. Instead, use the arrow keys to navigate, as well as the Home, End, Page Up, and Page Down keys, as needed. To select text, press and hold the Shift key while you use the arrow or navigation keys.

NOTE
> You *can* still use the mouse to select menu commands and toolbar buttons while you're recording a macro.

- You can click buttons on the Ribbon or the Quick Access toolbar and fill out the dialog boxes associated with the commands.
- You can open and close documents, and create new documents.
- You can choose Office, Word Options and set or change program options.

If you want to pause your recording session and return to it later, click the Pause Recording button. Any actions you perform while recording is paused are not recorded. Click Resume Recorder (same button as Pause Recording) when you're ready to resume your recording session. That button is available only on the Developer tab, so you must have displayed the Developer tab before you started recording. (You can turn it on during the recording, but the fact that you are turning it on will be recorded as an activity.)

Keep a few things in mind as you record your macros:

- The macro recorder captures the actions you perform, not the keystrokes you use to complete them. So, for example, if you open the Print dialog box, the macro does not notice which method you use to do so.

- If you record a command that displays a dialog box, such as clicking a dialog box launcher for a group on a tab, the dialog box doesn't reappear when you later run the macro. Rather, Word applies whatever settings you entered using the dialog box while you were recording the macro.

- Word records *everything* in the dialog box, so if you only want to turn on italic, it's better to press Ctrl+I or click the Italic button on the Formatting toolbar than it is to use the Font dialog box. Otherwise, Word also records other text attributes that apply to the current text—attributes you might not want to apply every time you run the macro.

- If you display a dialog box while you're recording, but you cancel the dialog box, Word doesn't record that command at all.

- Word records your actions literally. For example, if you record the Office, Open command and select a file, Word records the exact filename you opened. When you run the macro, Word attempts to open the same file. If the file is not found, an error occurs, and the macro stops running.

When you finish recording your macro, you can turn off the recorder in the following ways:

- Click the Stop Recording button on the status bar.
- Click the Stop Recording button on the Developer tab.

33

Creating Macros That Run Automatically

In most cases, you should give your macro a name that describes its function so that you can easily remember its purpose later. There are, however, several special names you can give your macros. These names cause your macros to run automatically when certain events occur in Word:

- A macro named AutoExec runs when you start Word. For this macro to work, you need to store it in your Normal.dotm template or another always-available template.

- A macro named AutoExit runs when you exit Word. If you want a macro to run every time you exit Word, store this macro in Normal.dotm or another always-available template.

- A macro named AutoNew runs when you create a new document. If you save this macro in a specific template, such as a memo template, then the macro runs each time you create a new document based on that template.

- A macro named AutoClose runs when you close a document. If you save this macro in a specific template, it runs when you attempt to close the template or any document based on the template.

- A macro named AutoOpen runs when you open the template that contains it or any document based on the template.

RUNNING A MACRO

Now that you have recorded and stored your macro, you can run the macro to perform the steps you have recorded. Use one of the following methods to run your macro:

■ If you assigned the macro to a button on the Quick Access toolbar, you can click the button to run the macro. If you have more than one macro on the Quick Access toolbar, point at a button to see its ScreenTip to determine which is which. (You cannot change the icon for a macro.)

■ If you assigned a keyboard shortcut for the macro, press the key combination.

■ To select the macro name from the list of available macros, click the Play Macro button on the status bar (green triangle), or click the Macros button on the Developer tab. The Macros dialog box appears, as shown in Figure 33.5. Select the macro name that you want to run and click Run to execute the macro.

Macros button

Figure 33.5
Use the Macros dialog box to select a macro to run.

Play Macro button

Running Word Commands as Macros

Word has more than 400 built-in commands that you can run as though they were macros. Many of these commands are the same as the commands already found on Word's Ribbon and menus. In some cases, though, there are commands that aren't found on any menu or toolbar button. In other cases, these commands provide a simpler or more effective approach to operations that you can perform with other commands.

To run a built-in command as a macro, open the Macros dialog box and select Word Commands in the Macros In box. Select the desired command in the Macro Name list and then click Run.

33

DEALING WITH MACRO ERROR MESSAGES

When your macro runs, the statements you recorded are performed just as you recorded them. Sometimes, though, an error can occur.

The most common problems are:

- Missing macros (for example, trying to run a macro from a Quick Access toolbar button where the macro has been deleted or is not stored in an available template)
- Security settings preventing a macro from running

Both of these situations result in the same error message, shown in Figure 33.6.

Figure 33.6
This error means the macro cannot run, either because it is missing or because your macro security settings will not allow it.

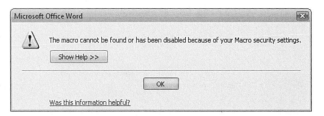

To check that the macro is available, open the Macros dialog box (shown previously in Figure 33.5) and set the Macros In setting to All Active Templates and Documents. If the macro does not appear there, you probably have stored it somewhere else by accident. You can either re-create it or copy it from the other document or template file. (To do the latter, see "Copying Macros Between Documents" later in this chapter.)

If the macro is available, then it's your security settings that need tweaking. See "Working with Macro Security" later in this chapter for help with that.

Another common error occurs when the macro cannot execute one or more lines of its code. This is called a *runtime error*. It happens when the conditions that existed when you recorded the macro no longer exist in some way. For example, perhaps the macro specifies opening a file that does not exist anymore in the referenced location. A runtime error looks like the one in Figure 33.7.

Figure 33.7
A runtime error points out a problem with the macro's code.

To correct a runtime error, you can edit the VBA code for the macro (if you are able), or you can delete and rerecord the macro.

If you want to delete the macro and rerecord it, click End to stop the macro and then delete it from the Macros dialog box (refer to Figure 33.5).

33

If you want to edit the code, click Debug to open the macro in the Visual Basic Editor (VBE) and then examine the code. The line that caused the error is highlighted, as shown in Figure 33.8.

Reset button   Highlighted code

Figure 33.8
The line of code that caused the error is highlighted.

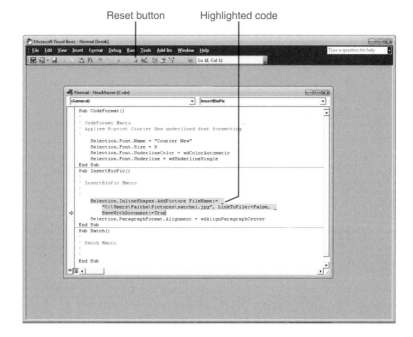

At this time, the macro is still running but is suspended in a state known as *Break mode*. After making the needed correction to the code, click the Reset button in the toolbar (see Figure 33.8). Then close the Visual Basic window and try running the macro again.

CAUTION

Occasionally, a macro runs out of control, repeating its actions over and over. This is not likely to happen with a recorded macro, but it sometimes happens when there is a programming error in a macro you have edited. In this case, you can stop the macro by pressing Ctrl+Break. Again, this puts the macro in Break mode, and you must reset the macro project.

MAKING ADDITIONAL MACROS AVAILABLE

If the macro you want to use is not available in the current document, but is stored somewhere else, there are several ways of making it available. The following sections provide some ideas.

OPENING ADDITIONAL TEMPLATES TO RUN MACROS

If you want to run a macro that is stored in a different template, you can open that template as a global template. There are two ways to make sure that a template is loaded globally:

- **Save the template in the Word Startup folder**—To determine where that folder is located, choose Office, Word Options. Click Advanced, then click the File Locations button in the General section, and then double-click Startup to see the location. Any template in this folder is opened invisibly, and as a read-only document, each time you start Word.

- **Open a template globally**—To do this, on the Developer tab, click Document Template. In the Global Templates and Add-Ins section of the Templates and Add-Ins dialog box, click Add and then select the template to load.

COPYING MACROS BETWEEN DOCUMENTS

Each Word document has a single VBA *project*, which is a collection of modules. A Word document can store many types of VBA code, not just macros, so it needs the capability of having multiple modules in its project. For macro purposes, however, you will work mostly with one module: the default module for storing macros, called NewMacros.

NOTE

> Modules can be renamed, and you can develop extra modules, so a template you receive from someone else might have multiple modules in them, and they might have different names than NewMacros.

Each macro is stored in the macro module as a VBA *procedure*, which is a set of step-by-step instructions to execute.

If a given document or template contains some useful macros, you might want to reuse them in some other template. One way to achieve this is to copy the macros from one project to another using the Organizer.

Follow these steps to copy one or more macros:

1. Open the source and destination templates or documents in Word.

2. On the Developer tab, click Macros, and then click Organizer. The Organizer dialog box opens (see Figure 33.9). This dialog box lets you display the modules in two templates or documents and copy modules from one list to another.

Figure 33.9
Use the Organizer to copy modules from one template or document to another.

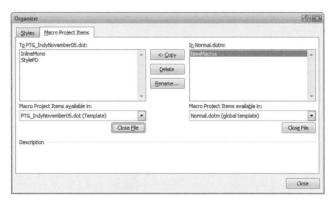

3. Under either list, if needed, display a different template:

   a. Click Close File.

   b. Click Open File.

   c. Select a different template or document.

   d. Click Open.

4. To copy a module from one list to another, select the module that you want to copy and click Copy. The macro is copied to the destination list.

NOTE

> If a module with the same name is already in the destination project, Word won't let you copy the module. If you still want to copy the module, you must rename it before copying it.
>
> To rename a module, select the module and click Rename. Type the new name for the module and click OK. For example, if both the source and destination locations call the module NewMacros, rename one of them.

5. (Optional) To delete a module from a project, select the module and click Delete. Word asks for confirmation that you really want to delete the module.

CAUTION

> After you delete a module and save the template that contained it, there is no way to recover the deleted module.

6. When you are finished using the Organizer, click Close.

RENAMING AND DELETING MACROS

The Organizer copies, renames, and deletes only entire modules, each of which might contain many individual macros. You might prefer to rename and delete individual macros instead.

To delete a macro, open the Macros dialog box (by clicking the Macros button on the status bar or the Developer tab) and then select the desired macro and click Delete.

To rename a macro, select the macro from the Macros dialog box and click Edit. The macro opens in the Visual Basic Editor. Find the line of code that starts with Sub and then shows the macro's name, and change the text following Sub to the desired name. Do not delete the parentheses.

ASSIGNING A KEYBOARD SHORTCUT TO AN EXISTING MACRO

As you saw earlier in the chapter, you can assign a keyboard shortcut to a macro as you create it. However, if you want both a keyboard shortcut and a Quick Access toolbar button for it, you must set up one or the other afterward.

To assign a keyboard shortcut to an existing macro, follow these steps:

1. Choose Office, Word Options.

2. Click Customize.

3. Click the Customize button. The Customize Keyboard dialog box appears.

4. In the Categories list, scroll down to the bottom of the list and click Macros. A list of the macros in the current document or template appear in the Macros list (see Figure 33.10).

Figure 33.10
Assign a keyboard shortcut to an existing macro.

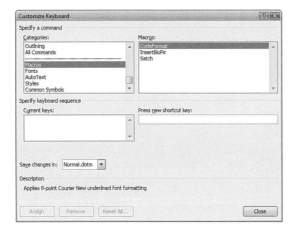

5. Click the desired macro. Any existing keyboard shortcut assigned to it appears in the Current Keys box.

6. Click in the Press New Shortcut Key box.

7. Press the shortcut key combination you want to use for the macro.

   You can create keyboard combinations that include function keys F1 through F12, the Ctrl key, the Alt key, and the Shift key (but not the Windows key). The key combination you choose is displayed in the Press New Shortcut Key text box. Under the Current Keys text box, the current assignment for this key combination is displayed, or the combination is shown as *[unassigned]*.

8. To accept the new keyboard assignment, click Assign. The new assignment appears in the Current Keys list.

   You can assign more than one key combination for each macro if you want to, but remember that a relatively limited number of key combinations is available for everything Word has to do.

   > **TIP**
   > Click Reset All to reset all key assignments.

9. (Optional) Assign keyboard shortcuts to other macros as needed by repeating steps 5–8.

10. Click Close.

11. Click OK.

TIP

If you find it difficult to identify unused keyboard sequences, try sequences that begin with the Alt key; most of these are unassigned.

Alternatively, you can obtain a list of shortcut keys assigned to existing Word commands. Open the Macros dialog box. From the Macros In drop-down list, select Word Commands. This presents you with a list of Word commands. Scroll down to and select the ListCommands entry. Click the Run button. From the List Commands dialog box, select Current Keyboard Settings. Click OK, and a new document is generated containing all the commands and associated shortcut keys and menu items.

CREATING A QUICK ACCESS BUTTON FOR AN EXISTING MACRO

Each individual macro can be added to the Quick Access toolbar. This can save you some time compared to opening the Macros dialog box and selecting the desired macro each time.

To add an existing macro to the Quick Access toolbar, follow these steps:

1. Choose Office, Word Options.
2. Click Customize.
3. Open the Choose Commands From list and select Macros. A list of the macros appears.
4. Click a macro and then click the Add button to add it to the toolbar (see Figure 33.11).
5. Add any other macros as needed; then click OK.

Figure 33.11
Create a button for a macro on the Quick Access toolbar.

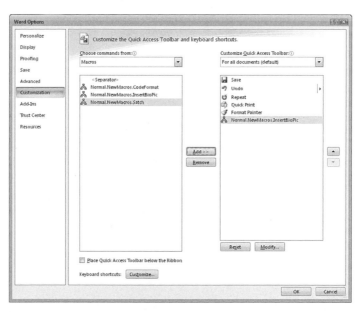

Each macro has an identical button on the Quick Access toolbar. To tell the macros apart, point to a button to see its ScreenTip.

EDITING MACRO CODE IN VBA

Macros are written in Visual Basic for Applications, a variant of the Visual Basic programming language designed for use within Office and other applications.

To write your own VBA code from scratch, you need to understand Visual Basic, and perhaps have taken a class or done some self-study in the language. However, if you just want to edit a macro, you can usually figure out what the various lines of code do and modify them in small ways or delete lines of code that are extraneous.

OPENING A MACRO FOR EDITING

To open up a macro in the Visual Basic Editor (VBE), follow these steps:

1. Click Macros in the status bar or the Developer tab, opening the Macros dialog box.

2. Click the desired macro and then click Edit. The macro opens in the Visual Basic Editor. If there are multiple macros, each one appears in a separate section within a single window for the module. In Figure 33.12, for example, there are two macros (CodeFormat and InsertBioPic) in the NewMacros module.

Figure 33.12
Use the Visual Basic Editor to make changes to macro code.

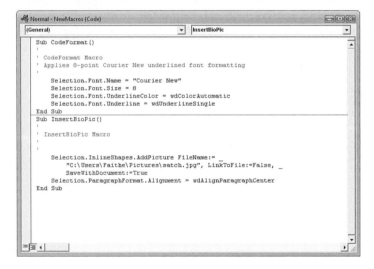

Here's a brief guide to what you see in Figure 33.12:

- Each macro's section begins with the statement Sub, followed by the macro name, and then empty parentheses (). For example:

```
Sub CodeFormat()
```

- Each macro ends with the statement End Sub.

- Lines with apostrophes (') at the beginning are comment lines and do not execute. These lines are there for reference purposes for someone who is examining the code. For example, in the CodeFormat macro in Figure 33.12, the following is a comment line, which came from the Description entered when recording the macro:

```
'Applies 8-point Courier New underlined font formatting
```

- Each command in a macro defines a part of the document or program, and then has an equals sign and a value for that item. For example:

```
Selection.Font.Name = "Courier New"
```

EXAMPLES OF MACRO COMMAND SYNTAX

The best way to understand macro code is to record some macros and then look at them in the Visual Basic Editor. Let's have a look at a few of the commands from Figure 33.12 as examples.

APPLYING CHARACTER FORMATTING

The first macro in Figure 33.12, CodeFormat, applies four types of character formatting to text:

```
Selection.Font.Name = "Courier New"
Selection.Font.Size = 8
Selection.Font.UnderlineColor = wdColorAutomatic
Selection.Font.Underline = wdUnderlineSingle
```

Each one begins with Selection, which tells it you are going to be acting upon the selected text (or the insertion point location). Next comes Font, which tells it you will be applying font formatting. After that comes the individual attribute being set, an equals sign (=), and the value for it.

Some of the values are no-brainers. For example, the font name appears just as it does on the Font list, in quotation marks because it is a text value. And the font size appears as a regular digit.

The other two values you would have to know how to write. (That's where experimenting with recording comes in handy.) The first one, wdColorAutomatic, specifies that the underline color will be the same as the text. The second one, wdUnderlineSingle, sets the underline style.

INSERTING GRAPHICS

The second macro in Figure 33.12, InsertBioPic, contains these commands:

```
Selection.InlineShapes.AddPicture FileName:= _
    "C:\Users\Faithe\Pictures\satch.jpg", LinkToFile:=False, _
    SaveWithDocument:=True
Selection.ParagraphFormat.Alignment = wdAlignParagraphCenter
```

The first three lines are actually one single command. Where the lines break, underscore characters are used to indicate that the command continues on the next line. Notice also that instead of the plain equal sign (=), this command uses a colon and an equal sign (:=) to separate the attribute from its value. Why? That's just the way the syntax works. The only way to know this is to take a course in VBA or study a lot of macro codes that you've recorded.

The final line of the macro is similar to the earlier examples except it sets a paragraph-level attribute rather than font-level.

PERFORMING THE SAME ACTION IN DIFFERENT WAYS

Now let's look at another pair of macros. Both of the macros in Figure 33.13 do the same thing: They make selected text bold and italic. However, they go about it in very different ways, and in certain circumstances could provide different results.

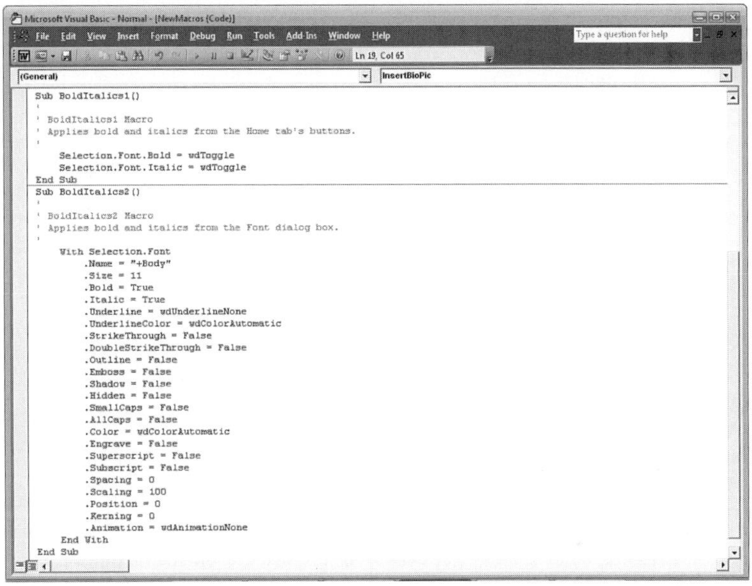

Figure 33.13
These two macros both make text bold and italic.

The first macro in Figure 33.13, BoldItalics1, toggles the Bold and Italic buttons on the Home tab with these lines:

```
Sub BoldItalics1()
' BoldItalics1 Macro
' Applies bold and italics from the Home tab's buttons.
'
    Selection.Font.Bold = wdToggle
    Selection.Font.Italic = wdToggle
End Sub
```

It appears to make the text bold and italic, but wait—does it really? Nope, it toggles the state of those features. Furthermore, it does not check their current states. If the text you selected before running the macro were already bold and italic, it would *remove* those attributes.

The second macro in Figure 33.13, BoldItalics2, creates a snapshot of the text's complete character-level formatting status. When I recorded this macro, I simply opened the Font dialog box, clicked Bold Italic, and clicked OK. I did not touch any of these other options; yet they are included in the macro because the macro records everything that was in that dialog box.

```
Sub BoldItalics2()
'
' BoldItalics2 Macro
' Applies bold and italics from the Font dialog box.
'
    With Selection.Font
        .Name = "+Body"
        .Size = 11
```

33

```
            .Bold = True
            .Italic = True
            .Underline = wdUnderlineNone
            .UnderlineColor = wdColorAutomatic
            .StrikeThrough = False
            .DoubleStrikeThrough = False
            .Outline = False
            .Emboss = False
            .Shadow = False
            .Hidden = False
            .SmallCaps = False
            .AllCaps = False
            .Color = wdColorAutomatic
            .Engrave = False
            .Superscript = False
            .Subscript = False
            .Spacing = 0
            .Scaling = 100
            .Position = 0
            .Kerning = 0
            .Animation = wdAnimationNone
        End With
End Sub
```

Obviously, BoldItalics2 is the less efficient macro in terms of the number of lines of code needed, but since macros execute nearly instantaneously, it's not a big deal. Furthermore, BoldItalics2 is actually a better macro if what I really want is for bold and italic to be turned *on* by the macro in all cases, even if either one is already on. BoldItalics2 also has the side effect of removing any other formatting from the text that happened to be applied already. For example, if the selected text had been set to AllCaps, that would be removed by running BoldItalics2.

Notice in the BoldItalics2 code that a new element is being used you have not seen yet: a `With` statement. It defines `Selection.Font` as a parent category, and then everything under that within the `With` statement inherits that prefix. So, for example, `.Italic = True` is really `Selection.Font.Italic = True`.

If you wanted to make sure that bold and italics were turned on by the macro—not toggled— but you did not want to specify formatting for those other settings, you could simply delete the unwanted lines of code, ending up with something more efficient but still effective, like this:

```
Sub BoldItalics2()
'
' BoldItalics2 Macro
' Applies bold and italics from the Font dialog box.
'
    With Selection.Font
        .Bold = True
        .Italic = True
    End With
End Sub
```

PERFORMING ACTIONS INVOLVING LOGICAL CONDITIONS

Some commands involve evaluating the document to see if a certain condition exists, and then acting accordingly. The Replace command is an excellent example of that. In the following code, the Replace dialog box is being used to replace all instances of "Sample" with "Example":

```
Sub FindReplace()
'
' FindReplace Macro
'
'
    Selection.Find.ClearFormatting
    Selection.Find.Replacement.ClearFormatting
    With Selection.Find
        .Text = "Sample"
        .Replacement.Text = "Example"
        .Forward = True
        .Wrap = wdFindContinue
        .Format = False
        .MatchCase = False
        .MatchWholeWord = False
        .MatchWildcards = False
        .MatchSoundsLike = False
        .MatchAllWordForms = False
    End With
    Selection.Find.Execute
    With Selection
        If .Find.Forward = True Then
            .Collapse Direction:=wdCollapseStart
        Else
            .Collapse Direction:=wdCollapseEnd
        End If
        .Find.Execute Replace:=wdReplaceOne
        If .Find.Forward = True Then
            .Collapse Direction:=wdCollapseEnd
        Else
            .Collapse Direction:=wdCollapseStart
        End If
        .Find.Execute
    End With
End Sub
```

Let's break this down a bit. First, there are two actions for clearing any existing formatting applied in the Find and Replace dialog box:

```
Selection.Find.ClearFormatting
Selection.Find.Replacement.ClearFormatting
```

Next, there's a With statement, just like before, but this time specifying the settings in the Replace dialog box:

```
With Selection.Find
    .Text = "Sample"
    .Replacement.Text = "Example"
    .Forward = True
    .Wrap = wdFindContinue
    .Format = False
    .MatchCase = False
    .MatchWholeWord = False
    .MatchWildcards = False
    .MatchSoundsLike = False
    .MatchAllWordForms = False
End With
```

33

Next, the actual operation is executed. Notice that it is acting only upon the selection at this point:

```
Selection.Find.Execute
```

Then there's something you haven't seen yet: a couple of If statements that determine what happens based on whether or not the searched-for text is found.

```
With Selection
    If .Find.Forward = True Then
        .Collapse Direction:=wdCollapseStart
    Else
        .Collapse Direction:=wdCollapseEnd
    End If
    .Find.Execute Replace:=wdReplaceOne
    If .Find.Forward = True Then
        .Collapse Direction:=wdCollapseEnd
    Else
        .Collapse Direction:=wdCollapseStart
    End If
    .Find.Execute
End With
```

Finally, it ends up with another Execute statement, this time in general (not just on Selection):

```
.Find.Execute
```

Of course, these examples have just scratched the surface of what you need to know to effectively write your own VBA code, or even to edit code with confidence. But they give you an idea of how to proceed as you learn more on your own.

WORKING WITH MACRO SECURITY

Back a few versions ago in Microsoft Office, macro viruses were prevalent. Some people figured out how to write executable virus code that could be stored in a macro; then whenever that macro was run as a document opened, the macro would copy itself into the person's Normal.dot template, and from there would replicate itself to all new documents. (There was a variant in Excel too.)

To counteract this, Microsoft developed macro security measures. They check a macro's source, author, and/or location and determine whether or not it is safe to run.

In the following sections, you'll learn how macro security works and how you can configure it to match your level of paranoia (er, *comfort with risk*).

NOTE

> Realistically, your chances of getting a macro virus these days are very low. Because Word has included macro virus security for several versions now, people who create viruses have lost interest in making them. The last time I actually saw a Word macro virus in a file was about 10 years ago. Better safe than sorry, though.

UNDERSTANDING TRUSTED PUBLISHERS AND LOCATIONS

At first the security was very simple: You could choose a level of security that applied to all macros in all files. But in Word 2007, macro security has become very sophisticated, enabling you to distinguish between different locations and different macro publishers.

Word's macro security clamps down on running most macros in a document or template. (See "Setting Security Levels for Macro Running" later in this chapter for details.) However, it relaxes its security when one of two conditions exist:

- The file containing the macro is stored in a trusted location.
- The macro has a digital signature from a trusted source.

A *trusted location* is one that Word recognizes as being your "home turf." When you place a file in a trusted location, you tell Word that it's okay to run whatever it finds in that file. This makes things much easier for amateur macro-writers who want to store their own macros in their own private templates, for example, and it makes it possible to run macros in files that friends and colleagues provide to you without having to go through the hassle of setting up digital signatures.

➔ To set up trusted locations, **see** "Specifying Trusted Locations," **p. 816**.

A *digital signature* is a code stored with the macro that compares itself to a code stored by an online or network signature authority to determine that it is really from the author it purports to be from and that it has not been modified since that author published it. Digital signatures are somewhat complex to set up, but worthwhile if you are planning to distribute your macros to a wide audience, such as from a public website.

➔ To set up digital signatures, **see** "Adding a Digital Signature," **p. 821**.

N O T E

> Both trusted locations and digital signatures are Office-wide features; they are not just for Word macros.

33

DETERMINING WHAT LOCATIONS ARE TRUSTED

Chapter 28, "Protecting and Securing Documents," deals with trusted locations in detail, but perhaps you're just curious at this point about what locations are already set up to be trusted on your system, so you can store your macro-enabled files there.

To find the trusted location list, follow these steps:

1. Choose Office, Word Options and click Trust Center.
2. Click the Trust Center Settings button.
3. Click Trusted Locations. A list of locations appears in the Path column.
4. Click OK to close the dialog box.

SETTING SECURITY LEVELS FOR MACRO RUNNING

There are two ways to access the macro security settings in Word:

■ On the Developer tab, click Macro Security.

■ Choose Office, Word Options, click Trust Center, click Trust Center Settings, and click Macro Settings.

The Macro Settings, shown in Figure 33.14, enable you to choose what happens when a file that is not in a trusted location contains macros. You can choose to enable or disable all, or you can differentiate between signed and unsigned ones.

Figure 33.14
Control how macros run (or don't run) when in files in untrusted locations.

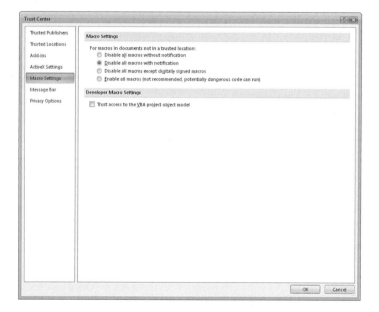

It's up to you what settings you want to use, but personally I leave this set to Disable All Macros with Notification most of the time. That way I can see when a macro is trying to run and I can then check it out and see if it's something I want.

If you regularly run signed macros, you might choose instead Disable All Macros Except Digitally Signed Macros. Neither of the other two settings—Disable All Macros Without Notification and Enable All Macros—are optimal since each is extreme in its own direction.

WORKING WITH ADD-INS

Add-ins are extra features that you can install for Word that extend its capabilities in some way. You can add, remove, or temporarily enable/disable the various add-ins in Word to control how it behaves.

Some of the add-in types you have already worked with in this book. For example, Smart Tags (Chapter 4), templates (Chapter 10), and XML schema (Chapter 32) are all add-ins.

NOTE

In Word 2007, you cannot save custom toolbars to a document or template, but you could in earlier versions. If you load a template containing custom toolbars, the toolbar buttons appear on an Add-Ins tab. One way to get a custom toolbar in Word 2007 is to develop it in Word 2003 and then move it over to Word 2007; another way is to use RibbonX, described in Chapter 35, "Using RibbonX."

One of the most powerful types of add-ins is a Component Object Model (COM) add-in. COM add-ins are supplemental programs that extend Word's capabilities by adding custom commands or features. COM add-ins can come from Microsoft or from third-party sources. They usually have a .dll or .exe extension and are written in a programming language such as Visual Basic or C++.

CAUTION

Many of the COM add-ins you'll find available for download on the Internet are written for earlier versions of Word, so their functionality in Word 2007 is uncertain.

If you find that a certain add-in crashes Word, see "Word Crashes After Enabling an Add-In" in the "Troubleshooting" section at the end of this chapter.

To view installed add-ins, follow these steps:

1. Choose Office, Word Options.

2. Click Add-Ins. A list of installed add-ins appears (see Figure 33.15).

Figure 33.15
See a list of installed add-ins here.

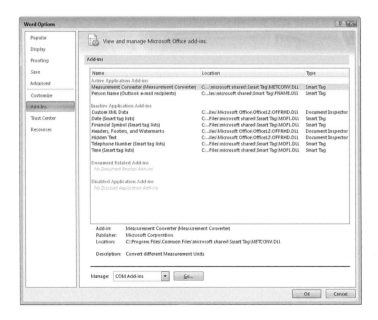

33

An installed add-in can be either enabled or disabled. Having the option of disabling an add-in rather than removing it entirely is handy because it allows you to turn one off temporarily without losing it. Disabling add-ins is also helpful for troubleshooting. If you are not sure what add-in is causing Word to crash, you can disable them all and then enable them one at a time until you find the problem.

To disable or remove an add-in, you need to know what type it is, because the steps are different for the various types. To determine a type, look in the Type column. In Figure 33.15, there are two types shown: Smart Tag and Document Inspector.

Based on the type, open the Manage drop-down list at the bottom of the dialog box and select the desired add-in type. Then click Go to open a dialog box interface specifically for that type of add-in.

ENABLING/DISABLING COM ADD-INS

Choose COM Add-Ins in the Manage drop-down list and click Go to display the COM Add-Ins dialog box. It lists the available COM add-ins; you can select one and click Remove, or you can change its load behavior. You can also click Add to add more COM add-ins, although most COM add-ins come with their own setup programs that do that part for you.

ENABLING/DISABLING SMART TAGS

Choose Smart Tags in the Manage drop-down list and click Go to display the AutoCorrect dialog box with the Smart Tags controls, just like in "Working with Smart Tags" in Chapter 4, "Using Spelling, Grammar, and Research Tools."

ENABLING/DISABLING OTHER ADD-INS

The four remaining types of add-ins are all controlled from the same dialog box. If you choose any of them and click Go, the Templates and Add-Ins dialog box opens. The dialog box contains separate tabs for each of the add-in types; add, remove, or enable/disable each type from its tab. Each of these is covered in more detail elsewhere in the book:

- **Templates**—See Chapter 10, "Using and Creating Project Templates."
- **Linked CSS**—See Chapter 31, "Developing Web Content."
- **XML schema and XML expansion packs**—See Chapter 32, "Preparing XML Content."

TROUBLESHOOTING

I RECORDED A MACRO BUT NOW IT'S NOT THERE

When you record a macro and save it in Normal.dotm, it is not actually saved there until you save Normal.dotm. So then if you start a new document, that macro might not be available until Normal.dotm has been saved. The easiest way to save it is to exit and reopen Word.

If that doesn't help, you probably saved the macro to the individual document rather than to the template. See "Copying Macros Between Documents" earlier in this chapter to learn how to move it over to Normal.dotm.

I MADE A MISTAKE WHILE RECORDING A COMPLEX MACRO

If you are in a dialog box and have made a mistake while the recorder is on, click the Cancel button of the dialog box or press Esc to close the dialog box. None of your selections in the dialog box will be recorded. If you have already completed the command or closed the dialog box, then choose Edit, Undo, and the last command will be removed from the macro.

If too many commands have been chosen, edit the macro when you are finished recording it. Remember which command you want removed. The macro statement you want to remove will have a similar name.

WORD CRASHES AFTER ENABLING AN ADD-IN

After a Word crash due to an add-in, Word will probably offer to start itself in Safe Mode the next time you start it. If it does not, hold down the Ctrl key as you click the icon or menu command to start Word to initiate Safe Mode. Then go to the list of add-ins (Office, Word Options) and remove the one causing the problem. See "Working with Add-Ins" earlier in this chapter.

You should not use Word in Safe Mode for normal document editing because the following limitations are in effect:

- Add-ins are not loaded.
- No customizations are loaded or saved.
- Preferences cannot be saved.
- You cannot save templates.
- The AutoCorrect list is not loaded and changes to it are not saved.
- Recovered documents are not automatically opened.
- Smart Tags are not loaded and new tags cannot be saved.
- Files cannot be saved to the Alternate Startup Directory.
- Documents with restricted permission cannot be created or opened.

CHAPTER 34

CUSTOMIZING THE WORD INTERFACE

In this chapter

CUSTOMIZATION: CHECK YOUR EXPECTATIONS

If you're a big fan of tweaking the interface, you're going to be a little disappointed at first with Word 2007. The Ribbon, and its many tabs, is not easily user-customizable.

NOTE

> In the next chapter, you will learn about RibbonX, which enables users to create customized tabs, but it's not straightforward and easy like it was in earlier versions of Word; you need to know something about XML to use it, and you need to be able to hack the data files or templates to implement your custom code. Chapter 35, "Using RibbonX," includes information about a utility by Patrick Schmid that makes ribbon customization a bit easier by automating the RibbonX process in a GUI environment.

What you *can* do with Word is add and remove buttons from the Quick Access toolbar and position the Quick Access toolbar either above or below the Ribbon. You can also assign shortcut keys and change various settings, from file locations to copy-and-paste options. In this chapter, you will learn about the various ways that you can customize Word.

CUSTOMIZING THE QUICK ACCESS TOOLBAR

The Quick Access toolbar is the row of buttons near the Office button in the top-left corner of the Word window. You can change its position (either above or below the Ribbon), add buttons to and remove buttons from it, as well as rearrange its buttons.

REPOSITION THE QUICK ACCESS TOOLBAR

Depending on how it's set up, the Quick Access toolbar is either at the very top (in the title bar) or below the Ribbon. In the title bar it's perhaps more easily accessible, but below the Ribbon there is more room for it, so you can have more buttons on it without interfering with the document name in the title bar.

To reposition the Quick Access toolbar, click the down arrow at its right end and choose Place Quick Access Toolbar Below the Ribbon (or Above the Ribbon, depending on its current position).

ADD BUTTONS THAT ALREADY EXIST ON THE RIBBON

Any button or control on any tab or menu can be easily added to the Quick Access toolbar via its right-click menu. Simply right-click it and choose Add to Quick Access Toolbar.

ADD BUTTONS NOT ON THE RIBBON ALREADY

Word is such a feature-rich program that not all its features are made available by default. Some of these are less common features that there was simply no room for on the Ribbon; others are features that pertain only to certain specialty types of documents, or are carry-overs from earlier versions of Word.

To browse the commands not already on the Ribbon, and potentially add some of them to the Quick Access toolbar, follow these steps:

1. Choose Office, Word Options.
2. Click Customize.
3. Open the Choose Commands From list and select Commands Not on Ribbon (see Figure 34.1).
4. Click a command and click Add>> to move it to the Quick Access toolbar.
5. Add more commands if desired.
6. Click OK.

Figure 34.1
Add buttons to the Quick Access toolbar that have no Ribbon equivalent from here.

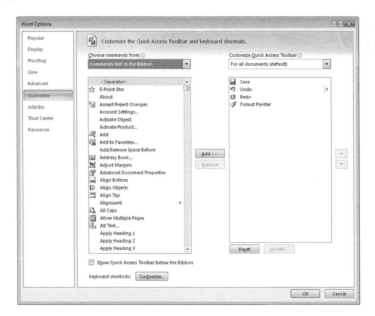

REMOVE BUTTONS

You can remove a button from the Customization options from the preceding section by clicking the command and clicking Remove (refer to Figure 34.1), but there's an easier way. You can simply right-click any button on the Quick Access toolbar and choose Remove from Quick Access Toolbar.

DEFINING SHORTCUT KEYS

Word has many shortcut keys predefined, such as Ctrl+C for Copy, Ctrl+S for Save, and so on. You can add to these assignments, and even change the assignments for key combinations. That way if any of the shortcuts are awkward for you to use, you can use keys that feel more natural for your most-used activities.

To define shortcut keys, follow these steps:

1. Choose Office, Word Options.
2. Click Customize.
3. Next to Keyboard Shortcuts, click Customize. The Customize Keyboard dialog box opens.
4. Select the command to which to assign the shortcut. Do this by first choosing a category at the left and then a command on the right (see Figure 34.2).
5. Look in the Current Keys box to see if there is a current key assignment for the command. That assignment will be removed if you do a new assignment.
6. Click in the Press New Shortcut Key box and then press the key combination to assign.
7. By default, the assignments will be stored in Normal.dotm. If you want them assigned somewhere else (such as in the current document only), select it from the Save Changes In list.
8. Repeat steps 4–6 for other keyboard shortcuts.
9. Click Close.
10. Click OK.

Figure 34.2
Define shortcut keys.

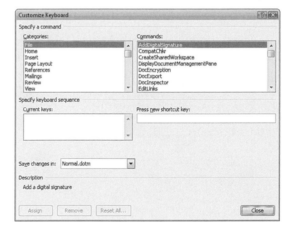

CHANGING VIEWING OPTIONS

There are lots of ways you can change how the Word window appears and how documents appear within it. These can be broken down into the following broad categories:

- **View settings**—These basic settings can be adjusted from the View tab at any time. These were covered in Chapter 1, "Introducing Word 2007," in the section titled "Working with Views."

- **Status bar content**—You can control what appears in the status bar, such as indicators for word count, page count, and macro controls.

- **Word Options settings**—You can use the Word Options dialog box to configure various settings that aren't available elsewhere.

CHANGING THE STATUS BAR CONTENT

The status bar is the bar at the bottom of the Word window, below the horizontal scroll bar. The status bar, by default, contains only a few pieces of information, such as the page count and word count, some view buttons, and a zoom slider. You can customize it by following these steps:

1. Right-click the status bar. A menu opens with check marks next to the displayed items.

2. Click an item to toggle it on or off (see Figure 34.3).

Figure 34.3
Choose what should appear on the status bar.

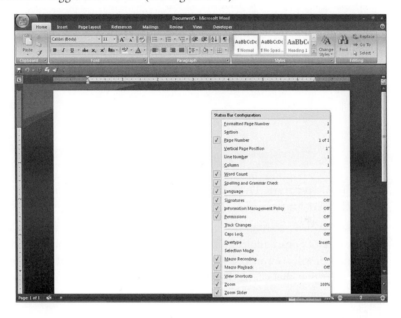

CHANGING PAGE DISPLAY AND FORMATTING MARKS

You can change page display and formatting marks settings from the Display options of the Word Options. Follow these steps:

1. Choose Office, Word Options. The Word Options dialog box opens.

2. Click Display.

3. In the Page Display Options section, mark or clear these check boxes (see Figure 34.4):

- **Show White Space Between Pages in Print Layout View**—If this is enabled, the pages will appear to be separated vertically; if disabled, they will run together like continuous-feed paper.

- **Show Highlighter Marks**—When this is enabled, highlighting appears both onscreen and when printed. You can disable it to hide highlighting temporarily without having to remove the highlighting.

- **Show Document ToolTips on Hover**—When this is enabled, ToolTips (pop-up messages) appear whenever you point the mouse at something that has a tip associated with it, such as a button on the Ribbon.

34

Figure 34.4
Set page display and formatting mark display options.

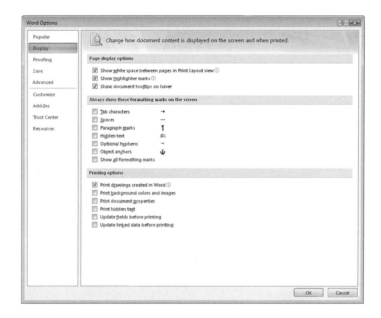

4. In the Always Show These Formatting Marks on the Screen section, mark or clear the check boxes for the various types of formatting marks.

   Note that these settings do not depend on the Show/Hide ¶ button's state (on the Home tab). For example, if you mark the check box here for Tab Characters, then tab characters will always be displayed, regardless of the Show/Hide ¶ button. However, if you clear that check box, then tab characters will be shown or hidden according to the button's status.

5. Click OK.

You can find additional display options under Advanced. Click Advanced and then scroll down to the Display section.

SETTING POPULAR OPTIONS

In the Popular section of the Word Options dialog box are two sections: Top Options for Working with Word, and Personalize Your Copy of Office (see Figure 34.5).

The Top Options for Working with Word is a compilation of miscellaneous popular settings with no special theme to them:

■ **Show Mini Toolbar on Selection**—When this is enabled, and you point at some text, the mini toolbar pops up for quick access to formatting buttons (see Figure 34.6).

Figure 34.5
Set personalization options.

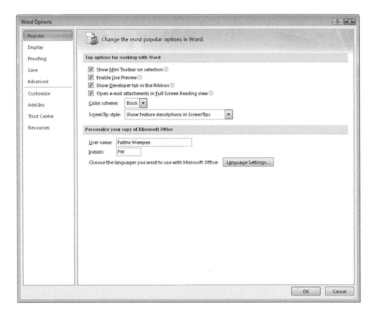

Figure 34.6
The mini toolbar, when enabled, appears when you point at text.

- **Enable Live Preview**—When this option is enabled, and you point to a setting on a gallery or menu from the Ribbon, a preview of that effect shows on the selected text.

- **Show Developer Tab in the Ribbon**—This toggles the Developer tab, which contains buttons useful for writing macros, creating forms, and working with XML content.

→ To learn about macros, **see** "Understanding Macros," **p. 906**.
→ To create forms, **see** Chapter 21, "Creating Forms," **p. 655**.
→ To work with XML content in Word, **see** "Using Word 2007 to Create XML Files," **p. 886**.

- **Open E-mail Attachments in Full Screen Reading View**—When this is enabled and you open a Word document from your email program (Outlook, Windows Mail, or other program), and the document opens in Word, the document opens in Full Screen Reading view. Otherwise, it opens in Print Layout view.

- **Color Scheme**—Here you can choose a color scheme for Office programs. This setting applies across all Office programs, not just Word. For example, the color scheme used for the figures in this book is the Windows Vista (Gray) scheme.

34

- **ScreenTip Scheme**—From this drop-down list, you can choose to show no ScreenTips, regular ScreenTips (small amount of information, small pop-ups), or enhanced ScreenTips (full information). Figure 34.7 shows the difference between a regular and an enhanced ScreenTip.

Figure 34.7
A regular (left) and enhanced (right) ScreenTip.

NOTE

Even though the scheme name has an operating system name in its title, it is not tied to the actual color scheme chosen in the OS.

CHANGING FILE LOCATIONS

Word has a variety of locations set up for saving different types of files, including documents, templates, AutoRecover files, saved themes, and so on. You can configure these file locations in the Word Options dialog box, but different types of files are set up in different places.

To set the default AutoRecover file location and the default location for saving regular Word files, follow these steps:

1. Choose Office, Word Options. The Word Options dialog box opens.
2. Click Save.
3. In the AutoRecover File Location box, type a path to the location where you want AutoRecover files stored (see Figure 34.8). Alternatively, you can click the Browse button and browse for a location.

Figure 34.8
Set the locations for Word documents and AutoRecover files here.

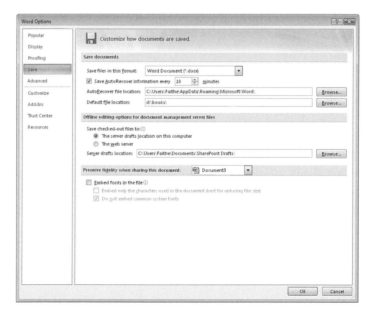

NOTE

> AutoRecover files are created automatically at the interval specified in the Save AutoRecover Information Every box. If Word crashes or terminates abnormally, the AutoRecover files are loaded so you can recover part of your unsaved work.

4. In the Default File Location box, type a path to the location you want to appear by default in the Save As and Open dialog boxes when saving or opening Word documents. Alternatively, you can click the Browse button and browse for a location.

5. (Optional) If you work with SharePoint server drafts, and you would like to set a location for those drafts on your local hard disk, enter or change it in the Server Drafts Location on This Computer box. Alternatively, you can click the Browse button and browse for a location.

6. Click OK to close the Word Options dialog box

   Alternatively, if you need to set the default locations for other types of files, continue the steps as follows:

7. Click Advanced, and then scroll down to the bottom of the window and click File Locations. The File Locations dialog box opens (see Figure 34.9).

Figure 34.9
Set locations for other file types here.

8. Click a file type and then click Modify.

9. Browse to the desired location and then click OK.

10. Repeat steps 7–8 for each location you want to change; then click OK.

11. Click OK to close the Word Options dialog box.

OTHER CUSTOMIZATION OPTIONS

Throughout this book, I've introduced you to bits and pieces of customization as it was applicable to various features in Word. Here's a list of where these are covered:

- "Setting File-Handling Preferences," **p. 54**
- "Customizing Spelling and Grammar Options," **p. 100**
- "Customizing and Extending the Research Tools," **p. 129**
- "Setting Print Options for Word Documents," **p. 137**
- "Setting Options for a Certain Printer," **p. 140**
- "Storing Different Properties for a Single Printer," **p. 141**
- "Customizing the Styles Pane," **p. 235**
- "Understanding and Configuring Collaboration Tools," **p. 784**
- "Adjusting Macro Settings," **p. 818**
- "Setting Privacy Options," **p. 820**
- "Specifying Trusted Locations," **p. 816**
- "Working with Trusted Publishers," **p. 818**
- "Options for Web Page Saving," **p. 863**
- "Setting Security Levels for Macro Running," **p. 930**

TROUBLESHOOTING

A BUTTON HAS DISAPPEARED FROM A TAB

When you resize the Word window so that it is narrower, sometimes groups collapse so that there is a single button representing the group. Click that button for a drop-down menu of the full set of buttons for the group. This is expected behavior. The button has not really disappeared.

HOW CAN I CLEAR THE RECENTLY USED FILE LIST ON THE OFFICE BUTTON MENU?

Choose Tools, Word Options and then click Advanced. In the Display section, set the Number of Documents in the Recent Documents List setting to zero.

CHAPTER 35

CUSTOMIZING WORD 2007'S RIBBON WITH RIBBONX

A New Way of Customizing Word

Word 2007 is full of new features, the most obvious one being the new Ribbon User Interface (UI). This new UI also comes with a new way of customization. In contrast to previous versions, though, the only thing that can be customized easily by a user is the Quick Access toolbar (QAT). Custom toolbars and menus, templates with a customized UI, and corporate-branded copies of Word are no longer a few mouse clicks away in version 2007. Instead, you need to resort to third-party tools or learn the XML-based *RibbonX* language. Because of this drastic change from previous Word versions, UI customization without third-party tools has become the realm of more advanced users.

This chapter describes in detail the use of RibbonX in customizing Word 2007's ribbon-based user interface. For a way around RibbonX, please see the section "Customizing Word 2007 Without RibbonX" at the end of this chapter.

→ For more on the QAT, **see** "Customize the Quick Access Toolbar," **p. 936**.

According to Microsoft's Office 2003 usage data, few users took advantage of the easy customizability of Word 2003. In fact, only a small percentage of all Office 2003 users ever customized their UI and the vast majority of those never changed more than three buttons. The Office 2007 team therefore created a static Ribbon UI that has the QAT to support the majority of customization needs. Nonetheless, some users still have the desire to customize this new UI. Users might disagree with the logic of how commands are distributed across the different Ribbon tabs. For example, users might consider header, footer and page numbering to be a page layout issue instead of an insertion issue. Users might want a unique corporate UI that hides features that should not be used according to corporate policies and highlights features that are frequently used within the particular company. Lastly, users might want to have a customized UI for a particular Word template or document.

All of these scenarios require the use of RibbonX, either directly or indirectly via third-party tools. You use RibbonX to tell Word what the UI should look like. In other words, you provide a description of the user interface changes to Word in RibbonX. Important to note is that you only describe the changes in RibbonX. For example, if you wanted to remove the Styles group from the Home tab, you would only describe that particular change in RibbonX to Word. In contrast, you would not describe to Word how the entire Home tab should look without the Styles group. Word loads your RibbonX description of the changes. If the description is error free, Word then applies the changes you specified to the Ribbon.

Loading the RibbonX changes into Word might be the most difficult step in customizing the new UI. RibbonX can either be loaded via a COM add-in or via a document or template. Developing COM add-ins is outside the scope of this book. You should consult a Word/Office programming book if you are interested in developing COM add-ins. Third-party tools for customizing Word 2007 generally are COM add-ins. The focus of this chapter is loading RibbonX via a document or template. Before discussing the loading of RibbonX however, let me first introduce RibbonX itself to you.

RIBBONX

RibbonX is an XML-based language defined by Microsoft for customizing the Word 2007 Ribbon User Interface. The first section gives a quick introduction to XML, which can be skipped by readers who have used it before. Following that, I introduce RibbonX itself. The last two sections deal with the tricky issue of loading RibbonX into Word 2007. I suggest that you read through the manual procedure to understand what is happening, but that you always use the Custom UI Editor introduced in the final section.

A QUICK INTRODUCTION TO XML

XML is the eXtensible Markup Language. XML is related to HTML, the HyperText Markup Language, which is the language used for websites. Both languages are under the auspices of the World Wide Web Consortium. A markup language augments a plain-text file with markups, which are nothing more than predefined text chunks. For a comparison of XML and HTML, see the "XML vs. HTML" sidebar. As the name implies, XML is extensible. This means that it is up to us to specify the markups for a particular scenario. The following line is a simple XML example:

```
<name>Bill Gates</name>
```

This line of XML shows one XML *element*. The element declares the data "Bill Gates" to be a name. It also shows the basic XML *syntax*. Syntax is the computer equivalent of the grammar of a language. For example, English grammar requires that each sentence end with a punctuation mark, that words are separated by spaces, and that a sentence should observe the subject/predicate/object order. XML syntax requires that all markup elements are opened by a less-than symbol (<) and closed by a greater-than symbol (>). Any text in an XML document enclosed between those two symbols is called a *tag*. XML differentiates between *opening* and *closing tags*. In our example, <name> is an opening tag that is closed by </name>. A slash followed by the name specified in the opening tag represents a closing tag.

XML vs. HTML

In HTML, the markups specify how the contents of the file should be presented. For example, you can specify with HTML whether text should be bold, italic, or underlined. A web browser then reads the HTML file and interprets the elements. It renders the website according to these elements.

In contrast to HTML's presentation focus, XML is focused on data. Or in other words, HTML is focused on how to display something whereas XML is focused on what something is. The difference between the two approaches is dramatic. In HTML, we describe that a particular piece of text should be bold, because we know (in our head only) that this text is the name of a person. In XML, we describe that this particular piece of text is the name of a person. Outside of our XML file, we then have a rule that says all names should be displayed in bold. With HTML, we need to make sure that we specify bold for every name. With XML, all we need to do is mark a name as such and the computer will handle the actual presentation of it.

In HTML, for example, you specify Bill Gates, which renders the words "Bill Gates" in bold. In XML, however, you could say <name>Bill Gates</name>, which would declare "Bill Gates" to be a name and present it according to a predefined rule for the presentation of names.

This data focus has made XML very popular. For example, most large shopping websites (for example, Amazon) are nowadays XML-driven. More importantly, the new file formats in Office 2007 are in the XML-based language OpenXML.

35

HTML has a limited set of predefined markups. XML, on the other hand, does not have any predefined one. It is extensible, as it leaves it up to us to define which type of elements are needed for a particular situation. This made it possible for the W3C to redefine HTML in XML. This resulted in the successor of HTML, called XHTML.

XML's syntax is strict about closing and opening tags. Any tag that was opened must be closed again. Most importantly, tags need to be closed in the reverse order in which they were opened. In the following example, `person` was opened first and hence has to be closed last. We also cannot interchange `</name>` and `</employer>`, as this would break the orders of how tags are *nested* in this example. It also shows that in XML there needs to be one *root* element that encompasses all other elements. In our case, `person` is the root element. Elements directly under another element are the *children* of the second one. In the following example, `name`, `employer`, and `rich` are children of `person`. The last new thing in this example is the `<rich/>` tag, where `/>` is a shorthand notation for `<rich></rich>` and can be used whenever there is nothing between the two tags.

```
<person>
    <name>Bill Gates</name>
    <employer>Microsoft</employer>
    <rich/>
</person>
```

Spacing and new lines between elements do not matter in XML. Therefore, the preceding XML example is identical in meaning, but different in what it looks like from the following example. Generally, properly indented and stacked XML is easier to read, understand, and write. If you are using a specialized XML editor, you probably have a feature that allows you to "pretty-print," meaning properly indent and stack, any XML. I will use pretty-printed XML for all RibbonX examples in this chapter.

```
<person><name>Bill Gates</name><employer>Microsoft</employer><rich/></person>
```

An element can be augmented by *attributes*. Attributes specify additional information for an element. In the previous two examples, information was represented as data enclosed by tags. In some cases, though, all information is encoded in attributes and there is no such data. RibbonX is such a case. To illustrate the difference, the following example provides the same data as the previous one, but only uses attributes. As you can see, an attribute consists of the attribute name (for example, `"name"`), followed by an equal sign and the value in quotes. Because there is no data within the `person` tags, I used the shorthand notation introduced previously for the `rich` tag. Please note that the names of XML elements and attributes—in the following example, person, name, employer, and wealth—are case-sensitive. For example, `name="Bill Gates"` is not the same as `Name="Bill Gates"`.

```
<person name="Bill Gates" employer="Microsoft" wealth="rich" />
```

If everybody just came up with the elements and attributes they liked the best and used them, as I did with my examples, XML would not be very useful as a means of exchanging data. For example, someone might decide that instead of calling the attribute `wealth`, she would call it `richness`. That means, though, that she cannot use the XML I created to describe a person—and I cannot use hers. In order to avoid this problem, we need to agree, ahead of time, on a set of rules that specify which elements with which attributes in what nesting order can be used. Such a set of rules is called an *XML Schema*, which is itself defined in a standardized XML format. An XML document that uses correct XML syntax is called *well-formed*. An XML document that is well-formed and conforms to an XML Schema is called *valid*. RibbonX is an XML Schema defined by Microsoft. When Word loads RibbonX, it checks it against the RibbonX Schema and only loads it if it is valid.

INTRODUCTION TO RIBBONX

Figure 35.1 shows the basic components of the new UI. The individual components are labeled with their RibbonX element names. The Ribbon consists of the officeMenu, the qat, and the tabs. An individual tab, in turn, has several groups.

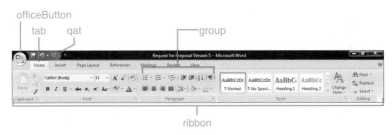

Figure 35.1
Basic components of the Ribbon UI.

This leads us to the first example of RibbonX code:

```
<customUI xmlns="http://schemas.microsoft.com/office/2006/01/customui">
    <ribbon>
        <tabs>
            <tab idMso="TabHome">
                <group idMso="GroupStyles" visible="false" />
            </tab>
        </tabs>
    </ribbon>
</customUI>
```

- In this example, you can see that the XML elements visible in Figure 35.1 are nested inside a customUI element that is not visible in the screen snapshot. This element serves as the root element for all RibbonX documents. Its attribute xmlns is a required attribute that specifies the XML Schema for this element, which in this case is a reference to the RibbonX XML Schema. All RibbonX files need to start with this tag, including the previously shown value for xmlns.

- The next two elements, ribbon and tabs, specify that this code deals with the tabs of the ribbon.

- The idMso attribute is used whenever a UI component (such as a tab, group, or control) built into Word by Microsoft is referenced. TabHome specifies the Home tab, whereas GroupStyles specifies the Styles group on the Home tab.

- The visible attribute for this group contains the only UI modification specified by the preceding RibbonX code. It hides the Styles group on the Home tab.

If you want to experiment with loading a RibbonX file manually into Word—something I suggest you avoid doing—you need to save your RibbonX code in a plain-text file with the

35

file extension .xml (for example, customUI.xml). You can use Notepad to create such a file. The preceding RibbonX example, similar to all the following ones, is also available on the book website as the file "customUI.xml".

LOADING YOUR RIBBONX CUSTOMIZATION INTO WORD

In order for Word to be able to load your RibbonX file, it needs to be embedded in a document or template in the new OpenXML file format. Documents in this file format use the extension ".docx" or ".docm," whereas templates use ".dotx" or ".dotm." Embedding a file in an OpenXML file is not a simple feat, and you should always use a tool—for example, the CustomUI Editor showcased in the next section—to do this. Doing this manually is a guaranteed way of inviting trouble, and I have not yet managed to get it right on the first attempt. The embedding process is identical for documents and templates, and also works the same way with Excel and PowerPoint 2007.

The book's website has a document called "customUI.docx" you can download that contains only the RibbonX shown and explained in the previous section. When loaded into Word, as you can see in Figure 35.2, it hides the Styles group as intended. I am going to use this particular file to illustrate how RibbonX is embedded in an OpenXML file.

Figure 35.2
The Ribbon after loading the customUI.docx file into Word.

As you learned in Chapter 2, "Creating and Saving Documents," a file in the new file format is a collection of XML and other files stored in a zip file, although with a different extension. You also learned how to change the extension to .zip and open the zip file. Using this procedure, I opened the customUI.docx file, the result of which you can see in Figure 35.3.

Figure 35.3
Folders of the unzipped OpenXML file.

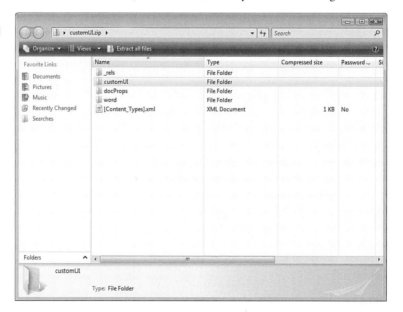

When Word opens any OpenXML file, it first takes a look into the _rels folder where it finds a file called `.rels`. This particular XML file specifies which of the other files in the OpenXML file contain the individual components of the file. For example, you can find the thumbnail of the document or the document itself referenced in the .rels file. The file containing the RibbonX example from the previous section is listed here, as you can see in the highlighted text in Figure 35.4. As you probably guessed from Figure 35.3, the "customUI.xml" file of the previous section is stored in the customUI folder.

Figure 35.4

The .rels file with the relationship to customUI.xml highlighted.

You might notice that the file is not pretty-printed. Word 2007 never pretty-prints this file, as pretty-printing introduces additional, unnecessary characters (normally line breaks, spaces, and tabs) that have to be read when opening an OpenXML file. Any additional character increases the load time for a document. Therefore for optimal load time, pretty-printing is not used. If you have opened the file in Notepad as I did, you might see the content only on one line. To have it look like it did in the preceding figure, you need to use Word Wrap from Notepad's Format menu. Now let's examine in more detail the lines I highlighted in Figure 35.4.

```
<Relationship
➥Type="http://schemas.microsoft.com/office/2006/relationships/ui/extensibility"
➥Target="/customUI/customUI.xml" Id="R73c090ee571e4cbf" />
```

The attribute `Type` specifies that this Relationship is for a RibbonX file. The `Target` attribute contains the correct path and filename of the RibbonX file. Notice that the value of the attribute starts with a "/" whereas none of the other Relationship elements have a similar slash. This particular slash is not needed, but the CustomUI Editor inserts it anyhow. The `Id` attribute specifies some unique ID for this Relationship. Any `Id` value can appear only once in a .rels file. As XML attribute names are case-sensitive, take note that `Id` is spelled with a capital *I*, which is different from the `id` attribute of RibbonX.

RibbonX files are not subject to the security settings in Word. This means that RibbonX will always be loaded no matter how restrictive the security settings are, as Microsoft does not consider RibbonX to have the possibility to cause any harm. Evidence of this is that you can embed RibbonX in non-macro documents and templates with the extensions "docx" and "dotx".

If you choose to embed a RibbonX file manually into an OpenXML document or template, you are probably going to need the following troubleshooting help.

 If you receive a message from Word that your Open XML file cannot be read due to problems with content, see "Modified OpenXML File Not Opening" in the "Troubleshooting" section at the end of this chapter.

 When you load a RibbonX file into Word, it can happen that you made an error in RibbonX. In order to see all such errors, follow the steps in "Catching RibbonX Errors" in the "Troubleshooting" section at the end of this chapter.

LOADING RIBBONX USING THE OFFICE 2007 CUSTOM UI EDITOR TOOL

Adding RibbonX manually is cumbersome and easily prone to errors. Microsoft recognized that and is providing a free editor to do this for you. This editor is called the Office 2007 Custom UI Editor Tool, which you can download via the author's website at http://pschmid.net/office2007/customize. After installing, launching the editor, and opening the "customUI.docx" sample, you see the screen shown in Figure 35.5.

Figure 35.5
The Custom UI Editor.

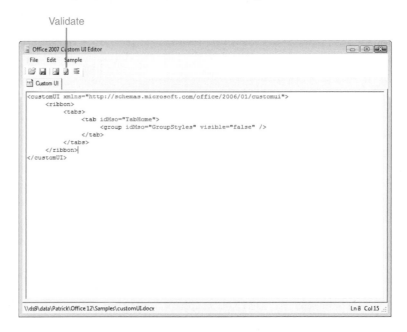

To use the CustomUI Editor, you need to create a document or template first and then open it in the editor. After that, the RibbonX code can just be entered into the editor window. It is inserted into the Open XML file when you save it. A very useful feature of the editor is the ability to validate a RibbonX document against the RibbonX XML Schema. This is an actual validation, even though the editor claims in the case of success that the document is only well-formed. I suggest that you use this editor all the time when working with documents and templates that contain RibbonX.

 When you load a RibbonX file into Word, it's possible that you might make an error in RibbonX. In order to see all such errors, follow the steps in "Catching RibbonX Errors" in the "Troubleshooting" section at the end of this chapter.

THE RIBBON UI STYLE GUIDE: DO'S AND DON'TS

RibbonX is a powerful language, and it allows you to change the Ribbon completely. However, not everything that can be done should be done. The Ribbon UI has a set of style principles that you should try to follow. Other users of your documents and templates with customized UIs will appreciate it, as it renders the behavior of your custom UIs in a predictable and familiar manner. Keep in mind that your UI modifications are specific to a document or template. Once a document or template is closed, those modifications are no longer applied to the Ribbon. In addition, a user might have multiple windows open with different documents/templates in them. In that case, the user will be faced with multiple different Ribbon UIs at the same time. The following discussion assumes that you will not be the only user of your documents/templates with customized UIs.

- Do not use RibbonX to create a Word 2003-like UI. It is tempting to do this to avoid training costs associated with Word 2007, but if you want a Word 2003-like UI, use Word 2003.

- RibbonX gives you the choice between modifying the Ribbon and creating your own Ribbon completely from scratch. Start from scratch only if absolutely necessary. Starting from scratch is a rather radical measure and only makes sense in a few cases.

- When you start from scratch, you can modify the Office button menu, the QAT, and all tabs. When you are only modifying the Ribbon, you cannot alter the QAT.

- The QAT belongs chiefly to the user. Word ships by default with only three items in the QAT, and the QAT can only hold up to 40. Place an item in the QAT only if it has to be absolutely available at all times, no matter what tab is active. In addition, I would suggest limiting the number of items that are preloaded into the QAT (including the Microsoft ones) to 15, so that all users can still add a significant number of controls.

- "Everything starts from the Ribbon." This was Microsoft's mantra for the new Ribbon UI. Microsoft did not follow it 100%, as you can see in the "Command not in Ribbon" list that exists in the QAT Customization dialog box. In addition, Undo and Redo are only on the QAT. When you are thinking about building your customized Ribbon, try to avoid providing a certain feature only on the QAT.

- The Office button menu is the place for the functionality that applies to a document as a whole, such as opening, saving, printing, encrypting, and so on.

- Functionality is grouped in tabs based on a logical scheme. For example, all features that deal with inserting things into a document can be found on the Insert tab. Try to respect this scheme as your users will be used to it.

- You can modify *core tabs* (the ones that are visible at all times) and *contextual tabs* (the ones that appear only when a certain object is selected). Some functionality might be best provided only in a contextual tab (for example, because it applies to a table).

- Only provide a feature in one place. For example, if you want to add the Address Book to the Ribbon, add it either to the Insert or the Mailings tab, but not both.

- The Home tab contains the 80% most-used commands. You should only add commands to it that are also used very frequently or are identical in nature to the ones on the Home tab.

- Do not waste space on tabs, as it is limited. As you can see by comparing Figure 35.1 and Figure 35.6 (shown later in this chapter), Microsoft groups collapse to a smaller size when your own group is added to an already full tab. The bigger your own group is, the more Microsoft groups collapse into single buttons. A group collapsed to a button means that a user now has to perform one additional click to use the commands of that group.

35

- Microsoft groups cannot be modified. That means you cannot remove or add buttons to a group that Microsoft created.

- It is tempting to replace Microsoft groups with your own groups augmented by a few buttons. You should do so sparingly as this might hide features from a user or cause conflicts with add-ins.

- You cannot change the order of Microsoft groups on the tabs where they were placed by default. That means, for example, that the Font group will always be after the Clipboard group on the Home tab. However, if you were to add the Font group to the Insert tab, you could freely decide where on that tab it should appear. You also cannot change the order of Microsoft tabs.

- You can use any Microsoft group, control, or tab in your own Ribbon. All you have to do is to specify in RibbonX where you want it to be. There are some limitations to this: You can use core tabs only as core tabs. That means a core tab cannot be used within a contextual tab set. In addition, a contextual tab cannot be used outside its original tab set. For example, the Chart Tools, Format tab can only be used as part of the Chart Tools. Last, the groups on the Add-Ins tab containing legacy add-in UI can only be on the Add-Ins tab or in the QAT.

- You can create your own groups. Controls cannot be directly added to tabs; they can only be added to groups. Hence, you need to create your own group if you want to add controls to any tab.

- You can create your own tabs. It only makes sense to create your own tab if you can fill it. A full tab has at least three groups and uses at least 70% of its area when viewed with a 1024×768 screen resolution.

- The first tab plays a special role in Word. It is the tab that Word opens with. It is also the tab Word returns to when a contextual tab is no longer in the foreground as the associated object was deselected. The first tab does not have to be the Home tab Word provides. Whatever tab you specify to appear in the tabs list before the Home tab will receive the special first tab treatment.

TIP

As explained in the beginning of this chapter, RibbonX can be provided by COM add-ins, documents, and templates. This means that multiple UI customizations might be applied at the same time. This raises the possibility that two different customizations alter the same UI element, but in a potentially contradictory way. For example, one customization might explicitly show the Styles group on the Home tab, whereas the other might hide it. In this sort of conflict, the last RibbonX customization to **load** wins. This can introduce a potentially problematic situation, as you cannot control what will load when on another user's computer, nor can you probably control what other Ribbon customizations are present. You should therefore always specify the absolute minimum RibbonX necessary to achieve your customization. The lesser RibbonX you provide, the lesser the chance for a conflict. Also note that if your RibbonX loads without any errors, but you do not see your customizations on the Ribbon, you should disable all COM add-ins and check that no other template or document is loading potentially conflicting customizations.

35

This section should have given you an idea of what you can do. The following two examples aim to give you a very concrete idea of what is possible with RibbonX. Once you have an idea of what you want to do, use the RibbonX Reference section to look up how to do it.

EXAMPLE: USEFUL OFFICE CONTROLS NOT IN THE RIBBON

When you scroll through the "Commands not in Ribbon" list of the QAT Customization dialog box, you might find some interesting controls there that you wished were on the Ribbon. For example, you might be interested in the Address Book control, which allows you to add a single address from Outlook to your current book.

Probably the most useful control in the Commands not in the Ribbon list is the "Styles" control. By default, Word 2007 does not have an equivalent to the Word 2003 control for picking styles. Instead, Word 2007 has the Quick Styles gallery in the Styles group. However it does not always tell you what the currently active style is. This is especially true if you are not using one of the default styles. In order to easily see which style is currently applied and to pick a different one, you have to use the Styles task pane, which takes up additional screen space. The Styles control solves this dilemma by providing the same way as Word 2003 for applying styles and determining the current one. This control would certainly be a good addition to the Home tab.

The following RibbonX code adds both controls to the Ribbon. You can find on the book's website a Word template called UsefulControls.dotx with this RibbonX code embedded.

```
<customUI xmlns="http://schemas.microsoft.com/office/2006/01/customui">
    <ribbon>
        <tabs>
            <tab idMso="TabHome">
                <group id="CustomStylesGroup"
➥label="Classic Styles" insertAfterMso="GroupStyles">
                    <labelControl id="emptyLabel1"/>
                    <labelControl id="emptyLabel2"/>
                    <comboBox idMso="StyleGalleryClassic"/>
                </group>
            </tab>
            <tab idMso="TabMailings">
                <group id="CustomAddressBookGroup"
➥label="Create/Insert" insertBeforeMso="GroupEnvelopeLabelCreate">
                    <button idMso="AddressBook"/>
                    <button idMso="EnvelopesAndLabelsDialog"/>
                    <button idMso="LabelsDialog"/>
                </group>
                <group idMso="GroupEnvelopeLabelCreate" visible="false"/>
            </tab>
        </tabs>
    </ribbon>
</customUI>
```

This RibbonX example introduces a few new attributes. The first one is id. Every group, tab, or control that you create needs an id attribute. The only requirement for the value of id is that it has to be unique in your RibbonX file. The label attribute specifies what label

35

will be displayed on the screen. The last two new attributes are `insertBeforeMso` and `insertAfterMso`. Those two attributes are used to specify where in relation to a Microsoft tab, group, or control your new element should appear.

The example shown above also shows a few new RibbonX elements. A `comboBox` is a control that has a text field that allows you to enter text, but also has a drop-down list from which to choose entries. The Styles control is a `comboBox`, and we therefore need to use the correct RibbonX element for it. A `button` is, as the name implies, simply a button that can be clicked. A `labelControl` is just a label that will be displayed on the Ribbon.

> **TIP**
>
> The Ribbon allows three controls to be on top of each other in one column. A column is filled from the top to the bottom in the order given in the RibbonX file. The two label controls in the example do not specify any "label" attribute. Hence, nothing will be displayed on the Ribbon. The only reason these two empty labels are there is to ensure that the Styles control is displayed at the bottom of the Ribbon. This is useful because it reduces the distance the mouse has to travel to reach the Styles control, hence allowing faster usage of the control. You should therefore place those controls at the bottom of your groups that are likely to be used the most.

Figure 35.6
The Word 2007 Home tab after loading the RibbonX file.

The Mailings tab also looks different (see Figure 35.7). For that particular tab, the preceding example hides the Microsoft Create group and creates a new group that contains both buttons from Create plus the Address Book. As pointed out in the style guide, you should hide Microsoft groups very sparingly.

Figure 35.7
The Word 2007 Mailings tab after loading the RibbonX file.

> **TIP**
>
> In order for these modifications to be applied to Word in general, independent of the opened document or template, you need to embed the RibbonX file into a Word template (.dotx). You then need to put this template into the Word Startup folder. You can determine where that folder is on your hard drive by going into Office, Word Options, Advanced, General, File Locations. Once you have the template there and close and reopen Word, you will see the changes to the Ribbon.

Remember to switch on RibbonX error detection as specified in "Catching RibbonX Errors" in the "Troubleshooting" section at the end of this chapter.

EXAMPLE: MEMO TEMPLATE

The second example is a template for a memo. As such, the template contains text that every new document will end up with, as you can see in Figure 35.8. Most importantly, though, the Ribbon is customized to provide only a limited set of features. Users of this template should spend most of their time on the content of the memo, and not its formatting. To that end, users are expected to only use styles for formatting text. This means that they should not see the controls for changing fonts, text size and font styles. The template already provides page numbers, which means that users should not have to worry about headers or footers. In addition, the memos should also do without pictures, charts, SmartArt, cover pages, equations, and so on. Tables are the only object that users should be able to insert. As this is a memo, users need to have access to all mailing-related controls. All the controls of the Review tab also need to be available, as multiple users might be working together on the draft. You can download the template called "Memo.dotx" with the embedded RibbonX from the book's website. Figure 35.8 shows the template opened in Word for a new memo.

> **NOTE**
> To learn more about formatting text with styles, please see Chapter 8, "Creating and Applying Styles and Themes."

Figure 35.8
Memo template with customized Ribbon.

The first piece of RibbonX code shows the startFromScratch attribute with a value of true. startFromScratch means that the entire Ribbon is reset. Therefore, we are starting with a blank slate. In contrast to the previous example, this means that we have to specify everything we want to be on the Ribbon, and not just the changes.

```
<customUI xmlns="http://schemas.microsoft.com/office/2006/01/customui">
    <ribbon startFromScratch="true">
        <officeMenu>
            <button idMso="FileNew" visible="true"/>
            <button idMso="FileOpen" visible="true"/>
            <button idMso="FileSave" visible="true"/>
            <splitButton idMso="FileSaveAsMenu" visible="true"/>
            <menuSeparator id="separator1"/>
            <splitButton idMso="FilePrintMenu" visible="true"/>
            <menu idMso="FileSendMenu" visible="true"/>
            <menuSeparator id="separator2"/>
            <button idMso="FileClose" visible="true"/>
        </officeMenu>
```

35

The preceding code customizes the Office button menu (see Figure 35.9). You might notice that `FileSaveAsMenu` is a split button, which means that the button itself can be clicked and that it has an arrow with a flip-out menu that appears in the right half of the Office button menu. In contrast, `FileSendMenu` only has a flip-out menu. I also used `menuSeparator` to visibly set several items apart from each other. As you can see in the figure, the customized Office button menu does not list the Prepare and Publish menu options, as both are not necessary for these particular memos.

> **TIP**
>
> Word inserts a Save button by default into the Office button menu when starting from scratch. If you do not want this button to appear, you need to explicitly hide it with
>
> ```
> <button idMso="FileSaveAs" visible="false"/>
> ```
>
> The changed Memo template is attached

Figure 35.9
Office button menu and the QAT of the Memo template.

Because this template starts from scratch, the following code is necessary to specify any QAT. `sharedControls` tells Word to use this particular QAT for all windows. The alternative, `documentControls`, would narrow the QAT customization to just the document. This distinction is meaningless, though, unless the template in question is located in the Word Startup folder. Because this particular template is not, I could have used either one. However, a QAT created via `documentControls` is visually different from the normal QAT. Hence, in order to make the QAT for this Memo template visually identical to the QAT a user is accustomed to, I used `sharedControls`. As you can see in the Figure 35.9, the Quick Print control is in the QAT, which is not the case in the default QAT.

```
<qat>
    <sharedControls>
        <button idMso="FileSave"/>
        <control idMso="Undo"/>
        <button idMso="RedoOrRepeat"/>
        <button idMso="FilePrintQuick" insertAfterMso="RedoOrRepeat"/>
    </sharedControls>
</qat>
```

A careful look at the preceding code shows the RibbonX element `control` for Undo. `control` is a generic element that can be used for any Microsoft control. In this case, Undo is actually a gallery. However, the QAT cannot contain any galleries, which means that you cannot use the following:

```
<gallery idMso="Undo"/>
```

In order to be able to add Undo to the QAT, you need to use the generic `control` element. You can use `control` whenever you do not know the actual control type.

Figure 35.8 shows the first tab of the Memo template. As you can see, the Home tab is not visible for this template. Instead, the first tab is a newly created Memo tab that includes a custom "Memo" group to highlight email as the preferred distribution method for these memos. As before for new groups, a new tab needs to be specified using an `id` attribute and needs to be named with the `label` attribute. We use the `insertBeforeMso` attribute to place it before the invisible Home tab to secure its spot as first tab.

```
<tabs>
    <tab id="TabMemo" label="Memo" insertBeforeMso="TabHome">
        <group id="groupMemo" label="Memo">
            <button idMso="FileSendAsAttachment" size="large"/>
            <button idMso="FileEmailAsPdfEmailAttachment" size="large"/>
        </group>
        <group idMso="GroupClipboard"/>
        <group idMso="GroupParagraph"/>
        <group idMso="GroupStyles"/>
        <group idMso="GroupEditing"/>
    </tab>
    <tab idMso="TabInsert" visible="true">
        <group idMso="GroupInsertPages" visible="false"/>
        <group idMso="GroupInsertIllustrations" visible="false"/>
        <group idMso="GroupInsertLinks" visible="false"/>
        <group idMso="GroupHeaderFooter" visible="false"/>
        <group idMso="GroupInsertText" visible="false"/>
        <group idMso="GroupInsertSymbols" visible="false"/>
    </tab>
    <tab idMso="TabMailings" visible="true"/>
    <tab idMso="TabReviewWord" visible="true"/>
    <tab idMso="TabView" visible="true"/>
</tabs>
```

You can also see that the Memo tab does not have the Font group. The associated RibbonX code is self-explanatory. The only thing worth pointing out is the `size` attribute. In the first example, I explained that there are normally three buttons per column on the Ribbon. If you want to have one single big button, though, you need to use the `size` attribute with the value `large`, as shown earlier.

35

NOTE

The button E-mail as PDF Attachment shown in Figure 35.8 with the idMso FileEmailAsPdfEmailAttachment will only be visible in Word, if you installed the Microsoft PDF add-in as described in Appendix B.

Figure 35.10 shows the Insert tab, which only allows users to insert a table. It would have been possible to place the Tables group on the Memo tab as well, but the Insert tab is the place users would expect to find it. As you can see, it was necessary to specify which groups to hide and which to show specifically once the Insert tab was added. The Mailings, Review, and View tabs are unchanged from their defaults.

Figure 35.10
The Insert tab of the Memo template.

> **TIP**
>
> RibbonX is language-neutral. This means, for example, that all customizations specified in this Memo template will be applied to a German Word 2007 as they are to a US-English Word 2007. Please note, though, that every text element you specify that is shown to the user is not language-neutral: Although this Memo template will load and customize a German Word 2007 the same way, all the labels specified in the RibbonX file will be in English. Labels for all Microsoft controls, however, will be in German.

Last, the template also limits what users can do with tables. The groups on the Design and Layout contextual tabs of the Table Tools that could lead users to spend more time on formatting a table than on its content are hidden. You can see this in Figures 35.11 and 35.12.

Figure 35.11
The Design tab of the customized Table Tools.

Figure 35.12
The Layout tab of the customized Table Tools.

These modifications to the contextual tabs are accomplished with the following RibbonX code. All contextual tabs are specified separately from the core tabs using the `contextualTabs` element. Contextual tabs are then grouped into tab sets. The figures show the tab set Table Tools with two contextual tabs. In RibbonX, the tab set is specified with the `tabSet` element. The actual tabs of a tab set are handled identically to all the tabs discussed so far.

```
<contextualTabs>
    <tabSet idMso="TabSetTableTools">
        <tab idMso="TabTableToolsDesign" visible="true">
            <group idMso="GroupTableLayout" visible="true"/>
            <group idMso="GroupTableStylesWord" visible="true"/>
            <group idMso="GroupTableDrawBorders" visible="false"/>
        </tab>
```

```
            <tab idMso="TabTableToolsLayout" visible="true">
                <group idMso="GroupTable" visible="true"/>
                <group idMso="GroupTableRowsAndColumns" visible="true"/>
                <group idMso="GroupTableMerge" visible="false"/>
                <group idMso="GroupTableAlignment" visible="false"/>
                <group idMso="GroupTableData" visible="true"/>
            </tab>
        </tabSet>
    </contextualTabs>
  </ribbon>
</customUI>
```

TIP

> An XML comment starts with `<!--` and ends with `-->`. Anything can be between those two symbols. Use XML comments to annotate RibbonX code so that it becomes easier to understand for others and that you can more quickly remember months later what a particular RibbonX code segment does. You can also use an XML comment to instruct Word to ignore a segment of RibbonX code. This can be useful in troubleshooting. For example, if you placed `<!--` in front of `<contextualTabs>` and placed `-->` after `</contextualTabs>` in the preceding code segment, Word would ignore all the RibbonX between those two tags. Hence, the Memo template would load without any customization of the contextual tabs.

RIBBONX REFERENCE

This section serves as your RibbonX reference. It first lists all RibbonX elements with a description and syntax. All relevant RibbonX attributes are showcased in the second section. The last section lists the idMso's for all tabs and teaches you how to determine the idMso for any Microsoft group or control.

This chapter does not discuss how RibbonX can be used in conjunction with VBA to create your own custom controls. RibbonX elements and attributes for this are therefore omitted in this reference. The full Microsoft documentation for RibbonX, as well as more information about RibbonX and customizing Word 2007, can be accessed via the author's website at http://pschmid.net/office2007/customize.

RIBBONX ELEMENTS

This section lists all relevant RibbonX elements. For every element, it gives a description, the attributes that can be used, its children (meaning all elements that can be nested directly within it), and an example.

NOTE

> Closing tags were included in the examples only when needed for clarity, mainly to show how subelements are nested within the opening and closing tags. Please keep in mind that every opening tag needs to have a corresponding closing tag, or be an empty tag, in XML.

35

customUI

Root element for RibbonX.

Attribute: xmlns

Example:

```
<customUI xmlns="http://schemas.microsoft.com/office/2006/01/customui">
```

Children: ribbon

ribbon

Top element for all Ribbon-related customizations. It is always nested directly under customUI, the RibbonX root element. You can see this previously as customUI specifies ribbon as its only child.

Attribute: startFromScratch

Example:

```
<ribbon startFromScratch="true">
```

Children: officeMenu, qat, tabs, contextualTabs

officeMenu

Contains all customizations of the Office button menu.

Children: control, button, checkBox, gallery, toggleButton, menuSeparator, splitButton, menu

qat

Contains all customizations of the QAT. Can only be used if ribbon is used with startFromScratch="true".

Children: sharedControls, documentControls

tabs

Contains all customizations for the core tabs.

Children: tab

contextualTabs

Contains all customizations for the contextual tabs.

Children: tabSet

35

tabSet

Contains the tabs for one contextual tab set (for example, Table Tools). You cannot create your own tab sets.

Attributes: idMso, visible

Example:

```
<tabSet idMso="TabSetTableTools" visible="true">
```

Children: tab

sharedControls

QAT elements common to all windows (if loaded via a template in the Word Startup folder).

Children: control, button, separator

documentControls

QAT elements specific to a document only.

Children: control, button, separator

tab

Attributes: id, idMso, label, visible, insertBeforeMso, insertAfterMso

Example:

```
<tab id="MyFirstTab" label="My first tab" visible="true">
```

Children: group

group

Attributes: id, idMso, label, visible, insertAfterMso, insertBeforeMso

Example:

```
<group idMso="GroupClipboard" visible="false" />
```

Children: control, labelControl, button, toggleButton, checkBox, editBox, comboBox, drop-down, gallery, menu, splitButton, box, buttonGroup, separator, dialogBoxLauncher

control, button, toggleButton, gallery

Attributes: id, idMso, label, visible, insertBeforeMso, insertAfterMso

Attributes (not in officeMenu or qat): size

Example:

```
<button idMso="Paste" visible="true" size="large" />
```

35

labelControl, checkBox, editBox, comboBox, dropDown

Attributes: id, idMso, label, visible, insertBeforeMso, insertAfterMso

Example:

```
<comboBox idMso="Font" />
```

menu

Attributes: id, idMso, label, visible, insertBeforeMso, insertAfterMso, imageMso

Attribute (not in officeMenu and splitButton): size

Example:

```
<menu id="newMenu" label="Copy and Paste" size="large" imageMso="Paste">
    <button idMso="Cut" />
    <button idMso="Copy" />
    <button idMso="Paste" />
</menu>
```

Children: control, button, checkBox, gallery, toggleButton, menuSeparator

Children (not in officeMenu): splitButton, menu

splitButton

Attributes: id, idMso, visible, insertBeforeMso, insertAfterMso

Attribute (not in officeMenu): size

Example:

```
<splitButton id="newSplitButton" size="large">
    <button idMso="Paste" />
    <menu id="newMenu" label="Copy and Paste">
        <button idMso="Cut" />
        <button idMso="Copy" />
        <button idMso="Paste" />
    </menu>
</splitButton>
```

Children: button or toggleButton (both optional; if omitted, first menu entry is used for button), followed by menu

box

Allows you to specify explicitly whether controls should be added vertically (in columns) or horizontally (in rows). The default without a box element is vertical. The default of the box element without the boxStyle attribute is horizontal.

Attributes: id, visible, insertAfterMso, insertBeforeMso, boxStyle

35

Example:

```
<box id="newBox">
    <button idMso="Paste" />
    <button idMso="Cut" />
</box>
```

Children: control, labelControl, button, toggleButton, checkBox, editBox, comboBox, drop-down, gallery, menu, splitButton, box, buttonGroup, separator

buttonGroup

Represents a button group. Buttons are grouped horizontally (in rows) and a frame is drawn around them.

Attributes: id, visible, insertAfterMso, insertBeforeMso

Example:

```
<buttonGroup id="newButtonGroup">
    <button idMso="Paste" />
    <button idMso="Cut" />
</buttonGroup>
```

Children: control, button, toggleButton, gallery, menu, splitButton

separator

Inserts a vertical separator.

Attribute: id

Example:

```
<group id="newGroup" label="Copy and Paste">
    <button idMso="Cut" />
    <button idMso="Copy" />
    <separator id="newSeparator" />
    <button idMso="Paste" />
</group>
```

menuSeparator

Inserts a horizontal separator into a menu.

Attributes: id, title

Example:

```
<menu id="newMenu" label="Copy and Paste" size="large" imageMso="Paste">
    <button idMso="Cut" />
    <button idMso="Copy" />
    <menuSeparator id="newMenuSeparator" title="Insert" />
    <button idMso="Paste" />
</menu>
```

35

`dialogBoxLauncher`

Adds a dialog box launcher to a group. A dialog box launcher is the little arrow symbol in the bottom-right corner of a group. You can see an example with the Clipboard group on the Home tab.

Example:

```
<group id="newGroup" label="Copy and Paste">
    <button idMso="Cut" />
    <button idMso="Copy" />
    <button idMso="Paste" />
    <dialogBoxLauncher>
        <button idMso="ShowClipboard" />
    </dialogBoxLauncher>
</group>
```

Children: `button`

RIBBONX ATTRIBUTES

As you can see in the preceding section, elements have many attributes in common. This section lists all attributes and explains their purpose as well as specifies what values you can use for them. Please refer to the previous section for examples and to find out which attribute can be used with which element.

`id`

Specifies an ID for an element created by the user. The value of each id element must be unique within a RibbonX file. That means, you can use any one ID only once in the same file.

`idMso`

Specifies the ID of a Microsoft control.

`label`

Specifies a label for an element. Cannot be used for Microsoft elements.

`visible`

Specifies whether or not an element is visible.

Values: `true`, `false`

`insertAfterMso`

Inserts the element after the Microsoft element specified by its `idMso` in the attribute value.

`insertBeforeMso`

Inserts the element before the Microsoft element specified by its `idMso` in the attribute value.

`size`

Determines whether a button is shown small (up to three buttons vertically) or big (one button vertically).

Values: `normal`, `large`

`startFromScratch`

Determines whether a RibbonX file specifies changes to the default Ribbon or specifies a completely new Ribbon.

Values: `true`, `false`

`imageMso`

Specifies a built-in icon. Provide the `idMso` of the control that already uses this icon.

idMsoS

Microsoft has published a list of all `idMsos` that can be used in Word 2007. The list, which was constructed in Microsoft Excel, has over 2,500 entries and specifies for every control its type and its location in the Ribbon UI. The list can be accessed via the author's website at http://pschmid.net/office2007/customize. Figure 35.13 shows the list in Excel with the entries for the Home tab.

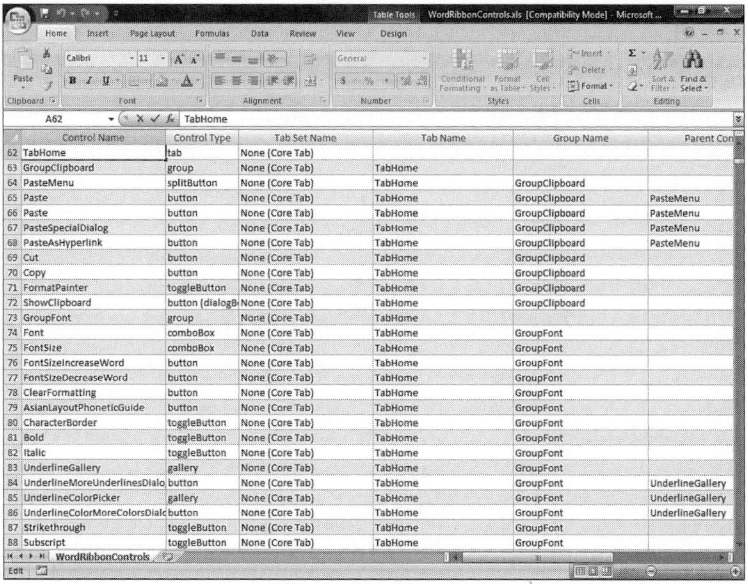

	Control Name	Control Type	Tab Set Name	Tab Name	Group Name	Parent Con
62	TabHome	tab	None (Core Tab)			
63	GroupClipboard	group	None (Core Tab)	TabHome		
64	PasteMenu	splitButton	None (Core Tab)	TabHome	GroupClipboard	
65	Paste	button	None (Core Tab)	TabHome	GroupClipboard	PasteMenu
66	Paste	button	None (Core Tab)	TabHome	GroupClipboard	PasteMenu
67	PasteSpecialDialog	button	None (Core Tab)	TabHome	GroupClipboard	PasteMenu
68	PasteAsHyperlink	button	None (Core Tab)	TabHome	GroupClipboard	PasteMenu
69	Cut	button	None (Core Tab)	TabHome	GroupClipboard	
70	Copy	button	None (Core Tab)	TabHome	GroupClipboard	
71	FormatPainter	toggleButton	None (Core Tab)	TabHome	GroupClipboard	
72	ShowClipboard	button (dialogB	None (Core Tab)	TabHome	GroupClipboard	
73	GroupFont	group	None (Core Tab)	TabHome		
74	Font	comboBox	None (Core Tab)	TabHome	GroupFont	
75	FontSize	comboBox	None (Core Tab)	TabHome	GroupFont	
76	FontSizeIncreaseWord	button	None (Core Tab)	TabHome	GroupFont	
77	FontSizeDecreaseWord	button	None (Core Tab)	TabHome	GroupFont	
78	ClearFormatting	button	None (Core Tab)	TabHome	GroupFont	
79	AsianLayoutPhoneticGuide	button	None (Core Tab)	TabHome	GroupFont	
80	CharacterBorder	toggleButton	None (Core Tab)	TabHome	GroupFont	
81	Bold	toggleButton	None (Core Tab)	TabHome	GroupFont	
82	Italic	toggleButton	None (Core Tab)	TabHome	GroupFont	
83	UnderlineGallery	gallery	None (Core Tab)	TabHome	GroupFont	
84	UnderlineMoreUnderlinesDialo	button	None (Core Tab)	TabHome	GroupFont	UnderlineGallery
85	UnderlineColorPicker	gallery	None (Core Tab)	TabHome	GroupFont	UnderlineGallery
86	UnderlineColorMoreColorsDialc	button	None (Core Tab)	TabHome	GroupFont	UnderlineGallery
87	Strikethrough	toggleButton	None (Core Tab)	TabHome	GroupFont	
88	Subscript	toggleButton	None (Core Tab)	TabHome	GroupFont	

Figure 35.13
Microsoft `idMso` list in Excel showing the Home tab controls.

You can see in this list that `UnderlineGallery`, for example, is located in the Font group on the Home tab and that it is a core tab. Core tabs are those specified in the "tabs" section of a RibbonX file. The names chosen for `idMsos` should be self-explanatory for the most part and reflect the labels in the US-English Word.

TIP

You can also determine the `idMso` for all controls and groups, but not tabs, directly in Word 2007. To do so, open the QAT Customization dialog box and hover your mouse over any control or group. The `idMso` is shown within parentheses in the ToolTip that appears, as you can see in Figure 35.14.

Figure 35.14
Determine the `idMso` via the QAT Customization dialog box.

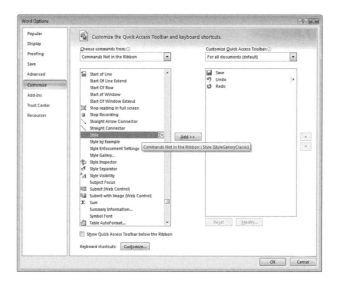

Because tabs are not shown in the QAT Customization dialog box, Table 35.1 provides you with the `idMsos` for all tabs and tab sets. Note that not all tabs listed here will be visible at all times. `TabSetPictureToolsClassic` is only used in Word's compatibility mode; otherwise, `TabSetPictureTools` is available. `TabSetSmartArtTools` is the counterpart of the compatibility mode tab sets `TabSetOrganizationChartTools` and `TabSetDiagramTools`. Word enters compatibility mode when you open a 97-2003 file format document or template. The effects of the compatibility mode are discussed in various chapters in this book. `TabSetInkTools` is only available on Windows editions with TabletPC support and an installed ink input device, such as a tablet pen.

TABLE 35.1   THE `idMso` FOR ALL TABS IN WORD 2007

Label	idMso	Tab Set idMso
Home	TabHome	None (core tab)
Insert	TabInsert	None (core tab)
Page Layout	TabPageLayoutWord	None (core tab)
References	TabReferences	None (core tab)
Mailings	TabMailings	None (core tab)

Label	idMso	Tab Set idMso
Review	`TabReviewWord`	None (core tab)
View	`TabView`	None (core tab)
Developer	`TabDeveloper`	None (core tab)
Add-Ins	`TabAddIns`	None (core tab)
Outlining	`TabOutlining`	None (core tab)
Print Preview	`TabPrintPreview`	None (core tab)
Insert	`TabBlogInsert`	None (core tab)
Blog Post	`TabBlogPost`	None (core tab)
SmartArt Tools, Design	`TabSmartArtToolsDesign`	`TabSetSmartArtTools`
SmartArt Tools, Format	`TabSmartArtToolsFormat`	`TabSetSmartArtTools`
Chart Tools, Design	`TabChartToolsDesign`	`TabSetChartTools`
Chart Tools, Layout	`TabChartToolsLayout`	`TabSetChartTools`
Chart Tools, Format	`TabChartToolsFormat`	`TabSetChartTools`
Picture Tools, Format	`TabPictureToolsFormat`	`TabSetPictureTools`
Drawing Tools, Format	`TabDrawingToolsFormatClassic`	`TabSetDrawingToolsClassic`
WordArt Tools, Format	`TabWordArtToolsFormat`	`TabSetWordArtTools`
Diagram Tools, Format	`TabDiagramToolsFormatClassic`	`TabSetDiagramTools`
Organization Chart Tools, Format	`TabOrganizationChartToolsFormat`	`TabSetOrganizationChartTools`
Text Box Tools, Format	`TabTextBoxToolsFormat`	`TabSetTextBoxTools`
Table Tools, Design	`TabTableToolsDesign`	`TabSetTableTools`
Table Tools, Layout	`TabTableToolsLayout`	`TabSetTableTools`
Header & Footer Tools, Design	`TabHeaderAndFooterToolsDesign`	`TabSetHeaderAndFooterTools`
Equation Tools, Design	`TabEquationToolsDesign`	`TabSetEquationTools`
Picture Tools, Format	`TabPictureToolsFormatClassic`	`TabSetPictureToolsClassic`
Ink Tools, Pens	`TabInkToolsPens`	`TabSetInkTools`

CUSTOMIZING WORD 2007 WITHOUT RIBBONX

As powerful as RibbonX might be, it is not the solution for everyone. The only way around RibbonX is to use third-party tools that provide a user interface and hide RibbonX from you. One such tool is RibbonCustomizer, which you can download from http://pschmid.net/office2007/customize. RibbonCustomizer allows you to customize all Office Ribbons, including Word's, with a simple user interface. The add-in can also create RibbonX code for you that you can paste into the CustomUI Editor to simplify the creation of your own

35

customized documents and templates. Once this tool is installed, you can find it on the View tab in Word by using on the large Customize Ribbon split button.

The UI customization dialog box shown in Figure 35.15 is modeled after the QAT Customization dialog box. It allows you to add and remove tabs, as well as create new ones. In addition, Microsoft groups can be removed and added to tabs. You can also change the order of groups and tabs, except when RibbonX does not support this, as explained in "The Ribbon UI Style Guide: Do's and Don'ts" section of this chapter. The program also has a feature that allows you to load customizations made by other people. Please note that this description and screenshot is for the Professional version of the add-in. Features, such as the ability to create your own group, will be added after this book went to print. Please check the website for up-to-date screenshots and feature descriptions. A free version of RibbonCustomizer with a more limited set of functionality is also available at http://pschmid.net/office2007/customize.

Figure 35.15
The UI customization dialog box of RibbonCustomizer.

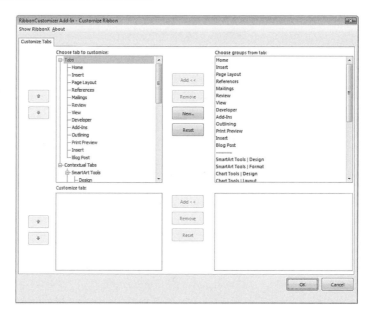

TROUBLESHOOTING

MODIFIED OPENXML FILE NOT OPENING

An OpenXML file that was modified to embed a RibbonX file is not opening in Word. Word states that there are problems with the contents of the file.

Embedding RibbonX code manually into an Open XML file is a cumbersome process that can fail easily. The following could be reasons why it failed:

- The RibbonX file does not exist at the position referenced in the `Relationship` element.
- You did not use the appropriate file extension. For example, you used a .docm extension even though the document was saved previously in Word as .docx.

■ You did not add the needed `Relationship` to the .rels file. If you did, you might have made a mistake, such as not capitalizing the `Id` attribute or not specifying a unique one.

CATCHING RIBBONX ERRORS

A RibbonX file can contain errors, even if it is valid. For example, you might have used a wrong `idMso`. In such cases, Word might not show some or all Ribbon modifications, but not give you an error message.

In order to receive an error message, you need to check "Show add-in user interface errors" in Office, Word Options, Advanced, General section (see Figure 35.16). This setting is at the bottom of the Advanced dialog box.

Figure 35.16
The Advanced Options dialog box showing the setting that enables the display of RibbonX errors.

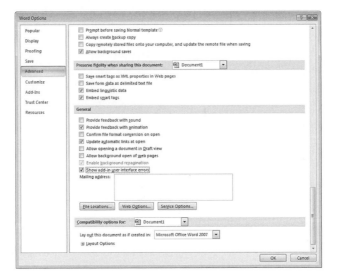

RESOLVING RIBBONX ERRORS

When you load a document or template with an embedded RibbonX file into Word, you receive one or several "Custom UI" error messages.

Here is what to do:

1. Verify that you used correct XML syntax and followed the RibbonX XML Schema. To do so, use the validation function of the Custom UI editor.

2. If you still receive error messages, troubleshoot one error message after the other. Once you fixed the first one, try loading the document or template again in Word and fix the next one. Fixing one error message might frequently fix some subsequent ones as well.

3. If the error message indicates that you used an incorrect `idMso`, verify the `idMso` against the Control ID list or the QAT Customization dialog box.

4. If the error message indicates that you cannot use a particular attribute with a Microsoft control, group, or tab, delete the attribute from your RibbonX code. Only a limited set of attributes can be used on built-in controls.

5. Go to the line indicated by the error message and interpret the error message in the context of the RibbonX code there.

CUSTOM UI EDITOR VALIDATION: INVALID CHILD ELEMENT ERROR

You receive an error that an element has an invalid child element when using the validation function of the Custom UI Editor.

There are several cases in which you could receive this error message:

- The RibbonX element cannot contain the element. For example, you cannot have the element `tab` directly as child of `ribbon`.

- You violated the required order of elements. This applies to the elements directly below `ribbon` and `qat`. The order has to be `officeMenu`, `qat`, `tabs` and then `contextualTabs`. You can leave elements out that you are not using, but you cannot use a different order. Also, `dialogBoxLauncher` needs to be the last element in a group.

- You repeated an element that cannot be repeated. For example, you have two `tabs` elements under `ribbon`. To resolve the error, combine the two elements into just one.

PART **VIII**

APPENDIXES

RECOVERING FILES AND REPAIRING WORD

In this chapter

RECOVERING DOCUMENT FILES

So your computer just crashed, or lost power, and you haven't saved your work lately. Nearly everyone who has ever used Word has experienced this now and then. It happens. Programs crash. Data gets lost.

However, with Word 2007, not *much* data typically gets lost because of the very good data-recovery features built in. As in Word 2003, Word saves your work in temporary files every few minutes, and after a crash, it attempts to load those temporary files so you can recover any unsaved changes to your documents. Therefore, the most you are likely to lose is a few minutes' worth of work.

In this appendix, you'll learn how to use and configure Word's data recovery features, how to repair problems with Word and with corrupted files, and how to safeguard your work by enabling Word to create automatic backup copies of previous versions.

USING THE DOCUMENT RECOVERY TASK PANE

As you work, Word silently creates AutoRecover versions of your document in the background. These are not regular saved files, but temporary files that store the edits you have made to the file since you last saved it. They are deleted when you successfully close the file or exit the program. If the program doesn't exit normally, though, the files are still hanging around, and the AutoRecover feature can use them to help you restore your lost work the next time you start Word.

NOTE

> AutoRecover files are stored separately for each user. So, for example, if one user crashes Word and then shuts down the PC before attempting to recover a lost document, and then another user logs in and opens Word, the second user will not see the first user's automatically recovered documents.

When you start Word after a crash, the Document Recovery task pane appears. It lists the files that Word was able to recover. For example, in Figure A.1, three files are available.

Notice in Figure A.1 that two of the files are actually the same file. One is tagged [Autosaved] and the other is [Original]. The Autosaved version is the more recent one, containing changes made since the last save.

To open one of the Autosaved versions, click it. When you are finished opening Autosaved files, click Close to close the Document Recovery task pane.

It's important to note that the Autosaved version is not a "real" Word document. It's a temporary version, and it won't exist anymore after you close Word, unless you save it. You can save it under a new name with Save As, or you can replace the original copy by clicking Save.

A

Figure A.1
Select Autosaved files to recover upon startup after a crash.

SETTING AUTORECOVER OPTIONS

By default, AutoRecover makes temporary copies of your open files every 10 minutes. If your time is very valuable and your work important, you might want to change the time to a smaller interval, such as five or even three minutes. Word slows down (very slightly) for a moment whenever it does a background save operation, but you lose less data in the event of a crash.

You can also change the AutoRecover file location. By default, it is in a user-specific location, so each user's Autosaved files are private:

In Windows Vista: C:\Users*username*\AppData\Roaming\Microsoft\Word.

In Windows XP: C:\Documents and Settings*username*\Application Data\Microsoft\Word.

If you would like one user to be able to access another user's Autosaved files, change the folder to one that's more easily accessible for all users.

To set the interval and the file location, follow these steps:

1. Choose Office, Word Options. The Word Options dialog box opens.
2. Click Save.
3. If desired, change the interval in the Save AutoRecover Information Every ___ Minutes box (see Figure A.2).

> **TIP**
>
> To turn off AutoRecover, clear the check box. But why turn it off? There's a tremendous upside to using it, and virtually no downside.

A

Figure A.2
Set AutoRecover
options here.

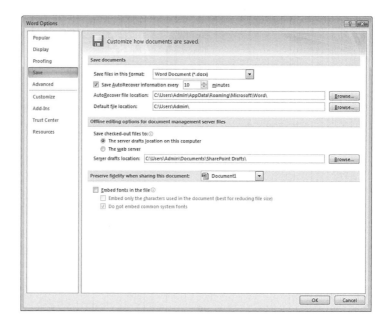

4. If desired, change the AutoRecover file location. You can either type a path or click the Browse button to browse for a location via the dialog box interface.

5. Click OK to save the changes.

RECOVERING DATA FROM AN UNREADABLE FILE

If Word can't open a file, and it's in the native Word 2007 format (that is, WordML format), you might be able to extract some of the text from it by deconstructing the file and browsing it as XML code.

Here's how to do this:

1. In Windows Explorer, rename the file to have a .zip extension instead of .docx.

2. Double-click the .zip file. A set of folders and XML documents appears.

3. Double-click the Word folder.

4. Double-click Document.xml. The text for the document appears in XML markup.

5. Copy the text to the Clipboard (select it and press Ctrl+C) and then paste it into a new document in Word or any text editor.

6. Clean up the text by deleting the XML codes.

A

CREATING AUTOMATIC BACKUP COPIES

Have you ever made changes to a document, saved your work, and then regretted it? You're in good company. Most people have. And because it's a user error, and not a program error, Word can't protect you.

However, you can configure Word to automatically save a backup copy of each document right before you save changes, so you'll always have the next-to-last version as well as the last one on hand. To set this up, follow these steps:

1. Choose Office, Word Options. The Word Options dialog box opens.
2. Click Advanced.
3. Scroll down to the Save section and mark the Always Create Backup Copy check box.
4. Click OK.

The backup copy is stored in the same location as the original, with the same name except with "Backup of" added to the beginning.

DEALING WITH WORD CRASHES

Word does occasionally crash, just like any other application. What do you do? The following sections provide some advice.

SENDING ERROR REPORTS

Depending on the way you have set up your system, when Word crashes you might also see a prompt to send Microsoft an error report. No personal information about you is sent with these reports; Microsoft simply wants the technical codes behind the crash so they can keep track of what's wrong with the program and fix it (see Figure A.3).

Figure A.3
Submit an error report.

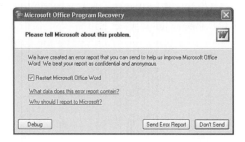

Occasionally, after you agree to submit an error report, an additional dialog box appears asking for more information about the crash. Typically it asks for your permission to upload portions of the document that was open when the crash occurred. You're free to say no to this if the data is sensitive, but rest assured that the people who see it at Microsoft have no interest in your personal or business life; they just want to stop the program from crashing.

One benefit of submitting the report is that sometimes a dialog box appears afterward with a hyperlink you can click to take you to the Microsoft support site where you can read an article that explains how to prevent that particular crash in the future. If you decline to send the error report, you don't get that information.

CHECKING FOR PROGRAM UPDATES

Most of the time a crash is a one-time deal. After a crash, you should recover your documents and then reboot your PC. Usually the problem doesn't return.

If the problem does return, try updating Word as follows:

1. Choose Office, Word Options. The Word Options dialog box opens.
2. Click Resources.
3. Click Check for Updates. The Microsoft Update web page loads.
4. Read the information on the web page and follow the instructions.

   If you are using Windows Vista, the update utility is built into the Control Panel; the web page opens the Control Panel for you and starts Windows Update.

If you are using Windows XP, the update utility is Web-based; follow the instructions on the web page to check for available updates.

FIXING CRASHES RELATED TO A CERTAIN DOCUMENT

If the problem reoccurs but only with a certain file, here are some things to try:

- Reboot. Until you've tried this, you can't assume that the document is at fault.
- If you can open the file in Word, immediately save it in a different format (such as Word 97-2003 format). Sometimes a different format will clear a corruption problem with a file.
- If saving in a different format doesn't help, select all the content from the file and copy it to the Clipboard; then start a new blank document, paste the Clipboard content into it, and save the file.
- If you cannot open the file in Word at all, see "Recovering Data from an Unreadable File," page 978.

DISABLING ADD-INS AND EXTENSIONS

Often, Word itself is not the cause of a recurring crash, but rather an add-in (an optional component, usually created by some company other than Microsoft). Add-ins are covered in Chapter 33, "Add-Ins and Macros."

If Word is able to identify a startup item that is causing a problem, it disables that item automatically the next time you start Word. This is called Automated Safe Mode. When this happens, a prompt typically appears, letting you know that the item is being disabled.

If Word starts up okay but then crashes frequently after it has been running a bit, it's possible the problem is occurring when a certain add-in or extension is executing its code in response to some action you are taking. In a situation like this, you at least have the leisure of examining what's loading and trying disabling some things. Follow these steps:

1. Choose Office, Word Options.

2. When the Word Options dialog box opens, click Add-Ins. A list appears of all your add-ins, both active and inactive (see Figure A.4). The add-ins on your system might differ from the ones shown in Figure A.4.

Figure A.4
Check what's loading automatically at startup.

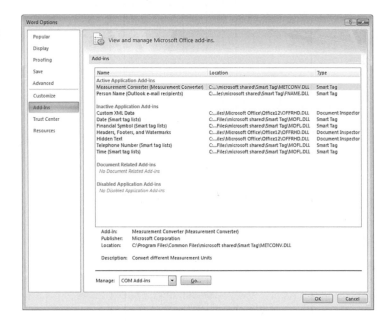

Some of the types you might see include the following:

- **Template**—A template can contain macros, so there's a possibility of a macro causing a problem or carrying a virus. However, Word manages templates pretty tightly, so they're not a likely suspect for a crash.

- **Smart Tag**—Smart tags are generally harmless and can be left enabled. To learn more about them, **see** "Working with Smart Tags," **p. 119**.

- **COM Add-Ins and Word Add-Ins**—Here's what's probably causing the error. A COM add-in is a mini application that runs within Word, usually written by a third party. A Word add-in is one that's specific to Word. Poorly written add-ins can cause crashes.

- **XML Schemas and Expansion Packs**—These help extend Word's XML capabilities. They're not likely to cause problems.

A

If you have a hunch about a particular add-in causing a problem, try disabling it. Note the add-in type in the Type column (see Figure A.4) and then open the Manage list, select that type, and click Go. The dialog box that appears depends on what type you've chosen. For example, Figure A.5 shows the one for Smart Tags.

Figure A.5
Check what types of add-ins are loading automatically at startup to track down a malfunctioning add-in.

You can disable the add-in by removing the check mark from the add-in's check box or by highlighting it in the dialog box and clicking the Remove button.

TIP

> It's best to disable an add-in by clearing its check box rather than removing it entirely. That way, if it turns out not to have been the culprit, you can get it back easily.

RUNNING OFFICE DIAGNOSTICS

If Word crashes frequently and you've already eliminated add-ins as the potential suspect, try using Office Diagnostics. The diagnostics take about 15 minutes to run, but can clear up most problems.

NOTE

> Office Diagnostics is the equivalent of the Detect and Repair feature used in previous versions of the Office Setup program.

If Word crashes frequently enough, it might automatically display a dialog box recommending that you run Office Diagnostics, in which case you can just follow the prompts. If that doesn't happen, do the following to run Office Diagnostics:

1. Choose Start, All Programs, Microsoft Office, Microsoft Office Tools, Microsoft Office Diagnostics.

   Alternatively, from inside Word (provided you can open it), choose Office, Word Options, click Resources, and then click Diagnose.

2. You'll see a dialog box that explains this feature; click Continue. The Start Diagnostics window appears, showing what will be tested.

3. Click Run Diagnostics. Then just wait for the tests to complete. Each test reports its findings as it completes, as shown in Figure A.6.

Figure A.6
Use Office Diagnostics to fix persistent problems with Word.

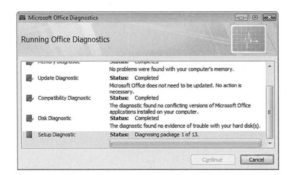

If repairs were made, a dialog box appears to that effect. In that dialog box is a Detailed Results hyperlink; click it to see exactly what happened during the repair process.

CONVERTING FROM OTHER WORD PROCESSING SYSTEMS

In this chapter

B

CONVERTING FROM PREVIOUS WORD VERSIONS

If you are upgrading to Word 2007 from any other version of Microsoft Word, you'll be pleasantly surprised at the ease with which your new program handles your old files. In most cases, they open seamlessly and automatically, with no warnings or decisions to make.

Ever since the earliest versions, Microsoft Word has standardized on the .doc extension for its files. Although Word 2007 changes this to .docx for its native-format files or .docm for macro-enabled documents, it can still open .doc files too.

To make sure .doc files are displayed in the Open dialog box, choose All Word Documents in the Files of Type list (see Figure B.1). If this setting is set to Word Documents (.docx), only the Word 2007-format files will appear.

Figure B.1
Make sure the Files of Type setting is All Word Documents to catch all the files from previous Word versions.

CONVERTING FROM MICROSOFT WORKS

Microsoft Works is an all-in-one suite of applications designed for casual or home use; it's like a scaled-down version of Office.

There are actually two versions of Works: the regular Works, which has its own proprietary word processor, and Works Suite, which has Microsoft Word as its word processor. If you use Works Suite, you're good to go with the instructions from the preceding section.

There have been many versions of Microsoft Works over the years, starting with an MS-DOS version; there have also been several Mac versions. They all use the same file extension: .wps. The actual file formats, however, have changed dramatically over the years. Word 2007 supports only the files from the post-2001 versions (6.0 and higher).

If your Works word processor file is version 6.0 or higher, you can open it from the Open dialog box by choosing Works 6.0 - 9.0 as the Files of Type setting.

If your Works version is lower than 6.0, you will need to perform an interim save step. In your version of Works, use the Save As command to save the file in Rich Text Format (.rtf); then open the resulting file in Word 2007.

TIP

> For an exhaustive description of the various Works versions and their files formats, see http://www.zimac.de/works/wkscmp.htm.

CONVERTING FROM WORDPERFECT

Earlier versions of Word included extensive tools and help for people upgrading to Word from WordPerfect. This was deemed necessary because WordPerfect was the most popular word processor in the world for over a decade.

However, nowadays WordPerfect is not nearly the powerhouse it once was, and people converting to Word from older versions of WordPerfect are now few and far between. Therefore, in Word 2007, Microsoft has drastically scaled back the WordPerfect transitional features. Gone are the special WordPerfect shortcut key conversion helpers from the Help system, for example.

Word 2007 will open WordPerfect files in either 5.x or 6.x format. WordPerfect 5.x files use the .doc extension (which can be confusing since that's Word's default extension); WordPerfect 6.x files use either the .doc or .wpd extension.

To open WordPerfect files, set Files of Type to the appropriate file type. If you are not sure which WordPerfect version file you have, choose WordPerfect 6.x because that includes both of the possible file extensions

CONVERTING FROM AN UNSUPPORTED FILE FORMAT

Occasionally you may encounter a file created in some really old, odd word processing system. Perhaps the original program that created it isn't available anymore, so there's no way of saving it in a more compatible format.

You might not be able to preserve all the formatting from such a file, but you can at least extract the text from it. To do so, in the Open dialog box set Files of Type to Recover Text from Any File (*.*). This enables Word to see every file type. Then select the file and click Open, and Word will do its best to extract as much text as possible.

CONFIRMING FILE CONVERSIONS

Word 2007 will convert files silently as it opens them whenever possible. If you would like to be notified when this happens, turn on the Confirm File Format Conversion on Open feature by following these steps:

1. Choose Office, Word Options. The Word Options dialog box opens.
2. Click Advanced.
3. Scroll down to the General section and mark the Confirm File Format Conversion on Open check box.
4. Click OK.

SHARING WORD DOCUMENTS WITH OTHER PROGRAMS

The default file format in Word 2007 is .docx, a proprietary XML-based format that is not compatible with any other version of Word or any other word processor on the market. (The macro-enabled version, .docm, isn't compatible with anything else either.)

NOTE

> For users of earlier Word versions, Microsoft has made a Compatibility Pack available for free download that enables those versions to open Word 2007 files. You can download it from http://office.microsoft.com. You can't assume that everyone who has an earlier version of Word will do this, however, so it's usually best to save files in Word 97-2003 format if you think others who don't have Word 2007 might want to read them.

If you need to share a document with someone who uses some other program, you'll need to use the Save As feature to save it in another file format. For Word versions from Word 97 to Word 2003, the Word 97-2003 format is your best bet; for earlier versions than that, use Word 97-2003 & 6.0/95 – RTF.

What's with the extremely long name for that format? Well, it's a hybrid file format that combines the features of all the older Word versions, all the way back to Word 95, and stores them in Rich Text Format (RTF). All that compatibility is achieved at the expense of file size; the files saved in this format are very large, but they're very backward-compatible. These files can even be opened in Windows WordPad and nearly all versions of WordPerfect.

→ To learn about saving in other different formats, **see** "Saving a Document," **p. 31**.

Word 2007 does not save in WordPerfect or other word processing formats (except Microsoft Works), but most of those programs will accept Rich Text Format (RTF) files and Word 97-2003 files, so in most cases it is best to try opening the file in the other word processing program. If it won't open, you can at least see what formats the program does accept and then try to find one that Word can save as.

CAUTION

> If you need to password-protect documents—or use protection for tracked changes, comments, or forms—you should know that these documents lose their protection when saved back to Word 97-2003 & 6.0/95 - RTF format.

SETTING A DEFAULT SAVE FORMAT

If not everyone in your group has upgraded to Word 2007, you will not be able to share Word documents in the default Word 2007 format with some people.

If you frequently share documents with others who use earlier versions, and you don't want to worry about whether they have the needed converter, your best bet is to set up Word to save by default in the Word 97-2003 format.

To specify a different file format as your default save format, follow these steps:

1. Choose Office, Word Options. The Word Options dialog box opens.
2. Click Save.
3. Open the Save Files in This Format list and select the desired file format (see Figure B.2).
4. Click OK.

Figure B.2
Choose a different format as your default save format.

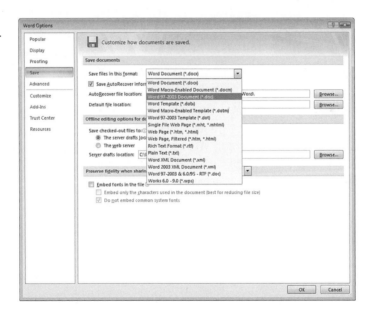

> **NOTE**
>
> The default format you specify affects only new files; when you resave an existing file, it is saved in its existing format.

DISPLAYING WORD FILES ON COMPUTERS WITHOUT ANY VERSION OF WORD

Microsoft Word isn't free, of course, and not all computers have it installed. If you encounter a system that doesn't have Word but needs to open Word documents, here are some options:

- Users can open Word 97-2003 documents in WordPad, the free word processing application that comes with Microsoft Windows. Some of the features of the Word document will not be visible, and you cannot save in Word format from WordPad. (However, you can save in Rich Text Format, which all versions of Word can open.) Note that WordPad cannot open Word 2007 files, so you need to save the files in an earlier format to share with these users.

- You can use Word 2007 to save in HTML format, which anyone using a Web browser can read.

- You can use Word 2007 to save in PDF format, which anyone with Adobe Reader can read. (Adobe Reader is free from www.adobe.com.)

- You can use Word 2007 to save in XPS format, which anyone with Windows Vista can read through Vista's XPS reader utility.

> **NOTE**
>
> In order to save a document as a PDF or XPS file, you need to download a converter from the Microsoft Office website, located at http://office.microsoft.com.

- You can save in a plain-text format, which can then be opened in any text application on any type of computer, including mainframes, Linux, Unix, Macintosh, and so on. Some of those systems might not accept disks formatted in the Windows/DOS file system, but you can transfer files to such systems as email attachments or via a network gateway.

- You can provide the Microsoft Word Viewer, a free application that can be copied and distributed. This small program, available for download from http://office.microsoft.com (search for "Word viewer"), enables any Windows user to view and print any Word 97-2003 document. It supports many, though not all, Word 2007 features. For example, it supports Print Layout view, Outline view, Web Layout view, Document Map, zooming, headers, footers, footnotes, comments, and hyperlinks.

You can't edit text in Word Viewer. However, you can copy the text into another application through the Windows Clipboard and then paste that text into some other text-editing program.

> **TIP**
>
> You can use Word Viewer as a helper application for viewing Word documents downloaded from the Internet. Word Viewer can also make it a little easier to work with customer and vendor organizations that have standardized on a different word processing platform.

> **CAUTION**
>
> Although Word Viewer can coexist with Word on the same computer, it works best on computers on which Word isn't installed. Even though the Word Viewer Setup program is designed to ask whether Word or Word Viewer should be the default for opening Word files, you may sometimes find that the wrong application loads if they are both installed.

ACCESSIBILITY TIPS AND TECHNIQUES

In this chapter

C

TYPES OF ADAPTIVE TECHNOLOGY

Imagine using your computer without a monitor, mouse, or keyboard. People with disabilities use computers every day without these devices. They do this by using what is called "adaptive" or "assistive" technology. Adaptive technology includes screen readers for people who are blind, screen magnification for people who have visual disabilities, Text-to-Speech (TTS) for people with learning disabilities, voice recognition for people with physical disabilities, and alternate input devices for people who can't use a standard keyboard.

In this appendix, you'll learn about the types of adaptive technology that people use, barriers to accessing documents, and specific techniques for designing and creating accessible documents that will assist everyone.

There are several types of adaptive technology that people can use to interact with computers and digital documents. The information listed here provides an overview of the categories of adaptive technology:

- **Screen readers**—Screen reading combines hardware (sound card) and software (synthesized speech) to provide auditory access to information displayed on a computer screen. A person using screen-reading tools uses the keyboard instead of a mouse. Examples of these tools are JAWS[1] from Freedom Scientific and Window-Eyes[2] from GW Micro.

- **Screen magnification**—This tool magnifies the screen, providing support for full-screen magnification, a lens-like tool, or various types of split-screen access. Most screen-magnification software also provide TTS support. Examples of screen magnification are ZoomText[3] from AiSquared or MAGic[4] from Freedom Scientific.

- **TTS or Text-to-Speech**—TTS tools provide auditory access to information displayed on the screen; however, it is not as complete as a screen reader. TTS is meant to provide supportive access rather than alternative access to a computer. One example of this type of tool is Read & Write Gold[5] from TextHelp Systems. Narrator is another example of a TTS tool and can be found in Windows Vista under Start, All Programs, Accessories, Ease of Access. In Windows XP, you'll find Narrator under Start, All Program, Accessories, Accessibility.

- **Voice recognition**—Voice recognition is software that works with a sound card to let the user interact with the computer using his or her voice instead of a mouse or keyboard. An example of this tool is Dragon NaturallySpeaking[6] from Nuance.

- **Alternative input devices**—For people who can't use a mouse, keyboard, or voice recognition, there are alternative methods of interacting with the computer. Examples of these tools would be an onscreen keyboard, IntelliKeys from IntelliTools,[7] single switches, and Morse Code.

These tools can be used in combination with each other. You can, for example, use screen reading and voice recognition together.

MICROSOFT OFFICE 2007 ACCESSIBILITY— BACKGROUND

Microsoft works with the developers of adaptive technology to ensure optimal accessibility of Microsoft Office applications. Within the applications are tools for document authors to use to create more accessible and usable documents. The user interface of Office 2007 makes it easier to find and use document structures. The accessibility and usability of documents depend on the use of a document structure and formatting.

The first tool provided in Office 2007 is an XML-based file format. XML, or Extensible Markup Language, allows document authors to move away from the traditional underlying structures of documents. It is the next step in the evolution of digital documents. The advantages to XML include the ability to separate the structure of a document from the formatting and content. In incorporating this separation, a document can have a structure; however, the person reading the document may choose how the formatting will be implemented and accessed. The structured content can then be repurposed to another XML-based file format, such as tagged PDF.[8] DAISY[9] (Digital Accessible Information System), or HTML, with little or no repair.

As we move toward XML-based content, we are also expanding our definition of accessible documents. The W3C WAI[10] (World Wide Web Consortium – Web Accessibility Initiative) created the first guidelines for HTML-based documents. These guidelines are being updated to include other document formats, such as PDF, word processed documents, presentations, and spreadsheets, as well as Flash, audio, and video files. Many countries, including the United States (Section 508[11]), are developing their own standards and guidelines for accessible digital information based on the W3C guidelines.

DOCUMENT ACCESSIBILITY BASICS

Although both Microsoft and adaptive technology developers work toward a more accessible document-authoring environment, the document author plays an integral role in the design and creation of accessible documents and information. Document authors have the skill to make information accessible or to create barriers to accessibility. The difference is in the tools used when designing templates and creating documents.

HEADINGS AND STYLES

One of the easiest tools to use when designing or creating a document is the use of headings and other styles to provide a navigational structure. Adaptive technology can "look" at a document and find paragraph text, headings, lists, tables, and other document structures based on the standard "definition" of each of these. It is here we begin to see the value of the XML-based structure. If we look under the hood of a document, the heading styles will be identified as <H1> for heading one, <H2> for heading two, and so forth. Adaptive technology can then let the reader know that the heading denotes a new topic or section of the document. Contrast that to what happens if formatting is manually applied to text to mimic a heading. Such a scenario forces the adaptive technology to instead look for a generic <P>

tag for paragraph, which presents the information as a paragraph, rather than as a heading. Imagine trying to find information in this book without the use of headings.

In previous versions of Word, if a document author wanted a heading style that was not the default heading style, a new style with a new name would be created based on the existing style. When working with styles, this is a key element to accessibility: base the new style on an existing one of the same structural element.

Word 2007 introduces themes to this process. Document authors can still create custom styles; however, there are built-in themes or color sets for documents that include structural elements such as headings, lists, and tables. For example, if you use the Foundry theme in a document that has already been formatted with the Office theme, your headings are still headings, even though they now have a different look and feel to them. If you create a custom theme, you can add it to the visible theme set and access it for any document you create.

There are two other navigational advantages to using headings:

- They are the basis for a table of contents, which assists all readers.
- They are the basis for creating bookmarks, if you convert a Word document to tagged PDF.

IMAGES, CHARTS, AND GRAPHICS

There are two ways to improve the accessibility of images in documents. The first is to ensure that images and other objects have Alt Text, or alternative text. Although this tool is identified as a "web" tool, current screen readers can also identify the Alt Text in Word documents.

However, if an image links to other information, it is more important to know where you are going than what the image is about. Combining information, for example, providing Alt Text such as "Photo of a rural landscape. Links to antique store home page," means that the readers have to listen to the description of the image before they can make the decision to follow it. This takes time and is less important than where the link is taking them.

The second way is to provide a caption for each image, equation, and table. Captions are important and often overlooked in digital documents. Why would we need captions for images, equations, and tables?

Alternative text is usable when someone is viewing the document on a computer; however, if the document is printed, the person reading the print version of the document also needs information about the image. Depending on the printer used, some critical details might not be as visible as they should be. It is also difficult to point your finger at an image on a printed page and have the Alt Text appear!

To use a caption, select the image, equation, or table and choose Insert Caption on the References tab, or press Alt+S, P.

HYPERLINKS

Hyperlinks or links can also present issues when trying to find information quickly in a document. How you approach links depends on the expected form of access to the document you are creating: print, print and digital, or just digital. Current screen readers have keyboard commands to list links in a document.

Imagine listening to http://www.freedomscientific.com, http://www.gwmicro.com, http://www.aisquaed.com, or http://www.texthelp.com/rwg.asp?q1=products&q2=rwg. Would you know where you were going? Would you want to listen to each piece of the URL to find out where it would take you? Similarly, for people with learning disabilities who might be confused by the "stream of letters," would you want to take the time to break down the URL in order to understand where it was going?

A better solution is to use contextual or text-based links. If we take the same links as in the preceding paragraph, but use words instead of the URL we find that we can go to Freedom Scientific, GW Micro, AiSquared, or TextHelp Read & Write Gold. We know exactly where we are going.

This will also create a barrier if all links start with phrases such as "go to," "select to," or "follow this link to go to...." When a person using adaptive technology asks for a list of links in a document, he or she will have the same problems as when all links begin with the web address: listening to unnecessary text and an inability to use the first character of a link to locate it in a list of links. Using the examples in the previous paragraph, the link to TextHelp can easily be located by pressing the letter "T" in a list of links. Even if there is more than one link that begins with the letter "T," it is a shorter list than having to move through every link in a document to find the one the user needs.

What about documents that are printed and viewed digitally? Typically, users will not be following a link with a printed document. If, however, they take the document with them to another computer and need to access a link, inserting the full URL as a footnote, endnote, or part of a bibliography will provide both forms of accessibility. All of these tools can be found under the References tab. The Ribbon commands are Alt+S, F (Insert Footnote); Alt+S, E (Insert Endnote); and Alt+S, C (Insert Citation) to create the citations, then Alt+S, B to insert the bibliography.

TABLES

Tables present a barrier to information when they are used to format an entire document. One of the items on the checklist of accessibility is the use of heading rows for tables. Why a table is being used in a document is also one of the best questions to ask yourself when starting to construct a table. Adaptive technology has keyboard commands for navigating tables. The person using the technology can get feedback on the column and row titles, cell locations, and formatting within a table cell. The Repeat Heading Rows command is found under the (Table Tools) Layout tab, or you can press Alt+J, L, J with your cursor in the heading row of the table.

C

Tables should also be inserted with a specific number of columns and rows identified rather than drawing them. Adaptive technology looks for the norm or standard. Document parts that are drawn present a barrier to access. To insert a table, choose Table on the Insert tab. From the keyboard, press Alt+N, T.

If a table starts out with six columns, is narrowed to five, then expands again with different cells merged along the way and different types of information presented in each section of the table, it is difficult to navigate visually and impossible to navigate with adaptive technology. It is even difficult to visualize this type of design as it is described in this paragraph!

Another accessibility issue involves allowing rows to break across pages. If the content in a row spans more than one page, a table might not be the best way of structuring a document. To turn off the rows breaking across pages, select the table, choose Properties from the (Table Tools) Layout tab, click the Row tab, and uncheck the Allow Row to Break Across Pages option. From the keyboard, with your cursor in a cell of the table, press Alt+J, L, K and choose T to select the table; then press Alt+J, L, O to open the Properties dialog box. You can now press Ctrl+Tab to move to the Row tab and press Alt+K to uncheck the Allow Row to Break Across Pages item.

When adjusting the spacing in cells to accommodate text or to provide a specific amount of spacing around text, document authors should modify the cell margins rather than insert blank lines in a cell. For someone using TTS or screen reading, each of those blank lines will be read to the user as "blank." This disorients the readers as they don't know if there is something wrong with the adaptive technology or the document, or both. It is also annoying to listen to seemingly endless instances of blank, blank, blank, blank…just to get to that one nugget of content. Cell margins can be found on the Cell tab in the Table Properties dialog box.

Often a document author will use a single cell table instead of paragraph borders to isolate and bring visual focus to an important concept. As document authors, we need to ask ourselves what the heading row of the table is each time we use a table structure. To access the paragraph borders, select the paragraph and choose the Borders button on the Home tab. You can adjust the color and effect of a paragraph border. You can also adjust the left/right indent of a paragraph by choosing the Paragraph dialog box launcher on the Home tab (or press Alt+H, P, G). If this is a style you will use often, you can add it to the Quick Style Gallery. From the keyboard, select the paragraph; then press Alt+H, B, O to open the Borders and Shading dialog (if the listed options aren't what you need). To adjust paragraph settings, with the paragraph selected, press Alt+H, P, G to open the Paragraph dialog box.

Table captions should also be used to provide a description of what the person reading the table data will find within the table. Sometimes an extra table row is used for this instead of the caption tool. To insert a caption for a table, choose Insert Caption on the References tab while your cursor is in a table. The "Table #…" is automatically filled in. From the keyboard, with the cursor in the table, press Alt+S, P to open the Caption dialog box.

There are complex data tables, and application developers and adaptive technology developers are working to try and improve access to these types of data tables. Access to information in tables begins with good design and the use of the table structure.

TEXT BOXES AND PARAGRAPH FRAMES

As mentioned in the previous topic on tables, often document authors use a single-cell table to isolate and direct attention to concepts. The other tool used to do this is the text box. Unlike a single-cell table, text boxes are completely inaccessible. They are objects that float over the document and are out of the "visual range" of adaptive technology. There may be instances where the use of text boxes is unavoidable; however, the same effect can often be achieved using paragraph borders.

Paragraph frames present the same degree of inaccessibility. They are objects that adaptive technology does not recognize. Paragraph frames aren't used as often as text boxes; however, it is worth mentioning their inaccessibility here as they resemble text boxes visually in a document and are equally inaccessible.

Information in this appendix is from *The Logical Document Structure Handbook: Word 2007* by Karen McCall (ISBN 0-9738370-9-8).

ENDNOTES

1. JAWS Headquarters at Freedom Scientific, http://www.freedomscientific.com/fs_products/JAWS_HQ.asp.
2. Window-Eyes from GW Micro, http://www.gwmicro.com/Window-Eyes/.
3. ZoomText from AiSquared, http://www.aisquared.com/index.cfm.
4. MAGic from Freedom Scientific, http://www.freedomscientific.com/fs_products/software_MAG100.asp.
5. Read & Write Gold from TextHelp Systems, http://www.enablemart.com/productdetail.aspx?store=10&pid=605&dept=20.
6. Dragon NaturallySpeaking from Nuance, http://www.nuance.com/naturallyspeaking/.
7. IntelliTools home page, http://www.intellitools.com/.
8. Adobe Systems Accessibility home page, http://www.adobe.com/accessibility/index.html.
9. DAISY (Digital Accessible Information System), http://www.daisy.org.
10. World Wide Web Consortium, Web Accessibility Initiative home page, http://www.w3.org/WAI/.
11. Section 508 of the Rehabilitation Act (U.S. government), http://www.access-board.gov/sec508/guide/act.htm.

COMMAND REFERENCE: WORD 2003 TO WORD 2007

In this chapter

Here are some tables that provide quick cross-references between Word 2003 and Word 2007. This same information is also available in the Word 2007 Help system, but you may find it easier to browse this content in print rather than onscreen. The onscreen version can be found in the article *Reference: Locations of Word 2003 Commands in Word 2007* in the What's New section of the Help system.

NOTE

> Any reference to "Office" in the Word 2007 column of the tables found in this appendix refers to the Office button located at the top-left corner of the Word 2007 window.

This reference includes the main menu system from Word 2003 and also the Standard and Formatting toolbars. For cross-referencing of other toolbars, see the version in the Help system.

FILE MENU

Word 2003	Word 2007	Notes
New	Office, New	
Open	Office, Open	
Close	Office, Close	
Save	Office, Save	Also available on the Quick Access toolbar.
Save As	Office, Save As	
Save as Web Page	Not available	You can do the same thing this command did by choosing Save As and setting the file type to a Web-based type.
File Search	Not available	Search instead from Windows.
Permission, Unrestricted Access	Not available	
Permission, Do Not Distribute	Not available	
Permission, Do Not Reply All	Not available	
Versions	Removed from product	This is not available because the Versions feature has been removed from Word. The only version management you can now do is via SharePoint or using the file version feature of Windows Vista.

Word 2003	Word 2007	Notes
Web Page Preview	N/A	This feature is no longer available in the default interface, but you can add it to the Quick Access toolbar if desired.
Page Setup	Page Layout tab, Page Setup group, dialog box launcher	
Print Preview	Office, Print, Print Preview	
Print	Office, Print	
Send To, Mail Recipient	Removed from product	You can still send documents to a mail recipient as an attachment. See Send To, Mail Recipient (as Attachment).
Send To, Reply with Changes	N/A	This feature is no longer available in the default interface, but you can add it to the Quick Access toolbar if desired.
Send To, Mail Recipient (for Review)	N/A	This feature is no longer available in the default interface, but you can add it to the Quick Access toolbar if desired.
Send To, Mail Recipient (as Attachment)	Office, Send, E-mail	
Send To, Routing Recipient	Removed from product	Routing is no longer supported.
Send To, Exchange Folder	N/A	This feature is no longer available in the default interface, but you can add it to the Quick Access toolbar if desired.
Send To, Online Meeting Participant	N/A	This feature is no longer available in the default interface, but you can add it to the Quick Access toolbar if desired.
Send To, Recipient Using a Fax Modem	Removed from product	To fax a document directly from Word, print to the Fax (or Microsoft Fax) printer driver provided by Windows.
Send To, Recipient Using Internet Fax Service	Office, Send, Internet Fax	
Send To, Microsoft Office PowerPoint	N/A	This feature is no longer available in the default interface, but you can add it to the Quick Access toolbar if desired.

D

Word 2003	Word 2007	Notes
Properties	Office, Prepare, Properties	
Sign Out	Removed from Product	
Exit	Office, Exit Word	

Edit Menu

Word 2003	Word 2007	Notes
Undo	On Quick Access toolbar	
Repeat	On Quick Access toolbar	
Cut	Home tab, Clipboard group, Cut	
Copy	Home tab, Clipboard Group, Copy	
Office Clipboard	Home tab, Clipboard group, dialog box launcher	
Paste	Home tab, Clipboard group, Paste	
Paste Special	Home tab, Clipboard group, Paste (drop-down arrow), Paste Special	Click the Paste button's drop-down arrow to see a menu from which Paste Special is available.
Paste as Hyperlink	Home tab, Clipboard group, Paste (drop-down arrow), Paste as Hyperlink	Click the Paste button's drop-down arrow to see a menu from which Paste as Hyperlink is available.
Clear, Formats	Home tab, Font group, Clear Formatting	
Clear, Contents	N/A	This feature is no longer available in the default interface, but you can add it to the Quick Access toolbar if desired.
Select All	Home tab, Editing group, Select, Select All	
Find	Home tab, Editing group, Find	
Replace	Home tab, Editing group, Replace	

Word 2003	Word 2007	Notes
Go To	Home tab, Editing group, Go To	
Links	Office, Prepare, Edit Links to Files	Available only when the file contains links.
Object	N/A	Still available from the right-click menu for the object itself.

VIEW MENU

Word 2003	Word 2007	Notes
Normal	View tab, Document Views group, Draft	
Web Layout	View tab, Document Views group, Web Layout	
Print Layout	View tab, Document Views group, Print Layout	
Reading Layout	View tab, Document Views group, Full Screen Reading	
Outline	View tab, Document Views group, Outline	
Task Pane	Removed from product	Some task panes are still available, but there is no longer a central way of accessing them all together.
Toolbars	Removed from product	There is no longer a way of customizing the interface by turning toolbars on/off.
Ruler	View tab, Show/Hide group, Ruler	
Document Map	View tab, Show/Hide group, Document Map	
Thumbnails	View tab, Show/Hide group, Thumbnails	
Header and Footer	Insert tab, Header & Footer group, Footer OR Insert tab, Header & Footer group, Header	
Footnotes	References tab, Footnotes group, Show Notes	

D

Word 2003	Word 2007	Notes
Markup	Review tab, Tracking group, Show Markup	
HTML Source	N/A	This feature is no longer available in the default interface, but you can add it to the Quick Access toolbar if desired.
Full Screen	View tab, Document Views group, Full Screen Reading	
Zoom	View tab, Zoom group, Zoom OR Zoom slider on status bar	

Insert Menu

Word 2003	Word 2007	Notes
Break	Page Layout tab, Page Setup group, Breaks OR Insert tab, Pages group, Page Break	
Page Numbers	Insert tab, Header & Footer group, Page Number	
Date and Time	Insert tab, Text group, Date & Time OR Design tab, Insert group, Date & Time	
AutoText, AutoText	Insert tab, Text group, Quick Parts, Building Blocks Organizer	
AutoText, New	Insert tab, Text group, Quick Parts, Save Selection to Quick Part Gallery	
AutoText, (list of entries)	N/A	The old AutoText entries that used to come with Word are no longer available, but you can re-create them using Building Blocks.
Field	Insert tab, Text group, Quick Parts, Field	
Symbol	Insert tab, Symbols group, Symbol	

Word 2003	Word 2007	Notes
Comment	Review tab, Comments group, New Comment	
Ink Comment		Only on Tablet PCs
Reference, Footnote	References tab, Footnotes group, Insert Footnote OR References tab, Footnotes group, dialog box launcher	
Reference, Caption	References tab, Captions group, Insert Caption	
Reference, Cross-Reference	Insert tab, Links group, Cross-reference OR References tab, Captions group, Cross-reference	
Reference, Index and Tables	References tab, Table of Contents group, Table of Contents OR References tab, Index group, Insert Index OR References tab, Table of Authorities group, Insert Table of Authorities	
Web Component	N/A	This feature is no longer available in the default interface, but you can add it to the Quick Access toolbar if desired.
Picture, Clip Art	Insert tab, Illustrations group, Clip Art OR Chart Tools Layout tab, Shapes group, Picture, Clip Art OR Header & Footer Tools tab, Insert group, Clip Art	
Picture, From File	Insert tab, Illustrations group, Picture	

D

Word 2003	Word 2007	Notes
Picture, From Scanner or Camera	Removed from product	Scan pictures from outside of Word and then insert or paste them in. The Scanner and Camera Wizard is still available from inside the Clip Organizer, however.
Picture, Ink and Drawing and Writing		Only on Tablet PCs
Picture, New Drawing	Insert tab, Shapes, New Drawing Canvas	
Picture, AutoShapes	Insert tab, Shapes group (drop-down list)	
Picture, WordArt	Insert tab, Text group, WordArt	
Picture, Organization Chart	Insert tab, Illustrations group, SmartArt	
Picture, Chart	Insert tab, Illustrations group, Chart	
Diagram	Insert tab, Illustrations group, SmartArt	
Text Box	Insert tab, Text group, Text Box	
File	Insert tab, Text group, Object, Text from File	
Object	Insert tab, Text group, Object, Object	
Bookmark	Insert tab, Links group, Bookmark	
Hyperlink	Insert tab, Links group, Hyperlink	

Format Menu

Word 2003	Word 2007	Notes
Font	Home tab, Font group, dialog box launcher	
Paragraph	Home tab, Paragraph group, dialog box launcher OR Page Layout tab, Paragraph group, dialog box launcher	

Word 2003	Word 2007	Notes
Bullets and Numbering	Home tab, Paragraph group, Bullets (drop-down list) OR Home tab, Paragraph group, Numbering (drop-down list) OR Home tab, Paragraph group, Multi-Level List (drop-down list)	Each type of bullet and numbering that was formerly a different tab in the Bullets and Numbering dialog box now has its own separate menu accessible from its button in the Paragraph group.
Borders and Shading	Home tab, Paragraph group, Borders (drop-down list) OR Home tab, Paragraph group, Shading (drop-down list)	Borders and Shading are separate buttons, each with its own drop-down list. To access the old-style Borders and Shading dialog box, choose Borders and Shading from the Borders button's menu. You can also add the command to the Quick Access toolbar for easier access.
Columns	Page Layout tab, Page Setup group, Columns, More Columns	
Tabs	Home tab, Paragraph group, dialog box launcher, Tabs button	Open the Paragraph dialog box and then click the Tabs button on it. Add the Tabs command to the Quick Access toolbar, if desired, for easier access.
Drop Cap	Insert tab, Text group, Drop Cap	
Change Case	Home tab, Font group, Change Case	
Background	Page Layout tab, Page Background group, Page Color	
Theme	Page Layout tab, Themes group, Themes	Themes are a different feature in Word 2007 than in Word 2003.
Frames	Removed from product	Two of the previous commands, Table of Contents in Frame and New Frames Page, can be added to the Quick Access toolbar.
AutoFormat	N/A	This feature is no longer available in the default interface, but you can add it to the Quick Access toolbar if desired.

D

Word 2003	Word 2007	Notes
Styles and Formatting	Home tab, Styles group, drop-down list, Apply Styles OR Home tab, Styles group, dialog box launcher	The Apply Styles pane is different from (and smaller than) the normal Styles pane that you get with the dialog box launcher.
Reveal Formatting	N/A	This feature is no longer available in the default interface, but you can add it to the Quick Access toolbar if desired.
Object	Removed from product	Formatting for an object is now accomplished via the object's right-click menu.

TOOLS MENU

Word 2003	Word 2007	Notes
Spelling and Grammar	Review tab, Proofing group, Spelling & Grammar	
Research	Review tab, Proofing group, Research	
Language, Set Language	Review tab, Proofing group, Set Language	
Language, Japanese Consistency Checker	N/A	This feature is no longer available in the default interface, but you can add it to the Quick Access toolbar if desired (in Asian versions only).
Language, Translate	Review tab, Proofing group, Translate	
Language, Thesaurus	Review tab, Proofing group, Thesaurus	
Language, Hyphenation	Page Layout tab, Page Setup group, Hyphenation, Hyphenation Options	
Word Count	Review tab, Proofing group, Word Count OR Status bar	
AutoSummarize	N/A	This feature is no longer available in the default interface, but you can add it to the Quick Access toolbar if desired.

Word 2003	Word 2007	Notes
Look Up Reference	Removed from product	
Speech	Removed from product	Speech services are now handled through the operating system and are available if you have Windows Vista.
Shared Workspace	Office, Publish, Create Document Workspace	
Track Changes	Review tab, Tracking group, Track Changes (drop-down list)	
Compare and Merge Documents	Review tab, Compare group, Compare (drop-down list)	
Protect Document	Review tab, Protect group, Protect Document OR Developer tab, Protect group, Protect Document	
Online Collaboration, Meet Now	N/A	This feature is no longer available in the default interface, but you can add it to the Quick Access toolbar if desired.
Online Collaboration, Schedule Meeting	N/A	This feature is no longer available in the default interface, but you can add it to the Quick Access toolbar if desired.
Online Collaboration, Web Discussions	Removed from product	
Online Collaboration, End Review	N/A	This feature is no longer available in the default interface, but you can add it to the Quick Access toolbar if desired.
Letters and Mailings, Mail Merge	Mailings tab, Start Mail Merge group, Start Mail Merge, Step by Step Mail Merge Wizard	
Letters and Mailings, Show Mail Merge Toolbar	Removed from product	
Letters and Mailings, Show Japanese Greetings Toolbar	Removed from product	

D

Word 2003	Word 2007	Notes
Letters and Mailings, Envelopes and Labels	Mailings tab, Create group, Envelopes OR Mailings tab, Create group, Labels	
Letters and Mailings, Letter Wizard	Removed from product	
Macro, Macros	Developer tab, Code group, Macros	To display the Developer tab, choose Office, Word Options, Personalize and then mark Show Developer Tab in the Ribbon.
Macro, Record New Macro	Developer tab, Code group, Record Macro / Stop Recording OR Status bar	
Macro, Security	Developer tab, Code group, Macro Security	
Macro, Visual Basic Editor	Developer tab, Code group, Visual Basic	
Macro, Microsoft Script Editor	Removed from product	
Templates and Add-Ins	Office, Word Options, Add-Ins	
AutoCorrect Options	Office, Word Options, Proofing, AutoCorrect Options	
Customize	Office, Word Options, Customize	
Show Signature	Removed from product	
Options	Office, Word Options	

TABLE MENU

Word 2003	Word 2007	Notes
Draw Table	Insert tab, Tables group, Table, Draw Table OR Table Tools Design tab, Draw Borders group, Draw Table	

Word 2003	Word 2007	Notes
Insert, Table	Insert tab, Tables group, Table	
Insert, Columns to the Left	Table Tools Layout tab, Rows & Columns group, Insert Left	
Insert, Columns to the Right	Table Tools Layout tab, Rows & Columns group, Insert Right	
Insert, Rows Above	Table Tools Layout tab, Rows & Columns group, Insert Above	
Insert, Rows Below	Table Tools Layout tab, Rows & Columns group, Insert Below	
Insert, Cells	Table Tools Layout tab, Rows & Columns group, dialog box launcher	
Delete, Table	Table Tools Layout tab, Rows & Columns group, Delete, Delete Table	
Delete, Columns	Table Tools Layout tab, Rows & Columns group, Delete, Delete Columns	
Delete, Rows	Table Tools Layout tab, Rows & Columns group, Delete, Delete Rows	
Delete, Cells	Table Tools Layout tab, Rows & Columns group, Delete, Delete Cells	
Select, Table	Table Tools Layout tab, Table group, Select, Select Table	
Select, Column	Table Tools Layout tab, Table group, Select, Select Column	
Select, Row	Table Tools Layout tab, Table group, Select, Select Row	
Select, Cell	Table Tools Layout tab, Table group, Select, Select Cell	

D

Word 2003	Word 2007	Notes
Merge Cells	Table Tools Layout tab, Merge group, Merge Cells	
Split Cells	Table Tools Layout tab, Merge group, Split Cells	
Split Table	Table Tools Layout tab, Merge group, Split Table	
Table AutoFormat	Table Tools Design tab, Table Styles group, Select a style	
AutoFit, AutoFit to Contents	Table Tools Layout tab, Cell Size group, AutoFit, AutoFit Contents	
AutoFit, AutoFit to Window	Table Tools Layout tab, Cell Size group, AutoFit, AutoFit Window	
AutoFit, Fixed Column Width	Table Tools Layout tab, Cell Size group, AutoFit, Fixed Column Width	
AutoFit, Distribute Rows Evenly	Table Tools Layout tab, Cell Size group, Distribute Rows	
AutoFit, Distribute Columns Evenly	Table Tools Layout tab, Cell Size group, Distribute Columns	
Heading Rows Repeat	Table Tools Layout tab, Data group, Repeat Header Rows	
Convert, Text to Table	Insert tab, Tables group, Table, Convert Text to Table	
Convert, Table to Text	Table Tools Layout tab, Data group, Convert to Text	
Sort	Home tab, Paragraph group, Sort OR Table Tools Layout tab, Data group, Sort	
Formula	Table Tools Layout tab, Data group, Formula	

Word 2003	Word 2007	Notes
Show Gridlines	Table Tools Design tab, Table Styles group, Borders, Show Gridlines OR Table Tools Layout tab, Table group, Show Gridlines OR Home tab, Paragraph group, Borders, Show Gridlines	When gridlines are already shown, the commands change to Hide Gridlines.
Table Properties	Table Tools Layout tab, Table group, Properties	

WINDOW MENU

Word 2003	Word 2007	Notes
New Window	View tab, Window group, New Window	
Arrange All	View tab, Window group, Arrange All	
Compare Side by Side With	View tab, Window group, View Side by Side	
Split	View tab, Window group, Split	
(Choose an open document to display)	View tab, Window group, Switch Windows, *document name*	

HELP MENU

Word 2003	Word 2007	Notes
Microsoft Office Word Help	Help button (top-right corner)	
Show the Office Assistant	Removed from product	
Microsoft Office Online	Office, Word Options, Resources, Go Online	
Contact Us	Office, Word Options, Resources, Contact Us	
WordPerfect Help	Removed from Product	
Check for Updates	Office, Word Options, Resources, Check for Updates	

Word 2003	Word 2007	Notes
Detect and Repair	Office, Word Options, Resources, Diagnose	
Activate Product	Office, Word Options, Resources, Activate	
Customer Feedback Options	Office, Word Options, Trust Center, Customer Experience Improvement Program	
About Microsoft Office Word	Office, Word Options, Resources, About	

STANDARD TOOLBAR

Word 2003	Word 2007	Notes
New Blank Document	N/A	No direct correlation, but Office, New starts a new document via a dialog box. You can add the New Blank Document button to the Quick Access toolbar if desired.
Open	Office, Open	
Save	Office, Save OR Quick Access toolbar	
Permission (Unrestricted Access)	Not available	
Mail Recipient	Removed from product	You can still send a document as a mail attachment with Office, Send, E-mail.
Print	Quick Access toolbar OR Office, Print, Quick Print	
Print Preview	Office, Print, Print Preview	
Spelling and Grammar	Review tab, Proofing group, Spelling & Grammar	
Research	Review tab, Proofing group, Research	
Cut	Home tab, Clipboard group, Cut	

Word 2003	Word 2007	Notes
Copy	Home tab, Clipboard group, Copy	
Paste	Home tab, Clipboard group, Paste	
Format Painter	Home tab, Clipboard group, Format Painter	
Undo	Quick Access toolbar	
Redo	Quick Access toolbar	
Repeat	Quick Access toolbar	
Insert Ink Annotations		Only on Tablet PCs
Insert Hyperlink	Insert tab, Links group, Hyperlink	
Tables and Borders Toolbar	Removed from product	Most of the tools can still be accessed from the Table Tools tabs (Design and Layout).
Insert Table	Insert tab, Tables group, Table, Insert Table	
Insert Microsoft Excel Worksheet	Insert tab, Tables group, Table, Excel Spreadsheet	
Columns	Page Layout tab, Page Setup group, Columns, More Columns	
Drawing	Removed from product	Many of the drawing tools are available from the Format tab when a drawing is selected.
Document Map	View tab, Show/Hide group, Document Map	
Show/Hide ¶	Home tab, Paragraph group, Show/Hide ¶	
Zoom	Status bar OR View tab, Zoom group, Zoom	
Microsoft Office Word Help	Help button (upper-right corner)	
Read	View tab, Document Views group, Full Screen Reading	

D

FORMATTING TOOLBAR

Word 2003	Word 2007	Notes
Styles and Formatting	Home tab, Styles group	
Style	Home tab, Styles group, dialog box launcher	
Font	Home tab, Font group, Font list	
Font Size	Home tab, Font group, Font Size list	
Bold	Home tab, Font group, Bold	
Italic	Home tab, Font group, Italic	
Underline	Home tab, Font group, Underline	
Align Left	Home tab, Paragraph group, Align Left	
Center	Home tab, Paragraph group, Center	
Align Right	Home tab, Paragraph group, Align Right	
Justify	Home tab, Paragraph group, Justify	
Line Spacing	Home tab, Paragraph group, Line Spacing	
Numbering	Home tab, Paragraph group, Numbering	
Bullets	Home tab, Paragraph group, Bullets	
Decrease Indent	Home tab, Paragraph group, Decrease Indent	
Increase Indent	Home tab, Paragraph group, Increase Indent	
Borders	Home tab, Paragraph group, Borders	
Highlight	Home tab, Font group, Text Highlight Color	
Font Color	Home tab, Font group, Font Color	

Setting Up and Modifying Office 2007

INSTALLING OFFICE 2007

Word 2007 is part of the Microsoft Office 2007 suite of programs. Although it is possible to buy Word as a standalone product, most people either buy it as part of Office or get it pre-installed on a new computer.

Installing Office is very simple. You just put the DVD into your PC and follow the prompts that appear. There are only two points at which you have significant interaction with the Setup program: You enter the product key, and you decide whether to do a standard or custom install. (Then if you choose the custom install, you pick the components to install and the folder in which you want to install them.)

NOTE

> If you click Customize, you can also choose what to do with any previous versions of Microsoft Word that the installer finds (keep them or remove them). You can keep all previous versions of all programs except Outlook; installing Outlook 2007 removes Outlook 2003 (and earlier versions) automatically.

Clicking Customize opens an extra screen with three tabs: Installation Options, File Location, and User Information. These tabs are detailed in the following sections.

INSTALLATION OPTIONS

On the Installation Options tab, you can choose which applications to install and also what subcomponents of each one you want and which overall shared components. Each item that appears in white on the list is set to be completely installed. Each item that appears in gray is set to be partially installed; click the plus sign next to such an item to see the sub-items and their statuses (see Figure E.1).

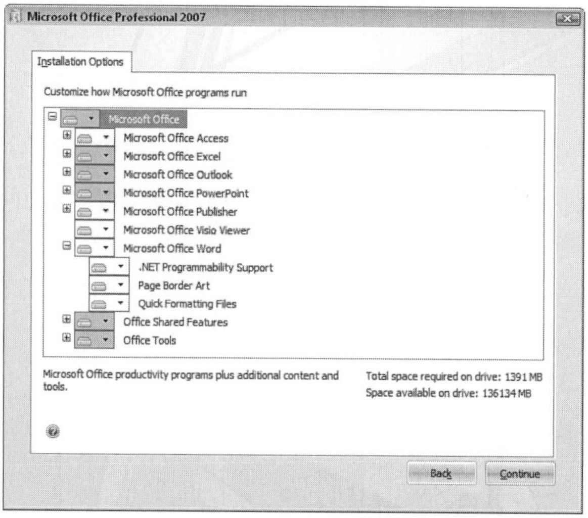

Figure E.1
On the Installation Options tab, choose which components to install.

To change the installation status of an item, click its down arrow and select the desired status from its menu. The choices are:

- **Run from My Computer**—This option will be installed.
- **Installed on First Use**—This option will be installed when you issue the command to use it for the first time. You might be prompted for the Office DVD at that point.
- **Not Available**—This option will not be available.

FILE LOCATION

On the File Location tab, enter the root path for storing the Office files. The default path is C:\Program Files\Microsoft Office. This is called the *root path* because it's the top level under which many subfolders will be created. For example, within that folder, an Office 12 folder will be created, and within that, folders for various helper files.

> **CAUTION**
>
> The main reason to change the file location is to store Office on another hard disk, either because your main hard disk is nearly full or because you prefer that Windows applications be installed on their own drive. When a hard disk gets too full, Windows starts having performance issues because there is not enough extra space to create the virtual memory the system needs. Therefore, if your hard disk is nearly full, it's much better to buy a new hard disk and install Word on it than to try to squeeze it onto your existing drive.

USER INFORMATION

On the User Information tab, enter your name, company, and initials. These are optional, but if you do enter them, Word will use them to assign Author properties to the documents you create, and Word will use your initials to sign revision marks and comments you place into documents.

MODIFYING OR REPAIRING YOUR OFFICE INSTALLATION

After Office has been installed, its Setup program can still be accessed from the Control Panel and can be used to modify, repair, or reinstall Office.

Follow these steps to access Setup:

1. From the Control Panel:
   - In Windows Vista, choose Programs, Programs and Features.
   - In Windows XP, choose Add or Remove Programs.
2. Click Microsoft Office 2007 (or Microsoft Word 2007) on the list of programs.

   The name varies slightly depending on the version you have, and includes the version name, such as Standard or Professional.

3. Click the Change button.

   In Windows Vista, if a user account control window pops up asking for permission to continue, click Continue.

4. In the Microsoft Office window, choose the option you want:

   - **Add or Remove Features**—Opens the Installation Options list, the same as with a custom install (refer to Figure E.1). Set each component to the desired setting: Run from My Computer, Installed on First Use, or Not Available.

   - **Repair**—Repairs the current installation without adding or removing any components.

   - **Remove**—Removes the entire program from your system.

5. Click Continue, and then follow the prompts to complete the Setup activity you chose to perform.

OPTIONAL TOOLS AND SHARED FEATURES

The steps for a custom installation in Office are fairly simple, as you just saw, and it's simple to change the options that are installed at any time. The tricky part is knowing which options you want and why.

Office 2007 comes with a variety of tools and shared features, none of which is necessary for using Word. Most of them are installed automatically in a default install, but not all of them. You might want to pick through them and remove the ones that you will never need, or add the ones that look interesting that aren't already installed. Table E.1 summarizes what's available.

TABLE E.1   OPTIONAL TOOLS AND SHARED FEATURES

Location in Setup	Option	Installed by Default?	Description
Microsoft Office Word	.NET Programmability Support	Yes	Allows Word programmability with .NET Framework version 1.1 or greater.
	Page Border Art	Yes	Graphics used for the Page Border feature (Borders and Shading dialog box).
	Quick Formatting Files	Yes	Theme files used for Quick Formats in Word.

Location in Setup	Option	Installed by Default?	Description
Office Shared Features	Clip Organizer	Yes	This is not actually the Clip Organizer utility itself, but rather the collections of art that are installed locally to your hard disk. There are two categories: AutoShapes and Themes, and Popular Clip Art.
	Converters and Filters	Yes	Conversion filters for various text and graphics formats. If you remove a converter for a file type and then try to open a file of that type, the open (or import) operation will fail.
	Digital Certificate for VBA Projects	Yes	A digital certificate for signing Visual Basic for Applications projects. If you remove this, you will receive security warnings when opening a VBA project that otherwise would have been signed.
	Fonts	Yes	Various fonts that come with Office 2007.
	International Support	Partly	This consists of two fonts. The Japanese Font is not installed by default; the Universal Font is.
	Microsoft Office Access Database Replication Conflict Manager	Yes	Primarily for Access, resolves conflicts between replicated databases
	Microsoft Office Download Control	Yes	The ActiveX control that enables clip art and templates to be automatically downloaded when selected. You'll probably want to keep this.
	Microsoft Office Themes	Yes	Provides access to the formatting themes that are consistent across applications
	New and Open Office Document Shortcuts	No	In earlier Office versions, shortcuts for creating new documents and opening existing ones were placed at the top of the Start menu by default. Most people didn't use them, so in Office 2007 they are not installed by default.

E

TABLE E.1 CONTINUED

Location in Setup	Option	Installed by Default?	Description
	Proofing Tools	Yes	There are four sets of proofing tools: English, French, Spanish, and Translation Core. For each of the three languages, you can enable/disable support for Find All Word Forms, Hyphenation, Spelling and Grammar Checking, and more. For French and Spanish, you can enable translation services to English.
	Visual Basic for Applications	Yes	VBA enables you to edit macros.
	Web Themes	Yes	There are two groups: Typical Web Themes and Additional Web Themes. Both are installed by default. Note that these are shared themes across all Office applications, not just for Word.
Office Tools	Document Update Utility	Yes	Keeps documents synchronized between the local PC and copies in online document workspaces.
	Equation Editor	Yes	Helps you create mathematical formulas with complex symbols
	Hosted Webs	Yes	Enables the use of Web folders on Office-compatible servers.
	Language Settings Tool	Yes	Provides an interface for setting language options across all Office documents.
	Microsoft Forms 2.0 .NET Programmability Support	Yes	Enables Microsoft Forms 2.0 programmability with .NET Framework version 1.1 or greater.
	Microsoft Graph	Yes	The utility that creates charts in Word, PowerPoint, and Access.
	Microsoft Office Document Imaging	On First Use	The utility that enables you to scan from within Office documents. It also installs the Microsoft Office Document Image Writer print driver.

E

Location in Setup	Option	Installed by Default?	Description
	Microsoft Office Picture Manager	Yes	The Picture Manager utility, for working with graphics.
	Microsoft Query	Yes	An add-in for Excel that provides direct database connectivity.
	Microsoft Script Editor (HTML Source Editing)	Partly	An add-in that allows HTML source editing when working with Web documents. The Web debugging tool is not installed by default.
	Research Explorer Bar	Yes	An add-in that enables you to use the Research tool from Word and other Office applications when you are in Internet Explorer.
	Smart Tag .NET Programmability Support	Yes	Allows smart tag programmability with .NET Framework version 1.1 or greater.
	Smart Tag Plugins	Yes	This is the main smart tag feature, providing intelligent recognition of data types from within Excel and Word. Various types are individually selectable.
	System Information	Yes	A troubleshooting tool that collects system information. Might be useful when talking with Microsoft technical support to diagnose an error.
	Windows SharePoint Services Support	Yes	Enables Office applications to interact with SharePoint Services.

E

INDEX

Symbols

: (colon) in indexes, 780

{=} field, 643

""(quotation marks) in indexes, 780

\ (backslash), 768

1.5 Lines (line spacing setting), 195

3-D (border type), 220

3-D charts, 503

3-D effects, 482-484

3-D rotation, 420-421, 549-550

A

About This Sentence option (grammar-check), 97

ABS() function, 386

absolute measurements (text boxes), 323

Absolute Position option (Picture Position settings), 407

accepting revisions, 792-793

accessibility, 992
  documents, 993
    charts/graphs, 994
    headings, 993-994
    hyperlinks, 995
    images, 994
    paragraph frames, 997
    styles, 993-994
    tables, 995-996
    text boxes, 997
  input devices, 992
  screen magnification, 992
  screen readers, 992

TTS (Text-to-Speech), 992
voice recognition, 992
XML-based content, 993

accessing workgroup templates, 304-306

ActiveX controls, 678

adaptive technology, 992
  document accessibility, 993
    charts/graphs, 994
    headings, 993-994
    hyperlinks, 995
    images, 994
    paragraph frames, 997
    styles, 993-994
    tables, 995-996
    text boxes, 997
  input devices, 992
  screen magnification, 992
  screen readers, 992
  TTS (Text-to-Speech), 992
  voice recognition, 992
  XML-based content, 993

Add Template dialog box, 313

Add Text command, 751

Add to Dictionary option (spell-check menu), 96

Add User – Webpage dialog box, 825

Add Users dialog box, 814

add-ins, 931-932
  COM add-ins, 931-932
  defined, 930
  disabling, 932, 980-982
  enabling, 932
  removing, 932
  Smart Tags, 932
  troubleshooting, 933
  viewing installed add-ins, 931

Add/Modify FTP Locations dialog box, 37

adding. See inserting

{AddressBlock} field, 567, 599, 647

addresses
  envelopes
    positioning, 336
    storing and retrieving, 338-339
    troubleshooting line spacing, 348
  mail merge
    blocks, 580-581
    validation, 589
  Smart Tags for, 119

{Advance} field, 643

Advanced Attributes dialog box, 808

Advanced document properties, 51-52

Advanced Layout dialog box, 501
  Picture Position tab, 406-407
  text wrap options, 404

After setting (paragraph spacing), 196-197

alerts
  document alerts, 828-829
  SharePoint Team Services, 843-844

aligning
  drawn objects, 471
  numbered lists, 210
  paragraphs, 206
  tables, 379
  text in table cells, 378
  WordArt, 488-489

Alignment option (Picture Position settings), 407

All Caps font effect, 173

alternate style names, 240-241

bibliographies
 bibliography fields, 732
 citations. *See* citations
 definition, 720
 fields, 732
 formatting, 729-730
 inserting from Bibliography
  Gallery, 730-731
 layouts, 730
 overview, 720
 removing from Bibliography
  Gallery, 733
 saving to Bibliography
  Gallery, 732-733
 sources
  creating when entering
   citations, 726-727
  deleting, 725
  editing, 724
  entering, 722-724
  inline references to,
   725-726
  temporary placeholders
   for, 727
  transferring to/from
   Master List, 725

Bibliography Gallery
 inserting bibliographies from,
  730-731
 removing bibliographies from,
  733
 saving bibliographies to,
  732-733

bit depth, 397-398

bitmaps, 396. *See also* **digital**
 photos
 fonts, 163
 images, 426

bits, 396

Black & white color mode, 413

blank documents, 28-29

blank entries, filtering for
 (mail merges), 586

blank pages, troubleshooting
 during printing, 151

blocking (Quick Style set
 switching), 232

Blogger, 850-851

blogs
 adding, 854-855
 categories, creating, 854
 compared to web pages, 848
 definition, 848

 deleting, 854-855
 pictures and graphics, adding,
  853-854
 posts
  creating, 853
  editing, 856
 services
  Blogger, 850-851
  community servers, 852
  MSN Spaces, 850
  registering, 849
  SharePoint 2007, 851
  troubleshooting, 856
  Word blogging interface,
   848-849

blue wavy lines, 96

body fonts, 16

bold text, 169-171

BoldItalics1 macro, 925

BoldItalics2 macro, 925-926

book folds, 268-269

Book Layout option (Picture
 Position settings), 407

Bookmark dialog box, 389,
 610-611

bookmarks, 610
 assigning to legacy form
  fields, 671
 creating, 610-611
 cross-references, 614-615
 hyperlinks
  another document, 613
  same document, 612
 jumping to, 611

borders
 adding
  clip art, 447
  drawings, 473-474
  pictures, 422
 pages, 294-295
 paragraphs, 217-218
  formatting, 219-221
  troubleshooting, 225
  types of, 218-219
 table cells, 374-376
 text boxes, 324-325

Borders and Shading dialog
 box, 219, 373-375

Box (border type), 219

box element, 964

breaking
 links, 329, 624
 paragraphs, 223-225

brightness (pictures), 412-413

browsers (Web page
 development), 861

Browsers tab (Web Options
 dialog box), 863-864

browsing clip art
 Office Online, 433-435
 Microsoft Clip Organizer, 436

bubble charts, 503

Building Block Gallery, 661

building blocks, 18, 276
 content control options, 664
 creating, 90-91
 definition, 90
 deleting, 93
 headers/footers, inserting,
  277-278
 inserting, 91-92
 properties, 93

Building Blocks Organizer
 dialog box, 92-93, 733

built fractions, 178

built-in commands, running as
 macros, 916

built-in watermarks, 288

bullet characters, 213-215,
 225-226

Bullet Library, 213

bulleted lists, 206-207
 AutoFormat As You Type,
  207-208
 bullet characters, 213-215,
  225-226
 Bullets or Numbering button,
  207
 list levels, 215-217
 SmartArt diagrams, 540
 spacing and indents, 217

Bullets or Numbering button,
 207

button element, 963

buttonGroup element, 965

buttons
 indenting paragraphs, 199
 Quick Access toolbar,
  936-937
 Stop Recording, 915

How can we make this index more useful? Email us at indexes@quepublishing.com

How can we make this index more useful? Email us at indexes@quepublishing.com

columns, 363-364

footnotes, 736

modified clips, 451

pictures between collections, 439

rows, 363-364

shapes, 449

subdocuments, 711

text, 72

Cut, Copy, and Paste commands, 73-74

drag-and-drop, 73

Office Clipboard, 78-79

Paste options, 76-77

Paste Special command, 74-76

text boxes, 322-324

MS-DOS names, 51

MSN Search, 125

MSN Spaces, 850

multicolumn layouts, 290

column presets, 291

custom column settings, 291-292

different column settings for selected text, 292

manual column breaks, 291

multilevel lists, 691

adding to Gallery, 696

creating, 692-695

custom list styles, 696-697

deleting, 698

list style presets, 691-692

numbers, including from higher outline levels, 695

multiparagraph text options (content controls), 663

Multiple (line spacing setting), 195

multiple pages per sheet, printing, 137

multiplier, line spacing as, 193-194

multisheet banners, 333-334

My Collections, 435

My Recent Documents shortcut (Favorites bar), 45

N

\n switch ({TOC} field), 756

names

macros, 909-910

styles, 240-241

user names, 787-788

navigating documents, 67

Click and Type feature, 68-69

keyboard shortcuts, 69-70

scrolling, 67-68

negative paragraph indents, 198

nested tables, creating, 366

nesting

fields, 652

lists, 215-217

subdocuments, 713-714

.NET Programmability Support, 1020

networks, saving documents to, 35-36

New Address List dialog box, 577

New and Open Office Document Shortcuts, 1021

New Blank Document button, 29

New Blog Account dialog box, 849

New Blogger Account dialog box, 850

New Column (section breaks), 264

New command (Office menu), 28

New Document command (Office Live workspaces), 826

New Document dialog box, 28

New MSN Spaces Account dialog box, 850

{Next} field, 648

Next Page (section breaks), 264

{NextIf} field, 648

{NextRecordIf} fields, 598

non-blank entries, filtering for (mail merges), 586

nonmodel dialog boxes, 523

nonprinting characters, viewing, 192-193

Normal style, 249

Normal view, 861

Normal.dotm template, 28-29, 298

restoring original, 317

saving changes to, 309-310

troubleshooting, 315-316

NOT() function, 387

note cards. *See* **folded note cards**

note separator lines, 740-741

Notepad, opening .lex files, 107

{NoteRef} field, 645

numbered elements (master documents), 706

numbered lists, 206-207

AutoFormat As You Type, 207-208

Bullets or Numbering button, 207

list levels, 215-217

number format, 210-212

restarting/continuing numbering, 208-209

spacing and indents, 217

starting at specific number, 209

number type (axis), 513-514

Numbering Library, 210-211

numbers

built fractions, 178

fields, 642-643, 649-650

footnotes/endnotes, 739

formats, 210-212, 388

outlines, 690-691, 698

styles, 210

O

\o switch ({TOC} field), 756

Object dialog box, 619

objects. *See also* **drawings**

converting SmartArt diagrams to, 558-559

embedding, 618-619

layering objects and text, 469-470

How can we make this index more useful? Email us at indexes@quepublishing.com

THIS BOOK IS SAFARI ENABLED

INCLUDES FREE 45-DAY ACCESS TO THE ONLINE EDITION

The Safari® Enabled icon on the cover of your favorite technology book means the book is available through Safari Bookshelf. When you buy this book, you get free access to the online edition for 45 days.

Safari Bookshelf is an electronic reference library that lets you easily search thousands of technical books, find code samples, download chapters, and access technical information whenever and wherever you need it.

TO GAIN 45-DAY SAFARI ENABLED ACCESS TO THIS BOOK:

- Go to **http://www.quepublishing.com/safarienabled**
- Complete the brief registration form
- Enter the coupon code found in the front of this book on the "Copyright" page

If you have difficulty registering on Safari Bookshelf or accessing the online edition, please e-mail customer-service@safaribooksonline.com.

Check out these great resources on Office 2007 and Windows® Vista™!

0789736403

560 pages

Want to become an Office 2007 power user? In this book, you get step-by-step instructions with accompanying 4-color visuals. This easy-to-use book includes optional practice files available on the web, a "Troubleshooting Guide" to assist with common problems, a "Project Guide" with real-world projects.

078973642x

448 pages

Discover visually how to make the most of the latest version of Excel. This book includes a NEW features icon highlighting what's new in Excel 2007, a troubleshooting guide to lend a hand with common problems, and a workshop section in the back of the book with projects to help you learn specific skills. Includes MCAS & MCAP exam objectives.

0789734729

1440 pages

Learn "from the trenches" advice on how to upgrade to Windows Vista—whether it is a handful of computers or an entire corporation. This book provides hands-on coverage of installing, configuring and surviving on a Windows Vista-based network. You will not only learn how to set up Windows networking features, but also how to install and set up basic networking software.

0789735970

1504 pages

Recognized Access expert, Roger Jennings, not only provides updates for the latest version, but also new chapters on application automation with Access macros and collaboration with Microsoft SharePoint Team Server. You will also find that all of the chapters have been updated for the transition from Jet to the new Access database engine.

0789735873

448 pages

Looking for the best way to cure an ailing Windows Vista PC? Look no further. You will be taken deep into the operating system to uncover expert level tools and techniques. The flowcharts cut through the problem right to the solution giving everyone the opportunity to find their way through Windows Vista.